The Rich, the Well Born, and the Powerful

ELITES AND UPPER CLASSES IN HISTORY

EDITED BY

Frederic Cople Jaher

The Citadel Press
Secaucus, N.J.

First paperbound printing, 1975
Published by Citadel Press
A division of Lyle Stuart, Inc.
120 Enterprise Ave., Secaucus, N.J. 07094
In Canada: George J. McLeod Limited
73 Bathurst St., Toronto 2B, Ontario
Manufactured in the United States of America

ISBN 0-8065-0505-2

Generous support from the University of Illinois, its Graduate College,
Center for Advanced Study, Research Board, and History Department facilitated the research for this book by providing released time, financial aid,
and research assistants.

Contents

The Rich, the Well Born, and the Powerful

Introduction

Appeals to equality and humility echo through the ages, but societies have almost invariably discriminated in distributing their assets. From remote beginnings to the present, power, wealth, and status have been unevenly spread among different social strata. The possession of one of these advantages has usually promoted acquisition of the others. History records widespread agreement on the nature and value of the rewards properly bestowed by the community. Focusing on groups that amassed a major share of these precious resources, we analyze the structure and strategy, tactics and thought, of groups in the upper orders of society. This perspective is important because the higher ranks have figured prominently in community decision-making. The top echelons have played key roles in initiating or implementing policies that shape the exercise of authority, distribution of resources, levels and modes of conflict and cohesion, and relations with other societies. Recent pleas to study the so-called inarticulate masses (unpublished might be a better word) should prompt even the most confrontation-minded historians to realize that they also need systematic analysis of upper classes and elites, if only to "know the enemy."

We have arranged these contributions chronologically to simplify the organization and to facilitate comparative references. Additional groupings may serve special analytical needs. Those interested in territorial scope of leadership will find that the essays fall into three categories. Robin Seager, Richard Mitchell, Richard Trexler, Walter Arnstein, and Paul Drake, respectively discussing the upper classes of classical Athens, the Roman Republic, Renaissance Florence, Victorian England, and Chile during the depression of 1929, write about enclaves exercising the broadest possible claims to community hegemony, and receiving deference, for varying time spans, from the societies they ruled. In the middle range of regional elites are Keith Hitchins' study of the eighteenth-century Rumanian Uniate hierarchy and Richard Jensen's analysis of twentieth-century midwestern elites. On the local level, Frank Foster focuses on sixteenth-century London merchants, and Frederic Jaher explores the fashionable Four Hundred of late nineteenth-century New York City.

These obvious geographical distinctions explain significant aspects of behavior in the upper orders. Regional and local leadership groups frequently mediate between their own sections and the larger society. Such relationships may create friction between the provincial elite and the national ruling class, or may cause internal disharmony over dualities of role and expectation. The conflict between the Rumanian Greek Catholic clergy and the imperial Habsburg court illustrates some of the difficulties involved in the interaction between intermediate elites and national ruling groups. Localized elites also may influence upper-class behavior by producing diversity in the higher ranks. Rooted in areas with different cultures or in different stages of social and economic development, these enclaves may encourage diversity and plurality and stimulate conflict or accommodation with the upper strata. In the Austro-Hungarian state, dissimilarity contributed to disintegration, for it reflected deep fissures in religious beliefs and national consciousness. In Elizabethan England, on the other hand, relations between the London merchants and the royal court were fundamentally harmonious.

Although territorial scope provides insights into the behavior of elites and upper classes, function is the essential measure of leadership: Where, how, and to what degree do groups establish and protect their dominance? To clarify these questions the upper strata can be divided into two orders of magnitude: upper classes and elites. Historically, upper classes have dominated the primary societal functions of religion, economics, politics, and war. The essays on the aristocracies of ancient Greece and Rome, Renaissance Florence, Victorian England, and twentieth-century Chile clearly deal with upper classes. Widely separated in time, these patriciates share the fundamental upper-class features of predominant power, wealth, and social status; their sovereignty is legitimized by community traditions and religious beliefs, and their membership is primarily determined by inherited rank. Despite disparities in time, place, culture, and social system, they exhibit remarkable uniformity in the sources, the means, and the structure of their preeminence.

These similarities are illuminated by comparing preindustrial upper classes with their counterparts in the age of industrialism, or by showing that ruling groups of preindustrial origins survived the social and economic changes wrought by industrialization. The studies of the Roman Republican ruling class (a preindustrial entity) and the aristocracies of Victorian England and twentieth-century Chile (leadership groups of preindustrial formation that maintained a large degree of hegemony in the industrial era) disclose many parallels in the relationship of kinship and status, reception of newcomers, and control over the same vital communal institutions. Perhaps this continuity of problems and policies in upper classes from different historical periods helps account for the ability of the British nobility and Chile's leading nineteenth-century families to retain much of their rank, wealth, and power despite radical upheavals in the technology and economy of their nations. It may be that fundamental alterations in the productive process are not accompanied by equally broad-ranging modifications in the ruling process. The alternatives and initiatives in gaining or maintaining place and power may vary within narrower limits; hence the techniques of leadership may not become as quickly or as completely outmoded as the techniques of production.

Those who exercise authority, accumulate wealth, and command respect may be called elites as well as upper classes. Conventional usage designates as elite all groups that wield power or possess high status and large fortune. The term also denotes all groups that demonstrate excellence: elite scholars, elite athletes, elite criminals, and so on. It is also applied to enclaves within classes. Not every member of the upper class, even in an aristocracy, is equal in power, wealth, or esteem, and those with a disproportionate share of these advantages become an intraclass elite when compared to less endowed members of the stratum. The elasticity of casual usage, however, makes the category too generic, and therefore imprecise. Elites exist at many levels and in many areas of society. But some levels do not have enough wealth, power, and legitimacy, and some areas are too narrow, to gain the celebrity and influence requisite for community leadership. Upper classes, on the other hand, assume generalized hegemony. Military, professional, political, economic, or intellectual elites may exist as separate entities, but upper classes must incorporate or control these groups. For the purposes of conceptual clarity—by distinguishing among different types of leadership groups dealt with in this collection—we define elite to mean those enclaves whose influence is primarily local and regional, whose functions are specialized, or that occupy auxiliary positions in the leadership hierarchy.

Regional or local elites defer to the upper classes and accommodate or rival other elites. The Rumanian Uniate clergy had to contend with the court nobility at Vienna, the London merchants with the crown, and the midwestern urban elites with each other and with the wealthier and more influential metropolitan patriciates along the Atlantic seaboard. Elite functions are limited in number as well as in magnitude. The Greek Catholic clergy dominated the religious and intellectual life of the Rumanians, but had limited influence on the politics and economics of the foreign-dominated principality in which they lived. The Four Hundred ran New York's high society, but though its membership overlapped with business and political elites, as a group it did not participate in major national or even local issues. John McKay's case study of the struggle for domination of the Briansk Ironworks Company underscores the inferior position of specialized or localized elites. Foreign capitalists were defeated because the tsarist government established Russian control in this turn-of-the-century contest.

Elites auxiliary to national ruling groups also act as intermediaries and competitors rather than as primary centers of power. David Ransel's investigation of the military and civil bureaucracy in eighteenth-century Russia shows the noble servicemen to be mediators and interveners, placemen and pleaders, rather than policy-makers or ultimate sources of authority. Similarly, in Thomas Krueger's and William Glidden's study, the New Deal intelligentsia occupies a secondary place in the hierarchy of power. As a political-intellectual elite 't influenced and helped implement, but did not govern, executive policy, it acted as a buffer between the Roosevelt administration and other political elites; and it was in frequent conflict with rival elites seeking to displace it.

Group hegemony is further determined by stage of development. Like other social organizations, elites and upper classes rise, peak, and fall; they experience periods of triumph, challenge, and defeat. By tracing life cycles, analyzing rivalries, and examining intragroup conflict, some of the authors highlight the dynamic dimension of their subjects. The writers on the aristocracies of the ancient world focus on the formation, consolidation, and, in the case of Athens, decline of the traditional ruling stratum—changes triggered by confrontations with emerging elites. Although concentrating on a single stage of development, the discussions of the Renaissance Florentine gentility, the Victorian nobility, and the twentieth-century Chilean upper class similarly emphasize the problems of group survival. The studies of regional, local, and specialized elites also concern themselves with life cycles and strategies of survival. The development, dominance, and decline of New York's fashionable set and the arrival and departure of the New Deal intelligentsia are portrayed from this point of view. While touching on origins, the explorations of the Rumanian Uniate hierarchy, the Russian civil service nobility, and the foreign capitalists directing the Briansk corporation focus in one phase of existence and on conflicts with competitors or on internal factionalism.

Politics is the arena of leadership most often emphasized in this collection, but the religious, familial, military, social, and economic aspects of hegemonic groups are also given close attention. Several of the contributors have made these aspects their basic theme. The essay on Renaissance Florence deals mainly with the attempt of the commune's gentry to retain its position by using charitable institutions to aid financially endangered members. The order saw its preservation as a whole involved in sustaining a declining part. The examination of the Greek Catholic hierarchy in Transylvania discloses that the basis of its authority was not political, but religious, intellectual, and educational. Political influence meant little in New York's fashionable set; power was defined as the ability to set social standards. The discussion of the conflict for control over the Briansk Ironworks, while not minimizing the important political implications, gives at least equal weight to economic forces and considerations.

These essays can also be distinguished according to three methods of analysis: compositional, operational, and intellectual. The authors have sought to ascertain who their groups were, what they did, and what they thought (and what was thought of them).

Although each study defines its group, the investigations of the London merchants, New York high society, the midwestern metropolitan elites, and the New Deal intelligentsia pay particular attention to the problems of constituent identification. They all include aggregate social profiles of membership, and the last two contain methodological discussions of collective trait analysis.

Several of the essays use role analysis to describe the activities and accomplishments of their subjects. Hence functional and institutional considerations are uppermost in the surveys of the aristocracies of antiquity, the Florentine patriciate, the London merchants, the Rumanian Uniate hierarchy, the Russian civil service nobility, the Victorian and Chilean upper classes, and the Briansk capitalists.

In the third approach the ideologies of these elites and upper classes are analyzed according to the mode of the history of ideas, and in functional terms as facets of group behavior. The ideology of the New Deal is treated as a system of ideas. The studies of the Athenian aristocracy and the Rumanian Greek Catholic hierarchy center on group consciousness; ideas are seen as a means of group cohesion, motivation for action, source of support for social position, or weapons against opponents.

The varied categories that integrate these essays do not coalesce into a general conception of the upper strata. The diversity of the past, as reflected in this collection, suggests once again that it may not be possible to formulate universally valid laws of history. Social theory is crowded with clashing and flawed models of leadership groups. Our hypotheses have more modest dimensions; they are historical in method, constructed to explain the structure, function, and thought of particular enclaves existing in specific time periods and cultures. We hope our analyses will contribute to more informed, elegant, and comprehensive theories, but the essential test of the value of our enterprise is the quality of the essays. To meet this standard we offer new topics of research, fresh interpretations of better-known subjects, and systematic and more complete treatment of material previously presented in fragmentary form.

Elitism and Democracy
in Classical Athens

ROBIN SEAGER

In *Politics* Aristotle repeatedly draws a distinction between the men of note in a community, *hoi gnorimoi*, and the masses.[1] The preeminence of the *gnorimoi* may be based on various grounds: moral excellence, noble birth, wealth, education.[2] The philosopher is naturally sympathetic to the claims of moral excellence, *arete*, but in terms of practical politics he sees wealth as the essential foundation for the predominance of any minority within the state.[3] The *gnorimoi* are frequently identified, directly or by implication, with the rich, *hoi euporoi, hoi plousioi, hoi tas ousias ekhontes*.[4] The justification for an elite of wealth may be distinguished from that for an elite of birth: the rich argue that they possess a greater share of the land, while the well-born urge pedigree, for high birth is excellence of breeding.[5] But elsewhere wealth and birth are closely associated,[6] and birth is even defined partially in terms of wealth: noble birth is old established wealth and excellence, and the well-born are those who possess ancestral excellence and wealth.[7] Education, too, like good birth, is more likely to be found among the rich.[8]

This paper investigates the conflict between the elitist values traditional in Greek society and the ideals of the most extreme democracy ever known in Greece or elsewhere, that of Athens in the fifth and fourth cen-

[1] Ar.*Pol.*1291b17, 1304a25, b33, 1305b13, 1307a30, 1309a1, 1310b9, 1313b18, 1315b3, 1318b34, 1319a3, 1320a14; see *AthP.*16.9, 28.2.
[2] Ar.*Pol.*1283a16, b1, 15, 1289b41, 1290b13, 1291b28, 1296b18, 1299b24, 1300a-16, 1313b39. See A. H. M. Jones, *Athenian Democracy* (Oxford, 1957), 45; J. K. Davies, *Athenian Propertied Families* (Oxford, 1971), 213.
[3] Thus wealth, however acquired, is the standard of oligarchs: Ar.*Pol.*1278a21, 1279b8, 18, 1294a11, 1318a20.
[4] Ar.*Pol.*1274a18, 1296a25, 1296b31, 1303b36, 1304b1, 22, 1305a4, 22, 1308b28, 1311a1, 1320b7; see *AthP.*26.1, 28.2, Plut.*Nic.*2.
[5] Ar.*Pol.*1283a31, 36.
[6] Ar.*Pol.*1209b19.
[7] Ar.*Pol.*1294a21.
[8] Ar.*Pol.*1293b37.

turies. The first section sketches the historical progress of the Athenian state, from the Eupatrid elite of birth through the elite of property established by the reform of Solon to the democracy of Pericles and his successors, in which, in theory at least, all citizens enjoyed the blessings of equality. The second section examines the ways in which democratic statesmen and orators sought, with only superficial success, to combat the continuing predominance of birth and wealth, in both the practical and ideological spheres. The final section illustrates how the democracy at the same time pursued a contrasting but more practical aim, trying to assimilate and render harmless the elitist tendencies it could not suppress, in order to effect a face-saving compromise between political theory and social fact.

1

The aristocratic Athenian state was controlled by an elite of birth, the Eupatrids, whose nobility, as Isocrates remarks, could be easily discerned from their very name.[9] The origin of the exalted position enjoyed by this group of families is veiled in legend, but the story Plutarch told in his life of Theseus may well bear some resemblance to the truth: these men had been the local dynasts of Attica; when the country was united under a single king, they became the royal council and founded Athens' only nobility of birth.[10] Their functions were those of the ruling class in any aristocratic state: to provide priests and, after the end of the monarchy, magistrates, to expound the laws and interpret the state religion.[11] Since the archonship was restricted to Eupatrids and the council of the Areopagus was composed of former archons, the Eupatrids had a monopoly of the only permanent element in the constitution. It may have been that the archons were selected by the Areopagus until the time of Solon, so that in choosing magistrates the council was in fact renewing itself by co-option. However, it is possible that even before Solon the archons were chosen by some form of popular election.[12]

Solon's reform of 594 put an end to the formally defined elite of birth.

9 Isoc.16.25. This is true even if the passage refers not to the Eupatrids as a caste but to a single *genos*. Against the existence of such a *genos*, see H. T. Wade-Gery, *Essays in Greek History* (Oxford, 1958), 106ff.; Davies, *APF*, 11f.; in favor: C. Hignett, *A History of the Athenian Constitution to the End of the Fifth Century B.C.* (Oxford, 1952), 315f.

10 Plut.*Thes*.32; see Wade-Gery, *Essays*, 86ff.

11 Plut.*Thes*.25.

12 *AthP*. 8.1f. claims that before Solon the archons had been appointed by the Areopagus but that Solon introduced the use of the lot; the latter can hardly be right. Ar.*Pol*.1274a1 says that Solon did not interfere with the method of choosing archons, but unfortunately does not indicate what he thought that was. See Hignett, *HAC*, 78ff.

Qualification for the highest office and consequently for eventual membership of the Areopagus was no longer to depend on membership of a family
recognized as Eupatrid, but on income derived from landed property.[13]
No doubt few Eupatrids were excluded by the change, since most of the
noble families owned large estates, and wealth had already been a consideration in determining which Eupatrids attained high office.[14] But the
reform was of great importance, for it is clear that there had existed for
some time a class of wealthy landowners who did not enjoy Eupatrid status
and so were excluded from political power.[15] It is said that when Theseus
defined the Eupatrid order, he distinguished it from two classes already in
existence, the *georgoi* or *geomoroi* and the *demiourgoi*.[16] These *georgoi*, or
farmers, must have been non-Eupatrid landowners, who under Solon's
reform received equality of privilege with Eupatrids except in the religious
sphere. A decade after Solon's archonship, the attempt of Damasias to establish a tyranny was followed by the rule of ten archons: five Eupatrids,
three *agroikoi*, and two *demiourgoi*.[17] These *agroikoi* would again have
been landowners of non-Eupatrid birth; the proportional representation exhibited here testifies both to the continuing prestige of Eupatrid blood
under the new order and to the end of exclusive Eupatrid power.

But the claims of birth were not forgotten, least of all by those who fulfilled them. The scions of noble houses still held the archonship under the
tyranny of Peisistratus and his sons, though many went into exile in 514,
when the assassination of his brother Hipparchus caused the rule of Hippias
to become increasingly harsh. The failure of the first attempt to overthrow
Hippias was commemorated in a drinking song that celebrated the fallen
heroes as men brave in battle and of noble birth, whose deed bore witness
to their pedigree.[18] The enduring influence of the noble families in politics
and religion receives eloquent attestation in the reforms of Cleisthenes,
who attempted in about 508, after the expulsion of Hippias in 510, to break
down the power of local dynasts and local cults in the interest of national
unity.[19]

[13] AthP.7.3, Plut.Sol.18, Ar.Pol.1274a18; see Wade-Gery, *Essays*, 99ff. Even for
the period before the reform the *Athenaion Politeia* equates the *gnorimoi* with the rich
(*AthP.*2.1f., 4.5, 5.1, 3). Solon himself in one of his poems contrasts the demos with
those who are looked up to for their wealth (Solon fr.5.3). In fr.4.9ff. he recognizes
that wealth does not always betoken excellence, but landed wealth appears to be the
standard again in fr.14.1ff.

[14] AthP.3.1, 6; see Ar.Pol.1273a23.

[15] See Hignett, *HAC*, 102f.

[16] Plut.Thes.25, Schol.Plat.Axioch.371d, Lex.Dem.Patm.152; see Wade-Gery, *Essays*, 89ff. On *demiourgoi*, see K. Murakawa, in *Historia*, 6 (1957), 385ff.

[17] AthP.13.2.   [18] AthP.19.3.

[19] For this aspect of Cleisthenes' work, see D. M. Lewis, in *Historia*, 12 (1963),
22ff.

The elite of property created by Solon was vulnerable on two fronts: the archonship and the Areopagus. In the long term, of course, these were inextricably linked, for as long as the Areopagus was composed of former archons, any diminution of the prestige of the archonship must ultimately weaken the influence of the Areopagus itself. As Athens evolved toward full democracy, the archonship was the first to come under attack. One blow was struck about 501 with the reform of the generalship, which made it possible for the generals eventually to replace the archons as the leading executive officials in the state.[20] But the coup de grâce came in 487 when the archonship fell victim to that lethal weapon of democratic egalitarianism, the lot.[21] Men of ability and ambition would no longer have any interest in holding an office that depended largely on chance; they would opt for the generalship, which remained elective and had another powerful advantage—it could be held repeatedly, the archonship once in a lifetime. So henceforth the Areopagus would no longer be recruited from the cream of Athens' ruling class, but would be composed of reasonably well-off, reasonably competent nonentities. Of course the effect was not immediate; the Areopagus no doubt contained sufficient ex-archons who had held office before 487 to be well worth attacking when Ephialtes stripped it of much of its traditional power in 462.[22]

But although neither birth nor wealth any longer supplied a formal qualification for political power, both still played a considerable part in determining the people's choice of leaders. The aristocratic descent of leading Athenian politicians is repeatedly attested by Plutarch: the extravagances of Cimon were tolerated because he was young and of a great family, Aristides was of a distinguished house, Pericles was of the highest descent on both sides, Phaeax had notable ancestors though he was otherwise insignificant, and one of Alcibiades' numerous claims to consideration was the distinction of his forebears.[23] Here again high birth is often complemented by wealth: Cimon was second to none in wealth as well as birth; Pericles had wealth, birth, and powerful friends; Nicias made good political use of the great wealth he drew from the silver mines of Attica; Hipponicus, the father-in-law of Alcibiades, had great renown and influence because of his wealth and birth; political doors were opened for Alcibiades by his birth, wealth, and bravery in battle.[24]

Isocrates also celebrates Hipponicus as first of the Greeks in wealth

[20] *AthP*.22.2.
[21] *AthP*.22.5; see Hignett, *HAC*, 173.
[22] *AthP*.25.1f.
[23] Plut.*Them*.5, *Arist*.1, *Per*.3, 7, *Alc*.13, 16.
[24] Plut.*Per*.9, 7, *Nic*.3f., *Alc*.8, 10; in general, see Plut.*Arist*.13.

and second to no Athenian in birth.[25] Xenophon speaks of the exaggerated self-esteem inspired by their birth in both Critias and Alcibiades.[26] Generals were elected, says the *Athenaion Politeia*, on account of ancestral renown.[27] Not until after the death of Pericles did the people first choose a leader not of the better sort.[28] So in extolling the great Athenian leaders of the past—Cleisthenes, Miltiades, Themistocles, and Pericles—Isocrates remarks that they excelled in birth, intelligence, and ability.[29] The leaders of the oligarchic revolution of 411, Peisander, Antiphon, and Theramenes, were men of high birth.[30] In *Frogs* Aristophanes appealed to the Athenian people to overthrow its low-born leaders in favor of those it knew to be of good birth and decent education.[31] The *Athenaion Politeia* characterizes the victims of the Thirty in 404 as those who excelled in wealth, birth, and dignity.[32]

On the other side, Demosthenes is always eager to sneer at the ancestry of his opponent Aeschines, whose father, if Demosthenes is to be believed, was a slave, his mother a whore.[33] Aeschines is equally ready to reply in kind—the people could hardly emulate the ancestors of Demosthenes, he remarks, for Demosthenes, whose mother was a Scythian, had no ancestors.[34]

The old association between birth and wealth had first been seriously undermined at about the time of the outbreak of the Peloponnesian War, when a new type of politician began to appear: the son of a wealthy factory-owner whose income had served to provide him with an education and now gave him the necessary leisure to engage in public life. These men were lampooned by their enemies for their vulgar origins: Cleon the tanner, Hyperbolus the lamp-maker, and Cleophon the lyre-maker were favorite targets of comedians and others.[35] In more general terms, Aristophanes makes the sausage-seller complain to the demos in *Knights* that it puts its trust in lamp-makers, cobblers, leather-workers, and tanners instead of in gentlemen.[36] Isocrates passes the overall judgment that the politicians of the old aristocratic type, Aristides, Themistocles, and Miltiades, were better men than Hyperbolus, Cleophon, and the leaders of the middle fourth century.[37]

[25] Isoc.16.31.
[26] Xen.*Mem*.1.2.25.
[27] *AthP*.26.1.
[28] *AthP*.28.1ff.
[29] Isoc.15.308.
[30] *AthP*.32.2.
[31] Arist.*Ran*.727ff.
[32] *AthP*.35.4.
[33] Dem.18.122, 129f.
[34] Aesch.2.171, 180; see Dein.1.111.
[35] Arist.*Eq*.136, *Pax* 270, 648 (Cleon); *Nub*.1065f., *Pax* 690 (Hyperbolus); And. 1.146, Aesch.2.76, *AthP*. 28.3 (Cleophon); on Cleon, see Davies, *APF*, 318; on Hyperbolus, see ibid., 517.
[36] Arist.*Eq*.738ff.
[37] Isoc.8.75; see 15.316 on the change.

Aeschines makes the point that a man was not forbidden to speak in the assembly simply because his ancestors had not held the generalship or because he followed some trade to provide himself with the necessities of life.[38] But Andocides had been forced to defend himself against attack because in extremity he had engaged in trade.[39] Demosthenes records that there was a law forbidding the uttering of insults against any citizen because he worked as a shopkeeper in the marketplace.[40] That such a law, more honored in the breach than the observance, was needed is sufficient proof that widespread prejudice existed. Certainly Demosthenes and Aeschines exchange slanders on this score too. Aeschines dismisses Demosthenes as the bastard son of a cutler and himself a writer of speeches for pay,[41] while Demosthenes sneers at Aeschines, whose father had been a lowly schoolmaster and who had himself served the people as an assistant clerk.[42] Even Plutarch finds Demosthenes' factory-owning father something of an embarrassment,[43] while of Phocion he remarks that his family cannot have been entirely without honor, for if he had really been the son of a pestle-maker, the hostile Glaucippus would not have overlooked this proof of low birth.[44]

But despite this prejudice and attempts to exploit it, the power of wealth, regardless of its source, is amply attested in fifth- and fourth-century Athens.[45] In the speech Thucydides puts into the mouth of the Syracusan Athenagoras, it is suggested that property-owners are best fitted to rule.[46] In the *Antidosis* Isocrates remarks that when he was a boy, wealth was a guarantee of security and respect, so that men pretended to own more property than they did, though now it was dangerous to be rich.[47] Demosthenes contrasts the poor man, who played little part in public life and could attain only those offices that were assigned by lot, with men the people elected as ambassadors, who were likely to be rich.[48]

2

The Athenian democracy was in principle opposed to any form of elitism.[49] In a democracy, as Aristotle remarks, the supreme goal is equality, *isotes*.[50]

---

[38] Aesch.1.27.   [39] And.1.137.   [40] Dem.57.30f.
[41] Aesch.2.93, 180, 3.173; so too Dein.1.111.
[42] Dem.18.127, 258ff., 19.70, 95, 199f., 249.
[43] Plut.*Dem*.4.   [44] Plut.*Phoc*.4.
[45] On sources of wealth, see Jones, *AD*, 88, and various examples in Davies, *APF*, 127, 181, 259ff., 385, 403f., 427ff., 459, 553, 562.
[46] Thuc.6.39.1; see Jones, *AD*, 54f.   [47] Isoc.15.159f.
[48] Dem.24.112. That those who held elective office were not always comfortably circumstanced is clear from the recital of Timotheus' financial difficulties in Ps.-Dem. 49.6, 11ff.
[49] See Jones, *AD*, 46f.   [50] Ar.*Pol*.1284a19.

In the most famous of all eulogies of the democracy, the funeral speech, Pericles insists that in democratic Athens all men are equal before the law, while honor is assigned not to wealth but to ability and merit, so that even the poor man is not prevented from doing what good he can for the city.[51] A client of Isocrates, who characterizes himself as a poor man, one of the people, exclaims that it would be a terrible thing if under a democracy all men did not receive equal treatment.[52] In a speech from the Demosthenic corpus it is said that if a man proposed that the right to speak in the assembly should be restricted to the youngest men, the richest, those who had performed liturgies, or any other such group, the people would condemn him to death, and rightly so, for attempting to overthrow the democracy.[53] Demosthenes himself asks what has become of equality and democracy if a poor man can be condemned while a rich man goes free.[54]

To enforce the ideal of democratic equality and combat the establishment of any elite, whatever its basis, the democracy had various practical weapons at its disposal. Aristotle gives a catalog in *Politics*: universal eligibility for office, the use of the lot in appointing magistrates, the denial of privilege to the wealthy, short-term magistracies with a ban on iteration, and payment for service on the council, in the assembly, in the courts, or as a public official or magistrate.[55] Universal eligibility had been the rule, in practice if not in theory, since 457, when the archonship had been thrown open to the third Solonian property class, the *zeugitai*;[56] it seems to have been that if any member of the lowest class felt inclined to put himself forward, his qualifications were not closely questioned. The most important development in the use of the lot had come in 487, when it replaced popular election in the appointment of the archons.[57] Its prominence in the full democracy of the fourth century is shown by the *Athenaion Politeia*.[58] Isocrates and Aristotle both saw as typical of the aristocratic state that the lot played no part in it,[59] and Aristotle again singles out the lot as a vital element of democracy.[60] However, it must be remembered that on this issue, at least, ideology was always tempered by reason: all military offices, from the generalship down, remained elective, and iteration, even in successive years, was always permitted.[61]

Payment for public service was even more important. Aristotle remarks that under the old aristocratic system, wealth as well as birth had to be

[51] Thuc.2.37.1.   [52] Isoc.20.19f.
[53] Ps.–Dem.25.29.   [54] Dem.51.11.
[55] Ar.*Pol.*1317b18ff.; for the various forms of pay, see *AthP.*62.2.
[56] *AthP.*26.2.   [57] *AthP.*22.5.
[58] *AthP.*43.1.   [59] Isoc.7.22, Ar.*Pol.*1273a17.
[60] Ar.*Pol.*1294b8; see Jones, *AD*, 48; Hignett, *HAC*, 228ff.
[61] *AthP.*61.

considered in the choice of magistrates, because the poor man has no leisure to engage in the work of goverment.[62] This could serve an aristocracy as a safeguard against encroachment by the lowly who had to earn their living; thus no payment for office, like no resort to the lot, is characteristic of an aristocratic polity.[63] Under a democracy compensation was essential if the poor were to be able to participate.[64] Payment for jury service was brought in by Pericles.[65] Payment for membership on the council, which was far more time-consuming than attendance in the courts or the assembly, must also have begun in the middle fifth century, though no evidence exists for the date. Ecclesiastic pay was introduced early in the fourth century, perhaps to combat increasing apathy.[66] The principle of payment for office was so essential to democratic thinking and practice that it was inevitably high on the list of targets when an attempt was made to overthrow the democracy. Its abolition was a major element in the program of the revolution of 411, which briefly established the oligarchy of the Four Hundred;[67] it was also rejected under the moderate constitution of the Five Thousand, which, even more briefly, succeeded the oligarchy before full democracy was restored.[68]

In addition to these practical weapons against elitism, the ideology of the democracy, rehearsed time and again by speakers in the assembly and the courts, was equally calculated to combat elitist notions. Sometimes the claims of birth and wealth were specifically rejected.[69] Pericles in the funeral speech had denied that wealth was the standard by which men were judged at Athens, and had insisted that poverty was no bar to talent.[70] Lysias complains about those who are capable of getting themselves out of trouble on the strength of their family.[71] There is nothing, Demosthenes insists, that should induce the people to put up with insolence in an individual: neither birth nor wealth nor influence.[72] He points to Midias' wealth as the origin and support of his lawless behavior, and urges the jury not to lose itself in admiration of the riches of Midias and his friends but to preserve its self-respect.[73] Later in the speech he again attacks those who think they are important just because they are well-off.[74]

---

[62] Ar.*Pol*.1273a23; for the importance of leisure, see also Isoc.7.26, though there the overall conception is very different.

[63] Ar.*Pol*.1273a17.   [64] Ar.*Pol*.1293a4.

[65] *AthP*.27.3, Ar.*Pol*.1274a8; see 1294a37 and 1297a36 on its importance; see Jones, *AD*, 49f.; Hignett, *HAC*, 219f.

[66] *AthP*.41.3; see Ar.*Pol*.1297a36, 1300a1.

[67] Thuc.8.65.3, *AthP*.29.5, 30.2.   [68] Thuc.8.97.1, *AthP*.33.1.

[69] See Dem.51.11, Hyp.4.32.   [70] Thuc.2.37.1.

[71] Lys.14.18.   [72] Dem.21.143ff.

[73] Dem.21.98, 210; for wealth as the cause of *hybris*, see Lys.24.16.

[74] Dem.21.213.

Apart from the outright rejection of elitist values, the positive virtues commended by democratic thought also militated strongly against any form of elitism. The interests of individuals and groups were expected to exhibit a total solidarity with those of the people, the democracy, and the city.[75] Andocides claims that his enemies attacked him because they knew that he, unlike them, had the city's interests at heart.[76] Such an attitude ran in his family: his father's grandfather Leogoras had plotted against the tyranny on behalf of the democracy and preferred exile with the people to a share in the tyrants' power.[77] Isocrates in his encomium of the elder Alcibiades maintains that the same men both overthrew the democracy and exiled Alcibiades; he and the democrats expelled by the Thirty had thus known similar sufferings. In exile Alcibiades chose to endure any hardship with the city rather than to prosper with the Spartans.[78] In short, he helped the demos, desired the same constitution as the mass of the people, suffered at the hands of the same men as the people, knew ill fortune at the same time as the city, and had the same friends and enemies as the people and shared its dangers.[79]

The family of Nicias showed similar constancy. Apart from Nicias' own goodwill toward the people, his brother Eucrates revealed his devotion by refusing to become a member of the Thirty, preferring to die in defense of the people's safety than to see Athens' walls destroyed, her fleet surrendered, and the people enslaved; his son Niceratus also died under the Thirty, unable to tolerate any form of government other than the democracy.[80] Demosthenes lectures Aeschines on this theme: it is not fine speeches and voice production that are valuable in an orator, he says, but the making of the same choices as the mass of the people and having the same friends and enemies as one's country.[81] Aeschines claims that his family satisfied the demand: his father, Atrometus, was exiled under the Thirty and helped in the restoration of the democracy, and his mother shared in the misfortunes of the city.[82]

Conversely, a standard way of attacking an opponent is to attempt to isolate him by denying his goodwill toward the people and suggesting that his interests and the city's are not the same.[83] Lysias' diatribe against Eratosthenes on this theme culminates in the charge that he thought of the

---

[75] Besides the passages cited below, see Ant.5.78, Lys.13.60, 16.10, 26.19; Ps.-Lys.20.1f., 27, 30, 33f.; for goodwill toward the people or the democracy, see Arist.Eq. 873f., Lys.16.3, 22.11, 30.18, 31.18.

[76] And.1.135.

[77] And.2.26.

[78] Isoc.16.4, 12, 17, 19, 38.

[79] Isoc.16.41.

[80] Lys.18.4ff.; see 12, 23f.

[81] Dem.18.280.

[82] Aesch.2.78, 147f., 3.191.

[83] Apart from the passages cited below, see Lys.12.42ff., 48, 50, 13.10, 20, Dem.8. 66, 10.74, 18.198, 292, 21.202, 24.173.

city as an enemy and the people's enemies as his friends.[84] The younger Alcibiades was not well disposed toward the people: he preferred to run the risk of a fine for evading military service than to join with his fellow citizens, since he cared nothing for the city.[85] In this he took after his father, who, at least according to the hostile Lysias, would have preferred to be a citizen of any city other than Athens.[86] The basic charge may take various forms: that the interests of a man or a group are different from those of the rest of the people,[87] that he profits from the city's misfortunes,[88] that he puts his own interests before those of the city,[89] or that he considers himself alien to the city.[90] Several of these themes are neatly combined in Lysias' attack on Philon, who put his selfish interests before the good of the city, did the opposite to all the other citizens, preferred to be a metic at Oropus than a citizen at Athens, profited from the city's misfortunes, robbed those who were well disposed toward the people, and in short behaved in a manner that was foreign to any conception of democracy.[91] Demosthenes uses similar tactics. Midias is consistently presented as the enemy of the city, the people, the laws, and the constitution.[92] Another enemy, Aristocrates, had not merely done the city no service, but he had not even chosen to regard the same men as enemies.[93] Timocrates had acted in opposition to the council, the demos, and the courts—to all the institutions of democracy.[94]

The good citizen had to keep control of his tongue and of his face. A client of Lysias proclaims that he is not open to the reproach that he looked with pleasure on the city's misfortunes.[95] Hyperides attacks Democrates for making jokes about the troubles of the city.[96] In the peroration of *De Corona* Demosthenes presents a vivid picture of Aeschines: he smiles or laughs at the successes of others, but at those of Athens he shudders and groans with downcast eyes.[97] Aeschines again responds in kind, accusing Demosthenes of wanting to be honored for policies that had brought misfortune to the city instead of rejecting the honor on that account.[98]

Solidarity and loyalty alone were not enough, however. Democratic ideology required the complete subordination of the individual to the state. In Demosthenes' idealized view of the fifth century, nobody stood out above the masses: Themistocles was banished when the people discovered

84 Lys.12.51.
85 Lys.14.9f., 15.10.
86 Lys.14.38.
87 Lys.22.13, 27.9.
88 Lys.25.25, 29.10, 31.17.
89 Lys.25.32.
90 Lys.28.6.
91 Lys.31.6ff., 17f., 34.
92 Dem.21.21, 26, 28, 31f., 34, 40, 61, 92, 96, 114, 126f., 134, 142, 201, 211.
93 Dem.23.214.
94 Dem.24.9, 29, 99, 102, 107, 110, 138, 204; see Ps.-Dem.47.41f., 59.44, 72.
95 Lys.21.18.
96 Hyp.2.2; see 9.
97 Dem.18.323.
98 Aesch.3.152, 211, 230.

that he thought he was greater than it.[99] The Pseudo-Andocides praises Callias, who by his personal efforts brought honor to the city.[100] Demosthenes accuses Midias of thinking it shameful to fear the people, smart to care nothing for it.[101] Apollodorus announces that he did not think more of his private affairs than those of the city, but was prepared to spend money and neglect his wife and ailing mother at home rather than desert his post as trierarch and render his ship useless to the city.[102] Hyperides exclaims at the paradox of a man who was ready to be a slave to tyrants yet presumed to give orders to the demos.[103]

The demand for subordination was expressed in various forms. A prime element was the requirement of absolute submission to the magistrates and the laws.[104] In the funeral speech Pericles claims that the Athenians always listen to the magistrates and the laws.[105] The most extreme of his successors, Cleon, argues that it is better for a city to have bad laws that are observed than good ones that are ignored.[106] Obedience to the magistrates and the laws, says the Pseudo-Andocides, guarantees the general security and is the greatest safeguard of the city.[107] A man can do the city no greater harm than to overthrow its laws.[108] Demosthenes even goes so far as to contrast law and oligarchy.[109] For Hyperides too, breaking the laws is tantamount to overthrowing the democracy.[110] Aeschines sanctimoniously instructs Demosthenes to follow the laws in public life, for this preserves the democracy.[111]

The behavior of Alcibiades could be criticized from this point of view. He refused to submit to the city's laws, expecting the people instead to bend to his whims, and used violence against his wife when she appealed for protection to the archon, as the law directed; thus he advertised his contempt for the laws, the magistrates, and his fellow citizens.[112] The speaker issues a general warning against those citizens who are stronger than the archons and the laws, and insists that he himself is not ashamed to be less powerful than the laws.[113] Antiphon attacks an opponent for break-

[99] Dem.23.205f.
[100] Ps.-And.4.32.
[101] Dem.21.201.
[102] Ps.-Dem.50.63.
[103] Hyp.2.10.
[104] For the supremacy of the laws, see Lys.22.10, Dem.20.90, 21.223ff., 24.134f., Ps.-Dem.26.5, 47.48.
[105] Thuc.2.37.3.
[106] Thuc.3.37.3.
[107] Ps.-And.4.19.
[108] Dem.24.31.
[109] Dem.24.75.
[110] Hyp.1.12; for the rule of law as characteristic of democracy, see Dem.21.30, 57, 223, 22.45, 24.5, 152, 156, 216, Ps.-Dem.25.16, 20f., 42.15; for the voice of the laws as the voice of the people, see Aesch.1.4ff., 33, 179, 3.23, 169, 196f., Hyp.4.5, 5.col.2, 6.25, Dein.3.16, Lyc.138, 150.
[111] Aesch.3.23.
[112] Ps.-And.4.19, 14, 39.
[113] Ps.-And.4.35, 42.

ing the established laws, inventing his own, and believing that his caprice should prevail over the laws.[114] It is neither just nor expedient, says Demosthenes, for the people to tolerate a man who demonstrates that his personal power is greater than that of the laws; yet Midias, far from submitting to the laws, turns them upside down as he pleases.[115] Deinarchus praises Timotheus, who, unlike Demosthenes, did not ask the people for such favors as would make him more powerful than the laws.[116] Dionysodorus is attacked for making his own laws,[117] and a jury is asked by what laws it has sworn to give judgment, those of the city or those that Phormio has laid down for himself.[118]

Aristotle repeatedly asserts in *Politics* that it is characteristic of democracies that the individual be able to do what he likes, since this is held to constitute freedom.[119] At Athens this was far from the case. To do what one likes is a token of insubordination.[120] Hence in the orators and elsewhere, doing what one likes is frequently contrasted with obedience to the laws.[121] Lysias goes so far as to say that it will destroy the laws.[122] The desire to do what one likes is always attacked;[123] its associations are arrogance, lawlessness, and injustice.[124] In democratic Athens only the Athenian people and its courts are free to do what they like.[125] The individual must conform and do what he is told, *to prostattomenon*.[126] On many occasions the phrase refers only to the various financial burdens—trierarchies, liturgies, and *eisphora*—imposed by the demos on the rich.[127] But it often connotes a more general abdication of the individual will.[128] Sometimes it is associated with obedience to the laws and decrees of the people,[129] and it is frequently linked with another virtue that similarly emphasizes the subordination of

---

[114] Ant.5.12f.   [115] Dem.21.66, 91.

[116] Dein.1.17; for further criticism of the desire to be stronger than the laws, see Dem.45.67, Ps.-Dem.35.54, 40.42, 44.36, 58.15.

[117] Ps.-Dem.56.12.   [118] Ps.-Dem.46.27.

[119] Ar.*Pol.*1310a33, 1316b23, 1317b11.

[120] Apart from the instances discussed below, see Isoc.15.164, Dem.23.201, 51.16.

[121] Xen.*Hell.*2.3.52, *Mem.*4.6.12, Lys.15.1, 3, 22.5, 30.34, Isoc.8.102f., Dem.21. 91, 23.32, 80, 24.18, 47; for opposition to obedience to the council and the people, see Ps.-Dem.25.20, 26, 35.28, 42.9, 59.112, Aesch.1.34.

[122] Lys.14.11.

[123] Ps.-And.4.36, Dem.22.16, Ps.-Dem.25.25f.: it is an outrageous assumption that a man should be able to say and do what he likes in a democracy.

[124] Lys.3.5, Dem.21.170, Ps.-Dem.25.26, 42.2.

[125] Dem.20.148, 24.151, Ps.-Dem.59.4, 88.

[126] See Arist.*Eccl.*758, 762, 766f., 944f., *Plut.*914, Ps.-Dem.50.3.

[127] Lys.7.31, 21.23, 25.13, Ps.-And.4.42, Isae.6.61, 7.39, 11.50, Dem.29.24, 38.26, 51.22, Ps.-Dem.50.13.

[128] Lys.12.20, 14.20f., 45, 16.17, 18.7, Isae.4.27, 7.35, 41, 10.25, Isoc.15.150, Dem.22.63, 54.44, Ps.-Dem.47.48.

[129] Isoc.5.14, Dem.24.112, Ps.-Dem.47.48.

the individual: being orderly, *kosmios*.[130] This is linked with justice,[131] obedience to the laws,[132] and minding one's own business,[133] and it also may be contrasted with doing what one likes.[134]

The strong emphasis on the supremacy of the state over the individual that permeated democratic notions of civic virtue extended to magistrates as well as private citizens, and this no doubt goes some way toward explaining why no elite of office, such as was constituted by the Roman *nobilitas*, ever developed at Athens. It is true that Demosthenes lists generalships among possible reasons why a man might be acquitted in court,[135] while another speech from the Demosthenic corpus suggests that the sons of generals might expect some consideration, remarking that a man had been condemned although he was not merely an Athenian citizen but also the son of a man who had held the generalship.[136] But Aeschines is expounding good democratic doctrine when he observes with approval that a man is not debarred from speaking in the assembly because his forebears were not generals.[137] The democratic attitude is eloquently summed up by Demosthenes: the people, he says, does not force any man to take part in public life, but when a man convinces himself that he has the ability and puts himself forward, it welcomes him, elects him to office, and puts its affairs in his hands, and if he proves successful it will honor him accordingly.[138]

This stress on the magistrate's dependence on the goodwill of the people made it difficult for the holders of office to conceive of themselves as a class superior to the masses. Isocrates is even more forceful: men who have the wealth and leisure to engage in government should manage the commonweal like slaves, with the demos as a tyrant over them.[139] In *Peace* he defines good men as those who are worthy of the highest honors but rest content with those bestowed on them by the mass of the people.[140] Magistracies are not something to be fought over; rather they are like liturgies, a burden on those who are forced to perform them though they bring a measure of honor.[141] Even successful generals must be cut down to size: those who defeated the Persians at the Strymon were granted permission to erect three Hermae, on condition that the inscription not mention their names, so that it would appear to celebrate the achievement of the demos,

[130] Lys.12.20, 14.21, Isae.4.27, 10.25; on *kosmios* in general, see Lys.7.41, 14.29, 41, 21.19, Arist.*Plut*.89, 386ff., 562ff., Isae.fr.131, Isoc.15.24, 144, 162, 228, 18.43.

[131] Isoc.7.70.
[132] Lys.1.26.
[133] Lys.26.3, Hyp.4.21.
[134] Lys.22.19.
[135] Dem.21.148, 151.
[136] Ps.-Dem.34.50.
[137] Aesch.3.127.
[138] Dem.19.99.
[139] Isoc.7.26f.
[140] Isoc.8.89; see Dem.20.108.
[141] Isoc.12.145.

not the generals as individuals.[142] Similarly, Demosthenes describes Salamis as a victory of the Athenians, Marathon as a triumph of the city.[143]

Nevertheless it is clear that in the late fifth and the fourth centuries those who made speeches and moved decrees in the assembly were regarded as a class apart, designated as speakers, *hoi rhetores* or *hoi legontes*, or politicians, *hoi politeuomenoi*, to be distinguished from and often specifically contrasted with the nonpolitical mass, *hoi idiotai*.[144] The *politeuomenoi* often held no office; it was therefore more difficult to subdue them to the will of the people. They did not need to be elected, they could not be dismissed, and they did not have to give an account of themselves at the end of their term. But the democracy was predictably hostile to the idea that they should be treated as an elite. Aeschines insists that in a democratic state the private citizen is king by virtue of the law and his vote.[145] He passionately urges the people to preserve its control over the politicians and to prick the bubble of their arrogance, for no man could ever try to overthrow the democracy unless he had proved himself more powerful than the people's courts.[146] Demosthenes too recalls the days when the people was master of the politicians and kept all benefits in its gift, while individuals were content to accept such honors and offices as the demos saw fit to bestow.[147] In the speech against Androtion, he complains that while the people tries to uphold the laws, the rhetors see to it that most criminals go unpunished, behaving like slaves who are ungrateful to their masters for their freedom, and urges the people to bring the politicians under the laws, regardless of whether this will hurt their self-esteem.[148]

3

Despite the democracy's theoretical rejection of elitism based on birth or wealth, rich men and men of distinguished descent continued to occupy

---

[142] Aesch.3.183.

[143] Dem.23.198; for Marathon, see Arist.*Eq*.1334.

[144] See Arist.*Ach*.38, 680, *Eq*.60, 325, 358, 425, 880, 1350, *Thesm*.292, 382, 530, *Ran*.367, *Eccl*.195, *Plut*.30, 379, 567; Lys. 18.16, 22.2, 30.22, 31.27; And.3.1; Isoc.5.2, 81, 140, 7.14, 8.5, 26, 54f., 124, 129, 12.12, 15, 13.9, 14, 14.3, 38, 15.30, 105, 132, 136, 138, 144, 185, 190, 200, 231, 234, 16.7, *Ep*.8.7; Dem.2.29, 3.22, 30f., 8.32, 10.70, 13.35, 18.45, 173, 308, 318f., 19.298, 20.74, 132, 21.189f., 207, 22.30, 36f., 66, 70, 23.4, 147, 184, 201, 209, 24.66, 112, 123f., 142, 147, 155, 173, 193; Ps.-Dem.25.40, 97, 26.3, 18, 48.24, 52.28, 58.23, 59.43; Aesch.1.7f., 25, 34, 165, 171, 186, 195, 2.74, 161, 3.2, 4, 7, 9, 20, 130, 231ff., 252f.; Hyp.1.20, 4.1, 4, 8, 22, 27, 30, 5.col.12, 24; Dein.1.4, 71, 88, 90, 98, 100ff., 112, 2.26, 3.19; Lyc.31; Ar.*Pol*.1305a10; Plut.*Phoc*.7. See Jones, *AD*, 128, 130.

[145] Aesch.3.233.   [146] Aesch.3.235.

[147] Dem.3.30, 23.209.

[148] Dem.24.123ff., 131; see 142, Ps.-Dem.26.23.

the highest positions in the state. So democratic ideology was forced to assimilate the claims of birth, wealth, and individual achievement to its own ideals of equality, conformity, and subordination. The notion of personal distinction conveyed by noble ancestors gave way to that of descent from men who had done some service to the city.[149] Thus Demosthenes praises the family of Hipponicus, which had to its credit many benefits conferred on the demos.[150]

To diminish the glory that an individual might derive from his personal successes in peace or war, these were praised only as evidence that their author was useful to the city, *khresimos tei polei*.[151] This is a far cry from the ideal of the young Athenian aristocrats at the end of the fifth century, as it is recorded in the works of Xenophon. Their aim, repeatedly stated in *Memorabilia*, is perhaps most eloquently expressed in *Symposium*: through manly courage to benefit one's friends and magnify one's country by defeating its enemies in battle, and so to achieve renown among Greeks and barbarians alike.[152] Here, though a man's accomplishments bring power and fame to his city, the old respect for personal qualities still survives; there is a spirit of pride, of unashamed delight in individual achievement and its rewards, that is a world away from the desire to be a useful tool of the state, which democracy put in place of the aristocratic ideal.

In *First Philippic* Demosthenes demands that every man make himself useful to the city.[153] In his speech for Phormio he instructs the clerk to read a list of the occasions on which his client has made himself useful to the city.[154] The various ways in which a man might be useful are cataloged in one of his tirades against Aeschines: the provision of horses, trierarchies, military service, the training of choruses, the performance of other liturgies, and the payment of *eisphora*.[155] Contrasting Aeschines and himself, he says that Aeschines never showed himself useful at all, whereas he had done everything that it behooved a good citizen to do.[156] Later in the speech he again judges himself by his services to the city before applying the same standard to Aeschines and ending with the rhetorical question "In what have you ever been useful at all?"[157] Others felt differently. Deinarchus remarks that the general Charidemus had made himself useful to the people and proposes to judge Demosthenes by the same standard.[158] His conclu-

---

[149] Cf.Aesch.3.169.   [150] Dem.21.144.
[151] Apart from the passages discussed below, see Lys.14.43, 20.23, And.2.18, Isoc. 15.161, 165, 305, Dem.20.48, 51f., 22.4, 36.57, 38.25, 54.44, Ps.-Dem.25.31, 50.2, 64, 58.64, Aesch.1.11, 3.161.
[152] Xen.*Symp*.7.38; see *Mem*.1.2.48, 2.6.25, 3.7.1f., 4.5.10, 5.3.4.
[153] Dem.4.7; see 8.70.   [154] Dem.36.56.
[155] Dem.19.282.   [156] Dem.18.180.
[157] Dem.18.301ff.; see 19.281.   [158] Dein.1.32, 35.

sion is that throughout his public career Demosthenes had been quite use-less.[159] Precedent was duly invented for the principle: Aeschines ascribes to Solon the aim of ensuring that a boy who had been properly brought up would, when he became a man, be useful to the city.[160] There is only one reason, he says elsewhere, for an honest politician to ask for rewards from the people: because he has been responsible for some benefit to the city.[161]

Demosthenes' list of ways of making oneself useful emphasizes the use of wealth. Aristotle even goes so far as to define the rich as those whose property is substantial enough to qualify them for the performance of liturgies.[162] Isaeus insists that a client is not a useless rich man, for he per-forms liturgies and pays taxes.[163] In the *Antidosis* Isocrates attacks men who inherit great wealth yet do not make themselves in any way useful to the city.[164] Elsewhere he argues strongly that wealth exists only for the benefit of the people.[165] A speech from the Demosthenic corpus also puts forward the view that the rich have a duty to make themselves useful to their fellow citizens, and attacks those who are wealthy but have never made themselves useful to the people.[166] Even when the rich staked a claim to special consideration, it was justified in terms of the services they per-formed for the people with their wealth.[167]

Under the constitution of the Five Thousand, after the fall of the Four Hundred, full civil rights were to be restricted to those who served as hoplites and supplied their own arms—the type of moderate system that Aristotle calls simply *politeia*.[168] The *Athenaion Politeia* preserves the so-called constitution of Draco, a propaganda document of the period which recalled that in the ancient Athenian state, before the time of Solon, this limitation of the franchise had been in force.[169] The champion of this form of government was Theramenes; Xenophon records his views. He was opposed, he says, to both extreme democracy and extreme oligarchy; he had always believed that the best constitution was that which gave power to those who could give useful service as cavalry or hoplites.[170] So too the propaganda of 411 claimed that the right to a say in public affairs should be reserved to those who were most able to make themselves useful with their property and their persons.[171] It is striking that what was clearly an

159 Dein.1.96f.
160 Aesch.1.11.
161 Aesch.3.236.
162 Ar.*Pol.*1291b33.
163 Isae.11.50.
164 Isoc.15.251.
165 Isoc.18.61ff.
166 Ps.-Dem.42.22, 31.
167 Dem.21.153; see 21.208.
168 Thuc.8.97.1, *AthP.*33.1f., Ar.*Pol.*1265b26, 1279b4, 1297b1.
169 *AthP.*4.2.
170 Xen.*Hell.*2.3.48.
171 Thuc.8.65.3; a similar formulation is in *AthP.*29.5; see 49.2.

attempt to create a formal elite was presented in terms that accept and indeed emphasize the democratic principle that the individual citizen existed only to further the interests of the city: the claim to privilege is defended on the ground that those who would enjoy it are best equipped to serve as instruments of the city's will.

The cliché of service with property and person, *tois khremasi kai toi somati*, is frequent in democratic contexts.[172] The best man, says Andocides, is he who has the courage to risk his property and person to do his fellow citizens some good.[173] Demosthenes makes the plea that all men be prepared *tois somasi kai tais ousiais leitourgesai*.[174] Elsewhere the political climate of his time, when the Athenians were becoming more and more reluctant to incur the dangers and discomforts of military service, leads him to place a premium on bodies and to praise those who showed their patriotism by means of personal service, not merely money or words.[175]

Personal courage also was brought within the democratic framework. To show bravery was to be prepared to incur danger on behalf of the people.[176] Aeschines quotes an epigram in praise of the men who had exposed themselves to danger to restore the democracy.[177] Conversely, those who are unwilling to face danger "with the others" are criticized.[178] The idea of solidarity in the face of a common threat is prominent in the formula "to share in the dangers of the city," which is particularly common in Lysias.[179] To have shared in the dangers of the city is proof of a properly democratic frame of mind, while to accuse a man of not playing his part is yet another way of isolating an opponent and demonstrating his ill will toward the people and the city. Thus Aeschines says that the Persian gold meant for Athens has all found its way into Demosthenes' pocket, while the people is left with the dangers.[180]

The quest for honor, *philotimia*, another aristocratic and individualist pursuit, was also redefined to conform with democratic requirements— enthusiasm in carrying out the tasks imposed by the people.[181] Thus Isaeus

---

[172] See Lys.19.58, 25.4, 31.15, Ps.-Lys.6.47, Ps.-Dem.42.25.
[173] And.2.18.
[174] Dem.10.28.
[175] Dem.21.145; there is a similar emphasis on service in person in 21.165, and by Apollodorus in Ps.-Dem.50.59.
[176] Lys.3.47, 4.13, 5.4, 16.18, 18.7, 21.3, 11, Isoc.8.47, 16.36, 41, Ps.-Dem.50.21, 59, 58.67, Aesch.2.147, 183.
[177] Aesch.3.190.
[178] Isoc.18.64, Dein.1.32, Lyc.5, 147; for the shame of avoiding danger when the city calls, see Lys.16.13, 17, 30.26 (when the people sailed out to face danger, Nicomachus stayed at home rewriting the laws of Solon), 31.7, 10.
[179] Lys.10.27, 14.7, 16.3, 12, 18.19, 24.25, 28.12f.; see also Lyc.48.
[180] Aesch. 3.240.
[181] See Lys.21.22, 26.3.

claims that a client did not lack *philotimia*, for he was willing to serve as trierarch, to train choruses, and to fight, to do everything he was told to do by the people.[182] Demosthenes too associates *philotimia* with training choruses, serving as a trierarch, paying *eisphora*, and being useful to the city.[183] One should not judge *philotimia*, he says elsewhere, on whether a man builds splendid houses or acquires many serving wenches and fine furniture, but on things that the mass of the people can share.[184] Midias claims that he gave the people a trireme; if he did so out of *philotimia*, then the people should show a proper degree of gratitude.[185] So in general *philotimia* is reduced to a readiness to spend money on the city.[186]

The only elite that spokesmen of the democracy were ever prepared to countenance was an informal one of merit. Pericles claims in the funeral speech that the Athenian way of life allowed for an elite of excellence.[187] Isocrates says that this had at least once been the case: those with the greatest ability had been entrusted with control of affairs by the people, though in his own day he saw fools giving orders to men more intelligent than themselves.[188] He celebrates the great leaders of the past—Cleisthenes, Miltiades, Themistocles, and Pericles—who excelled not only in birth and reputation but also in intelligence and oratorical skill.[189] Again in the *Panathenaicus* he remarks that any constitution is at its best when power is granted to those citizens who are most capable and intelligent.[190]

But despite these protestations, it is clear that far from accepting the claim of the talented to constitute an elite, even an elite whose position ultimately depended on popular approval, the Athenian people looked with the utmost suspicion on men of unusual intelligence and ability. Thucydides puts into the mouth of Cleon, the "watchdog of the democracy," the view that a mindless devotion to law and order is more useful than undisciplined cleverness.[191] Cleon goes on to attack men who want to prove that they are wiser than the law, and praises those who distrust their own intelligence and so accept the laws as cleverer than they are.[192]

The "Old Oligarch" confirms that the democrats thought in this way: the democracy, he says, valued goodwill much more highly than excellence that might be hostile.[193] Sometimes this attitude was justified by the event: the *Athenaion Politeia* observes that the leaders of the oligarchic revolution of 411, Peisander, Antiphon, and Theramenes, were all believed to excel

182 Isae.7.35; see 39.
183 Dem.18.257; see Ps.-Dem.42.25.
184 Dem.21.159.   185 Dem.21.160.
186 Dem.51.22, Aesch.3.19.   187 Thuc.2.37.1.
188 Isoc.7.22, 27, 15.72.   189 Isoc.15.308f.
190 Isoc.12.132f.; see 143.   191 Thuc.3.37.3.
192 Thuc.3.37.4.   193 Ps.-Xen.*AP* 1.7; see 2.19.

in intelligence and judgment.[194] Thucydides says that the masses regarded Antiphon with suspicion because of his talent.[195] Isocrates complains that the people rejects those who are more intelligent than itself, thinking that men devoid of brains must be more democratic than men of sense.[196] Thus Timotheus suffered for his talents at the hands of men who resented anyone naturally superior to themselves.[197] Even Isocrates was open to attack because of his ability as a writer and teacher.[198] Plutarch too offers several examples of the people's suspicion and distrust of ability. Pericles' music teacher, Damon, was ostracized because he was thought to be outstandingly intelligent, though he tried to use his profession as a smokescreen for his talent.[199] Nicias observed that the demos made use of those who excelled in oratory and judgment, but was suspicious of them and on its guard against their cleverness.[200]

This rejection of the idea of an elite of talent mirrors a wider distrust of excellence in any sphere that was fundamental to the outlook of democratic Athens. Themistocles, says Plutarch, was ostracized, for the people was accustomed to do this to any man whose power it thought to be so great as to be incompatible with democratic equality. The institution of ostracism he calls a sop to envy, which delights in cutting outstanding men down to size.[201] Again in *Aristides* he remarks that the demos disliked those who enjoyed a reputation greater than that of the mass.[202] There was a fear that Pericles would try to make himself a tyrant, for his superiority was thought to be too great to be accommodated within the confines of the democracy.[203] This fear of tyranny was the spur that drove the Athenian people to set its face against any form of elitism: prudent men, says the Pseudo-Andocides, are always on guard against those who rise too high, for of such are tyrants made.[204] It is ironic, but perhaps not surprising, that in proclaiming this watchword the guardians of democracy were only following the advice that one great tyrant had given long before to another: destroy any of the citizens who excel.[205]

[194] AthP.32.2.
[195] Thuc.8.68.1.
[196] Isoc.8.13.
[197] Isoc.15.138.
[198] Isoc.15.5, 15f., 33, 168. What the average man thought of the benefits of higher education as purveyed by Isocrates is nicely epitomized by a speaker whose opponent was one of his pupils: it does not worry him, he says, if a man wants to be a sophist and put money in Isocrates' pocket—he would be crazy to care about such things (Ps.-Dem. 35.15, 40).
[199] Plut.Arist.1, Per.4.
[200] Plut.Nic.6.
[201] Plut.Them.22; see Plut.Nic.11, Ar.Pol.1284a19, 37, 1302b15.
[202] Plut.Arist.7.
[203] Plut.Per.16.
[204] Ps.-And.4.24.
[205] Ar.Pol.1311a20; see 1284a30, 1313a40.

To summarize: first the aristocratic elite of archaic Athens had made way for the timocratic elite of Solon; then the twin bastions of the timocracy, the archonship and the Areopagus, had fallen, the first to the lot, the second to the reform of Ephialtes. Payment for service on the juries and the council meant that the equality proclaimed by the democracy could to some degree be enjoyed by the poor in practice as well as in theory. Meanwhile, to combat the hereditary belief in their own superiority still cherished by the noble and the rich, democracy fostered an outlook on life that was designed to undermine elitism and to propagate instead an ideal of subordination and uniformity. The attempt was only partially successful. The people still turned for leadership to aristocrats and men of substance; the repeated insistence of democratic speakers that birth and wealth deserve no consideration is ample proof that they continued to receive it. So the democracy salvaged its pride by redefining the old elitist virtues in terms that it found more acceptable. If a man based his claim to be a leader of the people on his noble lineage and ancestral wealth, that was plainly a flouting of equality. But if his ancestors had done some service to the people and he himself was prepared to be useful to the city, then the city might condescend without loss of face to reward him by exploiting his talents and drawing on his purse. In this way the Athenian democracy learned to reconcile its articles of faith with the social realities and practical demands of its day-to-day existence.

The Aristocracy of the
Roman Republic

RICHARD E. MITCHELL

Roman aristocrats, to borrow a phrase from C. Wright Mills, were "simply those who have more of what there is to have."[1] They were the wealthiest, the most influential, the most powerful, the most prestigious, and the best-educated citizens of the Republic. They were magistrates, commanders, governors, priests, and judges, not to mention poets and historians. In every respect they belonged to the upper class and were dominant in the Roman world. Principally, however, the aristocracy was concerned with politics, and success in politics determined status within the aristocracy.

Although they formed a homogeneous group when compared to the rest of society, not all aristocrats were equally potent. Senatorial families constituted the broader aristocratic group, but among senators the nobles were preeminent. Nobility was originally reserved for those whose ancestors obtained curule office, but by the second century B.C. only those families who reached the consulship were nobles. But aristocratic equality did not exist even among the nobles. Only a few families were continuously successful, holding a disproportionate share of the offices and shaping the decisions relating to domestic and foreign affairs. The elevation of non-aristocrats was controlled by the same families. Mobility into the aristocracy was stimulated by social, economic, and political changes, but was possible only for those wealthy citizens personally connected with established aristocrats who supported their elevation. In reality, mobility occurred as a consequence of the aristocrat's desire to retain control.

[1] *The Power Elite* (New York, 1959), 9. Citations of both ancient and modern literature will be kept to a minimum, and no attempt will be made to argue the many problems with which this essay deals. The notes are used primarily to direct the reader unfamiliar with the scholarship to modern literature where he will find additional bibliography and references to the ancient sources. Although my selection is arbitrary, my indebtedness to other scholars, often unnoted, will be obvious to ancient historians who chance to read the essay.

An elaborate network of personal relationships was the foundation of the dominant nobility's political influence and power. Supported by kin and client, they frequently intermarried or formed connections with other aristocrats or men of property. Some relationships were inherited and recognized by law, such as the patron-client, and in this sense aristocratic status was a birthright. Descendants claimed the fame, fortune, and following of ancestors, pointed to traditional practices and ancestral accomplishments to secure support, and insisted that success was justified by their high birth and merit. Societal, legal, and institutional practices also contributed to the maintenance of aristocratic control and privilege. The urban nature of the aristocrat, his position before the law, and his privilege and influence in assemblies secured his position. The Senate in particular was the mainstay of aristocratic control, but even it declined in power and influence in the second century as individual aristocrats carried their own personal politics to a logical conclusion.

Since support could be maintained or increased only by continued political success, aristocrats pursued personal goals often with ruthless self-interest. Personal connections with other aristocrats were informal, reciprocal, and fluid, but were effective in securing votes, passing bills, and obtaining favors. One acted responsibly toward one's followers and friends, and personal obligations determined political behavior, but few politicians practiced responsibility to citizens, allies, or provincials. Political decisions were often made in the interests of a clique, and the goals, policy, and general functions of government were similarly determined. The consequence of a politics based upon personal considerations was not merely personal but affected all of Roman society.

In early Roman society, with its noticeable absence of state regulations, legal and institutional safeguards, and protections for the individual, the weak naturally looked to the strong: son to father, kin to kin, client to patron, poor to rich, friend to friend, and noncitizen to citizen. As P. A. Brunt points out, such practices "could only have originated in a society in which economic and political power was very unevenly distributed."[2] Wealth, principally landholding, was the primary source of power. Throughout Roman Republican history, only the wealthy could afford to maintain an extended family unit and thereby derive support from kinsmen, have the economic and personal power and influence to obtain and support a large number of clients, or have the leisure to hold unpaid political and religious office. Similarly, military service in the cavalry or hoplite infantry was based upon one's property qualification, and the

[2] *Social Conflicts in the Roman Republic* (London, 1971), 49.

military units of the regal and early Republican period were virtually synonymous with the wealthier citizenry. The individual's economic status ultimately determined both his responsibility to the state and the extent of his power, influence, and privilege within the state. But among the wealthy, great weight was given to one's birth and to the number and nature of one's dependents. Those who traced their ancestry into the regal or legendary Roman past had the inside track on aristocratic positions. Both their aristocratic claims and their citizenship were based upon an ancient birthright.

In earliest Rome, membership in the community was determined by one's membership in a *curia*.[3] Later, before the Republic began, formal citizenship was based upon membership in a territorial unit, an urban or rural tribe.[4] Normally one was a citizen by birth, but one could also be a Roman citizen by one of many special governmental or individual grants. But in any period those whose citizenship was of recent vintage were at a disadvantage, and this was particularly true for the freedman and his descendants. Thus while citizenship and wealth were necessary to gain entry into the aristocracy, it mattered greatly whether one had old, inherited wealth or was a new citizen or a parvenu.

Most patricians must have been citizens of Rome by the beginning of the Republic. Tradition says that when Rome was ruled by kings, the kings appointed a council of elder advisers, senators, who were the heads (*patres*, or fathers) of the most prosperous and powerful *gentes*. These *patres*, or patricians, were aristocrats even under the monarchy.[5] As *paterfamilias*, the head of the family, each man exercised total control over his family,

[3] Originally the *curiae* had military, political, and religious functions most of which they eventually lost to other assemblies. To fight, to worship, and to assemble encompassed the rights of citizenship: *arma sumere, sacris adesse, concilium inire* (Tacitus, *Germania*, 6.6). See R. M. Ogilvie, *A Commentary on Livy, Books 1–5* (Oxford, 1965), 80, 408f.; Arnaldo Momigliano, "An Interim Report on the Origins of Rome," *Journal of Roman Studies*, 53 (1963), 108ff. (hereafter abbreviated *J.R.S.*); and the out-of-date but useful George W. Botsford, *The Roman Assemblies* (New York, 1909), 2ff., 168ff.

[4] L. R. Taylor, *The Voting Districts of the Roman Republic* (Rome, 1960).

[5] The problem of the origin of the patriciate is only part of the larger problem of the origin of the Republic. Discussions of ancient sources and modern theories are found in Botsford, *Assemblies*, 16ff.; H. J. Rose, "Patricians and Plebeians at Rome," *J.R.S.*, 12 (1922), 106ff.; *Cambridge Ancient History*, vol. 7 (Cambridge, reprint 1964); Hugh Last, "The Servian Reforms," *J.R.S.*, 35 (1945), 30ff.; Momigliano, *J.R.S.* (1963), 95ff.; Einar Gjerstad, *Legends and Facts of Early Rome* (Lund, 1962); Ogilvie, *Commentary*; Andrew Alföldi, *Early Rome and the Latins* (Ann Arbor, 1965); *Les origines de la république romaine: Entretiens sur l'antiquité classique*, 13, Fondation Hardt (Geneva, 1967). On the question of the patrician equation with the royal bodyguard, see Andreas Alföldi, *Der frührömische Reiteradel und seine Ehrenabzeichen* (Baden-Baden, 1952), and "(Centuria) procum patricium," *Historia*, 17 (1968), 444ff.; but cf. Arnaldo Momigliano, "Procum patricium," *J.R.S.*, 56 (1966), 16ff., and his review of Alföldi's *Early Rome*, in *J.R.S.*, 57 (1967), 211ff.

including adult married sons, over the religious rites and ceremonies practiced by the individual family, and over the family's collective wealth or
property.[6] Those upon whom others depended naturally institutionalized
these relationships, and the strong, influential men of property assumed
the positions of leadership once state institutions emerged and claimed
such positions as a right of birth. There is no truth to the argument that
patricians were the only original citizens, that they made up the complete
Roman aristocracy, or that they totally monopolized all governmental positions. However, as a group they were the most prosperous, the most
prestigious, and the most successful politically of the early citizens of
Rome, and the first to claim by right of birth the honors they received and
the privileges they enjoyed.

Possibly the patricians, in their capacity as military men or political
advisers, backed by their kin and clients, led the successful overthrow of
the last king, Tarquin. Perhaps, on the other hand, as members of his council, the Senate, they were merely in the best position to capitalize on his
exile and seize the reins of government. Once in command, certain patrician *gentes* began to develop their claims to exclusive power and tried
to establish their hereditary right to monopolize all important state positions and attendant privileges.[7] They reinforced their claims by appealing
to tradition, to their family's experience, expertise, and knowledge, and
to the propriety of their socioreligious standards and practices. As usual in
preindustrial societies, precedent, *mos maiorum* at Rome, was set forth as
the example to follow.[8] It dictated the acceptance of the status quo: if it
was good enough for the father, it was good enough for the son. The ancient
authorities clearly thought only patricians could be magistrates, senators,
and priests during the first years of the Republic. Certainly they were the
dominant group in society, and some patricians apparently tried to close
the ranks of the patriciate and thus the access of nonpatricians to public
positions. The last patrician *gens* created, the *gens Claudia*, was supposedly
added when Attius Clausus (Appius Claudius) moved to Rome from his
Sabine home about 504 B.C.[9] If other patrician *gentes* were added later,

---

[6] *Cambridge Ancient History*, vol. 7, 414ff.; H. F. Jolowicz, *Historical Introduction to the Study of Roman Law* (Cambridge, 1961), 112ff.

[7] Cf. Last, *J.R.S.* (1945), 31ff.; Momigliano, *J.R.S.* (1963), 117ff.

[8] For example, Cicero, *Epistulae ad familiares*, 4.3.1: *nam, quod exemplo fit, id
etiam iure fieri putant*—although Cicero is referring to a bad precedent having the force
of law (right). Cf. Gideon Sjoberg, *The Preindustrial City* (New York, 1965), 220ff.

[9] Livy, 2.16.4. See Ogilvie, *Commentary*, 273ff.; Taylor, *Voting Districts*, 6, 35ff.
The *gens Claudia* was *maior*, not *minor*, but the significance of the distinction is obscure
(cf. Ogilvie, *Commentary*, 145ff.).

they have left no record. It is safe to assume that the number of patrician *gentes* was fixed early in the Republican period.

On the other hand, according to popular myth, plebeians were all clients or dependents of the patricians.[10] But plebeians were citizens and had the same or similar religious practices as patricians.[11] Even if they were not originally magistrates, senators, or priests, the sine qua non of status in the community, wealth, could not be totally denied all nonpatricians, especially in the face of the territorial expansion of the state and the gradual sophistication of urban life. Thus wealthy plebeians also supported joint families, attracted a body of potentially powerful friends and clients, and used their ever-increasing importance to the state to win concessions from the patricians. The literary tradition, late in origin and much influenced by events of the post-Gracchan period, interpreted this period of conflict between patricians and plebeians as a contest between polar opposites: "The Struggle of the Orders" (509–287 B.C.). Normally plebeians are defined negatively, as nonpatricians and the reverse of what patricians are. Similarly, the application of the name *plebeian* to the poor, the great unwashed, of the late Republic resulted in this meaning's being applied anachronistically to those plebeians who led the struggle against patricians in the early Republic. But the struggle makes sense only if there were wealthy plebeians who desired a share of the privileges and honors that the patricians were attempting to monopolize, and if some plebeians were not so dissimilar to patricians as the sources maintain.

Evidence suggests that certain plebeians had been successful under the kings, and plebeian names are found among those who held magistracies in the early Republic.[12] This limited and debated evidence indicates that the gentilic pride and exclusiveness of the patricians were not totally effective against plebeians in the regal period or in the first half-century of the Republic, that the attempt by the patriciate to make itself a closed order and to claim a hereditary domination of the state positions originated later than did the Republic, and that this attempt was the consequence of plebeian threats to patrician power and influence.[13]

Moreover, the almost immediate repeal (445 B.C.) of a law of the

---

[10] Cicero, *De re publica*, 2.9.16; Dionysius of Halicarnassus, 2.9.12. Cf. Livy, 2.35ff., 55ff., and Ogilvie, *Commentary*, 293ff., 309ff.

[11] Rose, *J.R.S.* (1922), 106ff., has shown that the original distinction between patricians and plebeians was economic.

[12] Momigliano, *J.R.S.* (1963), 117f.; Ogilvie, *Commentary*, 293ff.

[13] Cf. Last, *J.R.S.* (1945), 30ff. Ogilvie, *Commentary*, 294, says, "the tribunate was created, not because the plebeians were politically weak, but because they were politically strong."

Twelve Tables (450 B.C.) that forbade intermarriage between patricians and plebeians[14] is obvious evidence for the acceptance of some plebeian mobility by the patrician aristocracy. Unquestionably some patricians held to a policy of exclusiveness and tried to monopolize the state machinery and attendant privileges, but they ran the risk of political failure in the face of combined patrician-plebeian opposition. Furthermore, even if not prohibited from intermarriage with plebeians, the limited number of patricians could not have maintained their original strength. Their ranks were depleted by shouldering a disproportionate share of the military responsibility during the early Republic, by the normal high rate of infant mortality, and by the fact that some must have slumped into poverty. In sum, the patricians could never hope to monopolize wealth, thus status, or to assume total responsibility for administering, expanding, and protecting the state. At Rome it would always be possible for some nonaristocrats to translate their wealth into social status, influence, and political office.

In fact as early as 494 B.C. plebeians had gone on strike, refusing to do military service until certain demands were met. The most important concession obtained was the right to elect their own plebeian officials, tribunes, who numbered ten by the middle of the century. By 400 B.C. plebeians had held the aedileship, quaestorship, and military tribunate with consular *imperium*, and more than likely some had been admitted to the Senate. The ancients viewed this trend from a distance and interpreted it, particularly the creation of the tribunate, as the beginning of a state within a state, the destruction of a previous stage of political harmony, and the advent of seditious activity.[15] Actually it was the foundation for the development of a plebeian aristocracy, which gradually coalesced with the patrician during the course of the struggle of the orders.

Many plebeian *gentes* successful in obtaining offices in the fifth and early fourth centuries apparently were established aristocrats, since they were among the first to obtain the consulship once it was opened to plebeians in 366 B.C. Of the nearly thirty plebeian *gentes* that obtained a consulship from 366 B.C. to the First Punic War, nearly two-thirds traced their ancestry to plebeians who held office prior to 380 B.C.[16] These *gentes* are among the most politically successful in the Republic. Even if this early evi-

---

[14] Consult T. Robert S. Broughton, *The Magistrates of the Roman Republic*, I–II (New York, 1951–52), for an extensive citation of ancient sources for dated events mentioned in this essay. F. Cornelius, *Untersuchungen zur frühen römischen Geschichte* (Munich, 1940), 113ff., is one of the few to attempt an analysis of the political groupings in fifth-century Rome.

[15] For example, Cicero, *De legibus*, 3.8.19.

[16] Unless otherwise noted, this and subsequent discussions on the extent and nature of officeholding by patrician and plebeian *gentes* are based upon lists compiled from Broughton, *Magistrates*.

dence is discounted, we must assume that certain *gentes* were already powerful enough to win considerable electoral success once offices were opened to them. In little more than a half-century following 366 B.C., plebeians gained a share of all the chief political and religious offices.

As a joint patrician-plebeian aristocracy developed, the tribunate, the source of power the plebeians used earlier to gain parity with the patricians, became little more than another "establishment" office. Though it was late in the second century that ex-tribunes were admitted to the Senate,[17] the office had long been used as a stepping stone to higher positions. There was certainly no stigma associated with holding the office. Patricians could not hold it, but established plebeian aristocrats did seek it, and many used the tribunate to protect senatorial supremacy and aristocratic advantage.

A quick reckoning from T. Robert S. Broughton's work shows that by the beginning of the Second Punic War, 10 ex-tribunes had reached the consulship, while the next 150 years produced over 50 tribunes who went on to the consulship and as many who reached the praetorship. Moreover, approximately 75 percent of all tribunes who became consuls belonged to *gentes* with previous generations of state service to their credit. Of the other 25 percent, few were successful beyond this single attainment of the consulship. As with other little-known consular *gentes*, such men needed assistance to win elections and could not sustain support beyond their own immediate person or generation. Of those who did not come from established *gentes*, C. Marius (consul, 107, 104–100, and 86 B.C.) and M. Curius Dentatus (consul, 290, 274–73 B.C.) stand out, but few of the others were independent sources of influence in their own day, and all needed aristocratic support on the way up. Indeed, Marius' connections with the aristocracy are well known.[18]

An aristocracy of officeholders had emerged, and plebeians merely continued what patricians had started: the hereditary domination of all important facets of Roman life by a few *gentes*.[19] It is a common assumption that at no particular period in Roman Republican history did the number

---

[17] See A. E. Astin, *Scipio Aemilianus* (Oxford, 1967), 354f.

[18] On Curius, see Friedrich Münzer, *Römische Adelsparteien und Adelsfamilien* (Stuttgart, 1920), 61f., 110. For Marius, see E. Badian, "Marius and the Nobles," *Durham University Journal* (1964), 141ff.; Thomas F. Carney, *A Biography of C. Marius: Proceedings of the African Classical Association*, supp. 1 (1961), 15ff.

[19] Münzer, *Römische Adels.*, 182, 322, argues that the patricians admitted some plebeians in order to remain in control and to avoid a greater influx of plebeians. F. Cassola, *I gruppi politici romani nel III secolo a.C.* (Trieste, 1962), 8ff., rightly insists that political conflicts were between aristocratic cliques, not between patricians and plebeians. Arnold J. Toynbee, *Hannibal's Legacy*, I (Oxford, 1965), 311ff., has a valuable discussion and bibliography but too much about democratic movements and radical politics.

of powerful *gentes* exceed 20. If we calculate the consulships obtained by the 22 most successful *gentes*, patrician and plebeian, the result will show that they monopolized nearly two-thirds of all Republican consulships.

Although plebeians were admitted as partners in virtually all state positions by the end of the fourth century, patricians continued to hold their share of the highest and most prestigious positions for some time despite a decrease in their numbers. Of the approximately 48 patrician *gentes* known in the fifth century, only 16 claimed consulships after 366 B.C. Of these, 3 held a single consulship or had a single generation of success, while 3 others virtually disappeared from public life for a century or more. But not all patrician *gentes* were equal in power and influence. Of those successful in the earlier Republican period, only 12 remained even moderately effective politically after 366 B.C. Members of these same 12 *gentes* held 80 percent of all consulships obtained by patricians and 45 percent of all Republican consulships. Furthermore, the 5 most victorious *gentes* monopolized over 25 percent of all consular offices and over 45 percent of those held only by patricians. During the first half of the first century B.C., only 8 patrician *gentes* were successful in winning the consulship; of these, only 5 held more than one. The many families of the *gens Cornelia* alone claim almost half of the patrician total in this period.

The evidence concerning plebeian *gentes* indicates a similar concentration of strength. Although there are more than 80 known plebeian *gentes* that claimed consular office between 366 and 49 B.C., 9 *gentes* held approximately 40 percent of all consulships held by plebeians after 366 B.C., and 6 of these claimed nearly 30 percent of that total. Such domination is surprising, since hardly a decade passed from 366 to 49 B.C. when a new plebeian *gens* did not rise to the consulship for the first time.

An analysis of the *gentes*, however, shows that continuous power and influence were retained by only a few clans. Only 5 *gentes* survived from the fourth century to the first century as consular, by which I mean they were able to claim at least one consulship in each century following the fourth. Similarly, only 5 *gentes* rising to the consulship in the third century continued to reach the consulship in each succeeding century. Yet 65 percent of all plebeian consulships were held by *gentes* that appeared as consular between 366 and 284 B.C. In fact the 8 most successful plebeian consular *gentes* had all held at least their first consulship less than a century after the consulship was opened to the plebeians. In a given century, the number of plebeian *gentes* to rise to the consulship for the first time was equal to the number that disappeared as consular. Of the plebeian *gentes* known from the fourth through the second centuries, almost half did not reach the consulship in any century subsequent to their initial appearance as consuls. Eighty percent of these *gentes* held no more than two consulships, and 45 percent acquired only a single consular post. The success of such *gentes* was frequently limited to a single individual or at most to a single generation.

Since no new patrician *gentes* were created, the plebeian aristocracy gradually became the majority group. Between the mid-fourth and mid-third centuries, Rome rapidly extended her franchise along with her territory in Italy, resulting in the relatively rapid growth of new plebeian *gentes*. Many were enfranchised Latins, Campanians, Etruscans, and other Italians.[20] By the end of the Second Punic War, plebeians had attained a clear majority. Due to the declining number of patricians, plebeians were elected to both consulships for the first time in 172 B.C., and held both consular positions fifty more times before the dictatorship of Caesar.

Through continuous political success a family or *gens* built personal connections and developed the broad reputation that guaranteed victory at the polls. Once well established, both patrician and plebeian *gentes* could again attain high office even after a decade, a generation, or, in a few cases, a century or more of obscurity. This must be attributed to their established personal connections and reputation, stimulated by a change in fortune.[21] Many an individual rose to preeminence, but for lack of off-spring, financial resources, or continuous political support, his *gens* dropped into obscurity in the next generation or so. Clearly the electoral success of such an individual was often not due to his own personal influence and reputation. Those who became the first of their *gens* to hold the consulship owed their success to the political clout of friends and associates. Even those few individuals honored for important activities or services or for particular talents would rarely have succeeded had it not been for aristo-cratic support or sponsorship. Decades or generations were usually spent occupying lower state positions and acquiring sufficient political support and public reputation to attain the chief magistracies.

The first member of a family to win election to public office was called a *novus homo*, a new man. Modern scholars too often apply the term loosely to the first in a family to obtain the consulship, although he often had ancestors who spent years in lower positions prior to the family's first

[20] Münzer, *Römische Adels.*, 47–97 passim, is helpful but widely speculative at times on the foreign origin of plebeian families. His comments on intermarriage among the orders, however, are sound, even if some of his examples are less than convincing.

[21] For example, the patrician *gentes* of Catiline (*Sergia*), Caesar (*Iulia*), and Sulla's family of the *gens Cornelia* were not continuously successful (cf. Broughton, *Magistrates*, II, "Index of Careers").

consulship.[22] By applying such a meaning to new men, scholars have created a false impression of mobility. Many plebeian families were represented on the consular *fasti*, but not many of these men were the first in their families to hold office or to be senatorial.

Given the lack of specific information concerning the ancestors of many of those who were the first of their *gens* to reach the consulship, perhaps we should strike a balance between the extremes of scholarly opinion. Matthias Gelzer lists 15 new men who became consuls between 366 and 49 B.C., while D. C. Earl maintains that "no fewer than twenty-nine consuls seem to come from new families," between 200 and 107 B.C. T. P. Wiseman probably comes nearer the truth. He knows of 11 new men between 191 and 49 B.C.[23] The total number of *novi* for the period between 366 and 49 B.C. was probably not greater than 25, approximately 4 percent of the total number of consulships.

Concerning entry into Roman aristocratic society, Earl says, "The Roman nobility was always of great vitality and ever in search of talent. Its attitude was not one of vigorous exclusion of outsiders but of carefully controlled inclusion."[24] Actually the Roman noble was "ever in search of" greater personal power and influence, but conceded entry into the aristocracy of officeholders to those numbered among his own real or potential supporters. Some new men, like Marius, doubtless found that even their own patrons would not support them if they carried their quest for office too far. Marius served Rome in various capacities, got as high as the praetorship, served with some of the most eminent men of his day, but found his noble patron unwilling to advance his candidacy for the consulship. This was the guarded preserve of the nobility, passed from hand to hand. Tradition tells that Marius was unwilling to keep to his proper station.[25] Even Cicero, so often the spokesman for the aristocratic cause, was considered a "foreigner" by some aristocrats. Catiline, for example,

22 T. P. Wiseman, *New Men in the Roman Senate, 139 B.C.–A.D. 14* (Oxford, 1971), 1ff., 105f.

23 Matthias Gelzer, *The Roman Nobility*, tr. Robin Seager (Oxford, 1969), 34ff., 51f.; D. C. Earl, *The Moral and Political Tradition of Rome* (London, 1967), 13; Wiseman, *New Men*, esp. 2f. and app. 5 ("Consular Novi"), 203. Earl does assume that some of his twenty-nine were senatorial.

24 Earl, *Moral and Political*, 13. Badian, *Durham Univ. Jour.* (1964), 142, says, "These great [Roman] patrons also kept an eye on local talent. . . . promising young men of the upper class in Roman cities were readily taken up by their great patrons and introduced to political life in the capital."

25 Sallust, *Bellum Jugurthinum*, 64.2. Metellus told Marius there was always time for him to seek the consulship with his (Metellus') son, who would be eligible in twenty years. Marius was about fifty at the time. For the new man's reliance on deeds and *virtus* compared to the noble's reliance on ancestors and clients, see Sallust, *Jug.*, 85. Marius' *imagines* are the scars on his chest. Cf. Earl, *Moral and Political*, 47ff.

thought Cicero's victory over him in 64 B.C. too great an insult to bear.[26]

To give an extreme example, the important Roman priesthoods illustrate the extent of the earlier patrician domination, the acceptance of wealthy plebeians as partners in the aristocracy, and the degree to which positions of influence were open to new men. Religious institutions are the least likely to change and the last to consider reform, but they are not immune to the strongest pressures of society. Appropriately, the last fortress surrendered by patricians to plebeians was their priestly stronghold. The election of plebeians to all major magistracies (by 337 B.C.), thus to the religious duties associated with the offices, helped to break down the patrician monopoly.

The growing complexity of society, which demanded a more sophisticated legal system, also played an important part in priestly control of the law. Plebeian admission to the priesthoods themselves was encouraged by C. Flavius' publication, ca. 304 B.C., of the forms of legal procedure, *legis actiones*, which had been the preserve of the pontiffs, all of whom were patricians. Publication hastened the law's separation from religious and patrician control.[27] Patrician domination of the law was a mainstay of their claim to exclusiveness, and their control over the *legis actiones* reinforced their position, since they alone could claim such knowledge and expertise. Given the connection of the *legis actiones* with ritualistic magic and religion and the conviction that such practices must remain unaltered, patricians claimed they should have exclusive knowledge of the holy writ, thus reinforcing their position and prestige in society. After publication, patricians could no longer make such claims, and plebeian pontiffs and augurs were added to the existing number of patrician priests (300 B.C.).

Patricians remained, for traditional religious practices demanded it, but the method of selecting the plebeians is revealing. Co-option, not election, was used. Perhaps the use of election to fill religious positions appeared unseemly, an affront to the gods, but all elections, indeed virtually all state business, were carried out with the auspices and thus with the knowledge of the gods.[28] More likely, since all important positions had been opened to the plebeians before this date, the two aristocracies, plebeian and patrician, had already coalesced into a single aristocracy by this

---

[26] Cicero, *Pro Sulla*, 21. Cicero is called the third foreign tyrant, a reference to his town's recent citizenship (Arpinum in 188) and his consular activities against Catiline in 63 B.C. The speech is a good example of the nobility's attitude toward *novi* and of the use of trials as a political device.

[27] Jolowicz, *Historical Introduction*, 88ff., 196ff.

[28] Botsford, *Assemblies*, 100ff. Officials of the plebeians did not require the auspices for their acts or election. Cf. L. R. Taylor, *Roman Voting Assemblies* (Ann Arbor, 1966), 62f.

time. Hence patrician priests carefully selected plebeian friends, political allies, or "safe" plebeians to hold such prestigious positions.[29] All four plebeian pontiffs initially selected had been consuls, while two of the five augurs were consular, and all were from established *gentes*. The only known new men to hold important priestly offices during the Republic were Ti. Coruncanius *pontifex maximus* in 254 B.C.; C Marius, augur, ca. 98 B.C.; and M. Tullius Cicero, augur in 53 B.C.[30] Generally the priesthoods went to the most prestigious Roman *gentes*, to consular families, and most often to younger sons. The latter indicates the control important *gentes* held over such positions.[31]

Even when the method of selecting the important priestly officials was changed to election by seventeen tribes in 104 B.C., little new blood flowed into the religious offices. When seventeen-year-old Julius Caesar entered the pontifical college in 83 B.C., for example, of the ten members in the college, four pontiffs had been consuls, one was consul, and five others, including Caesar, would be consuls. All were from *gentes* with long-established traditions of state service. The priests' power to nominate candidates and the aristocracy's influence in the tribes were the principal reasons the nobles continued to monopolize the priesthoods. Their wealth could also be used in less legal ways to influence the electorate—witness Caesar's elevation to the position of *pontifex maximus* in 63 B.C.[32]

The patricians lost their monopoly of the priesthoods, although their loss merely opened the way for monopoly by the patrician-plebeian aristocracy. Few new men ever obtained an important priesthood. Priestly positions not only endowed their holders with very real power and influence that were politically useful, but their activities, dress, and importance in state functions set the priests apart and added to their individual worth, *dignitas*.[33] In Rome there was no quarrel between those in the religious

---

[29] E. Stuart Staveley, "The Political Aims of Appius Claudius Caecus," *Historia*, 8 (1959), 410ff., esp. 416, 430ff.; Cassola, *I gruppi politici*, 8ff., 128ff., 149f.

[30] Wiseman, *New Men*, 169ff., and 169n5 for possible additions.

[31] David E. Hahm, "Roman Nobility and the Three Major Priesthoods (218–167 B.C.)," *Transactions and Proceedings of the American Philological Association*, 94 (1963), 73ff., has shown that pontiffs, augurs, and decemviri were for the most part co-opted before they obtained the consulship. Hahm calls the established *gentes'* control "patronage," but a better word would be "nepotism."

[32] L. R. Taylor, "Caesar's Early Career," *Classical Philology*, 36 (1941), 113ff., "The Election of the *pontifex maximus* in the Late Republic," *Classical Philology*, 37 (1942), 421ff., and "Caesar's Colleagues in the Pontifical College," *American Journal of Philology*, 63 (1943), 385ff.

[33] For the political activities of priests, see L. R. Taylor, *Party Politics in the Age of Caesar* (Berkeley, 1961), 76ff. On Roman religion generally, see Gaetano de Sanctis, *Storia dei Romani*, 2, pt. 2 (Florence, 1953), 121ff., on "Lo svolgersi e il declinare dell'antica tradizione religiosa."

sanctuary and those in the forum. The Middle Ages had separate bureaucracies that fought, governed, and prayed, but in the Roman Republic these functions, with few exceptions, were carried out by the same men. Regardless of the position held or activity engaged in, it was made the instrument of the aristocrat's political appetite and the token of his dignity.

Although as a group the Roman nobility opposed the election of new men as consuls, as individuals who based their political domination on a network of personal relationships they supported the mobility of some from their own clique, at least into the lower magistracies. In developing their power, influence, and interests at home and abroad, the aristocracy produced an increased demand for administrative and military personnel. In turn, more positions and opportunities opened to new men and contributed to their mobility. For example, beginning in the late fourth century, 16 military tribunes were elected, and in 268 B.C. the number of quaestorships was increased to 8. There had been but one praetor from 366 B.C. and only 2 from 241 to 227 B.C., when 4 were elected. In 197 B.C. the number increased to 6, and the praetorship clearly became subordinate to the consulship. Finally Sulla raised the number of quaestors and praetors to 20 and 8 respectively, and created a Senate with a membership of 600.

As a consequence of these additions, the senatorial aristocracy had more difficulty monopolizing offices. The nobility concentrated on the consulship, censorship,[34] and priesthoods, while a favored *novus homo* could often count on the praetorship. Between 138 and 70 B.C. approximately 17 percent of the known praetorships were held by new men, and from 89 to 49 B.C. the figure rises slightly to 25 percent.[35] Complete information is wanting on the officeholders and the careers of their ancestors, but apparently from 227 to 197 B.C., when the number of praetorships was raised to 4 and then 6, the number of new men who held the office of praetor was smaller than in the last hundred years of the Republic. Although a definite conclusion is impossible, given the fragmentary nature of the evidence, the figure is probably less than 15 percent.

We are poorly informed about the lower offices and the men who held

---

[34] Wiseman, *New Men*, 169, knows of two *novi* who held the censorship in the last 150 years of the Republic. Jaakko Suolahti, *The Roman Censors: A Study on Social Structure* (Helsinki, 1963), 80ff., has collected a great deal of information, but its interpretation and application are unhappy; cf. John Briscoe's review, *J.R.S.*, 56 (1966), 266f.

[35] Wiseman, *New Men*, 162f. Cf. Gaetano de Sanctis, *Storia dei Romani*, 2, pt. 1, 2nd ed. (Florence, 1969), 474. H. H. Scullard, *Roman Politics, 220–150 B.C.* (Oxford, 1951), 11, 306f., has shown that 151 of the 262 known praetors between 218 and 167 B.C. were from 20 *gentes*.

them, but as H. Stuart Jones said, "doubtless if we were more fully informed with regard to the holders of offices of lower grade than the consulship, we should find abundant evidence that expansion of the citizen body brought in its train an infiltration of fresh elements into the governing class."[36] Though the older plebeian *gentes* were still dominant, grants of citizenship did enable some *gentes* to translate their local power and influence into Roman offices. Beginning in the mid-fourth century, more information exists, indicating that for almost every subsequent stage of Roman Republican history, not only did new plebeian *gentes* claim Roman magistracies, but also many such *gentes* came from recently enfranchised districts. The Fulvian *gens* came originally from Tusculum, enfranchised about 380 B.C., and a Fulvius held the consulship in 322 B.C., the first of twenty his *gens* would claim. Tusculum was the original home of so many consular families, the *gens Porcia* to name another, that it was said to be packed with consulars.[37] Another example from the end of the Republic will suffice to establish the point. Arpinum, granted citizenship in 188 B.C., was the hometown of both C. Marius and M. Tullius Cicero. Both were exceptions in that they were new men, like M. Porcius Cato, the first of their *gentes* to be senators. All three, however, are known to have had influential aristocratic supporters.[38]

The Roman aristocracy's success in expanding the state and adding to its citizenry created a situation that could have threatened its own domination. There was an increase in the upward mobility of local aristocrats who came to Rome, but they were supported by Roman nobles desirous of increasing their own body of supporters. Within a generation or so, some of these men were found among the lower magistracies, and after considerable service, some obtained the consulship. The entry of these local aristocrats into the ranks of the Roman aristocracy served as "a device by which the Roman 'Establishment,' killing two birds with one stone, extended its own power over Rome and Rome's power over Italy simultaneously."[39] It is necessary to emphasize that this was also the method whereby those nobles from local municipalities entered the charmed circle at Rome. Roman aristocrats formed various types of associations and con-

[36] *Cambridge Ancient History*, vol. 7, 548.

[37] Cicero, *Pro Plancio*, 19. See Münzer, *Römische Adels.*, 48f., 64ff.; Taylor, *Voting Districts*, 301ff.; and Toynbee, *Hannibal*, I, 324f., for discussion and bibliography.

[38] For Marius, see n. 18. For Cato, see D. Kienast, *Cato der Zensor* (Heidelberg, 1954), and Scullard, *Roman Politics*, 110ff. On Cicero, see H. H. Scullard, "The Political Career of a 'Novus Homo,' " in T. A. Dorey, ed., *Cicero* (New York, 1965), 1ff.

[39] Toynbee, *Hannibal*, I, 340.

nections with these local aristocrats and thereby gained support for their own aspirations. The success of the local aristocrat is explained by the reciprocal nature of such relationships.[40]

Special grants of citizenship tell the same story. Some additions to the aristocracy came from Latin colonies, established in great number during the middle years of the Republic, since Latins could become Roman citizens by migrating to Rome.[41] And beginning in the last quarter of the second century, municipal magistrates obtained Roman citizenship for themselves and their families.[42] Citizenship grants were also made to individuals in the late Republic, especially for military service (as equestrians) and successful prosecution in the courts.[43] The men who obtained citizenship by these means were aristocrats in their own communities. Such grants are indicative of the privileged position enjoyed by such men and of the support they received from members of the Roman aristocracy.[44] The Social War (91–89 B.C.), during which the Italian peoples rebelled against Rome and as a consequence obtained the franchise, contributed to the rise of some local aristocrats to positions of importance at Rome. The vote was clearly desired by local aristocrats, and we must assume they used it in considerable numbers, although the established Roman aristocratic families did their best to turn a bad situation to their own advantage.[45]

The state's development was not all territorial; it was also growing richer and more sophisticated economically. The ever-expanding urban population and the urban aristocracy itself, increasingly given to conspicuous consumption, had to be cared for and provided many businessmen with a livelihood. State contracts, public works, and the economic needs of the administration and the developing empire generally were handled by private citizens, since the Republic never developed a civil service. Thus economic development made it possible for some to earn fortunes in such activities, and to use their wealth to form connections with

[40] Cf. Gelzer, *Roman Nobility*, 63ff., 101ff.; Sir Ronald Syme, *The Roman Revolution* (Oxford, 1960), ch. 2; Taylor, *Party Politics*, 25ff.; and Wiseman, *New Men*, 33ff.

[41] The privilege would of course apply to all those with Latin rights. Wiseman, *New Men*, 15ff., 29f. On citizenship generally, see A. N. Sherwin-White, *The Roman Citizenship* (Oxford, 1939).

[42] E. Badian, *Foreign Clientelae, 264–70 B.C.* (Oxford, 1958), 179f.; P. A. Brunt, "Italians Aims at the Time of the Social War," *J.R.S.*, 55 (1965), 90f.; cf. Donald W. Bradeen, "Roman Citizenship *per magistratum*," *Classical Journal*, 54 (1959), 221ff.

[43] Badian, *Foreign Clientelae*, 259ff., 281n6; Taylor, *Party Politics*, 114, and *Voting Districts*, 19.

[44] Wiseman, *New Men*, 18f., points out that grants to communities often lagged behind grants to individuals, an indication of a privileged position.

[45] See Taylor, *Voting Districts*, 101ff., and E. Badian's important review of the latter, *J.R.S.*, 52 (1962), 205f.; *Brunt, J.R.S.* (1965), 90–109, esp. apps. I and II.

those in power and thus acquire the wherewithal to make their way into the upper class.

The differentiation of *l'homme d'argent* began as the result of territorial and economic expansion, a process accelerated by the late fourth-century contact with Campania, Magna Graecia, and the more economically advanced and prosperous cities of Italy. It was further stimulated by Rome's success in the First Punic War and the creation of her first imperial possessions. The senatorial aristocracy, which controlled state finance and, through its monopoly of the office of censor, state business, gained considerable wealth and land as a consequence. But as the Second Punic War opened, the *Lex Claudia* (218 B.C.) was passed against the almost unanimous opposition of the Senate, limiting the size of a senator's ship (and those of his sons) to small vessels, useful only in marketing produce from senatorial estates. The senatorial class also seems to have been barred from participation in state contracts about this same time.[46] There is ample evidence that senators did not obey these laws but continued business as usual as silent partners, represented by their freemen or other front men.[47] And the Senate continued to control state finance, while the established *gentes* continued their monopoly of the censorship.

In spite of senatorial control, a group of men emerged outside the Senate who, among other pursuits, served the state, taking part in overseas commerce and trade, in the provisioning of troops, and in public contracts. Their rise was due more to economic and political developments than to the restrictions imposed on senators by the laxly enforced *Lex Claudia*. At least by the time of Cicero, these men were called *equites*, a title originally applied to those with a public horse who served as cavalry and voted in the eighteen equestrian centuries of the centurate assembly.[48] Apparently as early as the Second Punic War an *eques* was required to have a census rating of 400,000 *sesterces*. Senators had to have the same qualification, and until about 129 B.C. they voted in the eighteen equestrian centuries and retained their *equus publicus*.[49] Since some senators were too old for cavalry

---

[46] Cassola, *I gruppi politici*, ch. 2 (esp. 71ff., 81ff.), 215ff.; cf. H. Hill, *The Roman Middle Class in the Republican Period* (Oxford, 1952), 50f., 87ff.; and Z. Yavetz, "The Policy of C. Flaminius and the *plebiscitum Claudianum*," *Athenaeum*, 40 (1962), 324ff.

[47] For example, Plutarch, *Cato Maior*, 21.5–6; Cicero, *Actio secunda in Verrem*, 5.45.6–7.

[48] M. I. Henderson, "The Establishment of the *equestrian ordo*," *J.R.S.*, 53 (1963), 61ff.; Hill, *Roman Middle Class*, 113ff.; cf. C. Nicolet, *L'ordre équestre à l'époque ré-publicaine, 312–43 av. J.-C.*, 1 (Paris, 1966), 47ff.; Wiseman, *New Men*, 68ff., and "The Definition of 'eques Romanus' in the Late Republic and Early Empire," *Historia*, 19 (1970), 67ff.

[49] Cicero, *De re publica*, 4.2. The fragment refers to equestrian centuries, *in quo*

service, obviously there was no immediate connection between the *equites equo publico* and the cavalry. We do not know the relationship, if any existed, between the emerging class of wealthy men later called *equites* and those who voted in the eighteen equestrian centuries. Regardless, a group of wealthy individuals gradually became differentiated from the senatorial order, in part through obtaining powers once held by senators.

Polybius stated that one pillar of senatorial domination was that judges were taken from their number in the most important public and private suits.[50] In the second century the Senate began to hear charges of extortion, i.e., maladministration, brought against provincial commanders and governors, who of course were senators. In 149 B.C. a standing court (composed of senators) was established, but in 123 B.C. Gaius Gracchus strengthened the role of the *equites* by transferring the extortion court from senatorial to equestrian control.[51] The *iudices*, jurors, were now selected from those with equestrian census rating who had not held public office, and from those whose close relatives were not and never had been magistrates or senators. The relationship between the equestrian jurors and those *equites* who voted in the eighteen centuries is unknown, but *iudices* possibly belonged to the equestrian centuries.[52] Brunt has argued convincingly that *equites* obtained a share in other criminal and civil cases, and that the *iudices* for all judicial proceedings were selected from both *equites* and senators.[53]

The reasons for Gaius' reform were not narrow; the Senate's record of abusing its judicial powers was well known, and *equites* had little recourse against the power of provincial commanders and governors. The *equites* desired a more influential position in society, and Gaius could hope that after his reform they would follow his lead. The question of which group, equestrian or senatorial, was to control the extortion court was hotly contested for half a century after Gracchus' reform. Sulla enrolled many of the equestrians he left alive in the Senate and gave control back to that body.

---

suffragia sunt etiam senatus. The dramatic date of Cicero's *Republic* is ca. 129 B.C.; cf. Henderson, *J.R.S.* (1963), 70f.

[50] 6.17.7–9. See F. W. Walbank, *A Historical Commentary on Polybius*, 1 (Oxford, 1957), 695f., for discussion and bibliography.

[51] See E. Badian, "From the Gracchi to Sulla (1940–1959)," *Historia*, 11 (1962), 203ff., for an excellent review of the scholarship and not a few penetrating comments. See also J.P.V.D. Balsdon, "History of the Extortion Court at Rome, 123–70 B.C.," *Papers of the British School at Rome*, 14 (1938), 108ff.; and Erich S. Gruen, *Roman Politics and the Criminal Courts, 149–78 B.C.* (Cambridge, Mass., 1968), 87ff.

[52] Pliny, *Naturalis Historia*, 33.34, stated they were not called *equites* originally but *iudices*. Cf. Henderson, *J.R.S.* (1963), 72, with Nicolet, *L'ordre équestre*.

[53] "The Equites in the Late Republic," *Second International Conference of Economic History*, Aix-en-Provence, 1962, 1 (Paris, 1965), esp. app. 2, 141ff.

Finally in 70 B.C. the juries were selected from senators, equestrians, and *tribuni aerarii*.[54]

The fact remains that an equestrian order was increasingly distinguished from the senatorial class. Both were composed of wealthy men, but the former obtained status essentially by wealth, the latter by officeholding. Yet although equestrians clearly had an inherited upper-class status, just as praetorian families ranked lower in status than consular, so equestrian families were lower than senatorial families in the aristocratic hierarchy. To some extent equestrian control of the juries made them a political force,[55] but *equites* were often connected with aristocratic senators, and the political machinations of equestrians fit into the personal politics practiced by the nobility. Nothing would be further from the truth than to set *equites* and senators up as rival groups, one motivated by economic interests and the other by political.[56]

These rival forces appear in Republican history, but their lines are not so simply drawn. Specific issues could affect some among the equestrian order, and they could combine in defense of their common interests. This was particularly true of the *publicani*.[57] But many of the Italian municipal aristocrats were *equites*, often landed gentry, with stronger ties to Roman aristocrats of a similar type than to business-oriented *equites*, inside and outside Rome. Conversely, senators often engaged in "equestrian" activities, and equestrians frequently forsook the dangers of the sea for the security of the farm and the prestige of landowning.[58] No wealthy man was landless, nor could any man whose primary wealth was land avoid business activities relating to the marketing and sale of his goods.[59] The aristocracy's disdain for equestrian business dealings reinforced its own position in society by justifying its own superior style of life. As with many standards evoked by the aristocracy, practice differed from theory.

Thus on one level *equites* were virtually synonymous with the group

---

54 Presumably the *tribuni aerarii* had the equestrian census (cf. Cicero, *Pro Flacco*, 4) but not the title. They were lower in status than *equites*. See Henderson, *J.R.S.* (1963), 63f.

55 Gruen, *Roman Politics*, 91, 106. Cassola, *I gruppi politici*, 71ff., testifies to the earlier activity of businessmen as a pressure group, but cf. Brunt, "The Equites," 117ff., and app. 1, 138ff.

56 Brunt, "The Equites," 122; Christian Meier, *Res publica amissa* (Wiesbaden, 1966), 64ff. On senatorial business activity, see T. P. Wiseman, "The Potteries of Vibienus and Rufrenus at Arretium," *Mnemosyne*, 16 (1963), 275ff.; and M. W. Frederiksen, "Caesar, Cicero and the Problem of Debt," *J.R.S.*, 56 (1966), 131.

57 Brunt, "The Equites," 119, 122ff., and app. 1, 138ff.

58 Wiseman, *New Men*, app. 4, 197ff., "Business Interests of Senatorial Families."

59 See Cato, *De agri cultura*, 144–50, for the business dealings of landed aristocrats. See also Wiseman, *New Men*, app. 3, 191ff., "Estates of Roman Senators in Italy." Many of those listed are *novi*, i.e., from equestrian families.

of wealthy local aristocrats who often made their way to Rome, or who remained behind in the local community and together with their Roman counterparts constituted the Italian aristocracy. These aristocrats, within and without Rome, had more in common with one another than they had with the lower classes in their own regions. Economically, socially, or even politically, *equites* were not fundamentally different from senators. The difference was that the senatorial aristocracy had power and influence, while many among the equestrians desired an equal share. The relationship between the two orders, Brunt observed, "was not unlike that of the rich plebeians to the patricians before 366 B.C."[60]

Like the plebeians, the *equites* were the reservoir of new blood for the Roman aristocracy: the *novi homines* were equestrians.[61] That some *equites* became politically successful while others were treated with contempt and hostility by the aristocrats is best explained by the proximity of equestrian to senatorial status. The *equites*, nearest to the senators in social and economic status, were the group from which upward mobility was most possible. They presented the greatest threat to the domination of the established Roman aristocracy. On the other hand, if *equites* decided to give up, at least publicly, their nonpolitical role and espouse the ideology and practices of the Roman aristocracy, their aristocratic friends and enemies took an active interest in their candidacy. Supported by some, the *equites* found themselves opposed by most aristocrats.

Not all *equites* were members of local aristocracies or publicans. The *equites* most odious to the aristocracy were those of servile or lower-class origin. Many were artisans, businessmen, and civil servants. Wiseman states, "A considerable proportion of the equestrian order—we have no idea exactly how much—must have been composed of freedmen's sons, if not the freedmen themselves, and like other *equites*, they had the resources, if not usually the ambition, to stand for public office and the Senate."[62] As early as about 312 B.C., the censor Appius Claudius Caecus tried to enroll sons of freedmen in the Senate. Although they were not admitted, the attempt plus the successful political career of Appius' scribe, C. Flavius, attest to the mobility of some men of low birth.[63]

[60] *Social Conflict*, 72.
[61] Gelzer, *Roman Nobility*, 12f.
[62] *New Men*, 70f.
[63] Susan Treggiari, *Roman Freedmen during the Late Republic* (Oxford, 1969), 42f., 53ff. Flavius' colleague as aedile was Anicius Praenestinus, who must have recently moved to Rome (cf. Broughton, *Magistrates*, I, 168n2). Disregard Treggiari's statement (57n1) that Flavius was a *patricius*; the curule aedileship alternated between patricians and plebeians by this date.

Most evidence for mobility by humbler folk comes from the late Republic and Empire, and is difficult to assess because reports of servile or lower-class origin were frequently employed as rhetorical exaggerations to blacken the reputation of a political foe. Though information is limited, we know some descendants of slaves or *proletarii* moved up the ladder and eventually obtained public office. To accomplish this in one generation would have been virtually impossible, but in two or three it was not improbable. Some men, moreover, must have been far removed in time and circumstances from their original servile or common status by the time they reached office, and their backgrounds went unrecorded.

The increased sophistication and complexity of Roman life, administratively, economically, and socially, demanded more specialized and "professional" techniques and knowledge, and contributed to mobility. The need for specific officials or individuals to handle functions that became increasingly more numerous or more demanding of expertise resulted in the differentiation of groups of men who now could obtain wealth, acquire reputation, and form connections through the practice of their various skills.[64]

Just as certain higher offices were created and increased during the Republic, so a host of minor positions developed, some elective but most appointive, which some new men used as means of advancement into the senatorial aristocracy. Again Flavius, the scribe, is important since he was elected both tribune and aedile. Scribes and other so-called civil servants served magistrates and the *respublica* in ever-increasing numbers, and besides the obvious benefit of potential support from the aristocratic officials for whom they worked, they often employed illicit means to acquire considerable wealth. And positions such as moneyer or *tresvir capitalis* could be springboards to higher status.[65]

Military service was another means through which new men acquired public repute and aristocratic support for future advancement. Of course the wealth they obtained was not immaterial to their aspirations.[66] War was

---

[64] Especially helpful is K. Hopkins, "Structural Differentiation in Rome (200–31 B.C.)," in I. M. Lewis, ed., *History and Social Anthropology* (London, 1968), 63ff.

[65] Charles D. Hamilton, "The *tresviri monetales* and the Republican *cursus honorum*," *Transactions and Proceedings of the American Philological Association*, 100 (1969), 181ff.; but cf. Wiseman, *New Men*, 4, 147ff., who points out the advertising value of coin types. Andrew Alföldi, "The Main Aspects of Political Propaganda on the Coinage of the Roman Republic," in E. S. G. Robinson, ed., *Essays in Roman Coinage Presented to Harold Mattingly* (Oxford, 1956), 63ff., has interesting comments on the political importance of coin types.

[66] Wiseman, *New Men*, 121f., 143ff. Not all military tribunes were elected by the people. Others (and prefects) were selected by commanders. Personal associations played an important role in such selections.

Rome's biggest and most profitable business, and junior officers, serving as tent mates of influential Roman commanders, obtained handsome rewards for their service. In the mid-second century, Roman aristocrats were still required to do ten years of military service before entering the political arena, but by Cicero's day this was no longer the case. The work of Jaakko Suolahti on the junior officer corps shows that just as plebeians had earlier gradually replaced the patricians as the majority of military tribunes, by the first century those with equestrian status began to fill this post more frequently.[67] As the Punic Wars lengthened military service, a group of almost professional officers slowly developed. Men from established *gentes* still served in the military, but many *equites* now willingly gave extensive service, and some were rewarded late in their lives with public office and a seat in the Senate.[68]

The separation of law and legal procedure from religious and priestly control serves as the final example of the acceleration of upward mobility by the growing complexity of Roman society. Men without aristocratic backgrounds used legal expertise to gain fame, fortune, and following. Cicero's successful quest for the consulship, for example, was not incidental to his position as the foremost advocate of his day; nor was he the first or only new man to use the law as a means of elevation. As Roman law developed, so did its specialists, and jurisconsults began to appear in the third century.[69] The role of the advocate, with his expertise in rhetoric and oratory, became increasingly more important in the courtroom. Similarly, experts in the law, men who never entered the courtroom, also began to appear outside the immediate senatorial families. Such men counseled private citizens or public officials with jurisdiction over criminal or civil cases. The legal knowledge of such officials was often limited because Roman magistrates were first and last politicians, although law, literature, and agriculture were leisure-time pursuits for some.[70]

The law and the courtroom became a means of elevating or maintaining one's position, useful to aristocrat and nonaristocrat alike. The courtroom became the arena where enemies were attacked and friends defended, a place to begin a political career and build a reputation. For many

---

[67] *The Junior Officers of the Roman Army in the Republican Period: A Study in Social Structure* (Helsinki, 1955), 70ff., 108ff. Cf. Wiseman, *New Men*, 144, 176; and Hopkins, "Structural Differentiation," 72ff.

[68] Wiseman, *New Men*, 146ff.

[69] See Pomponius, *Digest*, 1.2.2.34, 38; *Cambridge Ancient History*, vol. 9 (Cambridge, reprint 1962), esp. 843ff.; Hopkins, "Structural Differentiation," 73ff.; Wiseman, *New Men*, 119ff.; and Jolowicz, *Historical Introduction*, 88ff. See Cicero *De officiis*, 2.55, for criticism of legal professionals once they let "anyone" practice.

[70] Jolowicz, *Historical Introduction*, 92; J. M. Kelly, *Roman Litigation* (Oxford, 1966), 97, 102f.; J. A. Crook, *Law and Life of Rome* (London, 1967), 79ff., 88ff.

it replaced the traditional method of obtaining *gloria* through military service.[71]

As new men in the military depended upon aristocratic commanders in the field, so new men in law were dependent. Traditionally some Roman aristocrats studied law, since the law and the courtroom were used to reinforce the aristocracy's societal and political norms and since patrons were legally obligated to aid their clients in civil and criminal cases.[72] A lucrative law practice facilitated upward mobility, but the aristocracy tried to inhibit the acquisition of wealth by lawyers. Aristocrats "freely" performed legal services for clients and friends, and considered monetary payment for services rendered degrading. Thus in 204 B.C. a law was passed forbidding gift-giving to those who extended legal aid, but it was effectively dodged by the new legal experts.[73] Often men, especially a local aristocrat's son like Cicero, studied with the most prominent Roman legal experts and were introduced into Roman aristocratic society at the same time.[74] Lawyers were not public defenders or champions of the poor, but championed one group of aristocrats against another. But that is merely another description of Roman politics.

The preceding pages give some indication of the origin, extent, and nature of the aristocracy's political dominance during the Roman Republic and present examples of the sources and types of mobility. The aristocracy developed naturally out of primitive society's reliance upon wealthy, powerful men. Patricians tried to restrict the number of privileged families, but failed because the development of the state compelled them to admit plebeian families and because some wealthy plebeians had never been completely excluded from influence. Subsequent increases in citizenry, territorial possessions, material prosperity, and administrative requirements and the growing complexities and necessities of social and political existence undermined the exclusiveness of the patrician-plebeian aristocracy and contributed to the rise of new men. It is a contradiction, but the Roman aristocracy's successful methods of guaranteeing its own continued hegemony were the greatest contributing factors in upward mobility. Mobility was the direct result of an attempt by the few to remain dominant. Aristocrats were both the guardians of the walls of privilege and the

---

[71] See Cicero, *Pro Murena,* 30; Nicolet, *L'ordre équestre,* 444ff.; Wiseman, *New Men,* 87.

[72] On the early patrician monopoly of the law and the patricians' protection of clients, see *Cambridge Ancient History,* vol. 9, 846f.; cf. Gelzer, *Roman Nobility,* 63f.

[73] Gelzer, *Roman Nobility,* 63f.; Cassola, *I gruppi politici,* 284ff. Specifically, the law forbade gifts over a certain amount to patrons; *patronus* was indeed the name applied to the early jurisconsult.

[74] Scullard, "The Political Career," 5f.

traitors who opened the gates. The established senatorial families retained their hold on the consulship, censorship, and the priesthoods, but their monopoly was achieved only through admitting their supporters to other magistracies.

As a group, the Roman aristocracy sustained its ascendant position by its control over the entire legal system, its favored position in the assembly of the centuries, its influence in the tribal assemblies, and its position in the Senate. In addition, the aristocracy's urban character and society's reliance upon oral communication were of equal importance to the continuation of aristocratic control.

Rome was the center of political activity. In fact the early patricians must have been primarily urban-based, which partly accounts for their success in taking power once Tarquin was exiled. All assemblies, elective and legislative, met there. Success in politics necessitated an urban residence, usually in the more fashionable, prestigious sections. The city attracted ambitious aristocrats from neighboring or newly enfranchised districts, and the younger generation of *domi nobiles* was not content, as Cicero's grandfather was, to exercise power and influence on the local level.

Naturally the greatest concentration of new men came from areas near Rome, from those that had had citizenship for some time, those near or on major roads leading to Rome, the larger, more prosperous districts, and those that had a number of villas or estates belonging to Roman aristocrats.[75] Some who came into the city for elections might support a native son over a Roman aristocrat,[76] but the aristocrat operated from the hub and had contacts with more regions. All roads led to Rome, but from Rome one could take a good road in any direction. Roman aristocrats traveled those roads. With the constant increase in the number of citizens, even the established politicians were constantly forced to form new alliances of marriage, friendship, and so on, to retain control of the government. The rich local aristocrat who frequently visited the city for the elections and accompanying festivities was courted by resident aristocrats who sought his support in the centuries, where the wealthy were dominant and where praetors, consuls, and censors were elected.

Men without such personal support might resort to coin and later to coercion, and the bribery laws of the Republic were designed to reinforce

[75] Wiseman, *New Men*, 13ff., points out that the lag between obtaining the franchise and possible admission to the Senate was often determined by such factors as those mentioned. The gap was often three generations.

[76] Cf. Cicero, *Pro Plancio*, 21–23, 39–45. Normally a tribe would vote for a member candidate, since he could legally present gifts (circus tickets and banquets) to his *tribules*; Taylor, *Voting Districts*, 15.

aristocratic standards. Once the electorate grew so large as to be unmanageable, even the nobility could resort to such measures. However, the laws of 139, 137, and 130 B.c. that established written ballots for elective, judicial, and legislative assemblies, although unpopular with the aristocracy, did not contribute greatly to an increase in bribery.[77] Personal connections formed by aristocrats were mutual assistance pacts and beneficial to both parties. While some clients (or debtors) might now be free from their patron's overseeing eye,[78] the growing population and complexity of society contributed to the weakening of the patron-client relationship more than did the laws that made voting secret. An aristocrat's influence and reputation had to keep pace with the growth in population.

In a society without developed communication media, possession of a name long known to the public was vital to a political aspirant. To be a Roman noble was literally to be "notable," but in a society dependent upon oral communication, it was also to be known. The *populus* preferred those it recognized to unknown quantities. Perhaps in this regard both ancient and modern writers give too much attention to the role played by *mos maiorum*, but it is probably correct to stress the basic conservative and poorly informed character of the *populus*. Even in modern society, a candidate for national office must work hard merely to have his name recognized by the people, and his chances of election are improved if his name is placed first on the ballot. A political pamphlet purportedly written for Cicero by his brother gives some indication of how difficult it was for an honest man without a noble background to make his way in Roman politics. Considerable time was spent merely making oneself known to the important people.[79]

An aristocrat was recognized in a Roman law court the same way the man in the street saw him—as a man of superior character, one of the best men in society, deserving of preferential treatment. At Rome, plaintiff, defendant, witness, judge, and jury knew that the wealth, connections, and prestige of the individual parties to a suit usually counted for more than the letter of the law.[80] Cicero praised the law's benefits to society, but he is

[77] See Taylor, *Roman Voting Assemblies*, 39, on the failure of the secret ballot: Marius' reform of 119 B.C. was helpful. Cf. Wiseman, *New Men*, 4ff., 129ff.

[78] Taylor, *Voting Districts*, 141, suggests that the citizens most affected by the laws were the freedmen. Cf. *Cambridge Ancient History*, vol. 9, 203.

[79] *De commentariolo petitionis*. See the discussion of Gelzer, *Roman Nobility*, 54ff.; Wiseman, *New Men*, 135ff.; and cf. M. I. Henderson, "De commentariolo petitionis," *J.R.S.*, 40 (1950), 8ff., who doubts the document is what it purports to be.

[80] Kelly, *Roman Litigation*, Crook, *Law and Life*, and David Daube, *Roman Law* (Edinburgh, 1969), have extensive treatments of the aristocrat's favored position in and before the law. In particular, see Kelly, 31ff., "Improper Influences in Roman Litigation."

our best witness to the effect of extralegal forces that affect its application.[81] His attempts to use his own influence or a friend's to win advantage in the courtroom for himself or a friend would be like attempts made by other Romans. Cicero perhaps never broke the law, but unlike so many others, his correspondence documents how he used his influence to take the blind-fold off Lady Justice.

That aristocrats had a favored position before the law is not surprising. They were the magistrates with jurisdiction over criminal or civil cases; they manned the juries; they supplied the advocates; they wrote the law and interpreted it.[82] They made extensive use of the law and the courtroom for strictly political purposes, to build a reputation, attract a following, and attack political opponents. Cato the Elder was no saint, but the fact that he was prosecuted forty-four times attests more to the persistence of his political opponents than to his illegal activities.[83]

The poor and politically impotent were literally powerless against their opposite numbers. It was virtually impossible for them to bring a wealthy, powerful man into court. Some might go quietly to avoid a scene or a scandal, or because the poor man had a wealthy, influential patron, but the powerful and influential did not willingly appear in court unless charged by a peer.[84] Hence even if the letter of the law was classless, which is debatable, its application was strictly along class lines. Having one law for all people, J. A. Crook observes, has always "put the poor at a disad-vantage against the rich."[85] It has also been said that "the poor break the law, the rich get around it (or at least try to)."[86]

Wealthy citizens, however, did not always have to go outside the law to receive advantages. Ancient sources associate riches with aristocratic status, and wealth obtained a privileged position for the aristocrat in the military assembly of the centuries, the *comitia centuriata*.[87] The assembly operated on the archaic principle, true to its original nature, that those who could afford to fight for their state should receive for their services the

[81] Much of Cicero, *Epis. ad fam.* 13, stands witness. See Kelly, *Roman Litigation,* 56ff.; cf. T. A. Dorey, "Honesty in Roman Politics," in T. A. Dorey, ed., *Cicero* (New York, 1965), 27ff.
[82] Kelly, *Roman Litigation,* 33ff., 66ff., 89ff.; Crook, *Law and Life.*
[83] Pliny, *Nat. Hist.* 7.100. See Gelzer, *Roman Nobility,* 85; Cassola, *I gruppi politici,* 347ff.
[84] Kelly, *Roman Litigation,* 1ff., 14ff.
[85] *Law and Life,* 93.
[86] Daube, *Roman Law,* 92.
[87] See Botsford, *Assemblies,* 66ff., 119ff., 201ff.; Taylor, *Roman Voting Assemblies.* Wolfgang Kunkel, *An Introduction to Roman Legal and Constitutional History,* tr. J. M. Kelly (Oxford, 1966), has a brief, admirable discussion of the constitutional position of the aristocracy.

greatest share of power and influence. This assembly was the chief elective, and originally the most important, legislative body of the Republic. Since the centuries elected the consuls, praetors, and censors, it is not surprising that most of these positions were filled by members of the established aristocracy. In the *comitia centuriata*'s developed but not final form, the wealthiest citizens of the state, *equites*, were placed in eighteen centuries, and of the five classes of citizens, those with a first-class census rating filled another eighty centuries: forty of juniors and forty of seniors. Thus the wealthiest members of society controlled a majority of the 193 centuries, while the most populous element was de facto powerless against their combined will.

Roman citizens also assembled in their tribal units to elect officials and to legislate. By 241 B.C. there existed thirty-one rural and four urban tribes. Thereafter, new citizens and new districts were added to existing tribal units. Each vote was theoretically equal in the tribes; there were no distinctions according to wealth or age as in the centuries, and the vote of the tribe was determined by the majority will within each unit. The assemblage of the entire citizenry or *populus* was called the *comitia tributa*,[88] and it elected quaestors, curule aediles, and military tribunes. When the plebeians alone gathered by tribes, the assembly was called the *concilium plebis tributim*;[89] here plebeians elected plebeian tribunes and aediles. Both assemblies could pass legislation, and after 287 B.C., when the *concilium plebis* obtained the right to pass legislation binding upon the entire state, the tribal assemblies replaced the *comitia centuriata* as the chief legislative bodies in the state.[90] Since plebeians far outnumbered patricians, little difference existed between the two tribal assemblies except for their presidencies. Tribunes presided over the *concilium*, while praetors and consuls conducted business before the *comitia tributa*.

After the creation of the last two tribes in 241 B.C., and before the Second Punic War, the centuries were reformed, except for the equestrian, and became divisions of the tribes; the centuries of the first class were reduced to seventy (thirty-five juniors and thirty-five seniors), and those in each tribe with first-class census qualification voted in a single century.[91] The arrangement gave the wealthy aristocrats—the urban nobles, most of

88 Botsford, *Assemblies*, chs. 12–14 passim; Taylor, *Roman Voting Assemblies*, 59ff.

89 Taylor, *Roman Voting Assemblies*, 59ff., maintains that patricians were always excluded from this assembly. Cf. Botsford, *Assemblies*, esp. 128ff., who presents the ancient evidence and interesting but not very acceptable conclusions.

90 See Taylor, *Roman Voting Assemblies*, 100ff., for references to the limited legislative activity of the centuries after 287 B.C.

91 Cassola, *I gruppi politici*, 96ff., 110ff.; and Taylor, *Roman Voting Assemblies*, 85ff., 159ff., have bibliographic discussions.

whom were enrolled in the rural tribes—much greater power. All attempts to interpret this as a democratic reform have failed. Possibly the centuries became divisions of the tribes because the aristocracy was more capable of influencing the vote in the tribal units. The Roman upper class continually invested in estates throughout Italy, resulting in their enrollment in the rural tribes.[92] Adopted sons, relatives, clients, or friends, spread throughout the tribal districts, gave their support to the noble Roman. Furthermore, only the wealthy from the various districts outside Rome could afford to come to the city for the elections, and the Roman aristocracy was tied to them by several types of personal relationships. Had not the centuries been changed to form units of the tribes, the nonaristocratic urban wealthy could have exerted considerably more influence on elections. But the change required those who had first-class census rating to be enrolled by the censors as landowners or residents of rural tribal districts.

Since censors enrolled citizens in their tribal units, the aristocracy used its control of the office to guard against any drastic shift in power. Still, beginning in 312 B.C. with the censorship of Appius Claudius Caecus, who tried to put urban dwellers into rural tribes and freedmen's sons in the Senate, attempts were made to shift freedmen and other citizens from urban to rural tribes and back again to increase or decrease their voting power. Censors were not above using their office to gain *clientelae*, or above giving their supporters a greater voice in the assemblies by assigning them to a tribe where their vote would count more heavily.[93]

The most important aristocratic institution of the Roman Republic and the foundation of aristocratic control of the state was the Senate.[94] Effective power rested with the Senate, and to be a senator was to be an aristocrat. The Senate was founded in the advisory *consilium* of the *paterfamilias*. Its members were selected first by kings, then by consuls, and finally, after 312 B.C., by censors. No law prohibited either king or consul from enrolling plebeians, whose numbers would increase in the Senate as they were admitted regularly to the higher offices, but for a century and a half the patrician members constituted a majority in the Senate. By the third century it was composed primarily of ex-officeholders.

We assume that membership was automatic for those who obtained a curule office, though enrollment by censors could result in a few exceptions. Following the heavy losses at Cannae in 216 B.C., the Senate's vacancies were filled with those curule officeholders not yet enrolled, plebeian of-

[92] Taylor, *Voting Districts*, esp. 277ff.

[93] See ibid., 132ff.; Cassola, *I gruppi politici*, 102ff., 119ff.

[94] P. Willems, *Le Sénat de la république romaine, sa composition et ses attributions* (Louvain/Paris, 1878–85); Jolowicz, *Historical Introduction*, 27ff.; Kunkel, *Introduction to Roman Legal and Constitutional History*, 18ff.

ficials, and those with distinguished military careers.[95] This was the normal order of selection, and the Senate was probably always open to some men who had not held a curule office.[96] Late in the second century, plebeian aediles and tribunes were regularly enrolled, though tribunes traditionally had the privilege of listening to Senate debates, vetoing its decisions, and convening the Senate (from the third century). Finally, the proscriptions and deaths caused by the Social War and civil wars (90–82 B.C.) necessitated a wholesale rebuilding of the Senate. Sulla accomplished this and raised the number of members to about six hundred.[97] Also the number of quaestorships was raised to twenty a year, and the office became the prerequisite for senatorial membership.

The entire population, voting in the *comitia tributa*, elected quaestors. When quaestors automatically became senators, in theory the entire population chose the members of the Senate, and this fact should have meant a more representative body. But since all voting was done in Rome and only the wealthy could afford to go there to vote, the Roman aristocracy still played a prominent role in determining the outcome of elections.

Crisis, calamity, and reform could change the membership of the Senate but rarely its character. Senators were the wealthiest men in the state. As early as the Second Punic War they had to have the highest census rating, and they voted in the eighteen equestrian centuries, though they were later removed. The standard used for recruiting senators thus remained consistent. Whether wealthy patricians, plebeians, equestrians, or local aristocrats sat in the *curia*, all belonged to the same upper-class stratum of Italian society: all were as sound as a denarius.

On the other hand, though *senator* was synonymous with *aristocrat* at Rome, within the Senate there was a gradation in status. One's status within the aristocracy was determined by the highest office obtained by one's family. Originally patricians were the nobles, but with plebeian entry into most public offices, the possession of the curule chair became the identifying mark of the *nobiles* and remained so until the early second century, when one had to be from a consular family to qualify as nobility.[98] Thus the noble families, the curule and subsequently the consular families, were the upper crust of the Roman aristocracy.

[95] Livy, 23.23. Since censors were elected only every five years, some curule magistrates would have to wait to be enrolled in the Senate. See Willems, *Sénat*, I, 153ff.

[96] Wiseman, *New Men*, 96f.

[97] Sir Ronald Syme, "Caesar, the Senate and Italy," *Papers of the British School at Rome*, 14 (1938), 1ff.; E. Gabba, "Il ceto equestre e il senato di Silla," *Athenaeum*, 34 (1956), 124ff.; Wiseman, *New Men*, 6ff., 100.

[98] Gelzer, *Roman Nobility*, 27ff.; cf. A. Afzelius, "Zur Definition der römischen Nobilität vor der Zeit Ciceros," *Classica et Medievalia*, 7 (1945), 150ff.

The difference in status among various senators is apparent in the Senate's deliberative procedure. The presiding magistrate, be he consul, praetor, or, later, tribune, had to recognize a senator before he could speak his opinion, and though preferences were doubtlessly often shown, generally custom dictated that the officer called first for the advice of those who obtained the highest office, consulship, beginning with the oldest patrician consular. As in the *comitia centuriata*, where the poor and those of modest wealth were seldom called to vote, so in the Senate the backbenchers, the *pedarii*, voted merely by joining those with whom they agreed.[99] Though the *pedarii* were not legally obligated, the power of a *pater*, a patron, or a friend (read also creditor) might well indicate the direction taken by many of those who voted only with their feet.

In the early Republic, patrician senators had the right to give their approval to the legislative and electoral measures of the *comitia*, but in the course of the struggle with the plebeians, measures were passed requiring patricians to give their approval, *patrum auctoritas*, before the vote, hence weakening their position. But this did not weaken the influence of the emerging patrician-plebeian aristocracy. They developed the custom of considering and debating the items that were to be placed before the people, until the practice became virtually a law and an important ingredient in their control of the state.

The magistrate, like the *pater*, was not bound to obey the advice, but the Senate's advice, *senatus consultum*, was seldom ignored, since senators held the keys to future political success or could readily find an official to veto unpopular measures. Through its *consulta* and the presiding magistrate's power over matters brought to an assembly's attention, in most instances the Senate could dictate the nature of those decisions on which the people voted. It could even compromise the sovereign power of the people to make war and peace. Though not empowered to make law, the Senate, by virtue of its traditional privilege of passing on the procedural propriety of the assemblies' measures, did possess the power to void actions taken by an assembly. The Senate also controlled the continuous affairs of state, foreign policy and finance, since it was the only institution with a consistent and continuous membership. Its members held their positions for life, while the power, *imperium*, granted to magistrates was for a year.

Some scholars assume a general increase in senatorial control over

---

[99] Willems, *Sénat*, I, 137ff.; L. R. Taylor and R. T. Scott, "Seating Space in the Roman Senate and the *senatores pedarii*," *Transactions and Proceedings of the American Philological Association*, 100 (1969), esp. 548ff. The article includes a valuable discussion of attendance (or possible attendance) at senatorial meetings.

magistrates and state functions in the late third and early second centuries. It is argued that the *populus* exercised considerable power following the end of the struggle of the orders in 287 B.C., electing and giving commands to some *novi homines*, one of whom was blamed for Cannae, but that after the disaster the people finally saw the wisdom of senatorial leadership, and consequently the Senate's power and influence were expanded and not seriously questioned until the Gracchan challenge.[100] Such assumptions are doubtful for several reasons. The *populus* did not have the power to choose consuls or allot commands before, during, or after the war; the wealthy were dominant in the centuries, the patron-client relationship was strong in the third century, and "popular" movements were motivated by the aristocrats they benefited. A democratic challenge to senatorial control never emerged. Moreover, conflicts in Roman politics were between aristocrats, most often between senators. Personal politics was as much at home in the *curia* as in the assembly or the forum.

The Senate was not a body united in mind and action; nor were its decisions determined by objective considerations of governmental responsibility.[101] The Senate's *auctoritas* rested upon the combined influence,

[100] In particular, Tenney Frank, *Roman Imperialism* (New York, 1914), 66ff.; *Cambridge Ancient History*, vol. 8, ch. 12 ("The Senate in Control"), 357ff.; J. Bleicken, *Das Volkstribunat der klassischen Republik* (Munich, 1955), 25ff., 35ff., 152f.; R. E. Smith, *The Failure of the Roman Republic* (Cambridge, 1955), 6ff.; Sir Frank E. Adcock, *Roman Political Ideas and Practices* (Ann Arbor, 1964), 36ff.; H. H. Scullard, *Scipio Africanus: Soldier and Politician* (Bristol, 1970), 162ff.; Toynbee, *Hannibal*, I-II passim; and U. Schlag, *Regnum in Senatu* (Stuttgart, 1968). These are but a few who refer to the democratic movement prior to the Second Punic War and the growth of senatorial power during and after. The struggle between patricians and plebeians was not a class struggle (*contra* Toynbee, *Hannibal*, I, 317); its resolution did not set Rome on the road to democracy, and to my mind to argue such is a misinterpretation of the Republic's aristocratic character in all periods. Scullard, *Scipio*, 175, says the Senate "had won undying prestige by its conduct of the war," although he elsewhere knows (*Roman Politics*, 26) that "the men who ruled the Senate ruled the State," and that the powerful nobles ruled the Senate (but cf. 233: "Problems and Policies of the Senate"). My quibble is with any statement that leaves the impression that the Senate had an independent identity or power, apart from the controlling nobles, that permitted it to formulate policy free from factional disputes.

[101] See Gelzer, *Roman Nobility*, 124ff.; and Cassola, *I gruppi politici*, for evidence of factionalism in the late third and second centuries. Frank, *Cambridge Ancient History*, vol. 8, 367f., says, "the Senate remained in power because it did its work well and fairly and because it retained the confidence of the voters. Not only does Cicero in his conservative days refer to this period as an era of harmony, but Sallust, the democratic [*sic*] historian, calls it a time of concord and good government." Smith, *The Failure*, expresses similar views. For a partial corrective, cf. R. M. Henry, "Roman Tradition," *Proceedings of the Classical Association*, 34 (1937), 7ff.; and Earl, *Moral and Political*, who has a thoughtful section on the ideology (propaganda) of the *novi homines* (44ff.) and their view of Roman historical development, but Earl at times seems to believe what the Romans thought about their pristine past. Cf. Meier, *Res publica amissa*, 152ff.; and Toynbee, *Hannibal*, II, 495, who says that before the revo-

power, and experience of all its members, but its decisions were determined by the most influential senators, the nobles backed by their followers. These cliques considered their own interests to be the interests of the *respublica,* and if they were influential enough, their interests became those of the state. Nobles had always acted this way, but as the Roman world became more complicated and sophisticated, problems arose that demanded some operative policy other than self-interest.

Senators could submerge their differences and combine against a fellow aristocrat, or, it is argued, senators might present a more united front in times of crisis at home or abroad.[102] In the former case, senators were united against a peer who threatened their *dignitas* or privilege and were not making or following a policy designed to increase senatorial control, and in the latter case, senators followed the lead of the more influential aristocrats. The iteration of offices and the protraction of commands as illustrated by the careers of Fabius Maximus, Claudius Marcellus, and Scipio Africanus attest more to the success and prominence of individual aristocrats than to the Senate's leadership and success as a body. In addition, the evidence of hostility among Rome's illustrious sons during and after the war does not suggest that the Senate was united in its policy of how or by whom the war should be fought or what to do once the war ended.[103] The Senate's chief concern, where it was of one mind, was the control of its own members. Aristocrats in pursuit of *gloria* and *honores* could overshadow their fellows, and so far as they could be controlled or held accountable for their actions, it was due to rival factions often working through senatorial machinery.

The Second Punic War created emergencies that resulted in the granting of exceptional powers to exceptional aristocrats. The unprecedented career and unmatched success of Scipio Africanus during the Second Punic War made him the most famous citizen of the Republic and a threat to

---

lutionary period the "Roman nobles . . . still retained enough of their order's traditional sagacity to keep the pursuit of their fraternal rivalries within limits." It was not tradition that kept them in check so much as lack of opportunity and other nobles.

[102] Toynbee, *Hannibal,* II, 494, believes "the Roman nobility presented a united front to the rest of the World," but "was divided internally by an intense competition, for offices and honours, between rival families and rival individuals." I question the "united front." Cicero, *De legibus,* 2.15.39, 3.14.32, following Plato, believes a change in music constitutes a change in the character of the state, and how much more did a change in command or magistrates result in an entirely different "policy" or governmental attitude. If the nobles presented a front, they were not united behind it. But cf. Meier, *Res publica amissa,* 8ff., 162ff., who argues that on major issues the nobles were in agreement: personal politics dominated the everyday questions only.

[103] See Scullard, *Roman Politics*; and Cassola, *I gruppi politici,* 259ff., 293ff., 361ff., 375ff., 405ff., for discussion and bibliography concerning factional disputes.

aristocratic politics. "Africanus's direct relation with the Roman people, as a popular hero . . . , threatened to undercut all the limited clientelae that rival Roman noble houses had been building up for themselves laboriously over the course of many generations. This was Africanus's unpardonable offence in the eyes of his peers."[104] Scipio was held in check by jealous nobles, not by a senatorial government desirous of increasing its control over magistrates.

With the extraordinary career of Scipio Africanus in mind, the aristocracy established qualifications for officeholders and regulated the magistracies in the hope that elevation would be more gradual and extraordinary careers avoidable. A biennium was introduced between holding a praetorship and a consulship, and finally the *Lex Villia Annalis* (180 B.C.) established a strict order of offices (*cursus honorum*) with a minimum age requirement for the praetorship and consulship.[105] The number of praetorships had been increased to six; the office became inferior to the consulship, and consular families alone were identified as nobility. Subsequently, toward the middle of the century, reelection to the consulship was forbidden.[106] The quaestorship with a minimum age requirement was added to the *cursus honorum* by Sulla, who also permitted patricians to hold the praetorship and consulship two years earlier than plebeians.[107] It was not uncommon for senatorial aristocrats to hold magistracies in the first year they were eligible, but apparently the only new man to do so was Cicero.[108] Those without reputation or sufficient support had to wait for an opening. Nobles could rely on their ancestral reputations and, as Cicero laments, be elected to office in their sleep.[109] Others had to work hard, often holding as many offices as possible, and spent lavishly on games and entertainment to win votes.

The aristocracy in turn sought to check what it considered unbridled

---

[104] Toynbee, *Hannibal*, II, 512.

[105] A. E. Astin, *The Lex Annalis before Sulla*, Collection Latomus, 32 (Brussels, 1958).

[106] Scullard, *Roman Politics*, 234. Meier, *Res publica amissa*, 309n3b, points out the gradual decline in the iteration of the consulship, with the remarkable exception of the Second Punic War. But the aristocracy now held promagistracies with more regularity, and they were often prorogued beyond a single year. *Gloria*, wealth, and following (see Badian, *Foreign Clientelae*) were more readily accessible: the promagistracies replaced the iteration of offices. The decline in the number of aristocrats who held more than one consulship does not indicate the weakening of an individual aristocrat's personal power or *dignitas*.

[107] See Astin, *The Lex Annalis*; on the privilege extended to patricians, see E. Badian, "Caesar's *cursus* and the Intervals between Offices," *J.R.S.*, 49 (1959), 81ff.

[108] Certainly he was the first in almost a century. Cf. Wiseman, *New Men*, 106, 166ff.

[109] *Actio secunda in Verrem*, 5.180.

ambition in candidates for office. The law directed at excessive electioneering (181 B.C.) should be seen in connection with the *Lex Villia Annalis*. Thereafter, bribery laws were common, as were laws directed at conspicuous displays of wealth. Men of wealth caused considerable anxiety to the aristocracy, since they could afford to display the physical and visible signs of status that nobles cherished because they reinforced the nobles' position in society. They could also engage in the same types of personal, social, economic, and political activities and maintain the same relationships as the nobility. Apparently the nobility wanted to prevent wealthy individuals from competing with them, by reducing the amount one could spend on gowns, banquets, and silver, hence stripping wealth of one of its trademarks.[110] Senators and equestrians, however, still retained their special togas, sandals, and rings that set them apart from other citizens.[111]

By checking electioneering and bribery of the electorate and by curbing the lavish, costly games of the aediles, the nobles attempted to further inhibit the direct use of wealth for political profit. There is no evidence that such laws were passed because they were in keeping with the true aristocratic "Roman character." The idealized picture we have of Rome's pristine past and of her poor, simple, honest peasant consuls is a product of the second century, not the fifth. There is little evidence that the laws successfully controlled *ambitus*, or that the laws establishing qualifications and regulations for officeholding could not be set aside if circumstance and influential aristocrat demanded. But in normal times the laws did put politicking back on ground familiar and favorable to the aristocrat, where clients and friends were more important than hired votes, and an influential patron the most effective means of elevation. Such practices also guaranteed the continuing domination of politics by the patrons.

Following the disaster at Cannae, the door of the Senate was opened to many new men, and after generations in the lower offices, some of their descendants reached the higher magistracies. The plebeians who were the first of their families to appear as consuls during the course of the second century came mostly from senatorial families. Important noble *gentes* held their own, but the declining number of patricians admitted some new families to the consulship. Also the number of *novi homines* who reached the praetorship rose gradually in the second century.[112] Mobility was on the

---

[110] Daube, *Roman Law*, 117ff., esp. 123ff.

[111] Meyer Reinhold, *History of Purple as a Status Symbol in Antiquity*, Collection Latomus, 116 (Brussels, 1970), presents an interesting picture of the use of purple (and other status symbols) and shows how Roman aristocrats tried to restrict its use to their own group, just as they attempted to curb displays of wealth.

[112] Wiseman, *New Men*, 162ff.; and see above, p. 39. The increase in the number of praetorships made competition for the consulship more intense, but the nobility

rise, but the nobility was not in decline. Nobles controlled the consulship by either tenure or patronage. The most important reason for the advance of certain senatorial plebeian *gentes* was the support they received from nobility who promoted their candidacy to add to their personal following and to avoid an influx of new men. Senatorial and noble exclusiveness were not strictly maintained, but few *novi homines* before Marius reached the consulship. The nobility attempted to close ranks at the top because it could no longer successfully control the bottom rungs of the hierarchy. The new consular families were supported by the *nobiles* whose interests they served. Mobility functioned in the interest of the noble factions.

The senatorial court was another arena in which the aristocrats played at politics. It is assumed that the Senate usurped the judicial power of the people, and thereby tried to control promagistrates by senatorial rule and to punish those who did not obey by bringing them to trial.[113] Yet I find no evidence that the introduction of the senatorial extortion court was a consequence of the Senate's desire to arrogate more power, or that the court was instrumental in making commanders and governors more obedient to senatorial advice. The only certainties are that the court was not introduced out of any humanitarian feelings of responsibility toward Rome's provincials, and that it was excessively used as the setting for factional struggles.[114]

Although tribunes are often regarded as the "chattels of the nobility," they also played a notorious role in the divisiveness of Republican politics.[115] In the second century, not all tribunes were docile followers of the

---

continued to hold it or to determine the successful candidates. Scullard, *Roman Politics*, 56f., argues, rightly I believe, that the selection of so many new senators after Cannae resulted in the strengthening of the nobility, since they normally determined decisions. It must have also contributed to factionalism, inasmuch as few of the *novi praetorii* obtained the consulship: the nobles promoted their senatorial followers. Wiseman (182) lists over 300 possible *novi homines* who entered the Senate in the last 100 years of the Republic: 3 percent became consuls.

[113] Bleicken, *Das Volkstribunat*, 140, 146; Scullard, *Roman Politics*, 201f., 235ff.; cf. Toynbee, *Hannibal*, II, 492ff., who has too much about the moral standards of the "establishment" and its desire to control "black sheep." See also Smith, *The Failure*, 78f.

[114] E. Badian, *Roman Imperialism in the Late Republic* (Pretoria, 1967), 10, says, "The Roman oligarchy, like other oligarchies, was not efficient at protecting its subjects against its members." Concerning the *lex Calpurnia* of 149 B.C., Badian says (11) that the senators "made an honest attempt to protect their subjects against the worst effects of misbehaviour on the part of magistrates." As I see it, the Senate had no such policy, but was dominated by the nobles who might turn to the courts to check or punish a rival. See Gruen, *Roman Politics*, with whom I agree in theory but find much to question in detail.

[115] See Livy, 10.37.11, where some tribunes are called *mancipia nobilium*. Bleicken, *Das Volkstribunat*, 47ff., lists tribune activity in the service of the Senate during the war with Hannibal. Tribunes also engaged in prosecution (131ff.) for factional advantage.

senatorial aristocracy or protectors of their vested interests. Tribunes agitated against aristocratic leadership as practiced by consul and Senate, and were extremely active against and abrasive to the "establishment" decision-makers even before the Gracchi.[116] The contradiction was that many of those who opposed the collective will of the Senate were members of that august body, and were backed by other aristocrats. The Gracchi serve as an excellent illustration of this point. Certainly both were considered anti-senatorial, yet both were nobles with noble senatorial supporters. As L. R. Taylor points out, "It was not an alignment of senate against people, but an opposition between groups of men of noble or senatorial rank."[117] Moreover, as Sallust recognized, Roman politicians worked for their own interests, whether maintaining the rights and benefits of senatorial government or advocating a return of power to the people. Both oligarchs and *populares* compromised the *libertas* of citizens in their quest for *dignitas*.[118]

The oligarchic factions of the Senate, acting as a mob in defense of their privilege, were the first to shed blood in 133 B.C., and they legalized the deed the following year.[119] The *auctoritas* of the fathers failed, and they appealed to force. Then in 121 B.C. the Senate passed for the first time a *senatus consultum ultimum*: the final decree, tantamount to martial law. The senatorial oligarchs empowered the magistrates to take measures to see that the state should suffer no harm. Its employment caused controversy in both the ancient and modern worlds, since it was a device used by senators to protect the state against other aristocrats they considered

---

[116] L. R. Taylor, "Forerunners of the Gracchi," *J.R.S.*, 52 (1962), 19ff.; cf. Bleicken, *Das Volkstribunat*, 101ff., 152.

[117] *Party Politics*, 12.

[118] Sallust, *Bellum Catilinae*, 38.2–4; Taylor, *Party Politics*, 12f. Ch. Wirszubski, *Libertas as a Political Idea at Rome during the Late Republic and Early Principate* (Cambridge, 1960), 16f., points out that "the Roman citizen sought to assert and safeguard his rights, not against the overriding authority of the State, or the tyranny of the majority, as it is sometimes called, but against other citizens who were stronger than himself, or against the officers of the State who, in the pursuit of their own private interests, might encroach upon his rights, abusing the power . . . entrusted to them."

[119] See D. C. Earl, *Tiberius Gracchus: A Study in Politics*, Collection Latomus, 66 (Brussels, 1963); Astin, *Scipio*, 191ff., 211ff., 227ff.; and the more general Henry C. Boren, *The Gracchi* (New York, 1968). Smith, *The Failure*, 5, says, "the Gracchi by the means they adopted in pursuit of their ends precipitated a spiritual crisis in Rome which was the first cause of all that followed." H. H. Scullard, "Scipio Aemilianus and Roman Politics," *J.R.S.*, 50 (1960), 74, adds, "Any hope of an amicable settlement was shattered by [Ti.] Gracchus' methods . . . his actions in fact alienated sympathy and created distrust among senators of varying outlook . . . not only among Optimates but also among moderates like Scipio [Aemilianus]." That Scipio was not a moderate, cf. Astin, *Scipio*. Too much emphasis is placed on the methods of the so-called *populares*. Certain proposals and certain individuals could not succeed by "traditional" methods. It is not easy to determine who is more the adherent of *mos maiorum*, Tiberius with his agrarian plan or the oligarchs led by Scipio Nasica.

dangerous.[120] It was used not to safeguard the *respublica* but to guarantee the control of some senatorial aristocrats over the state. These senators would agree that "extremism in defense of liberty [or *dignitas*] was no vice," but such extremism was always employed in the name of public good.[121] For chaos to reign, it remained only for a single aristocrat to apply this defense to his own individual activities.

Aristocratic objectives were personal power and influence; wealth, tradition, institutional privilege, personal politics, and personal following were the means used to accomplish these objectives. Personal relationships opened doors closed by tradition and upper-class ideology, but while strengthening the hand of the individual aristocrat, they undermined aristocratic control. Aristocrats might collectively oppose the concentration of power or influence in a single pair of hands, but opposition did not mean they followed a consistent policy or were united and cooperative in more than their opposition. The personal nature of Roman politics precluded the development of governmental policy. Individual advancement outweighed constitutional and traditional practices, which were pillars of aristocratic domination. In this respect, Scipio Aemilianus is an excellent example. Conservative by nature, Scipio's methods of self-promotion were popular, even revolutionary. As A. E. Austin states, "It is one of the characteristics of his career that, with conspicuous success, he places his own advancement above both usage and the law, that in the furtherance of his own ambitions he cultivated and exploited popular favor as an instrument with which to defy the Senate."[122]

I concur, but Scipio is singled out only to indicate what many a noble would have done if given the opportunity. Exceptional conditions, created by the failures and inconsistencies of state practices, advanced individual

[120] Jolowicz, *Historical Introduction*, 34; Gruen, *Roman Politics*, 96f. A. H. J. Greenidge, *The Legal Procedure of Cicero's Time* (Oxford, 1901), 406, states the problem plainly: "no amount of treasonable design can legally make a citizen into an enemy, unless that treason has been proved in a court of law." "Every decrease in power is an open invitation to violence—if only because those who hold power and feel it slipping from their hands, be they the government or be they the governed, have always found it difficult to resist the temptation to substitute violence for it"; Hannah Arendt, *On Violence* (New York, 1969), 87. Cf. A. W. Lintott, *Violence in Republican Rome* (Oxford, 1968).

[121] Wirszubski, *Libertas*, 16: "just as dignitas became a watchword of 'vested interest' so could libertas be used as a battle-cry—sincere or feigned—of social reform." As rightly observed by M. I. Finley, "Athenian Demagogues," *Past and Present*, 21 (1962), 19, "Politicians regularly say that what they are advocating is in the best interests of the nation, and, what is more important, they believe it. Often, too, they charge their opponents with sacrificing the national interests, and they believe that."

[122] Astin, *Scipio*, 243.

aristocrats beyond their fellows. Aristocrats in search of preeminence were a heavy burden for the Republican constitution to carry. Julius Caesar was not the first scion of a noble family to desire and obtain through offices, talent, and intrigue a greater *dignitas* than other aristocrats, but when he crossed the Rubicon in defense of his dignity, the blend of existing conditions and his unique talents determined he would be the last. As I began with Mills, so I conclude, "All politics is a struggle for power; the ultimate kind of power is violence."[123] The Roman Republic came to a violent end.

[123] *Power Elite*, 171.

Charity and the Defense of
Urban Elites in the
Italian Communes

RICHARD C. TREXLER

Giù nei slums
c'è la miseria
Non è come la povertà. . . .
Giovanna Marini singing "Vi parlo dell'America"

To the modern age it seems strange to find members of an elite characterized before the law as poor, and entitled to charity. Yet such was the case
in medieval and early modern Europe. While the governments of the
Italian city-states were long restrained from direct governmental aid to
members of the governing class by pressures for sustenance from the lower
classes, private confraternities took up the task of aiding those who could
not beg because of their social position: the Shamed Poor. This confraternal
task, as well as other more traditional practices in the division of charity,
suggests that medieval and early modern charity served as an instrument
for maintaining the governing class. This paper will examine the nature
of "poverty" and then analyze the early practice of sustaining the lifestyle
of one's brothers within the "honorable" segment of Florentine society.

The late medieval and Renaissance Italian equivalent of the term
"elite" was *uomini di stato* and, in a looser sense, *uomini da bene.* The *stato*,
or status, extended to these men's families: they had held political office,

Research for this paper was done while I was a Fellow at the Harvard University
Center for Italian Renaissance Studies (Villa I Tatti). I would like to thank Signora
Maria Ludovica Andreucci Lenzi for her paleographic help, and professors Sergio
Bertelli, Riccardo Fubini, and Giorgio Spini for their help in obtaining access to a key
document.

paid taxes, were entitled to ambassadorial work, figured in the ceremonies of the communes, and so forth. In Florence they were citizens, sometimes noble but commonly *popolani*.[1] Below this group were the small independent artisans of little social worth, sometimes citizens but often not matriculated in a guild and thus completely outside the political class. Finally came the *popolo minuto*, the salaried residents and journeymen. This substantial portion of the general population included skilled and semiskilled, but also the mass of unskilled, labor in the medieval city. The *minuti* were not considered part of the political fabric of the city at all. They bestowed no honor on it, had no status, indeed were called the *popolo di Dio*. They belonged, that is, only to the celestial body politic.[2]

The elite studied here consists of the first of these groups, the *cittadini*, or citizens, as many called them. Unlike a modern member of an elite, whose appurtenance is not clear from his dress or bearing, his medieval and early modern counterpart was distinguished by his honorable deportment and bearing and the customary deference accorded him by the lower middle class and by the *minuti*. Such an individual was not necessarily powerful in any measurable form. Yet his physical presence marked him as a member of a group of honorable men, the group that embodied secular authority and social order. This "honor elite," therefore, was more visible and no less socially crucial than a contemporary elite. Lower ranks deferred to its right to rule and represent, to embody the honor and power upon which the commonwealth was based.

This honor elite cannot be precisely circumscribed. Lauro Martines has recently summarized the contemporary criteria for honor as financial status, public office, marriage alliances, and family tradition.[3] An Infangati or a Bisdomini could command respect in the city though his star had long since fallen. The wealthy Panciatichi, on the contrary, were a byword for dishonestly acquired goods, and for that they were viewed with less honor even though they were politically active. Thus the honor elite can be partially distinguished from those men who governed the commune. A

---

[1] The political struggle between the noble *magnati* and the *popolani* ended in victory for the latter. A common practice in the period after 1343 was for nobles to change their family name and take on popular status, the only status possessing full political rights in Florence after 1293; see M. Becker, *Florence in Transition*, I (Baltimore, 1967), 5–8.

[2] On the social content of the *minuti*, see E. Werner, "Probleme städtischer Volksbewegungen im 14. Jahrhundert, dargestellt am Beispiel der Ciompi-Erhebung in Florenz," in *Städtische Volksbewegungen im 14. Jahrhundert*, ed. Werner and Steinmetz (Berlin, 1960), 11–55; and the recent work by Gene Brucker, "The Ciompi Revolution," in N. Rubinstein, ed., *Florentine Studies* (London, 1968), 317–23.

[3] L. Martines, *The Social World of the Florentine Humanists* (Princeton, 1963), 10, 18–84.

common criterion for *political* respectability was whether one had been considered for potential officeholding in the magistracies—the number ran to about 5,000 in 1382, about one-eighth of the population.[4] But there is no exact formula that allows us to predict the holder of a position of honor.[5]

In the late medieval Italian communes, elevation into a position of honor was statistically rare, but occurred often enough to have attracted the attention of contemporaries. An established family generally considered its rise an admirable part of its past. In Florence, where books of family *ricordanze* were common during this period, it was normal for the head of the household to recognize his ancestors' humble but honest beginnings, and then chronicle the improvements in the family's political, social, and economic fortunes.[6] Long-established families frequently blamed civic disasters on the influence of these new people, but their rise was considered regrettable rather than unnatural.

Downward mobility was another matter. With status came honor, and for medieval and early modern man, a family that once attained respectability had a virtually natural right to retain status. The disappearance or collapse of once-established families was not thought of as a natural result of a mobile merchant society. Sometimes fate was blamed, and just as often the reckless squandering of capital by blameworthy sons. There was no God-given reason for such tragedies.

Honored families in economic straits were not just a private matter. The word "commune" also meant a fraternal grouping of these families. Thus destitution of members of this community involved the dishonor of the city itself. It was a civic and social as well as familial tragedy. The *uomini da bene* owed nothing to the new men because they were new; they did owe something to established families because they were old.

[4] A. Molho, "The Florentine Oligarchy and the *Balìe* of the Late Trecento," *Speculum*, 43 (1968), 26–27. For the quattrocento, see N. Rubinstein, *The Government of Florence under the Medici (1434 to 1494)* (Oxford, 1966), 53–67.

[5] The right to bear arms in the city was a crucial mark of social status, two thousand being licensed in 1393; Molho, "Oligarchy," 27. Statistics on other common denominators of status are in A. Molho, "Politics and the Ruling Class in Early Renaissance Florence," *Nuova Rivista Storica*, 52 (1968), 404–8. All Florentine historical literature refers to some aspect of this problem of reputation. In addition to ch. 2 of Martines' above-mentioned book, I have found most helpful G. Brucker, *Florentine Politics and Society, 1343–1378* (Princeton, 1962), 27–56; P. J. Jones, "Florentine Families and Florentine Diaries in the Fourteenth Century," *Papers of the British School at Rome*, 24 (1956), 183–205; and C. Bec, *Les marchands écrivains à Florence* (Paris, 1967), pt. 1. I have generally renounced the use of the term "patriciate" in this essay in referring to Florentine society. Its connotation is too narrow for the group I want to describe. "Honor elite" has the advantage of being just as vague but more attuned to the social conceptions of the society I am describing.

[6] See, e.g., Giovanni di Pagolo Morelli, *Ricordi*, ed. V. Branca (Florence, 1956), 81–90.

A fundamental test of the cohesion and operativeness of a social order is the ability of the dominant group to protect its own. This paper deals with the developments in charity by which the *uomini da bene* of the republic of Florence (ends 1530) sought to prevent their fellows' decline from status through financial reverses. This aid was motivated by some thoroughly functional considerations: preservation of capital and tax base, maintenance of social order, and the principle of authority. Ideationally and institutionally, however, such alms were conceived as charity to the poor. Initially, then, we must find the charitable niche into which these "poor" people fit.

Contemporaries tended to conceive of three different social corporations deserving of alms: the religious, the lay miserable, and the lay poor. Each of these groups was identified by a social function and by a social psychology. Each formed a legal category as well, and the lawyers' definitions of religion, misery, and poverty helped to form popular notions through exposition in the pulpit and through their influence on charitable and testamental matters. Let us consider the first two categories, and then the third, within which we will find the embarrassed elite.

The clergy was a natural recipient of charity for one was, in effect, giving to God. This corporation was favored by the legal dictum that when deciding to whom poor money should be given, the distributor should prefer the virtuous if need were equal.[7] The clergy was virtuous by definition. Consequently when wealth was left in general "for the poor" and "for pious causes" and was motivated by the love of God, executors often distributed it to the clergy. The neediest received it, and this usually meant the mendicant friars such as Franciscans and Dominicans, who were bound by oath to own no real property.[8]

In exchange for this charity, the secular clergy ministered to parishioners; the mendicants preached while the monks and nuns prayed. There was a strong sense of implicit contract by which the religious protected the city by their example, preaching and prayer, and received alimentation in exchange.[9] The Franciscan Salimbene affords an insight into this sense of contract when he rails against the beggars who, part of no religious order,

---

[7] "Nam etsi omnibus debetur misericordia, tamen iusto amplius"; *Corpus Iuris Canonici*, d. LXXXVI, c. 14. Subsequent references to the canon law consist only of the abbreviated legal citation.

[8] On the practical implications, see Bartolus de Saxoferrato, *Tractatus Minoricarum*, in his *Consilia, Quaestiones, et Tractatus* (Venice, 1567), II, ff. 129 seq. At Florence the annual communal alms for the poor were divided during the trecento between lay miserables and pious entities; A(rchivio) di S(tato), F(irenze), *Provvisioni* 25, ff. 76rv (30 Oct. 1329). In the quattrocento, religious were commonly excluded from these alms; *Provv.* 107, f. 106v (21 June 1417).

[9] "Dignus est operarius mercede sua"; X.3.28.1.

simply stood in front of churches and begged without saying a word. They did no work, said the good mendicant, and should be forcibly disbanded.[10] The miserable constituted another object of charity. According to law the miserable were unable to defend or take care of themselves.[11] But within this group, two quite distinct social types can be distinguished. There were the indigent: poor resident handworkers plus a floating population of dayworkers, both of whom were unable to provide themselves with food and shelter if adversity struck. These miserables are those we today call "the poor," except that the economically indigent were often thought to be coterminous with beggars.[12] In addition to this group, certain categories of the population were miserable by law, whether they were hungry or wealthy. Widows, orphans, prisoners, and the mentally disturbed were miserable because they had an inferior legal position, were too young, could not move about, and so on.[13] Because of legal liabilities, members of the clergy were also often termed "miserable."

The complexity of this category makes it difficult to classify the charity and motivations of these burghers. The *misericordia* due the miserable cut across class lines; the concept of misery was not fully our own. Hence a charitable donation to an undefined miserable person, or even to a "genuinely miserable person," tells us next to nothing about the economic class or social group to which the donor or testator intended to contribute. For this we need to know to whom such wealth was actually given.[14]

The economically miserable or indigent were equivalent to the *popolo minuto* mentioned above. Their function was to provide the hand labor for men of substance. St. Bernardina da Siena spoke of this group when he said, "The rich are necessary to the commune, and the poor to the rich."[15] If such a man could work and did not, he was entitled to no alms, added the Florentine archbishop Antonino (1446–59). Idleness encouraged all man-

[10] Salimbene De Adam, *Cronica*, ed. G. Scalia, I (Bari, 1966), 369, 374, 406, 416, 419.

[11] "Miserabilesque personas, concilio et auxilio destitutas"; R. Trexler, *Synodal Law in Florence and Fiesole, 1306–1518* (Vatican City, 1971), 239:15.

[12] In Florentine tax lists, *miserabili* designated those who were too poor to pay taxes; Brucker, *Politics*, 48.

[13] In so many words, Innocent IV made this distinction in his *Apparatus*; see the text in B. Tierney, *Medieval Poor Law* (Berkeley, 1959), 18. The 1517 Florentine synodal constitutions contain the typical formulation: "Viduis, pupillis, mentecaptis, furiosis, caeterisque miserabilibus personis"; J.-D. Mansi, *Sacrorum Conciliorum nova et amplissima collectio* (Florence and Venice, 1759–98), XXXV, c. 305.

[14] Failure to take account of these complexities has marred the conceptual framework of the various works of W. K. T. Jordan on English charity. For an evaluation, see J. A. F. Thomson, "Piety and Charity in Late Medieval London," *Journal of Ecclesiastical History*, 15 (1964), 179, 194; and most recently, B. Pullan, *Rich and Poor in Renaissance Venice* (Cambridge, Mass., 1971), 13f., 197–202.

[15] I. Origo, *The World of San Bernardino* (New York, 1962), 110.

ner of vice, and the indigent were attracted enough to villainy as it was.[16]

A definite group psychology attributed to the indigent explains why charitable distribution to them usually amounted to a fraction of that tendered to other needy groups. The poor were accustomed to eating less refined foods; they should receive them.[17] To feast them with delicacies was a sin, for it encouraged boisterous behavior.[18] To bequeath a large generic gift to the poor was presumptive evidence that it was not meant for the indigent. A meager gift was presumably for this group.[19] In the age of the fall, property was to be protected: "Otherwise human society could not stand, for goods would lack, and [those who are] evil would seize everything."[20] Charity aimed at preserving corporative identification, not at fostering interclass mobility.

The third category of charity, "the poor," has bedeviled the history of medieval charity. Catholic historians have tended to equate them with "the poor in our normal everyday sense of the word," while an antagonist like G. G. Coulton pointed out that substantial sums of poor money went to the clergy, including quite substantial monasteries.[21] Very few historians

---

[16] As a general rule the canonists and theologians agreed that the starving were entitled to minimum sustenance before any other distribution—with the exception of the idler. If we consider the present age's persistent enlightened belief that "anyone can get work if he really wants to," we will have little difficulty imagining medieval urban man's attitude. Tierney believes that the open job market of the High Middle Ages may have shrunk in the fourteenth and fifteenth centuries, implying that the harshness toward the idler suited to an earlier age was inadequate for this scarcer age. A quattrocento Italian would have found this argument as unempirical as do those today who insist there are jobs for those who want them. Except at times of disaster, medieval laws and chronicles yield little evidence that the hungry of otherwise sound body were preferred in the distribution of poor monies. In Venice, for example, as today, a lay beggar had to be physically disabled to deserve alms; Pullan, *Rich and Poor*, 301–3. On the new structuralization of poor categories in the 1520s, see ibid., 239f.

[17] St. Antoninus, *Summa* (Paris, 1521), p. 4, t. 3, c. 5, § 2. For the similar views of earlier canonists, see B. Tierney, "The Decretists and the 'Deserving Poor,' " *Comparative Studies in Society and History*, 1 (1958), 366.

[18] "Quinimmo peccare dicuntur, qui pauperibus lauta convivia exhibent"; Cornelius Benincasii, *De paupertate, ac eius privilegiis*, in *Tractatus universi iuris* . . . (Venice, 1584), XVIII, f. 146va. This important tract was first printed in Perugia in 1562.

[19] Ibid., f. 164v.

[20] "Bonum esset ut aliqua essent propria, alioqui[n] non staret humana societas, quia bona egerent, at mali omnia raperent, et ita secundum diversos status ius naturae communionem, et divisionem dictat"; ibid., f. 141v, citing the early trecento canonist Guido da Baysio.

[21] Brian Tierney, for example, takes this Catholic view: "The poor who were to be provided for by the bishop of the diocese according to the decretist texts were the ordinary indigent lay folk and clergy, 'the poor' in our normal everyday sense of the word"; Tierney, *Medieval Poor Law*, 69. Of help on this question is M. Mollat, "La notion de pauvreté au moyen âge: Position de problèmes," *Revue d'histoire de l'église de France*, 52 (1966), 5–23.

have examined its meaning in regard to the lay world. The easy equation of modern with medieval "poverty" has been fostered by the fact that in the past the word was used in a wide sense that could include the miserable. Given this confusion, it will be well to look at some historical background. Who were the medieval poor?

Two Belgian scholars have recently examined the use of the word *paupertas* in Carolingian Europe of the ninth and tenth centuries and in Anglo-Saxon sources from the seventh to the eleventh centuries. Their conclusions are quite striking. The poor were those who were not rich, or those who could not defend themselves from the attacks of the rich. They were weak, not poor in our sense. Further, the poor were always free men; there is no case of a poor serf. In the 183 cases in Anglo-Saxon sources where the significance of the word *pauper* is indicated, 72 times it meant the opposite of rich, 45 times the contrary of powerful, and 66 times the opposite of unfree.[22]

The actual financial condition of the *pauperes* reached from "ease to the most absolute distress." Dufermont believes that the *pauperes* were generally small proprietors. Their feeble condition was separated from indigence only by time: "The feeble became poor; the feeble are a reservoir of poor."[23]

Thus the poor were a large social group, defined only by their powerlessness vis-à-vis the rich, their moderate means, and their freedom. Most important, they were men of property. The pauper emerges in these documents usually in the defense of his wealth.

The term *miserabilis persona* was apparently unknown to these documents. But when urban societies with no serfs arose, the judicial vocabulary responded. Roughly, the distinction between free poor and serf yielded to one between *pauper* and *miserabilis persona*.

The development of urban legal institutions did not replace the earlier understanding of poverty. In the hagiographical literature of the Middle Ages, one of the most persistent examples of saintly charity is aid to fallen nobles. St. Nicholas aids a noble so that his daughters will not become prostitutes; St. Dominic helps another noble retrieve his daughters from the heretics to whom he had been forced to give them so that they could be fed.[24] Why did charity toward nobles or gentlemen so often exemplify charity per se? Basically it was because a natural link between high social standing and virtue was assumed. Conversely, medieval writers were wont

[22] J.-C. Dufermont, "Les Pauvres, d'après les sources anglo-saxonnes du VIIe au XIe siècle," *Revue du Nord*, 50 (1968), 189.

[23] Ibid., 190. See also R. Le Jan-Hennebicque, "'Pauperes' et 'Paupertas' dans l'occident carolingien aux IXe et X^e siecles," *Revue du Nord*, 50 (1968), 170.

[24] Antonino, *Summa*, p. 4, t. 5, c. 18, § 1.

to point out how seldom the humble had achieved sainthood.[25] Florence's archbishop Antonino, for example, did not believe that Mary Magdalen had been a prostitute; corrupted, yes, but a public woman, no. She was of noble family, he reasoned, and therefore relatives would have prevented poverty from driving her into the streets.[26] What then was more desirable than to prevent girls who did not have to become prostitutes from entering that life?

Aid to those of gentle birth has a firm foundation in the law. In the late Middle Ages and early modern period, poverty was conceived as the condition of not being able to meet the living standards of one's social group. Three examples will quickly suggest implications of this important fact.

Baldus (d. 1400) was asked about "a noble who had alimentation, but could not preserve his dignity, and perhaps had daughters whom he could not marry." "Could something be given to him by the bishop or executor in subsidy of life or of dowries as if to a poor person?" The lawyer responded, "Yes, since although not like a beggar, he nevertheless lacks sustenance according to the state of his birth, and therefore is to be numbered among the poor."[27]

The canon lawyer Petrucci (d. 1348) examined the case of a nunnery whose inhabitants had sufficient room and board, but could not build a cistern or cloister without disposing of capital. His decision that "the nunnery can be numbered among the poor" was influenced by this reasoning: "If it is said that the nunnery has many possessions, we respond that it also has many expenses. Once one considers the nunnery's social and religious position, it can rather be said that the nunnery is more indigent than the poor mendicant, who is accustomed to begging for his bread in the marketplace. Only after considering the quality of the poor should alms be distributed accordingly."[28]

---

[25] G. G. Coulton, *Medieval Village, Manor, and Monastery* (New York, 1960), 241, 523–27.

[26] "Cioè, in che modo s'intende Maria Maddalena essere stata peccatrice. E perchè secondo il volgare si dice peccatrice quella che sta nel mal luogho, alcuni dicono, lei essere stata meretrice, la quale opinione non mi piace, nè credo, perocchè era ricca e nobile. Come è da credere il fratello nobile et dabbene avessi sofferto tanto suo vituperio?" *Lettere di Sant' Antonino, arcivescovo di Firenze* (Florence, 1859), 113.

[27] "Et respondo quod sic, quia licet non ut omnino mendicans, tamen statum natalium suorum aliqua sustentatione eget, et ideo inter pauperes connumeratur"; Baldus degli Ubaldi (d. 1400), *In primum, secundum et tertium cod. lib. commentaria* (Venice, 1577), lib. I, lex XXXVII (f. 53r). This was also the opinion of the canonist Hostiensis (mid-dugento); Petrucci refers to him in his *consilium* cited below.

[28] "Et si dicatur monasterium habet pluries possessiones, responditur et habet plurimos expensus et onera. Unde considerato statu suo, plus debet dici indigens quam pauper mendicans consuetus per publicum questum sibi victum querere. Consideratis

In the same vein the canonist Giovanni d'Andrea remarked that a canon of the cathedral of Bologna could live without absolute penury on 25 florins a year, but not becomingly on less than 100 florins; "and I might say the same of myself."[29]

Poverty did not mean misery, the lawyers said, "but a necessity of those things required to live rightly." Even with alimentation, "unless he has enough to live well and blessedly, he is called poor."[30] There was a difference between indigence (*egestas*) and poverty. The first lacked food, the second that necessary to live correctly. "He who has no goods at all is said to be in the most extreme poverty." This condition was better called "indigence and pauperism than poverty."[31] With this legal terminology in mind, we can grasp the significance of references in testaments and communal laws to persons "not so much in poverty but in the greatest misery," "not so much poor as in extreme necessity," for what they are: not rhetoric, but important operative distinctions in everyday life.[32]

It is evident from the opinions of the legists that poverty reached far up the social and financial hierarchy. These jurisprudents were often faced with the practical problem of determining whether a party to a suit was poor. The determinations below represent not fanciful scholastic constructions, but precedential rulings in the administration of charity.

They were poor who could not pay their debts. The declaration of bankruptcy and the sale of property by creditors were other hallmarks of poverty. The civil law included among the poor those who could scarcely live by their daily labor, but some jurisprudents extended this to "anyone who lives by his labor and by his own occupation." This sweeping definition of poverty included anyone dependent on daily work rather than on rents for his sustenance. Consequently the sale of lands on which rents were based was presumptive evidence of poverty.[33]

---

quidem personis pauperum sic eroganda est . . . "; F. Petrucci, *Disputationes, Questiones, Consilia* (Siena, 1488), q. 282.

[29] Tierney, *Poor Law*, 37.

[30] "Paupertas est rei ad recte vivendum pertinentis necessitas. Quam quidem diffinitionem comprobo, quoniam is qui habet unde alimenta percipiat, nisi tamen abunde ad bene beateque vivendum habeat, pauper nuncupatur"; Benincasa, f. 139vb, with references to Guido da Baysio and the early quattrocento lawyer Paolo da Castro.

[31] "Is qui nil prorsus in bonis habet dicitur in arctissima paupertate constitutus, et sic non simpliciter, sed plusquam pauper est ex quibus omnibus simul iunctis colligit plus egestatem, et mendicantem, quam paupertatem esse"; ibid., ff. 139vb–140ra, citing Baldus. "Down the scale to destitution might be listed: *paupertas, inopia, penuria, egestas, indigentia, necessitas*"; M. Mollat, "Pauvres et Pauvreté à la fin du XII. siècle," *Revue d'ascetique et de mystique*, 41 (1965), 307.

[32] See, e.g., ASF, *Provv.* 101, ff. 196rv (14 Oct. 1412); 109, ff. 207r–208r (27 Dec. 1419).

[33] "Mercatores decocti dicuntur pauperes, quia coguntur propriis laribus carere";

We commonly encounter "poor" with servants. Fathers ordinarily were required by law to dower their daughters. They were relieved of this duty "if they did not have the resources to dower, or if not enough would remain to them thereafter to enable them to live commodiously according to their quality and dignity." "One must consider not only the dowerer, but as well those without whom the dowerer cannot live honorably according to his state. For the privilege conceded to one person is extended also to the servants without whom he cannot maintain himself. . . ."[34] This meant that a man whose status required servants was considered poor if he had to give up those servants. The critical point was not that the servants might be reduced to destitution by being dismissed—the poverty of *servi* was as seldom the subject of jurisprudence in the fourteenth century as it had been a juridical subject in Anglo-Saxon times—but that such a master transferred his quality of poverty to his servants. Thus all had to be maintained, given his status as master. The canonist Oldradus (d. 1335) said: "Under the appellation of 'the poor' are also included those who are accustomed to serving the poor. Thus whatever is given to the servants of the poor is said to be arrogated to the poor."[35]

Rentiers provide a final example of the types of poor found in the social hierarchy. In the case of a father who was assigned rents by his sons, or a mother who was supported by rich sons, Baldus ruled that this support

---

Benincasa, f. 146va, citing Angelo degli Ubaldi. "Vel non posse suis creditoribus satisfacere"; ibid., citing Baldus. "Vel cesisse bonis"; ibid., citing *communis opinio*. "Et hinc notanter dicebat Bartolus in l. tres tutores, num. 4, ff. de administ. tuto, quod quando bona alicuius venduntur a creditoribus praesumitur, quod ille sit pauper et non solvendo, et quod alias non permitteret distractionem. Item dicitur ab effectu probata paupertas eo ipso, quod probatum est aliquem ex suis laboribus proprioque artificio vivere, c. quod super, et ibi not. Abb. extra de voto, vel inde vivere non posse, Baldus in l. paupertas, ff. de excusa. tut . . ."; ibid. "Aliquando eum qui suo quotidiano labore, quotidianisque operibus vix vivere potest, l. paupertas . . . "; ibid., f. 147rb. Jurists also extended the appellation to exiles because they could not live at home; ibid., f. 146va. As we remember how common banishment was in the Italian commune, this legal dictum throws light on the propensity of Italians automatically to call exiles "poor." The biographer Vespasiano da Bisticci gives a description of the "poor" banished Felice Brancacci, "sendo in esiglio e povero e fuori della patria"; *Vita di uomini illustri del secolo XV* (Florence, 1938), 26 (*Vita* of Eugenius IV).

[34] "Dicuntur autem praedictae persone inopes ad effectum, ut dotare non teneantur quando dotando non haberent, nec eis superesset tantum, quod commode secundum earum qualitatem et dignitatem vivere possent; ita tenet Dynus . . . Angelus . . . et Imola . . . ut refert subtilis Aretinus. . . . Et consideratio non solum habetur dotantis, verum etiam aliorum sine quibus dotans honorifice secundum statum suum vivere non potest. Cum privilegium alicui pro se concessum, extendatur etiam ad ministros sine quibus ille stare non potest"; Benincasa, f. 156vb, citing Bartolus and Baldus.

[35] "Et Oldradus in consilio 11 ubi dicit quod pauperum appellatione, veniunt etiam ii qui pauperibus servire solent, itaque pauperibus dicitur arrogatum quod servientibus pauperum datum est"; ibid.

did not by itself prevent the parents from being termed poor, "since he who has alimentation does not always cease to be poor."[36]

The unifying characteristic of these examples is that the poor in question are propertied. This is not surprising, since the court cases from which these rulings emanate arose from doubt that persons of this condition could be termed poor. The point is that not property, but sufficient property, was the decisive criterion for determining poverty. Poverty was not simply a deprivative entity, said Benincasa. It was "deprivation in respect to riches and goods," and his mid-cinquecento colleagues were going so far as to accept Plato's definition: "poverty is not the decrementation of possessions, but the incrementation of insatiability."[37] Many of the privileges that were permitted *favore pauperum* dealt with the insufficiencies of the propertied. Freedom from dowering daughters, the right to alienate inalienable property, freedom from civil taxation "except in dire necessity,"[38] even the privilege of being excused from one's contractual obligations to one's tenants: all referred to the propertied.[39]

The judicial categories of poverty thus included the miserable, divided between those who were economically destitute and those who were legally *miserabiles personae*, and the poor, those propertied individuals who could not live according to their social position. These terms were by no means precise; a difference existed between the generic and legal uses of the term. In the division of alms, however, whether the distributor was a private testator, a confraternity, the commune, or a religious, the proper use of the term was what counted.

We now focus on the aid rendered the fallen of good family. It was assumed that they had a special claim on the consciences of Christians. "It is the greatest type of misfortune to remember that one had once been happy," said the moralist and archbishop Antonino.[40] A mendicant was ac-

---

[36] "Nec obstare, quod pater ususfructuarius sit in bonis filorum, et mater a filiis divitibus sit alenda, quoniam ex eo solo non desinit pater, aut mater pauper esse, quia is, qui habet alimenta non semper desinit esse pauper"; ibid., f. 163rb, citing Baldus. On the broad meaning given the word *alimentum* by Bartolus in his tract, see the summary, ibid., f. 149rb.

[37] Ibid., f. 139vb.

[38] Ibid., f. 143vb.

[39] Ibid., ff. 143rb–143va. See ibid., f. 159rb, for the right to sell vassals if one needed food or clothes. It is significant that while contemporary legal tracts on the privileges of the poor show a preoccupation with those rights which permitted the "poor" *Herr* to deprive his *Knecht*, modern commentaries on the rights of the poor sooner mention those more improbable privileges such as the right to steal if starving; see the exhaustive and solid work of G. Couvreur, *Les Pauvres ont-ils des droits? Recherches sur le vol in cas d'extrême nécessité depuis la concordia de Gratian (1140) jusqu'à Guillaume d'Auxerre (1231)* (Rome, 1961).

[40] Antonino, p. 4, t. 5, c. 18, § 1.

customed to begging for his bread, but the natural condition of good folk prevented them from doing the same. Such honorable people "would rather die than beg." The Venetian prelate Contarini (1483–1542) believed that the charitable bishop had to prefer to all others "those for whom, because of their noble origins, poverty was ignominy. Without calumny they cannot take a salaried position. One must contribute to them before anyone else. Since it is not to be expected that they will seek alms, one must give them without being asked, sometimes even to the anonymous. After these have been cared for, [the bishop] should tend to other poor persons."[41] Unable to take gainful employment, dowerless girls from respectable families often chose prostitution, while the men squandered what they had, involved themselves in gang wars, and became involved in conspiracies and the like.[42]

As a whole, this group was called the "shamed poor," the *poveri vergognosi*. In its simplest sense it referred to the needy who did not beg. Early documents using the term in a practical context do not explicitly identify the *vergognosi* as belonging to any particular class, even though shame was a quality more class-oriented than existential: "Shame, which betrays the well-born."[43] In 1311, for example, the archbishop of Ravenna distinguished between the poor who would publicly receive alms at the periodic episcopal distribution and the *poveri vergognosi* who had to be sought out at home and helped. For this purpose he ordered his suffragan bishops to appoint a group of *uomini da bene* for each section of their cities who would collect and distribute alms to this group.[44] In 1333, in Florence, when a testamentary disposition required alms to be given to the beggars and the *poveri vergognosi*, the beggars were all gathered in the churches and given six pence apiece, while the shamed were sought out and given twice as much.[45] Later the term became more clearly attached in practical matters to those of honorable birth, or even nobility. What had never been far below the surface—the tendency to equate mendicancy with

---

[41] "Omnibus vero in hoc officio anteferendi sunt illi, quibus nobili genere ortis paupertas ignonimiae esse solet; neque expectandum, ut eleemosinas petant; verum his etiam non petentibus largiendum, et quandoque insciis. Post hos alios curet pauperes"; Gasparo Contarini, *De officio episcopi*, in his *Opera* (Paris, 1571), 429.

[42] Pullan, *Rich and Poor*, 229.

[43] "Verecundia, quae ingenuous prodit natales"; *Corpus Iuris Canonici*, d. LXXXVI, c. 17.

[44] "Et ut pauperibus verecundis valeat provideri, in quolibet quarterio vel sexterio cujuslibet civitatis, et aliis insignibus locis nostrae provinciae, quolibet anno eligantur quatuor vel sex, sicut videbitur episcopis esse sufficiens, catholici et devoti et honorabiles viri, qui questam requirant pro eleemosyna hujusmodi pauperibus facienda; et dividant, prout discretioni eorum videbitur expedire"; J.-D. Mansi, XXV, c. 473.

[45] *Croniche di Giovanni, Matteo e Filippo Villani*, I (Trieste, 1857), X, 165.

economic misery—became more overt in the quattrocento: the lower classes beg, and the good families were too shamed to plead for help.

How did the Florentines subvent their shamed poor, those downwardly mobile families, during the period up to the fall of the republic in 1530? Three resources were open to these poor: their families, charitable confraternities, and the communal government itself.

Familial or consorterial self-help was the most durable means for aiding fallen citizens. Preference for one's *familia* (including relatives and servants) was built into the law, following Ambrose's dictum that love should be given, in descending order, to God, parents, children, other members of the *familia*, and finally strangers.[46] The shame of family members having to ask for necessities brought dishonor to the family. Other things being equal, said Antonino, indigent *familia* should receive the largest share of alms.[47] Testamental bequests are the most obvious source for examining the import of this preference accorded relatives. Yet testamental execution was so complex, the avidity of the communal and episcopal fiscs so predictable, that a shrewd Florentine testator who desired to bequeath part of his estate to needy relatives did not leave the sums to them through direct legacies or the creation of partial or universal inheritances.[48] Inheritances were liable to charges on the estate: taxes past, present, and future, and all debts. Simple legacies were subject to a tax on notarial contracts, and were difficult to collect because of litigation over the estate.

Such litigation brought with it the danger that the testator would be determined to have been a usurer, thus threatening to consume the estate in paying back the thefts. Testators commonly sought to forestall such an eventuality by recognizing and "repaying" thefts while they were still alive and healthy, thus gaining absolution from all claims to usury incurred up to that point. This defense, however, entailed the disadvantage of ad-

---

[46] Tierney, *Poor Law*, 57. Tierney makes clear that while this influential text with its emphasis on *familia* did not enter the concordance of Gratian, being first cited in the ordinary gloss, Gratian's work contains a passage from Ambrose of great social significance. It instructs the bishop to favor shamed old people of good birth and those who have fallen from riches to indigence (*egestatem*); d. LXXXVI, c. 17. Scarcely a generation later the anonymous *Summa Elegantius in iure divino* (ca. 1169) recommended giving alms "sooner to your own than to strangers, to the sick than to the healthy, to him ashamed to beg rather than to the bold, to the indigent rather than to the possessing, and among the indigent to the just before the unjust"; Tierney, "Deserving Poor," 365.

[47] "Debet etiam elemosyna dari propinquis indigentibus et magis quam aliis ceteris paribus"; Antonino, p. 4, t. 5, c. 18, § 10.

[48] For the following, see my "Death and Testament in the Episcopal Constitutions of Florence (1327)," in *Renaissance Studies in Honor of Hans Baron* (Florence, 1970), 29–74, and "The Bishop's Portion," *Traditio*, 28 (1972), 397–450.

mitting a past crime, thereby weakening the chances for a flawless execution of the subsequent testament.

The most common means used to avert the dangers of taxation and accusation was to diminish radically the size of the inherited estate, that part most accessible to attack. The remainder could then be divided up in legacies to pious causes. Such pious bequests were privileged by virtue of their right to first payment. There was, generally speaking, no contract gabelle on them. The estate could also be depleted by leaving some amount as restitution of dishonest gains taken from unknown persons (*incerti*).

These legacies might be left to specific pious entities such as a hospital or a male or female religious house, or they could be left generically for the poor and for pious causes, without specifying a recipient. The testator had to be able to rely upon the executors of the will to act in the interest of the testator's *familia*. If a certain pious entity could serve as the fictitious recipient of a fictitious sum, then the testator could name that entity. Otherwise he would leave the sum generically, placing upon the executor the burden of distributing to the *familia* the sums for poor and pious causes. The executors also had the task of distributing the *incerti* that had been left to the poor. The result of these practices was that substantial sums left for pious causes in Florentine testaments found their way back into the *familia* through executor action in favor of the testator's *familia*. It is evident from the foregoing that generic sums without a specific recipient, whether the purpose (e.g., marrying girls) is stated or not, do not give a reliable indication of testamental intent or of the nature of the charity itself. To a lesser extent this is also true of legacies (or inheritances) left to specified entities, for these entities sometimes served as fictitious property-holders in exchange for a donation.

Before about 1400 there is no systematic way to determine just what part of pious donations was directed back into the family.[49] But fragmentary records of the episcopal curia give some idea of how common the practice was. Since the bishop was legally responsible to insure that pious monies were used for pious purposes, executors would attempt to obtain a ruling in his curia determining the family of the testator to be poor. Sometimes the family's condition resembles our modern definition of poverty, but usually these records deal with families of substance. This is not surprising, since the bishop was more interested in the testamentary dispositions of these families than in those of modest estate. What is surprising, namely that families of rank, name, and substance were designated poor, reaffirms data cited in the legal cases discussed above. Consequently

[49] For about a century after this point, the deposit *Pupilli* in the ASF affords this possibility.

a testamentary sum for restitution or for the poor was often returned in toto to the family. In cases where executors stipulated the recipients of poor monies, they were relatives of the deceased. Thus a Nerli and an Altoviti were found to be in need.[50] A Manieri's[51] and an Agli's[52] poor money goes to help dower the girls of these clans. Three daughters of Berto di messer Stoldo de' Frescobaldi were designated "poor shamed girls" and their dowries were subsidized.[53] And the bishop acting as father of the poor assigned the whole inheritance of a Mozzi, which belonged to the poor, to two other Mozzi for the remainder of their lives.[54]

A certain amount of this traffic was undoubtedly fraudulent. In fact the notarial acts by which the bishop absolved poor heirs from paying *incerti* or legacies to other poor regularly contain a section in which the bishop as father of the poor recognized the receipt of a sum perhaps a quarter of that he returned to the family.[55] Or he would recognize this imbursement and accept the executor's promise to distribute the rest. The episcopal curia often went so far as to exempt specifically the executors or heirs from having to prove notarially in the future that they had in fact paid such sums.[56]

Moralists commonly voiced their repugnance of such fraud, but the manipulations were based on the twin assumptions already examined: preference was due to the family and to those whose estate was endangered. And these examples rested on an accepted definition of the poor. It was the best of law, for example, for the bishop of Florence to absolve the Florentine patrician Sassetti from the debt he owed the poor for his usury, for the latter argued convincingly that "he had come on such poverty that he could not commodiously and decently live with his *familia* according to his status and condition."[57]

In the fifteenth century the shamed poor ceased to be largely a matter

---

[50] Jacopo di Berto Vantugi de' Nerli, Piero di messer Odo degli Altoviti; A(rchivio) A(rcivescovile) di F(irenze), *Libro di Contratti*, 1335, f. 172v, at 26 Jan. 1336.

[51] Ibid., ff. 12v–13r.

[52] Ibid., ff. 47v–48r. The relationship cannot be determined in either case.

[53] Ibid., ff. 147r–148v. The girls were nieces of the testator; their father, one of the seven executors, was an important political figure; G. Villani, *Cronica*, XII, 17.

[54] *ASF, not. antecos.* L 35 (1363–73), 22 Feb. 1370 s(til). f(lor).

[55] See, for example, the Altoviti reference above, n. 50.

[56] An instance is a testament executed by two Guidalotti in 1337. The bishop recognized the reception of £50 (16.8 florins) of the 300 florins owed from the estate for "egenis verecundis, et carceratis et piis locis." He conceded the remainder to them to distribute: "nec de distributione et erogatione ipsa fidem facere teneantur per publica instrumenta"; *AAF, Libro di Contratti*, ff. 160v–161r.

[57] Cecco di fu Azzone "ad tantam paupertatem devenit quod secundum suum statum et conditionem commode et decenter vivere cum sua familia non potest . . . "; *AAF, A–IV–2* (1299–1317), f. 11v (1 Dec. 1299).

to be dealt with either by the bishop or by the individual family, and became the object of specific concern to communes and citizenry. This development raises two questions. Why did downward mobility of established classes become so pressing as to require an extrafamilial institutionalized aid? Given the financial straits of these families, were there credit institutions that could come to their aid?

Local conditions strongly influence any response to the first question. In Florence, taxation was certainly an important factor. In a recent monograph, Anthony Molho has shown the extent to which the commune was forced to levy the capital resources of the tax-paying citizenry in order to meet the war costs of the years 1423–33.[58] By the time Cosimo de' Medici came to power in 1434, many family fortunes had disappeared and scores of citizens suffered open shame. The political proscriptions that followed increased the misery of many families that had already incurred heavy financial burdens in the attempt to maintain the status of the old, anti-Medicean regime.

In more stable Venice, the explanation of the rise of the poor gentility as a social problem is more complex. The problem inhered in the nature of the political system of the *Serenissima*, which rested on a hereditary aristocracy. From its beginnings in the late thirteenth century, this nobility depended heavily on a monopoly of communal magistracies to support its progeny. There were never enough of these offices, and their scarcity increased during the fifteenth century.[59] The republic being constituted in its nobility, it was to be expected that Venice would witness the most forthright attempt at direct communal subvention of its poor aristocracy. In a highly original bill submitted to the Venetian legislature in 1492, certain nobles proposed that the commune pay 70,000 ducats each year in welfare to poor nobles who were without office. Those over sixty years of age were to receive 100 ducats a year, while men from twenty-five to sixty should receive 50 ducats.[60]

The Venetian *Collegio* opposed this bill. Status should not be increased through the expenditure of public money, they asserted. The bill would encourage faction in the city, and attract poor nobles from the Venetian colony of Crete. When two nobles of the Bon and Falier families persisted with the recommendation, the Council of Ten banished them.[61]

Each commune and signory had such peculiar reasons for familial

[58] A. Molho, *Florentine Public Finance in the Early Renaissance* (Cambridge, Mass., 1971).
[59] J. C. Davis, *The Decline of the Venetian Nobility as a Ruling Class* (Baltimore, 1962), 15–53, with emphasis on the sixteenth century.
[60] Pullan, *Rich and Poor*, 230.
[61] Ibid.

decline, but two general explanations may be offered. First, the conditions of international commerce during the quattrocento were not expanding in such a way as to absorb the sons of the Italian communal elites. Increased use of birth-control methods among the propertied is evidence of this decline. Family budgets could not support large families unless one were of the minuscule group of already established families whose wealth actually increased during the quattrocento.[62] The second general element contributing to the decline was the ubiquitous rise in dowry prices for marriage, and an increased population in the nunneries.[63] To support or marry off a daughter in the quattrocento demanded a great deal of money, and the expenditures seriously weakened many families.

But the costs did not stop there. With a diminishing supply of virgins, the number and average age of unmarried males rose rapidly. The result was a continuing strain on the finances of the fathers. The sons faced a restricted field of commercial investment and difficulties in procuring wives whose dowry money might set them up in business. Many of them consequently squandered their money in games and whoring and in the plush entertainment of Renaissance society. When bankruptcy came, the sequence of debt and degradation revolted the honorable citizens. The excesses of the *giovani* (men under forty) in the quattrocento included insurrection against civil authority[64] and goon squad attacks on religious ceremonies,[65] not to mention the more prosaic pest of gambling. The shame of these men reached its nadir when a youth of honest family was discovered begging, previously protected in his shame by a mask to disguise his birth. At the beginning of our period the *vergognoso* was considered confined to his house because he could not beg; by the early sixteenth century the same term could refer to those who begged—in disguise.[66]

Confronted with this social problem, citizens of a fifteenth-century Italian commune began to look to the communal fisc for alleviation. In general, however, Italian communal governments, as in the case of Venice, did little to formally aid the established poor during the period under study, despite the fact that these unfortunates belonged by family and order to the sovereign groups in the cities.

[62] D. Herlihy, "The Tuscan Town in the Quattrocento," *Medievalia et Humanistica*, n.s. 1 (1970), esp. 88–89, 94–95, 97–98, 108–9.

[63] R. Trexler, "Le célibat à la fin du Moyen Age: Les religieuses de Florence," *Annales*, 27 (1972), 1329–50.

[64] Pope Pius II gives a vivid account of the situation in Rome; *Memoirs of a Renaissance Pope*, ed. L. C. Gabel (New York, 1959), 158–59, 169–80.

[65] On the *Compagnacci* and the services organized by Savonarola, see P. Villari and E. Casanova, *Scelta di prediche e scritte di fra Girolamo Savonarola* (Florence, 1898), 481–86.

[66] Pullan, *Rich and Poor*, 221.

The noble monopoly of the magisterial positions in the government of Venice is a striking example of the unquestioned privilege accorded those of antiquity and wealth in the republican and signorial communes of Italy. A recent historian has seen an increasing objectivity in the administration of the mid-trecento Florentine commune,[67] but if it ever did exist, such objectivity was fleeting. Privilege in the closed society of Venice was legal; in "open" Florence it was operative. By and large, government existed for the protection and furtherance of the *principali*. When the Medici replaced oligarchy with a more signorial rule, Cosimo cultivated his power by systematically placing old families in his debt by loans and other favors. In these difficult times when many families were shamed by their financial difficulties, the new regime of the Medici maintained the reign of privilege by preserving many families that otherwise might have disappeared.[68]

The forces in Florence that maimed any attempt to formalize aid to the gentility and those of honest condition rose from below. Great numbers of salaried workers and wandering indigents created an overriding political need to channel formal communal charity to the noncitizenried population. Lack of grain for indigents hastened social disturbances. Medical care and housing for the economically miserable were necessary for the same reasons, and the government of Florence supported an elaborate system of hospitals, hospices, bread lines, and the like to minister to this segment of the population.[69] The threat of unrest among the *popolo minuto* might not diminish de facto privilege in the administration of government, but it inhibits a communally directed welfare system for the propertied classes.

Florentine society was not without social welfare, but it was private and associative, administered within each guild. Unaided by government, guilds attempted to redeem their members from hard times. Since membership in the Florentine *arti* was restricted to the middle and upper classes, this charity was equivalent to class self-help, yet it was institutionalized by occupation rather than by class.[70]

Only one lay group with status was specifically subsidized by the

---

[67] Becker, *Florence in Transition*, I, 203–13.

[68] On Cosimo's patronage, see N. Machiavelli, *History of Florence and of the Affairs of Italy* (New York, 1960), 315. For an authoritative evaluation of the relative position of new men and established families in the government of Florence during Cosimo's life, see Rubinstein, *Government*, 62–67.

[69] L. Passerini, *Storia degli stabilimenti di beneficenza e d'istruzione elementare gratuita della città di Firenze* (Florence, 1853). There is a pressing need for monographs on these charitable institutions.

[70] A. Doren, *Le arti fiorentine*, I (Florence, 1940), 353–55. Doren indicates that such charitable activities for brothers were not well developed within the Florentine guilds, most of the alms going to ecclesiastical entities. For an early guild statute (1332) assigning alms to the *poveri vergognosi*, see ibid., 354.

quattrocento Florentine commune, ex–civil servants, the so-called *famiglia* of the commune. The first trace of pensions for this group appears in a law of 1378.[71] The commune, it stated, had a special duty toward its longtime familiars and domestic servants. Accordingly, the hospital of San Gallo was charged to care for them in their sickness and poverty. Expenses were paid by two eleemosynary companies in town. Half a century later, we find a special sum of more than a thousand florins spent annually for "the poor who have alms for life," that is, those familiars retired because of age or illness.[72] They received £6 or 8 per month as a pension. Subsequent laws spelled out those who were eligible and the preconditions of a pension.[73] This pension to civil servants represents an important development in the origins of modern social welfare. Yet the motivation given for the communal disbursements demonstrates a tenaciously associative or corporative, rather than a modern statist, conception of welfare. These pensioners were in fact members of a family, the family of the communal lords. The laws promulgating the aid repeatedly state that servants not receiving aid would have to beg. If this happened, it would be to the shame of the commune. This is essentially indistinguishable from the motivation for the head of a household to provide for his old servant woman, or for a confraternity to aid its deprived brothers.[74]

It is difficult to find formalized aid by the communal fisc for any segment of the propertied class. Although the creation in 1425 of a communal dowry-investment fund for young girls and boys was intended to maintain the tax-paying stratum, no specific aim of preserving the honor of old families seems to have inspired this institution. Investment was open to all who could buy in. It is true that rising dowries caused the government in the late quattrocento and early cinquecento to limit investments in the dowry fund, hoping in this way to control the size of dowries. Behind this

---

[71] *Provv.* 66, ff. 37r–38r (12 June 1378).

[72] References to this practice abound after about 1413. See this selection: *Provv.* 102, ff. 8r, 140r–141r; 106, ff. 22r, 162r (cited in Brucker, "Ciompi," 324); 119, f. 268v; 122, f. 156v; 136, ff. 15rv.

[73] For example, *Provv.* 143, ff. 250r–251v (30 Oct. 1452).

[74] Despite its associative nature, this communal pension system is significant because the association was the government. Modern social welfare history represents a continuing enlargement of the concept of the "family" or clientele of the state. The Florentine pension system has never been studied. Its principles, however, meet the criteria set up by A. Sapori for a social welfare system, but in a purer form than the later Venetian "previdenza" thought by Sapori to be innovative. In all probability the practice of communal pensions became generalized in northern Italy in the second half of the trecento, becoming to the civil service what the life rent had long been to the *commessi* of the monasteries; see my "Une table florentine d'espérance de vie," *Annales*, 26 (1971), 137–39; A. Sapori, "I precedenti della previdenza sociale nel medioevo," in his *Studi di Storia Economica*, I (Florence, 1955), 426–41.

and like laws was the desire to preserve the honor of the establishment, for as the law asserts, sons and daughters of elevated condition were being forced to marry social inferiors.[75] Yet these actions of the signoria do not represent any direct use of the fisc to aid a particular class of citizens as was recommended at Venice at the end of the quattrocento. The commune worked for those who invested in it, but was inhibited from aiding the fallen "poor" as a class by the continual eleemosynary pressures exerted on the fisc by the lower elements of society.

Honorable families might have coped with their financial difficulties if they had been able to borrow at reasonable rates. But a crisis of credit accompanied the stagnation of the commercial market during this period, and this affected not only the honest families but the entire middle class. Small shopkeepers needed adequate credit, and for most of the quattrocento, Jewish pawnbrokers provided the only available credit for these little men of property. The high interest charges destroyed the limited patrimony of many of this class. The plight of a gentleman victimized by the Jew might more readily bring tears to the contemporary observer, but the commune realized that once again political charity had to have preference over Christian alms.

Much attention has been focused on this credit crisis because two significant institutions of quattrocento Italy were closely related to it, the Jewish moneylenders and the *Monti di Pietà*, or communal pawnshops. From their first institution at Perugia in 1462, the new *Monti* were intended to supplant the high charges of the Jews with a low, even nominal, interest charge. Unfortunately the new institution's historians, mostly Franciscans, have primarily conceived of the *Monti di Pietà* as another example of aid to "the poor."[76] Little serious inquiry has been directed toward who was aided, scholars simply assuming that the traditional poor were assuaged: The "lower class," the *popolo minuto*, had been victimized by the Jews and saved by the *Monti*.[77] Scant attention has been paid to the credit crisis of the gentility, and it has even been asserted that they had easy credit access through the banks run by fellow Christians.[78] Historians have treated the

[75] "Assai dissimuli in qualità e conditione"; *Provv.* 201, ff. 12v–13v (11 Apr. 1511).

[76] The latest work on the *Monte di Pietà* contains an extensive bibliography; S. Majarelli and U. Nicolini, *Il Monte dei Poveri, periodo delle origini (1462–1474)* (Perugia, 1962).

[77] F. R. Salter, "The Jews in Fifteenth-Century Florence and Savonarola's Establishment of a *Mons Pietatis*," *Cambridge Historical Journal*, 5 (1936), 194–95. Pullan also fails to discriminate, calling the borrowers "genuinely poor" and "poor and ordinary people"; *Rich and Poor*, 470, 582.

[78] Salter, 195.

Monti di Pietà's relation to the poor in twentieth-century terms and have ignored the possibility that the *Monti* also provided relief for deprived gentility. The *Monti di Pietà* did not in fact aid the salaried working class, the *popolo minuto*, but the majority of the possessing class. Poverty must be understood in its contemporary context; hence the problem of the fallen rich must be considered as part of the general credit crisis of the quattrocento.

An earlier historiographic tradition saw more clearly the social strata that stood to benefit from cheaper credit. With his strong proclivities toward social Darwinism, the Capuchin De Besse perceived that it was not the proletariat and day laborers who were aided, but those who had something to pawn.[79] De Besse's assertion leads to the conclusion that the strata victimized by the Jews and later aided by the new *Monti* included the downwardly mobile middle class and the "poor" gentility of the communes.[80] In Florence, pawn inventories of a Jewish pawnbroker indicate that the propertied were the ones borrowing from the Jews,[81] and one chronicler said that "the things [the Jewish pawnbrokers] possessed belonged to poor Florentine gentlemen."[82]

The same pattern is found in the new *Monti*. A Perugian pawn inventory lists items that certainly did not come from the destitute.[83] These *Monti* were created to aid the "fatter poor" (*pauperes pinguiores*), the shop-owning middle class, the citizen class.[84] Defenders of the *Monti* almost uniformly stressed that *citizens* were to be helped by the new institutions: "The *Monte* provides for one's poor brother citizens, so that they abstain . . . from thieving, to which they often come because of poverty, soiling and perturbing civil life and association."[85] The following juxtaposition is characteristic: "Beggars [should receive] the perpetual subsidy of hospitality, while poor citizens [should receive] prompt and perpetual

---

[79] L. De Besse, *Le bienheureux Bernardin de Feltre et son œuvre*, II (Paris, 1902), 24–28. De Besse's translation of texts is faulty, and such terms as "social groups" and "middle class" are his own invention. A modern work on Bernardino's social significance has unfortunately accepted these translations; G. Barbieri, *Il beato Bernardino da Feltre nella storia sociale del Rinascimento* (Milan, 1962), 58.

[80] For a recent assessment of the utility of the Jewish moneylenders and the *Monti* of the Veneto, see Pullan, *Rich and Poor*, 470, 474f., 493, 573, 604–21.

[81] U. Cassuto, *Gli Ebrei a Firenze nell'età del Rinascimento* (Florence, 1918), 171.

[82] Cited from the Florentine history of Giovanni Cambi, in ibid., 370–71.

[83] Majarelli and Nicolini, 337–58.

[84] Those in extreme need, ran the argument, had their own charitable institutions; De Besse, II, 25; H. Holzapfel, *Die Anfänge der Montes Pietatis* (Munich, 1903), 116–19.

[85] "Mons fratribus suis civibus pauperibus providet, honeste ut vivant, et a rapinis . . . abstineant, quae saepe ob paupertatem . . . proveniunt, et civilem vitam atque conversationem maculant et perturbant"; De Besse, II, 26, quoting the same defender.

loans for use in their necessities."[86] We are reminded of a like juxtaposition in the law. Beggary and citizenry were mutually exclusive. In Florence the profit made by the *Monte di Pietà* (instituted in 1496) was assigned to the shamed poor. Communal laws explained that the *vergognosi* were, after all, the same people who pawned to the *Monte*.[87]

The credit crisis that gripped Italy in the quattrocento affected propertied individuals from varied social levels. But pressure from the economically miserable and the economic malaise affecting its shopkeeping middle class in themselves prohibited formal aid from the Italian commune to its fallen families of repute. In the quattrocento and cinquecento, confraternities, associations formed for charitable ends among those united not by occupation but by pious ideals, provided the alms to maintain status. Not loans—the point in the early period was to keep the declining gentility from the clutches of the pawnbrokers.

Confraternal aid to the *vergognosi* was not unknown when the Florentine *Compagnia de' Buonomini di San Martino* was established in 1442. Contemporary to the injunctions of the archbishop of Ravenna mentioned above (1311), a group existed in Bologna called the *fratres verecundorum*, which may have served the shamed.[88] Testamental grants for the shamed entrusted to confraternities appear about the same time.[89] At Florence the important lay alms company of Or San Michele started to earmark some of its alms for the *vergognosi*. Its mid-century records of pious distributions show a distinction made between alms to the poor and to the shamed poor, alms to the individual shamed poor given in substantially greater amounts than the pittance conferred on others; and in grants to families and to marriageable girls, a tendency to equate shame and gentility.[90]

[86] "Hoc est igitur a fine civilis societatis praeceptum obligans episcopos et rectores, et magistratus urbium providendum mendicis quidem de perpetuo subsidio hospitalitatis, et pauperibus civibus de perpetuo, promptoque mutuo ad usum necessitatis ipsorum"; ibid., 28, quoting the same.

[87] Passerini, *Beneficenza*, 742–43.

[88] P. Tacchi Venturi, *Storia della compagnia di Gesù in Italia*, I (Rome, 1950), pt. 1, 401.

[89] See, for example, above, 75 and n. 56.

[90] S. La Sorsa, *La compagnia d'Or San Michele overo una pagina della beneficenza in Toscana nel secolo XIV* (Trani, 1902), 88–89, 93. The quantitative disparity between alms to the *vergognosi* and the indigent was due to the disparity in social standing of the recipients, but it was encouraged by the fact that a family's shame was a sufficient excuse to omit that family's name from the alms records. This invited excesses on the part of the distributors, and was inveighed against as early as 1333 in the group's statutes: "It is not enough to write: 'To a poor and shamed family'"; ibid., 192. The confraternity's alms registers for the 1350s reflect the distinction between small and large alms given to common and honest social types. Reg. 254, for example, lists the names of those aided by petty alms; reg. 225 lists the names of those agents

Alms to the shamed became an acceptable confraternal activity during the trecento, but not yet a statutized activity. Only in the 1420s have I encountered constitutions of an Italian confraternity that specify aid to the shamed poor as a formal charitable duty alongside the more traditional one of feeding beggars and caring for the sick and imprisoned. The Milanese confraternity of the Misericordia prefigures formal attention to the shamed in its 1422 statute:

Item. Since, according to the injunction to charity, one is required to more strongly subvent relatives, and especially [those related by] spiritual bonds;

And so that the associates of this honorable society of Mercy are united in the exercise of works of piety by the bond of devotion, that is toward the poor sick and beggars;

We ordain that if anyone of the said society becomes sick or falls into a need which he cannot meet by himself or with his goods, he is to be afforded by the associates of the said confraternity with goods set aside for other needy, according to [its] possibilities and [his] need.[91]

The twenty-five "men of good fame" who comprised this confraternity were to aid their spiritual brothers when any of them came upon hard times. The statutes certainly consider this contingency fortuitous, for the limited membership of Milanese confraternities was recruited from the cream of Milanese society, overwhelmingly men of standing and mostly of wealth, men whose honesty might be assumed and whose faculty to give to the poor assured.[92] Thus the contingency of aid to brothers might seem remote. There is little novelty in this goal. It is true that matriculation in the confraternity was not occupationally but socially determined, and that in Milan it was becoming fashionable to limit membership to the upper class. But the principle remained associative: aid to the fallen was due members of the confraternity.

The statute of 1422 is significant because just seven years later in the same city an important departure was made from these traditional associative principles. The statutes of the Scuola della Divinità (1429) sustain the traditional duty of sending each day one or two beasts loaded with grain and wine to a different part of the city. But if the brotherhood prospered, the statutes continue, the brothers might use the increased income to

---

who received substantial sums to give to unnamed persons; *ASF, Or San Michele,* regs. 254, 255. I owe this information to Gene Brucker.

[91] A. Noto, ed., *Statuti dei luoghi pii elemosine amministrati dall' Ente Comunale di Assistenza di Milano* (Milan, 1948), 13.

[92] Ibid., ix, 14.

marry poor girls, liberate prisoners, "or subvent poor nobles who are ashamed to beg."[93] Thus the primary aim of the scuola was to feed those who issued from their houses to solicit food openly. With luck, the brothers would then be able to aid those who could not beg (prisoners) and those who were ashamed to (poor nobles).

By 1429, then, charity to the shamed poor (equated with nobles) had been recognized as a definite, if secondary, duty of a lay eleemosynary group. This obligation was owed to fellow nobles who were not members of that confraternity. Confraternal charity toward the shamed poor no longer rested strictly on the associative principle. It had become charity for others as well as for brothers, or more precisely, charity for brother nobles. Perhaps social class was now being conceived of as a spiritual bond, a *cognatio spiritualis*.[94]

The decisive step toward an organization with the primary purpose of aiding the shamed poor was taken in Florence in 1442. Stripped of all legend and tradition, little is known about the foundation and early history of this confraternity. The oldest account book of the company starts in 1442 (Florentine style, 1441).[95] The first rule of the company might seem to have been written before the death of Pope Eugenius IV (1447), for the introductory invocation honors him by name.[96] But the codex containing these rules dates from the late quattrocento or even the cinquecento. Consequently the oldest document that indicates the probable goal of the group dates from at least forty years after the foundation. While probably containing older sections, the original rule had already been emended.[97]

According to the prologue, the group first met in February 1442 with the blessing of Eugenius (who was resident in the city at this time).[98] Tra-

---

[93] "Aut subventionem pauperum nobilium qui mendicare erubescant . . . "; ibid., 35.

[94] Benjamin Nelson's extensive consideration of brotherhood as it relates to the usury prohibition does not relate the concept of *cognatio spiritualis* to urban class-structure; *The Idea of Usury* (Chicago, 1969).

[95] C. Torricelli, *La congregazione dei Buonomini di S. Martino in Firenze. Notizie Storiche* (Florence, n.d. [after 1942]), 3.

[96] See below, 106.

[97] See below, 105. From contracts with the *Badia*, we know that the move into these quarters took place between 1478 and 1482; Torricelli, *Congregazione*, 4; T. Rosselli-Sassatelli-Del Turco, *La congregazione dei Buonomini di San Martino* (Florence, 1930), 9–11. Further evidence of the document's lateness is the invocation of St. Martin (below, 106); apparently the confraternity chose him as its protector only after the move into the oratory; N. Martelli, *I Buonomini di S. Martino* (Florence, 1937), 12. Indeed the only reason to ascribe any part of the document to the period of its foundation is the salutation to Pope Eugenius.

[98] See below, 106.

dition to the contrary, this document does not suggest that Antonino Pierozzi (not yet archbishop) played any role in bringing the first Buonomini together, stabilizing their rule, or acting in the role of spiritual father.[99]

It is difficult to ascertain the original aims and procedures of the company, so encrusted are they with pious traditions. Modern historians have described the contents of a memorial on the company written in 1622 as if the document were original, supposedly on the basis of its assertion that the procedures it summarized in thirty-two points had long been practiced by the group.[100] The quattrocento codex gives a sparser picture.

This codex leaves little doubt that the company was founded primarily "for the utility of the shamed poor" of the whole Florentine dominion, those "who are not accustomed to beg," and at a time when the cost of bread caused much suffering to these shamed men and their families.[101] The company helped this group by requiring each of its twelve "procurators of the shamed poor" to contribute a minimum of three bushels of grain each year. Ideally this donation was to be distributed weekly within successive months.[102] Second, the procurators were to solicit aid and alms from spiritual and temporal lords and from citizens and other persons.[103]

This meager harvest of information from the codex can be supplemented by ascertaining the quality of the original procurators of the company. This will give some indication of who was to be aided. Once again, certain traditional assumptions have to be set aside. For example, the eighteenth-century Florentine historian Richa said that St. Antonino had picked the procurators from the membership of the established confra-

[99] No archiepiscopal approval of the confraternity is extant. Neither Antonino's writings nor the account books of his curia mention the group. The first three biographers of Antonino fail to mention his supposed special tie to the company. While not ascribing the foundation to Antonino, the historian Buoninsegni, writing within six years of the archbishop's death, does link the archbishop and the confraternity. Until better evidence is produced, the tradition tying them together must be considered a typical example of ascribing to a saint any significant charitable foundation started during his life; R. Morçay, *St. Antonin Archevêque de Florence (1389–1459)*, (Paris, 1914), iv–ix; D. Buoninsegni, *Istoria Fiorentina* (Florence, 1637), 125. For a variant passage of Buoninsegni, see Torricelli, *Congregazione*, 3, without reference. The first direct statement that the Buonomini had been instituted by Antonino is contained in the first papal indulgence to the group, dated 1476; *Codex S. Martino*, ff. 1v–2r. The first assertion that he had written the rule of the Buonomini is in a municipal law of 1502; Passerini, *Beneficenza*, 933. For the late quattrocento linkage of the archbishop and the Buonomini by Vespasiano da Bisticci, see below, 93.

[100] All biographers of Antonino have done this. The memorial is at ff. 38–49 in the codex. The 32 "rules" are at ff. 45–49. This memorial ascribes the foundation to St. Antonino of course, but does not attribute a written rule to him.

[101] See below, 106.

[102] See below, 108.

[103] See below, 106.

ternity of San Girolamo.[104] I cannot corroborate this statement. More significant is Passerini's assertion that the real motive for "St. Antonino's promotion" of the group was the familial suffering caused by the political proscriptions against anti-Medicean families after Cosimo's return in 1434.[105] I can find no basis for his assurance that the original Buonomini were of the party opposed to Cosimo.

The twelve men were not "among the principal citizens," although the requirement of personal alms set forth in the oldest rule demanded respectable condition. Only four had family surnames, and of these only Francesco di Benedetto di Caroccio degli Strozzi had significant financial standing in the commune.[106] Another, Michele di messer Piero Benini, held a magistracy in 1444.[107] A third worked in 1447 as a syndicator of the accounts of the archiepiscopal curia.[108] The last of the four patricians, Bernardo di Marco di messer Forese Salviati, remains completely faceless.

Of the remaining eight, six were identified in the quattrocento codex as small merchants (four in wool, a silk merchant, and a shoe salesman), one as a notary, while the eighth was not occupationally identified.[109] Ser Alessio di Matteo Pelli functioned in 1447 as notary of the important magistracy of the *Consuli del Mare*.[110] In 1453 the woolmaster Jacopo di Biagio dell'Ancisa was the governor of a religious sodality for boys and

[104] G. Richa, *Notizie istoriche delle chiese fiorentine* (Florence, 1754), I, 209. A liaison to this prestigious confraternity can, however, by no means be excluded. It met in the hospital of Lemmo, and a document written between 1447 and 1458 tells that the *infermi vergognosi* preferred this hospital "because one isn't visited so often there"; *Seminario maggiore di Firenze, codex Rustici*, f. 51v; Vespasiano da Bisticci, *Vite*, 145 (*Vita* of Niccolò degli Albergati).

[105] Passerini, *Beneficenza*, 502f.

[106] He ranked eighteenth in net capital in his quarter of the city in 1427; Martines, *Social World*, 372. The brother of the famous miniaturist Zanobi Strozzi, Francesco was fifty-four years old when the confraternity was founded in 1442; M. Levi d'Ancona, *Miniatura e Miniatori a Firenze dal XIV al XVI secolo* (Florence, 1962), 263.

[107] Rubinstein, *Government*, 264. Michele was a personal friend of S. Bernardino. Vespasiano da Bisticci, who also knew him, called him "uno uomo da bene e di buona coscienza . . . uomo litterato e nel quale erano molte laudabili condizioni"; Vespasiano, *Vite*, 205 (*Vita* of Bernardino).

[108] Luigi d'Urbano di messer Francesco Bruni, "revisore dei conti dei camarlinghi"; S. Orlandi, *S. Antonino*, I (Florence, 1959), 62. Bruni was also a benefactor of the men's confraternity of S. Paolo and the boys' confraternity of the Vangelista; see my "Adolescence and Ritual Salvation in Renaissance Florence," in C. Trinkaus and H. Oberman, eds., *The Pursuit of Holiness* (Leyden, 1973), 212f.

[109] They were ser Alessio di Matteo Pelli, *notaio;* Onofrio d'Angnolo and Giuliano di Staggio, *drappieri;* Giovanni di Baldo, *lanaiuolo;* Jacopo di Biagio dell'Ancisa, *cimatore;* Pasquino d'Ugolino del Vernaccia, *setaiuolo;* Primerano di Jacopo, *calzaiuolo;* Antonio di Maffeo da Barberino; Passerini, *Beneficenza*, 503.

[110] G. Uzielli, *La vita e i tempi di Paolo dal Pozzo Toscanelli* (Rome, 1894), 500f. Pelli served as a legal procurator for Cosimo de' Medici; see Trexler, "Adolescence," 213.

young men.[111] The draper Giuliano di Stagio attempted in 1458 to obtain the governance of a local asylum for abandoned children. The archbishop's intercession characterized him as a *buonuomo* and recommended Giuliano and his wife to the hospice, but it was unsuccessful, and this modest plum fell to a Florentine priest.[112]

These were respectable men but not among the *principali*. Their families do not seem to have been tied to the proscriptions of Cosimo or to the later plots against the family. It is true that in 1497 three of the six new "helpers" who had been added to the company signed the famous letter to Alexander VI defending Savonarola,[113] and one of these, Bernardo di Inghilese Ridolfi, spoke in council in favor of the death penalty for the alleged pro-Medicean conspirators.[114] But this is probably related more to Savonarola and his friarate of San Marco than to long-standing anti-Medicean rancors. Anyway, Lorenzo the Magnificent himself had been one of the Buonomini.[115]

The social status of the procurators indicates that the aid was not originally intended only for those with family names—the thin stratum at the top. The quattrocento codex gives little information on this point, except for this vague designation: "Especially the Shamed Poor." But it does tell us that the procurators were to deliberate and vote on recipient families.[116] This probably rules out traditional disbursements to nameless beggars. The first direct evidence of the Buonomini at work bears out this exclusion. A series of frescoes painted in the hall of the oratory of San Martino around 1480 has as its motif the traditional corporal works of mercy.[117] Strikingly, however, the aid recipients in these paintings are solid individuals. None is ragged, none miserable. While this can in part be explained by artistic conventions—quattrocento painters tended to represent the poor in a more dignified guise than did their trecento pre-

[111] S. Orlandi, II, 313.

[112] Antonino, *Lettere*, 196f. Pasquino d'Ugolino Del Vernaccia matriculated in the silk guild in 1436 as a *setaiolo minuto*, one permitted to sell silk but not manufacture it. The family was apparently not prosperous, and his heirs assessed modest taxes in 1457. Florence Edler de Roover was kind enough to pass on this information.

[113] Villari and Casanova, *Scelta*, 515, 518.

[114] F. Guicciardini, *The History of Florence* (New York, 1970), 132.

[115] Torricelli, *Congregazione*, 7.

[116] See below, 107. I have been unable to consult the business books of the confraternity that probably would furnish some exact information on who received aid. In any case, a solution to this problem lies beyond this paper's scope. It is to be hoped that when this problem is attacked, both these books and the now flooded account books of many other eleemosynary groups in Florence will be easily available.

[117] See the reproductions in Rosselli-Sassatelli-Del Turco, *Congregazione*. I have been unable to obtain the monograph by L. Desideri-Costa, *La chiesa di S. Martino del Vescovo e l'oratorio dei Buonomini* (Florence, 1942), which deals with the problem of attribution.

decessors—the regular dignity of these clients suggests the artist intended to represent respectable people: a widow whose estate is being inventoried by the Buonomini; a gentle couple espoused with their aid, the groom dressed in the latest styles, the father of the bride a merchant; those "hungry" being fed and those "naked" being clothed, all other than destitute. In the painting showing the Buonomini ministering to a woman who has recently given birth, the mother's servant receives food and wine from the procurator. Even the pilgrims being lodged are well dressed; clearly the artist wanted to accent the aid given to responsible and virtuous social types.

Despite this primary intention, the confraternity did not ignore the destitute poor. Perhaps it did not disperse alms to unknown miserables, but the whole cast of this fresco cycle and other circumstantial evidence surrounding the foundation of the group is so traditional in nature as to rule out an exclusive concern for the shamed poor. Even the paintings suggest this by their lack of evidence of masks or of a desire to hide one's identity. The shamed received their aid at the warehouse of the Buonomini. Only when necessity required (taking of an inventory, a marriage, help to women in childbirth) are they pictured abroad.

Another piece of visual evidence, this one from the brush of Lorenzo Lotto in Venice in 1542, shows more precisely the intent of the Venetian company for its *vergognosi* a century after the foundation of the Florentine Buonomini.[118] Since the Venetian group was modeled on the Florentine, we can surmise from this painting the intent and caritative conception of the earlier group: founded primarily to aid the shamed, but doubtless preserving a series of secondary, more traditional aims designed to alleviate those of lesser social quality.

Lotto's painting shows two altar boys on either side of an apotheosized St. Antonino. On the viewer's right, one of them either gives or receives small bundles of chits from a group of respectable women. The altar boy on the left, on the contrary, gives money to a group of ragged and maimed individuals, the traditional beggar types known so well from trecento paintings.

The new Venetian confraternity conceived of itself as ministering to the traditional miserable and to the respectable shamed. Money was given to the former, while the latter received chits that entitled them to a steady ration of grain meals and like alimentation.[119] The early Buonomini prob-

---

[118] Reproduced in B. Berenson, *Lorenzo Lotto* (London, 1956), pls. 327–29.

[119] This reading of the painting does not agree with that of Berenson, who says that the clerk on the right is receiving petitions, while the one on the left is giving charity; ibid., 115.

ably proceeded in much the same way, except that if the Buonomini's original intent was maintained, there were no public alms given to nameless beggars. Help for the lower classes there was, but it was discreetly given. Only in the cinquecento were the Florentine confraternity and its daughters able to move toward a more single-minded dedication to the "more shamed" and away from the traditional charitable effort to do a little bit of everything.[120]

The element of conservatism in the early years of the company of St. Martin can be partly understood as a projection of traditional communal attitudes toward alms companies. The primary eleemosynary consideration of Florence's republican regimes had always been provision for the economically miserable: the salaried, the drifters, and the miserable disabled. To that end the Signoria supported hospitals for the sick and the miserable handicapped. To feed the indigent population during times of want, however, communal officials during the trecento had often relied on the administration of the old confraternity of Or San Michele. Commonly the captains of this group received assignments in money or kind from these officials, which they would then distribute.[121] After the Black Death of 1348 this group became enormously rich, for numerous legacies and estates flowed into its hands through testamentary substitution. The commune stepped in and assumed such an active role in ordering the group's affairs that its private confraternal character was finally undermined.

A decline in the income of the group accompanied this increasing control. The growing reluctance of citizens to contribute to this confraternity, the most important eleemosynary institution in Florence during the trecento, in part resulted from the bad reputation the captains built up after the Black Death—they aided themselves and not the poor—but it also stemmed from the fact that the organization had become semiofficial. Citizens knew that a commune in economic straits would quickly lay hands on Or San Michele's money, thus violating the donor's intent.[122] By the beginning of the quattrocento Or San Michele could no longer dispense substantial alms to the indigent, and the commune had no central eleemosynary institution for that purpose. This is evident in the legislative provisions for the indigent. During the trecento, communal alms for the laity normally moved through Or San Michele. By 1400 public commissions appointed by the commune were necessary to help the starving, and this practice con-

---

120 This interpretation accords with the early seventeenth-century memorial written by Vincenzio Pitti and mentioned above; see below, 98.

121 See, for example, *Provv.* 25, ff. 76rv (30 Oct. 1329).

122 For an analysis of this development, see my "Florence, by the Grace of the Lord Pope . . ." *Studies in Medieval and Renaissance History,* 9 (1972), 166–69.

tinued for decades.[123] These commissions, or *balie*, remained short-term, and no durable communal bureaucracy for charity was established during the quattrocento.

In November 1456 this practice was significantly modified. Communal grain officials were instructed to give Archbishop Antonino 250 florins each month for the coming eight months, and the following August the commune assigned some 255 bushels of grain to him. Under pain of conscience Antonino was required by the commune to distribute this wealth, at his discretion, to poor and miserable persons in the city of Florence.[124]

In Vespasiano da Bisticci's *Vita* of Antonino, written toward the end of the century, it is suggested that the Buonomini played a part in effectuating this charity:

It happened that there was great want in Florence at that time, and the multitude of the poor was large, both in the city and in the *contado*. [Antonino] had a large quantity of bread made, and appointed certain persons over these alms who gave them not only to the public poor, but provided for the shamed poor in their every necessity. He instituted this company of the shamed poor which exists today. He could not meet such a demand with the thousand florins which they advanced to him from their incomes, and it was necessary for him to write Pope Eugenius several times, who sent him money; [Eugenius] often sent him money to prosecute this work. Similarly, [Antonino] asked some citizens for some alms, and each gave to alleviate such great need.[125]

This passage indicates that during Antonino's lifetime the Buonomini assumed a role in communal eleemosynary procedures, perhaps originally through the mediation of the archbishop. While the first historical mention of the Buonomini (by the historian Buoninsegni in the 1460s) stressed the aid given by the company to the shamed, the perception that the new company might serve as a conduit to aid the indigents of Florence as Or San Michele had done in the trecento was not missed by the government of the city.

With the materials at hand, it is difficult to follow the early steps by which this approach between confraternity and commune took place. We know that Lorenzo the Magnificent (d. 1492) was one of the procurators of the confraternity. This is a sure sign that the confraternity was of polit-

[123] See, for example, *Provv.* 89, ff. 94v–95v (25 June 1400); 98, ff. 112v–113r (7 Dec. 1409); 107, f. 106v (21 June 1417).

[124] *Provv.* 148, ff. 5r–6r (16 Feb. 1456 sf); 148, ff. 301r–302r (30 Aug. 1457). For the simultaneous initiatives for *poveri vergognosi* during famines elsewhere in Italy, see below, 99.

[125] Vespasiano, *Vite*, 191f.

ical significance in the city at that date, for it was a policy of the Medici to hold office in confraternities to prevent their harboring conspiracies.[126] Given the political significance of the Buonomini's assistance to established families, Lorenzo's decision to become one of the twelve suggests that the confraternity was disposing of sizable funds by this time, and that he could have influenced their distribution to loyal Mediceans.

A further step toward communal utilization of the Buonomini was taken in 1492, the year of Lorenzo's death. One of the small plums the commune traditionally disposed of was the right to designate some pious entity as the recipient of debts owed to the commune of which the commune itself was not aware. Remittances came from those conscience stricken over malfeasance in office, or because of the usurious rates at which they lent money to the city, or for a variety of other reasons that would bring unsuspected citizens to pay the commune. From the thirteenth century on, the commune had absolved those who gave what they felt they owed. Provisions were made for secrecy to enable the debtor to repay without risking prosecution.[127]

The traditional recipient of such debts had been the *Opera* or building lodge of the cathedral. But in 1492 a periodic renewal of this type of law directed the money to the Buonomini di San Martino.[128] The commune maintained this arrangement thereafter, and the first Grand Duke Cosimo continued the practice into the principate.[129]

The disposition of 1492 was, as far as I can determine, the first reference to the confraternity among the communal laws. Clearly, on the eve of the great Dominican preacher Savonarola and at the death of Lorenzo the Magnificent, the confraternity of San Martino had become the most fostered eleemosynary confraternity in Florence. In quick succession communal monies came pouring into the company. In 1495, 3,000 florins from the sum collected through an impost on the clergy were diverted to the Buonomini.[130] The following year saw incomes from the communal office handling the control of rebels assigned to them. And in that year came the assignment of the profit from the new *Monte de Pietà* to the Buonomini.[131] The confraternity was now accomplishing for the commune in the difficult 1490s what Or San Michele had done during mid-trecento. From his pulpit

---

[126] On the political ramifications of the confraternities, see the documents in R. Hatfield, "The Compagnia de' Magi," *Journal of the Warburg and Courtauld Institutes*, 33 (1970), 143, n. 168.

[127] The first record I found of this practice in Florence is from 1295; A. Grote, *Das Dombauamt in Florenz. 1285–1370* (Munich, 1959), 31.

[128] *Provv.* 205, ff. 6v–7r (27 Mar. 1520), referring to the earlier law.

[129] Torricelli, *Congregazione*, 7.

[130] Martelli, *Buonomini*, 13.

[131] Torricelli, *Congregazione*, 5.

the fiery Savonarola encouraged Florentine lawmakers to give to the Buonomini the communal funds traditionally spent on carnivals and races. Giving it to the shamed poor would please the saints more than the running of a race, he said.[132] The same friar encouraged youth confraternities to gather funds for St. Martin, and two monumental processions garnered thousands of florins to feed the coffers of the confraternity.[133] During the period of this friar's ascendancy in the city, the company undoubtedly reached the peak of its financial strength.

As Vespasiano was writing at about the same time, the confraternity cared for the "public poor" as well as for the shamed.[134] It filled a political need. The extent of its semiofficial aid to the indigent is shown by a communal law of May 1497 that assigned to "those of San Martino, namely of the Society of the Shamed," the old papal quarters near the Dominican church of Santa Maria Novella, "so that those poor and beggars in the city of Florence who have no domicile or hospice in which they can be quartered can be quartered in them."[135] Immigrants were not the only people being subsidized through the group. The diarist Landucci tells that in the wake of the French invasion (late 1494) the salaried work force lived off the alms of St. Martin.[136]

Like the now decrepit society of Or San Michele, the Buonomini had attained this preeminent position while still largely a private and independent entity. Like Or San Michele, its greatest wealth had been generated during a period of plague, penury, and scarcity. Finally, like its predecessor, great wealth and position made it irresistible to the communal fisc.[137] By a law of 18 May 1498, the confraternity of San Martino was nationalized.

The conflict between communal needs and the goals of a private confraternity primarily dedicated to preserving the *uomini da bene* could not be more glaring than in the reasons given by the commune for this action. The Buonomini had risen to fame because of the strict privacy in discreetly aiding the shamed and—if we can believe a later tradition—

[132] Ibid., 5f.
[133] P. Ginori Conti, ed., *La Vita del beato Ieronimo Savonarola* (Florence, 1937), 122f., 132, 134.
[134] "Non solo a' poveri pubblici, ma a' poveri vergognosi provedessino in ogni loro necessità, segretamente"; see the full translation above, 93.
[135] "Illis de Sancto Martino, videlicet societatis de vergognosi, stabula quae nuncupantur *del Papa*, posita in via della scala, ut in eis hospitentur pauperi et mendicantes existentes in civitate Florentie, non habentes domicilium vel hospitium in quo possint hospitari"; cited in Luca Landucci, *Diario Fiorentino*, ed. I. Del Badia (Florence, 1969), 150.
[136] "Così non può stare; e' poveri che vivono solo di manifatture si morranno di fame, àranno a stare colle limosine di San Martino"; ibid., 97f.
[137] Printed in Passerini, *Beneficenza*, 929–31.

because the group never accumulated a corporate estate, but promptly auctioned off any personal or real estate it received and distributed the proceeds immediately.[138] In its decision to nationalize the group, the commune saw things from a different angle. The help the Buonomini gave to the "poor shamed citizens" was so useful and necessary, it said, that it was advisable for "some public magistracy" with a limited term in office to determine who should receive what. Broadly hinting that the previous determinations had not been equitable, it argued that the new magistracy, by distributing the alms of the confraternity to those who most needed them, would encourage everyone to contribute more willingly to this work of mercy. If everyone knew his alms were dispensed with all due discretion and equity to "the shamed poor and other needy of the city of Florence," charity would increase.[139]

The wording of this law conceals the political reality that had called it into being. The Buonomini were in effect being criticized for serving as tools of Savonarola, favoring with alms those circles friendly to the friar. The Dominican had been executed the month before, and the law books of May 1498 contain several measures directed against the friar's followers. In any case, the commune clearly wanted to use the group's immense resources for those most in need, and that meant the homeless, the hungry, and the indigent.

It is curious that in the very decade when new companies to aid the shamed poor of good family were being founded in other areas of Italy, the mother group's original goal was successfully subverted by the Florentine commune. The nationalization of the Buonomini occurred because of the marked republican spirit of the Savonarolan period and that immediately succeeding it. Florence in this decade was the wonder of Italy, having expelled the Medici and created a new Grand Council whose distinguishing aim was representativeness.

The confraternity did not long remain a public organization. In 1502 the commune rescinded the law of 1498, and the group again assumed its formally private character. What caused this swift turnabout? One of the purposes of the seizure had probably been accomplished: the books of the

---

[138] Though the wording of the oldest rule suggests such a practice by providing for the distribution of all alms, it does not specifically state this to be so. In fact at one point it obliges the procurators to pay for their warehouses "from the goods which come into their governance in the exercise" of their office; see below, 108. This lack of capital was a fact at the time of Grand Duke Cosimo (mid-cinquecento); Torricelli, *Congregazione*, 7, giving no source. In his memorial of 1622, Pitti laid great emphasis on this practice as being original and the basis of the health of the confraternity; *Codex S. Martino*, f. 42 n.p.

[139] Passerini, *Beneficenza*, 930.

company had no doubt been screened for political content. Four years after Savonarola's death, the commune could feel that continued absorption served no further purpose. Another reason was stated in the rescission law:

The said company has lapsed into great decline, and those alms which used to be given it before the [nationalization] are no longer given to it. This law has changed the original mode of governance of the said company, by which [the Buonomini] had been appointed for life. They had sound intelligence on the poor shamed citizens, and they took care of their needs. Now, these [poor shamed citizens] would sooner support the direst necessity than want to manifest their misery and poverty to some office.[140]

Alms given to the confraternity had declined substantially—as had happened after the nationalization of Or San Michele. An equally interesting argument for reprivatizing was that the shamed citizens (note throughout the term "citizen") were not coming forward to receive alms. We are again reminded that the particular clientele of the confraternity was neither penniless nor starving. The commune had decided that the utility of the confraternity in ministering to the indigent had not, after four years, equaled the traditional utility of the Buonomini to the shamed citizens.

The decision was made easy by the group's prohibition of accumulating capital. While the commune had been able to profit by seizing Or San Michele in the 1350s because of the enormous landed patrimony possessed by that confraternity, its profit from San Martino depended more on day-to-day gifts and legacies than on rents. When alms decreased, the commune found the group a liability.

From that day to this, the Buonomini di San Martino has remained a private confraternity. But its return to private hands did not end encouragement by the commune. The group continued to receive tax revenues, and at least in the early years of the cinquecento it continued to aid the city by ministering to immigrant *uomini da bene* during times of scarcity.[141] Yet from that time on, the company increasingly emphasized its private aid to the shamed. Assistance to the lower elements continued

---

140 Ibid., 932f.
141 For subsequent assignments of the profit from the *Monte di Pietà*, see *Provv.* 196, ff. 39r–40r (30 Nov. 1505); 199, ff. 47r–48r (8–12 Jan. 1508 sf). For the extension of the "secret debt privilege," see *Provv.* 205, ff. 6v–7r (27 Mar. 1520), and Torricelli, *Congregazione*, 6 (1537). On help to immigrants: "considerata la moltitudine di poveri vergognosi huomini da bene che pe temporali adversi si truovano nella città di Firenze"; *Provv.* 199, ff. 47r–48r (8–12 Jan. 1508 sf).

but played the lesser role. This is in keeping with the general history of the confraternities for the shamed in Italy during the cinquecento, which functioned from then on as eleemosynary groups specifically for the gentlemen of the cities. Thus the 1622 memorial of the Buonomini tells that the confraternity gave up the practice of distributing daily bread and limited itself to monthly distributions of meal to those voted upon.[142] Subsequently, alms were clearly divided between meal and money. The meal, "always our best alms," went to "the citizens and the more shamed shopkeepers," the money to the "shopkeepers of lesser condition"—a characteristic juxtaposition.[143] While the sick and women in childbirth were to be aided regardless of social class,[144] the *vergognosi* were also to be helped in educating their children, paying for servants, and the like.[145]

The Buonomini had found their place in the increasingly rationalized administration of charity in early modern Europe.[146] In its beginnings the group had been primarily intended to aid the shamed. Found to be invaluable to the commune, in the latter part of the quattrocento it became the main conduit for the commune's eleemosynary aid to the destitute. Following its peak of financial strength during the Savonarolan period, it turned toward a more conscious policy of aiding the shamed poor, that term being ever more indicative of the higher class of families of the city—

[142] "In cambio di dar pane nelle gionate destinate vollero che si desse farina mese per mese a queste famiglie che da loro erano conosciute, et giudicate meritevoli di tale elimosina"; *Codex S. Martino*, f. 42 n.p.

[143] "La qual limosina di farina fu dipoi con lunghezza di tempo destinta in farina e danari, la farina lasciata alli Cittadini, et Artieri più vergognosi, et i danari assegnati ad Artieri di minor conditione"; ibid. In the same memorial, Pitti stated as a principle of the confraternity: "In [the distribution of] alms, the citizens with the most shame are always to be preferred"; ibid., f. 45 n.p.

[144] "Non per questo lasciando di havere pensiero delle povere genti di più bassa conditione con aiutarli ne parti delle loro donne, et ne casi di infermità"; ibid., f. 41 n.p.

[145] "Perchè, oltre che ella aiuta coloro che per i migliori del popolo sono reputati, col supplire al vitto di tante famiglie le sostienne che all' ultimo esterminio non precipitino, et che le donne in pudicitia, et castità si conservino et che le fanciulle o con impiegarle al servizio di Dio, o con maritarle non si conducono con miserabile vita ad invecchiarsi nelle Case con infinito dispiacere, e pensiero di loro parenti, et con pericolo dell'offesa de Dio, et dell'honore delle famiglie loro, et alli figluoli maschi potendo i padri con queste elimosine allevargli et fare insegnare loro in qualche parti [*sic*] le virtù danno cagione poi col sapere, e con l'industria di rilevare le case, et acquistare reputatione alle famiglie loro, se come più volte è avvenuto, e quasi come buon padre di famiglia non ad un solo bisogno del prossimo come le altre opere pie indirizzate, a tutte le necessità de suoi figluoli per quanto ella può ha provveduto"; ibid., f. 44 n.p. See also Richa, *Notizie*, I, 211.

[146] The declining gentleman and merchant seem to have been the focus of attention in northern Europe as well. I have not pursued the subject. Imbert points to the number of hospices specializing in the housing of "bourgeois et bourgeoises déchus de leur chevance"; J. Imbert, *Les hôpitaux en droit canonique* (Paris, 1947), 127. On the whole subject of rationalization in Italy, see Pullan, *Rich and Poor*, pt. 2.

as the 1622 memorial put it, those who have long brought honor to the city through their exercise of public office.

This return to and "ennobilization" of the original function of the Florentine group came at a time when confraternities modeled on the Buonomini were springing up throughout Italy: Vicenza in 1492, Bologna in 1495, Faenza in 1517, Rome and Genoa at about the same time, Venice in 1537, and innumerable cities thereafter.[147] The organization and distribution of charity in the Italian city-states were influenced by a class conception of shame from the foundation of the Buonomini through the middle of the sixteenth century. In the same year that Antonino was receiving grain to distribute to the poor and miserable, fra Cherubino da Spoleto obtained alms at Perugia for the shamed poor who might otherwise die of hunger.[148] The following year a *Monte di Pietà* was set up at Ascoli Piceno —the first charitable institution bearing that name in the quattrocento—to sustain and feed those citizens who could not, given the general want of the moment, sustain their children and familiars, and who were too ashamed to beg.[149]

If this is reminiscent of the legal poverty of the nobles with servants, our minds will be attuned to the modes of poverty examined earlier. Throughout the period under consideration, the identification between shame and honest condition proceeded apace. Contemporary to the Buonomini foundation, for example, an admirer of the Florentine hospital of Santa Maria Nuova stated that the hospital "gives alms to shamed poor and helps girls marry, and if some infirm gentleman in necessity sends to the minister stating what he needs, the minister, who is full of charity, sees to medicine, providing secretly for the sick man."[150] Buoninsegni in his recollection of the company of the *poveri vergognosi* described the latter as those "poor who, born of an honest line, were ashamed to ask for alms."[151] In the 1490s the decision was made to donate any profit of the

---

[147] Tacchi Venturi, *Compagnia di Gesù*, I, pt. 1, 401–4; P. Paschini, *Tre ricerche sulla storia della chiesa nel cinquecento* (Rome, 1945), 5–8.

[148] Majarelli and Nicolini, *Monti dei Poveri*, 95.

[149] "Pro substentatione et alimentatione pauperum civium dicte civitatis et aliunde et maxime verecundorum et eorum qui erubescunt et verecundantur hostiatim elemosinas querere et se, filios et familiares non valent nutrire et substentare inopia presenti"; ibid., 129.

[150] "E anchora in que luogo sempre vi si fae limosine a poveri vergongniosi e da fanciulle per maritare; e danchora se alchuno gentile huomo nella sua necessitae e infirmitae mandasi al ministro dicendo il suo bisongno, il ministro, che e pieno di charitae, soperisce a medicine, provedendo sagretamente a tale infermo"; *Seminario Maggiore di Firenze, Codex Rustici*, f. 50r.

[151] See above, n. 99.

Monte di Pietà to the Buonomini because the *vergognosi* were those who were pawning to the *Monte*. The *vergognosi*, said a 1502 law, were citizens who would support every necessity rather than manifest their misery to communal bureaucrats.[152] A 1509 law spoke of the "multitude of *uomini da bene* in the city of Florence who because of the difficult times are poor and shamed."[153]

The shamed poor to whom the Buonomini ministered, said the mid-cinquecento historian Varchi, were "all those who, being noble and in extreme need, do not have the means to live, or the resources to sustain their *famiglie*."[154] His contemporary Michelangelo equated "the poor citizens of Florence who are ashamed to beg" with the nobility.[155] At about the same time, the English priest Gregory Martin described aid given in Rome to the "men and women which are of good families decaied," "poore Gentlemen and Gentlewomen called Vergognosi, because they may not begge for shame."[156]

At Venice as well, the term *poveri vergognosi* by early cinquecento had come to refer mainly to the gentility. In 1506 the *Provveditori della Sanità* spoke out against rogues and persons of low and wretched condition who covered their faces with cloaks or sacks so they would not be recognized and masqueraded as good citizens of excellent family reduced to poverty.[157] In approving the Venetian company for the *vergognosi* in 1537, the *Provveditori* referred to "the great multitude of shamefaced poor and other sick and afflicted persons of various social ranks, some concealed and others revealed, noblemen and others, dispersed throughout the city."[158] Not surprisingly, in Venice it quickly became a mark of honor to aid one's fellow nobles. Marino Sanudo tells in early cinquecento: "If you

---

[152] "E' quali hora più tosto sopportono ogni necessità che voglino scoprire ad ogni ufficio la miseria et poverta loro"; Passerini, *Beneficenza*, 932.

[153] See above, n. 149. Note also the terminology of this papal letter (1511) addressed to the Bolognese company for the *vergognosi*: "... in civitate vestra bononiensi erant quamplurimi etiam cives Bononienses etiam nobiles familiae gravati et adeo ad paupertatem reducti quod eorum filios et filias sustentare ac illos et illas maritare [non possunt] et mendicare erubescebant ac aliae miserabiles et pauperes personae que elemosinis christifidelium indigebant"; P. Paschini, *La beneficenza in Italia e le "Compagnie del Divino Amore" nei primi decenni del Cinquecento* (Rome, 1925), 93.

[154] Dànno segretamente ogni mese la limosina a tutti i poveri vergognosi, cioè a tutti quelli che nobili e mendici essendo, non hanno nè da viver essi, nè donde sostentare le loro famiglie"; B. Varchi, *Storia Fiorentina* (Florence, 1963), I, 608 (IX, 49).

[155] The sculptor's letters are very instructive, for their disarmingly simple identification of shameful poverty with good family is unreflective; cf. the Speroni translations in I. Stone, ed., *I, Michelangelo, Sculptor* (London, 1962), 209–11, 225, 238, 247 (letters of 9 Feb. 1549, 29 Mar. 1549, 20 Dec. 1550, 26 Jan. 1555, 8 May 1556).

[156] G. Martin, *Roma Sancta*, ed. G. B. Parks (Rome, 1969), 207f.

[157] Pullan, *Rich and Poor*, 221.

[158] Ibid., 267.

want honor, you have to give to some poor gentlemen. . . ."[159] And give they did. In 1501 some thirty rent-free houses were furnished to poor noblemen by the terms of a will,[160] while around 1537 another testator left a house to eight "seekers" of the *vergognosi* confraternity, those who collected alms for the shamed.[161]

No greater model of Christian charity existed than the rich openly begging for the poor.[162] But was this intent sustained? Who were the "seekers" for the *vergognosi*? We have seen that the archbishop of Ravenna in 1311 had entrusted this task to honorable men of substance. The same intent is found in the Milanese statutes of 1429 and in the rule of the Florentine Buonomini. Yet we may doubt that the well-to-do publicly begged for their shamed brothers. One of the events that contemporaries of Savonarola found phenomenal was that respectable youth (mostly nobles, some said) would openly solicit for the *vergognosi*. One old man, when confronted by these youth, chastised them: "What do you think you are doing? After all, you are the sons of respectable men. Why are you disgracing them, going around collecting like the poor?"[163] The poor begged; *uomini da bene* did not, unless they were masked.

A cinquecento Paduan painting depicts what may have been more customary: poor nobles attached to a confraternity begging in the streets with veils over their faces.[164] The caption reads, "A poor gentleman seeker at alms." It shows a masked man in confraternal frock carrying his tin box and holding his mask firmly in place. Contemporary to this painting was a Genoese confraternity called "of the veil," whose members apparently collected alms while disguised by masks.[165]

This review of the contexts of the word "shame" shows a firm connection in the popular mind by 1500 between shame and gentility. The

[159] B. Pullan, "Poverty, Charity, and the Reason of State: Some Venetian Examples," *Bollettino dell'instituto di storia della società e dello stato veneziano*, 2 (1960), 37.

[160] Ibid.

[161] Pullan, *Rich and Poor*, 268.

[162] Antonino in his *Summa*, for example, had spoken of St. Martin, "who served his servant in the military when he should have been served by him"; *Summa*, p. 4, t. 2, c. 5, § 7.

[163] Ginori Conti, *Vita . . . Savonarola*, 124.

[164] "Pobero Gentilomo Zirgato Æleemosena"; *Museo Civico di Padova, Codicetto Bottacin* (MB 920). My thanks to Signora Andreucci Lenzi, who was kind enough to send me a photocopy of this.

[165] "Compagnia del Mandiletto." The daughter of its founder quotes his interest in the *poveri vergognosi*: "cioè quelli che si hanno viste del bene già et poi divenuti poveri, si vergognano mendicare": "This year I gave my poor shamed three syrups and some medicine, but next year, God willing, I'll give them hens, because they need them." Also at Genoa, it would appear, if one wanted honor one gave to one's own poor gentlemen; Paschini, *Tre ricerche*, 26f.

concept of shame relates to a decline in social respectability. Respectability and financial difficulties were not and are not mutually exclusive. But a distinction must be made between the impoverished *vergognoso* trying to maintain a face of respectability and those miserables of the lower class who, far from entertaining the luxury of shame, begged to maintain body and soul. Even today many of us can more easily be moved by the tragedy of the single son of good family who comes on hard times than by poverty without tragedy and without flaw: the grinding misery of those born to want. The reason for our emotion is not much different from that which affected our middle-class forebears: brotherhood. We recognize ourselves beneath the veil.

The sixteenth century brought with it a rationalization of charitable institutions unknown in previous ages. Privilege was as much a part of that age as the previous, but it too was part of a plan. The Venetian aristocracy got pensions of a sort.[166] The higher the social class, the more dignified the aid. In both eras shame was greater if one was honorable. The age of absolutism, however, formalized these assumptions into law. In Padua, for example, the profits from the *Monte di Pietà* could be used after 1534 to dower the girls of guild families. Subsequently those same dowries were rationalized in a way which reminds us of a much older tradition, that of the medieval law, Or San Michele, the men of St. Martin. A daughter of a patrician could be dowered by these *Monte* profits with fifty ducats, one of a guild family with a maximum of twenty-five. The profits were to be divided equally between the two groups.[167] Thus one girl of the patrician class received as much as two of the honest guildman's daughters. Both were deemed poor, for the profits from the *Monti di Pietà* continued to be considered as reverting to the poor in this way.

The persistence and intensification of the shame-gentility nexus with its attendant privilege are best illustrated by the execution of a will in Venice in 1609. The famous Scuola di San Rocco had been entrusted with a substantial sum to dower young women as it thought best. It was decided to give fifty ducats each to the daughters of governors of the scuola who had encountered financial reverses. "The daughters of other unfortunate citizens, so long as they had never in their father's lifetime exercised any

---

[166] Davis, *Venetian Nobility*, 50–51, who cautions that they were reserved for needy cases and were unlike those given to noblemen in some European courts. Social welfare had advanced by mid-cinquecento to the point that Contarini could ascribe the famed Venetian stability in part to the poor relief accorded "such that eyther presently do, or at any time have employed themselves in honest trades of use and service to the commonwealth, and grow at length eyther by age or weaknesse unable to persever therein . . ."; Pullan, *Rich and Poor*, 7f.

[167] De Besse, *Bernardino*, II, 88–91.

'mechanical trade' but had respected the demands of their social position, were entitled to a dowry of 25 ducats each." In order to even qualify for dowry help from this bequest, a daughter had to bring proof of her abstention from manual labor. In this manner the famed caritative institution dowered young women as it thought best.[168]

This article has attempted to determine what "poverty" meant in medieval and Renaissance Florence and to trace the attention given to the downwardly mobile segment of the established families. The "establishment" was initially privileged in an informal way. In the quattrocento a confraternity sprang up in Florence to cater to the shamed. During its first half-century it competed with the demands of those truly indigent and their patron, the commune. In the cinquecento the future role of the *vergognosi* confraternities became set. They were to minister to the fallen elite with the encouragement of the state, but not under its control. This development accompanied increased attention to the maintenance of the livelihood of the whole tax-paying segment of the population.

It had been the idea of certain of the propagators of the *Monti di Pietà* to operate the pawnshops without any interest at all. This profoundly conservative side of the *Monti* reflected the persistent notion that money did not naturally fructify. The true charity involved in the *Monte* were the alms freely given by the Christian to build up the capital of the "mountain." This was traditional in means, if not in ends. As with simple alms to the *vergognosi*, someone had to lose in order for another to gain. The Jews might make thousands of florins out of fifty, but this was unnatural and criminal. The good society was one of scarcity and parsimony. But not only money was scarce; so were honor and respectability. These as well as lucre had to be jealously maintained, for the loss of either was an absolute deprivation. Italy entered the early modern period committed to both ideas.

This article complicates rather than solves some of the problems of medieval and early modern charity. It argues that charity was an instrument for preserving the families of the communal elites, but without determining to what extent that was the case.[169] The fundamental point is that "the poor" included all those who could not live according to their corporatively defined life status. The more "honest" their status, the higher their priority among the legions of the needy. The primary argument among historians of medieval charity has been the theoretical one of whether Christian writers favored "creative" charity or indiscriminate

---

[168] Pullan, *Rich and Poor*, 81f.

[169] Professor Pullan's new book is rich in information and insights, yet in practice he also mistakes present and past conceptions of poverty.

giving. The assumption generally made is that laymen who received charity were of the lower classes. This conception has remained largely unquestioned because historians have consulted source materials of a generally theoretical nature, unleavened by the practical consideration of who actually received aid. I refer not only to the emphasis placed upon the tracts on poverty. Historians assessing testamental charity have preferred easily available testaments to scarcer executions. Those examining the account books of confraternities have dealt in the eleemosynary categories furnished them by their sources rather than in the names and conditions of the fostered. Finally, works dealing with governmental charity do not permit us to assess the role of class in official disbursements of charity. In terms of social history, however, a more realistic research strategy would determine the division of charitable funds between the indigent poor of low condition and the downwardly mobile of honest or preeminent condition.

In Florence, extensive sums were spent on the indigent. But by whom? An in-depth study of patterns of charity emphasizing who actually received aid might show that like the divisions of charitable sums described above, as much was given to the relatively few *uomini da bene* as to the economically miserable multitudes. Such a finding would accord with the legal and theological guidelines for charitable giving examined here. As distinct from many of their modern interpreters, medieval jurists and theologians saw such preference as natural and just. Medieval and early modern charity was not only a tool to control the *popolo minuto* through ameliorative charity; nor can its intent be conceived of as simple Christian love for the less fortunate. It was also an instrument to preserve political and social authority by maintaining the honor of the elite that governed and administered. What remains to be determined is the political and financial interplay between these two procedures: on one side, the preservation and fructification of the *uomini da bene*, and on the other, the alimentation of the disquieted, miserable indigents, the first a Christian ideal, the second a political practice.

Where did the money go is the most pressing question. Yet to evaluate testamental executions properly, a firm grasp of the language of charity is imperative. The alternative is an anachronistic choice between simplistic acceptance of Christian ideal as practice and of a materialism that eschews the spiritual motivations that pervasively informed medieval charity. "Poverty" is only the most important of these terms; "pious causes," "for the soul," "shame"—there are many others. Certainly one of the most important is the basic concept of brotherhood. In this paper we have seen the classical associative principle at work in the Milanese statutes: brothers of the confraternity deserved preferential aid. Subsequently, noble citizens of the same city instituted aid for "nobles ashamed to beg" who were not members of the group. Moves in this direction imply a redefinition of brotherhood: class affiliation created "spiritual brotherhood." Brotherhood traditionally defined as *familia* was enlarged to include class mutuality. "If one wants honor," we recall, "it is necessary to aid some poor noble."

The roots of class-conceptualized brotherhood may stem from the ethos of the knightly orders, importations from abroad into urban Italy. Or such a conception may be indigenous to the urban merchant class: "Brothers betray each other; partners do not." In any case, the search for origins must not lead us to assume evolutionary development in the conception of brotherhood.[170] From the crisis of the feudal cosmology in the eleventh century, caused in part by the development of a merchant class, western European history has been marked by a constant search for "natural" social bonding agents. In recent Florentine historiography, Richard Goldthwaite has argued that the modern nuclear family was victorious over consorterial "brotherhood" in fifteenth-century Florence.[171] His thesis will be challenged by those who see a revival of the consortery. The present paper goes further. By showing the growing institutionalized concern for class affiliates, it suggests that social and economic brotherhood—never absent but now institutionalized and fitted with an ideology—was an increasingly powerful "familial" force. Castiglione's courtier and Alberti's *Famigliari* cohere primarily not to the social institutions of court and family—the Alberti in Leon Battista's hands exude little cohesive warmth—but to a social code common to a wider unit or brotherhood: the Gentlemen.

APPENDIX

The inedited text of the oldest *capitoli* or rule of the Buonomini printed below comes from a codex in the *Archivio dei Buonomini di San Martino, Firenze*. It is preceded in the codex by (1) the record of the donation made 21 Nov. 1482 through which the Buonomini purchased their meeting place in the church of S. Martino (c. 1); (2) the text of the indulgence given the

---

[170] On the whole question of brotherhood and otherhood, the work of Benjamin Nelson, *The Idea of Usury* (Chicago, 1969), is fundamental. Perhaps because his departure point is the biblical injunctions on "stealing" or usuring from brothers and others, Nelson nowhere refers to a class-oriented conception of brotherhood in his sources, which range from the Decretal Glossators to the eighteenth century. In light of Nelson's formidable silence on a class-oriented conception of brotherhood, I offer my hypothesis with deliberate caution.

[171] R. Goldthwaite, *Private Wealth in Renaissance Florence* (Princeton, 1968), 251–75.

group by Sixtus IV, dated 1 Mar. 1476 (cc. 1v–2r); (3) an antiphon and a prayer to St. Martin (c. 2v); (4) a miniature showing an enthroned bishop welcoming a poor man under his cloak (c.3). The *capitoli* follow (cc. 3–7). The hands recording the previous are of the late quattrocento or early cinquecento. Following the *capitoli* (cc. 8–37) is a list in various hands of the names of the procurators and their helpers who acceded at various times to those positions in the company. There follows (cc. 38–49 unnumbered) the memorial of 1622 written by Vincenzio Pitti.

My thanks are due Maria Ludovica Andreucci Lenzi for her transcription, and the Compagnia dei Buonomini for access to this codex.

Ad laude et gloria del nostro signore iesu christo, et della sua gloriosa madre vergine maria et del beato sancto martino nostro protectore et advocato, et di tuta la celestiale corte. Ad honore della sancta chiesa di Roma, et del sanctissimo in christo padre at Signore papa Eugenio IIII et del reverendo in christo padre et signor messer l'arciveschovo della città di firenze. Ad utilità de poveri vergognosi della detta città et contado et distretto, et ad salute dell'anime degl'infrascripti principiatori delle infrascripta [sic] opera de misericordia; et di chi ci porgerà aiuto, alla quale l'onnipotente idio presti gratia et augmento connperseveranza.

Considerando la carestia presente et la moltitudine de poveri della città et contado di firenze, maximamente di quegli che non sono consueti a mendicare et il sinistro che patischono molti colle loro famiglie; spirati da dio dal quale i sancti desiderii et le giuste operationi procedono; gl'infrascripti Dodici citadini dilibirorono colla benedictione del sanctissimo padre et Signore papa Eugenio quarto negli anni domini 1441 del mese di Febraio pigliare lo essertitio d'essere procuratori de detti poveri vergognosi, et a quello attendere con diligentia et fede durante la vita loro, salvo giusto impedimento. Et cerchare tutti insieme et divisamente secondo parrà alle loro discretioni ogni aiutorio et limosima da cischuno signore spirituale et temporale et da ogni cittadino et altre persone per distribuire di tempo in tempo ai detti poveri vergognosi per li modi vie et forma che dissotto saranno annotate.

Prima deliberono d'eleggere uno religioso sacerdote il quale sia loro correctore o vero directore; acciò che continuamente avessino dove ricorrere per consiglio et spiri[c.4]tuale aiutorio. Il quale religioso abbi auctorità d'elegere uno altro sacerdote in istato secolare di matura età et di buona vita il quale sia come suo vicario; che continuamente s'abbi a ritrovare coi detti procuratori in ogni partito s'avesse a fare, se con chomodità aver si può, acciochè in ogni loro opera sia il consiglio spirituale et la fede del detto sacerdote, sendo non dimeno approvato per la magiore parte de detti procuratori. La electione del quale correctore sia in questo modo: cioè ch'el proposto nomini tre huomini spirituali et di buona fama, et disaminato tralloro si metta appartito et chi a più fave rimanga correctore. Et manchando detto correctore o suo vicario per morte o per altra cagione oppe [opperchè] detti procuratori si mutassino si provegha come dissopra si dice.

Anchora ch'el numero de detti procuratori non sia nè possa essere più che dodici, et manchandone per morte o altro giusto impedimento alchuno o per alchuno difetto si commettesse che dio lo diliberi del quale si stia al giudicio de sacerdoti che per li tempi fussono in detto asserticio deputati et della magiore parte s'abbia examinare per secreto partito a fave de detti dodici procuratori il quale giudicio s'abbia examinare per secreto partito a fave bianche et nere. Et in tal caso s'abbia a nominare in luogo di quello manchasse uno per ciaschuno de detti procuratori, et quegli mettere appartito, et quello che avesse più fave nere abiendo il numero de due terzi s'intenda essere in luogo di quello manchasse et se si fussono concorrenti si gitti le sorte, et chi toccha la sorta s'intenda essere electo, et non possa essercitare detto ufficio se prima non si confessa per essere più abile alla divina grazia; et fedele a questa opera principiata.

Item che nella chiesa di sancto martino di firenze sia al presente la loro residenza la quale concede loro l'abbate della badia di firenze a beneplacito di lui et suoi successori che possino andare; sanza averne a fare alchuna recognitione alla detta ba[c.5]dia et quivi fare condure diurnamente pane e ogni altra cosa s'avesse a distribuire. Intendendo non dimeno per detto uso non acquistare alchuna giuriditione in su detto luogo ma a ogni voluntà et richiesta dill'abate o suo successore lascialla libera et spedita come al presente l'a.

Anchora ch'el modo del dispensare le limosine si debba dare di concordia della magior parte de detti procuratori insieme col sacerdotte, se con chomodità aver si può, divise in mese secondo richiederanno i bisogni e tempi e a quagli poveri che per la magior parte sia deliberato.

Anchora ch'el detto sacerdote cioè vicario tenga una borsa in che siano inborsati i detti dodici procuratori et ogni mese traga uno propossto il quale tenga conto di tutto quello li perverà nelle mani in danari et roba et cosi di tutto quello distribuirà per entrata et uscita et de partiti si farà a suo tempo. Et finito il mese suo infra octo dì sia tenuto rendere ragione al suo successore con dargli ogni resto di danari et roba gli avanzassi in mano, il quale proposto si debba trarre octo dì innanzi che l'altro esca, et possa detto proposto ragunare il resto de compagni quando et come alla sua conscientia parrà bisogni et ciaschuno de detti compagni sia tenuto per amore di dio a ubidire, aiutare, et puramente consigliare secondo si richiede a detto essercitio.

Anchora che infermando achuno de detti procuratori debba il proposto che sarà in quel tempo farlo vicitare da compagni quando et come allui parrà; et se avesse bisogno sovenirlo. Et manchando di vita sieno tenuti e compagni in fra uno mese fargli dire uno uficio mortuario per l'anima sua nella quale si spendi fiorini due.

Item che ciaschuno de detti dodici procuratori debbeno ogni anno dare del loro proprio per distribuire a poveri et per dare buono exemplo di loro al proximo staia tre di grano o quel più volessi dare, et detto grano sia la prima partita ch'el proposto metta a entrata distribuendo le dette tre [c.6] staia o quel più avessi per ciaschuna settimana durante el tempo suo acciò che continuamente ogni settimana si facci qualche limosina; et se caso fusse che per alchuno sinistro alchuno de detti procuratori non potessi darlo chiedendolo per amore di dio se egli lasciato.

Anchora che i detti procuratori debbano vivere honestamente, fuggire ogni contrarietà di bene vivere, non giucare nè stare a vedere, non usare a taverne nè alluochi disonesti, non fare contratti inleciti, usare alle chiese, andare alle messe, alle prediche, a divini ufici come è debito a veri christiani; et sieno tenuti ciaschuno de detti una volta il mese o per lo meno di due confessarsi, et communicarsi oltre all'obrigo della chiesa tre volte l'anno, cioè per la natività di Christo; per la pentecoste, et per l'assumptione di nostra donna. Et debba ciaschuno de dodici dire ogni dì l'oratione di sancto martino coll'antiphona et col versetto acciò che dio mediante le intercessioni di sancto Martino proveghi a poveri et loro conservi in pace. Et dire ogni dì sette pater nostri coll'ave maria, ricordandosi dell'ore di Christo patì passione, in caso che altro uficio o divotione non dicesse. Et se alchuno de detti procuratori non si portasse honestamente come di sopra si dice, et essendo amonito et non si emendi, sendo dichiarato per la magior parte de detti procuratori et di consiglio de detti due sacerdoti, s'intenda essere privato et cancellato di detto numero. Et se scadesse che alchuno de detti procuratori non volesse o non potesse essercitare detto ufficio, sendo dichiarato nel modo detto pe detti procuratori insieme co sacerdoti, rimanghi fuori del numero, et in suo logo s'elega uno altro come pel capitolo se dispone.

Item che i sopradetti dodici procuratori col detto sacerdote per le due parti di loro habino auctorità et balia di giugnere et diminuire quello che paresse loro a questi capitoli secondo le occurrentie de temporali et etiam de elegere ministri per aiutorio del loro essercitio multiplicando le facende como potrebbe acchadere et premiare quelli tali [c.7] elegessono per loro aiutorio come per le due parti dilloro si disponesse, et torre case et luoghi a pigione per conservare le cose et roba avesseno a guardare, tutto a spese de beni pervenissono in loro governo per detto essercitio. Intendendosi non dimeno che per detta auctorità et balia non si possa accrescere o diminuire il numero de detti dodici procuratori. Ma continuo stare fermo come al presente è scritto; i quali si debbeno scrivere da piè a questi capitoli di mano del sopradetto correctore.

Item s'adomandi al sancto padre per rimedio de peccati de sopradetti procuratori per essre più solleciti nel bene operare in questo misericordioso essercitio quella indulgentia annuale che parrà alla sua beatitudine e a quelgli che persevereranno fino alla morte simile mente li parrà secondo la consueta largità della sancta chiesa. Et a quegli che porgeranno aiutorio a questa opera pia quella indulgentia, che parrà alla sua sanctità. Le quali indulgentie si debbeno fare notare in su certo libro diputato. Et se alchuno de detti procuratori, o di quegli che saranno manchasse in fare o observare i detti capitoli o alcuna parte d'essi o obmettesse alcuna delle cose avessi affare, che per questo non intenda essere tenuto o obligato a peccato mortale.

Politics and Community
in Elizabethan London

FRANK F. FOSTER

During the sixteenth century London experienced a period of unprecedented growth. Since the fourteenth century, houses had been springing up beyond the walls, those medieval ramparts that delineated the City of one square mile. In the sixteenth century these clusters of homes grew into suburbs that seeped even farther from the walls, and from the traditional jurisdiction of the City. Expansion went hand in hand with a dramatic upsurge of population, which for the preceding two or three centuries had held at between thirty and forty thousand. By the Reformation about sixty thousand lived there, at mid-century around ninety thousand, and at the end of Elizabeth's reign in 1603 nearly a quarter of a million. The birth rate was no higher in early modern London than in the counties, the death rate substantially higher; thus a larger population meant higher immigration, especially after the Reformation, and, above all, greater internal mobility in favor of the cities.

The attraction of London lay in the concentration of talents and opportunities that had always existed in the largest and wealthiest city, the center of government, business, and fashion. London intensified its predominance during the sixteenth century with the revitalization of royal government under the Tudors and the development of overseas trading companies. Also contributing to its preeminence was the emergence of a more articulate and active group of landowners, the gentry, who increasingly came to London to sit in Parliament, to seek profitable investments in land or trade, to find favor with the crown or their titled cousins, to quarrel with each other, to display themselves magnificently, and to gobble up property suitable for town houses. Always influential in the realm, henceforth London determined in ever larger degree the directions of English history. By the end of the sixteenth century it had truly become the "behe-moth on the Thames."[1]

So much growth caused changes in London, changes that affected even the great merchants of the City. As wholesalers became aware of the opportunities in foreign markets, they extended the basis of their wealth by multiplying their investment in overseas trading companies. At the same time, as if to prove that fortunes made in trade were no bar to social respectability, they bought country estates from the lands of the dissolved monasteries. For the rest of the century they invested in the land market, and gradually came closer to families of gentle birth (the true upper class of England), through mutual interests in Parliament, in trading ventures, in London itself, and even through intermarriage. The particular London merchants who entered City politics took part in all these activities, yet these political merchants were remarkable for their overwhelming interest in the City, and their extraordinary loyalty to the small circle of men active in civic politics. This group, constituting a local elite within London, will be the focus of this essay.

City politics over the two preceding centuries had developed tradi-tions of its own, traditions strong enough to withstand the winds of change that were blowing in London and throughout the realm. Social change caused some men to lose their bearings, and it threatened their personal fortunes, but the political merchants found a bedrock of stability and con-tinuity in City government. Political institutions and procedures changed very little, and in devoting themselves to City government, these merchants became a part of that conservatism. For example, civic magistrates usually ignored the new suburbs. Rather than meet the challenges of an expand-ing London, they condemned growth and fought to retain ancient privi-leges. Though they mingled with the gentry and nobility, they were careful not to invite them into the councils of the City, the exclusive pre-

---

[1] Especially useful for the London background are Eliza J. Davies, "The Trans-formation of London," *Tudor Studies Presented to A. F. Pollard* (1924), ed. R. W. Seton-Watson, 287–314; Norman G. Brett-James, *The Growth of Stuart London* (1935); F. J. Fisher's three articles, "The Development of the London Food Market, 1540–1640," *Economic History Review*, 5:2 (Apr. 1935), 46–64; "Commercial Trends and Policy in Sixteenth-Century England," *Economic History Review*, 10:2 (Nov. 1940), 95–117; "The Development of London as a Center of Conspicuous Consumption in the Sixteenth and Seventeenth Centuries," *Transactions of the Royal Historical Society*, 4th ser., 30 (1948), 37–50; Valerie Pearl, *London and the Outbreak of the Puritan Revolution: City Government and National Politics, 1625–43* (1964); Lawrence Stone, "Social Mobility in England, 1500–1700," *Past & Present*, no. 33 (Apr. 1966), 16–55; E. A. Wrigley, "A Simple Model of London's Importance in Changing English Society and Economy, 1650–1750," *Past & Present*, no. 37 (July 1967), 44–70. Unless noted otherwise, all books mentioned in this essay were published in London.

serve of merchants. Meanwhile, in order to keep London loyal, the crown favored its rulers with contracts, patents, and numerous advantages, which sustained them as individuals and encouraged their dominance in the City as a governing class. Not surprisingly, under these circumstances, the political merchants found traditional methods of government quite satisfactory.

In the long run their commitment to City government had even deeper implications, for the threads of politics were woven across the whole web of their lives. The purpose of this essay is to examine the civic rulers in some detail, and to illustrate the close relationship that existed between City politics and their lives.[2] In part 1, government and political structure in the City will be described, and the various ranks, or levels, of political activity will be defined. Part 2 will show that a ruler's political rank was a close measure of his place and connections in London society.

1

Government in Tudor London was a cooperative enterprise between the monarch, whose traditional supremacy was as undisputed as it was formal and distant, and the great City merchants, whose authority rested on an autonomous and energetic administration. As the monarch's chief representatives in London, the mayor, aldermen, and common councilmen thought first of keeping the peace and enforcing all laws. They also raised troops, collected subsidies, contributed to loans, and gathered information on the activities of Jesuit missionaries, for example, or the number of new buildings. They worked closely with royal officers on numerous commissions—most often as arbitrators of commercial disputes. In return, the crown endorsed the City's internal autonomy and assisted periodically in ransacking the countryside for London's food, or in supporting the City in jurisdictional disputes. Within the twenty-six wards of the City, the mayor and twenty-five other aldermen came together regularly in the Court of Aldermen. This court held the highest civic authority. The larger Court of Common Council was subordinate and supportive; it met at the pleasure

---

[2] My intention here has been to look at London from an internal position, from the viewpoint of its greatest citizens rather than from the perspective of those who happened to be there but were not intimately bound up with London's destiny—men like royal officers, country gentlemen, lawyers, and even most other merchants. Therefore the chief sources used were the rich manuscript collections of the Guildhall Library, the Corporation of London Records Office, and the City livery companies. From these it has been possible to reconstruct the intricacies of City government as well as the political attitudes of the civic rulers. This approach has led me to conclusions about the rulers' assumptions and behavior that would not have been so apparent had I been looking only at urban social structure, say, or the operation of London markets. This essay summarizes some of the results.

and behest of the aldermen, who were indispensable members of Common Council. The local authorities—the courts of wardmote, the parish vestries, and the courts of assistants in the guilds (i.e., livery companies)—supplemented the central authority of the Court of Aldermen, both by executing its directives and because aldermen and/or councilmen sat on, and always carried the initiative in, these local bodies.

Like other conciliar bodies in the sixteenth century, the Court of Aldermen understood its jurisdiction in broad terms. Construction of tenements, leasing of property, and the cleanliness of streets came within its purview. So did the disposition of those who told lies, slandered officials, beat their mothers, ate flesh during Lent, or were found abroad by the night watch. Idlers, masterless men, prostitutes, aliens, orphans, the poor, shopkeepers, craftsmen, merchants, City officers, and foreign dignitaries constantly demanded their attention. Aldermen did not divide their responsibilities according to specialized functions; they mixed together and handled simultaneously the executive, judicial, legislative, financial, and electoral. But broad powers of initiative and supervision did not excuse them from a high degree of humdrum detail: on the same day he visited the queen, an alderman might check the accounts of a cornmonger or confer with his constables about stray dogs.

Two fundamental concerns of the Court of Aldermen were the regulation of trade and economic practices. The mayor established and enforced a number of prices, particularly for such essential goods as bread, ale, wood, grain, and coal. Aldermen launched frequent inspections, usually through the wardens of the crafts, to assure high standards of quality in manufactured goods. The Court of Aldermen exercised wide powers of regulation over the water supply, the Thames, markets, and shops. But the court was judge as well as policeman, and heard appeals from both tradesmen and consumers who felt mistreated. Probably their most serious concern was the actual supply of certain provisions. The aldermen frequently summoned poulters, woodmongers, and coal suppliers, and decreed specific requirements concerning the time and place to deliver these goods.

Obviously civic government was burdensome. Why did anyone want to become an alderman or common councilman? The eternal attractions of power operated in Elizabethan London: some men have always found it more pleasant to rule than be ruled. The pride of becoming lord mayor, the dignity of an alderman, especially in his capacity as magistrate, the honor of representing one of the greatest cities in Europe, the thrill of mixing with royalty and nobility—all are motives of importance, especially in an age that loved display and revered hierarchy. At the same time, an age that concerned itself so much with order, almost obsessively, also saw in ruling a great duty. But to the political merchants of London there existed something beyond duty, something approaching a calling, and one the more compelling for being invested with the glorious accretions of tradition, for merchants had always ruled in London. Ruling London contributed to personal satisfactions, and bolstered feelings of confidence and belonging that accompanied membership in a recognized ruling group. The sense of continuity so prevalent in City government doubtless provided a welcome island of tranquillity in a sea of change and uncertainty.

The community of rulers also offered more tangible rewards to its members. As a result of friendships formed through politics, marriages were arranged, personal loans were given, leases to civic property were granted, and other favors were exchanged. Connections in City politics facilitated entrance into the exclusive overseas trading ventures and enjoyment of their monopolies. Such advantages became particularly important in the absence of regular compensation for discharging civic affairs. The rulers came from among the more prosperous merchants, to be sure, but after beginning their political routines they devoted less time to their own commercial endeavors. Furthermore, the expenses necessary in the higher places, especially mayor and sheriff, ran into thousands of pounds. Even maintaining the dignity of an alderman or a leading common councilman required hundreds of pounds a year, and these places were for life. It was vital to belong to a group that sustained its members by lucrative social and business connections. Indeed these connections constituted a further incentive to enter civic politics. At the same time, neither the pull of group favor from above nor the push of personal ambition from below ever operated the same way for all concerned. Favor naturally discriminates, and ambition varies from man to man. As a result, while similar patterns of behavior existed, even men of similar wealth and position sometimes rose to different levels.

Promotion in civic office depended mostly on favor. Despite a wide franchise in London (all citizens, or freemen, could vote in some elections), the ballot yielded to favor on all crucial occasions. The potential power of massive numbers was dissipated by a ruling oligarchy that nominated in advance the men who would stand for formal elections. In view of these practices the freeman's vote meant little. He could vote in the annual assembly of his ward, which elected common councilmen, constables, and other ward officers, but this amounted to a ratification of choices previously made by vestry leaders. (The precincts of a ward often coincided with parishes; even where parish and precinct lines were not identical, parish vestries administrated nearby precincts.) The freeman also voted in the ward whenever aldermen were nominated. Invariably, however, the candidates put forward were, if not selected by the establishment, at least representative of it; anyway, the Court of Aldermen made the final elections.

The freeman might also vote in his parish and his guild, whenever the ruling vestrymen or assistants permitted, but he took no part in nominating officers or setting policy. The freemen who attained the dignity of liverymen in their guilds (the wholesale traders and richer retailers who held the governing positions) were entitled to vote for one of the two sheriffs of London, the chamberlain, the two bridgemasters, the City auditors, aleconners, and M.P.'s. But the rulers nominated the candidates who went before the liverymen. The co-optive character of City elections is emphasized by the fact that at all levels—in the wards, parishes, guilds, and on the Common Council and Court of Aldermen—the aldermen and influential common councilmen made the important choices.

To an outsider the rulers were a cohesive and exclusive group. Within the ruling class, ties of common interest came first, but differences existed, particularly in the amount and kind of political activity, and these differences accounted for the various levels or ranks among the rulers. Contemporaries distinguished only two ranks—aldermen and common councilmen—but a close examination of the rulers' political activity suggests that four would more accurately fit the circumstances. I shall call them wardmen, leaders, notables, and the elite. These are my own terms and are used in order to clarify more precisely the relationship between political activity on one hand, and social position and connections on the other. Each group will be defined by certain characteristics that reflect the experiences of most men in the group, but the characteristics are not complete descriptions of all members.

The first and least important of the four are the wardmen, who may have numbered as many as a thousand at any particular time during the second half of the sixteenth century.[3] These men acted in several capacities at the same time. In their wards they were the chief assistants to the foreman of the wardmote inquest, whose job was to investigate and correct common nuisances. In their parishes they assisted with the business of their church, and since the parish was understood to be both a spiritual and a secular jurisdiction, they performed a number of duties appropriate to local urban government. In their livery companies they carried out the private business of their guilds as well as certain public duties for London. Essentially these were three different sorts of wardmen: those active only in the

[3] This estimate is based on the approximate number of offices that existed in the 26 wards, the 25–30 most important parishes, and the 25–30 leading livery companies; allowance has been made for the fact that often the leading officers of a vestry were simultaneously ward and livery officers.

local context of a ward, a parish, or a livery company (these were the most numerous); a middling group who by virtue of election to the Common Council became officers for the whole City but continued to work mostly through the local institutions; and the rising men who later became the aldermen and more important councilmen, and served the entire City more than any part of it. Except for this small third group, the wardmen were not important in the political hierarchy of London. The heart of the ruling class therefore consisted of a group of moderately active common councilmen (leaders), a mixed group of prominent councilmen and lesser aldermen (notables), and the most prestigious aldermen (the elite).

The leaders emerge from the third group of wardmen. They are distinguished from the wardmen below them and the notables above them by the quantity and quality of their political experience. Several things are considered here: the offices they held, the committees they served on, and the length and intensity of service. Personal wealth was another consideration because size of fortune identified those who shared the kinds of connections that encouraged and accompanied wider political experience. The leaders were distinct in at least one of these ways: (1) they held at least two civic offices; (2) they had moderate committee experience; (3) they were sureties for civic bonds at least twice, showing they possessed sizable wealth.[4] There were only about 118 leaders during Queen Elizabeth's reign. Men who were active on only a few committees or who held only one office cannot be called leaders, though they are among the more prominent wardmen just because of their occasional City-wide service. During the early part of the reign, before the pressure of civic work grew so heavy, many councilmen took no part as civic officeholders or committeemen. Only a little over half the council's members during the first half of the reign, and never more than 60 percent, were active beyond their own wards. In later years events forced an increase in the number of active men, approaching 90 percent of the council's membership at times, but most of them held only a single office, usually hospital governor, and sat on only a few committees, if any.

Despite the larger volume of business in later years, most of it was handled by the permanent or ad hoc committees of either the Court of Common Council or the Court of Aldermen. The crucial business of committee work remained in the hands of a few, and from year to year the minority tended to consist of about the same men. Considering only the councilmen, 60 percent of the committeemen of 1559 reappeared in 1560;

---

[4] In borrowing money abroad, the queen found it enhanced her credit to have City merchants stand as guarantors of repayment. This evidence concerning level of wealth is confirmed by subsidy payments and the other assessments mentioned in n. 33.

by 1599–1600 there was a 77 percent continuity. During the busiest times of the reign only about one-third of the council, or 70 men, were active in committee work; usually it was considerably less. Probably only a little over a quarter of the councilmen had much committee experience; perhaps half the total had a limited amount. If committee work was handled by a minority, an even smaller group provided the leadership. Forty-one men were active on committees in 1559, yet 12 of them muscled their way into two-thirds of the assignments. In 1600, 11 of 66 committeemen carried 40 percent of the load.

The 12 committeemen of 1559 and the 11 of 1600 who dominated committee work in those years are more than just leading councilmen; they are the notables. Adding two more categories to the three mentioned, it can be said that notables were those who (4) were very active committeemen and (5) held at least four civic offices. Greater officeholding was closely associated with greater committee work, because committee work provided that wider view of City affairs which was helpful for effective office management; conversely, the experienced officeholder contributed more to his committees. Forty-one councilmen can be called notables.

Among the 138 Elizabethan aldermen,[5] 9 were leaders or notables while on the Common Council, but having been elected aldermen, they paid fines to avoid serving, were then discharged, and took no permanent part in the work of the Court of Aldermen. Fourteen others who were discharged had insufficient political experience to deserve any ranking; another died within a few months of his election. The rest served at least a year; 50 aldermen can be called notables and 64 the elite. The elite were set apart from the notables by even greater political experience. They were the men with the most offices, especially more of the highest ones, and the greatest committee work. Since aldermen moved into the places available to them by seniority, the elite can be defined as the most senior aldermen. To put it another way, the elite are the 64 aldermen who became mayors.[6]

The political behavior of the two chief ranks, the notables and the

[5] For the number of aldermen, see Alfred B. Beaven, *The Aldermen of the City of London* (1908–13), vol. 2, 29–48. The figure 138 was reached by beginning with the men on the Court of Aldermen when Elizabeth's reign began and adding each one sworn during her lifetime.

[6] Seven of the 64 elite actually held the mayoralty before Elizabeth's accession, but they are considered Elizabethans because they continued to serve under her until their deaths; 10 others who reached the court before the queen's death did not hold the mayoralty until after 1603.

An apt demonstration of the importance of seniority for advancing aldermen is the fact that only 4 of the 64 elite served less than the average tenure of all Elizabethan aldermen: eleven years. The shortest tenure was that of Thomas Curtes, pewterer and later fishmonger, who served eight and a half years. Conversely, only 3 of the 50 other aldermen (the notables) had a tenure on the court exceeding the eleven-year average.

elite, can be illustrated in some detail, beginning with the notables. Of what did their political activity consist? Since both councilmen and aldermen were notables, how much difference existed between these two degrees of notables? Table 1 compares the experience of 32 notables: 16 councilmen and 16 aldermen. The table is arranged (from top to bottom) to show the approximate order of holding offices that was normal for most men.[7] Counting the number of their City offices reveals that councilmen held somewhat more places, if the position of alderman itself is discounted.

TABLE 1. *Political Experience of the Notables*

OFFICE	HELD BY THE 16 ALDERMEN	HELD BY THE 16 COUNCILMEN
Hospital governor	8	15
Tax collector	3	4
Aleconner	0	2
Auditor of Bridgehouse and Chamber	9	13
Hospital auditor	4	9
Grain Committee	1	4
Bridgehouse Estates–City Lands Committee	8	7
Unsuccessful nominee for bridgemaster	0	1
Unsuccessful nominee for chamberlain	0	1
Hospital treasurer	5	4
Auditor general of hospitals	4	1
Sheriff	16	1[a]
M.P. (burgesses)	0	4
Bridgemaster	0	1
Provost marshal	1	0
Alderman	16	2[b]
Total	75	69

[a] Roger Jones became sheriff after his election to the Court of Aldermen. See note b.
[b] Roger Jones was an alderman for fourteen months, but since he became an alderman after the terminal dates for this study (1558-1603), he is considered a councilman. The other alderman is Richard Staper, who served three days.

[7] The experiences of all notable aldermen were largely the same, but among notable councilmen there were greater differences. Some of the councilmen never held an office higher than hospital auditor, or sat on a committee of greater importance than the Bridgehouse Estates–City Lands Committee. For the comparison in this table, therefore, the councilmen selected were those whose experience came closest to that of the notable aldermen.

But the busiest individuals were the aldermen. By the time an alderman had earned his fourth or fifth office, he had gone further than most of the notable councilmen, and a large part of his career still lay before him. A councilman reached a fourth or fifth office, if ever, in the late part of his career.

While serving in similar beginning posts, those who became aldermen gained a larger share of the higher offices. Of greater significance is the speed of their rise. Using the office of hospital treasurer as an example, all five future aldermen secured this important place within six years of their first recorded appearance in City politics, whereas no councilman took less than six years, all but one requiring over ten. Aldermen had a similar edge in committee work. Despite the fact that councilmen found increasing responsibility on committees during Elizabeth's reign, committee work remained largely in the hands of the aldermen. They were, and had always been, the nucleus of all civic committees, most of which were formed by the Court of Aldermen. The court itself met at least twice nearly every week; it centralized and supervised all civic administration.[8] In the hands of this small body were both the creation of policy by its senior members and its execution by seniors and juniors.[9] Thus the notable aldermen were more important politically than the notable councilmen. While some of the younger aldermen could not count as many offices or as much experience as some councilmen, they sat at the center of power, and if they lived long enough, they would direct that power.

Elite aldermen, while councilmen or junior aldermen, inevitably occupied the leading places. Table 2 shows a nearly complete digest of the offices these sixty-four men held.[10] The table is divided into five columns to show that men with the longest tenure did have more places, especially

[8] It consisted of the twenty-six aldermen, a few permanent assistants, and other advisors who were summoned irregularly.

[9] Senior aldermen (the elite) were those who had served as mayor.

[10] If it were possible to show a complete record of each man's career on this table, a few additions could be made, mostly among the offices in the first half of the table. But while the table will not show every City position, it is about 95 percent complete. The men who extended beyond 1558 and 1603 (the terminal dates for gathering information) fall about equally into each of the seniority groupings; therefore the comparison among these groups in the number and kind of offices they held and when they held them is not distorted. Furthermore, from an acquaintance with many careers it is possible to assume certain things that are lacking in the table; for example, that more men might have been governors of hospitals, since that was a typical way to begin a career. Perhaps two or three more would have been chief auditors of the Bridgehouse and Chamber, but all the other auditors are included. It is unlikely that many more would have been tax collectors, because this kind of place (unlike governor or auditor) did not help a man advance. Finally, by extending the terminal dates, all the hospital treasurers, auditors, and auditors general have been searched out, and in other respects the table is complete.

TABLE 2. *Political Experience of the Elite*

OFFICE	HELD BY MEN WHO SERVED OVER 24 YEARS (12 MEN)	20–23½ YEARS (12)	17–19 YEARS (14)	12½–16½ YEARS (14)	8½–12 YEARS (12)
Hospital governor	4	6	1	5	4
Tax collector	0	2	0	1	1
Auditor of Bridgehouse and Chamber	4	6	2	5	3
Hospital auditor	0	2	2	4	3
Grain Committee	0	1	0	1	0
Bridgehouse Estates–City Lands Committee	12	9	7	8	7
Hospital treasurer	3	4	4	1	4
Auditor general of hospitals	1	1	3	4	2
M.P. (burgesses)	0	1	0	1	1
Company master	12	10	10	12	8
Sheriff	12	12	14	14	12
Provost marshal	1	0	0	0	0
Mayor	12	12	14	14	12
Hospital president	14*	13*	10	7	11
Chief auditor of Bridgehouse and Chamber	7	10	10	8	5
Surveyor general of hospitals	8	6	3	0	0
Comptroller general of hospitals	6	2	0	0	0
M.P. (knights)	5	3	5	0	0
Colonel of Trained Bands	1	1	0	1	0

* One or more men held more than one presidency.

in the offices open only to senior aldermen. The elite were conspicuously less active in the early or beginning offices than men who never became aldermen, but all of them had some early places. Having gained sufficient political experience to advance to the Common Council, they had a number of other choices to make before moving further. A candidate had to consider his age, health, personal aspirations, and business endeavors before taking up the aldermanic gown. Desire to be an alderman and willingness to serve a long time were also important. The average tenure of all aldermen was eleven years (averaging to the nearest year); for men who did not pay to be quickly discharged, it was thirteen years.

Men who decided to move up to the Court of Aldermen had to clear another hurdle, the mayoralty, before ranking as the elite of the City. Some aldermen preferred to pay fines rather than serve. William Masham was discharged from the court on 8 January 1594 for £600, because of being "grievously tormented with gout, colic, and stone, unwieldiness and disability of body."[11] Despite his plea of bad health, he lived another six years. In 1594 Masham was the most senior of the junior aldermen, which meant he was next in line to assume the mayoralty in October of that year. Part of his desire for the discharge can be attributed to his unwillingness to take the next step in City politics. Thomas Starkye was discharged on 20 September 1588 for a similar reason. Since the end of October 1587, when George Barne completed his mayoral year, Starkye had been the next in line and should have taken the chair immediately after Barne, but he did not; George Bonde, the next in line after Starkye, took the chair instead. The pressure on Starkye to take his turn was not relieved, nor was it ever in these cases, and his discharge came just nine days before George Bonde's successor was to be chosen. The standard excuse of "age and infirmity"[12] is less credible in view of the pressure on him to serve. It was an unwritten law that if a man was unwilling to become mayor, he must leave the court, and there is no case among the Elizabethan aldermen of a man allowed to stay on the court after refusing to accept the mayoralty.

The decision to become mayor was an important one, and five men delayed this responsibility in order to arrange their affairs. Others weighed unfavorably the costs that would result against other interests, needs, and ambitions. Eighteen aldermen in this period served for several years but left the court in time to miss the mayoral year, nine of them just before they would have had to face election. These refusals to serve do not seem to have been based on political struggles within the ruling class. David Woodroffe, for example, was Catholic and may have felt uncomfortable about sitting with a majority of Protestants, but he was not deprived because of his religion. Thomas White before him and later Thomas Offley were also Catholics, and no one tried to ease them out of office.[13] Had Woodroffe's brethren been trying to oust him, they could have done so conveniently in a much shorter time, but they stretched out their dealings with him for over three years, giving him every chance to stay on the court.

[11] Corporation of London Records Office, rep(ertory) 23, f. 146; Beaven, vol. 1, 115.

[12] Rep. 21, f. 590; Beaven, vol. 1, 115.

[13] On White, see *Dictionary of National Biography*; W. J. Loftie, *A History of London* (1883), vol. 1, 325–26; A. G. Dickens and Dorothy Carr, *The Reformation in England to the Accession of Elizabeth I* (1968), 127. On Offley, see a list of "papists" drawn up for Secretary Walsingham around 1578: C(alendar) of S(tate) P(apers) D(omestic), Addenda (1566–79), 25/118.

His turn as mayor should have commenced in October 1556, but he was allowed a delay, and Thomas Offley succeeded as the next most senior alderman. When Woodroffe was still not willing to take the chair in 1557, committees of the court began to call on him. On 19 November 1558 a committee of three aldermen and the recorder finally urged him to "serve the City according to his vocation or else to give some reasonable sum to the use of the City and to give up his cloak and room of aldermanship that there may some other be elected to serve in his place."[14] Woodroffe had not been attending the court for over a year, and had he been more conscientious about his duties, the discharge would have taken much less time. He agreed with the tradition that he must serve or resign, and when the committee spoke with him, it was clear that only the amount of his fine was a subject of controversy.[15] Other committees kept after Woodroffe throughout 1559, but no agreement was reached until he finally paid £100 and was discharged on 5 January 1560.[16] The long delay was caused by haggling over a fine: £100 was considerably less than most men were allowed to pay.

But the great majority of aldermen who lived long enough accepted the mayoralty. Considering the average period they spent on the Common Council—seven to eight years—and the normal tenure as junior aldermen— eight to twelve years—about eighteen years as councilman and alderman were required before becoming mayor. Having served as mayor, senior aldermen undertook varying activities. Although Henry Rowe in four years past the chair gained no new positions and Thomas Lodge in three years gained but one, Rowland Heyward assumed three new position- in his first year as a senior alderman. In general, having decided to stay on in order to serve the mayoralty, most men remained as senior aldermen until their deaths.[17] They filled the several offices open to them by rotation. These offices were important in the City and often demanded a considerable investment of time. While not sinecures, these places also brought prestige to the holders. With one exception, the chief auditor of Bridgehouse and Chamber, who served only a year, all offices open to senior aldermen were held for an indefinite time.[18] Since there were not many of these offices, and

---

[14] Rep. 14, f. 90[b].
[15] Ibid., f. 104.
[16] Ibid., f. 273.
[17] The only exceptions between 1542 and 1643 are William Chester, Thomas Lodge, Nicholas Woodroffe, John Braunche, Thomas Pullyson, Richard Martin, and Nicholas Mosley. From the wording of their discharges, and the supplementary material gathered by Beaven or found in the Remembrancia volumes, it seems four of the seven were forced to leave the court because of financial inadequacy or unwillingness to assume the offices held by senior aldermen; the others left for disciplinary reasons.
[18] The chief auditors of the Bridgehouse and Chamber succeeded in the order

since the elite often held them until death, senior aldermen sometimes went several years without a new position.

Because aldermen held the offices open to them largely by rotation, the number of offices occupied does not necessarily mark the active elite or distinguish them from those content to do the minimum expected of them. Filling offices merely meant responsibility for rather specific duties, and while all the elite held such offices, some were much more active on committees and more regular in attendance at court. Attendance records for the aldermen who were the most active on committees reveal that they also attended the court more often.[19] For example, in 1569, a year of plague in the City, Rowland Heyward attended 56 of 84 courts, about average for the year; in 1577 he attended 84 of 100, way ahead of the average; and in 1593—the year of his death—he still managed to go to 62 of 97 courts, also over the average. Richard Martin in 1593 and 1599 was far ahead of the average attendance, and was probably the most active senior alderman in the 1590s. Thomas Offley displayed the same pattern: in 1559 and 1569 he was well over the average attendance, and he was just over average in 1577. Among the junior aldermen, with individual exceptions, there is less often the same direct relationship between attendance and committee work.

Some junior aldermen attended the court more faithfully than some seniors, yet seniors made committee assignments, chaired the committees, and provided leadership in the court and the City. During particular years individuals might be unable to assume their usual active roles, but over a number of years senior aldermen as a group remained the most active. Individual examples stand out. In the early part of the reign, Martin Bowes, William Garrarde, and Thomas Offley were the exceptional men; Lionel Duckett, John Ryvers, Wolstan Dixie, and George Barne were in the middle years; Richard Martin and John Harte were in the later years. The most remarkable alderman of this time, Rowland Heyward, was extremely active throughout the reign until his death in 1593. These men constituted a kind of elite within the elite; by virtue of their greater involvement, they were the most influential rulers of London.

2

The remainder of this essay will focus on the rulers' behavior beyond politics: their status, training, business activity, wealth, affiliations, and family

---

that they had served as mayor; this position was usually taken as soon after the mayoral year as possible.

[19] Each day's court minutes are preceded by a list of the aldermen attending that day.

connections. All ranks of the ruling class were closely integrated by a number of overlapping connections, especially through the livery companies, in trading ventures, and through family links. The elite shared more of these connections, the notables and leaders proportionally less. At the same time, there was a relationship between the number and quality of these ties and political rank. The elite were the most politically active, and simultaneously the greatest men in London mercantile society. Political rank also reflected social position among the notables and leaders. In London this particular combination of social integration and political stratification produced a ruling class that was interested above all in unifying and advancing the whole group. There was no attempt to use the greater ties and influence of a few to create a dominant faction within the ruling class.

Considerations of status were implicit in nearly everything the rulers did. They knew that their achievements, whether in City politics, in business, or in other endeavors, were partly the cause and partly the result of their status, and they recognized that status was unequally distributed. Titles are an obvious reflection of the gradations of status.[20] Each of the elite, except Thomas Skinner, became a knight; he failed because he died a month after beginning his mayoralty, the completion or near completion of which was the usual requirement for knighthood.[21] However, only one leader (Baptist Hicks), one notable (Roger Jones), and perhaps two other notables (Thomas Bramley, the haberdasher, and Thomas Piggott, later of Buckinghamshire) were ever knights. Forty-nine percent of the notables and 25 percent of the leaders were declared armigerous at the London visitation of 1568.[22]

Membership in one of the Inns of Court also indicated status rather than an interest in studying or practicing the common law, for most of these connections were begun well after men had risen in the hierarchy of London government. Thirty-nine percent of the elite (25 men) were affiliated with an inn, but only 17.1 percent of the leaders and 16.6 percent of the notables.[23] Those interested in formal education might spend time at

[20] In order to make comparisons among the elite, notables, and leaders, I have selected 36 leaders from the total of 118. These 36 were selected at random. Therefore in the various comparisons that follow, leaders means the select 36. Notables refers to the 41 commoners only, not the 50 aldermen who also qualify as notables; elite means all 64 mayors.
[21] At least that was the case until the "inflation of honors" of 26 July 1603, when James I knighted all members but one of the Court of Aldermen who were not already knights (Beaven, vol. 1, 255–56).
[22] William A. Shaw, *The Knights of England* (1906); The Harleian Society, *The Visitation of London, 1568*, 1 (1869) and 109–10 (1963).
[23] Joseph Foster, *The Register of Admissions to Gray's Inn, 1521–1889* (1889);

Oxford or Cambridge, but university experience had no perceptible impact on subsequent careers in London. Perhaps something of family status is suggested for those who attended a university before settling down in London, but in view of the small number who attended, one cannot say that the ruling class took much stock in the universities. Only two of the elite (Henry Billingsley and William Chester) probably went to Cambridge, and only one leader (Baptist Hicks). Namesakes of 28 other rulers appear in the records of Oxford or Cambridge or both, but even assuming all these are our Londoners, the total is not impressive. Twelve are elite (19 percent of the elite), 8 are notables (20 percent), and 8 are leaders (22 percent).[24]

So far as the rulers themselves were concerned, residence in London was one of their greatest claims to status. There they began an apprenticeship. There they entered into other associations, especially through the livery companies, which might result in a favorable marriage or open the door to City politics. And London was the center of their foreign business ventures. In view of their extensive lands in the counties, it is revealing of London's importance to the rulers—and to their own status—that they preferred to live in town.[25] Probably no other group of merchants was as much in evidence there. Measured by their attendance at the Court of Aldermen and the Common Council, and at a lower level the courts of wardmote, the parish vestries, and the wardens' courts and courts of assistants in the livery companies, their abundant interest in the City and its life is obvious. Their interest, it should be remembered, was voluntary. No one had to become an alderman or councilman, and having become one, no one was required to endure the tedium of civic affairs with the enthusiasm so typical of the rulers. A few found the routine unfruitful and retired to country estates. But nearly all who retired did so before ever reaching the pinnacle of political influence. Progress in politics meant an increasing commitment to London. There were good reasons for this, for business and social connections multiplied with the passing of time. Doubtless some men retired from

---

Students Admitted to the Inner Temple, 1547–1660 (1877); W. P. Baildon, ed., The Records of the Honourable Society of Lincoln's Inn, 1: Admissions, 1420–1799 (1896); H. A. C. Sturgess, ed., Register of Admissions to the Honourable Society of the Middle Temple, 1 (1949).

[24] John Venn and J. A. Venn, Alumni Cantabrigienses (Cambridge, 1922); Joseph Foster, Alumni Oxonienses (Oxford, 1891).

[25] Whenever records of landowning were found, the elite were much more likely to mention county as well as City property. Eighty-eight percent of the elite mentioned county lands in their wills (or it is recorded in inquisitions post mortem), but only 59 percent of the notables and 67 percent of the leaders held lands outside London. Ironically, the men who might most easily have retired were the ones least likely to do so, since it was the elite who more often stayed in London.

City life because they failed to establish ties that would have made staying on more profitable or interesting. Even the less prestigious rulers, however, mostly stayed in London.

A testament to the great attraction of London in this period is the fact that most rulers, from elite to leader, were not native Londoners. Only 12 of the elite (19 percent) were certainly or probably born in London, whereas 34 (53 percent) were not, or very likely not.[26] Among the notables and leaders there is greater uncertainty about place of origin, making any statistical survey less useful; yet where the evidence exists, the tendency was the same: most were not born in London. Those born in London had a decided advantage in two respects that were essential to successful political advancement. They had, at least at the beginning of their careers, more ties with families already or soon to be involved in civic politics, and they were more often able to secure an apprenticeship with a prominent ruler as a result.[27]

Apprenticeship, or servitude, had been the main avenue to the freedom of the City since the early fourteenth century; it was also the process whereby craftsmen qualified for entry into their profession. But by the sixteenth century, among the merchants who ruled the City, most men entered an apprenticeship not to become qualified craftsmen—these men were merchants, not craftsmen—but to gain the freedom and attach themselves to an important personage who might further their careers in trade, politics, and perhaps marriage. Often apprenticeship was the prelude to more lasting associations. In both domestic business and foreign trade, apprentices found entry into the companies facilitated by association with patrons. So commonly were apprentices brought along by their patrons in the major trading companies that in 1591 Lord Burghley complained about apprentices who became members of the Turkey Company even before they could provide any stock or engage in the trade.[28]

London ties like these undoubtedly accounted for the rapid rise of

---

[26] Place of birth has usually been determined by the residence of a man's father at the time of some particular documentation: a herald's visitation or the drawing up of a will, for example. Needless to say, this is not a completely reliable guide to the places their children were born, for there may have been family mobility before or after any of the documents that have survived were compiled. Nonetheless, a number of men took the trouble to reveal their birthplace in their wills, and this source confirms that most rulers were not born in London.

[27] The names of apprentices and masters are found in the records of the livery companies, usually in apprenticeship registers, or freedom registers, or in the wardens' accounts. To determine family relationships I have relied primarily on wills, heralds' visitations, and Beaven's work. I have also used the *Dictionary of National Biography* and the unexpected notes in a City minute book or a livery company record that clarify relationships.

[28] *C.S.P.D.* (1591–94), 239/140.

such men as Henry Billingsley, John Braunche, John Garrarde, Henry Rowe, and Nicholas Woodroffe. Twenty-one of the elite, a third of them born in London, served their apprenticeship with a man who was or soon became important politically. But these initial advantages were not indispensable, and certainly not relied on exclusively. Another twelve of the elite (among whom at least half, and probably all but one, were not born in London) had masters who were never politically prominent. Therefore considerations other than place of birth, apprenticeship, and early family connections contributed to the success of a substantial number of the elite. Considering the men who ultimately became the most powerful politically —those I called the elite within the elite—the pattern of their early careers was not markedly different from that of other men who became the elite. By comparison with the notables or leaders, however, the distinctness of the elite as a group is clear, and the elite made far better use of early connections such as apprenticeship. Most notables and leaders served their apprenticeship with political bigwigs, but a large minority had masters of no political consequence. What was important was not just to gain an apprenticeship with a ruler, but with a very influential one, and in this respect the masters of the elite were, with little exception, men of much greater political and social prominence than those of the notables and leaders.

Among the other considerations that led to political prominence, business and social connections were vital. They integrated the ruling group and encouraged the achievement of a level of wealth appropriate to the rulers. Overseas trade ranked first among the elite's business activities. Of the 22 men named by John Strype as the greatest merchants of the early Elizabethan years, 20, most of them merchant adventurers, were rulers of London. Interest in foreign commerce grew as opportunities increased during the queen's reign; for the Jacobean period it has been estimated that between one-third and one-half the aldermen had their principle source of income from foreign trade, while perhaps 70 percent of them joined in a venture occasionally.[29]

No institution was more instrumental in advancing these connections than the livery company, which indeed was the center of social life. Rulers commonly married into the families of their liveried brethren. Those whom

[29] John Strype, Survey of London (1720), vol. 2, bk. 5, 291; Robert G. Lang, "The Greater Merchants of London in the Early Seventeenth Century," D. Phil. thesis (Oxford University, 1962), 94–96. The particular trading activities of many rulers are already known; see especially Astrid Friis, Alderman Cockayne's Project and the Cloth Trade (1927); T. S. Willan, The Muscovy Merchants of 1555 (Manchester, 1953); the Lang thesis just cited; and T. K. Rabb, Enterprise and Empire: Merchant and Gentry Investment in the Expansion of England, 1575–1630 (Cambridge, Mass., 1967), esp. bibliography and appendix.

they remembered most fondly in their wills were fellow liverymen. Livery-men usually served as overseers of each other's estates, and it was the rare ruler who neglected to give his guild a present, perhaps a silver cup or a memorial dinner. Largely through their livery companies the rulers dispensed donations to the poor, to schools, and to other young merchants. Livery companies were usually the trustees that administered most of the lands and capital endowments left by the rulers, and they provided a nucleus for other business enterprise. Particular companies were especially valuable: of the 44 elite who are known to have invested in overseas trade, 35 (or 80 percent) belonged to only six livery companies. Among the notables, 51 percent of the investors in foreign trade were members of the same six liveries; among the leaders, 83 percent.[30] The significance of this small group of livery companies and the connections they engendered is underscored by the fact that approximately 70 percent of the men who rose to the highest political standing in the City were members of these same six liveries. Also suggestive of the concentrated, and doubtless deliberate, character of their connections is the rulers' preference for three particular trading ventures—the Spanish Company, the Merchant Adventurers' Company, and the Muscovy Company. Forty-one percent of their investment was in these three companies alone.

Membership in the charmed circle of six liveries, however, was not requisite to become an investor in overseas trade; witness the numerous activities of Thomas Cambell, an ironmonger, or Richard Saltonstall, a skinner.[31] But such men also illustrate the general importance of livery and family connections. Cambell was the son-in-law of a wealthy and politically active councilman and ironmonger, Edward Bright, while Saltonstall was a close friend and associate of an even more prominent councilman, William Towerson, also a skinner, who had a part in several overseas ventures.[32] Nine of the fourteen notables who invested in more than one venture belonged to one of the six chief liveries. Of the five who did not, the first was William Towerson, just mentioned; the second was his friend, business

---

[30] The six were Grocers, Haberdashers, Merchant Taylors, Mercers, Clothworkers, and Drapers. The figures on investment are primarily from Rabb, 233–410, though especially for the period before 1575 it has been necessary to supplement Rabb by reference to the standard printed material on overseas trade. The percentage is lower among the notables due to the large number of skinners (21 percent) among the notables who invested.

[31] Cambell was a member of the Spanish, Eastland, Levant, East India, Irish, and French companies. Saltonstall was a merchant adventurer, backed a privateering venture, and was a member of the Muscovy, Spanish, Levant, and East India companies.

[32] Towerson's activity was similar to Saltonstall's: he was a merchant adventurer, backed a privateering venture and one of the Frobisher-Fenton voyages, and was a member of the Muscovy, Spanish, and Eastland companies.

associate, and relative by marriage, John Harbie, another skinner; Thomas Bannyster and Geoffrey Walkedon were also skinners, Bannyster the son-in-law of an alderman, Walkedon the apprentice of one alderman and the close friend of another; the last, Thomas Fettiplace, ironmonger, was a friend and neighbor of one of the most prominent councilmen of the Elizabethan period, Robert Offley.

Livery affiliations were vital for business and political advancement, since apprentices commonly moved into the same political circles as their masters. The business success and political rank of the master gave a fair indication of the future prospects of his clients, with the result that dependents of a great man would often become great men themselves, as both higher-ranking politicians and more prosperous entrepreneurs. It followed that greater success in one endeavor usually led to the same in the other. Considering foreign trade, more of the elite invested (69 percent) than either notables (44 percent) or leaders (50 percent). It did not follow, however, that the greatest businessmen were exclusively the most active politicians, or vice versa. Of the ten most active politically, only four were also among the ten most active traders. Rather than overlapping extensively in the leadership roles, the elite exhibited some specialization of behavior—some preferred politics, some trade—showing how little they desired to create a dominant faction in the City.

A comparative measure of wealth clearly indicates that the councilmen and aldermen were among the richest citizens of London.[33] Subsidy assessments are a useful guide to the various levels of wealth in the City, where £50 and up was the top bracket. Most of the leaders and notables and all the elite were in this bracket, and the aldermen and wealthier coun-

---

[33] I have examined three subsidies as a guide to wealth: for the 1559 subsidy, see MS 2859 at the Guildhall Library Muniment Room; for 1572, MS 2942; for 1589, see *The Publications of the Harleian Society*, 109–10 (1963), 148–64. Various other local records have also been consulted from the wards, parishes, and livery companies. Here are the details of one. It is from the court book of the Ironmongers' Company for 14 November 1569 (f. 76ᵇ), and is an assessment on the assistants. The highest assessment was £8 on William Rowe, who was a warden that year but not a councilman until 1574 or alderman until 1581. Another warden, Richard Morris, councilman since the early 1560s, also paid £8. Edward Bright, councilman for about the same time as Morris, paid £6. James Harvye paid £5 (he was an alderman two years later); two other future aldermen (Thomas Cambell, alderman beginning 1599, and Robert Chamberlain, elected alderman in 1596) were wealthy enough at this time to be assessed at 30 shillings each. Two other prominent ironmongers escaped assessment because of the high city office they held: Alexander Avenon, then mayor, and William Dane, then sheriff. What is significant here is that the men then on the Court of Assistants who were or were to become aldermen or councilmen were the ones who paid the most. Parish and ward assessments also show that councilmen and aldermen invariably paid more than most other men, and that men on their way to higher office in the City also rated the higher assessments.

cilmen were often assessed at over £200. Aldermen in particular were reluctant to admit to their court any man who was not of financial independence, and the most common excuse for rejecting the nomination of a candidate for the aldermanry was "insufficiency" of estate. Other men, once successfully elected to the court, considered the burdens of office too great and preferred to pay a substantial fine instead of serving. There were other reasons for declining to serve, but sheer material inability should not be overlooked as the motive of many, since there was no formal monetary compensation for aldermen. The records of aldermanic elections reveal that the "wealthier and wiser" men had always been chosen, and by 1469 there was a specific requirement that the candidate's goods, chattels, and expectant debts amount to £1,000.[34] By 1525 this qualification was 2,000 marks (£1,333),[35] and by the 1640s it was £10,000.[36] No specific valuation was required for councilmen's estates, but substantial levels of wealth were expected. Councilmen were also not paid, and from their ranks came the aldermen.

Two examples can illustrate the variance in personal wealth between men of different ranks. Elite alderman James Harvye, an ironmonger, owned a house with a garden and nine tenements in Lime Street, as well as unspecified lands in the Old Jewry and in the parish of St. Benet Gracechurch. Outside London, he held a manor and other assorted lands in Wiltshire, a manor in Staffordshire, and various lands in Essex, some in Hornechurch near London. A large part of his business was through the Antwerp market, and he had found it convenient to purchase a house there. At his death he was able to settle 2,000 marks on each of his five children still unadvanced.[37] In 1572 he had been assessed at £300 toward the subsidy voted in 1571. One of the leaders, councilman William Chelsham, a mercer, was assessed at £80 for the same subsidy. He had a share in the tenure of five City tenements and shops, in addition to a leasehold in St. Mary-le-Bow. He held a manor in Clapham that he reckoned to sell for £1,366.13.4. He was able to settle £600 on his wife outright, over and above the third portion of his personalty to which she was entitled. His eldest son, already advanced, received £550; two married daughters were given £200 each, and his only unadvanced child, Magdalen, had £300 set aside for her on the day of her marriage.[38]

[34] Reginald R. Sharpe, ed., *Calendar of Letter-Books Preserved among the Archives of the Corporation of the City of London* (1899–1912), *Calendar of Letter-Book L*, 85. This was an order of the Court of Aldermen on 29 July 1469.

[35] Rep. 7, f. 45[b]; Letter-Book N, f. 287[b].

[36] Pearl, *London and the Outbreak of the Puritan Revolution*, 60.

[37] P(rerogative) C(ourt) of C(anterbury). 39 Rowe.

[38] P.C.C. 25 Peter.

Charitable donations are another indication of wealth. A common pattern existed in these bequests, a pattern established by the wealthier merchants and followed whenever possible by others. Aldermen and wealthier councilmen carefully adhered to the mode and invariably appeared among the most generous givers.[39] The rulers commonly supported the poor of their own livery company, the several parishes they had been affiliated with in London, often particular wards, and sometimes their place of birth. Nearly all of them provided for a number of poor who would follow their funeral cortege. Scholars at the universities, colleges, schools, and other towns were frequently supported, but the bulk of the rulers' munificence was poured into London itself: to hospitals, prisons, and livery companies; to churches for sermons or lectures; to friends, relatives, servants, and apprentices; and to other City charities.

In analyzing the distribution of wealth among the rulers, considerable variation is found. Generally the elite were richer than the notables, who were in turn richer than the leaders. But there were sometimes steep differences within the same group. More important, the relationship between political power and wealth was close, even fundamental, but it was not rigidly defined around a particular group of men. The men of greatest political power, for example, did not all share the same level of wealth; nor did the very richest exercise a proportionate influence in politics. Considering again the ten most active politically, six appear only once among the top ten in one of the three subsidies examined; thus only 20 percent of the richest were simultaneously the most politically active. Furthermore, men of equivalent wealth were found at all levels of civic politics, and some of the richest Londoners were never active politically, even at the lowest echelons.[40]

Occasional crown contacts were another experience shared by the rulers. A few had family connections with royal officers. Francis Walsingham, the queen's secretary of state, married a sister of alderman George Barne and was the stepfather of alderman Christopher Hoddesdon's wife. Walsingham was also a cousin of a notable councilman, Blaise Saunders.[41] The great William Cecil, through his second wife, Mildred Cooke, was related to two aldermanic families of an earlier generation, the Cookes and Fitzwilliams. Neither had descendants in Elizabeth's reign who were active in politics, but through his sister-in-law, Anne Cooke, wife of Nicholas

---

[39] Wilbur K. Jordan, *The Charities of London, 1480–1660* (1960), deals at length with the patterns of charitable giving and specifies the bequests of quite a few rulers.

[40] Witness Sir Thomas Gresham, who founded the Royal Exchange and was probably the most famous Elizabethan merchant; he never entered City politics.

[41] Beaven, vol. 2, 173, 175; Conyers Read, *Mr. Secretary Walsingham and the Policy of Queen Elizabeth* (Oxford, 1925), vol. 3, 370.

Bacon (Elizabeth's lord keeper), Cecil was related indirectly to alderman James Bacon and councilman Thomas Bacon, both brothers of Nicholas Bacon and therefore uncles of the famous Francis Bacon. The Caesar brothers, Julius and Thomas, both crown attorneys and judges, married daughters of aldermen: Julius to the daughter of alderman Richard Martin, Thomas to that of alderman William Ryder. There were other, less prominent matches, not to mention the ties that developed between the rulers and various members of the gentry, or the friendships that grew out of mutual associations through Parliament or the trading companies. Yet a general view of the rulers' connections discloses an impressive degree of interrelationship with other liverymen of London, usually fellow rulers.

Aside from such personal connections, virtually all the elite—most other aldermen, and some notable and leading councilmen—loaned money to the crown and performed a number of services for the queen. The amount of activity was greater among those already more influential in civic politics. Those who held crown offices engaged in much more than the traditional associations with Westminster, yet considering the rulers' availability and the crown's need, it is noteworthy how few of the London rulers held such positions. Among the aldermen, Henry Billingsley, Richard Saltonstall, and William Ryder were customs officials; Ryder and John Swynnerton were farmers of various imposts. Martin Bowes and Richard Martin were leading officials at the mint.[42] But there were few, if any, others. Among the leaders and notables, only seven held offices under the crown. London was clearly the center of the rulers' attention.

In family as in other connections, a close pattern of relationships existed among all the rulers with variations among the ranks. Most of the elite and their children found spouses among the wealthiest mercantile families of London, families that shared their interests in the same overseas trading companies and were members of the same small circle of City livery companies. Despite the spectacular success individual aldermanic families had in marrying their kin into houses of the aristocracy or squirearchy,[43] the elite were more inclined than the notables (and the notables more than the leaders) to intermarry with other merchant families, especially with others who were involved at some level in the politics of the City. Among the leaders, just over half (56 percent) had definite or probable family links with other political families; two-thirds of them (67 percent) had close ties of friendship among the same families.[44] The extent

---

[42] Beaven noticed most of these offices; for the rest, and for the royal offices of the councilmen, I have consulted the several printed calendars of papers deposited in the Public Record Office.

[43] Beaven, vol. 2, 168ff. for examples.

[44] It is not possible to identify all the friends of these men, but their wills do

of connections varied considerably among the leaders, from John Gresham the younger (son of an alderman, nephew of another, and cousin of the famous Sir Thomas Gresham) or William Hewet the younger (son of an alderman) to the sixteen who had no known links to political families, and the twelve apparently without even close bonds of friendship or business association with other rulers.

The same kinds of connections were more abundant among the notables, and even more so among the elite. Ninety-one percent of the elite had at least one relation who was or became involved in City politics (notables 61 percent, leaders 53 percent); 69 percent of the elite had more than one (notables 39 percent, leaders 31 percent). Eighty-nine percent of the elite had at least one close friend who was or became a ruler (notables 78 percent, leaders 64 percent); 72 percent had more than one (notables 54 percent, leaders 44 percent).[45] Each of the three groups had extensive links within each of the other two, but it is clear that the elite were more often associated with other aldermen, especially other elite. It is suggestive of the importance of the aldermen in civic life that even the leaders and notables had more of their connections with them than with other notables and leaders, especially where family ties were concerned. These findings confirm the importance that was attached to family by those men who sought to make the most of their careers.

Family became increasingly useful at higher rungs of the political and social ladders. Kinship ties on the Court of Aldermen in 1580 illustrate this.[46] A number of close links existed between several of the 28 men who sat together for part or all of that year. Four of them served with a brother-in-law; 3 others had a son-in-law on the court; one of them, alderman

---

mention a number of their closest friends; the figures on friendship have been established from these names in wills. Individuals that were both relatives and close friends of another ruler were counted for the statistics here as either a friend or a relative, not both.

[45] Because it was not possible to discover the totality of each individual's connections, these figures are only approximate and are best used as a guide to the relative standing of one group with regard to another, not as an absolute measure of connections. There may be slight distortions in these figures, even when used as relative measures among groups. Concerning relations and friendships, the proportional edge of the elite may be in part because more of them left wills in which to look (84 percent) than either notables (73 percent) or leaders (72 percent). Virtually all the elite without a will were found in some visitation, as were 83 percent of the notables and 92 percent of the leaders. It is difficult to see how even complete data would alter the conclusion that leaders and notables had far fewer connections than the elite, thus I have let the figures stand for comparative use. To offset the absence of a man's will or pedigree, I have examined a number of other wills and pedigrees of London merchants through which the family connections of the rulers themselves can be partly filled in.

[46] The year was selected because it demonstrated more connections than 1560 but less than 1600; it was not an untypical year.

Draper, had 2 sons-in-law with him. One of the 3 sons-in-law, alderman Starkye, had been married twice; both his fathers-in-law were also aldermen during 1580. These close relations among the aldermen of 1580, as well as their ties with other aldermen, past and future, can be summarized as follows:

> One was a grandson of an alderman.
> One married the granddaughter of an alderman.
> Three were sons of aldermen.
> Nine were sons-in-law of aldermen.
> Two were brothers of aldermen.
> Six were brothers-in-law of aldermen.
> One married the widow of an alderman.
> Two were fathers of aldermen.
> Seven were fathers-in-law of aldermen.
> One was a grandfather of an alderman.
> One's granddaughter married an alderman.

Indirect or more distant links existed between members of the court in 1580. The son of alderman Avenon had married a daughter of alderman Harvye. Thomas Offley and Nicholas Woodroffe were linked through Offley's brother-in-law, former alderman Stephen Kyrton, who somewhat later became the father-in-law of Woodroffe. Another example is aldermen Avenon and Ramsey. Avenon's daughter, Alice, married John Farrington (the brother of alderman Richard Farrington), and she was referred to in the will of Ramsey as a cousin. Avenon and Ramsey had no blood tie and no very direct links of affinity, yet they considered their tie to be close. Such relationships, based on ties through marriage, were considered by the rulers to be as important as more traditional blood bonds—which is clear enough by the deliberate way they went about building such connections. It is remarkable that the English language has never produced a word to recognize such ties specifically. "Cousin" and "kin" were sometimes used to indicate such relations, as well as other vague connections, but such words were primarily used to describe traditional blood ties. In order to identify families linked together through marriage, I have used the word "compernupt."[47] Searching out these compernuptial ties discloses that there

---

[47] Affinity is not satisfactory either, because it usually refers to very close marriage ties, as between a husband and his wife's blood relations, or vice versa. Compernupt stretches affinity to encompass those whom the rulers actually recognized as closely linked. Whether they saw these ties as strictly family does not matter much; what matters is that they saw themselves closely bound to groups made up partly of blood relations and partly of extended affinity connections.

were no fewer than twenty different pairs of men on the court with these connections, though some may not have been established by 1580.

Family links were especially important because they had so much to do with business success. In the 1590s alderman Robert Lee took his two sons, Henry and Robert, Jr., into the wine-importing business with him. James Cambell, a future alderman, followed his father, alderman Thomas Cambell, into various enterprises that included wine imports and export of woolens and draperies.[48] The same occurred in domestic companies. George Barne, a future alderman, owed his rise in the Haberdashers' Company to his father, also an alderman before him, but his interest and rise in the Company of Mineral and Battery Works was through his father-in-law, alderman William Garrarde.[49] Through their wills some individuals even assigned to relations their memberships in overseas trading companies.[50]

The older generation of a family was an important source of capitalization to the younger, first because of the traditional dowry, but also due to the custom of London whereby one-third of a citizen's estate had to be divided among his orphaned children. Family and business were not independent of social advancement; associates often became friends, and families of friends and associates intermarried. One example can serve to emphasize the role of the livery companies in nourishing all of these connections. Three compernupts—councilman Richard Springham, future councilman Mathew Field, and Geoffrey Duckett, probably a relative of alderman Lionel Duckett—were each shareholders and directors of the Company of Mines Royal in 1568. They had each married a daughter of alderman William Lok, mercer, and all three were themselves mercers.[51] Among the thirty directing shareholders of the same company were five other members of the Mercers' Company: George Nedham, Francis Nedham, Sir Thomas Revett, Richard Barnes, and the governor of the company, alderman Lionel Duckett.[52]

The benefits of family connections were not shared equally by all, not even among the elite. In Elizabethan London fifteen families stood out above the rest because of the sheer number of their marriage ties, their large progeny, and their good fortune in surviving. For these reasons the fifteen were related to more rulers than any other similar group of families.

[48] Lang, "The Greater Merchants of London," 174–76, 189–94.
[49] M. B. Donald, *Elizabethan Monopolies: The History of the Company of Mineral and Battery Works from 1565 to 1604* (1961), 37.
[50] For example, the will of Richard Malorye (P.C.C. 9 Stonarde) and of Thomas White (36 Stonarde).
[51] M. B. Donald, *Elizabethan Copper: The History of the Company of Mines Royal, 1568–1605* (1955), 91–92.
[52] Ibid., ch. 3.

Neither the Pakyntons nor the Whitmores produced Elizabethan aldermen, though the Pakyntons had been represented by an M.P., and they married into eight aldermanic families. George Whitmore, son of a wealthy merchant adventurer of Elizabeth's reign, did become an alderman in 1621; his family was linked to at least seven aldermen. The Gore, Chamberlain, and Quarles families produced Elizabethan councilmen and aldermen, though in each case the aldermen paid fines instead of serving a normal tenure on the court. The other ten families were more intimately tied to civic politics because each had at least one representative who became mayor.[53] Each of these fifteen families can be considered the center of a cluster of families, the indirect ties of which (compernupts) ultimately extended to 67 percent of the elite, 39 percent of the notables, and 42 percent of the leaders.[54] The Offley cluster was certainly the most extensive, for in addition to its patriarch, Sir Thomas Offley, there were his two brothers, alderman Hugh Offley and councilman Robert Offley, and three other Offleys, probably his nephews or sons, who were lesser councilmen. Between them the Offleys were related to twelve aldermanic families and had marriage ties with no fewer than nineteen others, including representatives of seven of the other fourteen cluster families.

The fifteen cluster families are another illustration of the tendency among the elite for different groups to show specialized behavior. But it would be wrong to say these fifteen were the most powerful or influential families. The cluster families had more ties with other eminent families, but they were no more cohesive than many other groups of families. They had no particular unity through trade, wealth, or political activity. Only three of the fifteen ranked in the top fifteen in trade; only three had an equivalent ranking in wealth; five were among the fifteen more active politically. Many other families had ties to individuals of the highest rank and maintained extended clusters only slightly less impressive than any of those among the fifteen. At least twenty additional families had direct blood ties with three or more aldermanic families, and their compernupts included still other aldermen and councilmen. Any number of families, when collected together, could show ties with two-thirds of the elite or a high percentage of all aldermen and councilmen.

Though some important marriage ties were useful for families of politi-

[53] The other ten families, with given names of elite aldermen in parentheses, are: Heyward (Rowland), Lee (Robert), Offley (Thomas), Draper (Christopher), Hewet (William), Rowe (Thomas, father of Henry and cousin of William), Lowe (Thomas), Garrarde (William and his son, John), Weld (Humphrey), and Barne (George and his father, George).

[54] In working out these figures I counted as compernupts those families that were joined by only one intervening family.

cal consequence, nothing as impressive as what the fifteen cluster families arranged was mandatory. Five of the elite had no known connections to other political families, and numerous others had only one or two such ties, frequently to the more humble ruling families. Even greater numbers of notables and leaders had few family connections. Nor were family ties, even among the most politically prominent, exclusively built up among those of equivalent influence: even the cluster families absorbed a number of obscure connections, and within any family of consequence there were ties with notables and leaders, not just other members of the elite. Similarly, the personal friends and business associates of the elite cut across a broad section of London mercantile society, embracing different levels of wealth, trading activity, and political rank.

The four ranks of the ruling class of Elizabethan London (wardmen, leaders, notables, and the elite) shared much beyond their commitment to civic politics. At least the top three ranks possessed great wealth and high status. They took part in similar trading activities, developed common links of family and friendship, and enjoyed connections through the same livery companies. Their similar experiences distinguished them from all other social groups in London, and encouraged a sense of community because of their internal loyalties and their exclusiveness regarding outsiders. These close affiliations not only united the rulers but also enabled them to remain politically dominant in the City. Their ties varied, but they varied in similar ways for men in the same political rank. Rank was an accurate measure of the quality and extent of other ties.

As the top rank, the elite built up more of the associations common to all rulers. The several specialized groups that developed among them symbolized their greater personal success: one was the most active politically, another the wealthiest, another engaged in more overseas trading ventures, still another arranged the largest number of marriages. But the specialized groups lacked the traits of cohesive cliques. No single cluster of families stood out as the greatest traders or the wealthiest or the most active politically. The wealthiest men did not have distinctive links in business, family, or politics—or no more than the other elite. The greatest traders were not necessarily the wealthiest or most politically active, and so on. A few men, like Rowland Heyward, Thomas Offley, and George Barne, Jr., excelled simultaneously in trade, in politics, and in accumulating wealth, but their eminence resulted from personal achievement and the same kind of favor all rulers mutually enjoyed, not exclusive recruiting by some dominant clique within the ruling class. Nor did greater personal success lead to aloofness from the group. Group loyalty was especially strong among the elite, who maintained close bonds with even the more humble rulers. Unlike some historical elites, these privileged few never attempted to translate their greater advantages into factional domination of City politics. Their achievement was a model and inspiration to the other ranks. And since the elite rose higher by virtue of their wider connections among all the rulers, their personal success further solidified the close community that ruled London.

An East European Elite in the Eighteenth Century: The Rumanian Uniate Hierarchy

KEITH HITCHINS

For the greater part of the eighteenth century the higher clergy of the Rumanian Uniate (or Greek Catholic) church in Transylvania largely determined the spiritual, cultural, and political development of their people. They had no rivals. They performed the ceremonies—baptism, marriage, and last rites—which the great mass of the population believed essential for happiness in this world and indispensable for salvation in the next; they were responsible for education, established and staffed the village schools, the gymnasia, and the seminary, and devised the curricula; they explained the past to their people; they roused the national psyche and became the principal bearers of national consciousness; and they represented their newly discovered nation before the imperial Habsburg court in Vienna and the privileged estates of Transylvania.

Their multifarious role owed much to the nature of Transylvanian society. In the first half of the eighteenth century its political and economic structure was still largely what it had been in the Middle Ages; the same could be said of the mentality of its leading classes. The church remained the dominant intellectual and cultural force. The vast majority of the population was composed of peasants, or serfs, who often found their only consolation in the rituals and promises of religion.

The Rumanians of Transylvania were preeminently a peasant people. We cannot speak of a Rumanian merchant class or aristocracy, for since the fifteenth century the Rumanians had gradually been excluded from political power and economic privilege by a system of government that reserved such things to members of the so-called three nations[1]—the Mag-

[1] In the medieval sense of *natio*, that is, a larger or smaller group having special rights and privileges.

yar nobility, the Saxon[2] bourgeoisie, and the upper-class Szeklers[3]—and their churches—the Calvinist, Lutheran, Unitarian, and Roman Catholic. Most of the Rumanian nobility had been assimilated by the Magyar *natio*, and a bourgeoisie had simply failed to develop. As peasants the Rumanians were on the lowest rung of the social scale, hence could not form a *natio*, and as Eastern Orthodox they did not enjoy freedom of religion but were merely tolerated by the estates; consequently, there were no places for them in the diet or the Gubernium.[4] Separate Rumanian political bodies never developed, and by the end of the seventeenth century only the Orthodox church remained as a purely Rumanian institution, and only its higher clergy was in a position to provide some semblance of national leadership.

The Uniate elite and indeed the Uniate church owed their existence to the peculiar combination of circumstances attendant upon the extension of Habsburg rule over Transylvania in the last decade of the seventeenth century. For reasons of its own, the court of Vienna promoted a church union of the Orthodox with Rome; in so doing, it invested the new Uniate bishop and his chief aides with powers that, together with the religious authority they already enjoyed among the devout peasantry, raised them to a position of leadership within Rumanian society that they were to hold almost unchallenged for nearly eight decades. But it must be stressed that this was a local elite; it was never a part of the Transylvanian elite, which it continuously aspired to join, or the imperial elite.

The advent of Habsburg rule following a long period of Transylvanian independence did not at first presage any significant changes in the structure of government and society. In 1691 Emperor Leopold I, whose armies had only recently driven the Turks from Transylvania, confirmed the privileges of the three nations and the four established churches and solemnly promised to respect the principality's venerable constitution. But actually he intended to reduce the independent-minded estates to obedience to Vienna and to make his new possession an integral part of a centralized empire. The Roman Catholic church, whose value as a unifying force Leopold had long appreciated, was to play a major role in bringing these plans to fruition.

For the first time the Orthodox Rumanians became the special object of the court's attention. Comprising nearly one-half the total population of Transylvania, they could if managed properly, so the court thought, become a bulwark of both Catholicism and the *Gesamtmonarchie*. The first step was to bring about their conversion, a task entrusted to the pri-

---

[2] The name by which the Germans of Transylvania are generally known.
[3] A people closely related to the Magyars and speaking Magyar.
[4] The central executive council of Transylvania headed by a governor.

mate of Hungary, Leopold Cardinal Kollonics, archbishop of Esztergom. He was ably assisted by the Jesuits, who had returned to Transylvania in 1693 after almost a century of banishment. From the beginning they concentrated their efforts on the clergy rather than the masses, for they knew from the failure of Calvinist missionaries how deeply attached the peasantry was to Orthodoxy. Nor was the clergy inclined to abandon the faith of their fathers. The Jesuits therefore wisely passed over matters of dogma and ritual and took advantage instead of the widespread discontent of the Orthodox clergy with their tolerated legal status and their abiding poverty.

Treated for centuries as an outcast, the Orthodox church possessed too little property or other wealth to provide adequate livings for the parish clergy and most of the protopopes.[5] The state of course gave no aid, and it even forbade the Orthodox clergy to collect a tithe from the faithful. As a consequence, the priest had to depend upon fees from parishioners for baptisms, weddings, and other services rendered, or upon manual labor performed for some nearby landlord. His training was often rudimentary. If he were lucky, he would attend a brief course of study at one of the small monasteries that dotted Transylvania, but usually he had to be satisfied with what he could glean from his own village priest. In education, dress, and way of life there was little to distinguish him from the other inhabitants of the village.[6] The higher clergy—the metropolitan, his aides, and some protopopes—lived in somewhat easier circumstances, but chafed under the indignities to which they were subjected and longed for a place among the estates that befitted their station.

The Jesuit missionaries came forward with a plan that would improve the material existence of the clergy and at the same time preserve the essentials of Orthodox doctrine and ritual: Orthodox priests would enjoy the same privileges and immunities as Roman Catholic priests in return for accepting the Four Articles of the Council of Florence of 1439, which had briefly reunited the Latin and Byzantine churches. If they would recognize the pope of Rome as the visible head of the Christian church, use unleavened bread in the communion, accept the existence of Purgatory, and acknowledge the procession of the Holy Spirit from the Father and the Son, then they would be received into the estates. The Four Points of Union, as they are commonly called, actually required little change in the religious life of the Orthodox: canon law and the liturgy remained the same; Rumanian continued to serve as the liturgical language; priests could marry;

---

[5] A priest who has administrative responsibilities over other priests in a given church district.

[6] The condition of the Rumanian clergy before the union is amply described in Ştefan Meteş, *Istoria bisericii româneşti din Transilvania*, I, 2nd ed. (Sibiu, 1935), 445–504.

and most important for the mass of believers, all the outward observances were left unaltered. The pledges made by the Jesuits were given official sanction in an imperial diploma of 16 February 1699.[7]

With their religious scruples appeased and with the prospect of material gain irresistible, the head of the Orthodox church in Transylvania, Metropolitan Atanasie Anghel, and most of his clergy (54 protopopes and 1,653 priests) signed the Final Act of Union at an imposing synod held in Alba Iulia on 5 September 1700. But soon afterward Atanasie began to have second thoughts about the court's intentions of fulfilling its promises, and demanded a more explicit and binding declaration than that contained in the 1699 diploma. On 19 March 1701 the court obliged by issuing a lengthy document known as the Second Leopoldine Diploma. It went much further than Leopold and Kollonics had intended. The third article was truly revolutionary in its implications, for it offered laymen—even peasants (*plebiae conditionis homines*)—and priests who would "unite" with the Roman church the same rights and privileges enjoyed by Roman Catholics. The Uniate clergy interpreted this to mean their elevation to the rank of a fourth nation, and it provided the legal basis for their subsequent political activity.[8]

Neither Leopold nor Kollonics intended to create a new nation, certainly not one of such a mixed and plebeian character. Social experiment was foreign to them, and very likely they did not grasp the full implications of their own words. Article five was a more accurate reflection of their sentiments toward the Uniates. It created the post of *teologus*, who was ostensibly to act as adviser to the new Uniate bishop on matters of doctrine and procedure. But in practice his real function was to act as a sort of imperial proconsul over the new church in order to ensure that its ministers served the best interests of the court. Consequently his permission was needed before the bishop could make a tour of inspection, convoke a synod, or appoint a priest to his parish. In time the *teologus* became the despised symbol of "Latinization" and "foreign domination" of the Uniate church.[9]

But these were problems for the future, and Atanasie was sufficiently reassured to proceed with his reconsecration as Uniate bishop of Transyl-

[7] The most recent scholarly account of the church union with Rome is David Prodan, *Supplex Libellus Valachorum* (Cluj, 1967), 114–36. The relevant documents have been published in Nicolae Nilles, *Symbolae ad illustrandam Historiam Ecclesiae Orientalis in terris Coronae S. Stephani*, 2 vols. (Oeniponte, 1885), I, 161–232.

[8] The diploma is analyzed in Zoltán Tóth, *Az erdélyi román nacionalizmus elsö százada, 1697–1792* (Budapest, 1946), 34–44.

[9] The question of the *teologus* is thoroughly discussed in Zenovie Pâclişanu, "Din istoria bisericească a românilor ardeleni. 'Teologul' vlădicilor uniţi (1700–1773)," in Academia Română, *Memoriile Secţiunii Istorice*, ser. III, vol. I (Bucharest, 1923), 149–92.

vania in Vienna on 24 March 1701, and to accept the jurisdiction of the archbishop of Esztergom over his diocese. The court assumed that the religious union was now complete and that the Orthodox church had ceased to exist. But in many villages and even in whole districts the peasants had no idea that they had "united," and their priests carried on as before.

By their promotion of the union of the Rumanian Orthodox with Rome, the Habsburg emperor and the Roman Catholic hierarchy of Hungary had created the conditions necessary for the formation of the elite dealt with here. The Uniate clergy's special relationship to the deity had already established its immense prestige and moral authority among the pious peasantry; now the court, to attain its ends, began to deal exclusively with the bishop and his aides in all matters affecting the Rumanians, both secular and religious, and thus conferred upon them a semblance of political power as well. In order to consolidate the union, the court took steps to create a numerous and well-educated clergy, and for the first time began to spend large sums of money on the training of Rumanian priests, on church construction, and on priests' salaries, and channeled this aid through the bishop. As a result of these changes, every aspect of social life came within the competence of the Uniate hierarchy, and it gradually assumed the role of national leadership.

The Uniate higher clergy may be considered primarily an intellectual elite. Its position of leadership depended mainly upon spiritual and moral authority rather than the actual exercise of political and economic power. Although they were members of the imperial elite, they had little to do with the formulation of policy and were expected merely to carry out instructions from Vienna. The members of this elite were chosen on the basis of ability and motivation rather than inheritance or class origins. They came from quite diverse social groups—the gentry, the clergy, and the peasantry—but the gentry, i.e., what remained of the Rumanian nobility, predominated. The principal bond that united them, besides holy orders, was a common educational experience, and as time passed, a growing national consciousness and a consequent awareness of the special responsibilities incumbent upon them. Their cohesiveness also owed much to the fact that they were Rumanian, and as such were detached from the economic and social structure of Transylvania and stood apart from its ruling classes. Largely because of this separateness their view of society was highly critical, but they never consciously aimed at revolutionizing or destroying it. Instead they sought places for themselves and their people within the existing structure. Among their own people their views generally prevailed, for they had no competition from other Rumanian elites; the undifferentiated nature of Rumanian society precluded the development of specialized elites. Within their own ranks there was remarkably little conflict on fundamental issues.

The Uniate elite consisted of the bishops, the principal administrative officers of the diocese, and the monks of the monasteries of Blaj, the diocesan see. In establishing the existence of the elite and determining its functions, certain individuals have been selected as being most representative of the whole. They are the bishops Ioan Patachi (1721–27), Ioan Inochentie Clain (1729–51), Petru Pavel Aron (1751–64), Atanasie Rednic (1764–72), and Grigorie Maior (1772–82), and the monks Silvestru Caliani (dates of birth and death unknown) and Gerontie Cotorea (1720–?), who held numerous administrative and teaching positions and were themselves on several occasions candidates for bishop. Before their election as bishop, Aron, Rednic, and Maior had occupied the post of episcopal vicar or had been close advisers of their predecessors, and like Patachi and Clain, they were monks, a status that until Joseph II's reign was a prerequisite for high church office.

These men, with one exception, came from the gentry; several were the heirs of a long priestly tradition in their respective families. Aron came from one of Transylvania's poorest regions, the Munții Apuseni (Western Mountains), where his father and several of his brothers were Uniate priests. Rednic was from Maramureş, in the far north beyond the borders of the principality of Transylvania, where whole villages of peasants retained the noble privileges bestowed upon them centuries before by the kings of Hungary. Caliani was from the village of Sînmartinul de cîmpie in the broad plateau of central Transylvania, where his father was a parish priest. Cotorea was brought up in the village of Totoiu in southern Transylvania. Little is known about the early life of Patachi and Maior, but judging from their exceptional educational opportunities, they too were probably members of the gentry. Only Clain, of the sample chosen, was of peasant stock. He was born and raised in the village of Sad in southern Transylvania, where an enterprising and prosperous Rumanian peasantry had survived the encroachments of the great manors. He was ennobled in 1729 after he had been named bishop, and possessing the rank of baron, he was the only one of the seven (and of the Uniate clergy and the Rumanian nation generally) to have a seat in the Transylvanian diet.[10]

Whatever their exact social status was, we may assume that their families were better off materially than most Rumanians, and were therefore able to assure their sons important cultural advantages. The most important was enrollment in one of the Roman Catholic gymnasia or colleges of Transylvania. Many Rumanians, usually the sons of priests or gentry

[10] Tóth, *Erdélyi román nacionalizmus,* 169–70.

who possessed some privilege or had some pretension to culture, attended the Piarist gymnasium in Bistriţa or the Jesuit colleges in Braşov, Sibiu, Alba Iulia, and Cluj. The best graduates of these schools were sent abroad to complete their education, take holy orders, and then return to Transylvania to promote the union.[11] Each of the selected seven men attended the Jesuit college in Cluj and then studied theology and philosophy at Roman Catholic institutions in Vienna, Rome, or Trnava (Hungarian: Nagyszombat), in present-day Slovakia. Here they were drawn into the currents of European humanist thought and acquired the intellectual breadth to create a unique synthesis of Western and Eastern Orthodox culture. Patachi, Aron, Caliani, and Maior attended the College for the Propagation of the Faith in Rome. Patachi received his doctorate in philosophy there, the first Rumanian to be awarded this degree, and Aron and Maior were ordained as priests in Rome in 1743 and 1745, respectively. Clain, Aron, and Cotorea studied theology at Trnava, which was known as "Little Rome" because of the zeal with which the Jesuits, who had established a seminary there, trained missionaries for service all over eastern Europe. Patachi, Rednic, and Cotorea took courses in theology and philosophy offered by the Pazmaneum in Vienna, a college established in 1623 for the purpose of strengthening Catholicism in Hungary.[12]

The recruitment and tenure of the members of this elite, especially the bishops, depended largely upon their willingness and ability to promote the union and to further the political aims of the court. Clain and Maior were forced to resign their offices because they had grown too independent, and the court had consequently come to doubt their worth. Neither they nor their colleagues were ever recognized officially as the spokesmen of the Rumanian nation for the simple reason that the court and the Transylvanian estates never acknowledged the existence of a Rumanian nation. The emperor considered the Uniate bishop one of his subordinates and reserved his appointment to himself, while the estates adamantly refused to tamper with the constitution of the principality, and repeatedly rejected all requests of the Uniate bishops for implementation of the First and Second Leopoldine Diplomas. But the Uniate hierarchy's place in Rumanian society did not depend as much upon the attitude of the ruling classes in Vienna and Transylvania as upon its own sweeping social functions.

This elite performed the two main services of any clergy in a society like that of Transylvania—the religious and the educational. Its uniqueness

[11] V. Şotropa, "Românii la gimnasiul latino-catolic din Bistriţa, 1729–1779," *Transilvania*, 32 (1901), 3–17; Iacob Radu, *Foştii elevi români-uniţi ai şcoalelor din Roma* (Beiuş, 1929), 8–17; Nicolae Comşa, *Dascălii Blajului* (Blaj, 1940), 16–19; Coriolan Suciu, *Arhiereii Blajului* (Blaj, 1944), 9–41.

[12] Tóth, *Erdélyi román nacionalizmus*, 182–87.

lies not in this traditional role but in its intellectual and political functions, whereby it created a national ideology by synthesizing the Rumanians' Latin historical heritage and their Eastern Orthodox faith and directed the campaign to make principles and promises a reality.

The Uniate hierarchy was first of all responsible for the efficient operation of church government from the smallest unit, the parish, to the diocesan synod. The chief executive of the diocese was the bishop, who exercised considerable discretionary powers and who by the middle of the eighteenth century presided over a numerous bureaucracy. There were some 2,100 parish priests, 47 protopopes, and the diocesan consistory, a sort of executive committee appointed by the bishop and composed of three members, always monks, and responsible to him; on extraordinary occasions it could be expanded to include the twelve most important protopopes. There were also the *teologus*, the episcopal vicar, and the notary of the clergy, and finally the diocesan synod, which, composed of all the protopopes, had final authority in all internal church matters and advised the bishop in his dealings with the state.[13] The bishop frequently entrusted the members of the consistory with special assignments; Silvestru Caliani, Atanasie Rednic, and Grigorie Maior, who were on the consistory in 1754, at the same time held important teaching positions in the recently established schools of Blaj. The bishop bore ultimate responsibility for the welfare of the church. A steady flow of reports from the protopopiates, communications from the Transylvanian chancellery in Vienna and the Gubernium, and frequent tours of inspection kept him informed about the condition of his diocese in general and the performance of his priests in particular.

The Uniate elite, it is important to remember, was primarily concerned with the heavenly, not the earthly, kingdom; hence it devoted most of the diocese's resources to the strengthening of religious faith, especially through study and teaching. The monasteries of the Holy Trinity and the Annunciation at Blaj were intended both as retreats where the individual might seek his own spiritual perfection and as institutions where young people could receive a Christian education and where propagators of the faith could be trained. In them, especially under bishops Aron and Rednic, whose asceticism was renowned, no worldliness was tolerated and the regime was severe, but it was accepted as befitting an institution dedicated to the service of God. Subordinate to the monasteries were the seminary and the other schools of Blaj, which were the only Rumanian institutions

13 Augustin Bunea, *Episcopii Petru Paul Aron și Dionisiu Novacovici* (Blaj, 1902), 375–83.

of higher learning in Transylvania until the beginning of the nineteenth century.

As teachers in these schools the higher clergy exercised its greatest influence over the talented young men who it hoped would help fill its own ranks. Sometimes they did their teaching without benefit of buildings or books and took their knowledge and faith directly to the people. With Bishop Aron's accession, preaching became a regular part of the higher (and parish) clergy's duties. He, Maior, and Caliani were gifted orators who made extended forays into the countryside to bring the word of the true faith to even the most remote peasant villages. At the most elementary level they tried to correct the exaggerations and falsehoods about Christianity that circulated in the folklore and superstitions of the people and that were widely accepted as gospel by them.[14] These sermons make clear that this elite dimly viewed popular creativity in matters of faith and morals as harmful to the proper development of a Christian community. The people, in their view, had nothing to teach the learned; rather, they had to be taught if they were to achieve happiness in this world and salvation in the next. This attitude did not change significantly until the end of the century, when the intellectuals—of another generation—realized that the people had something useful to contribute and, instead of condemning folklore, began to collect and study it.

The schools of Blaj, planned in the early 1730s by Bishop Clain, were dedicated by his successor, Aron, in 1754. There were three: the seminary, where future priests were trained; the middle school, which soon developed into a lyceum with a curriculum similar to others in the Austrian empire, and where classical languages, German, Hungarian, mathematics, geography, ancient history, and the history of Transylvania were taught; and the elementary school, where pupils learned the fundamentals of reading, writing, and religion.[15] Between 1754 and 1772 an average of three hundred students attended the schools each year.

The curriculum was typical for the period and was planned by the bishop and the consistory. They also chose the teachers, who initially, at least in the seminary, were monks from the Monastery of the Holy Trinity who had had advanced theological and philosophical training abroad; Grigorie Maior was the first director of the middle school, and Caliani taught religion and Rednic taught dogmatics and church history at the

[14] Ibid., 386–88.
[15] Timotei Cipariu, *Acte și fragmente latine romanesci pentru istoria bisericei romane mai alesu unite* (Blaj, 1855), 217–24; Nicolae Albu, *Istoria învățământului românesc din Transilvania până la 1800* (Blaj, 1944), 173–87.

seminary. This practice continued under Aron's successor, Rednic. When he introduced courses in logic and metaphysics at the middle school in 1772, he chose as teachers two young men who had recently returned from the Pazmaneum in Vienna, Ştefan Pop and Samuil Clain, a nephew of the bishop. Lectures, often based upon courses taken in Vienna or Rome, and religious books printed in the Rumanian principalities—or in Blaj, after the establishment of a Uniate printing press about 1750—were the usual teaching materials until regular textbooks began to be introduced in the 1770s. In this way young Rumanians were for the first time brought into contact with Western thought. As we shall see, those who had the additional good fortune to study abroad fused their new knowledge with their native Orthodox traditions to create the ideology of modern Rumanian nationalism.

The Uniate elite probably saw its own role in Rumanian society as primarily that of pastors and teachers. But its immense contribution to the development of religious life and education notwithstanding, it owes its special place in Rumanian history to its role as pioneers of a new concept of nationhood and as political leaders.

In elaborating what may be called a national ideology, Uniate intellectuals between 1720 and 1780 combined the elements of folk consciousness that had been present in the mass of the Rumanians of Transylvania since at least the fifteenth century[16] with their own learned theories about the Roman descent of the Rumanians. They regarded Orthodoxy as the essence of the Rumanian community. But the outward forms of worship —the liturgy, icons, fasts, and holidays—not the theology, provided the framework within which the homogeneity, and eventually the national self-consciousness, of the Rumanians first expressed itself.[17] The idea of "Rumanian" before the eighteenth century was synonymous with "Orthodox"; it was an ethnic rather than a legal or political concept, but it was not yet wholly a national concept, the mass of Rumanians still considering themselves a part of the greater Orthodox community that included the Russians and Serbs. The union with Rome in 1700 did not alter these intuitive beliefs, but it did provide Uniate intellectuals with a means by which they could justify historically the existence of a Rumanian nation in Transylvania, and of even greater significance for the development of a national ideology, it enabled them to disengage their own people from the international Orthodox community.

The union reinforced their belief in the Rumanians' direct descent

16 The most recent discussion of the problem is Ştefan Pascu, *Marea Adunare Naţională de la Alba Iulia* (Cluj, 1968), 9–20.
17 Tóth, *Erdélyi román nacionalizmus*, 70.

from the Romans. Gerontie Cotorea gave the clearest expression to the idea of the connection between Latin consciousness and the religious union with Rome in his *Despre articuluşurile cele de price*, written in 1746.[18] Cotorea identifies the Roman people with the Roman church, and treats the union of the Rumanians with the latter as a return to the church of their forebears, in effect as a reaffirmation of their intrinsic Latinity. He attributes the decline of the Rumanians and their domination by the three nations to their separation from Rome, which had resulted from the schism between the Eastern and Western churches, and he predicts that a new age of glory will accompany the renewal of old ancestral ties. These ideas were common among Uniate intellectuals in the middle of the eighteenth century and provide the best explanation for the paradox that these same men, while stressing their Latin heritage, obstinately opposed the Latinization of their church.

Uniate intellectuals vigorously promoted the union by deed and word. For example, when Rednic and Maior became bishops, they were so forceful in their proselytizing that even the court of Vienna felt obliged to urge moderation, out of fear that the unrest it had caused among large numbers of Orthodox might lead to a general uprising. They also wrote numerous books[19]—*Floarea adevărului* [The Flower of Truth] (1750), a joint work of Aron and the monks of Blaj; *Despre schismaticia Grecilor* [The Schism of the Greeks] (1746) by Cotorea; *Păstoricească datorie* [Pastoral Duty] (1759) by Aron; and *In contra schismaticilor* [Against the Schismatics] by Rednic—all of which explained the validity of the Four Points of Union and justified the action taken by Atanasie Anghel and his clergy. Like the court, the Uniate hierarchy maintained the fiction of the completeness of the union, but at the same time they were utterly opposed to "foreign" influences in their church. From the episcopate of Clain on, they tried to rid themselves of the *teologus*, whom they considered an agent of Roman Catholicism, and resisted any infringement of the canon law or ritual of the Eastern church by the Roman Catholic hierarchy of Hungary.

The explanation of the foregoing lies in the idea of nation that Uniate intellectuals had elaborated by the middle of the eighteenth century: Orthodoxy—its spirituality as well as its popular practices and beliefs—remained the basis of national identification. But under the influence of the union and the direct contacts with the West that it facilitated, the second generation of Uniate intellectuals had taken an enormous step forward in delimiting the concept of Rumanian nation. When Cotorea,

---

[18] Zoltán Tóth, "Cotorea Gerontius és az erdélyi román nemzeti öntudat ébredése," *Hitel*, 9:2 (1944), 90–91.

[19] Bunea, *Episcopii Aron şi Novacovici*, 368–71.

Aron, and Maior refer to it, they use the term "Romano-Valachus," by which they are clearly differentiating the Slavic members of the Orthodox international—the Russians and Serbs—from themselves.[20] The same idea is expressed in the contest between Bishop Aron and the Serbian Orthodox metropolitan of Carlovitz over jurisdiction of the counties of Zarand and Hunedoara in southern Transylvania. Aron argued against the pretensions of Carlovitz not only by invoking the claims of the Uniate church but also by citing the overwhelmingly Rumanian ethnic character of the region.

Self-awareness, at least among the intellectuals, had clearly progressed beyond the spontaneous recognition of common traits. But it had not yet evolved into a modern national consciousness characterized by the idea of a state encompassing all members of a specific group. For example, the Uniate intellectuals were well aware that the Rumanians of Transylvania, Moldavia, and Wallachia shared a common origin and spoke the same language, but they did not draw any political conclusions from this knowledge. It may be that under the impress of the union with its emphasis upon the Rumanians' ties with Rome rather than Constantinople, the center of Eastern Christendom, a separate Transylvanian Rumanian consciousness was in process of formation.

The Uniate elite's level of national consciousness may be measured by examining their political activity. It begins with Bishop Clain, a person of extraordinary intellect and boundless energy, who almost single-handedly fought to obtain recognition of the Rumanians as a fourth nation.[21] To succeed, he thought it necessary to convert all the Rumanians to the union. His motives were political, not religious: to bring them under the provisions of the Second Leopoldine Diploma. Catholicism was not the goal but merely the means by which the Rumanians might achieve full equality with the three nations.

In numerous petitions to the court between 1729 and 1744 Clain invoked precedent and imperial writ in support of his claims.[22] But he also used quite modern arguments based upon the inherent qualities of the Rumanians and the services they had rendered the throne and society. In a petition to Emperor Charles VI in 1735, he cited their numbers (85,857 families according to his own census of 1733), their payments to the imperial treasury (greater, he was careful to note, than the contributions of any other nation), and their deliverance of Catholicism in Transylvania

20 Tóth, Erdélyi román nacionalizmus, 285–86.

21 The best short account of Clain as a national leader is David Prodan, "La lutte de Inochentie Micu pour le relèvement politique des Roumains de Transylvanie," Revue Roumaine d'Histoire, 4:3 (1965), 477–96.

22 Augustine Bunea, Din istoria românilor. Episcopul Ioan Inocenţiu Klein (1728–1751) (Blaj, 1900), 28–30; Nilles, Symbolae, II, 512–17.

from what he judged to have been almost certain destruction.[23] In a second petition of the same year, this one to the Transylvanian chancellery, he set forth as proof of the Rumanians' right to equality with the three nations their direct descent from the Romans who came to Dacia (Transylvania) in the second century A.D. and their uninterrupted presence there ever since. He was the first to use the theory of Daco-Rumanian continuity, as it came to be called, as an argument on behalf of national rights. Through him a truism accepted by the folk consciousness for centuries had become a political weapon.[24]

As Clain pursued his campaign, his use of the union as a mere instrument became obvious to all concerned. Finally, at a synod held at Blaj on 6 July 1744, which included laymen as well as priests and many Orthodox, he could apparently contemplate abandoning the union altogether unless his demands were met. The synod was almost unanimous in voting support for such a course of action.[25] The composition of the synod itself, which Clain undoubtedly intended as a national assembly, and the priority he gave to national as opposed to more limited religious goals established his conception of nation as essentially ethnic. He included in it everyone who had a common heredity, cultural tradition, and folk consciousness and who spoke the same language, and especially important, he made demands on behalf of the Rumanian nation as a whole not simply for a privileged *natio* like the clergy but for the peasant masses as well. In his most recent petitions to the court before the synod, he had insisted that the Rumanian nation have representation in the Gubernium, and the implication was that eventually account be taken of population and contributions to the general welfare in determining its size, and he urged that the burdens of the peasantry be lightened, in particular by reducing the number of days of labor service they owed their landlords.[26]

The court itself had finally become convinced of Clain's true feelings toward the union, and fearing that its work of nearly half a century would be undone if he remained as bishop, it summoned him to Vienna for an accounting in July 1744. Clain's sojourn in Vienna convinced him of the court's changed attitude, and in December he fled to Rome, presumably to seek the pope's aid. But no one there would support him, and he remained in exile until his death in 1768.[27]

Clain resigned as bishop in 1751, and his successors—Aron, Rednic,

[23] Bunea, *Klein*, 37–38.
[24] Tóth, *Erdélyi román nacionalizmus*, 92–97.
[25] Nilles, *Symbolae*, II, 563.
[26] Ibid., 518–19.
[27] G. Bogan-Duică, *Procesul episcopului Ioan Inochentie Clain* (Caransebeş, 1896), 59–71; Bunea, *Klein*, 170–76.

and Maior—carried on his struggle with the same persistence but without his audacity. They continued to press for the recognition of the Uniate clergy as a fourth nation as a necessary first step in the emancipation of the whole Rumanian people. They were at the same time indefatigable in promoting the union, but, like Clain, not from a desire to become more Catholic but in order to achieve their political objectives. Theirs was essentially a nationality struggle, especially during Maior's episcopate. Maior wanted to bring all Rumanians—Orthodox as well as Uniates—under his direction and eventually to create a state within a state, without precise boundaries but united in its allegiance to a Rumanian bishop.[28] The court was not receptive to such manifestations of independence, which called to mind the case of Clain, and in 1782 it forced Maior to resign.

Maior's resignation coincided with a decline of the Uniate elite's position in Rumanian society, and in the decades immediately following, its dominance of cultural and intellectual life was permanently undermined. The causes were many and complex. Not least among them were the court's grudging acknowledgment of the existence of an Orthodox church and the appearance of competitors. Emperor Joseph II, who ascended the throne in 1780, was not especially concerned with advancing the cause of the union, but he had political and economic goals that required an end to religious hostilities and the inclusion of the Orthodox Rumanians as active subjects of the centralized state he wished to create. He therefore appointed a regular Orthodox bishop in 1784 and took the first important steps in organizing an Orthodox school system. These measures marked the beginning of a regeneration of the Orthodox church, which by the middle of the nineteenth century was to attain an influence at court and in Transylvania equal to that of the Uniate church. An Orthodox intellectual class, lay and ecclesiastical, came into being during this period, and making their own the national ideology that had evolved in the eighteenth century, they assumed an elitist role among their own faithful.

While this outside challenge was growing, the Uniate elite was confronted by an equally serious threat to its leadership within its own church. Later generations of Uniate intellectuals, trained in the schools of Blaj and in Rome and Vienna, were far more secular-minded than the generation that preceded them. Many found employment in the civil service or the liberal professions and thereby formed the nucleus of a lay intellectual class, which, together with their Orthodox counterparts, took the leadership of the national movement out of the hands of the clergy in the second half of the nineteenth century. Some remained in the church and were faithful servants of it, but even they were concerned more with actual

[28] Tóth, *Erdélyi román nacionalizmus*, 261–62.

social and political problems than with heavenly paradise. Such changes were directly related to the accelerated modernization of economic and social life that the Habsburg monarchy was undergoing during the nineteenth century. The Rumanians participated in it, and in Transylvania this led inevitably to a differentiation of Rumanian society and the gradual emergence of numerous specialized elites.

Bureaucracy and Patronage:
The View from an
Eighteenth-Century Russian
Letter-Writer

DAVID L. RANSEL

The study of social relations among the service nobility of eighteenth-century Russia presents special difficulties. While ostensibly adopting Western values of legality and rational order, the educated elite of service nobles continued throughout the century and beyond to organize itself on traditional patterns of personal relations and patronage. The conflict of the new ideal and the traditional reality created a painful ambiguity for the servicemen. On one hand, they had no choice but to engage in the patronage organizations that formed the foundation of social and political life in the state service. On the other, they were becoming increasingly aware of how little this reality corresponded with the new values to which they were outwardly committed.

It was certainly no secret that Russians commonly organized themselves in personal and kinship patronage groups cemented by bribery and nepotism. The members of the nobiliary service elite made their careers and way in the world by adherence to one or another of the patronage hierarchies operating at court, in various branches of the central administration, or in the provincial bureaus. All this is fairly well known from negative evidence: decrees forbidding such behavior; criticism leveled at it from the throne as well as from intellectuals, notably in critical works by the famous satirists Denis Fonvizin and Nikolai Novikov; and in the straightforward, impassioned denunciations of Alexander Radishchev.

Conspicuously lacking, however, has been an unbiased presentation of the patronage system. Having become imbued with the new values of rational order and legality, educated Russians of the late eighteenth century were usually unwilling to say anything in justification of the system of personal relations. Instead they engaged in almost universal condemnation of patronage, bribery, and favoritism. They regarded the prevailing pattern of social relations as an abuse, the root cause of most evils in government and society. One must therefore look beyond the usual sources in order to obtain a balanced picture. The second section of this essay introduces an unpretentious document of the period, a simple letter-writer or style manual, which in its small way makes a contribution to such a picture. In the circumstances of the elite's common moral rejection of its own organizational behavior, the letter-writer proves to be an interesting and revealing source. As a practical guide to making one's way in the world, it unselfconsciously reflects the persistence of the traditional patronage system and discloses as do few other sources the essential operative social relations of the time.

Before turning to the letter-writer itself, I must comment on three aspects of the question of bureaucracy and patronage: the structure of the elite, the genesis of its criticism of traditional relations, and the positive role of the patronage system as it came into conflict with the new value of legality.

Since this essay focuses on behaviors characteristic of the bureaucratic nobility as a whole, no attempt will be made to subdivide this group into specific functional categories or to separate it from a supposed power elite at the top. In eighteenth-century Russia up to 1762, all members of the nobility were obligated to serve the state for at least twenty-five years. The usual pattern was to begin in the military service and then shift to a civilian post. There was little differentiation until late in the century of the talents and abilities for these two spheres of activity, and personnel could easily be transferred from one to the other. In practice this meant that the methods and behaviors adopted in the military administration were often employed in the civil bureaucracy, and even in estate management by those nobles who after 1762 transferred out of the state service altogether and retired to their landed estates.[1]

As for the matter of defining a "power elite," historians have worked at the problem for some time without arriving at a consensus. Legal distinctions were of no help. The term "nobility" (*dvorianstvo*) as a juridical category included all state servitors above a specified rank, comprising everyone from the wealthiest and most politically influential dignitaries down to impecunious commissioned officers and propertyless civil ser-

[1] This is a central theme of Marc Raeff's excellent essay *Origins of the Russian Intelligentsia: The Eighteenth-Century Nobility* (New York, 1966).

vants. Consequently other standards have been tried. One author may locate the elite in the guards regiments of the capital. Another may include only the first four ranks in the state service hierarchy, known collectively as the *Generalitet*.[2] Soviet historiography speaks of intraclass strata that replace one another in social and political leadership at various times through coups d'etat.[3] As helpful as all these interpretations are, none can be regarded as conclusive. Typically they stress horizontal lines of elite organization and rightly recognize the enormous discrepancies of wealth and status characteristic of the noble estate as a whole. Unfortunately no clear legal or social standards have been found to delineate such horizontal categories. In this paper, therefore, emphasis will be placed upon vertical lines of cohesion: the social relations of the patronage hierarchies that gave expression to social and political power in Russia.

Traditional patronage relations came under criticism by articulate members of the nobility for the first time in the eighteenth century. Contributing most directly to the critical attitude was the state's decision to adopt rational legal organization as part of a conscious modernizing enterprise forcefully imposed from above. This decision was symbolized by Peter the Great. Although his seventeenth-century predecessors showed the way, Peter was the first to galvanize efforts to establish a rational order in Russian administration. He replaced the ancient council of aristocrats, the *Boiar Duma*, with a Governing Senate appointed by the emperor without regard to class and functioning as overseer of the state administration on the basis of a legally defined jurisdiction and competence. Then he threw out the forty-odd Muscovite administrative departments (*prikazy*), with their multitude of confusing and overlapping spheres of action and revenue sources, and substituted nine collegial boards. Activities of the collegia were regulated by and coordinated with those of the Senate and subordinate bureaus according to procedures defined in the General Regulations of 1720. Provincial administration likewise underwent a major reorganization. This reform, at least on paper, established uniform regulations for all provincial bureaus.

These changes made a striking contrast with the traditional patrimonial system based on personal delegation of authority. In addition, Peter revamped the entire reward and recruitment structure. State officials were to receive salaries instead of land grants or payments in kind for their

[2] There is now a detailed study of this group by B. M. Meehan, "The Russian Generalitet of 1730: Towards a Definition of Aristocracy," Ph.D. diss. (Rochester, 1970).

[3] See, for example, S. M. Troitskii, "Istoriografiia dvortsovykh perevorotov v Rossii XVIII v.," *Voprosy istorii*, 21:2 (Feb. 1966), 38–53; Ia. Ia. Zutis, *Ostzeiskii vopros v XVIII v.* (Riga, 1964), 184–200.

service. Both salary and status were to be determined by one's place on the Table of Ranks, a device Peter created by borrowing the Muscovite practice of ranking according to heredity and then shifting it to the bureaucratic principle of merit. Henceforth, through meritorius service a commoner could advance up the ranking table to a point where he automatically acquired the privileges of hereditary nobility.[4]

The crowning achievement of Peter's efforts to implant legal relations in Russian administration was to be the creation of a code of laws. The tsar devoted twenty-five years to this very ambitious and ultimately unsuccessful enterprise. From 1700 to 1725 he organized three separate commissions to work on the task. When the last one met in 1719, Peter, desperate for success, simply ordered the members to translate the Swedish codex, amend it to fit Russian conditions, and complete the job within a few months. Needless to say, this method created more difficulties than it resolved. The traditions and concepts informing Swedish law had so little in common with Russian conditions that amendment proved at least as troublesome as producing an entirely new code. Six years later when Peter died, the commission was still struggling to bend and shape the foreign code into a usable instrument for Russian jurisprudence.[5]

Several of Peter's other efforts shared a similar fate. His successors soon began interpreting the Table of Ranks, for example, in such a way as to favor the already ennobled. Although these measures did not work as well as intended, patronage connections and enlistment at birth allowed sons of nobles to monopolize the higher ranks. But recent evidence has shown that advancement of commoners into the lower ranks conferring nobility occurred more frequently than was previously believed.[6] In the

---

[4] The most readily available study in English of the reforms is V. O. Klyuchevsky, *Peter the Great*, tr. Liliana Archibald (New York, 1961; original Russian ed., 1910); for more recent accounts, see R. Wittram, *Peter I, Czar und Kaiser (Peter der Grosse in Seiner Zeit)*, 2 vols. (Göttingen, 1964), and James Cracraft, *The Church Reform of Peter the Great* (Stanford, 1971). On the provincial reforms, still most valuable is M. M. Bogoslovskii, *Oblastnaia reforma Petra Velikogo: Provintsiia 1719–1727* (Moscow, 1902). The Table of Ranks is explained in a recent article by J. Hassell, "Implementation of the Russian Table of Ranks during the Eighteenth Century," *Slavic Review*, 29:2 (June 1970), 283–95.

[5] V. N. Latkin, *Zakonodatel'nye kommissii v Rossii v XVIII stoletii* (St. Petersburg, 1887), 20–38. For attempts to use foreign, especially Swedish, models and their distortion when filtered through Russian reality, see H. Hjärne, "Svenska reformer i Tsar Peters välde," *Ur det förgångna* (Stockholm, 1912), 123–31, and the valuable documentary collection on the same subject, N. A. Voskresenskii, *Zakonodatel'nye akty Petra I*, 1 (Moscow, 1945); a reevaluation of Scandinavian influence may be found in E. Puttkammer, "Einflüsse schwedischen Rechts auf die Reformen Peters des Grossen," *Zeitschrift für ausländisches öffentliches Rechts und Völkerrecht*, 19 (1958), 369–84.

[6] S. M. Troitskii's groundbreaking research has just opened this question anew. The previous view, based mainly on legal records, held that advancement of men in lower

case of provincial government, retreat from Petrine norms was much clearer. Just two years after Peter's death, local administration returned to the seventeenth-century system of military governors with their undifferentiated executive, judicial, and police authority.[7] Finally, in regard to the Governing Senate, which Peter had instituted as the depository of state law and highest judicial instance, even before his death the tsar complained about the persistence of traditional "vices." The senators, he noted sadly, were merely "playing [with the laws] as with cards, lining up one suit to another" while in fact they "strive mightily to place mines under the fortress of justice." Even the most merciless beatings and threats failed to uproot corruption, which often involved the tsar's most trusted lieutenants. Peter moaned that even his closest associate, Alexander Menshikov, wallowed in lawlessness: "His mother conceived him in sin and he is ending his life in knavery; if he doesn't straighten up, he'll be missing his head."[8]

Despite considerable setbacks, Peter's efforts did bear some fruit. If he failed to establish the substance of legal relations, he at least implanted an aspiration.[9] Through ukases and manifestos he projected the new values of open and orderly administrative procedure, functional division of responsibility, and hierarchical subordination. In the institutions of the Senate and central collegia he embodied at least the pretense of rationality and legal system. With these models to look to, the Russian elite of the eighteenth century began to recognize the new value as desirable and superior to traditional ways. At the same time, predominantly Western

---

offices to a rank conferring nobility met with tough restrictions until 1762. Thereafter it became easier, except for a brief slowing of the trend following the Pugachev Rebellion (1773–74). See A. Romanovich-Slavatinskii, *Dvorianstvo v Rossii ot nachala XVIII veka do otmena krepostnogo prava* (St. Petersburg, 1870), 14–15, and N. F. Demidova, "Biurokratizatsiia gosudarstvennogo apparata absoliutizma v XVII–XVIII vv.," *Absoliutizm v Rossii* (Moscow, 1964), 228–39. However, Troitskii's investigations into the social background of over 5,000 bureaucrats raise serious questions about this view. His painstaking researches have shown that roughly one-third of the bureaucrats in 1755 were of nonnoble origin. "Sotsial'nyi sostav i chislennost' biurokratii Rossii v seredine XVIII v.," *Istoricheskie zapiski*, 89 (1972), 295–352.

[7] Iu. V. Got'e, *Istoriia oblastnogo upravleniia v Rossii ot Petra Velikogo do Ekateriny II*, 1 (Moscow, 1913), esp. 18–48.

[8] Quoted in I. I. Ditiatin, *Ekaterininskaia kommissiia 1767 g. "O sochinenii proekta novogo ulozheniia"* (Rostov on Don, 1904), 41–44.

[9] This theme is superbly elucidated in George Yaney's study on the growth of system in Russian administration, *The Systematization of Russian Government: Social Evolution in the Domestic Administration of Imperial Russia, 1711–1905* (Urbana, Ill., 1973). For a concise summary of the development of this ideal and its expression in Peter's work, see A. Lappo-Danilevskii, "L'idée de l'état et son évolution en Russie depuis les troubles du XVIIᵉ siècle jusqu'aux réformes du XVIIIᵉ," in *Essays in Legal History*, ed. Paul Vinogradoff (London, 1913), 356–83.

educational institutions (also introduced by Peter) gradually deepened and fortified these values to the point that articulate members of the elite could find nothing to defend in the traditional system of personal relations with the bribery and toadyism that sustained it.[10] This sentiment failed, however, to produce a substantive change in the system of personal relations. Such a change required much more than a recognition of its desirability and the enactment of decrees. Client-patron and kinship hierarchies continued to form the basic units of social-political organization. Not only weie they vital to the functioning of the tribute-collecting hierarchy that was the administration, but also they served, in the absence of an operative legal system, as a means of achieving a measure of personal security, freedom of action and expression, advancement, or any other social value.[11] What the aspiration implanted by Peter did produce was a critical attitude toward the traditional system of relations, as well as a belief that standards for such criticism existed in Russian society as native Russian values. Peter did not complete a legal code, but his successors did not shelve the idea. Throughout the century monarchs and leading ministers made repeated efforts to compile a systematic code, and they regarded its absence as a great misfortune for government and society.[12] On another plane, leading institutions continued to serve the interests of personal favorites and their clients, but no one willingly defended such conditions. On the contrary, they were widely deplored. Typical of

[10] Marc Raeff presents an excellent résumé of the intent of Peter's reforms in *Imperial Russia, 1682–1825* (New York, 1971), 71; he discusses the education and Westernization of the elite in *Origins of Russian Intelligentsia*, esp. chs. 3 and 4.

[11] Yaney, *Systematization of Russian Government*, develops this point in some detail.

[12] See, for example, Peter Shuvalov's comments in Latkin, *Zakonodatel'nye kommissii*, 82; Denis Fonvizin's and Nikita Panin's ideas in E. S. Shumigorskii, *Imperator Pavel I, zhizn' i tsarstvovanie* (St. Petersburg, 1907), app., 1–35, the most important section of which has been translated by Marc Raeff, *Russian Intellectual History: An Anthology* (New York, 1966), 96–105. These men, among others including the rulers, shared the common notion of the period that the state needed clear "fundamental laws" to operate efficiently. Historians have frequently seconded this idea. James Hassell, "The Vicissitudes of Russian Administrative Reform, 1762–1801," Ph.D. diss. (Cornell University, 1967), 92–96, cites the case of a pensioner in Paul's reign who took a regular government position. A question arose whether he should be paid in addition to his naval pension. Through a six-week process the Senate discovered that the only pertinent law—that of 1763—was perfectly clear: pay the pension plus a sum equal to it. Despite the clarity of the law, the affair was delayed and finally decided by the emperor. Why? A practice had developed to pay such persons in addition to pension the remainder up to the regular salary of the office in question. Paul resolved the issue in favor of paying the full salary of the office. Hassell regards the problem as the lack of adequate law to guide administration, and cites Radishchev's critique on the shortcomings of Russia's legal code. But this is not the point at all. As this example demonstrates, clear laws would not make procedures less arbitrary. The law here was crystal clear, yet other practices developed.

such critics was Catherine II's senior minister Nikita Panin, who decried the fact that "government business was determined by the influence of individual persons rather than by the power of state institutions."[13]

Not surprisingly, the rulers themselves were the most vigorous opponents of bribery and personal patronage. They realized that the patronage hierarchies below interfered with their control of the state machine and effective articulation of their own power.[14] Catherine II waged a major campaign against graft in the first years of her reign. Looking at the Senate, the depository of law, she noted that it "often promulgated laws, dispensed ranks, titles, money—in a word—nearly everything, and restricted other judicial offices in [the exercise of] their laws and prerogatives." The lower officials' arrant dependence on the powerful men above had caused such servility in the lower offices that they had completely forgotten the regulations by which they were to make representations against Senate ukases not in conformity with the law. Catherine remarked sadly that "the slavishness of persons working in these [lower] offices is indescribable, and no good can be expected from them so long as this evil is not stamped out."[15] In result, "justice was sold to the highest bidder, and no use was made of the laws except where they could benefit the most powerful."[16]

In order to correct the situation, Catherine promised at her accession "to enact such state laws according to which the government . . . would carry on its activity within its power and proper bounds, so that in the future every state office would possess its limits and laws."[17] But this ad-

[13] From his decree for the establishment of a state council (1762) in *Sbornik Imperatorskogo Russkogo Istoricheskogo Obshchestva*, 7 (St. Petersburg, 1871), 209, where the author includes numerous examples of this abuse. An excellent case in point from an earlier period is the independence of the War Collegium under the powerful favorite Count B. C. Münnich. This subordinate institution received the right not to execute Senate decrees it found in conflict with imperial ukases. Its reports and promotion proposals went directly from the collegium to the empress, bypassing the Senate and cabinet, and it even made dispositions altering foreign policy without consulting the Foreign Affairs Collegium. V. G. Shcheglov, *Gosudarstvennyi Sovet v Rossii*, 1 (Moscow, 1892), 624–25.

[14] Max Weber's comment, although made in reference to the more highly developed bureaucracy of late nineteenth-century Russia, provides a picture of this dilemma. "The Russian Czar of the old regime was seldom able to accomplish permanently anything that displeased his bureaucracy and hurt the power interests of the bureaucrats. His ministerial departments, placed directly under him as the autocrat, represented a conglomerate of satrapies . . . [which] constantly fought against one another by all the means of personal intrigue and, especially, they bombarded one another with voluminous 'memorials,' in the face of which, the monarch, as a dilettante, was helpless." *From Max Weber: Essays in Sociology* (New York, 1946), 234.

[15] Ditiatin, *Ekaterininskaia kommissiia*, 42.

[16] Catherine II, *Sochineniia imperatritsy Ekateriny II*, ed. A. N. Pypin, 12, pt. 2 (St. Petersburg, 1907), 567.

[17] V. A. Bil'basov, *Istoriia Ekateriny II*, 2 (Berlin, 1900), 91.

mirable intention, even if carried out, could do no more than reinforce the pretense of system. Without a corresponding change in the officials' attitudes and practice of organizing themselves in informal hierarchies, the pretense of law could in the short run do as much to facilitate abuses as to diminish them. As one of Catherine's advisers was quick to point out, this condition had in the reign of Empress Elizabeth allowed a mere secretary (Dmitrii Volkov) "to perform the functions of a prime minister under the pretext of administering a bureaucratic order that did not exist."[18]

Criticism of favoritism and patronage grew even sharper after the 1760s when popular nongovernment journals began to appear in print. Although this criticism emanated mainly from the liberal nobiliary intelligentsia, it was by no means confined to that side of the political spectrum.[19] The ultraconservative social critic Prince M. M. Shcherbatov was likewise among the discontented. While Shcherbatov idealized pre-Petrine Russia, he depicted utopia as not so much a patrimonial society based on patronage networks as a class-bound totalitarian state in which each social group would have assigned uniform apparel, living quarters, and even flatware.[20] And of course the rulers themselves and their ideological supporters in the press continued at intervals to attack abuses. Hence articulate Russians, political leaders and publicists alike, were virtually unanimous in their disdain for the methods that perforce they themselves employed daily in order to survive and achieve success.[21]

The conflict inherent in this conjuncture of the new value of legality with the persistence of traditional modes of elite organization was by no means an entirely negative phenomenon. While the tension may have been personally painful for the noble servicemen, it also acted as a positive, crea-

---

[18] From Panin's memorandum on the state council decree (1762), *Sbornik IRIO*, vol. 7, 207.

[19] A. V. Zavodov, ed., *Istoriia russkoi zhurnalistiki XVIII–XIX vekov* (Moscow, 1963), 41–69.

[20] See his "Puteshestvie v zemliu Ofirskuiu g-na S . . . , shvetskogo dvorianina," *Sochineniia kn. M. M. Shcherbatova*, 1 (St. Petersburg, 1896), 748–1059; there is an excellent summary and analysis by A. A. Kizevetter, "Russkaia utopiia XVIII stoletiia," *Istoricheskie ocherki* (Moscow, 1912), 29–56. On Shcherbatov's plan for putting a stop to bribery, see S. M. Solov'ev, "Rasskazy iz russkoi istorii," *Russkii Vestnik*, 35 (1861), 337–38.

[21] For the comments of one pro-government publicist, see Richard Pipes, ed., *N. M. Karamzin's Memoir on Ancient and Modern Russia* (Cambridge, Mass., 1959), 147–56, 182–90. With respect to this critical view, the stress is on articulate. In the rare instances when evidence appears on the attitudes of rank and file nobles, as in the cahiers of the Legislative Commission of 1767, they express a preference for the personal or familial nature of authority, although even in this case the assumption seems to be that paternal authority will remove abuses. For a very able discussion of this question, see Wilson Augustine, "Notes toward a Portrait of the Eighteenth-Century Russian Nobility," *Canadian Slavic Studies*, 4: 3 (Fall 1970), esp. 384–86.

tive force in the growth of Russian administration. Several aspects of this question deserve comment.

First, the assumed existence of a legal rational framework imposed standards altogether incompatible with the prevailing pattern of organization in patronage hierarchies. The legally instituted standards called for promotion by merit (Table of Ranks), administrative rationality (Senate and subsidiary organs operating according to legally established procedures), and judicial due process (Reforms of 1775). In other words, the normal patterns of bribery and patronage belonged clearly to the area of criminal behavior. Since the persistence of this pattern forced administrators charged with accomplishing practical ends to engage in such activities, they were bound to suffer many of the insecurities commonly associated with criminal behavior.[22]

A second circumstance mitigated this condition. In practice, prosecution seems to have been rare. So long as a patronage hierarchy managed to carry out its assigned tasks without producing major disruptions, the central authorities had every reason to protect it for the useful services it performed. Moreover, the groups themselves, especially those in the central government and at court, constituted considerable social power. They were not mere cliques but powerful family alliances that extended their tentacles into many areas of government and society. Among the most prominent family groups in high government at mid-century were the Vorontsov clan in Elizabeth's reign, which, in cooperation with the favorite Shuvalov and his family, dominated the leading institutions for foreign and domestic affairs as well as Moscow University and the principal cultural organs.[23] In Catherine II's reign, two hierarchies—one based on the Panin family with its collateral ties to the Kurakin and Nepliuev clans, and another formed around the five Orlov brothers and their intimates—divided authority until the mid-seventies, when both were supplanted by a new hierarchy organized under the favorite G. A. Potemkin. In addition to dominant position at court, Potemkin could boast a substantial territorial base in New Russia, where he and his clients ruled with little interference from

---

[22] The positive aspects of this dilemma are discussed by George Yaney, "Bureaucracy and Freedom: N. M. Korkunov's Theory of the State," *American Historical Review*, 71: 2 (Jan. 1966), 468–86. The penalties for bribe giving were much less severe than those for bribe taking. Peter I had equalized them, showing again with what determination he set out to introduce legal relations. The government had to abandon this as impractical later in the century, as it recognized that in many cases the offer of bribes was a necessary means of acting. S. A. Korf, *Dvorianstvo i ego soslovnoe upravlenie za stoletie 1762–1855* (St. Petersburg, 1906), 380–81.

[23] A study recently made of the role of the Vorontsovs is L. J. Humphreys, "The Vorontsov Family: Russian Nobility in a Century of Change, 1725–1825," Ph.D. diss. (University of Pennsylvania, 1969).

the central government.[24] Hence the reach of these groups was often impressive.

There was also considerable internal cohesion in the patronage hierarchies. They were cemented by strong personal and kinship loyalties that rendered them difficult to penetrate. Even in the absence of material sanctions from, for example, a group in decline, personal allegiances were frequently strong enough to cause members to scuttle their own careers in preference to switching loyalties and bringing down on their heads the hostility of the group.[25] Under these circumstances, rulers had great difficulty uncovering abuses and determining the validity of accusations brought against officials. Disrupting a patronage network usually involved accepting the word of an outside plaintiff, or of representatives of a competing network in a subordinate hierarchical position, over that of the government's highest officials backed by friends and relatives in many areas of the administration and society. Even then, any action ran the risk of weakening a mechanism that, however corrupt, was the only one the ruler had to carry out his commands. An attack on one member of a network of relations frequently produced resistance up and down the line, from superiors who relied upon his services as well as from demoralized subordinates who depended upon his protection. Consequently it required great determination, if not reckless daring, to root out abuse.

When Catherine II at the outset of her reign decided to punish offending officials, she found that her only means of compelling the Senate to convict was to appear personally at its deliberations.[26] The senators were in no mood to point the finger, because the corrupted hierarchies often reached to the highest echelons of administration. Much to her dismay, Catherine's close supervision revealed only that one of the biggest grafters was her own procurator general.[27] Therefore, to reform meant to court disaster. Once a purge began, there was no telling how far it would lead. As a result, energetic rulers who set out to cleanse their administrations of graft and corruption quickly discovered that insofar as they achieved success, they did so at the risk of undermining the instruments of their own

[24] David Ransel, "Nikita Panin's Imperial Council Project and the Struggle of Hierarchy Groups at the Court of Catherine II," and David Griffiths, "The Rise and Fall of the Northern System: Court Politics and Foreign Policy in the First Half of Catherine II's Reign," both in *Canadian Slavic Studies*, 4: 3 (Fall 1970), 443–63 and 547–69, respectively.

[25] Hassell, "Vicissitudes," 123; David Griffiths, "Russian Court Politics and the Question of an Expansionist Foreign Policy under Catherine II," Ph.D. diss. (Cornell University, 1967), 65–66.

[26] S. M. Solov'ev, *Istoriia Rossii s drevneishikh vremen*, 15 vols. (Moscow, 1959–66), vol. 13, 215.

[27] Ibid., 215–17.

power. Wise rulers soon learned to respect these limitations and adjust their expectations to an unpalatable reality. Those more daring or foolish, like Peter III and Paul I, enjoyed but brief and stormy careers cut short by assassination.[28]

The considerable obstacles to exposure and prosecution did not, however, provide foolproof protection to the patronage hierarchies and their participating officials. They occasionally still found themselves in serious trouble, which usually occurred when an important superior fell victim to a court intrigue or was caught by a major shift in government policy. At such times the full force of the law was brought to bear against officials who had done no more than engage in normal modes of political and social organization.

A notorious case of this sort involved cabinet minister Artemii Volynskii, who in 1739 attempted to replace the ruling clique of Baltic Germans with his own leadership and personal following. The attempt failed, and unfortunately for Volynskii and his clients, the threatened Germans, much shaken by the challenge, reacted with unwonted severity and refused to limit prosecution to issues of graft and patronage abuse. To these they added charges of high treason, and extended the penalties to horrible tortures and capital sentences. All those associated with Volynskii and his reform plans shared in his disgrace.[29]

More to the point were the accusations leveled against Empress Anne's powerful favorite Johann Ernst Biron two years later when he fell from power. His judges denounced him for "always maintaining Bestuzhev in favor and bringing him into the Cabinet of Ministers with great contempt and slander toward the former ministers."[30] The client in question, A. P. Bestuzhev-Riumin, himself had to face charges of seeking out and accepting Biron's patronage. The court's list of accusations against Bestuzhev included these:

1) while in Copenhagen [as ambassador], he had corresponded with Biron and at the time of his first return trip to St. Petersburg sought him out so that he might receive through him the Order of Alexander Nevskii and an increased salary, which he in fact received. When he was again sent to Copenhagen, Biron

---

[28] Marc Raeff, "The Domestic Policies of Peter III and His Overthrow," *American Historical Review*, 75:5 (June 1970), 1289–1310, demonstrates this point on the basis of thorough archival investigations, and draws some interesting conclusions about the imperial period as a whole. For Paul, see M. V. Klochkov, *Ocherki pravitel'stvennoi deiatel'nosti vremeni Pavla I* (Petrograd, 1916).

[29] Iu. V. Got'e, "'Proekt o popravlenii gosudarstvennykh del' Artemiia Petrovicha Volynskogo," *Dela i Dni*, 3 (1922), 1–31.

[30] Solov'ev, *Istoriia Rossii*, vol. 11, 39.

promoted him to privy councilor and furthermore promised to promote him to Cabinet Minister and to obtain a pardon for his father; 2) on an order from Biron he attempted to persuade the Danish court to give [Biron] the title of Illustrious Prince; 3) after Bestuzhev's second return trip to Petersburg Biron promoted him to Cabinet Minister.[31]

For these crimes both men were deprived of their goods and sent into exile.

Similar, though in some cases less severe, fates befell leading hierarchies that were supplanted by changes in regimes or major policy shifts in 1727, 1730, 1758, 1762, and 1780. Members of the formerly powerful groups were hauled before a court and indicted for favoritism and patronage abuses.[32] At the very least they received punishments of demotion, honorable exile, or service in some post distant from the capital.

One noteworthy feature of all these indictments and legal proceedings was that while they pretended to encourage legal standards in elite organization, their effect was in certain respects the opposite. The legal proceedings were triggered by patronage contests. Since a recently victorious personal or kinship hierarchy employed the legal mechanism to remove a discredited competitor and solidify its own authority, the action only superficially represented an endorsement or furtherance of legal rational system. One might argue that the effect of such an action was simply to reinforce the practice of patronage and favoritism in government, for here again the pretense of law and system was turned into an instrument for facilitating continued abuses. But this was not the whole story. The maintenance of pretense was in itself very important, and over the long run contributed to a belief in the efficacy of legal relations. Since the patronage contests were expressed in terms of a bureaucratic facade, they upheld this all-important pretense and thereby played a positive role in the development of legal rational relations, a point worth returning to.

But first something must be said about other positive aspects of the patronage system. Patronage groups performed indispensable functions

[31] Ibid., 38–40.

[32] R. V. Ovchinnikov, ed., "Krushenie 'poluderzhavnogo vlastelina' (Dokumenty sledstvennogo dela kniazia A. D. Menshikova)," *Voprosy istorii*, no. 9 (Sept. 1970), 94–95; D. A. Korsakov, "Sud' nad Kniazem D. M. Golitsynym," *Drevniaia i novaia Rossiia*, no. 10 (1879), 20–62; Herbert Kaplan, *Russia and the Outbreak of the Seven Years' War* (Berkeley, 1968), esp. ch. 7, on the background of Bestuzhev's fall; on the change in 1781, in which the dispersal of the Panin hierarchy was handled with a minimum of indictments, see Griffiths, "Rise and Fall," 560–69. Soviet historians have attributed these changes to struggles among "interclass strata" (*prosloiki*) within the nobility. A recent example is Troitskii, "Istoriografiia dvortsovykh perevorotov v Rossii XVIII v."; but as there was no evidence of conflicting socioeconomic programs or an attack on class (or interclass) values, Eisenstadt's model of court or bureaucratic clique would seem more appropriate; *Political Systems of Empires*, 215–17.

not provided by other institutions. Their persistence and vitality reflected substantial success in fulfilling these services. Favoritism and patronage facilitated a degree of social mobility. This was especially true at the upper reaches of the state hierarchy. Rulers usually chose their favorites from among the middle gentry and raised these happy individuals and their families to unexpected heights of titled eminence and wealth. A list of only the most noted of each reign included A. D. Menshikov (son of a stable tender), E. J. Biron (minor gentry of Courland), A. G. Razumovskii (son of a registered Cossack), A. I. Shuvalov (son of a Petrine *arriviste*), and G. A. Potemkin (minor gentry of Smolensk province).[33]

But not only these persons profited. In the train of each favorite came a considerable number of additional families who through friendship with the principal also increased their fortunes. In view of the large number of favorites rewarded by empresses Elizabeth and Catherine, the aggregate social and economic mobility provided by this factor was far from trivial. One historian has reckoned it as the principal contribution to capital accumulation among the leading families of the empire.[34] Furthermore, established aristocratic clans drew into their patronage networks able servitors from the lesser nobility and from commoners. The Panin-Kurakin group, to cite one prominent example, was responsible for raising several well-known commoners, including diplomats I. M. Simolin and A. S. Stakhiev, as well as two leading ministers, D. M. Troshchinskii and State Secretary M. M. Speranskii.[35] The famous radical A. N. Radishchev got his start with the Vorontsov family. The foreign minister of late Catherinian times, A. A. Bezborodko (of the Ukrainian lesser gentry), came along in the baggage of Prince Potemkin, who himself owed his rise to Catherine's personal favor. As a result of this co-option of able low-ranking men and the infusion of new blood, the patronage system did not rigidify.

But a more significant factor in its vitality was the continuing insecurity of the service elite. This insecurity was largely a product of the tension between the ideal of legality introduced by Peter I and the reality of meeting demands imposed by a modernizing absolutist state. The tension was a creative force, both a cause and an effect of the dynamic development of

---

[33] Catherine II's favorites from Orlov forward, including Vasil'chikov, Zavadovskii, Potemkin, Zorich, Korsakov, Strakhov, Lanskoi, Mordvinov, Ermolov, and Zubov, were all from the poorer gentry, and before being raised by the empress they scarcely had adequate means to support themselves in the guards. Romanovich-Slavatinskii, *Dvorianstvo v Rossii*, 161.

[34] Ia. L. Barskov, "Pis'ma imp. Ekateriny II k gr. P. V. Zavadovskomu," *Russkii istoricheskii zhurnal*, no. 5 (1918), 240–41. A detailed list of populated estates granted by eighteenth-century monarchs to their favorites may be found in Romanovich-Slavatinskii, *Dvorianstvo v Rossii*, 159–63.

[35] Hassell, "Vicissitudes," 114–15.

the Russian state, and it could have acted only once the pretense of legality had been established. With no satisfactory method of resolving this tension, short of the leadership's abandoning its commitment to remold society in a modern image, patronage groups served as a necessary cushion between the superhuman goals the leadership defined for the country and the all-too-human materials set in motion to achieve them. On one hand, patronage groups functioned as an effective protection for the basic social values of personal security, career, and status, which were constantly threatened by the violence of the modernizing enterprise, while at the same time, they interfered with that enterprise by placing entrenched hierarchies in the path to its fulfillment. On the other hand, these informal groups also acted as the principal means of articulating and executing the ruler's goals. Destroying them would only have increased insecurities and fragmented society further, possibly paralyzing the ruler's ability to act at all.

Consequently the maintenance of the mediating hierarchies of patronage, even while they constituted a moral outrage to many social critics and a hindrance to the rulers, nevertheless served important interests of both sides. Until some new institution emerged that could facilitate government action while providing a reasonable measure of personal security, the increasing demands on the participants in the modernizing enterprise would tend to reinforce rather than remove the influence of patronage groups. Looking back on their contribution, one can see that they managed with some degree of success to adapt themselves to the difficult process of modernization in Russia.

2

In order to give concrete form to the values and principles underlying the patronage system, we may now turn to an investigation of the Russian letter-writer. It provides an excellent view of the rituals and unspoken assumptions governing formal social relations among the service elite.

First, a word about the source. Letter-writers appeared in large numbers in eighteenth-century Europe. For nearly two hundred years they had been coming out in England, France, and Germany in steadily increasing quantity and variety. Their history may be traced back to the Latin formularies and etiquette books of the Italian Renaissance. In each country the appearance of such handbooks seems to have been associated with two phenomena: the growth of a general postal system, and a period of expansion and prosperity giving rise to upward social mobility. The letter-writer—as well as handbooks of science, art, and history that appeared at the same times—was designed as a shortcut to learning and polish for those who had acnieved prosperity or new position without a commensurate level of culture.[36] The first Russian letter-writer followed this pattern. Although appearing much later than its European counterparts, it came at just the time one would expect, in the reign of Catherine II when the civil bureaucracy expanded to three times its previous size. Many new officials from the lower nobility and commonality were for the first time taking positions in the state service and must have found this concise guide to proper style very useful.[37]

The value of the letter-writer for the historian lies in its complete lack of concern for the quality of social relations. As a practical guide to "getting along" in the world of eighteenth-century Russia, the manual had no cause to criticize social relations. It simply accepted them as given. The editor's pretensions extended only to the improvement and refinement of the prevailing style. For this reason the letter-writer is more useful than authentic correspondence in illuminating the mores of the era. Being designed as models, the letters in such a handbook had to reflect typical generalized patterns. As Charles Haskins has noted in reference to form letters from an earlier period, "The hundreds of student letters which have reached us in the manuscripts of the Middle Ages have come down through the medium of collections of forms or complete letter-writers, shorn of most of their individuality but for that very reason reflecting the more faithfully the fundamental and universal phases of university life."[38] The same could be said of the Russian letter-writer's faithfulness in representing the quality of formal social relations among the eighteenth-century service nobility.

The manual in question was richly bound in leather in a compact duodecimo format that could serve admirably as a practical and attractive reference book for the desk or be easily portable for taking along on business trips or foreign sojourns. Although research has failed to reveal the name of the editor, there is some information on its publication background. The manual first appeared in 1788 as one of the earliest publications of the later wealthy and renowned Glazunov publishing firm. The Glazunovs specialized in the printing of belletristic and historical works

---

[36] There is a considerable literature on letter-writers, but it has remained entirely in the province of literary scholars tracing the origins of the epistolary novel. Some recent examples are: Katherine Hornbeak, "The Complete Letter Writer in English, 1568–1800," *Smith College Studies in Modern Languages*, 15:3–4 (1934); François Jost, *Essais de littérature comparée* (Fribourg and Urbana, 1968), esp. 118–19; Reinhard Nickisch, *Die Stilprinzipien in den Deutschen Briefstellern des 17. und 18. Jahrhunderts* (Göttingen, 1969).

[37] Demidova, "Biurokratizatsiia," 238–40.

[38] Charles Haskins, *The Rise of Universities* (New York, 1923), 103, cited in Hornbeak, "The Complete Letter Writer," viii.

aimed at the nobiliary and intellectual elite.[39] The firm made a wise choice in selecting the style manual as one of its first efforts. Judging from its publication history, the work enjoyed considerable popularity. A second edition came out within a year of the first, and a third, slightly expanded edition followed in 1793.[40]

In this connection it would be helpful to note one major difference between the Russian letter-writer and the European model after which it was undoubtedly patterned. European letter-writers were usually directed at the rising bourgeoisie. This early Russian manual, while including several items of interest to merchants, allotted much more space to matters concerning noble servicemen. In Russia, where the bourgeoisie was little developed, the servicemen provided the natural market for such a manual. Many of them in the late eighteenth century still had a relatively low level of culture and were often only semiliterate. They could well use a manual that would help their correspondence make the right impression on a superior, and it was for these servicemen that the book was designed. But the title did not directly convey this emphasis. It read: "A Letter Writer containing various letters, requests, business notes, contracts, testimonials, authorizations, vouchers, identification passes for serf peasants, order to an overseer, form of mercantile assignation, receipts, vouchers [sic], letters of transmittal and credit."

At first glance, the work might appear to be a handbook for merchants. Scrutiny of the content would not sustain this opinion. Of 84 examples of written style presented in the book, less than a third (27) were devoted to technical questions, and these would have interested nobles as well as merchants. Among the examples were letters of credit and exchange, payment orders, travel permits, and internal passports, also specimens of affidavits, leases, a will, and a number of contracts relating principally to the transfer of serfs. The content of most of these form letters reveals that they directly concerned the interests of the nobiliary elite, since they refer to serfs and populated estates, the ownership of which was the exclusive privilege of nobility.

The largest part of the letter-writer, the remaining two-thirds, was taken up with communications passing exclusively among the elite of serving nobles. And most significant for purposes of this discussion, 60

[39] A. A. Sidorov, ed., *400 let russkogo knigo-pechataniia 1564–1964*, 1: *1564–1917* (Moscow, 1964), 270; "I. P. Glazunov," *Russkii biograficheskii slovar'*, vol. 5, 265–66.

[40] *Svodnyi katalog russkoi knigi grazhdanskoi pechati XVIII veka 1725–1800*, 2 (Moscow, 1964), 417. Unfortunately the tirage is not indicated for any of these editions. Citations in this article will refer to the second edition, 1789.

percent of these examples (34 of 57) dealt directly with the attainment, maintenance, and loss of patronage connections.[41]

Preceding these samples of written style were two introductory sections of general interest. The first presented comments on various types of letter-writing: business letters, letters of recommendation, of advice, of thanks, and others. The quality of the advice may be judged from this selection on letters of courtesy: "Letters containing mere politenesses are more difficult than other types, since for the most part they have nothing of substance to convey. It requires some imagination to fill them up. The usual expressions are so commonly known that no one dares to use them any longer. However, propriety demands that we write something. Thus, it is necessary to apply our intelligence."[42] However trivial the content of such letters, the editor expressed not the slightest doubt as to their importance; in fact he devoted the longest segment of his introduction to this type of letter.[43] And with good reason. Such empty communications played an important ritualistic role in the prevailing system of social relations; they influenced the mode of communication among members of patronage hierarchies and thereby helped to maintain cohesion and morale within those elemental building blocks of society.

The second introductory section provided a brief and very useful list of proper titles to be employed in salutations and complimentary closings of letters to persons of various ranks in the state service. The reader then arrived at the main substance of the manual, the samples of proper written style for typical communications of the day.

A considerable range and variety of patronage letters were presented.

---

[41] Given the nature of the source, further categorization for purposes of analysis would not yield useful results. Even if one were to divide the samples neatly into communications exhibiting patronage relations, legal rational behaviors, and various degrees of mixture to show the intrusion of legal rational relations into the prevailing system of personal relations, the comparison would reflect only the number of different types of communication, not the quantity or frequency of any particular type.

[42] *Pis'movnik soderzhashchii raznye pis'ma, prosheniia, zapiski po delu, kontrakty, atestaty, odobreniia, rospiski, propuski i pis'mennoi vid krepostnym liudiam, prikaz staroste, formu kupecheskikh assignatsii, kvitantsii, rospiski, pis'ma posylochnye i kreditnye* (St. Petersburg, 1789), 12–13.

[43] At this point the editor uncharacteristically offered one small criticism of the prevailing practice. "It often occurs," he wrote, "that having a need to write something to someone, we do not ourselves know what to say to him. We compose a letter, filling it solely with words of respect, affection and the like, which in this case mean next to nothing, and we conclude with the offer of our services. This practice is altogether unreasonable. But what is one to do when it has already been so firmly implanted?" *Pis'movnik*, 13; for the entire discussion of this type of letter, see 12–19. The editor did, however, include such letters in the collection, showing that he recognized their value in certain situations.

Among the 34 samples devoted exclusively to such matters, the largest number belonged to these three categories: requests for jobs and job transfers (7 letters), requests for outright grants-in-aid (5 letters), and requests for intervention and protection in court cases (5 letters). Several others could possibly be included in these categories. They represented appeals for patronage protection without specifying the precise nature of the favor required. But more important than any particular request was the action of the patronage link, which bore common characteristics in all the letters.

In patronage hierarchies, powerful persons bestowed favors or advanced requests from a subordinate client to be promoted to a higher rung on the patronage ladder. In this way the superior maintained the respect and gratitude of the subordinate so vital to the continuance of services required by the superior. The subordinate, who through bribery and particular services manipulated his patron to keep his favor, came to expect these benefits. This expectation derived from the subordinate's belief in his patron's power and personal influence; the subordinate relied quite explicitly on the assumed and somewhat mysterious power of his protector. While this understanding was seldom openly expressed, it ran through nearly all the style manual's letters in subtle yet unmistakable terms. This may be seen in the examples presented below of the principal types of patronage letters appearing in the manual: patron seeking a job for a client, aid requested in a court action, patron asking help for a client in trouble, appeal of a destitute widow, subordinate attempting to regain lost favor, and a young man opening a patronage contact.

A relatively modest expression of the dependency relationship may be observed in this first letter, in which a patron requests the placing of a client in a new position.

Anyone else would consider my boldness inexcusable; but Your Excellency will of course not count me guilty in consideration of the fact that, despite [my boldness], I have reserved my most dutiful esteem for the merits and virtues of your personage. In such hope I venture to request most humbly of Your Excellency to take the bearer of this [letter] Major I. under your protection and place him in the vacancy now opening at N. Knowing your discernment in fairly evaluating persons, gracious lord!, I can strongly assure you of his abilities as well as his complete gratitude to you as his true benefactor; wherefore with great confidence in entrusting him to your favor with my deepest respect I remain always. . . .[44]

[44] Pis'movnik, 83-85.

More often a client in making a request recorded some specific instance of his worthy service. Or at the very least there was a clear statement of the dependency relationship, as with the following introduction in a request for protection in a court case. The petitioner began: "If you respect my humble request as much as I have respected your orders, then I may rely fully on receiving your help in a court action I am now engaged in with a noble living in my area."[45]

Occasionally a letter could be quite direct without ritual bows to services previously performed. This was the case in the following letter, which shows a patron appealing to a third party for action on his client's behalf. The example is revealing also for its attitude toward legal justice (*pravosudie*); it was something employed to victimize people, and a patron was therefore duty-bound to protect his clients from its depredations. The letter eloquently conveys the values and attitudes underlying the patronage system.

I am altogether certain that you have a humanitarian spirit and a charitable heart, which sympathizes with human need, gives aid to the unfortunate and protects and frees them from misfortune. For this reason I present you with an instance in which you might easily display this virtue of yours and demonstrate it by action. It is well known to you that a certain P. K. is leading a miserable existence in the city of N. I won't explain his case; you yourself have a clear conception of it. It only remains for me to remind you of his misery which has long since deserved to be an object of your charity. I ask sincerely that you would rescue this man, whom a certain person *has made a sacrifice to legal justice* and severity, from the ominous situation now threatening him.[46]

More often the examples given in the letter-writer showed a subordinate appealing to a superior, and these letters bore two unfailing characteristics. They were exceedingly deferential, if not obsequious, and contained more or less subtle reminders of the superior's obligations.

Among the most candid were petitions from widows and dependents of former servicemen. Since the subordinate was deceased and could manipulate no longer, the desperate petitioners had to spell out the superior's obligations in some detail in order to obtain his essential support. The following sample and two other equally poignant letters from widows included in the manual indicate that even after Catherine II's provincial

---

45 Ibid., 164–65.
46 Ibid., 71–73 (italics added). *Pravosudie* could mean justice in senses other than that obtained through legal process. In such cases the word was usually followed by a genitive modifier, e.g., *pravosudie Bozhi* (God's justice). The context here makes clear its meaning as legal justice.

government reform (1775),[47] which established local organs for the protection of widows and orphans, dependents continued to rely on the favor of powerful persons in order to receive survivor benefits. Such appeals would usually go to the dead man's former chief, as in this letter to a brigadier.

In my present extremity I make bold to approach you as my sole protector. Extend a helping hand to an unfortunate widow deprived of subsistence by her husband's death, [a man] who sacrificed his life for the fatherland following his duty and your orders. Take pity, kind sir, on my distress, remembering my husband's devotion to you; as he lay dying he pronounced your name as his true benefactor. And if in thinking of his survivors he went to the grave with this hope in you, would you then leave his poor widow and children to perish. I enclose herewith my petition to His Excellency Count N. Be my protector. Testify to my husband's service and with the firmness characteristic of you when defending truth and acting for the unfortunate, present my husband's debts. Kind sir, his service and death in the war . . . your protection, my misfortune, my three children, are they not sufficient to obtain for me some charity, with which I might provide my unhappy family some sustenance, and without which in all honesty, I must perish.[48]

Another letter represented the appeal of a subordinate who had lost his patron's favor and was desperately trying to regain it. As in the case of the widow, this model letter conveys the painful insecurity of the Russian serviceman. Even with all the usual benefits granted on retirement, the less exalted servicemen seem to have had difficulty holding body and soul together without the additional protection and benefaction of a powerful patron.

Most Excellent Count. . . . Upon entering my position in 1759, I had as my sole object the advancement of the work and I eagerly tried to carry out my duties with exactitude and to gain your favor. For 20 years I had the pleasure of enjoying it before all my fellows; and this was my sole priceless reward. Your Excellency, being fair in all things, will not refuse to grant me due justice in recognizing the zeal with which I was always attached to your person and my perfect gratitude for your most gracious disposition toward me [as may be seen from the fact] that I never dared trouble you by asking any special reward for myself even at those times when you may have encouraged me by lavishly praising my actions.

[47] V. Grigor'ev, *Reforma mestnogo upravleniia pri Ekaterine II* (St. Petersburg, 1910), 271–75, 283–87.
[48] *Pis'movnik*, 68–70.

Having relied solely on your favor, I and my family hoped to be honored by your protection forever. But to my misfortune I was suddenly deprived of it when Your Excellency decided to entrust my position to another. Although I was by your gracious recommendation released at that time with all benefits that could be expected, nevertheless to this time I still feel anxiety and am plagued with doubts as to whether I had given you some cause to be displeased with me. For this reason I venture most humbly to beg Your Excellency to return to me, a decrepit old man, your eminent patronage. For without it my days may end unbetimes; without it, Most Excellent Count, shall I, already burdened by a numerous family, continue to suffer want, from which only you can rescue me.

Instead of the considerable rewards that have been granted to others thanks to your generous intercession, to me it would be a priceless treasure if you but restored your eminent favor, whose beneficent result would reinforce my strength exhausted by the burdens of age and serve me and my poor family as a blessing; accepting it we shall praise you as our benefactor, to whom I had and have now the deepest respect and true devotion.[49]

This letter did not stand alone in the manual as evidence of the impoverishment of state servicemen. A considerable number of the model letters involved cases of threatened destitution. The appearance of these letters no doubt reflected a serious crisis for the lesser servicemen, who in the late eighteenth century were suffering from the ravages of a steady inflation and the heavy costs of meeting the social demand to maintain a Westernized lifestyle.[50]

The manual also included letters from people in serious trouble with the authorities. One particularly striking example concerns a retired staff officer who was arrested while on a visit away from home. He was appealing to a titled superior: "I served honorably all my life, possessing the rank of staff officer and now owing to the petition of the provincial registrar N., based neither on law nor decency . . . I have been held under arrest for nearly a half year, and the first month I was treated as severely as if I were a common criminal."[51] During this time the local authorities made no effort to bring the case to trial. The imprisoned man could not even obtain

---

[49] Ibid., 63–67.

[50] Among such letters were these: two letters request job transfer or release from service due to debts incurred from the high cost of living in St. Petersburg (53–57, 57–60); request to patron to help pay large personal debt (74–78); petitioner who served in both military and civil bureaucracies has lost villages due to debts (103–7); additional examples (115–19, 153–55, 162–64, 167–68, 168–70, 186–88). On the nobility's economic position, see the groundbreaking article by Arcadius Kahan, "The Costs of 'Westernization' in Russia: The Gentry and the Economy in the Eighteenth Century," *Slavic Review*, 25:1 (Mar. 1966), 40–66.

[51] *Pis'movnik*, 78–83.

a temporary release, despite the fact that two officers of repute volunteered to stand surety for him. The registrar, in cooperation with the provincial chancellery, refused to settle the case until the prisoner paid what the registrar demanded.

One might wonder at the reason for including such a letter in a style manual,[52] but a close look at provincial government in eighteenth-century Russia would quickly dispel any doubts about its usefulness. The tyranny of local officials was notorious. And little wonder. In the absence of a systematic legal code and with the central government unable to exercise effective control over its agents, the power that those agents necessarily possessed could be employed for whatever purposes they found most beneficial. As a result, innocent citizens frequently found themselves at the mercy of avaricious local authorities or any powerful person who could buy the authorities' cooperation. Faced with such conditions, a Russian responded not by appealing to a legal system that did not operate, but as in the case of the arrested staff officer, by turning to a powerful protector who could exert influence on the hierarcy that was responsible for his miseries.[53]

Established procedures for appeal did exist. An injured party could send a complaint to the appropriate department of the Governing Senate in the capital and, theoretically at least, obtain a judgment against the offending local officials. But even a cursory investigation of such actions would reveal less about the operation of the legal process than about the inability of the central government to enforce its decisions outside the capital city.

Take, for example, the actual case of a soldier Alekseev who was victimized (*sechenie na domu*) by a certain Major Mordvinov in Novgorod province. Alekseev obtained a judgment against his attacker for 50 rubles

[52] In fact European letter-writers of the seventeenth and eighteenth centuries frequently included a model letter to a friend in prison. The letter usually conveyed condolence and bore an assumption of the imprisoned person's guilt. For an English letter of this type, see Hornbeak, "The Complete Letter Writer," 88. The modification that took place in the Russian example is again very revealing. The letter was from the imprisoned man and carried a presumption of innocence, an unfortunate soul victimized by local officials.

It is necessary to do much more by way of comparing the pretenses of the Russian letter-writer with those of western Europe. In preparing this article, I was unfortunately unable to obtain actual letter-writers from western Europe and had to rely on the information in literary monographs, whose interest in social questions and law was limited.

[53] See Yaney's comments on the peasant's legal consciousness, which may for this period be generalized to the rest of Russian society, in "Law, Society and the Domestic Regime in Russia, in Historical Perspective," *American Political Science Review*, 59:2 (June 1965), 380–81.

in damages. Instead of receiving payment, he got a surprise visit from the enraged major and several of his fellow landlords, who treated the unfortunate man to a merciless thrashing for the audacity of filing a complaint against their friend. A brave soldier, Alekseev then appealed to the Senate, which ordered the Novgorod chancellery to levy a second fine on Mordvinov and 10 rubles in damages on all participants in the beating. The Senate further directed its Novgorod office to report promptly on its action in the case. Weeks went by with no report. The Senate issued yet another order. Finally it became apparent that the Novgorod chancellery was simply sabotaging the Senate's decision and had no intention of implementing it. Nearly a year had passed since the first judgment against Mordvinov was handed down. It was painfully obvious to the Senate officials that the provincial authorities in Novgorod were beholden more to criminal elements among the local nobility than to their own superiors in St. Petersburg. As a last resort the Senate decided to pay Alekseev directly for the damages and withhold that amount from the salaries of the Novgorod officials.[54] Needless to say, had Major Mordvinov enjoyed connections at court or in the Senate, the good soldier Alekseev could have expected only further abuse for his efforts.[55]

The letter-writer provided examples of more fortunate occasions as well. In a society where personal patronage made careers while the bureaucratic principle of advancement by merit, however firmly expressed in law, remained a pious counsel of perfection, a young man starting out in life had to know how to make the proper contacts. A letter-writer could therefore scarcely boast completeness without including examples of introductory letters to potential patrons. The manual recommended this approach as typical:

Dear Sir,

The respect and devotion which I feel toward worthy persons moves me to write to you, even though I do not have the honor of knowing you personally. Your good inclinations and sincere feelings have made your name known to all; and this very fact compels me to seek [written] correspondence with you. . . . Do not refuse me this wish. Do not give as a reason my lack of acquaintance with you and be assured that I am moved to it for no other reason than by respect and

[54] Case from the First Department of the Governing Senate, quoted at length in G. P. Makogonenko, *Radishchev i ego vremia* (Moscow, 1956), 137–39.

[55] In this connection it is indicative that the letter-writer offered few examples of appeals to law. Only four letters refer to such matters, and three of them have to do exclusively with obtaining the personal intervention of a patron in a court case; the fourth is a threat of foreclosure. *Pis'movnik*, 159–60, 164–68.

love of virtue and merit; giving you all justice in this, I desire to possess sincere friendship and acquaintance, remaining always with my complete respect . . .

Your Excellency's . . . humble servant. . . .

The manual then offers a proper reply to such a request.

Dear Sir,

You anticipate me in what I have for long since sincerely wished, having known of you by reputation from my truest friends. Your proposal gives me the fullest satisfaction and for this reason I all the more gladly promise you my friendship, which you may be assured I shall endeavor to preserve eternally by showing you my sincerety, kindness and sincere benevolence, with which being now filled, I have the honor to be unshakably with complete esteem. . . .[56]

Such an exchange could create a new patronage alliance beneficial to both sides. The first writer found a new patron, and the second was pleased to take on obligations to a person he expected to be a useful client.

As these few examples demonstrate, the letter-writer captures a picture of Russian social relations in a revealing phase. The manual shows the transferral of habits and associations characteristic of the face-to-face informal relations of previous eras to a society in which written communication had become increasingly important. The letters reveal not only the undiminished vigor of the patronage system, but more interesting, the ritualistic forms of various types of patronage relations. The publication of the letter-writer testifies to a growing literacy and Westernization among the elite, but the content of the model letters makes it clear that the earlier style had not yet been altered in the direction of legal relations. Despite strong legal proscriptions and the moral sanction of enlightened social critics, patronage remained the foundation of relations among the noble servicemen. Until Russian society could provide more than the pretense of legality to protect values of property, status, and personal security, the patronage system would continue to fulfill this essential social function.

Patronage groups continue to be a feature of modern Russian and Soviet elite organization. Although literature on the topic is limited, the

[56] Ibid., 97–100. It was probably more common to make such desirable connections through informal face-to-face contacts. In this regard the Freemasonic lodges, which grew rapidly during the seventies and eighties, played a very important role. See, for example, Ivan Elagin's explanation of why he first joined the Masons, "Zapiska I. P. Elagina: novye materialy dlia istorii masonstva," *Russkii Arkhiv*, 2:1 (1864), 93–110.

presence of such groups is confirmed by frequent Soviet press attacks on the bureaucratic practice of "familyness" (*semeistvennost'*).[57] This observation poses some interesting questions for researchers in Soviet studies. For example, it would be useful to know the extent to which the present phenomenon has its roots in earlier similar forms or might resemble them in structure or motivation. Such a study could yield important insights into the impact of revolution and industrialization upon traditional institutions, as well as help identify problems and institutional survivals closely associated with the function of patronage groups.

[57] Raymond Bauer et al., *How the Soviet System Works* (New York, 1961), 87–94. Several other authors have commented on this. Leon Trotsky naturally singled it out for criticism, in *The Revolution Betrayed* (New York, 1965), 99–101, 253–54; J. S. Berliner, "The Informal Organization of the Soviet Firm," *Quarterly Journal of Economics*, 66:3 (Aug. 1952), 342–65, esp. 356–60; David Granick, *The Red Executive: A Study of the Organization Man in Russian Industry* (Garden City, 1961), 149–50; Merle Fainsod, *Smolensk under Soviet Rule* (New York, 1958), is in some respects a case study of one such hierarchy group operating in the western province; Barrington Moore, Jr., *Terror and Progress—USSR* (New York, 1955), 154–78, contains an excellent analysis of the dynamics of patronage groups under conditions of intermittent terror; but only Yaney, "Law, Society and the Domestic Regime," attempts to set this behavior in a historical context.

Elites in Conflict in Tsarist Russia: The Briansk Company

JOHN P. MCKAY

A striking peculiarity of Russian economic life before the revolutions of 1917 was the prominence of foreign businessmen in industry and finance. This was especially so in the case of "big business" in the generation before World War I, when foreigners, a small minority of all businessmen in Russia, were relatively numerous, effective, and significant. One may reasonably think of these leading foreign businessmen as a subgroup within the functional economic elite of all big businessmen operating in Russia.

If the business elite in Russia lacked homogeneity because of the large foreign component, so the foreign group itself was far from unified. By 1900 French, Belgian, German, and English business leaders were all well represented, in line with the large Russian investments of each of these nationalities. The foreign group at any given moment in the nineteenth century was also marked by differences in the degree to which members had been assimilated and merged into the indigenous Russian group. For example, by 1900 businessmen of German origins, whose ancestors had migrated to Russia in the early part of the nineteenth century, were often Russian citizens by birth or naturalization and "russified" to a considerable extent. Yet in common with other largely assimilated foreign businessmen, they retained a certain cohesiveness as well as close ties with their ancestral homeland and its representatives in and outside Russia.

Leading French capitalists in Russia held on to the link with the home country more tenaciously. This was in part because their Russian interest was of more recent origins, and also because they already were well-established members of their own national economic elite before investing in Russia. Commanding both large financial resources and advanced industrial technology, French businessmen often sought out native Russian capitalists and managers for their ventures, but retained them as junior partners with linguistic and administrative skills while the French themselves jealously guarded ultimate decision-making authority.

As far as I can tell on the basis of histories of many French firms in Russia, this desire to be the primary decision-makers meant that the top strata of French businessmen seldom cooperated with their counterparts from the Russian business elite on the basis of equality in specific business enterprises. Temporary combinations between equals might be possible, but long-term division of authority and responsibility was not. The Russian business elite also sought to harness foreigners, but in subordinate capacities more in tune with ties often going to the aristocracy and upper bureaucracy. Should the two business elites come together as equals in a given venture, the seeds of conflict were already sown.

This was precisely what happened in the case of the Briansk Company, the investigation of which provides a rare detailed view of the interaction of the foreign and Russian subgroups of the business elite in Russia. It should be noted that this focus on the interaction of elites, as opposed to the study of a single elite, is an atypical approach to elite study, as the essays in this volume testify. Yet this maverick attempt to probe relations between separate elites corresponds to countless historical and contemporary situations, and I think it will prove suggestive regarding practical and conceptual problems of elite study.

The Briansk affair is also significant in terms of understanding relations between foreign businessmen and the Russian state under capitalism. For the development of the Briansk embroglio modified the initial confrontation and saw a clear clash between the French business elite in Russia, actively supported by the French government, and the Russian state. Thus it relates directly to charges that foreign investment, which even most Soviet scholars admit quickened the pace of industrialization, particularly in the 1890s, also resulted in the loss of Russian political dependence.

In my work on foreign entrepreneurs in Russian industry before 1914, I reached rather unorthodox conclusions regarding this question. Simply stated, the evidence suggests that the Russian state effectively managed foreign businessmen and used them to help implement the government's basic policy of more rapid economic development for greater political power.[1] With this in mind I wish to add hitherto unpublished evidence that contributed to my original findings and that stands as a sort of test case for my conclusions concerning the nature of relations between foreign businessmen and the Russian state.

---

[1] See John P. McKay, *Pioneers for Profit: Foreign Entrepreneurship and Russian Industrialization, 1885–1913* (Chicago, 1970), esp. 268–86 and 379–89.

Exceptional dynamism was the distinguishing characteristic of the Briansk Ironworks Company from its inception. Founded in 1873 with its plant at Bezhitsa in Orel province of central Russia, the firm began as a producer of iron rails for railroad construction. Unlike the famed but decadent integrated iron producers of the Ural Mountains, Briansk was essentially a processor, converting imported English pig iron into finished rails. As such, Briansk was one of a small number of companies that aggressively seized the profit opportunities inherent in rapid railway construction and a more sophisticated policy of state protection in the 1870s.[2] That policy permitted duty-free importation of pig iron while taxing imported rails heavily, thereby breaking with both the almost prohibitive protectionism of the early nineteenth century and the free or nearly free importation of rails and equipment in the 1850s and 1860s.

The founders, P. I. Gubonin and V. F. Golubev, were directed by a wealthy noble businessman, Prince V. Tenishev, who was the firm's top administrator until his retirement in 1896. Representative of the aristocratic entrepreneur often found in eastern Europe, Prince Tenishev had the personal connections with court and bureaucracy necessary for the success of a firm based upon a new tariff policy and expanded, state-supported railroad construction. Under his leadership, dividends averaged 15 percent from 1875 to 1880, while capital stock increased more than fourfold. The owners felt that a large portion of their success was due to their superior management. And if their self-congratulatory histories of the firm must be read with a critical eye, they also portray an entrepreneurial dynamism rarely found in Russia before the 1890s.

Perhaps most indicative of this quality was the rapid and continuous metamorphosis of the firm's product mix in the face of changing market conditions in the first ten years. While it was exclusively a producer of iron rails in 1873, other products accounted for two-thirds of total sales prior to production of steel rails after 1876. Steel rails then grew very rapidly to account for three-fourths of sales in 1879, before falling to only one-quarter of sales in 1883 as speciality products—bridges, elevators, bars, etc.—were developed to take the place of the shriveled market for rails.[3] The directors thus managed to meet the cyclical demand for rails of improved quality, while developing rapidly diversified products when demand for rails fell sharply.

[2] Two company publications have been particularly useful for the early history of the firm: Aktsionernoe Obshchestvo Brianskogo rel'soprokatnogo, zhelezodelatel'nogo i mekhanicheskogo zavoda, *Obzor desiatiletnei deiatel'nosti Obshchestva Brianskogo . . . Zavoda, 1873–1883 g.* (St. Petersburg, 1885), and *Kratkii istoricheskii ocherk prinadlezhashchikh obshchestvu zavodov, zheleznogo rudnika i ugol'nykh kopei* (Moscow, 1896).

[3] Briansk, *Obzor*, 2–4.

This responsiveness to changing conditions was tested more dramatically in the 1880s. As demand for metallurgical products in general and rails in particular contracted during this depressed decade, profits and dividends fell sharply, one major steel company (Putilov) went bankrupt, and in 1882 the first syndicate or cartel was formed in the Russian steel industry to prevent competition and divide the market.[4] This cartel prevented disaster, but it certainly did not bring prosperity. In the words of a leading Soviet authority, "The position of all members of the rail syndicate remained difficult until the beginning of the 1890s."[5] Briansk did better than most: it was one of only two firms in the cartel paying any dividends whatsoever at this time, although the rate fell continuously from 25 percent in 1882 to 12 percent in 1888.

Had the basic structure of the Russian steel industry been established, Briansk might have been able to ride out this cyclical contraction of a cyclical industry with a certain equanimity. Yet an informed and realistic observer knew this was impossible. The industry was on the verge of its most revolutionary period since the growth of iron production in the Urals under Peter the Great in the early eighteenth century. Not until the Stalin era would innovations of such magnitude recur. This revolution involved a massive shift in the geographical center of the Russian steel industry, from the old northern regions to the completely new southern industrial area in the western Ukraine and Donets Basin, the most exciting and significant development of Russia's prerevolutionary industrial spurt and "take-off."

This development began in 1870, when the Englishman John Hughes established the first integrated steel producer in southern Russia, the New Russia Ironworks Company.[6] In spite of sizable subsidies, however, Hughes's success was not assured until 1884, when the long-discussed Catherine Railroad finally linked high-grade Krivoi Rog iron deposits with Donets coal, providing Hughes with much better ore than he had found near his plant in the Donets Basin. The completion of the road reflected state support for southern metallurgy. Just as the government had encouraged new producers, such as Briansk, to build modern steel plants to process imported pig iron in the 1860s and 1870s, so it promoted linkage backward to steel with southern-produced pig iron from the mid-1880s.

The challenging opportunity of creating a modern integrated steel industry was successfully met. Whereas there were only two steel com-

[4] Fuller discussion of these problems may be found in McKay, *Pioneers for Profit*, 112–19, 299–303, 340–49, and the sources cited there.

[5] I. F. Gindin, *Gosudarstvennyi bank i ekonomicheskaia politika tsarskogo pravitel'stva, 1861–1892 gody* (Moscow, 1962), 259.

[6] In English, see J. N. Westwood, "John Hughes and Russian Metallurgy," *Economic History Review*, ser. 2, 17 (1965), 564–69.

panies in the southern area in 1885, producing 8.6 percent of total Russian pig iron, there were at least eighteen in 1900, producing 57.8 percent of all pig iron made in Russia (excluding tsarist Poland). Most striking were the almost complete dominance of firms with foreign capital, technology, and management in this movement and the secondary role played by indigenous Russian firms. Yet there was the exception that proved the rule: the Briansk Company alone seized this opportunity by itself and contributed markedly to this movement. Thus it continued to distinguish itself as a Russian firm of unusual resourcefulness and remained a source of pride and profit in the face of foreign triumphs and leadership. Briansk represented, in effect, the most dynamic elements of the Russian business elite, receiving in turn the support of the bureaucracy and thereby the entire Russian political elite.

The period between serious consideration of an integrated southern steel mill (1884) and further expansion on the Kerch Peninsula (1897) saw a complex and total transformation of the Briansk Company. To do justice to all the factors involved would carry me far from the crisis of conflicting elites I seek to analyze. Yet two key points should be made if that conflict is to be understood.

First, Briansk's long-standing relations with the Russian state resulted in a privileged position. One keen and impartial observer felt that Briansk had always been an object of marked favor on the part of the state, and with an "exclusively Russian management always receives state orders more easily than its competitors."[7] Certainly the publications of the company, particularly that of 1885, spoke of the great need for government support in the form of premiums and large orders if the company were to build a southern plant. It is also clear that large state orders eased the strains of the company's difficult transformation, which led to grave problems in 1890–92.

Briansk had originally decided that the southern plant would refine only pig iron, which would then be shipped by river hundreds of miles north to the Bezhitsa plant. There existing equipment would refine and process the pig iron into steel ingots and finished steel products. Yet when the new southern blast furnaces at Ekaterinoslav were finished in 1890, this original plan proved impractical, almost disastrously so. The thin lifeline between the two plants clogged along the upper Desna, freezing in winter and drying to a trickle in summer. While the northern mills lacked

[7] Crédit Lyonnais, Paris, France, Études Financières (hereafter cited as C. L.), Briansk, Étude, Jan. 1903, and Note, Apr. 1900. This extremely important source for late nineteenth-century economic history has several excellent manuscript analyses of Briansk. This source and the other archival sources used in this study are discussed in McKay, *Pioneers for Profit*, 396–400.

pig iron, the southern plant stockpiled enormous quantities. No doubt state support strengthened the resolve of Prince Tenishev and his assistants to modify completely their initial conception. They added steel-refining capacity and at least finishing mills for rails in the south, while phasing rails out at Bezhitsa, where they henceforth concentrated production of more highly finished articles. The completely transformed plant at Bezhitsa became the largest producer of locomotives and freight cars in Russia—another example of Briansk's "relations," since such equipment was sold principally to state-owned railroads.

Second, the company was able to use foreigners as subordinates in several capacities. The Crédit Lyonnais engineer in Russia noted with admiration that most of the vast southern plant at Ekaterinoslav was excellent and embodied the plans and suggestions of the high-quality foreign technicians the Russian directors had used intelligently.[8] Thus Briansk's directors obtained indispensable Western techniques without relinquishing leadership. Similarly, Briansk was one of the first Russian firms to tap successfully Western financial markets in the early 1890s without simultaneously surrendering control. For although the Russian owners increased Briansk's joint-stock capital and their investment from 1,800,000 rubles in 1886 to 5,400,000 in 1889, the need for even more funds was a critical problem during the wholesale transformation of the firm.

In January 1890 the company succeeded in placing 6,000,000 francs (2,200,000 rubles) of 5 percent first-mortgage bonds in France through the Crédit Mobilier. A year later the company tried to place about 11 percent of its capital in France through a secondary offering, an offering undoubtedly emanating from Russian insiders seeking to reduce their increased commitments in the face of uncertainty. These shares went begging in France, and the question of control was already posed. One French financial journal concluded that Briansk's bonds were well secured and fitted the desires of small French capitalists, but that these small investors would long be wary of the shares of an exclusively Russian company.[9]

Actually there were merger discussions with the famous French-owned Huta-Bankova Steel Company, the largest producer in tsarist Poland and the oldest, brightest jewel of the Bonnardel Group in Russia. The Bonnardel Group, an informal grouping of firms around the very wealthy Lyons capitalist Jean Bonnardel, was the most consistently successful and

---

[8] C.L., Briansk, Note, Apr. 1900.

[9] *Le Pour et le Contre*, 24 Aug. 1891, in Archives Nationales, Paris, France (hereafter cited as A.N.), 65 AQ, K 30. This box contains literally hundreds of clippings on Briansk from French-language financial journals over more than twenty-five years. It was of the greatest usefulness in clarifying certain points in Briansk's evolution.

largest amalgam of foreign-controlled firms in Russia.[10] This group was clearly Briansk's equal. Perhaps that was the problem. So nearly equal, though with somewhat different assets, that there was no agreement concerning who would absorb whom and which group of managers would step aside.[11] So Briansk expanded its plants, while the Bonnardel Group's Huta-Bankova Company founded its own large integrated producer in the Donets Basin.

Yet collaboration if not merger continued, even if we cannot trace every step of the relationship with exactitude. While the possibilities of merger were being explored, the Russian and French businessmen examined the problem of raw materials necessary for southern production. This resulted in the formation of the Dubovaia Balka Mining Company in late 1892, after fifteen months of negotiations to purchase the extremely rich Krivoi Rog iron deposits from the heirs of Alexander Pol'. The Bonnardel Group's Huta-Bankova agreed prior to incorporation to buy from Dubovaia Balka for fifteen years all ore needed by its new southern subsidiary, built in part because the merger talks with Briansk had failed. Alexis Goriainov, the director of Briansk's Ekaterinoslav plant, was one of the founders of the new mining firm. Yet the mining firm's tie to Huta was clearly stronger, even though Huta took only 5 percent of the mining firm's capital. The two French firms (Dubovaia Balka and Huta-Bankova) were apparently closely associated, though ownership and management were not identical.

These details are important for understanding Briansk's evolution leading to the 1900–1902 confrontation. As the tempo of industry and speculation quickened in 1895, the ties between Briansk and Dubovaia Balka Mining Company grew tighter in three joint ventures. The first of these was the Ekaterinovka Coal Mining Company, directed by the Frenchmen from Dubovaia Balka (Paul Bayard, Theodore Motet, René Raoul-Duval), with two directors from Briansk (Alexis Goriainov, the southern plant manager, and his top assistant, the Frenchman Modeste Pierronne). Briansk soon became a major customer of this coal company. A second firm founded in early 1895, the South Russian Mechanical Engineering Company, contained the same cast, plus another Goriainov from St. Petersburg.[12] The third firm was the Kerch Metallurgical Company, which ushered in the third stage of Briansk's development.

Briansk's interest in yet a third major plant was symptomatic of the boom conditions of the late 1890s, conditions that Briansk enjoyed as much

[10] McKay, *Pioneers for Profit*, 337–67.
[11] The financial press believed this the case; for example, *Le Journal Financier*, 31 July 1892, in A.N., 65 AQ, K 30.
[12] McKay, *Pioneers for Profit*, 357–60.

as any of the foreign firms in southern Russia. Profits rose more than threefold, from 1,220,000 rubles in 1892 to a peak of 4,010,000 rubles in 1897. Capital had necessarily been increased, but by only 50 percent in the same period. Demand for metallurgical products was firm and so were prices. Except for a few pessimists worried about the consequences of such rapid expansion, the biggest uncertainty for the steel industry seemed to be on the supply side, specifically the availability of adequate iron ore.

The exceptionally rich and easily mined ore of Krivoi Rog had served well for ten years, but by 1895 fears of rapid exhaustion of and high prices for Krivoi Rog ores encouraged leading firms to seek alternative supplies in the south, which in practice meant the enormous low-grade deposits on the Kerch Peninsula on the Sea of Azov. With reserves estimated at 700,000,000 tons in 1903, or ten times those of Krivoi Rog at that time, Kerch ores resembled those of the Luxembourg field of western Europe, although they were actually more difficult from a technical point of view. But they were cheap: not more than 30 or 40 percent of the price for Krivoi Rog ore per unit of pure iron.[13] That Briansk became interested in this alternative source of supply while most firms continued to focus on Krivoi Rog, and then sought to reap large gains from these low-quality ores, shows the company's undiminished aggressiveness and imagination. Yet the project failed, and we must look closely to understand why.

Preliminary investigations in 1895 had led Briansk to lease almost 20,000 hectares of iron ore deposits at Kerch for thirty-six years, with the right of renewal for an equal period.[14] Initially Briansk used some of these ores in briquette form after shipping them by water and rail to the main plant at Ekaterinoslav. Judging by the experiences of the two Belgian companies on the Kerch Peninsula, and the Kerch Company itself later on, this involved technical difficulties that made such shipments of doubtful value. With market conditions excellent, the Russian directors then decided in 1897 that Briansk should build another vast integrated steel mill at Kerch itself to utilize the great quantities of cheap ore there. It was soon apparent, however, that Briansk by itself would lack the financial resources for such an expensive undertaking.

In these conditions the top Russian directors of Briansk, who had previously used foreign technicians and investors in subordinate positions, followed the lead of employees like plant manager Goriainov and moved much closer to foreign businessmen. They formed the kind of implicit Russian-foreign partnership often seen in new firms in Russia during the surging 1890s. Although the contours of this specific pooling of interests

13 Ibid., 129–31.
14 A.N., 65 AQ, K 118, Kerch, Prospectus, 1895.

are at points somewhat obscure, it is possible to think of this cooperative effort as a tenuous fusion of foreign and domestic business elites, both supported by their respective political elites, with which they overlapped. Concretely this meant an agreement between Briansk and the directors of Dubovaia Balka and the South Russian Mechanical Engineering Company to incorporate and complete the Kerch undertaking jointly.

There was apparently some hard negotiating, but the Kerch Metallurgical Company was incorporated in late 1898 with the joint-stock capital of 10,000,000 rubles divided equally between the partners. Yet whereas the Banque Suisse et Française subscribed one-half of Kerch's capital for the French founders and insiders in cash, the Briansk Company received 5,000,000 rubles in shares and 1,350,000 rubles in debt for purchases and investments made prior to incorporation. Briansk was no doubt overpaid for its contribution, and could expect a large profit if Kerch shares could be sold in France at anything near par. Such was the case when soon after incorporation the French bank sold 3,000,000 rubles of Briansk's Kerch shares to French investors for 3,600,000 rubles.[15] This rapid liquidation of Kerch shares suggests that Briansk's directors regarded the whole affair more as a short-term speculation than a long-term investment. Yet Briansk certainly remained involved. And when the Kerch Company increased its capital by 5,000,000 rubles in 1899, Briansk subscribed almost one-third of the issue, with funds borrowed specifically for that purpose from the Banque Suisse et Française.

This increase was also insufficient. By 1900 Kerch's second mammoth blast furnace neared completion, and more funds were required. Briansk, however, was beginning to have problems of its own. Profits were off sharply in 1899 and even more so in the economic crisis of 1900. The company's expansion program at its two existing plants also required funds. Little wonder, then, that once the Russian central bank, the State Bank, decided to make exceptional loans to major Russian firms to help them through the crisis, Briansk received such a loan. Under the close supervision of Finance Minister Sergei Witte, the State Bank advanced Briansk 5,000,000 rubles in November 1899 on the security of 8,000,000 rubles of its authorized but unsold first-mortgage bonds. The pride of the steel industry, from the Russian point of view, deserved government support at another critical moment.

At the same time Briansk was securing a state loan, however, its "Russian" character was fading fast. Rapidly rising profits in the steel industry had brought an even faster rise in stock prices. The price of

15 I. F. Gindin, "Neustavnye ssudy Gosudarstvennogo banka i ekonomicheskaia politika tsarkogo pravitel'stva," *Istoricheskie zapiski*, 35:107–8.

Briansk common advanced from a high of 133 rubles as late as 1893 to a high of 557 rubles during 1896, with a yearly high of 523 rubles in 1899, after fluctuating between 450 and 550 rubles in the three preceding years.[16] These fantastic moves, coupled with inside knowledge of anything but a sky-blue future, led Briansk's owner-managers to liquidate their holdings. Prince Tenishev led the way in 1896, when he retired from the company with a great fortune; Golubev and other insiders followed suit in 1899. With the aid of clever but unscrupulous intermediaries, they passed their shares to small investors in France at very high prices for great profits.[17] No doubt the French partners in the Kerch Company helped in these secondary distributions. The result was that Briansk, the pride of Russian metallurgy, was approximately 90 percent French-owned by 1900.[18]

Yet the Russian directors had no intention of meekly turning over leadership to an army of small foreign investors. Therefore, to provide Briansk with funds for current operations, perhaps to pay inflated dividends, and certainly to maintain a lever for control, the Russian insiders advanced from their own pockets short-term loans of at least 5,000,000 rubles at high interest rates. The calling, or threat of calling, these loans would at least allow continued and profitable control of the company, and quite probably would provide a means of manipulation and improper if substantial gains at the expense of French shareholders in the worsening economic crisis.

This strategy might well have succeeded if the fate of Briansk had been the sole consideration. French banking and financial circles in general, and the men from Dubovaia Balka in particular, were certainly not above shearing the French investing public. And that public seldom succeeded in defending its own interests, unless they coincided with those of the rich and the powerful. Yet this was precisely the case. The Dubovaia Balka and Mechanical Engineering companies and their directors Motet and Gorjeu, with their connections with leading brokers and bankers in Lyons and Paris and frequent participations in the loosely constructed Bonnardel Group, were very much concerned with the Kerch Company,

---

16 Ibid., 106.

17 One of many articles planted in the French financial press burns with an excitement that the investor was, and no doubt is, almost invariably ill advised to follow. Noting that Briansk shares were certain to rise, "We are making a pressing appeal for our readers and subscribers to buy without delay. For they would regret to see pass by without profit the great rise which this stock is going to take and which will carry it rapidly, in a few months, [from 1,407 francs] to around 2,000 francs [750 rubles]." Profits would be all the greater since a margin of 35 percent would require investment of only 500 francs per share. *Le Portefeuille Français*, 1 Jan. 1899, in A.N., 65 AQ, K 30.

18 A.N., F 30, 343, Briansk, Delcassé to Caillaux, 18 Dec. 1900.

where their money and reputations were invested. Briansk's Russian directors felt otherwise, for they had recouped much of Briansk's original investment. They preferred to sever their ties with Kerch and its French directors now that possible losses there clearly exceeded probable gains.

In the face of these divergent aims and interests, the original partnership of the two business elites exploded in bitter and violent estrangement. In the first months of 1900 the French financial press began to attack the secret dealings and alleged incompetence of Briansk's Russian management, and called for a committee of foreign shareholders to place French representatives upon the board of directors.[19] The French group leading Kerch (Motet, Gorjeu, etc.) was preparing a power play extremely rare under nineteenth-century capitalism, and probably unique in Franco-Russian business relations. Mobilizing disgruntled stockholders, they ousted Briansk's Russian management in a successful proxy fight. Petrovskii and Golubev were forced to resign at the annual meeting in late June 1900. Alexis Goriainov, who had long been cooperating with Motet and Gorjeu while Briansk plant manager at Ekaterinoslav, was chosen president. Motet and Gorjeu became board members and the powers behind the throne.

The displaced Russians promptly called in all their loans to Briansk. These loans now totaled 8,000,000 rubles and had to be repaid at any cost if the firm were not to go into bankruptcy, where the Russian creditors would again take control.[20] Motet, Gorjeu, and their associates then tapped their enormous financial resources and paid in full. They also negotiated with the Société Générale of France an 8,000,000-ruble increase of Briansk's capital to reimburse themselves and their bankers. This successful increase came at the beginning of 1901, near the very depth of the panic, and its success is indicative of the power, resources, and determination of the French group.

The former Russian directors fought back. "The projected capital increase raised a veritable tempest of protest" from them at what must have been an extraordinarily wild meeting in January 1901.[21] First the ousted Russians challenged the powers of foreign shareholders, pointing to article 55, which stated that no participant could represent more than two shareholders. Indeed, agreed the French, but only insofar as this did not contradict article 57, which allowed shareholders with less than twenty shares to choose a single representative to vote up to one-tenth of the firm's total capital. When criticized for continuing Briansk's investments, particularly

[19] For example, *Paris-Bourse*, 11 June 1900, in A.N., 65 AQ, K 30.
[20] A.N., F 30, 343, Delcassé to Caillaux, 18 Dec. 1900.
[21] *Banque Privée*, 30 Jan. 1901.

those in the Kerch Company, the French administrators explained how and why their hand had been forced by the previous Russian directors. Unalterably opposed to the increase of capital, the Russians said that even if the French majority voted affirmatively, it made no difference, implying that they would secure an administrative veto after taking their case to the minister of finance. As one French financial sheet put it, "in reality they still consider themselves the sole proprietors of the company; the foreigners are permitted to put in their money and nothing more. They regard the intervention of foreigners on the board of directors as an intrusion, and for a little they would decree that profits are to be distributed only among Russian shareholders."[22]

The increase in capital and continued investment in the faltering Kerch Company were the immediate and ostensible source of conflict between the two business elites. Whereas the French sought to hold Briansk and Kerch together so that neither would be sacrificed, the previous Russian directors felt an otherwise sound Briansk was being compromised in stubborn folly. But there was more involved. As I have suggested, Briansk was the great all-Russian success in the southern steel industry, a firm intimately linked to state policies and administrators. Kerch was a hastily conceived unfinished Franco-Russian speculation, a product of a fleeting insatiable foreign demand for Russian securities. From the point of view of the former Russian directors, Briansk was the lasting concern and Kerch only a momentary excess.

As the special meeting showed, the determined and resourceful former Russian directors encouraged their old collaborators in the Russian administration to take up the gauntlet and reverse the foreign decisions. In the light of subsequent developments, we can see that they found a sympathetic hearing in the bureaucracy, though we do not know to what extent they created such support or only tapped it. Most probably the Russian political elite already shared the feelings of the old directors and willingly took their place vis-à-vis the French. The French business elite had won the first round, but the contest was far from over.

The state and its energetic minister of finance, Sergei Witte, were already deeply involved. One legacy of the Russian directors was the large loan of November 1899 from the State Bank. The French interests quite naturally sought to maintain or extend such credit as the financial needs of Briansk and Kerch were met as a whole, while Witte and the State Bank looked toward recovering their advances. Thus a series of discussions between the French and the State Bank resulted in firm proposals in October 1901.

[22] Ibid.

The French conceded that French firms in Russia could not expect long-term loans from the State Bank, and agreed to repay the State Bank as soon as possible. In the meantime they sought temporary advances for both firms through Briansk. The actual proposal was this: The 8,000,000 rubles of Briansk obligations held by the State Bank would be sold in Paris for 7,000,000 rubles, of which 2,000,000 would go to reduce the State Bank's advances from 6,000,000 to 4,000,000. Of the remaining 5,000,000 rubles, Briansk would loan 2,500,000 rubles to Kerch. The State Bank's loan of 4,000,000 rubles to Briansk was to be secured by 6,000,000 rubles of authorized but unsold first-mortgage bonds of the Kerch Company.

Yet Kerch had at least three strikes against it as far as the state was concerned. It was an overcapitalized and poorly executed speculation; it was now largely French and should therefore depend on Frenchmen for financial resources; and its completion only promised to exacerbate the overproduction crisis in the steel industry. Therefore Witte and the State Bank refused to finance Kerch in any way, directly or indirectly, and made any further loans to Briansk dependent upon Briansk's agreement to stop financing Kerch as long as any loans from the State Bank were outstanding.

This ran counter to the French group's fundamental goal and was thus unacceptable. In a complicated set of moves, the French group then provided new money for Kerch while making Briansk underwrite the considerable risks of such an operation—exactly what the Russians, both private and official, had sought to prevent. In essence the mechanism was the following: Briansk bought the 6,000,000 rubles of unsold Kerch first-mortgage bonds for 4,500,000. Since Briansk had no funds for such a purchase, it borrowed the money it paid Kerch from the French bankers. (Kerch already owed Briansk 1,500,000 rubles, so received only 3,000,000 rubles in cash.) Kerch thus received funds from the French, but the money first passed by way of Briansk, by far the stronger credit risk.[23]

[23] Gindin, "Neustavnye ssudy," 108; 65 AQ, K 118, Report to Kerch Shareholders, 11 Feb. 1902. Actually the matter was a good deal more complicated, and although the French archives are apparently fuller than the Russian ones in this respect (Gindin, 111), some questions remain regarding these contracts. As the Crédit Lyonnais engineer said, the ties between Kerch and Dubovaia Balka (Motet, Gorjeu, and associates) were "exceedingly close and exceedingly obscure," no doubt intentionally so.

Briansk apparently "bought" the Kerch bonds for 4,500,000 by borrowing that sum from the French. Specifically, the Banque Suisse et Française, representing the Motet group of insiders, advanced the down payment of 1,500,000 rubles to Briansk, with 18,000 shares of Kerch common stock owned by Briansk as security. Then a syndicate headed by the Société Générale guaranteed that Briansk would pay Kerch the remaining 3,000,000 rubles, and immediately advanced that sum to Kerch for Briansk's account. The key was what would happen if Briansk were unable to pay this 3,000,000 rubles that the Société Générale had advanced Kerch on Briansk's behalf. Almost assuredly Briansk was to pay a penalty of 1,000,000 rubles to the Banque

This arrangement left Briansk holding the bag and was actually a qualified victory for the French point of view. Since the State Bank's initial loan of November 1899 to Briansk was for only nine months, the bank had to agree, at the very least, to renew its credit. If not, Briansk might well come crashing down not only with Kerch but with other firms sucked into a wave of bankruptcies. The State Bank grudgingly renewed its credit three times before the final solution of the whole question in late 1902.

For a time it was touch and go, and the French Foreign Office felt it necessary to exert very strong pressure on the Russian government, at the request of the Kerch and Société Générale directors, to secure these renewals. In October 1901 Motet complained bitterly of the Russian government's hostility, in a private audience with the French minister of finance, Caillaux. Motet claimed that Witte had maliciously refused Kerch the right to import coal duty-free from Turkey for that portion of pig iron that would be sold abroad and for which Kerch had a large order. "There is," he said, "an implacable desire to ruin the industries in which French capitalists are interested. Thus some Russians want the crisis in metallurgy to worsen."[24]

These incidents, combined with as yet unsuccessful attempts to gain approval of the metallurgical syndicates, led to formal requests to aid Briansk when Vishnegradskii, the director of credit operations at the Russian Ministry of Finance, spoke with Caillaux in Paris in October 1901. Vishnegradskii subsequently wrote that he had spoken to Witte, who said he would do what he could for the French in Briansk, in contrast to previous refusals to do anything.[25] The scarcely veiled threat was that the collapse of French industrial societies would lead the French to close or restrict their credit markets to future demands from their Russian ally.[26] Thus the State Bank's reluctant extension of its loan to Briansk was a real achievement for the French directors, who refused to sever the Briansk-Kerch tie.

The French chargé d'affaires in St. Petersburg, Boutiron, summed up the results of the temporary agreement in a November 1901 note to the

---

Suisse et Française, the original agent for the Kerch bonds, which then had the option to fulfill Briansk's original contract with Kerch. In that event the Société Générale syndicate would receive its original 3,000,000 rubles, while the Banque Suisse et Française would purchase the Kerch obligations from Briansk for 2,000,000 rubles (3,000,000 minus the 1,000,000 penalty from Briansk). Thus the Banque Suisse et Française would end up paying a total of 3,500,000 rubles in all for the Kerch bonds and 18,000 shares of Kerch stock. Admittedly these arrangements are complex, but they must be spelled out if one is to understand the intricacies of subsequent negotiations.

[24] A.N., F 30, 343, Caillaux, undated note [Oct. 1901].
[25] A.N., F 30, 343, Vishnegradskii to the French director of funds, 29 Oct. 1901.
[26] A.N., F 30, 343, notes, 10 and 22 Nov. 1901.

minister of foreign affairs, Théophile Delcassé. Noting that he had seconded the Société Générale's director Dorizon in his last negotiations in St. Petersburg with the State Bank, he exulted that "there is reason to think that at this moment the sum necessary to save Kerch from imminent collapse is already united. . . . The support which it has just received from your excellency makes it possible to believe that at the least it will be able to exist long enough to reform itself, sell its assets, or merge with another firm." Boutiron noted that Kerch's previous mistakes would always make it the justified object of suspicion, whereas the saving of Briansk was much more appreciated by Russian officials.[27] Yet whatever the uncertainties, there was only a "little more hope for Briansk than for Kerch." The implication was clear: the two might sink or swim, but they would do so together.

This credit arrangement in late 1901 permitted the Kerch Company to complete almost all of its plant by the middle of 1902. Open-hearth furnaces for Thomas steel-refining and most of the rolling mills of an enormous integrated producer were then finished. The company was no longer pursuing panic exportation of pig iron at sacrifice prices, but was beginning to produce finished products for the domestic market. If Russia had not been in the midst of a depression, and if the firm's resources had not been exhausted, there would have been reason for cautious optimism.

The situation was in fact desperate, and some type of financial reorganization of Kerch was inescapable. Such a reorganization, a common enough occurrence under nineteenth-century capitalism and particularly endemic in early twentieth-century Russia, would have forced shareholders to take losses to attract new capital on preferred terms.[28] Once again negotiations were inevitable, since Kerch's major creditor, Briansk, was in turn dependent upon the Russian state and the French capitalists.

In July 1902 Dorizon of the Société Générale advanced new propositions. Although Kerch would be completed in September, he said, it would close its doors due to lack of working capital, and Briansk's investments there would finally end. Yet Briansk's outstanding short-term debt to French bankers of almost 6,000,000 rubles was a "grave threat."[29] If no arrangement were reached, then Briansk itself would also suspend payments, and lengthy bankruptcy proceedings would begin. Kerch would pass for a very low price to the foreign syndicate holding Kerch bonds. Neither development was desirable, according to Dorizon, so he proposed that the state

[27] A.N., F 30, 343, Boutiron to Delcassé, 11 Nov. 1901.
[28] On financial reorganization in Russia, see McKay, *Pioneers for Profit*, 225–32.
[29] A.N., F 30, 343, Louis Dorizon to Witte, 1/14 July 1902 (July 1 by the Russian calendar, July 14 by the Western).

buy the Kerch bonds from Briansk at their face value of 6,000,000 rubles, and receive the 18,000 shares of Kerch from Briansk as a bonus. Witte refused, noting the unsatisfactory financial condition of Kerch and reiterating his earlier demand of a clean break between the two steel companies.

At this point the French again applied heavy political and financial pressure. A rumor that both the State Bank and the Société Générale would shortly call in their loans to Briansk sent Briansk's battered stock plunging again from 113 rubles to 90 rubles on the Paris exchange. Caillaux, the French minister of finance, warned again of the seriousness of such a bankruptcy for Russia's general credit-rating and for the French government as well, since it had permitted the official listing of Briansk in France.

In the face of these pressures Witte was seemingly forced to make new offers. He now agreed that the State Bank would advance Briansk an additional 3,000,000 rubles on the security of an additional 4,000,000 rubles of first-mortgage bonds. But there were conditions: the Société Générale was to guarantee the sale of the Kerch bonds for what Briansk had originally paid (4,500,000 rubles), and also guarantee to sell the State Bank's old Briansk obligations for what the State Bank had paid.[30] Witte had been forced to retreat, as Gindin cautiously puts it. Others would say this was a prime example of French diplomatic pressure and financial blackmail of a dependent tsarist government.

The question requires careful scrutiny. Certainly there was pressure and a subsequent Russian offer. The difficulty lies in appraising the offer. Here the views of the other side in the negotiations, the French businessmen of the Société Générale, strongly suggest that Witte had shrewdly retreated—to a quite unacceptable offer. In doing so he could appear to yield to pressure, while in fact he maintained his basic position: the separation of Briansk and Kerch, which would permit him to support Briansk better and block Kerch more effectively.

Witte's "concessions" emphatically rejected any arrangement permitting Kerch to receive another million from Briansk as a penalty payment, a payment coming indirectly from the State Bank. Moreover, the Société Générale was asked to guarantee emissions of bonds amounting to 11,-500,000 rubles in order that Briansk might receive an additional 3,000,000 rubles. Put another way, the Société Générale would through its guarantees increase its commitment from 3,000,000 rubles to 14,500,000, while the State Bank would reduce its commitment from 7,000,000 to 3,000,000. In reporting this offer, Rocherand, the Société Générale representative in St. Petersburg, boiled over in anger:

[30] A.N., F 30, 343, Rocherand to Dorizon, 14 Sept. 1902.

The honorable governor of the State Bank [Pleske, a close Witte associate] was certainly right in saying in July that he would not treat the Société Générale as an equal [in this matter]! And today the State Bank informs Briansk that discussions concerning the sale of some rights to mines at the Krivoi Rog would be very bad for the loan negotiations. They do not want Briansk, a *Russian company*, to sell its minerals to a *French company;* they do not want that sale to serve to reimburse a French creditor!

Believe me, my dear director, the national question first, and the hostility against the Société Générale second, play a dominating role in all this affair. They want to push us out of Briansk and they would like to have us reimburse them before we go, which is outrageous. They don't say it openly—that would be too maladroit—but they prepare the ways.

Thus Pleske discreetly praises our financial control of Briansk but he has Kokchorov [the State Bank's representative on Briansk's board of directors] tell me twice that such control runs counter to the company's statutes and that the State Bank will ask that it be lifted before the 3,000,000 ruble loan. No doubt they will allow me on the Board, but only after renouncing my appointment as [financial] auditor.

In closing, Rocherand summed up the discouragement of a frustrated man: "Wednesday I return to Paris, where I am called by family duties and affections which have been all too long sacrificed to the deceitful fantasies of Russian bureaucrats."[31]

Two weeks later an only slightly less discouraged French diplomatic representative in St. Petersburg reported that all the efforts of the financial groups interested in Kerch had failed after a year of constant work. Kerch had just filed for bankruptcy, and its great plant stood silent. The causes, he felt, were multiple. There had certainly been a lack of scruples on the part of the founders, French and Russian alike; a lack of adequate initial capital, which was difficult to remedy subsequently; the bad quality of the first products; and the chimerical vision of large export sales. "But also, and above all perhaps, Kerch falls because of the implacable will of Witte who, they say, wanted to make an example [of it]. Now Kerch lies a great dead body that a little breath would bring to life again. The company closes at the very moment it has purified its management, finished its installations, and transformed its production methods. . . . But the suspension of payments of this firm which became French, tied—whatever people may say—to the Société Générale, is a serious occurrence."

As for Briansk, "that other company tied even more tightly to the

31 A.N., F 30, 343, Société Générale, Rocherand to Dorizon, 14 Sept. 1902.

Société Générale," its credit was certainly threatened. If Briansk were to avoid following Kerch, "sacrifices" would be necessary at Paris and St. Petersburg. For the French owned the shares, and Briansk's insolvency would bring down other companies. "And the Imperial Administration cannot see 20,000 workers thrown out of work in the dead of winter, or the price of state bonds experience the effects of the fall of Briansk." Indeed the bankruptcy of Kerch had already caused the Ministry of Finance to change its position and advance important credits to Briansk, as a number of Russian banks were calling all their loans.[32]

With Kerch in bankruptcy, negotiations over Briansk resumed. There was a sense of urgency since part of Briansk's 3,000,000-ruble loan to the syndicate headed by the Société Générale fell due in November 1902. Dorizon could anticipate that some of the lenders in the syndicate would refuse to extend or modify the terms of Briansk's indenture, given the greater risk now involved. Similarly, Briansk still owed 1,500,000 rubles to the Banque Suisse et Française. Thus Dorizon and the Société Générale were not free agents, and the French Foreign Ministry was correct in stating that a lack of any agreement would mean bankruptcy or receivership for Briansk.[33]

A series of telegrams between Dorizon and Rocherand, which were passed to the anxious French Ministries of Finance and Foreign Affairs, allow us to follow the November negotiations between the Société Générale and the State Bank in detail. The following coded telegram was typical and marked a step toward agreement: "If Paul [code name for Pleske of the State Bank] will advance Bertha [Briansk] 3,000,000 rubles, would you prolong existing [Société Générale] loans for a period to be discussed, with the promise to sell Catherine [Kerch] bonds [to the public] for 4,500,000 rubles if [market] conditions permit, and buy for 3,000,000 if they do not?" Rocherand asked Dorizon.[34] Dorizon agreed on extending the credit, but refused to guarantee sale of the Kerch bonds for 3,000,000 rubles.

The terms of sale for the Kerch bonds were the key. In essence, was Briansk to be freed once and for all from Kerch with no additional loss, as the State Bank demanded, or was it going to be forced to honor contracts requiring it to pay yet one more million to disengage itself completely? (See n. 23, above.) At this point the Société Générale agreed to reimburse Briansk the 1,000,000-ruble penalty if the Société Générale were to sell the 6,000,000 rubles of Kerch obligations for even 2,000,000 rubles. Such a sale was extremely likely, and Rocherand reported that this concession made

---

[32] A.N., F 30, 343, Boutiron to Delcassé, 29 Sept. 1902.
[33] A.N., F 30, 343, Delcassé to Rouvier, 15 Nov. 1902.
[34] A.N., F 30, 343, 4 Nov. 1902.

a good impression on Pleske.[35] Agreement seemed likely as both sides awaited Witte's return to St. Petersburg ten days later. A relatively strong Briansk would stand alone once again, as the state had wished, and Motet and his associates in the Banque Suisse et Française would have the Kerch bonds and shares necessary for painful and unaided reorganization of Kerch.

Then thunder broke. To the amazement of all, Witte repudiated Pleske and went back to his original offer of September, which included guaranteeing the sale of the Kerch bonds for 4,500,000. "Paul [Pleske] considers this decision [of Witte's], taken after studying the matter and long discussion with him, as irrevocable. He seems quite shocked. At least this unbelievable decision ought to have the effect of disengaging our responsibility from the now inevitable consequences. Without instructions to the contrary I shall present bills of 450,000 rubles [to Briansk] the 20th Russian style and protest [their nonpayment] the 23rd."[36] Briansk was nine days from suspending payment—and the road to bankruptcy or receivership.

Witte's alleged reason for his about-face was a series of violent attacks in the Russian press criticizing the meddling of bureaucrats in private business matters.[37] In the light of past and future action, in Briansk and other firms, the historian would be forced to suppose that this reason was a smoke screen, but in this case he may be certain, because there is another telegram to Dorizon that is extremely instructive: "I have it from an intimate associate of Valentin's [Witte] that there is nothing to the refusal that it is the opposition to state control. Everything will work out if you succeed in having Rouvier [the minister of finance] wire Valentin demanding in the interest of French shareholders and the French stock exchange to support the Bertha and Catherine [Briansk and Kerch] affair. Act urgently. Obtain that request no matter what it costs. It is Valentin who asks it. Reply immediately. Alexis [Goriainov]."[38] One might say that Briansk's president, the talented flunky of the French, had every reason to push for such intervention and may have been manipulating on his own, although this seems very unlikely. For when he presented the whole question ten days after Briansk's bills were protested before the Committee of Ministers, Witte showed himself very much in control.

Witte's first arguments before the committee were familiar enough.

[35] A.N., F 30, 343, Société Générale, Dorizon to Rocherand and Rocherand to Dorizon, 11 Nov. 1902.
[36] Ibid., Rocherand to Dorizon, 26 Nov. 1902.
[37] Ibid., Rocherand to Dorizon, 24 Nov. 1902.
[38] A.N., F 30, 343, undated telegram [probably 27 or 28 Nov. 1902] to Dorizon.

Briansk's fall would hurt the credit of Russian firms in foreign markets and embarrass the French government. Briansk was also one of the best firms in Russia, not one of those that ought to disappear in the depression. Its collapse would bring big losses to other firms and would increase unemployment. So some intervention was necessary.

Shifting gears, Witte then turned to Kerch, the key to the matter as much for him as for the French. The French, he argued, must not be allowed to buy the Kerch bonds for 2,000,000 rubles and thereby obtain a plant in which 20,000,000 rubles had been invested. In the interests of the inflow of foreign capital, the tsarist government never intended that Russia's national patrimony would go into foreign hands for almost nothing. And if the French bought the Kerch plant, it could be completely finished by adding a few rolling mills. "This would deal a most severe blow not only to Briansk but also to our other metallurgical firms, since it is well known to all that in view of favorable natural conditions the Kerch Company is able to manufacture products cheaper than all the other plants, which would have very weighty consequences for the present overproduction in the iron industry." Thus Witte concluded that "support for the Briansk Company ought to be taken in such a way that it would remove at the same time the danger of a rapid reopening of the Kerch affair."

This indefinite mothballing of the Kerch Company could best be done by having the State Bank buy the Kerch first-mortgage bonds for 4,500,000 rubles. "But it will be extremely inconvenient for the State Bank to take on itself the role of creditor seeking the declaration of insolvency for the Kerch Company, all the more so since in the present case insolvency will result in the loss of the shareholders' capital, which was realized for the most part in France." Thus "it follows to acknowledge as preferable that the declaration of Kerch's insolvency result from the demand of the present owner or the creditors"—that is, the demand of Briansk or the French banks.[39]

The final agreement, reached in St. Petersburg after Witte called Dorizon there, apparently follows Witte's recommendation to the Committee of Ministers to the letter. The State Bank agreed to buy the Kerch obligations from Briansk for 4,500,000—but only after Kerch was formally declared bankrupt. Briansk agreed to break all ties of any kind with its ill-fated foundling immediately, and received an additional loan of 5,000,000 rubles from the State Bank, 1,500,000 of which was used to pay off at once the Banque Suisse et Française. The Société Générale extended its credit of 3,000,000 rubles to Briansk. It also promised to float Briansk's bonds "as

39 Witte's presentation is in Gindin, "Neustavnye ssudy," 111–12.

soon as the market permitted," thereby permitting Briansk to pay off the Société Générale loan and most of its indebtedness to the State Bank. Thus Briansk bonds were to be sold abroad to pay off the State Bank and the Société Générale, while Briansk was to sell the Kerch mortgage bonds to the State Bank without loss. Briansk's financial position and prospects were thereby considerably improved, while Kerch, the "great dead body waiting only for a breath to resurrect it," was to decompose gradually in the hands of the state for the foreseeable future. The conclusion was certainly much different than anyone had expected, as Boutiron noted, but it fitted Witte's final plan very closely.

What did this extraordinary denouement signify? A victory for the forces of foreign financial capital in embryonic stage, a fair compromise, or, as I suggest, an extremely forceful defense of Russian interests by Russian public authority in the face of combined foreign economic and political pressure? Alternately, in terms of conflicting elites, it is reasonable to see the outcome as representing the ultimate triumph of the native Russian elite, vanquished at the private level but successful at the public level, over the foreign economic elite, supported by the foreign political elite.

This is clearly the implication of Witte's action, which was explained to the Committee of Ministers in the extraordinary document excerpted above. To the moment of Kerch's suspension of payments, Witte followed the line indicated by the ousted Russian directors and sought to liquidate Briansk's investments in order to insure the survival of one of "our oldest and most important firms," and the only major southern producer of totally Russian inspiration. To do so, the State Bank used its advance to Briansk to prevent Briansk and Kerch from being grafted together. This goal was realized with Kerch's suspension of payment. But that was not enough. Not only was Kerch to go bankrupt, but also the French must be denied the possibility of reorganizing their company and forced to accept a total loss on their investment. The State Bank's original loan to help the Russian firm was thus ultimately used to expropriate the Kerch shareholders and managers.

The State Bank paid 4,500,000 rubles for the Kerch bonds, as opposed to the 2,000,000 but most probably 3,000,000 the French were willing to pay. Yet all of this payment went to Briansk, whereas any reorganization by the French would have involved the participation of the original shareholders as well as the bondholders. This was so a fortiori since the bondholders (through the Banque Suisse et Française) and the shareholders were basically the same group—the French interests clustered around Motet and the Bonnardel Group.

There were at least three reasons for Witte's action. He had been seeking all along to make an example of Kerch as the type of unbridled speculation and undirected entrepreneurship the tsarist government would not accept, and certainly the lesson would be all the stronger if a leading foreign group learned that the most clever contracts were no match for the resolute hostility of the government. Second, Kerch was an ultra-modern plant, and its output would indeed weigh heavily on Russian metallurgical prices and complicate efforts to shore up the industry.[40] Third, there was the desire to give the appearance of compromise in order that relations with French capitalists might not deteriorate unnecessarily. All three might be considered aspects of the general policy on foreign capital and entrepreneurship, which sought to employ but direct the outsider.

Witte of course fell from office. Yet despite assertions to the contrary, unpredictable but effective government control of foreign business remained. Again Briansk is exemplary. Foreign investors, mainly French, increased their holdings to at least 95 percent of all the firm's capital in 1909. They subscribed to almost all of the 120,000 shares of 5 percent preferred stock in 1906, which doubled Briansk's outstanding capital and which paid back the loans of the State Bank and the Société Générale. (The Société Générale had concluded that preferred shares could be sold more easily than bonds.)

Yet there was no foreign control. A Crédit Lyonnais observer noted in February 1904 that "for several years the predominant influence in Briansk lay with the French represented by M. Motet and Gorjeu and with the Société Générale which had her own men [on the board]—Rocherand, Ferand, Kolb-Bernard. But since the State Bank intervened and took the Kerch obligations for its own account, the Russian element has taken the leadership, with Ivanov as the representative of the State Bank." Speaking of two French directors, in 1913 the same source stated that "it seems that these two personalities [from the Société Générale] ought to be without any influence on the management of the Briansk . . . where the Société Générale no longer has any loans and probably few shares or bonds."[41]

Apparently the fears of the French ambassador Bompard had been realized: "It should not be the case that now [1906] that the Société Générale's advances have been repaid that it relinquishes interest in the management of the Company."[42] Another analysis in 1906, from Pierre Darcy of the Banque de l'Union Parisienne, concluded that there was

---

[40] The technical reports from the Crédit Lyonnais make this clear. Gindin is mistaken to suppose the contrary ("Neustavnye ssudy," 112).

[41] C.L., Feb. 1904; Note, Jan. 1913.

[42] A.N., F 30, 340, Boutiron to the minister of foreign affairs, 30 Nov. 1906.

little risk in underwriting a public subscription of shares, since the commitment would be liquidated before Briansk's Russian managers might very well compromise the company again. Even so, it did not seem wise to seek any permanent control over Briansk, as that would bring responsibility for the management's actions. "If our Bank took that responsibility, simple surveillance would not suffice. We would need absolute control. In other words, the Bank would then need to substitute itself for all the old management, and that responsibility would be far from being compensated by the possible profits of such an action."[43] The lesson of Kerch had been learned well. Whoever might determine the ultimate destiny of Briansk—the representatives of the government, the increasingly autonomous and completely Russian managerial elite, or even the violent and discontented workers and their spokesmen—it would not be foreigners.

I think the successful defense of Russian interests in the face of French pressure has bearing on the general study of elites. As I suggested at the beginning, this episode may be conceived of as a particularly well documented example of the interaction of conceptually and factually distinct elites in conflict. On one hand there was the French business elite, supported by the French political elite, and on the other hand the Russian business elite, which was subsequently replaced by the political elite. The members of these elites interacted and came into conflict on a specific issue as they sought incompatible goals. And in the end the Russian political elite imposed its will upon the foreign business elite.

In placing this case study within the framework of interacting elites, we have approached elite study in an atypical manner. As the essays in this book indicate, studies on elites normally focus on a single elite or compare elites separated by time and space. This is convenient of course, and to the extent that investigators see themselves as studying functional elites there is no particular problem. The elite is simply the upper portion of the many groups making up a society—the military elite, the business elite, the religious elite, the cultural elite, the labor elite, and so on.[44] "Elite" is an elegant term for the leadership group—not much more, not much less—and therefore is useful in historical and empirical research.

Opposed to this demystified view of society as containing many leadership nuclei drawn from the various areas of human activity, which are labeled (functional) elites, there is the grander concept of a dominant or hegemonial elite at the top of society. This dominant elite draws upon different subordinate functional elites, but it is the *real* elite—the power

---

[43] Banque de l'Union Parisienne, Russie, no. 47, Report on Briansk, 12 July 1906.
[44] For example, the studies in Seymour Lipset and Aldo Solari, eds., *Elites in Latin America* (New York, 1967).

elite, the military-industrial complex elite, the ruling class, or whatever. While it is impossible to delve into the relationship that may theoretically or empirically exist between functional elites on one hand and a ruling class on the other, I point out that the two concepts are very different. Thus one finds the rubric "elite" covering dissimilar if not contradictory concepts of multiple interacting elites, which may compete for status and power, even though only one is studied at a time, and a ruling elite, homogeneous enough to concentrate status and power capable of dominating a society.

It seems to me that students of elites have not adequately elucidated this ambivalent and ambiguous character of elite study. Perhaps they never will, since the intellectual antecedents of elite study draw from highly divergent schools of thought.[45] In any event, historians and contemporary investigators should recognize the somewhat uncertain conceptual, or theoretical, underpinnings of elite study, and should not assume a conceptual elegance that does not exist. They should also remember—as economic historians like myself, both "old" and "new," now acknowledge in private if not always in public—that such clarification and elegance will come as much from empirical investigations as from increased speculative activity, which must not be allowed to wander oblivious to concrete and complex data.

With this in mind, Briansk emerges as a good example of the inadequately analyzed process of the interaction between conceptually distinct elites that overlap in practice with other elites. These elites may be seen initially as the foreign and indigenous business elites, and subsequently as the foreign business elite and the Russian political elite. The process of interaction between these elites shows how difficult it is, at least in this case, to think of some real elite mysteriously merging and dominating the subordinate elites that conflict so sharply. It is also an example of how a political elite may impose its will on the economic elite, contrary to what a vulgar economic determinism would suggest. In the Briansk affair, as elsewhere, the political tail is quite capable of wagging the economic dog.

[45] See T. B. Bottomore, *Elites and Society* (New York, 1964), for one interesting discussion of the whole question.

The Survival of the Victorian Aristocracy

WALTER L. ARNSTEIN

The British aristocracy has been at once the most easily definable and one of the most elusive of historical upper classes.[1] An individual either was a member of the hereditary peerage or was not. Thus it is possible to state with confidence that in 1830 there were 304 peers of the realm (i.e., dukes, marquesses, earls, viscounts, and barons with the right to sit in the House of Lords) and that in 1896 there were 502.[2] Yet as J. H. Hexter observed in connection with the historical controversy over the "rise of the gentry" in Tudor and early Stuart England, the difference between peers and other landed gentlemen was a legal rather than a significant social one: "Neither a distinctive economic class nor a clear-cut prestige group, peerage was a legal status constituted as a consequence of the past favor of English monarchs. Collectively, but not individually, the peers were the first gentlemen of England in honor and wealth, clearly distinct from the rest neither in source of livelihood nor in way of life."[3] The distinction Patrick Colquhoun drew in 1814—between the 576 families in the United Kingdom who constituted the "Highest Orders," and the "Second Class" of 46,861 families of "Baronets, Knights, Country Gentlemen, and others having large incomes"—remained socially and economically equally elusive. It is well to remember, moreover, that both classes combined made up less than 1.4 percent of all the families in the kingdom.[4] The English aristocracy,

[1] I am grateful to the members of the graduate research seminar in British history at the University of Illinois during the spring semester of 1970 for exploring with me many of the questions raised in this essay.

[2] The 26 bishops, the 16 representative Scottish peers, the 28 representative Irish peers, and the royal princes are excluded from this tally. *British Almanack* (London, 1830), 35; (1896), 48.

[3] J. H. Hexter, *Reappraisals in History* (Evanston, Ill., 1961), 128.

[4] Patrick Colquhoun, *A Treatise on the Wealth, Power and Resources of the British Empire* (London, 1814), cited in J. F. C. Harrison, ed., *Society and Politics in England, 1780–1960* (New York, 1965), 7–8. Discussing the late seventeenth-century

F. M. L. Thompson has suggested, is "only another word for the greater owners of land."[5]

Foreign observers like Alexis de Tocqueville in 1833 have been most impressed by the ease with which the British aristocracy opened its ranks, in contrast to continental aristocracies,[6] and it remains true that over the centuries the makeup of the peerage was continually altered by new accessions. William Pitt the younger suggested in the 1780s that any man with an income of £20,000 a year ought to be made a peer, and during his prime ministership he recommended ninety-two new creations to King George III, partly as a substitute for more materialistic forms of political reward.[7] In the process, Pitt did more to bring political power and social prestige to men who were already landed gentlemen than to give distinction to commercial or industrial wealth (except at second or third remove). J. H. Plumb has indeed recently suggested that it was easier for "men of new wealth" to unseat or amalgamate with established elites in the early eighteenth century than in the late eighteenth or early nineteenth centuries.[8] In the nineteenth century, even as the total British population increased more rapidly than ever before, the rate of creations to the peerage declined to an average of little more than four a year between 1837 and 1866.[9]

Whatever may be said about the accessibility of the peerage—and it is well to keep in mind that accessions from below were more than balanced by the "downward mobility" of untitled younger sons—few historians have questioned the predominance of the aristocracy during the first decades of the nineteenth century. Elie Halévy's description is characteristic: "The aristocracy controlled all the machinery of government. It was supreme in both Houses of Parliament and disposed at pleasure of every

---

aristocracy, Peter Laslett agrees that "the peerage in England was for all purposes except the details of their status at one with the rest of the ruling segment," and that "the gap between those who were within and those who were outside the ruling group was greater than the gap between any two orders within the ruling group itself"; *The World We Have Lost* (London, 1965), 40–41.

[5] F. M. L. Thompson, *English Landed Society in the Nineteenth Century* (London, 1963), 28.

[6] Alexis de Tocqueville, *Journeys to England and Ireland*, ed. J. P. Mayer (New Haven, 1958), 43.

[7] G. M. Trevelyan, *British History in the Nineteenth Century and After* (London, 1937), 109f.; Archibald S. Foord, "The Waning of 'The Influence of the Crown,'" in R. L. Schuyler and H. Ausubel, eds., *The Making of English History* (New York, 1952), 406.

[8] J. H. Plumb, *The Origins of Political Stability in England, 1675–1725* (London, 1967), 6. See also W. L. Guttsman, *The British Political Elite* (London, 1963), 117.

[9] Ralph E. Pumphrey, "The Introduction of Industrialists into the British Peerage," *American Historical Review*, 65:1 (Oct. 1959), 4.

government office. All the local administration of the country was in its hands."[10]

What happened to the aristocracy thereafter? The customary verdict of English historians has been simple enough: the aristocracy gave way to the middle classes. For certain Marxist historians, the English "bourgeois revolution" had already taken place in the middle of the seventeenth century,[11] but most other historians have focused on the year 1832. That year marked "the bourgeois revolution" for Esmé Wingfield-Stratford. The middle class remains for Sir Charles Petrie the "dominating feature" of the Victorian scene. Yet another historian, J. F. C. Harrison, has noted recently that within the span of a single lifetime (of a man like Robert Owen, 1771–1858), "England passed from a small, agrarian, aristocratic society to an expanding, urbanized, middle-class nation. . . ."[12] American textbook authors have been happy to agree that 1832 "definitely established the supremacy of the middle class."[13]

At first glance, the facts do seem to speak for themselves. Did not the repeal of the Corn Laws in 1846 symbolize the subordination of agricultural to manufacturing interests? Was not the extension of the suffrage achieved by the Reform Act of 1832 multiplied several times over in the Reform Acts of 1867 and 1884? Did not the Secret Ballot Act of 1872 free the workingman from the fear that his vote might antagonize his employer, and the tenant from concern that his vote might anger his landlord? Did not the County Councils Act of 1888 democratize local government in the rural areas as it had been earlier democratized in the urban?

The generalizations of twentieth-century historians concerning the waning of the aristocracy and the waxing of democracy in Victorian England are not figments of fancy. They rest, in the first instance, upon an awareness of a long list of legislative reforms, and second, upon the express expectations, fears, and prognostications of the participants in what often seemed to be momentous constitutional battles.

Before the great Reform Act of 1832 was a fact, Radicals like Francis

[10] Elie Halévy, *England in 1815* (vol. I of *History of the English People in the Nineteenth Century*), tr. E. I. Watkin and D. A. Barker (London, 1961), 221 [first published in 1913].

[11] E.g., Christopher Hill, *The English Revolution* (London, 1955).

[12] Esmé Wingfield-Stratford, *Those Earnest Victorians* (New York, 1930), 102; Sir Charles Petrie, *The Victorians* (London, 1961), 29; Harrison, *Society and Politics*, 50.

[13] Edward McNall Burns, *Western Civilizations*, 6th ed. (New York, 1963), II, 715. For Goldwin Smith "the shift from landed aristocratic control to control by the commercial and industrial middle classes continued steadily" after 1832; *A History of England*, 3rd ed. (New York, 1966), 582. J. H. Hexter sees the middle class as receiving "a sort of hegemony over English society"; *Reappraisals in History*, 113.

Place had predicted that an aristocracy they described as "foolish and malicious" would "not govern this nation much longer, for the great moral and intellectual improvement of the masses has prepared them for assuming charge of the nation."[14] A youthful John Stuart Mill foresaw with surprising complacency the prospect of a revolution that would "exterminate every person in Great Britain and Ireland who has £500 a year."[15] Thomas Babington Macaulay characterized the national debate of 1832 as "the struggle which the middle classes in England are maintaining against an aristocracy,"[16] and according to John Wilson Croker, the leading Tory publicist of the day, the result would be "no King, no Lords, no inequalities in the social system; all will be levelled to the plane of petty shopkeepers and small farmers."[17] The events of 1832 were seen by some as a prelude to the horrors of the French Revolution, an era during which no institution would be safe. Even the less excitable Sir Robert Peel, Tory leader in the House of Commons, termed the act "a fatal precedent," and speculated that the British monarchy might last five years more at most.[18]

Even when the passage of the measure was followed by domestic peace, the duke of Wellington was convinced that "the revolution is made, that is to say power is transferred from one class of society, the gentleman of England professing the faith of the Church of England, to another class of society, the shopkeepers being dissenters from the church, many of them being Socinians [i.e., Unitarians], others atheists."[19] The young Tory Radical Benjamin Disraeli was persuaded that the measure had destroyed forever the "aristocratic principle" in England and had "virtually conceded the principle of Universal Suffrage."[20]

Foreign observers like the astute Alexis de Tocqueville, who visited England in 1833, did not discern a revolutionary beneath every parliamentary bed, and speculated that a cataclysmic transformation might yet be avoided. Yet Tocqueville saw the British Isles pervaded by "a spirit of discontent with the present and hatred of the past." Aristocracy was in decline, and in Britain as in America, "the century is primarily democratic. Democracy is like a rising tide."[21]

---

[14] Francis Place to John Cam Hobhouse (19 Dec. 1827), British Museum Add. Ms. 35,148, f. 8. I owe this quotation to Prof. Robert Zegger.

[15] Cited in Michael St. John Packe, *John Stuart Mill* (London, 1954), 103.

[16] Cited in Harrison, *Society and Politics*, 103.

[17] L. J. Jennings, ed., *The Croker Papers* (London, 1885), II, 113.

[18] *Hansard's Parliamentary Debates*, 3rd ser., 13 (1832), col. 426; Sir Denis LeMarchant, *Life of Althorp* (London, 1876), 255.

[19] Jennings, *Croker Papers*, II, 206.

[20] Benjamin Disraeli, *What Is He?* cited in B. R. Jerman, *The Young Disraeli* (Princeton, 1960), 180; cited in J. R. M. Butler, *The Passing of the Great Reform Bill* (London, 1914), 245.

[21] Tocqueville, *Journeys to England and Ireland*, 52, 54.

How fascinatingly different was the verdict of foreign observers fifty years later. For the American consul Adam Badeau, writing in 1885,[22] aristocracy remained the pivot of English social and political life, and for Grant Allen, an American critic of 1900, aristocracy persisted as a "genuine and powerful living dragon."[23] Thoughtful English observers did not disagree. "In the constitution of English society at the present day," T. H. S. Escott wrote in 1879, "the three rival elements—the aristocratic, the democratic, and the plutocratic—are closely blended." But, Escott went on, "the aristocratic principle is still paramount, form[ing] the foundations of our social structure. . . ." Twenty-five years later Sidney Low agreed that it was singular how little the advance of democracy had led to the actual control of affairs by "persons belonging to the most numerous classes of the population."[24]

The best evidence for the manner in which the Victorian aristocracy had in typically feline fashion resisted its oft predicted extinction is furnished by Lord Salisbury's cabinet of 1895, "the last government in the Western world to possess all the attributes of aristocracy in working condition. . . ."[25] The British cabinet united the day-by-day management of the national government with the leadership of the legislature. At a time when the cabinet was indeed "gaining in political weight at the expense of the House of Commons,"[26] its head was Robert Arthur Talbot Gascoyne-Cecil, ninth earl and third marquess of Salisbury. He lived at Hatfield, the immense country estate north of London that had been the childhood home of Elizabeth I. Salisbury's distant ancestor William Cecil had served as Elizabeth I's chief minister; William's son Robert served in a similar capacity under King James I, who in due course named him first earl of Salisbury and granted him the royal residence at Hatfield.

Although the Salisbury of the 1890s was all too fearful that "now democracy is on top, and with it the personal and party system,"[27] he somehow managed to be secretary of state for India twice, foreign secretary twice, and now prime minister for a third time without ever cultivating or acquiring the common touch or even concealing his dislike for mobs of all

---

[22] Adam Badeau, *Aristocracy in England* (New York, 1885), esp. 5.

[23] Grant Allen, "The British Aristocracy," *Cosmopolitan*, 30 (1900), 657.

[24] T. H. S. Escott, *England: Her People, Polity, and Pursuits* (London, 1879), I, 22; Sidney Low, *The Governance of England* (London, 1904), 173.

[25] Barbara Tuchman, *The Proud Tower* (New York, 1966), 3. The first chapter of the book, "The Patricians," provides an instructive and elegant group pen-portrait. It is the source for much of the information in the paragraphs that follow.

[26] A. L. Lowell, *The Government of England* (New York, 1908), II, 513.

[27] Salisbury to Herbert Bismarck, cited in James Dukes, "Heligoland, Zanzibar, East Africa: German Politics and the Colonial Issue, 1884–1890," Ph.D. diss. (University of Illinois, 1970), 110.

kinds, "not excluding the House of Commons."[28] Salisbury served as prime minister and led the Government in the House of Lords. Leader of the House of Commons was Salisbury's nephew and eventual successor, Arthur James Balfour. Balfour was the epitome of the detached and urbane gentleman, a philosopher by avocation, a bachelor by preference. Balfour was of ancient Scottish lineage on his father's side, and both the namesake (Arthur) and the godson of the first duke of Wellington. Family marriages of his numerous aunts and uncles enabled him to "call cousins with half the nobility of England."[29]

Salisbury's secretary for war was the fifth marquess of Lansdowne and twenty-eighth lord of Kerry in a direct line. Lansdowne's grandfather had served as one of George III's prime ministers, and his father had been a member of seven cabinets between 1827 and 1857. Lansdowne himself had already served as governor-general of Canada and viceroy of India and was, the *Spectator* suggested in 1895, one of those Anglo-Irishmen "who can rule by a sort of instinct."[30] Another of Salisbury's leading colleagues was Spencer Compton Cavendish, the eighth duke of Devonshire and one of the nation's leading landlords and wealthiest men. He owned estates in Yorkshire, Lincolnshire, Cumberland, Sussex, Middlesex, and Ireland as well as his native Derbyshire, which he served as lord lieutenant. He had been a major parliamentary figure in the House of Commons from the 1860s until his father's death in 1891, and in 1895 he was also chancellor of Cambridge University and president of the British Empire League.

Although nine members of Salisbury's cabinet were members of the House of Lords, ten were elected members of the House of Commons. Thus it seems at first glance as if the commoners did constitute a narrow majority of the cabinet. But one of these "commoners" was A. J. Balfour, another was the chancellor of the exchequer, Sir Michael Hicks-Beach, eighth baronet, and a third was the home secretary, Sir Matthew White Ridley, ninth baronet. The rank of baronet, since its creation by King James I in 1611, had been fully as hereditary and as connected with landownership on a large scale as had the ranks of the peerage proper (barons, viscounts, earls, marquesses, and dukes in ascending order of degree). Two of the other "commoners" were Henry Chaplin, a country squire par excellence who prided himself on owning two packs of fox hounds (he also had a duke for a brother-in-law and a marquess for a son-in-law), and his colleague Walter Long, president of the Board of Agriculture, who was equally representative of the country squirearchy.

[28] Henry W. Lucy, *Memoirs of Eight Parliaments* (London, 1908), 114.
[29] Cited in Tuchman, *Proud Tower*, 45.
[30] Cited in ibid., 37.

The only true commoner in the cabinet was Joseph Chamberlain, the onetime screw manufacturer and radical mayor of Birmingham. Back in 1883, Chamberlain had condemned Salisbury as spokesman "of the class to which he himself belongs, who toil not, neither do they spin."[31] Now a common antipathy to Gladstone's home-rule proposals for Ireland and a common devotion to the British Empire had brought Chamberlain and Salisbury into coalition, but as Balfour on one occasion confided to Lady Elcho, "Joe, though we all love him dearly, somehow does not absolutely or completely mix, does not form a chemical combination with us."[32]

Not only was the British government of 1900 predominantly aristocratic, but it was predominantly landed aristocratic. The duke of Devonshire could boast landed estates totaling 186,000 acres. Although few peers could rival him in this regard, he was not alone; even William Ewart Gladstone, the great Liberal leader whose role in the democratization of the franchise and in the opening of civil service positions to merit rather than heredity and patronage remains unchallenged, died in 1898 as owner of a 7,000-acre estate with 2,500 tenants and a rent toll of over £10,000 per year. Nor did Gladstone himself, great as was his oft expressed faith in the ultimate rectitude of the people, believe that society could "afford to dispense with its dominant influences."[33] Over a hundred Englishmen still owned estates totaling 50,000 acres or more; 2,500 owned more than 3,000 acres. Country homes like Chatsworth of the Devonshires and Blenheim of the Marlboroughs contained over three hundred rooms; during the London season, the city's houses and squares were still inhabited by the families whose names they bore, Devonshire House and Lansdowne House, Grosvenor Square and Cadogan Place.[34] Titled ladies like Elizabeth Balfour, daughter of the earl of Lytton, set the tone of London life and were involved in the type of matchmaking that caused so many members of the cabinet of 1900 to be related to one another. Thus Lord Lansdowne was married to a sister of Lord George Hamilton, the secretary of state for India, and his daughter was married to a nephew (and heir) of the duke of Devonshire.[35]

The persistence of the aristocratic and squirearchical tradition was accompanied by the persistence of domestic service. Of four million English workingwomen in 1901, a million and a half were servants, the largest single

[31] Cited in Alfred Havighurst, *Twentieth-Century Britain*, 2nd ed. (New York, 1966), 21.
[32] Cited in Kenneth Young, *Arthur James Balfour* (London, 1963), 129.
[33] Cited in Philip Magnus, *Gladstone* (London, 1954), 433.
[34] Tuchman, *Proud Tower*, 26, 14.
[35] Ibid., 20; Thompson, *English Landed Society*, 301.

occupational group.[36] What makes H. G. Wells's *Wonderful Visit* (1895) so delightful a satire of late Victorian squirearchical life is the fact that country ways had altered so surprisingly little since the eighteenth century, and that Wells, himself the son of a housemaid, had been able to draw freely upon personal experience.[37] According to one recent estimate by a social historian,[38] the ratio of annual income between the average nobleman and the average farm laborer, which Gregory King had estimated at £3,000 to £15 in 1695, was virtually identical in 1901.

TABLE 1.[39]   *The Aristocratic Element in British Cabinets, 1830–1900*

CABINET	PARTY	PEERS	LESSER ARISTOCRATS	TOTAL ARISTOCRATIC ELEMENT	COMMONERS
1830 Grey	L	70%	23%	93%	7%
1834 Melbourne	L	44	38	82	18
1834 Peel	C	58	25	83	17
1835 Melbourne	L	46	38	84	16
1841 Peel	C	57	36	93	7
1846 Russell	L	50	38	88	12
1852 Derby	C	54	15	69	31
1852 Aberdeen	LP	46	46	92	8
1855 Palmerston	L	50	43	93	7
1858 Derby	C	46	31	77	23
1859 Palmerston	L	40	40	80	20
1865 Russell	L	53	13	66	34
1866 Derby	C	33	47	80	20
1868 Disraeli	C	36	43	79	21
1868 Gladstone	L	40	7	47	53
1874 Disraeli	C	50	17	67	33
1880 Gladstone	L	44	6	50	50
1885 Salisbury	C	50	38	88	12
1886 Gladstone	L	44	6	50	50
1886 Salisbury	C	50	36	86	14
1892 Gladstone	L	29	12	41	59
1894 Rosebery	L	38	12	50	50
1895 Salisbury	C	47	21	68	32
Average for 1830–1900		47%	24%	71%	29%

[36] Laslett, *World We Have Lost*, 226.
[37] Cf. Lovat Dickson, *H. G. Wells: His Turbulent Life and Times* (New York, 1969), 65–66.
[38] Laslett, *World We Have Lost*, 203–4.
[39] This information is derived primarily from the *Dictionary of National Biography* and the volumes of *The Annual Register*. I am grateful to my graduate student Andrew Thomas Southam for doing the laborious spadework.

As Table 1 makes clear, the aristocratic element had dominated every previous cabinet of the 1830–1900 period as well, with the possible exception of Gladstone's governments of 1868 and 1892. Until 1867 the domination had been virtually complete in Liberal and Conservative cabinets alike; thereafter, Liberal cabinets became appreciably less aristocratic, while Conservative cabinets like that of 1895 (technically "Unionist" rather than "Conservative") remained characteristic of an earlier pattern. For purposes of Table 1, "lesser aristocracy" is defined as including Irish peers, baronets, and sons or sons-in-law of peers. Untitled country gentlemen and cabinet members related to the peerage in other ways are defined as "commoners."

Table 1 makes clear how muted the "middle-class triumph" of 1832 was at the highest levels of government, how all but invisible before 1868. Thus Peel's cabinet of 1841 included "eight peers, two heirs to earldoms, three baronets, one knight, and only one plain 'Mr.'"[40] When the Conservative Lord Ellenborough taunted the Palmerston cabinet of the late 1850s with being nothing more than a family party, Earl Granville, one of its members, replied: "My Lords, I must make a clean breast of it at once. Some of those who went before me had such quivers full of daughters who did not die old maids that I have relations upon this side of the House, relations upon the other, and that I had the unparalleled misfortune to have several in the last Protectionist [i.e., Conservative] Administration."[41]

W. L. Guttsman's studies of the makeup of late Victorian and early twentieth-century British cabinets corroborate the impression Table 1 provides. He discerns a similar pattern among the junior ministers; among 107 of those in the 1886–1916 period whose background Guttsman studied, 58 (54 percent) proved to be the direct descendants of aristocrats.[42] In general the pattern holds true for Victorian prime ministers as well. Men like Sir Robert Peel, Benjamin Disraeli, and William Gladstone were doubtless atypical, as the sons, respectively, of a cotton manufacturer, a Jewish literary critic, and a Scottish businessman, but their contemporaries were more conscious of their atypicality than are recent historians viewing their educational and wider social background. It remains a fair generalization that the first prime minister not from a landed family was Herbert Henry Asquith, who took office in 1908.[43]

From Lord Salisbury's vantage point the House of Commons may at times have resembled a mob, but the traditional lower chamber of Parliament even in 1900 was in no sense characteristically "middle class." Its members may no longer have relied on aristocratic patronage for election,

[40] Robert Blake, *Disraeli* (London, 1966), 160.
[41] Cited in T. H. S. Escott, *Great Victorians* (London, 1916), 265.
[42] Guttsman, *British Political Elite*, 33, 102.
[43] Thompson, *English Landed Society*, 295.

as did a vast number in the eighteenth century, but so long as parliamentary service was unpaid, M.P.'s required an independent source of income. Of 670 M.P.'s in 1895, some 420 were gentlemen of leisure, country squires, retired army officers, and barristers.[44]

The area of public life in which the landed classes retained sway in least disputed fashion throughout the Victorian era was county government. As a long-range consequence of the Municipal Corporations Act of 1835, municipal government did fall into middle-class hands, though even here the strength of gentry representation remained high: 51 percent in 1842 and 24 percent in 1885.[45] The composition of the county magistracies, the unpaid justices of the peace who in petty and quarter sessions continued to conduct a host of judicial and administrative functions, remained consistently squirearchical. The lord lieutenant of the county, appointed by the crown, served as presiding officer over quarter sessions and was invariably a peer. His regional significance is reflected in the portentous tone in which the demise of one was announced in the *Newcastle Journal* in 1865: "The Duke of Northumberland is dead. It will spread a gloom and sorrow in the north, whose dark shadow will fall upon a generation to come."[46] The lord lieutenant in turn appointed the justices of the peace, who tended to be predominantly country squires. There were, after all, not enough peers or sons of peers to fill the number of positions open.

Thus the county magistracy may fairly be said to have remained "the most aristocratic feature of the English government."[47] The duke of Wellington set forth the specifications of the ideal justice of the peace in 1838: "Magistrates must," he declared, "as required by the Act of Parliament, be gentlemen of wealth, worth, consideration, and education . . . they should have been educated for the bar, if possible and . . . above all, they should be associated with, and be respected by the gentry of the country."[48] Few had acquired the prescribed legal training, but all received the requisite income from land of at least £100 a year, and almost all were accepted members of country society. In 1833 the magistrates of Merionethshire "went on strike" because there had been appointed to sit among them a wealthy local landowner who had once kept a retail shop and remained

[44] Tuchman, *Proud Tower*, 14.

[45] The percentages are based on a study by former graduate student Carl Zangerl, founded on *Parliamentary Papers*, 1842, XXXIII, "The Return of the Clerk of the Crown in Chancery of All Persons Appointed as Justices of the Peace in Each and Every County in England and Wales," and *Parliamentary Papers*, 1888, LXXXII, "Return Giving the Names and Professions of All Justices of the Peace for the Counties of England and Scotland."

[46] Cited in Thompson, *English Landed Society*, 81.

[47] K. B. Smellie, *A History of Local Government*, 3rd ed. (London, 1957), 36.

[48] *Hansard's Parliamentary Debates*, 3rd ser., 43 (1838), col. 1280.

by religious conviction a Methodist. Their action was defended by a local observer: "The refusal of the County Magistrates to act with a man who has been a grocer and is a Methodist is the dictate of genuine patriotism; the spirit of aristocracy in the country magistracy is the salt which alone preserves the whole mass from inevitable corruption."[49]

How "uncorrupted" the county magistracy remained is demonstrated by a comparative study of the social background of the county magistrates of England and Wales in 1842 and 1887.[50]

YEAR	PEERS AND HEIRS	GENTRY	CLERGY	MIDDLE CLASSES	OTHERS	TOTAL
1842	8.4%	77.1%	13.4%	–	1.2%	100%
1887	7.5%	80.7%	6.1%	4.0%	1.7%	100%

Some of the functions of the county magistracy were taken over by new agencies—poor-law boards, sanitary boards, and highway boards, among them—and the number of paid professional officials also increased, but as Anthony Brundage has recently demonstrated,[51] aristocratic influence on poor-law administration was more direct after the act of 1834 than before. Justices of the peace were assigned to ex officio membership on most of the new boards and remained governmentally predominant, at least until the passage of the County Councils Act of 1888. That measure deprived the J.P.'s of their nonjudicial functions, but it appears to have been less than dramatic in its impact upon the rural social structure. Perhaps half the newly elected county councillors were old nominated magistrates writ large.[52]

The purpose of this essay thus far has been to propose that in defiance of the hopes and fears of contemporaries, and in contradiction to the generalizations still often encountered in survey histories of Victorian Britain, the Britain of 1900 remained, from the prime minister down, in many respects a remarkably aristocratic country. Accordingly, during the past decade a number of historians and sociologists have suggested that the most fundamental questions to be asked about Victorian Britain may not be "How and why did it become democratic?" and "How did the middle class come to predominate?" but "How can one account for the remark-

[49] Cited in Sidney and Beatrice Webb, *English Local Government from the Revolution to the Municipal Corporations Act*, I (London, 1906), 385.

[50] See Carl Zangerl, "The Social Composition of the County Magistracies in England and Wales, 1838–1887," *Journal of British Studies*, 11:1 (Nov. 1971), 113–25.

[51] "The Landed Interest and the New Poor Law: A Reappraisal of the Revolution in Government," *English Historical Review*, 87 (Jan. 1972), 27–48.

[52] The statement is based on my graduate student Prudence Ann Moylan's survey of county election returns as reported in the *Times* (London).

able survival in prestige and influence of the aristocrats and squires?"

"The central problem," according to F. M. L. Thompson, "is to discover how it came to pass that the social order based on landed estates survived far into an age in which the initial superiority of the landed classes in possession of the material sinews of power had evaporated."[53] The historian of imperialism, A. P. Thornton, has observed that although "the story of English liberty" has been oft retold, the accompanying story of the English "tradition of successful paternalism" has not.[54] From a different vantage point, sociologist W. L. Guttsman has called attention to the fact that "the persistence of aristocratic rule in a country which, thanks largely to its entrepreneurial middle class, had reached a position of economic and industrial eminence in Europe is an extraordinary phenomenon."[55]

Although a number of scholars have directed notice to various facets of this "extraordinary phenomenon," what has been lacking is a systematic framework of historical explanation. The purpose of the remainder of this essay is to propose such a framework.

One avenue of explanation is the suggestion that the acts and the years —1832, 1846, 1867, 1884—that have served as neat signposts pointing first to middle-class rule and then to democracy have been in part deceptive. The great reform acts—even the abolition of the Corn Laws—prove on examination to have been not so much successive installments of a single principle enacted into law as the complex products of often contradictory social pressures.

Of no legislative measure was this more true than of that oft touted first installment of democracy, the Reform Bill of 1832. The tendency of the bill was in some senses "democratic." The redistribution of parliamentary seats took cognizance of population movements. The size of the British electorate was increased by 70 percent, from 478,000 to 814,000.[56] The bill had a democratic tendency also in that the outcome was determined by a threat to swamp the House of Lords, in that the bill, having once broken with tradition, invited similar breaks with customs in decades to come, and in that the stormy debates and popular demonstrations associated with the measure came to symbolize resistance to oligarchical rule

[53] Thompson, English Landed Society, 2.
[54] A. P. Thornton, The Habit of Authority (London, 1965), 7, 13. The volume is tied together more by theme than by thesis, but it remains a fascinating if somewhat miscellaneous collection of quotations and data.
[55] Guttsman, British Political Elite, 60.
[56] These are the customary estimates. See Anthony Wood, Nineteenth Century Britain (New York, 1960), 453. Since the act also introduced the first system of electoral registers, the formal size of the electorate after 1832 is much easier to determine than its formal size before.

in the minds of hundreds of thousands of lower-class Englishmen scarcely affected by its provisions.

This capsule summary fails, however, to do justice to all the pre-1832 survivals—pocket boroughs, large-scale bribery, aristocratic predominance —that Norman Gash discerned two decades ago in his analysis of the political structure of early Victorian England.[57] Nor does it do justice to what D. C. Moore has called "the other side of reform."[58] Moore recalled that the original stimulus to the reform movement of 1829–32 had been given not by Whigs like Grey or by extraparliamentary leaders like Francis Place but by anti-Wellington Tories, disenchanted with a ministry and a House of Commons that would surrender a fundamental Tory principle by granting "Catholic Emancipation." Moore has reiterated more recently that not merely did such Tories set the movement under way, but also many of their hopes were realized by the bill that ultimately became law, and in general the political powers of the landed interests were strengthened rather than weakened.[59]

Historians have never denied that the reform government of Earl Grey, with its eleven peers and four commoners, was far from middle class, especially when we consider that one of its "commoners" was the heir to an earldom and another the younger son of a duke. And although Grey and the Whigs have been praised for realizing that concession rather than obstruction was the proper mode of meeting middle-class demands, Grey's colleagues were little noted for their affection toward the middle class per se. "I don't like the middle classes" was the offhand comment of Lord Melbourne, Grey's home secretary and successor. "The higher and lower classes, there's some good in them, but the middle classes are all affectation and conceit and pretence and concealment."[60]

Grey was convinced from the start "that the more the bill is considered, the less it will be found to prejudice the real interests of the aristocracy."[61] To the extent that the number of pocket boroughs was cut, it was argued, so far could the danger be reduced that bourgeois capitalists or Roman Catholics might buy parliamentary seats. The framers of the bill saw their purpose as strengthening the "legitimate" influence of rank, position, and property while diminishing "corrupt" influence as well as the extraparliamentary political associations the struggle over the measure had inspired.[62]

[57] *Politics in the Age of Peel* (London, 1953), esp. x, xi.
[58] *Victorian Studies*, 5:1 (Sept. 1961), 7–34.
[59] E. P. Hennock and D. C. Moore, "The First Reform Act: A Discussion," *Victorian Studies*, 14:3 (Mar. 1971), 321–37.
[60] Cited in David Cecil, *Melbourne* (London, 1953), 161.
[61] Cited in Butler, *Passing of Great Reform Bill*, 255.
[62] Ibid., 256; Thompson, *English Landed Society*, 48.

The extension of the suffrage is often too readily equated with the promotion of political democracy, but the uses to which Napoleon III and Bismarck were to put universal manhood suffrage in 1852 and 1867, respectively, ought give us pause. Thus the so-called Chandos clause of the Reform Bill of 1832 enfranchised wealthy tenant farmers in such a manner as to add to the electoral influence of their landlords. The transfer of seats from "rotten" boroughs to counties can itself be interpreted as strengthening the landed interest.

The relationship of the House of Lords to the bill is also often oversimplified. We all too readily ignore such paradoxes as the Whig earl of Radnor's bringing pressure upon his nominees in the House of Commons to vote in favor of the disfranchisement of the borough they represented.[63] More fundamental is the little-known fact that opposition to the reform bill in the House of Lords came almost exclusively from new creations. Of the 112 holders of peerages created before 1790, no less than 108 voted *for* the bill in 1831.[64] Even the threatened swamping of the recalcitrant upper house would have done remarkably little to "democratize" the lords. Grey's plan was to call up the eldest sons of peers in their fathers' baronies, to grant English peerages to certain Irish and Scottish peers, and to ennoble a number of elderly and childless landed gentlemen.[65]

One of the main errors of prognostication committed by the fearful opponents of the Great Reform Bill was to assume that the new middle-class electorate would be primarily interested in electing to Parliament men precisely like themselves, that £10 householders would prefer to see other £10 householders in charge at Westminster. The new electorate proved to be interested far more in having its government operated in businesslike fashion than in operating it directly.[66] Close to one hundred proprietary parliamentary seats remained after 1832, and landed families continued to furnish a majority of the House of Commons, a substantial one until 1868, a small one until 1885.[67] The commercial or industrial interests accounted for at best a fourth of the seats before 1868. To call the parliament of 1842 a "middle-class Parliament," as did two reputable historians, would appear to be a very loose playing with words.[68] As has already been established, middle-class representation in the cabinets of the 1840s and

---

[63] Emily Allyn, *Lords versus Commons* (New York, 1931), 18f.

[64] Butler, *Passing of Great Reform Bill*, 286f.

[65] Thompson, *English Landed Society*, 59.

[66] Gash, *Politics in Age of Peel*, 438–39.

[67] J. H. Hanham, *Elections and Party Management: Politics in the Time of Disraeli and Gladstone* (London, 1959), xv-xvii.

[68] J. L. and Barbara Hammond, *Lord Shaftesbury* (London, 1925; reprinted 1969), 84.

1850s was even more minimal. Guttsman could identify only three genuine "middle-class" politicians, representing the specific aspirations of their class" among the 103 men who held cabinet office between 1830 and 1868.[69]

It is no wonder that Alexis de Tocqueville could return to England in 1857 on his last visit and find to his astonishment that the anticipated democratic revolution had failed to occur and that it was still the same old England.[70] "The aristocracy," Matthew Arnold agreed four years later, "still . . . administers public affairs; and it is a great error to suppose, as many persons in England suppose, that it administers but does not govern."[71] The aristocracy governed, which is not to suggest that it therefore governed as a single political party with a single point of view or that it failed to take cognizance of the desires of other groups in what had become economically an increasingly sophisticated society.

The sense of complexity that may be evoked by an examination of the events of 1832 seems at first glance altogether absent from the events of 1846. The Corn Laws during the post–Napoleonic War years had to many Englishmen come to symbolize governmental preference for one traditional interest, the landed, and corollary discrimination against another, the industrial—paradoxically the very economic interest that was providing the foundation for British power and prestige. In 1846 surely, if not before, the class issue was joined, the middle class versus the aristocracy, with the middle class emerging triumphant. The Anti–Corn Law League, founded in industrial Manchester in 1838, was clearly a middle-class institution founded by nonaristocrats, and by general admission it proved to be the best organized and most persistent extraparliamentary pressure group Britain had yet encountered. It combined an appeal to Smithsian reason—for a government to interfere with the free flow of international trade by artificial import tariffs was a violation of the first law of economics—with an emotional appeal for cheap bread reminiscent of the Old Testament prophets. And its victory of 1846, the death knell—immediate or prospective—of all protective tariffs, was so complete as to leave it without a cause and bring about its triumphant dissolution.

Further examination discloses that the events of 1846 were far more complex than a simplistic triumph of manufacturer over landlord. The historian of the Anti–Corn Law League has demonstrated that the league by itself was not able, and might never have been able, to bring about the repeal of agricultural protection in the circumstances of the 1840s.[72] By

[69] Guttsman, British Political Elite, 38–39.

[70] David Paul Crook, American Democracy in English Politics, 1815–1850 (Oxford, 1965), 201.

[71] Cited in Guttsman, British Political Elite, 34.

[72] Norman McCord, The Anti–Corn Law League, 1838–1846 (London, 1958).

supporting the Whigs in the general election of 1841, the league leadership backed the wrong political horse; it failed to establish itself as a significant separate political force at by-elections during the years that followed, and by the start of 1845 a sense of frustration pervaded its ranks. It was the independent judgment of Peel and his Conservative cabinet, which followed closely the decision of the leader of the Whig opposition, Lord John Russell, to opt for free trade, which turned the balance. Although Peel may to some extent have been gradually converted by the articulate league leader, Richard Cobden, and although he was certainly conscious of and concerned with the social divisions the Corn Law issue was creating, the coincidence of the Irish potato blight provided the immediate motivation. "Rotten potatoes have done it all; they have put Peel in his damned fright," commented the duke of Wellington in disgust; but the duke proceeded loyally to push repeal through a predominantly Tory, and landed, House of Lords.[73] It was thus a predominantly landed parliament that repealed the Corn Laws.

That the Corn Laws provided a noisy clash of symbols for protectionists and free traders alike cannot be denied, but several economic historians in the course of the last decade have challenged the notion that the Corn Laws were ever particularly effective in stabilizing the income of the landed classes, as they were intended to do. They might prevent or restrain the importation of foreign grain, but they could hardly prevent domestic grain prices from fluctuating widely from one harvest to another. The Corn Law reformers tended to assume that large quantities of cheap foreign grain were ever available, ready to be imported into the British Isles, but by the mid-1840s this was a false assumption. German and French grain prices were in fact only a little below British prices. Whereas the average price for wheat was 58s. 7d. per quarter during the ten years preceding repeal, it fell less than 7 percent (to an average of 55s. 4d.) during the ten years following repeal.[74]

It was becoming clear by the 1840s, and was to become more clear in retrospect, that agriculturist and manufacturer increasingly tended to prosper and to encounter depression in concert rather than one prospering at the expense of the other.[75] Dairy farmers had already become aware

[73] Cited in Philip Guedalla, *Wellington* (New York, 1931), 463.

[74] G. P. Jones and A. G. Pool, *A Hundred Years of Economic Development* (New York, 1940), 83. See also D. C. Moore, "The Corn Laws and High Farming," *Economic History Review*, 2nd ser., 18:3 (Dec. 1965), 544-61. Susan Fairlie has argued, however, that the tendency was in part caused by Corn Law repeal; "The Corn Laws and British Wheat Production," *Economic History Review*, 2nd ser., 22:1 (Apr. 1969), 88-109.

[75] F. M. L. Thompson, "The Countryside," in Asa Briggs, ed., *The Nineteenth Century* (London, 1970), 156.

that their prosperity depended upon full employment in nearby factory towns,[76] and the landed aristocracy had become increasingly divided on the continued merits of agricultural protection. Earl Fitzwilliam was urging the ineffectiveness of the Corn Laws and the desirability of their repeal as early as the 1820s; and by 1843 and 1844 Whig landlords like the marquess of Westminster were making sizable monetary contributions to the Anti-Corn Law League. The repeal of the Corn Laws was to injure the small marginal farmer far more than the owner of large and efficient estates; it was the former, not surprisingly, who remained the more consistent in supporting politicians opposed to repeal.[77] A survey of House of Commons divisions by William Aydelotte indicates that squire M.P.'s voted for and against the Corn Laws in almost equal numbers; he is persuaded that the events of 1846 did not represent "an economic and political victory of the middle classes over the aristocracy and the gentry."[78]

However influential the Corn Law crisis may have been in breaking up Peel's Conservative party and in leading to two decades of relative political confusion, it clearly did much less than has often been assumed to shake the economic strength or social prestige of the landed classes. The 1850s and 1860s proved to be years of farm prosperity; land prices and rents rose, and the concentration of landholdings tended to increase. Thus the dominance of the landed classes in either the cabinet or the political system generally had not in any significant degree been broken by the 1860s.[79]

Comparable paradoxes pertain to the Reform Bills of 1867 and 1884. The abortive Reform Bill of 1866 did provide *the* great debate in the annals of the English—or any other—parliament on the philosophical merits or demerits of democracy; but democracy as a political ideal was not the motive of the men who initiated the reform movement of the mid-1860s. Their purpose was merely to add some 400,000 skilled artisans, as a form of reward rather than as a measure of right, to the electorate of approximately 1,360,000 registered voters.[80] As a consequence of parliamentary

[76] Thompson, *English Landed Society*, 239.

[77] See David Spring, "Earl Fitzwilliam and the Corn Laws," *American Historical Review*, 59:2 (Jan. 1954), 287–304; G. Kitson Clark, "The Electorate and the Repeal of the Corn Laws," *Transactions of the Royal Historical Society*, 5th ser., 1 (1951), 125.

[78] William Aydelotte, "The House of Commons in the 1840s," *History*, 30 (1954), 248–62, and "The Country Gentlemen and the Repeal of the Corn Laws," *English Historical Review*, 82 (1967), 47. Betty Kemp reaches a similar conclusion in "Reflections on the Repeal of the Corn Laws," *Victorian Studies*, 5:3 (Mar. 1961), 189–204.

[79] Cf. G. Kitson Clark, *The Making of Victorian England* (London, 1961), 209–10, 214.

[80] F. B. Smith, *The Making of the Second Reform Bill* (Cambridge, 1966), chs. 1 and 3.

confusion and of a desperate desire on the part of the minority Derby ministry to retain office, a great many more men were enfranchised (approximately 1,100,000). Derby admittedly described the measure as "a leap in the dark," yet the fact that it is possible to make this statement, "Democracy was established in England by the 14th Earl of Derby," without being literally absurd demonstrates the paradoxical nature of the bill.[81] Clearly Disraeli would not have piloted the measure through the House of Commons or Derby through the Lords if either had anticipated the political demise of his social class or party.[82] The most searing opposition to reform in 1866 and 1867 came from a nonaristocrat, Robert Lowe, who saw the question not as upper class versus lower class but as intelligence versus ignorance.

Nor did the post-1867 House of Commons or cabinet bear out the worst fears of the measure's opponents. The limited nature of seat redistribution left at least 108 M.P.'s who "still owed their seats to the combined power of influence and long purses."[83] The increase in the number of English county seats—from 144 to 172—and the decrease in the number of borough seats—from 323 to 286—also aided the landed interest.[84] The Whiggish *Edinburgh Review* observed complacently in 1869, "The English House of Commons still remains the most aristocratical body in the world; and its power is all the greater in that it is not derived from aristocratical privilege, but from the free choice of the whole people."[85] The French visitor Hippolyte Taine concurred: "enfranchised or not, the labourer and the 'shopkeeper' agree in wanting a man of the upper classes at the helm."[86]

The Reform Act of 1884 was a step toward democracy, and the Redistribution of Seats Act, which accompanied it, subtly introduced the ideal of "one man, one vote" by the philosophical back door and gave a boost to national party organizations. Although the act is credited with the establishment of universal manhood suffrage in England, it may more properly be said to have established "household suffrage" in the rural areas as in the cities. Forty percent of adult males remained disfranchised by residence and other requirements, and Great Britain remained the only one of the

[81] Escott, *Great Victorians*, 235.
[82] So argues Gertrude Himmelfarb, "The Reform Bill of 1867," in *Victorian Minds* (New York, 1970), 333–92.
[83] Guttsman, *British Political Elite*, 82.
[84] Thompson, *English Landed Society*, 225.
[85] "The New Ministry," *Edinburgh Review*, 129 (Jan. 1869), 291.
[86] Cited in Hippolyte Taine, *Notes on England*, tr. Edward Hyams (London, 1957), 165.

major western and central European powers not to have established universal suffrage for the election of the members of the lower house of its parliament before World War I.[87]

The setting up of the civil service system in 1870 represented a sharp ideological break with aristocratic tradition, yet "it was arguable that the change to competitive examinations merely replaced the patronage of the older universities."[88] The Secret Ballot Act of 1872 may also have been influential,[89] yet the specific effect of the act has always been difficult to measure, and the long-held assumption that it was largely responsible for the development of the late Victorian Irish nationalist movement has been largely disproved.[90] Suspicions concerning the actuality of electoral secrecy may also have been more widespread than is generally believed. And although Henry Pelling could discern the origins of the British Labour party in the 1880s and 1890s, the party as such remains a twentieth-century phenomenon. As Grant Allen phrased the matter in 1900, in a characteristically condescending American manner, "In spite of the reform bills and everything else that has been done to popularize the representation, English voters, out of pure ingrained snobbery, continue to return in vast numbers unknown young men of aristocratic families, and to reject in their favor distinguished politicians of tried and proved ability."[91]

A second avenue of explanation for the survival of the aristocracy in Victorian Britain may well lie in the persistence of the House of Lords as a recognized and significant component of the British constitution. At first glance this seems a substitution of cart for horse. Was not the survival of the House of Lords itself merely a function of the persistence of the aristocracy? Had not the House of Lords been mocked even in its eighteenth-century heyday as a "hospital of incurables"?[92] Did not the traditional upper chamber seem ever more isolated from the rest of the life of the nation by the early 1830s,[93] and had not the duke of Wellington, its leader

---

[87] See Neal Blewett, "The Franchise in the United Kingdom, 1885–1918," *Past and Present*, no. 32 (Dec. 1965), 27–56. Admittedly the German, Austrian, and Italian parliaments exercised less power than did the House of Commons.

[88] Thompson, *English Landed Society*, 74.

[89] So thought at least one observant French visitor. See Emile Boutiny, *Le développement de la constitution et de la societé politique en Angleterre* (Paris, 1898), 369–71.

[90] See R. C. K. Ensor, *England, 1870–1914* (Oxford, 1936), 24. Cf. Michael Hurst, "Ireland and the Ballot Act of 1872," *Historical Journal*, 8:3 (1965), 326–52.

[91] Allen, "The British Aristocracy," 661.

[92] Lord Chesterfield, cited in William B. Willcox, *The Age of Aristocracy, 1688–1830* (Boston, 1966), 100.

[93] Cf. Tocqueville, *Journeys to England and Ireland*, 45.

for a generation, complained that "nobody cares a damn for the House of Lords. The House of Commons is everything in England, and the House of Lords nothing."[94] In the 1860s Walter Bagehot did describe the traditional upper chamber as appertaining, for the most part, to the "dignified" as opposed to the "efficient" elements in the British government. Gilbert and Sullivan, in the 1882 operetta *Iolanthe*, found it possible to mock the peers in a fashion they would not have dared apply to the monarchy. They played with notions such as that "a duke's exalted station be attained by competitive examination," and in recalling the lengthy history of the peers' chamber, they remarked: "The House of Lords throughout the war / Did nothing in particular / And did it very well."

All of this would seem to suggest that whatever significance the House of Lords possessed depended on the individual prestige of its members. No doubt the relationship worked both ways, but I suggest here that the House of Lords continued to be highly respected and that the manner in which—as the primary institutional expression of the political power of the landed aristocracy—it conferred and continued to confer prestige upon the aristocracy en masse may well be a neglected yet significant explanation for aristocratic survival. In the early 1830s the survival of the House of Lords did seem to be in genuine danger,[95] and there were to be rumbles of discontent with the body in the early 1860s and again in the mid-1880s; but one of the remarkable aspects of Victorian history is the manner in which an ever-growing electorate appeared to reconcile itself to the persistence of a hereditary governing chamber. Thus the Liberal Lord Granville could suggest in 1860 that the House of Lords "stands as high now in popular favour and esteem as it did at any period of its existence," and the marquess of Clanricarde noted with pleasure the absence of any agitation directed against the peers.[96] A full generation later, the English expatriate and editor of the American weekly the *Nation*, E. L. Godkin, concurred that "the bulk of Englishmen are rather proud of the Peers as an institution [although] they are every now and then provoked with them. . . ."[97]

Nor ought the relative absence of criticism during most of the Victorian years be attributed to the failure of the House of Lords to exercise power. Attendance at many of its sessions might be low—thirty to forty members showed up regularly in the 1830s and 1840s, perhaps fifty in the

94 Cited in Butler, *Passing of Great Reform Bill*, 286.
95 Cf. Norman Gash, *Reaction and Reconstruction in English Politics, 1832–1852* (London, 1965), 30ff.
96 *Hansard's Parliamentary Debates*, 3rd ser., 158 (1860), cols. 1462, 1496.
97 E. L. Godkin, "The Reform of the House of Lords," *Nation*, no. 1579 (1895), 236.

1890s[98]—yet low attendance at formal sessions, as the history of the U.S. Congress demonstrates, is not incompatible with the exercise of formal power. Not only did the peers still initiate legislation, but they also revised and amended, and often their amendments were accepted by the Commons. Since foreign secretaries like Granville and Salisbury were peers, major discussions of foreign policy often took place in the upper chamber. Finally, the House of Lords exercised power by successfully vetoing legislation. It did not choose to exercise such power ultimately in halting the enlargement of the electorate—it did not reject the Reform Act of 1867 or of 1884 (though in the latter case it insisted upon prior agreement to an appropriate redistribution act)—and it treated benignly many early attempts to regulate factory hours and prohibit women and children from working in the mines.

On questions concerning religion and Ireland—the two necessarily overlapped—the House of Lords remained a profoundly conservative force. It blocked the admission of non-Anglicans to Oxford and Cambridge in the 1830s and the admission of Jews to the House of Commons in the 1840s and 1850s. It played a predominant role in the private divorce acts that were necessary to sever marriage ties legally before 1857.[99] It consistently opposed the diminution of the privileges of the (Anglican) Church of Ireland, and was skeptical of local government reform efforts there. Legislation aimed at increasing the privileges of tenant farmers—English or Irish—was repeatedly blocked. During Gladstone's last ministry, 1892–94, the Lords vetoed an employer's liability bill, a parish councils bill, and most significant, the goal of Gladstone's final legislative crusade, the Irish Home Rule Bill of 1893.[100] That the motives of the peers were often self-interested may well be true; that the peers tended to equate their own interests with those of their nation is equally likely. However, that the peers continued to exercise real power throughout the nineteenth century appears indisputable.

Another source of lordly power confirmed by the Judicature Act of 1873 was the role of the upper chamber as the nation's supreme court. In practice, the chamber's judicial functions were by the late nineteenth century exercised almost exclusively by the "law lords," a group of trained judges appointed to the peerage for life. Yet the press—and constitutional historians—continued (and continue) in confusing fashion to attribute

[98] Ralph Waldo Emerson, *English Traits* (Boston, 1856), 91; Tuchman, *Proud Tower*, 36.

[99] Petrie, *The Victorians*, 207.

[100] Cf. Allyn, *Lords versus Commons*; Eric Strauss, *Irish Nationalism and English Democracy* (New York, 1951), esp. 111.

such decisions to the House of Lords without further explanation. It seems reasonably clear that most Englishmen persisted in praising or blaming the chamber as a whole for the actions of a small and specially appointed fraction of its membership.[101]

The exercise of power by the House of Lords throughout the Victorian era might well be interpreted in a different light if the makeup of the peerage had profoundly altered during that time period. But the fact remains that, certainly until 1885, it did not. The first lesson to be drawn from Ralph E. Pumphrey's study, "The Introduction of Industrialists into the British Peerage,"[102] is how remarkably few industrialists were introduced. A few lowly lawyers rose to the lord chancellorship during the pre-1885 period; but of the 139 new peers created between 1833 and 1885, only one-fifth possessed less than 3,000 acres of land yielding at least £3,000 a year in rents. Alfred, Lord Tennyson, sole representative of the arts in the group, was also the only new peer to be virtually landless and bereft of close aristocratic connections.[103] It continued to seem appropriate for men with insufficient landed wealth to refuse a peerage even when offered—as Sir Robert Napier, leader of a successful military expedition to Abyssinia, did in 1868, and as Gladstone himself did, when offered an earldom by Queen Victoria in 1885.[104]

When Disraeli recommended a barony for the relatively landless banker Lionel Rothschild in 1868, Queen Victoria noted that she "could not think that one who owed his wealth to contracts with foreign governments for loans, or to successful speculation on the stock exchange, could fairly claim a British peerage."[105] Lionel Rothschild's son Nathaniel, a substantial country gentleman, attained in 1885 the peerage that had eluded his father, and much has been made of Lord Salisbury's decision that same year to recommend a barony for Henry Alsopp, a self-made brewer with but a modest country estate. Yet even if one accepts that approximately a third of the two hundred new peers created between 1886 and 1914 "represented the new wealth of the industrial revolution," it must be recalled that many of these same peers were second-generation

---

[101] Walter Bagehot argued in 1867 that "the supreme court of the English people . . . ought not to be hidden beneath the robes of a legislative assembly," but it continues so. *The English Constitution* (Garden City, N.Y.: Doubleday Dolphin ed., n.d.), 167–68.

[102] Pumphrey, "The Introduction of Industrialists," 1–16.

[103] Thompson, *English Landed Society*, 60, 62.

[104] *Spectator*, 2 May 1868; Magnus, *Gladstone*, 330; cf. Guttsman, *British Political Elite*, 118.

[105] Cited in Thornton, *Habit of Authority*, 255. Austrian emperors apparently had fewer scruples in these matters, since Lionel Rothschild was already a baron under Austrian law.

industrialists who lived on country estates. The true "self-made men" represented at most a quarter of the new peers;[106] among the total number of peers, they were scarcely noticeable. As late as 1900 the premier industrial nation could continue to boast (or confess to) a predominantly landed aristocracy.

The long-lived House of Lords helped maintain the tradition of public service in the British aristocracy. Disraeli was far from alone in his belief that although "the leaders of the mob will become the oppressors of the people," a hereditary aristocracy could be counted upon to be swayed by less selfish motives.[107] Public office for aristocrats was less a way of making money than a way of occupying time once money had been inherited. It cost an individual perhaps £500 a year to be a member of Parliament for a borough and closer to £1,100 to represent a county.[108] Lord Palmerston told the seventh duke of Devonshire when wishing to give office to his son, the young marquess of Hartington: "Young men in high aristocratic positions should take part in the administration of public affairs and should not leave the working of our political machine to classes whose pursuits and interests are of a different kind."[109] Hartington, the eventual eighth duke of Devonshire, accepted for the remainder of his life the notion that he owed a debt to his country that had to be paid in the form of public service.

This attitude contrasted sharply with that of certain mid-Victorian middle-class Radicals like John Bright who were perpetually fearful that holding political office might by definition be incompatible with upholding political principles.[110] Young men of aristocratic background were unlikely to be troubled by such scruples. When it came to entering the House of Commons and when it came to securing ministerial and eventually cabinet office, they possessed the additional advantages of economic independence and family influence and connections. Even the most successful businessmen could not compete on even terms. In a conversation of the 1850s John Arthur Roebuck, a veteran Radical M.P., compared the situation of such a man with the youthful Lord Stanley (the future fifteenth earl of Derby). "Know you, my Lord," Roebuck told Stanley, "his case and yours are very different. Such a man's goal is your starting point, where other men end you begin. You step right into the business of government; he has to conquer his way up to that. By the time he has conquered his way to where you start from, old age comes upon him and he is unfitted for his office."[111]

---

[106] Thompson, *English Landed Society*, 293–94.
[107] Cited in Guttsman, *British Political Elite*, 63.
[108] Ibid., 81.
[109] Cited in ibid., 206.
[110] Cf. G. M. Trevelyan, *The Life of John Bright* (London, 1913), 283, 395–96.
[111] *Times* (London), 4 Sept. 1859, cited in Guttsman, *British Political Elite*, 55.

Foreign observers like Tocqueville and Taine agreed. In the 1830s Tocqueville suggested that an aristocrat might well be "infinitely more skilled in the science of legislation than a democrat can ever be."[112] In the 1860s Taine saw England as becoming "a republic wherein the aristocratic institution is engaged in turning out the requisite supply of Ministers, Members of Parliament, Generals and Diplomats just as a polytechnic school turns out the requisite supply of engineers."[113] In a land that continued to cherish the unpaid amateur as opposed to the cog in a paid, centralized, bureaucratic wheel, such an arrangement might well continue to flourish. In ministries like the Foreign Office, in which even after 1900 "men from families totally unknown to Lord Salisbury or his private secretary did not need to apply," an independent private income was taken for granted as a way of supplementing relatively low annual salaries.[114] A political career that involved service in local government and in the House of Commons and ultimately promotion (active or passive, according to preference) into the yet prestigious House of Lords was thus the hope, and frequently the reality, for many a Victorian aristocrat. The continued significance of the House of Lords helped give institutional meaning to, and may provide partial explanation for, the survival of that aristocracy.

Whatever the role of the House of Lords and of the tradition of public service in fostering aristocratic survival, would that survival have been possible without a firm economic base? By general consensus, the economic base upon which the aristocracy rested was land. Land gave prestige, and position as the head of a huge estate with a great park and dozens of servants made one the natural social leader of a community involving numerous gentry neighbors, tenants, and village folk—all this was clear enough. Some aristocrats possessed several large estates and traveled from one to the other like medieval kings—mostly in search of new game to hunt. (Hunting was the bond that tied the aristocracy and gentry and the wealthier farmers together in a single rural society, however much it may have alienated the tenant farmers whose crops were trampled on and who, if caught poaching, were severely punished.[115]) Other aristocrats possessed estates they scarcely knew. When visited by an impecunious French friend in 1848, Lord Hertford noted: "I have a place in Wales which I have never

112 Alexis de Tocqueville, *Democracy in America*, ed. J. P. Mayer and Max Lerner (New York, 1966), 214.
113 Taine, *Notes on England*, 155–56.
114 Zara S. Steiner, *The Foreign Office and Foreign Policy* (Cambridge, 1970), 19; Rupert Wilkinson, *Gentlemanly Power: British Leadership and the Public School Tradition* (London, 1964), 23.
115 Thompson, *English Landed Society*, esp. 136, 147.

seen but they tell me it's very fine. A dinner for twelve is served every day and the carriage brought round to the door, in case I should arrive. It's the butler who eats the dinner. Go and settle down there."[116]

For an aristocrat, selling land was less a business transaction than a social disgrace. When the debt-ridden sixth duke of Devonshire was strongly considering such a step in 1845, the third Earl Fitzwilliam counseled caution. The relative gain would be minimal.

But what do you lose in order to gain this small proportionate addition to your disposable income? Why, you lose greatly in station—You are now, taking all circumstances into consideration, the first gentleman in the East Riding of Yorkshire . . . the alienation of one of the great masses of your landed property is a very different affair, and cannot fail to make a sensible inroad upon the position which you hold in the great national community.[117]

Not only was the land not sold, but if at all possible it was kept together in a single estate. Younger sons and daughters might receive a dowry and allowance charged upon the income of the estate, but the estate itself descended to the eldest son by means of entail. Since English law "abhorred a perpetuity" and allowed land to be tied up for three generations only, an entail generally involved a father, his eldest son, and his (unborn) eldest grandson until he was twenty-one. Since by tradition each landowner once of age entered upon a new legal arrangement of this type, the effect was to perpetuate family ownership to the extent that there were heirs. In his more romantic moments, the owner of an estate therefore could—and doubtless did—see himself as "for the time being . . . steward of a trust for unborn generations and temporary recipient of the fruits of his forbears' endeavours."[118] Numerous foreign visitors to Victorian Britain were convinced that aristocratic influence was founded upon primogeniture and entail.[119]

That land ought to have provided the economic basis for aristocratic and gentry life seems clear; in the words of an anonymous contributor to *Fraser's Magazine*, "The riches of trade come and pass away; they fluctuate

---

[116] Cited in W. L. Guttsman, ed., *The English Ruling Class* (London, 1969), 71.

[117] Cited in David Spring, "The English Landed Estate in the Age of Coal and Iron: 1830–1880," *Journal of Economic History*, 11:1 (Winter 1951), 17.

[118] Thompson, *English Landed Society*, 6, 64, 70.

[119] Cf. Frederick Law Olmstead, *Walks and Talks of an American Farmer in England* (London, 1852), 215; Adam Badeau, *Aristocracy in England* (New York, 1885), 42–51, 239, 245. As F. M. L. Thompson reminds us, primogeniture was, except in cases of intestacy, perpetuated by custom rather than law. "Law and Politics in England in the Nineteenth Century," *Transactions of the Royal Historical Society*, 5th ser., 15 (1965), 23–44.

in dependence on a thousand accidents of human affairs: the riches of the earth alone are sure and permanent, unless we abandon them by wilful blindness, obstinacy, and neglect."[120] Yet what of Lady Bracknell's plaint (in Oscar Wilde's *Importance of Being Earnest*) that "land has ceased to be either a profit or a pleasure. It gives one position, and prevents one from keeping it up."

During much of the nineteenth century, English landowners in their role as rent collectors (only 10 percent of the land was farmed by owner-occupiers[121]) did make money—though probably never as much as they might have made from selling their land and investing their capital in more venturesome industrial enterprises (or even, during much of the century, from investing their funds in government bonds). The period of the Revolutionary and Napoleonic wars had been a good time for landowners—many a debt-ridden estate was reprieved by the rises in rents that followed.[122] Temporary fluctuations aside, this prosperity continued into the 1820s, 1830s, and 1840s. Agriculture was more than ever an avocation as well as a source of wealth for aristocrats, and the Corn Laws helped spur a "managerial revolution" on many estates. There was much new investment in farm improvement schemes, especially in the field drainage made possible by the mass production of clay drainpipes.[123]

Until the 1870s the value of land continued to rise steadily and the concentration of landownership to increase subtly. According to the "New Domesday Book" of 1873, half the land in England was owned by the aristocracy, one acre in eight by a duke. Four-fifths of the land was owned by but 7,000 individuals, and of the sixteen who received more than £100,000 a year in rental income, all except two were peers.[124] Yet if the estimated value of English land rose 29 percent between 1814 and 1868 (from £37 million to £48 million), it hardly kept pace with the 169 percent rise in the value of all real property (land, houses, railways, etc.) during the same period.[125] Nor did large-scale investment in agricultural land prove profitable. Thus the estimated annual rate of return on the duke of Northumberland's investments in farm improvements between

---

[120] "Ancient Country Gentlemen of England," *Fraser's Magazine*, 7:42 (June 1833), 657.

[121] Thompson, *English Landed Society*, 116.

[122] Ibid., 212.

[123] Ibid., 158–61, 247–48; David Spring, "Aristocracy, Social Structure, and Religion in the Early Victorian Period," *Victorian Studies*, 6:3 (Mar. 1963), 272–73.

[124] See review of Douglas Sutherland, *The Landowners* (London, 1969), in *Times Literary Supplement*, 27 Feb. 1969, 202; cf. John Bateman, *The Great Landowners of Great Britain and Ireland*, 4th ed. (London, 1883).

[125] J. H. Clapham, *Economic History of Modern Britain* (Cambridge, 1930–32), II, 278.

1847 and 1878 was 1.5 percent.[126] As F. M. L. Thompson observes, "an industrial capitalist who survived for many years with no return on his fixed capital, and eventually began to receive under 2½ per cent would have been a great curiosity in Victorian England."[127] Among the owners of agricultural land, he was the rule rather than the exception.

Whatever the vicissitudes of farm income earlier in the century, there is little question that "the great depression" of 1873–96 caused that income to decline. The period was marked by a general deflation and a widespread lowering of profit margins. As a result of American competition, English wheat prices fell by half between 1870 and the mid-1890s, and the total acreage devoted to raising grain declined by more than a third. Rent rolls declined by 30 or even 50 percent, and almost all incentive for making additional rural improvements disappeared. The same processes often aided cattle and dairy farmers, for whom the late Victorian years were years of stability or growth rather than of decline. The agricultural depression was above all a depression in wheat, and to a lesser extent in barley and wool.[128]

Many landowners clearly suffered from the depression, and their place in the rural social structure deteriorated accordingly; yet when we learn that the duke of Northumberland had a more opulent standard of living in 1895 than in 1870, we must look at the total situation once more. Land is too often equated with agricultural land on which grain is grown or cattle are pastured. The truly profitable land for many Victorian landed aristocrats, however, was urban land, upon which towns and cities were being built. Large sections of London, for example, were owned by the dukes of Bedford, Portland, Norfolk, and Westminster, large sections of Liverpool by the earls of Derby and the marquesses of Salisbury, large areas of Sheffield by the dukes of Norfolk and the earls Fitzwilliam. The list is lengthy.[129] By 1844 the duke of Portland was receiving half his net income—£50,000 a year—from rentals on his London properties. The duke of Bedford attributed 72 percent of his net estate income of his London properties.[130] The Grosvenors and the Russells fell into a similar category. When such property was sold, the profit was likely to be considerable.

[126] Thompson, *English Landed Society*, 250.
[127] Ibid., 252.
[128] Ibid., 303, 308–9, 315; T. W. Fletcher, "The Great Depression of English Agriculture, 1873–1896," *Economic History Review*, 2nd ser., 13:3 (Apr. 1961), 417–32.
[129] Thompson, *English Landed Society*, 267; Spring, "The English Landed Estate," 9.
[130] Thompson, *English Landed Society*, 267; David Spring, *The English Landed Estate in the Nineteenth Century: Its Administration* (Baltimore, 1963), 141. See also Frank Banfield, *The Great Landlords of London* (London, 1888), 73–92.

Thus when the Metropolitan Board of Works acquired Northumberland House in the Strand in 1874 for street widening purposes, the duke of Northumberland received £497,000 in compensation.[131]

Land could provide income in another way. If minerals lay below—especially coal—the landowner could lease out the mines or collect annual royalties or even set up and operate the collieries himself. The duke of Northumberland received about 20 percent of his net income from coal mines in the mid-Victorian years; by 1914 the proportion had risen to 60 percent.[132] The duke of Bedford owned the most valuable copper and arsenic mines in Britain, and the duke of Cleveland and the marquess of Bath owned valuable lead mines. The earl of Durham's income from his coal mines was twice as high as his income from agricultural land.[133]

Although the coming of the railway during the early and mid-Victorian years might disturb the placidity of the countryside and bring to a close the ducal processions, which resembled royal progresses with their vast retinue and air of ceremony, they also brought mostly gain to aristocratic purses. Thus the duke of Northumberland received £23,000 in compensation for railway rights-of-way between 1847 and 1851. It was generally agreed that a railway increased the rentable value of nearby farmland by 5 to 20 percent.[134]

Other, if relatively minor, sources of aristocratic income were provided by the sale of timber, bark, and venison, by the leasing of pasture land, and even—in anticipation of more recent times—by charging admission for conducted tours of a country estate. Thus the mid-Victorian earl of Pembroke made up to £50 a year from conducted tours of his Wilton House.[135]

Asked by a young nobleman in the middle of the eighteenth century what had become of the gallantry and military spirit of the old English nobility, Dr. Samuel Johnson replied: "Why, my Lord, I'll tell you what is become of it: it is gone into the city to look for a fortune."[136] The notion is an inviting one—that the nineteenth-century aristocracy survived economically by going into industry—but by and large the evidence would seem to point the other way. Individual aristocrats did own and operate canals and mines, and in a few instances even iron foundries and docks connected with their mines. But the degree of aristocratic entrepreneur-

[131] Thompson, *English Landed Society*, 105.

[132] Ibid., 266, 317.

[133] Ibid., 266; Spring, "The English Landed Estate," 22, and *The English Landed Estate: Administration*, 43.

[134] Thompson, *English Landed Society*, 65, 256, 262.

[135] Ibid., 97.

[136] *Boswell's Life of Johnson*, ed. G. B. Hill and L. F. Powell (Oxford, 1934), II, 126.

ship should not be exaggerated. In 1869 only 5 percent of all the collieries in England were operated as well as owned by landowners.[137]

Bagehot, writing in the 1860s, felt certain that "there is no educated human being less likely to know business, worse placed for knowing business than a young lord."[138] Railway directorships were pressed upon often reluctant aristocrats as a way of gaining prestigious names and local sympathy for such enterprises, but actual aristocratic investments in such railways tended to be relatively small. The 1850 edition of Bradshaw's *General Railway Directory* listed only twenty-four peers and twenty-five sons of peers as railway directors. During the late Victorian years the number of railway directors in the House of Lords at any one time did not rise above fifty-nine.[139] Some aristocratic funds had always been invested in government bonds, but until the 1880s there was no general movement by landowners to diversify their assets by investing in stock exchange securities. There were extremely well-to-do peers in the England of 1900. The seventh duke of Devonshire left a fortune of over £1,790,000 upon his death in 1891; the sixth Earl Fitzwilliam's fortune upon his death in 1902 was close to £3 million.[140] The landed gentry dependent upon rents from agricultural land alone had obviously done much less well, but the great landowners had for the most part kept pace with economic change by remaining dependent upon land in its widest sense—the rent tolls it provided in town as well as country, the mines that lay beneath it, the railway rights-of-way that traversed it.

One explanation for the survival of the Victorian aristocracy to which historians have paid far too little attention is the failure of businessmen to acquire the prestige as businessmen that one might well have anticipated in the land that pioneered industrialization and became the nineteenth-century "workshop of the world." In the most prominent recent reassessment of Victorian society, Harold Perkin reiterates the notion that "the ideal citizen for the bulk of the middle class was, naturally, the capitalist, and the ideal society a class society based on capital and competition."

[137] Thompson, *English Landed Society*, 264. According to Charlotte Erickson, "It cannot be fairly said that [landowners] played an important part in the development of the steel industry"; *British Industrialists: Steel and Hosiery, 1850–1950* (Cambridge, 1959), 17.

[138] Bagehot, *English Constitution*, 161.

[139] J. T. Ward, "West Riding Landowners and the Railways," *Journal of Transport History*, 4:4 (Nov. 1960), 245–47; Philip S. Bagwell, "The Railway Interest: Its Organisation and Influence, 1839–1914," *Journal of Transport History*, 7:2 (Nov. 1965), 83–84.

[140] Thompson, *English Landed Society*, 307; G. E. Cockayne, *The Complete Peerage* (London, 1916–26), IV, 350; V, 525.

Perkin points out that the capitalist was visualized as the enterprising self-made owner-manager, and he goes on to celebrate the "triumph of the entrepreneurial ideal" in mid-Victorian England.[141] Yet the impact of Perkin's conclusion is immediately and almost completely vitiated by his admission that the "entrepreneurial class ruled, as it were, by remote control, through the power of its ideal over the ostensible ruling class, the landed aristocracy which continued to occupy the main positions of power down to the 1880s and beyond."[142]

Capitalist (or entrepreneurial) values such as thrift, duty, and character were certainly hailed in Victorian Britain. Samuel Smiles could recount a number of Horatio Alger success stories in his *Lives of the Engineers* (1861–62) and in kindred volumes. Yet the elevation of ideals was not accompanied by the placing of businessmen on pedestals, and it would never have occurred to Queen Victoria or any of her prime ministers to proclaim (à la Calvin Coolidge) that "the business of the British Empire is business." When Earl Russell invited middle-class manufacturer John Bright to his home for dinner in 1866, upper-class English society was shocked—even though Bright had by then been a public figure for a generation.[143]

Walter Bagehot suggested in the 1860s that the newspapers "give a precedent and a dignity to the political world which they do not give to any other. The literary world, the scientific world, the philosophic world, not only are not comparable in dignity to the political world, but in comparison are hardly worlds at all."[144] Bagehot was editor of the *Economist*, the foremost business journal of the day, yet it did not occur to him even to suggest the business world as a candidate for, much less the triumphant recipient of, such journalistic apotheosis. Trade was persistently scorned as crass, materialistic, undignified; and the fictional Soames Forsyte was speaking for several generations of upper-class Victorians when he cautioned his new wife that "the English are fearful snobs. . . . Look, Annette! It's very simple, only it wants understanding. Our professional and leisured classes still think of themselves a cut above our business classes, except of course the very rich. It may be stupid, but there it is, you see. It isn't advisable in England to let people know that you . . . kept a shop or were in any kind of trade. It may have been extremely creditable, but it puts a sort of label on you."[145]

---

[141] Harold Perkin, *The Origins of Modern English Society, 1780–1880* (London, 1969), esp. 221, 271.
[142] Ibid., 271–72.
[143] Thompson, *English Landed Society*, 209.
[144] Bagehot, *English Constitution*, 100.
[145] John Galsworthy, *The Forsyte Saga* (New York, 1932), II, 424.

It was a label one preferred to hide rather than advertise. In turning down a business offer in 1875, young Frederick Lugard, the future empire-builder in Africa, observed: "Of course 'a gentleman is a gentleman wherever he is,' but still the Lugards have been in the Army and in the Church, good servants of *God* or the *Queen*, but few if any have been tradesmen."[146] A decade later another empire-builder, Sir Herbert (later Lord) Kitchener, was congratulated for ignoring "the narrow tradesman's point of view" in his administration of the Sudan and for concentrating instead upon "the main questions which concern us as a nation."[147] Top businessmen did not move in the highest social circles, either in the far reaches of the empire or at home, and most Victorians would rather have sat down to a bad meal with a stupid aristocrat than to a good meal with an intelligent businessman.[148] "In Britain," wrote Stephen Aris in 1971, "the businessman enjoys a somewhat ambiguous position. . . ."[149] It has always been so.

"The merchant," T. H. S. Escott noted in his acute temporary appraisal of late Victorian England, "represents an interest which is *almost* deserving of a place among the estates of the realm." They ranked so high, Escott suggested, because they had learned to minimize or conceal the speculative elements in their enterprises and because they had allowed themselves time to devote attention "to the pursuits of society and the affairs of the country." Unlike the far less trustworthy stockjobbers, they drove to their places of business in horse-drawn carriages rather than catching commuter trains to the city.[150] Obviously the businessmen most highly thought of in Victorian England were those who acted least like businessmen or who, ideally, had ceased to be businessmen altogether.

Gladstone once wondered "why commerce in England should not have its old families, rejoicing to be connected with commerce from generation to generation. It has been so in other countries; I trust it will be so in this country."[151] Yet it was not to be, except perhaps among distinctive religious groups such as the Quakers (with the Barings, Gurneys, and Cadburys) and the Jews (with the Rothschilds). "The once enterprising manufacturer," complained Arthur Shadwell in 1910, "has grown slack, he has let the business take care of itself, while he is shooting grouse or

[146] Cited in Margery Perham, *Lugard* (London, 1956), I, 35.

[147] Cited in Philip Magnus, *Kitchener* (New York, 1958), 71.

[148] Cf. D. C. M. Platt, *Finance, Trade, and Politics in British Foreign Policy, 1815–1914* (London, 1968), esp. xviii, xx.

[149] Aris was comparing the role of the businessman in England with his role in Japan; "For the Greater Glory of the Company," *Sunday Times* (London), 9 May 1971, 53.

[150] Escott, *England: Her People*, II, 40–41.

[151] Cited in John Morley, *The Life of William Ewart Gladstone* (London, 1903), I, 7.

yachting in the Mediterranean." A few years earlier G. B. Dibblee had noted sorrowfully that the "best brains of our upper classes will go anywhere but into industry—into a bank or a merchant's office perhaps, but not into horny-handed manufacture." Members of the middle class had increasingly acquired the same antibusiness prejudices: "the attractions of dignified and cultured ease, of politics or the learned professions are too dazzling. . . ." [152]

The phenomenon of the merchant seeking to become a landed gentleman was not new in Victorian England; what is easily ignored is how strongly such a Tudor phenomenon persisted. In his *Culture and Anarchy*, Matthew Arnold wrote somewhat disdainfully of "industrialists in search of gentility." [153] "See," wrote Richard Cobden, the exemplar of the oft touted middle-class triumph, "how every successful trader buys an estate!" [154] The most extreme Victorian example of that process was Lord Overstone, a member of the Ashburton branch of the Baring family, who between 1823 and 1883 spent £1,670,000 in the purchase of landed property. [155] By purchasing Canford in 1845 for £345,000, Sir John Guest began "the transformation of Dowlais iron into Dorset aristocracy," and laid the groundwork for the peerage conferred upon his son in 1880. [156] Innumerable other examples could be cited of successful businessmen with their families who in the course of half a century gradually withdrew from the arena of their financial success in order to become country gentlemen. [157] The new country gentlemen were far more likely to assimilate the tastes and attitudes of their new connections than to impose a capitalist or entrepreneurial spirit upon them.

But what of the public schools? Did not these institutions, reformed by Dr. Thomas Arnold of Rugby and his disciples, do their share in impos-

[152] Cited in A. L. Levine, *Industrial Retardation in Britain, 1880–1914* (New York, 1967), 3, 73. Levine concludes that "social-psychological" and "social-cultural" phenomena rather than purely economic disadvantages were ultimately responsible for Britain's relative industrial decline during the period in question. Although he cites conservatism, the "deification of amateurism," and the relative neglect of both science and "scientific management," he pays perhaps too little attention to the relative lack of prestige (e.g., vis-à-vis the United States) that a business career provided (see 21, 57–58, 61–62, 68). He concedes that the origins of Britain's technological lag went back to the 1850s or even the 1830s (17).

[153] (London, 1969), 210.

[154] Cited in O. F. Christie, *The Transition to Democracy, 1867–1914* (London, 1934), 147–48.

[155] Cited in Thompson, *English Landed Society*, 39.

[156] Ibid., 40.

[157] Ibid., 129, 298. See also D. H. Aldcroft, "The Entrepreneur and the British Economy, 1870–1914," *Economic History Review*, 2nd ser., 17:1 (Aug. 1964), 128–29. Peter Laslett discerned the same pattern in seventeenth-century England; *World We Have Lost*, 48.

ing middle-class values upon the aristocracy? Harold Perkin has recently reiterated the notion that the public school reform movement was "a response to the bludgeonings of middle-class critics," and that the reformers "embraced the new entrepreneurial ideal and its morality and instilled them into the sons of the aristocracy and gentry."[158] Can the reform of such elite educational institutions as Eton, Harrow, and Rugby thus be viewed as epitomizing the Victorian triumph of middle-class ideals?

The alternative point of view put forth by Rupert Wilkinson is both better documented and more persuasive. He suggests that the reformed public school system "'captured' middle-class talent in the promotion of gentry-class power." "By indoctrinating the *nouveau riche* as a gentleman, the public schools really acted as an escape-valve in the social system. They helped avert a class conflict which might have ended the reign of the landed gentry."[159] It could be argued that the typical eighteenth-century aristocrat was as likely to have been educated by a private tutor as by any school, however prestigious, and that the emphasis on religion and competitive sports that was part of Dr. Thomas Arnold's program of "muscular Christianity" was more middle class than aristocratic. Yet during the first half of the nineteenth century the number of tradesmen's sons at schools like Eton was declining rather than rising.[160] Even when the proportion began to grow again in the mid-Victorian years, the businessman's ethos would not predominate. "Look at the bottle-merchant's son and the Plantagenet being brought up side by side," wrote Thomas Arnold's son Matthew in the late 1860s. "Very likely young Bottles will end by being a lord himself."[161]

Public school life was austere and could be cruel. Its purpose was to subordinate individualism and foster an almost mystical fondness for the community that might in later life be transferred to the House of Commons, an army regiment, or the queen as symbol of the British Empire. Even the prosaic *Times* sounded romantic when it described Eton as "a continuous body of gentlemen of all ages, having one common centre at school, and only leaving it for active life, to return to it, as it were, in their sons."[162] Sharp differences in rank were emphasized, but so were notions of fair play, self-restraint, and leadership relying on consensus. The goal

[158] *Origins of Modern English Society*, 297–98.
[159] Wilkinson, *Gentlemanly Power*, esp. viii, 4, 24.
[160] E. L. Woodward, *The Age of Reform, 1815–1870* (Oxford, 1938), 465; Wilkinson, *Gentlemanly Power*, 12.
[161] Cited in Asa Briggs, *Victorian People* (Chicago, 1955), 145.
[162] *Times* (London), 6 June 1861, 8, cited in Edward C. Mack, *Public Schools and British Opinion since 1860* (New York, 1941), 20f. See also Edward C. Mack, *Public Schools and British Opinion, 1780–1860* (New York, 1939).

of the system was to produce a boy who loyally obeyed his superiors and who at the same time could command a regiment or head a government.

The gentlemanly ideal of the mid-Victorian educator was not identical with earlier aristocratic ideals; Bertrand Russell—himself a third earl—was to suggest that "the concept of the gentleman was invented by the aristocrats to keep the middle classes in order."[163] Yet the ultimate amalgam incorporated more of the dicta of Lord Chesterfield than the maxims of Samuel Smiles. The public school also continued to emphasize the non-utilitarian virtues of a classical education: in 1884 Eton had twenty-eight classics masters, six mathematics masters, no modern language teacher, no science teacher, and one historian.[164] It emphasized the virtues of continuity and tradition far more than the advantages of a utilitarian rationalism. It stressed hierarchy rather than social equality. It formed "a citadel against the materialism and selfishness generated by the new capitalism of the Industrial Revolution."[165] The reformed public school reinforced the aristocratic cult of the amateur and the aristocratic tradition of public service. It bred a sense of self-assurance analogous to "the certainties generated by the aristocratic family."[166] To be an Etonian, recalled Shane Leslie, was to "imbibe a certain sense of effortless superiority. . . ."[167] Not least of all, the public school helped develop a uniformity of accent, which in twentieth-century England became "the most sensitive delineator of social class."[168]

A public school education fostered a career in Parliament, the civil service, the army, India, or the Church of England. It discouraged careers in science, technology, and industry. A survey of 524 steel manufacturers active between 1850 and 1950 indicates that only 33 attended Eton or Harrow.[169] A survey of 651 members of the House of Commons in 1869 indicates that at least 156 had graduated from one of the two schools.[170] At a time when at least 50 percent of the members of the House of Commons were graduates of Oxford or Cambridge, only 9 out of 164 steel manufacturers active between 1875 and 1895 could call one of these institutions their alma mater.

Numerically the public schools and the universities—which even in the 1860s continued to provide special gowns and special dining privileges for

[163] Cited by Alan Brien, *Sunday Times* (London), 1 Aug. 1971.
[164] Wilkinson, *Gentlemanly Power*, 64.
[165] Ibid., 91–92; see also 38–42, 110.
[166] Ibid., 61.
[167] *The End of a Chapter* (New York, 1916), 40.
[168] Thompson, *English Landed Society*, 85.
[169] Erickson, *British Industrialists*, 35.
[170] The estimate is based on an analysis of *Dod's Parliamentary Companion* (London, 1869).

aristocrats[171]–formed only a minute portion of Britain's increasingly complex educational structure; but when it came to prestige and to the training of political leaders, it was these institutions that counted. And whatever their virtues in staffing a distinguished and often admirably disinterested civil service, they did little to foster industrial enterprise; they were friendly neither to creative imaginations nor to innovation generally. They looked upon business as a fundamentally crass and ungentlemanly occupation. "If the Industrial Revolution began in Britain," concludes Rupert Wilkinson in a characteristic gentlemanly understatement, "it was not because of the public schools."[172] Soames Forsyte's reflections upon the passing of the Victorian age are similar: "Sixty-four years that favoured property, and had made the upper middle class; buttressed, chiselled, polished it; till it was almost indistinguishable in manners, morals, speech, appearance, habit, and soul from the nobility."[173] By absorbing members of the business class rather than being vanquished by them, the Victorian aristocracy and gentry survived.

The ultimate goal of most businessmen was to become, or to have their sons and grandsons become, landed gentlemen and perchance landed aristocrats; and the accepted tradition for the sons of such aristocrats and gentlemen was to enter the prestige professions. "There is no other body of men in the country," wrote James Caird in 1878, "whose influence is so widely extended and universally present. From them the learned professions, the church, the army, and the public services are largely recruited."[174] It was easy enough for early nineteenth-century middle-class radicals to denounce the aristocracy as fundamentally parasitic, the exploiters of toil of others, the recipients of private and public patronage. Yet one of the reasons for the survival of the Victorian aristocracy must surely be the fact that many of their sons continued to fill positions that were not mere sinecures but enabled their holders to gain and confirm prestige in the eyes of their countrymen.

The continued involvement of the landed classes in the largely unpaid positions as members of Parliament and as county magistrates has been dealt with earlier. There was a similar continuity in the social background of the holders of paid civil service positions of an administrative nature. The substitution of competitive examinations for older methods of patronage between 1854 and 1870 may justly be regarded as a triumph for the

---

[171] Arthur James Balfour, *Retrospect: An Unfinished Autobiography, 1848–1886* (Boston, 1930), 20–21.

[172] Wilkinson, *Gentlemanly Power*, 215.

[173] Galsworthy, *Forsyte Saga*, II, 413.

[174] James Caird, *The Landed Interest and the Supply of Food* (London, 1878), 58.

entrepreneurial ideal. Yet the examinations themselves were geared to the kind of education the public schools and universities provided. Gladstone, the minister most responsible for bringing the examination system into being, predicted happily to a colleague in 1854 that the change would confer "an immense superiority [upon] all those who may be called gentlemen by birth and training."[175] Recent students of the subject concur that "the patrician status of many civil servants was a fact of the first importance."[176] Permanent secretaries usually had an education and social standing equal to, in a few cases superior to, the cabinet members they served; the higher civil service posts were therefore seen as far more respectable than positions in banks, insurance offices, or business offices. In the words of one observer of 1888, they were "able to deal with persons outside the office as gentlemen."[177]

Two areas in which patronage continued to hold sway even after 1870 were the Church of England and the army. Like the House of Lords, the Church of England was under attack in the 1830s, and its leaders were criticized, among other things, for paying less attention to preaching the gospel than to providing the children of aristocrats with good incomes.[178] The specter of disestablishment hovered over the church, but except in Ireland (and, in the early twentieth century, in Wales), it remained a phantom. Bishops, whatever their individual merits, continued to come from aristocratic or gentry backgrounds. The right to appoint a majority of parish priests remained in the hands of individual patrons, who almost invariably were landed gentlemen.[179]

Noble lineage counted even more in the army than in the church, and commissions in the best regiments remained the preserve of the scions of aristocratic families. Criticism of aristocratic mismanagement during the Crimean War did lead several years later (in 1871) to the abolition of the system of purchasing commissions. Other reforms were largely thwarted by the second duke of Cambridge, first cousin to Queen Victoria, who retained the post of commander in chief of the army from 1856 to 1895, and for whom the military organization that won the battle of Waterloo remained good enough. The late Victorian army was noted for the absence

---

[175] Cited in Wilkinson, *Gentlemanly Power*, 23. The paradox that a Victorian tendency toward professionalization in law, medicine, and architecture coexisted with the persistence of a fundamentally nonutilitarian—indeed non-"middle-class"—education is explored by W. J. Reader, in *Professional Men: The Rise of the Professional Classes in Nineteenth-Century England* (London, 1966), ch. 7.

[176] Henry Parris, *Constitutional Bureaucracy* (London, 1969), 145.

[177] Sir Thomas Farrer, cited in Geoffrey Kingdon Fry, *Statesmen in Disguise* (London, 1969), 86; see also 46, 68, 72.

[178] Cf. Owen Chadwick, *The Victorian Church*, I (Cambridge, 1966), 173.

[179] Thompson, *English Landed Society*, 71.

of a general staff, a lack of specialization, and a spirit of gentlemanly amateurishness. Writing privately from South Africa at the time of the Boer War, the newly created Lord Kitchener complained that "people here do not seem to look upon war sufficiently seriously. It is considered too much like a game of polo, with intervals for afternoon tea. . . ."[180] Some significant reforms were to take place in the early years of the twentieth century, but in the middle of World War I, veteran journalist Thomas Escott could still observe complacently: "From Wellington to Kitchener, the continuity of the military succession has been without a break."[181]

Professionalism was more apparent in the British navy, but there too one could discern a keen awareness of social class distinctions. When Disraeli wished in 1877 to appoint as first lord of the Admiralty William Henry Smith, a man who had aided his father in building a gigantic newspaper distribution and railway bookstall business, Queen Victoria was sorely troubled. She reminded her prime minister that "it may *not please* the Navy in which service so many of the *highest rank* serve, & who claim to be equal to the Army—if a man of the Middle Class is placed above them in that very high Post. . . ." Disraeli assured the queen that in addition to his other virtues, Smith displayed "a perfect temper & conciliatory manners." The queen accompanied her ultimate acquiescence with a final warning that Smith must not "lord it over the Navy (which almost every First Lord does) & be a little modest & not act the Lord High Admiral which is offensive to the Service. . . ."[182] Smith was to be satirized by Gilbert and Sullivan in *H.M.S. Pinafore* as "the office boy in an attorney's firm" who polished up the handle of the big front door so carefully that he eventually became "the Ruler of the Queen's Navee." He remained so conscious of his lowly station that in 1885 when Queen Victoria offered to confer the Grand Cross of the Bath upon him, Smith declined the honor. Lord Salisbury attributed the refusal to Smith's "peculiar position with respect to his extraction and the original avocation of his family."[183] By 1885 Smith had been a member of Parliament for almost two decades, had served twice as a cabinet member, and had long since withdrawn from the active management of his eminently respectable family business.

The British Empire was closely connected with the military services in offering outlets for the ambitions of aristocrats, and it can hardly be doubted that the nineteenth-century expansion of that empire played a major role in the preservation of the Victorian aristocracy. Early in the

[180] Cited in Magnus, *Kitchener*, 162.
[181] Escott, *Great Victorians*, 145.
[182] Cited in Viscount Chilston, *W. H. Smith* (London, 1965), 94–95.
[183] Cited in ibid., 205.

nineteenth century James Mill had sarcastically referred to British colonies as constituting "a vast system of outdoor relief for the upper classes."[184] ("Outdoor relief" was the poor-law expression for assistance granted outside the parish workhouse.) The colonies continued to provide opportunities for income and occasional glory throughout the century. The institution of the competitive examination system for the Indian civil service in 1854, like the subsequent institution of the same for the civil service at home, had relatively little effect upon the social background of successful applicants.[185] When Disraeli, in his Crystal Palace speech of 1872, sought to reawaken what he considered a slumbering pride in empire among his fellow Englishmen, he stressed this very theme: "The issue is not a mean one. It is whether you will be content to be a comfortable England . . . or whether you will be a great country—an Imperial country—a country where your sons, when they rise, rise to paramount positions. . . ."[186]

Imbued by an elitist public school ethos that caused the fledgling imperial administrator to see himself above his native charges in civilization and morality as well as above bribery and graft, England's sons did rise to paramount positions all over the world. "From the standpoint of gentlemanly values, the principle of 'the white man's burden' was really an imperial extension of *noblesse oblige*."[187] In India, the British in effect imposed a caste of administrators upon the complex caste system already in existence; most of them had received a classical education, and in their approach to India they resembled the "guardians" of Plato's Republic. They were forbidden to own land in India or to engage in trade.[188] The British Empire was fundamentally an aristocratic enterprise, and even in the 1920s two of every three Indian civil servants and colonial or dominion governors hailed from the same small number of public schools. School friends became administrative associates, and the empire could justly be said to be governed on a first-name basis.[189]

The late Victorian imperial revival went hand in hand with a revival of monarchical popularity that the critics of George IV and William IV in the 1820s and 1830s would hardly have anticipated. Monarchical power had diminished, if not so much as is commonly believed,[190] but monarchical

---

184 Cited in John A. Hobson, *Imperialism: A Study* (London, 1902), 51.

185 J. M. Compton, "Open Competition and the India Service, 1854–1876," *English Historical Review*, 88 (Apr. 1968), 265–84.

186 T. E. Kebble, ed., *Selected Speeches of the Late Right Honourable the Earl of Beaconsfield* (London, 1882), II, 534.

187 Wilkinson, *Gentlemanly Power*, 100.

188 Philip Woodruff, *The Men Who Ruled India* (London, 1954), II, 75–78.

189 Wilkinson, *Gentlemanly Power*, 102; Guttsman, *British Political Elite*, 319.

190 Cf. Frank Hardie, *The Political Influence of the British Monarchy, 1868–1952* (London, 1970), ch. 2 and 3.

prestige was at an all-time high by the 1880s. Queen Victoria may have been bourgeois in her daily habits and her disapproval of gambling and sexual indulgence, but at her court she was the most punctilious promoter of distinctions in rank. At receptions for debutantes the queen would kiss the daughters of dukes, marquesses, and earls on the forehead while merely extending a hand to the daughters of lesser nobles; tradesmen's daughters were not invited at all. When at one reception the queen seemed inadvertently about to kiss the daughter of a mere knight, an observant gentleman-in-waiting was so shocked that he burst out in alarm: "Don't kiss her, Your Majesty; she's not a real lady!"[191]

What of yet another explanation for the survival of the Victorian aristocracy: that aristocrats adjusted with sufficient success to middle-class morality so as to appease the widespread early nineteenth-century criticism of their extravagance, their self-indulgence, their lechery, and their frivolity. The notion that they adapted their manners to the dictates of Victorianism has often been advanced. Edmund Burke had suggested in the 1790s, "Manners are more important than laws. Upon them in a great measure the laws depend. The law touches us but here and there and now and then. Manners are what vex and soothe, corrupt or purify, exalt or debase, barbarize or refine us, by a constant, steady, uniform and insensible operation, like that of the air we breathe in."[192]

If Burke was right, then surely a significant alteration in manners—though requiring explanation in turn—may become a significant explanatory strand. Half a century ago, Halévy wrote of the early nineteenth-century middle class: "dogmatic in morals, proud of its practical outlook, and sufficiently powerful to obtain respect for its views from the proletariat on the one hand, from the aristocracy on the other."[193] G. K. Chesterton was to phrase the matter more succinctly: "The great lords yielded on prudery as they had yielded on free trade." A disillusioned Karl Marx struck an analogous note during the mid-Victorian years: "The ultimate aim of this most bourgeois of lands would seem to be the establishment of a bourgeois aristocracy and a bourgeois proletariat, side by side with the bourgeoisie. . . ."[194]

In the 1830s there may indeed have been at least briefly a conscious desire to appease criticism by mending manners. Thus in an 1834 article entitled "Hints to the Aristocracy," *Blackwood's Magazine*, a Tory journal,

[191] Cited in Petrie, *The Victorians*, 51–52.
[192] Edmund Burke, *Letter on a Regicide Peace*, cited in Maurice J. Quinlan, *Victorian Prelude* (New York, 1941), 69.
[193] Halévy, *England in 1815*, 590.
[194] Cited in Magnus, *Gladstone*, 163.

recommended less social exclusiveness, greater seriousness, and fewer field sports.[195] Aristocrats reduced their expenditure on servants' liveries, acquiesced in the closing of gambling clubs and the decline of dueling in the 1840s, and became less dandified in dress and involved less frequently in publicized sexual adventures and misadventures.[196] They drank less and swore less; they also became more hypocritical, but as the *Morning Chronicle* observed as early as 1827, "hypocrisy is, at all events, an homage offered to public opinion, and supposes the existence of a fear of the people."[197]

The conclusion that the mid-Victorian aristocracy was made up mostly of earnest and prudish puritans would do more to support a thesis of aristocratic suppression than of aristocratic survival. It would also be very wide of the mark. Lord Frankfort did not hesitate to sue his former mistress in the courts in order to regain some jewels.[198] Lengthy if largely unpublicized liaisons with married women did not injure the career of Lord Palmerston in the early Victorian era, of the marquess of Hartington in the mid-Victorian years, or of Arthur J. Balfour as the century drew to a close.[199] When a club steward forgot to take the fifth earl of Glasgow a drink he had ordered and went to bed instead, the earl sought out the steward and set his bedclothes afire.[200]

The favorite novel of young aristocrats in the 1850s was George Alfred Lawrence's now forgotten *Guy Livingstone*. They admired the novel's hero, according to whom "the world consists of soldiers, the aristocracy, and others. Of these classes the first two treat as they please the third, which duly submits, and even rather likes it." To chase women and chase foxes and allow frequent intervals for card playing—"Such," according to Guy Livingstone, "is the whole duty of man."[201] Horse racing remained the vocation as much as the avocation of the fourteenth earl of Derby, who served three times as prime minister during the 1850s and 1860s. Robert Peel's eldest son once suggested that to most Victorian aristocrats, "politics and racing seemed things which Providence had joined and which man ought not to put asunder."[202] Despite the shame that Victorians associated

---

[195] *Blackwood's Magazine*, 25 (1834), 68–80.

[196] Thompson, *English Landed Society*, 190; Quinlan, *Victorian Prelude*, 264; Gordon Rattray Taylor, *The Angel-Makers* (London, 1958), 252–53, 278.

[197] Cited in Quinlan, *Victorian Prelude*, 119.

[198] John W. Dodds, *The Age of Paradox: A Biography of England, 1841–1851* (London, 1953), 70.

[199] Cf. H. C. F. Bell, *Lord Palmerston* (London, 1936), I, 97; Tuchman, *Proud Tower*, 39, 49.

[200] Petrie, *The Victorians*, 192.

[201] Cited in Escott, *Great Victorians*, 331.

[202] Cited in ibid., 233.

with bankruptcy, the duke of Newcastle, the earl of Winchilsea, and Lord De Mauley were all involved in bankruptcy cases in 1870. Even the wealthiest aristocrats occasionally lived beyond their means, and their sons were yet more likely to be extravagant.[203]

The Victorian era was a complex one, and class influences did not make themselves felt in simplistic fashion. The aristocratic influence upon middle-class attitudes toward education and business has been noted above. Admittedly there was a middle-class influence that subtly altered aristocratic mores, yet many aristocrats never became Victorian in the stereotyped sense now often attached to the term. For much of the century they felt themselves separated from Victoria's court. While Albert was alive, he preferred the company of businessmen and scientists; after his death, the "Widow of Windsor" chose for two decades to be separated from almost all society. Victoria upheld distinctions in rank, but she tended to hold suspect the conduct of many aristocrats. Such people were all too likely to exert an unfortunate influence upon her son and heir, the Prince of Wales, and his "Marlborough House set."[204]

A thesis of aristocratic embourgeoisement during the Victorian era is also open to criticism, because the changes of manner it involved clearly preceded the 1830s. The initial decline in drunkenness, profanity, gambling, and obscenity may have been more immediately a response to the French Revolution of 1789 than to the English Reform Act of 1832. If so, it clearly coincided with, rather than followed, the last age of unquestioned aristocratic supremacy.[205] Events in France, the *Annual Register* of 1798 observed, had done more to persuade the upper classes of the connection between good morals and social order "than all the eloquence of the pulpit and the disquisition of moral philosophers had done for many centuries." The common people were startled to see the avenues to churches filled with the carriages of aristocrats and gentlemen.[206] The custom of church attendance among the upper classes, a rarity in the eighteenth century, continued into the early Victorian years, as did the custom of daily prayers at home for the family and household servants. The evangelical bluestocking Hannah More, who had addressed the aristocracy with *Thoughts on the Importance of the Manners of the Great to General Society* in 1788, was comforted in her old age—in the 1820s—to "have lived to see such an increase of genuine religion among the higher classes of society."[207] A House

[203] Thompson, *English Landed Society*, 286.
[204] Elizabeth Longford, *Victoria, R.I.* (London, 1964), 472.
[205] Such is, in part, Quinlan's argument in *Victorian Prelude*, esp. 262.
[206] Cited in ibid., 96.
[207] Cited in ibid., 256.

of Commons committee noted with satisfaction in 1832 the increasingly decorous nature of Sunday observance among the upper classes. Such a state of affairs was taken for granted by the 1850s.[208]

Such religiosity was admittedly the product of self-interest as well as of evangelical conversion. The duke of Wellington, who hardly ever attended church in London, did so faithfully once a week in the country. "I consider," he explained, "that the attendance at divine service in publick is a duty upon every individual in high station, who has a large house and many servants, and whose example might influence the conduct of others."[209] Aristocrats did indeed influence the conduct of others, and philanthropic organizations that failed to attract the patronage of one or more titled noblemen were equally unlikely to attract monetary contributions. Aristocrats were the taste-makers of society. They preserved the manners, art, books, and gardens that gave meaning to civilization. The visiting French observer Hippolyte Taine was impressed in the 1860s by the manner in which aristocrats were "expected to be first in opening their purses as the feudal barons were expected to be in the forefront of the battle." They fulfilled these expectations, Taine concluded, in devoting as much as 10 percent of their annual income to charitable purposes.[210] A more recent historian estimates 4 to 7 percent as the customary standard among aristocrats, and but 1 to 2 percent among the gentry.[211]

Evangelical ideas added a new patina to traditional notions of noblesse oblige. Upper-class women, who were placed by early nineteenth-century educators upon a pedestal that precluded gainful employment, were still expected to succor the poor; in Hannah More's words, "every young lady should become an amateur social worker."[212] Most aristocrats concentrated their paternalistic impulses upon their own estates. Such parochialism was insufficient for Anthony Ashley Cooper, the seventh earl of Shaftesbury and the most eminent evangelical layman and aristocratic social reformer of the Victorian era; in 1844 he wrote: "We must have nobler, deeper and sterner stuff; less of refinement and more of truth; more of the inward, not so much of the outward, gentleman; a rigid sense of duty, not a 'delicate sense of honour'; a just estimate of rank and property, not as matters of personal enjoyment and display, but as gifts from God, bringing with them serious responsibilities, and involving a fearful account."[213]

[208] Chadwick, *Victorian Church*, I, 325, 366, 456.
[209] Cited in ibid., 515.
[210] Taine, *Notes on England*, 141–42.
[211] Thompson, *English Landed Society*, 210.
[212] Cited in Quinlan, *Victorian Prelude*, 155.
[213] Cited in Edwin Hodder, *Life and Works of the Seventh Earl of Shaftesbury, K.G.* (London, 1887), II, 77.

Few Victorian aristocrats would have met Shaftesbury's test, but the very fact that there were some—that men like Shaftesbury could devote a political lifetime to the alleviation of the lot of the factory worker, the miner, and the chimney sweep—elevated the prestige of the aristocracy as a group among the other classes of society. It has also had an impact upon the twentieth-century chroniclers of English working-class life. John L. and Barbara Hammond, after recounting the woes of the early nineteenth-century lower classes, turned to a sympathetic, and frequently reprinted, life of Lord Shaftesbury. It would never have occurred to them to write a biography of Richard Cobden or John Bright. Shaftesbury emphasized the duties of rank, not its abolition; he expected the gratitude of those he aided, not their self-help. Shaftesbury's notion of social reform was clearly paternalistic;[214] but have twentieth-century notions of social reform been fundamentally different? The fact remains that Victorian aristocrats aided their own survival by an adroit if partial (and in large part pre-Victorian) transformation of image, by their charities, and occasionally by their espousal of social reform.

Shortly before his death in 1852, the duke of Wellington attended a social gathering at which a local clergyman led the assembly in this traditional song: "God bless the squire and all his rich relations / And keep us poor people in our proper stations." "By all means," murmured the old warrior under his breath, "if it can be done."[215] To a significant degree it *was* done throughout the nineteenth century. The observations of several generations of foreign visitors and domestic commentators support the conclusion that English society exhibited a keen sense of social hierarchy, accompanied by a feeling of deference toward those who stood on a higher rung. When Englishmen encountered, in stagecoach or railway carriage, fellow countrymen of whose rank they were uncertain, they preferred silence to social error.

Prince Pückler-Muskau, a German who toured the British Isles in the late 1820s, expected to find republican realities beneath the trappings of nobility. Instead he found English life "ultra aristocratic" and indeed "caste-like."[216] An American visitor to the Great Exhibition of 1851 noted that as soon as the admission fee was reduced from ten shillings to one, popular attendance fell off, because of the lesser likelihood of seeing an aristocrat on the premises. In the 1860s Hippolyte Taine observed that

---

[214] Cf. Michael E. Rose's review of the most recent reprint of the Hammond biography, in *Economic History Review*, 2nd ser., 23: 3 (Dec. 1970), 587–88.

[215] Cited in Escott, *Great Victorians*, 53.

[216] E. M. Butler, ed., *A Regency Visitor* (London, 1957), 333.

English aristocrats seemed to receive from lower-class people a spontaneous respect that their continental counterparts failed to obtain.[217]

Domestic observers, whether critics or upholders of the status quo, concurred that Englishmen somehow combined a love of individual liberty with an elaborate system of privilege and precedence. Richard Cobden noted in the 1830s that whereas Frenchmen seemed continually concerned with "privileged inequality in their social system," Englishmen were little troubled.[218] Though Walter Bagehot's pragmatic *English Constitution* (1867) differed significantly from John Stuart Mill's more theoretical *Representative Government* (1861), Bagehot and Mill agreed on the significance of deference in English politics, on the willingness of most Englishmen to let themselves be governed by members of the upper classes. Nor had the taste run dry by the 1890s. "Every Englishman dearly loves a lord," Joseph Chamberlain noted with perplexity. To be a lord, Lord Ribblesdale agreed with satisfaction, "is still a popular thing."[219]

The survival of the Victorian aristocracy was aided not only by the acute sense of status that pervaded all classes in society; also the willingness to subordinate oneself to those of higher rank was matched by the expectation that those of lesser rank would defer to one in turn.[220] "The insatiable love of caste," complained Cobden in 1835, "pervades every degree from the highest to the lowest."[221] The process is illustrated to perfection in the several available versions of Mrs. Beeton's cookbook, first published in 1861 as *Beeton's Book of Household Management*. The original complete edition sold for 7s. 6d. For those who required "in a Cheaper form, complete and reliable information in the culinary department," there was Mrs. Beeton's *Everyday Cookery and Housekeeping Book* at 3s. 6d. For "Households and Families with more Moderate Means and requirements" there was *Mrs. Beeton's All About Cookery* at 2s. 6d. Mrs. Beeton's *Englishwoman's Cookery Book* was at 1s. directed to "the very numerous Middle-class Households where, with limited incomes, economy and good management are imperatively necessary"; the 600-recipe volume was also "well adapted for Presents from Mistress to Servants." *Mrs. Beeton's Sixpenny Cookery Book for the People* was expressly designed "for the great Working Classes of Britain." At the lowest end of the social scale, *Beeton's*

[217] Warren Isham, *The Mud Cabin* (New York, 1853), 116; Taine, *Notes on England*, 162.

[218] Cited in Thornton, *Habit of Authority*, 42. Cf. Grenville Fletcher, *Parliamentary Portraits*, 3rd ser. (London, 1862), 198.

[219] Cited, respectively, in Giovanni Costigan, *Makers of Modern England* (New York, 1967), 201, and Tuchman, *Proud Tower*, 15.

[220] See, e.g., Walter L. Arnstein, ed., "A German View of English Society: 1851," *Victorian Studies*, 16:2 (Dec. 1972), 185.

[221] Richard Cobden, *England, Ireland, and America* (London, 1835), 34.

Penny Cookery Book with its 200 "useful recipes" was recommended "for Distribution to every Cottage Home, as an incentive to improved domestic arrangements, and as a gift in Parish Schools."[222]

That the domestic staff of an aristocratic family had its own hierarchy was one of the truisms of Victorian life.[223] That domestic servants evaluated their own status by the social rank of their masters was another. Thus the American consul Adam Badeau relates the story of the domestic who went to work for a baronet but promptly gave notice: her new employer turned out to be a mere physician, whereas she was accustomed to working for true gentry.[224] That social rank continued to be measured in large degree by the number of servants a man had at his command is illustrated by a *Punch* cartoon of 1872. This conversation takes place:

PASSENGER: And whose house is that on the top of the hill there?
BUS DRIVER: Oh that's Mr. Unbeknownst, Sir. He's what they call a R.A. [member of the Royal Academy]
PASSENGER: O'Indeed! Ah a magnificent Painter! You must be rather proud of such a great man living amongst you down here.
DRIVER: Great Man, Sir? Lor' bless you, Sir, not a Bit of it! Why, they only Keeps one Man-Servant, and he don't sleep in the 'Ouse!!![225]

Assumptions of social hierachy remained most obvious in the social and political relations of landlord and tenants. The dependents of the duke of Northumberland avowed their position with frankness and with apparent enthusiasm at the annual dinner of 1859:

> Those relics of the feudal yoke
> Still in the north remain unbroke:
> That social yoke, with one accord,
> That binds the Peasant to his Lord . . .
> And Liberty, that idle vaunt,
> Is not the comfort that we want;
> It only serves to turn the head,
> But gives to none their daily bread.
> We want community of feeling,
> And landlords kindly in their dealing.[226]

---

[222] Cited in Steven Marcus' review of the facsimile edition of *Beeton's Book of Household Management*, in *New York Times Book Review*, 14 Dec. 1969, 3.
[223] Cf. Tocqueville's description of family prayers with servants at the house of Earl Radnor, in *Journeys to England and Ireland*, 68; also Badeau, *Aristocracy in England*, 103–4.
[224] Badeau, *Aristocracy in England*, 163.
[225] *Punch*, 20 Jan. 1872, 32.
[226] Cited in Thompson, *English Landed Society*, 291.

Though Victorians deplored blatant bribery, they acknowledged the role of "legitimate influence" in politics, the proper respect that tenants might and generally did pay to the advice of their landlords.[227] Perhaps the most extreme example of such influence was the election address Erle Drax, member of Parliament for a borough in Dorset, issued just prior to a general election: "Electors of Wareham! I understand that some evil-disposed person has been circulating a report that I wish my tenants, and other persons dependent on me, to vote according to their conscience. This is a dastardly lie; calculated to injure me. I have no wish of the sort. I wish, and I intend, that these persons shall vote for me."[228]

The political loyalty of economic dependents appears to have been as often the consequence of hope for future advantage or of ancient habit as of fear.[229] It was also the major reason why Liberals like Walter Bagehot opposed the drive toward universal manhood suffrage in the 1860s. In the rural areas, Bagehot feared, "the parson and the squire would have almost unlimited power. They would be able to drive or send to the poll an entire labouring population."[230]

During the 1830s and 1840s, the age of the anti–Corn Law League and the Chartist movement, the structure of deference seemed for a time to be on the verge of disintegration. Its persistence into the middle and late Victorian years represents in part a revival, a revival buttressed by the relative economic prosperity of the 1850s and 1860s and by the ability of Lord Palmerston to subordinate domestic divisions to a widespread sense of national community.

The habit of deference was fostered by religion, by education, and by yet other forces. From the 1790s on, the Religious Tract Society peddled hundreds of tracts—fifteen million per year by the 1840s—one of whose major lessons was that the humble ought to be content with the station to which God had been pleased to call them.[231] Miss Humphreys' *Hymns for Little Children*, published in 1848, included:

> The rich man in his castle,
> The poor man at his gate
> God made them, high or lowly,
> And ordered their estate.[232]

227 Cf. Clark, *Making of Victorian England*, 211–12.
228 Cited in Sir William Fraser, *Disraeli and His Day* (London, 1891), 218.
229 Cf. Thompson, *English Landed Society*, 201–7.
230 Bagehot, *English Constitution*, 185.
231 Quinlan, *Victorian Prelude*, 120.
232 Cited in Chadwick, *Victorian Church*, I, 347. *The Penguin Dictionary of Quotations* attributes the poem to Mrs. C. F. Alexander (1818–95).

Many Anglican churches seated worshipers in precise accordance with their social rank, and Victorian doctrines of degree and place are exemplified by the Anglican clergyman who warned his parishioners against the farm labor union organizers who promised them an earthly millennium. The fate of irreligious Paris, briefly in the hands of the Commune in 1871, presented an awful warning to those who would tamper with the different grades of society. "Let us take warning by her fate," the rector concluded, "and as God has been pleased to constitute various ranks of society by placing some in the higher, some in the middle, and some in the lower ranks, let us cheerfully accept the position He has assigned us, and be thankful for His mercies."[233]

The education system, which was voluntary and largely in Anglican hands until 1870, tended in a similar direction. The English history the fledgling scholars were taught—filtered into primers from the weighty volumes of Hallam, Macaulay, Froude, Freeman, and Stubbs—boasted a cast of kings, knights, and princesses playing their allotted roles in an epic reaching its apogee in the Victorian era. The kings and aristocrats were by no means all portrayed as heroes, yet they dominated the historical stage. The tone of these histories "was paternalistic, and they approved the successive paternalisms of English governments."[234]

Other forces may well have intertwined to perpetuate both the attitudes of deference and the belief in social hierarchy. Emigration provided a safety valve for the most restless and the most frustrated; at least a million and a half people per decade departed from the British Isles from the 1840s through the 1890s.[235] The revival of imperial interests in the popular press gave increased and generally favorable publicity to soldiers, and the army was by tradition the most obviously hierarchical of social institutions. The aristocracy continued to provide ordinary Englishmen with a vicarious romance and excitement that Hollywood movie stars were to provide in the 1930s and 1940s and pop singers and TV idols in more recent years. The survival of the aristocracy was based in significant part on the persistence of a sense of deference that itself was associated with notions of social hierarchy accepted to a greater or lesser degree by all members of Victorian society.

A last avenue of explanation deserves investigation as a clue to the survival of the Victorian aristocracy—the Irish Question. A generation ago,

[233] Cited in Wingfield-Stratford, *Those Earnest Victorians*, 307–8.
[234] Thornton, *Habit of Authority*, 262.
[235] Brian Mitchell and Phyllis Deane, eds., *Abstract of British Historical Statistics* (London, 1962), 47–48.

Sir Robert Ensor in a notable interpretative essay[236] called attention to one of the most significant and at the same time most paradoxical transformations of late Victorian Britain: in 1870 the Liberal party, the party of the left in terms of the political spectrum of the day, was dominant in Parliament and in the kingdom. In 1895—after the passage of the Secret Ballot Act and after the electorate had been made 63 percent larger as a result of the Reform Act of 1884—the party of the right, a Unionist coalition of Conservatives and ex-Liberals, was dominant in Parliament and the country. The fashionable Marxist answer would suggest that the early nineteenth-century bourgeoisie, which had first joined the Liberal party in order to struggle against the landed class that dominated the Conservative party, had subsequently made common cause with its erstwhile rivals in order to struggle against a rising proletariat. As Ensor went on to demonstrate in persuasive detail, however, the immediate cause of the late Victorian changes in party allegiance and predominance was the Irish Question. The Irish Question—in the form of agrarian depression and agrarian violence, of newly awakened national aspirations scarcely appeased by the occasional "carrots" of successive British governments and only sharpened by the "sticks" of repeated coercive acts—transformed many an English Liberal into an English Conservative.

It may be argued with equal justice that the same Irish Question fortuitously played a highly significant role in abetting the survival of the Victorian aristocracy. During the 1870s and early 1880s, a subtle process of class differentiation was increasingly delineating the Liberal and Conservative parties. The Conservatives were becoming not merely the party of country squires but also the party of urban businessmen and suburban white-collar workers, though for the moment the latter two groups were scarcely represented in the party's leadership.[237] In the meantime the Liberal party, though similarly led by landed gentlemen and to a lesser extent by lawyers and businessmen, was in the process of having its mass base increasingly made up of urban and rural laborers. The "Lib-Labs" of the late Victorian era (i.e., Liberal M.P.'s of laboring-class background) had no real Conservative counterparts.[238]

The traditional Whig faction was increasingly uncomfortable in the Liberal party of the 1880s, but it was still well represented in the cabinet

[236] R. C. K. Ensor, "Some Political and Economic Interactions in Late Victorian England," *Transactions of the Royal Historical Society*, 4th ser., 31 (1949), 17–28.

[237] See E. J. Feuchtwanger, *Disraeli, Democracy and the Tory Party* (New York, 1968), and James Cornford, "The Transformation of Conservatism," *Victorian Studies*, 7:1 (Sept. 1963), 35–36.

[238] See, e.g., G. D. H. Cole, *British Working Class Politics, 1832–1914* (London, 1941), esp. 98–99.

assembled by Gladstone after the Liberal electoral triumph of 1880. The marquess of Hartington was secretary of state for India, the duke of Argyll was lord privy seal, Earl Granville was foreign secretary, and the cabinet included four additional peers. The Whigs may have been unhappy about the radical proclivities of social reformer Joseph Chamberlain, the president of the Board of Trade, but it was the Irish Question that led to their separation from the Liberal party. An abortive bill of 1880 to compensate evicted Irish peasants led to the resignation from the ministry of the fifth marquess of Lansdowne. Gladstone's Irish Land Act of 1881 provoked the resignation of the duke of Argyll. The Home Rule Bill of 1886, Gladstone's proposal that a domestically autonomous parliament be restored to Ireland, brought on the mass exodus of the Whigs led by the marquess of Hartington.[239]

Although a handful of hereditary Liberal peers remained after 1886, from then on the political weight of the aristocracy was consolidated beneath the Unionist banner. The derisory margin of 419–41 by which the House of Lords vetoed Gladstone's Second Home Rule Bill of 1893 illustrates how low Liberal fortunes had fallen in the traditional upper chamber. Yet such aristocratic consolidation might well have proved a source of weakness rather than of strength if it had enabled the Liberal party to rally the populace in a political battle against entrenched privilege. It did not do this, because Gladstone's Home Rule Bill alienated not merely the Whig aristocracy but also substantial segments of the middle-class and lower-class electorate. That segment of English life which Noel Annan has dubbed "the intellectual aristocracy,"[240] the educators, editors, publicists, and scientists of late Victorian England, were as opposed as the hereditary aristocrats to a policy that they interpreted as a reward for criminal behavior. The men who had repeatedly disrupted the proceedings of the House of Commons and who had seemingly given countenance to murder, mayhem, and arson in the Irish countryside were now to be rewarded with a government of their own. That government was to be not merely in the hands of criminals but also in the hands of Roman Catholics, for did not "home rule" mean "Rome rule"? The fitfully slumbering passion of anti-Catholicism was reawakened,[241] and many a faithful Methodist and Baptist

[239] Gordon L. Goodman, "Liberal Unionism: The Revolt of the Whigs," Victorian Studies, 3:2 (Dec. 1959), 173–89; Donald Southgate, The Passing of the Whigs, 1832–1886 (London, 1962).

[240] See Noel G. Annan, "The Intellectual Aristocracy," in J. H. Plumb, ed., Studies in Social History: A Tribute to G. M. Trevelyan (London, 1955), 241–87.

[241] E. R. Norman, Anti-Catholicism in Victorian England (London, 1968). See also the review article by Walter L. Arnstein, "Victorian Prejudice Reexamined," Victorian Studies, 12:4 (June 1969), 452–57.

severed his allegiance to the Liberal party, the traditional party of religious dissent. The home-rule struggle was only the last of numerous Victorian episodes that united peer and peasant, Anglican and dissenter, and right-wing Tory and left-wing Liberal beneath the common banner of anti-Catholicism.

The home-rule struggle involved yet more. In Lord Salisbury's words, it "awakened the slumbering genius of Imperialism."[242] This in turn helps explain why the Gladstonian Liberals were deserted not only by the marquess of Hartington but also by Joseph Chamberlain. The erstwhile reform mayor of Birmingham, the Radical politician par excellence of the early 1880s, took a giant step on the road to the colonial secretaryship of 1895. In the process he retained the loyalty of his Birmingham constituents and of numerous Liberals in other parts of the British Isles. The Home Rule Bill was a response to an awakened Irish nationalism, but it is too easily forgotten that the resultant political battle helped arouse a more fervent British nationalism, a spirit that manifested itself in notions of imperial expansion and consolidation and in the patriotic fervor exhibited at Queen Victoria's Golden Jubilee in 1887 and her Diamond Jubilee in 1897.

Gladstone succeeded, to the satisfaction of many Englishmen, in defending home rule as a plausible as well as high-minded resolution of an otherwise insoluble problem, but to a larger number of Englishmen the proposal remained an affront to their Protestantism, their patriotism, and their sense of propriety. The fear of home rule strengthened party discipline among House of Commons Conservatives,[243] and for two decades it contributed to the political subordination of issues of social reform to issues of empire. In the process it helped to bring the Salisbury ministry of 1895–1902 to power and to foster the continued survival of the Victorian aristocracy.

The thesis of this essay has been that in spite of the still widespread belief that Victorian Britain represented a triumph of middle-class people and values, the hereditary landed aristocracy displayed a remarkable ability to survive the vicissitudes of three generations of economic and ideological change. This survival took place in defiance of the expectations of both the radicals and the reactionaries of 1832. It can be accounted for on the basis of a combination of several factors: the ongoing tradition of public service among aristocrats; the surviving prestige and significance

---

[242] Cited in *Cambridge History of the British Empire*, III (Cambridge, 1959), 157.
[243] Cf. Hugh Berrington, "Partisanship and Dissidence in the Nineteenth-Century House of Commons," *Parliamentary Affairs*, 21:4 (Aug. 1968), 338–74.

of the House of Lords and the continuing domination of local government in much of the British Isles by the aristocracy and the squirearchy; the preservation of an economic base primarily in the form of urban real estate holdings, income from mines, and land values enhanced by railway building; the failure of businessmen to gain the social prestige they might have been expected to call their own in "the workshop of the world"; the manner in which the public schools tended to inculcate predominantly aristocratic rather than predominantly middle-class values; the continuing prestige accruing to aristocrats for their charities and their patronage of philanthropic causes and occasionally of political and social reform measures; the manner in which the British Empire provided careers for them and their younger sons and in which its existence reinforced paternalistic habits of mind; the continuance of a tradition of deference as part of a society distinctly conscious of hierarchy at all levels. Finally it has been suggested that one of the incidental consequences of the late Victorian "Irish Question" was to consolidate the aristocracy under one political banner and to cause questions of religion and patriotism—which cut across class boundaries—to take precedence over political questions that might otherwise have accentuated class distinctions.

My purpose has not been to suggest that because the English aristocracy survived, Victorian society was therefore unchanging, or that the political and economic and ideological battles that add fascination to a study of the period were therefore sham battles. A single essay can by necessity concentrate on only one strand of what is by general consensus a complex tapestry. This essay does imply that the Victorian era was for the aristocracy a period not so much of disintegration as of relative stability. Those analysts from Bagehot on who emphasize the plutocratic elements in Victorian society at the expense of the aristocratic forget that for centuries English nouveaux riches had been transforming themselves or their descendants into hereditary aristocrats; the process was probably less obvious during the mid-Victorian years than during the age of the Tudors, the turn of the eighteenth century, or the age of William Pitt the younger. While political miscalculation might well have cost a Tudor aristocrat his head or forced an early eighteenth-century aristocrat to seek refuge in France, and while steep inheritance and income taxes were to force twentieth-century aristocrats to guide tourists through ancestral estates (or more often to sell them), the Victorian aristocrat was essentially free from either threat.

The other side of the thesis here advanced is that the still widespread notion that Victorian Britain was the site of a "middle-class triumph" is more myth than reality.[244] The British Isles may have pioneered the Industrial Revolution, but their inhabitants never completely accepted industrial values. It seems plausible (if at first glance farfetched) to contend that Britain moved from the values of aristocratic paternalism to those of Fabian socialism without ever undergoing a period of distinct middleclass rule. Who, after all, were the businessmen prime ministers of Great Britain? A case might be made for Sir Henry Campbell-Bannerman (1905–8), for Stanley Baldwin (1923–24, 1924–29, 1935–37), and for Neville Chamberlain (1937–40), though in all three cases involvement with business took up a very brief portion of a lengthy public career, and according to A. J. P. Taylor, Baldwin was "the only industrial capitalist who has ever been prime minister."[245] Yet before either Baldwin or Chamberlain ever reached the pinnacle, the prime ministership had gone to David Lloyd George (1916–22), the nephew of a Welsh shoemaker, and before Baldwin had completed two years as head of the cabinet, it went to Ramsay MacDonald (1924, 1929–35), the illegitimate son of a Scottish domestic servant.

In *Responsible Government* the prolific Labour party ideologue Harold Laski declared that he would much rather have been governed by an aristocrat like Lord Shaftesbury than by Richard Cobden, "by the gentlemen of England [rather] than by the Gradgrinds and Bounderbys of Coketown."[246] Imperialists like Alfred Lord Milner and socialists like Sidney Webb were equally paternalistic and equally likely to justify power on the basis of service.[247] Even though the Webbs resented the drawing of such analogies, they were quick to note the manner in which their fellow socialists MacDonald and Philip Snowden felt a kinship to aristocratic values and to aristocrats as individuals.[248] MacDonald, the first socialist prime minister of England, "liked pomp and ceremony: he had an intense and abiding sense of the picturesque and a deep love of the ordered and ancient and the hierarchical."[249]

If the historical evidence here presented has proved convincing, this question will necessarily arise: why have so many general historians, British and American alike, been so insistent on seeing a middle-class triumph in 1832? Two answers suggest themselves in the case of British

244 "I have been tempted to write a chapter . . . on the 'Myth of the Middle Class in mid-Victorian England,'" wrote the late W. L. Burn, in *The Age of Equipoise* (London, 1964), 8. The chapter was never written, but the volume contains much of the evidence that would have gone into it.
245 *English History, 1914–1945* (Oxford, 1945), 236.
246 Cited in Thornton, *Habit of Authority*, 252.
247 Cf. ibid., 28.
248 See, e.g., Beatrice Webb, *Diaries, 1912–1924* (London, 1952), 263, 279.
249 Mary Agnes Hamilton, *Remembering My Good Friends* (London, 1934), 128.

historians. First, a feeling, conscious or unconscious, that a Marxist analysis demanded a British equivalent to the French Revolution of 1789. If 1640 did not fit the bill because it required an explanation for the aristocratic revival of the late seventeenth and early eighteenth centuries, then 1832 would have to do. A second answer is that the concept of "middle class" has remained consistently hazy. Obviously if it is stretched, say, to include the younger sons of peers (like Lord John Russell in 1832), then middle-class victories can indeed be discerned by the enterprising historian in the most unlikely places. The historian who confines the phrase to the urban nonlanded manufacturer or merchant and his relations will find such victories more elusive. The trouble, A. P. Thornton has recently reminded us, is that "no one can yet safely assume that his definition of 'middle class' corresponds with anyone else's."[250]

American historians have been no more precise than their British counterparts in defining the phrase "middle class." It seems safe to suggest, however, that the phrase is likely to conjure up in the mind of an American student of the 1960s and 1970s a group constituting 80 percent or more of his own society. That clearly is not what the phrase represented for those Englishmen who used it in the 1830s, who were probably thinking of a small group—perhaps no more than 5 percent of the population—immediately beneath the landed gentry in rank.[251] Alexis de Tocqueville, who foresaw the demise of the aristocracy, admitted in 1833 that "the aristocracy in England has . . . a power and a force of resistance which it is very difficult for Frenchmen to understand."[252] What has proved difficult for Frenchmen may well have proved equally difficult for Americans. Some American historians may have been subconsciously impelled, by a form of Anglophilia found only in the United States, not merely to extol (legitimately enough) the English traditions of constitutionalism and of personal liberty but also to discern political democracy and a spirit of social equality when they were at most a prospect rather than a reality. In the Declaration of Independence, liberty and equality are held to be analogously "self-evident," but Tocqueville may have written more profoundly when he observed, "The taste which men have for liberty, and that which they feel for equality, are in fact two different things."[253]

If the British aristocracy survived until the onset of the twentieth century, when did it die? It would require another essay to do that subject

[250] Thornton, *Habit of Authority*, 264

[251] See John Horace Round, *Peerage and Pedigree* (1903), cited in Thornton, *Habit of Authority*, 183; see also Asa Briggs, "Middle-Class Consciousness in English Politics, 1780–1846," *Past and Present*, no. 9 (Apr. 1956), 65–74.

[252] Tocqueville, *Journeys to England and Ireland*, 43.

[253] Cited in Thornton, *Habit of Authority*, 161.

justice, but a few remarks may not be amiss. Sir Winston Churchill once suggested that a "definite and recognizable period in English history ended when Salisbury resigned in 1902."[254] A better case may be made for the general election of 1906 and the Liberal government of the pre–World War I era that permanently relegated the aristocracy to a minority role in the cabinet.[255] Lloyd George's budget of 1909 was the first to seriously threaten to make it economically impossible to keep up a large landed estate, and the battle over the Parliament Act of 1911, which deliberately pitted "the Peers" against "the People," has been proclaimed as marking "the death of the aristocracy."[256] Yet the House of Lords and the aristocracy persisted in most respects until the First World War. F. M. L. Thompson suggests that the true watershed may be found in the war and its immediate aftermath: the scarcity of domestic servants; the spirit of social equality; the income tax, which had absorbed 4 percent of the gross rents at one estate in 1914 and took 30 percent in 1919. The budget of 1919 also increased the inheritance tax on estates above £2 million in value to 40 percent; the deaths of numerous young aristocrats in the war meant that the same estate might change ownership twice or more during the same decade. Between 1917 and 1921 one-fourth of all the land in England may have changed hands, and the large estates were generally bought by their former tenants or by urban real estate developers.[257]

During the years that followed, old aristocratic traditions such as public service tended to ebb. In 1928 the House of Commons still contained fifty-eight sons of peers and baronets; by 1955 the number had shrunk to twelve.[258] World War II only confirmed the social changes set into rapid motion by World War I, and the farmer replaced the squire in the countryside.[259]

Yet it would be erroneous and presumptuous to suggest that the British aristocracy is literally dead even in the 1970s. The prime minister's grandson, the fifth marquess of Salisbury, leader of the House of Lords during the 1950s, presided at Hatfield House until his death in 1972. A fourteenth earl (the earl of Home; since 1963 Sir Alec Douglas-Home) found it possible to serve as foreign secretary and as prime minister during the 1960s and as foreign secretary once more during the 1970s. Neither the Labour government of Clement Attlee nor that of Harold Wilson, its electoral

---

[254] Cited in A. L. Kennedy, *Salisbury* (London, 1953), 5.

[255] Cf. Havighurst, *Twentieth-Century Britain*, 85.

[256] George Dangerfield, *The Strange Death of Liberal England* (London, 1934), 66.

[257] Thompson, *English Landed Society*, esp. 327–35.

[258] Guttsman, *British Political Elite*, 94, also 136.

[259] Petrie, *The Victorians*, 38.

promises notwithstanding, ever found it opportune to abolish the yet largely hereditary House of Lords. The English journal the *Tatler* still carries pictures of "men in tweeds talking to their game-keepers, and the sons of viscounts in full evening dress enjoying a joke with the daughters of baronets at charity balls."[260] Country house life still persists on a diminished scale, and at least one recent inheritor of a ducal title was heard to explain: "Being a duke is like having a birthday every day of the year."[261] The total abolition of the aristocracy remains a possibility rather than an actuality. Should that day ever arrive, British life would certainly become duller; and a society that grants distinctions solely because of merit rather than because of accidents such as birth is likely to be more discontented rather than less, for the same reason that chess is a more frustrating game than bridge. The loser cannot blame the luck of the draw.

During the middle of the nineteenth century the British aristocracy still constituted a distinct social and political upper class. Contemporary British society is made up of a number of overlapping elites of which the hereditary landed aristocracy remains one. It provides us with a significant link to the past and with a fascinating illustration of that element of continuity that British history so abundantly supplies.

[260] Review by Christopher Booker of Roy Perrot, *The Aristocrats* (London, 1968), in *New York Times Book Review*, 10 Nov. 1968.
[261] Cited by Cyril Connolly in the *Sunday Times* (London), 24 Mar. 1968.

Style and Status: High Society in Late Nineteenth-Century New York

FREDERIC COPLE JAHER

Elites may vary from city to city and, where several groups contest leadership, within the same city. Urban patriciates that maintain hegemony over a long period neutralize the challenge of new men by either co-option or effective exclusion. Longevity creates a stable, homogeneous elite structure. Rapid social change, extensive institutional and technological innovation, large infusions of new blood, and spectacular economic growth, on the other hand, make it difficult for these groups to perpetuate themselves through family firms and ties and patrician social and political organizations.

Postrevolutionary patriciates in Philadelphia, Boston, and New York initially developed similar life patterns. A residue of the colonial elite combined with new men emerging from the political and economic disruptions of the 1770s and 1780s to fill the gap left by the departed Tories. Formerly great provincial ports, these cities developed into major national commercial centers. Social prominence in Boston, Philadelphia, and New York derived from wealth and power accumulated in foreign trade, banking, real estate, law, and politics. By the first decade of the nineteenth century an enclave of eminent politicians and businessmen associated with prestigious religious, educational, and professional groups constituted high society in the three cities. In Boston and Philadelphia the members of these mercantile-Federalist elites founded dynasties. Their descendants perpetuated inherited status by dominating subsequent industrial, financial, and cultural enterprises in their localities. To this day, Boston Brah-

I wish to thank the American Philosophical Society for a 1967 grant that enabled me to accumulate some of the material for this essay. I am also indebted to Jocelyn Ghent for her research assistance.

mins and Philadelphia gentlemen influence the membership and policy of many business and professional firms, and honorific social, cultural, charitable, and educational institutions. They help direct prestigious law offices and banks, art museums, symphony orchestras, historical societies, and many of the older charitable organizations. For generations the Cadwaladers, Ingersolls, Rushes, Hopkinsons, Whartons, and Peppers of Philadelphia, and the Higginsons, Cabots, Lowells, and Adamses of Boston have maintained influence in the commercial and cultural life of their cities. After the Civil War, declining resources, social change, and immigration weakened their ability to withstand challenges from rising elites, but they still retain a significant share of property, power, and prestige.[1]

New York elites developed in a different way. Post–Civil War descendants of New York's prominent colonial and federal families, the knickerbocker set, and of the great overseas merchants, most of whom moved down from New England in the first quarter of the nineteenth century, gave way to railroad and banking clans. New York elites, lacking the institutional and kinship protection of patriciates in the other two cities, fragmented, or at best occasionally overlapped when the rare family or individual preserved its position for more than a generation or two. Separate enclaves dominated trade, politics, culture, and fashion, although some common membership existed among these groups. New York's elites possessed neither solidarity nor continuity. Fading elites risk disintegration as renegade members desert to more powerful and wealthier *arrivistes*. Conversely, power, solidarity, and continuity enable urban elites to expand their original domain (usually commercial) into social, intellectual, cultural, and political areas; to increase group cohesion by monopolizing leadership roles; and to develop an aristocratic dimension by bequeathing predominance to descendants. New York, unlike Boston or Philadelphia, retained no single nineteenth-century group with the generalized hegemony necessary to form an upper-class structure; nor did any group in that city develop into an aristocracy by perpetuating a multifaceted urban leadership over several generations.[2]

[1] The best studies of patrician Philadelphia are E. Digby Baltzell, *Philadelphia Gentlemen: The Making of a National Upper Class* (Glencoe, Ill., 1958); Nathaniel Burt, *The Perennial Philadelphians: The Anatomy of an American Aristocracy* (Boston, 1963). The best general account of the Boston Brahmins is Cleveland Amory, *The Proper Bostonians* (New York, 1947). See also Frederic Cople Jaher, "The Boston Brahmins in the Age of Industrial Capitalism," in Jaher, ed., *America in the Age of Industrialism: Essays in Social Structure and Cultural Values* (New York, 1968), 188–263. The most convenient collection of proper Boston family biographies is Mary Caroline Crawford, *Famous Families of Massachusetts*, 2 vols. (Boston, 1930).

[2] Studies of post–Civil War New York society appear in the following volumes. Frederick Townsend Martin, *The Passing of the Idle Rich* (Garden City, N.Y., 1911),

This study focuses on one enclave, the "beautiful people" of late nineteenth-century New York. This elite sought to establish its leadership by determining social style and prestige in fashionable New York. The strategies of the smart set were based on the conviction that status derived from repute, i.e., from a well-publicized role and image that served to integrate the group and to create and keep followers. While the techniques for the Four Hundred were consciously designed by social arbiters and society leaders to accomplish this purpose, their values were less autonomous. Notions of priority, propriety, and society frequently reflected the confusing and conflicting forces of amorphous upper-class New York.

The conditions that made turn-of-the-century New York society celebrated or infamous (depending upon the observer) began to attract attention in the 1840s, when Philip Hone and George Templeton Strong, observers with impeccable social credentials, bemoaned the advent of a "commercial aristocracy . . . a fluctuating, mushroom aristocracy."[3] Yet Hone had achieved his own social position, and Strong was only second-generation establishment. The diaries of Hone and Strong, the writings of Charles Astor Bristed, and the reminiscences of Ward McAllister, all well-connected men-about-town in the 1840s and 1850s, repeatedly report

---

and *Things I Remember* (New York, 1913); Henry Collins Brown, *In the Golden Nineties* (Hastings-on-Hudson, 1928); Gabriel Almond, "Plutocracy and Politics in New York City," doctoral diss. (University of Chicago, 1938), 92–96, 150–59, 272, 275–78; Albert Stevens Crockett, *Peacocks on Parade* (New York, 1931); Wayne Andrews, *The Vanderbilt Legend* (New York, 1941), 198–99, 227ff.; Andrew Tully, *Era of Elegance* (New York, 1947); Harvey O'Connor, *The Astors* (New York, 1941), 55ff.; Elizabeth Drexel Lehr, *"King Lehr" and the Gilded Age* (Philadelphia, 1935); Ward McAllister, *Society as I Have Found It* (New York, 1890); Helen Worden, *Society Circus* (New York, 1936); Lloyd Morris, *Incredible New York* (New York, 1951); May King Van Rensselaer and Frederic Van de Water, *The Social Ladder* (New York, 1924); Stuyvesant Fish, *1600–1914* (New York, 1942), 213–24, 290; Ralph Pulitzer, *Society on Parade* (New York, 1910); Robert Roosevelt, *Love and Link* (New York, 1886); M. E. W. Sherwood, *An Epistle to Posterity* (New York, 1897), 85–86, 175–200, 363–80.

General studies of American social elites are Dixon Wecter, *The Saga of American Society: A Record of Social Aspiration, 1607–1937* (New York, 1937); Cleveland Amory, *Who Killed Society* (New York, 1960), and *The Last Resorts* (New York, 1952).

For a comparative study of Boston and New York City elites, see Jaher, "Nineteenth-Century Elites in Boston and New York," *Journal of Social History*, 6 (Fall 1972), 32–77.

[3] Bayard Tuckerman, ed., *The Diary of Philip Hone*, 2 vols. (New York, 1889), vol. 2, 271, 297; Allan Nevins, ed., *The Diary of Philip Hone* (New York, 1936), 648, and *The Diary of George Templeton Strong*, 4 vols. (New York, 1952), vol. 1, 236, 269; vol. 3, 509. These are the best accounts of New York society between 1830 and 1860. For another contemporary society figure who shared their views, see Charles Astor Bristed, *The Upper Ten Thousand: Sketches of American Society* (New York, 1852). For similar observations from foreign observers, see Francis J. Grund, *Aristocracy in America* (New York, 1959); Bayard Still, *Mirror for Gotham* (New York, 1956).

splendid dances, parties, and sumptuous dinners at which old families mixed with wealthy newcomers.[4] The porousness of high society, a consequence of the rapid turnover of its personnel, and lavish expenditure prefigured the next generation of fashionable New York.

Relatively stable elites along the eastern seaboard, in Charleston, Philadelphia, and Boston, did not receive this type of criticism from disgruntled gentlemen. Patrician Philadelphia's historian, Nathaniel Burt, cites only one antebellum aristocrat hostile to the city's upper class. This critic, Sidney Fisher, found Philadelphia society dull, vulgar, and undermined by upstarts who crowded out old families. Despite this condemnation, he felt that "the difference between the best Philadelphia and New York society" lay in the "unpretending, elegant, cordial and friendly" ways of old Philadelphia. Fisher attributed this atmosphere to the scarcity of "families [who] have not held some station for several generations, which circumstance had produced an air of refinement, dignity and simplicity of manner wanting in New York and also a great degree of intimacy among the different families who compose our society as their fathers and grandfathers knew each other."[5]

The sense of group decline expressed by some New Yorkers as early as the 1840s awaited, in Boston, the late nineteenth-century nostalgia of Charles Francis Adams, Jr., James Russell Lowell, and Charles Eliot Norton, the irony of Henry and Brooks Adams, and the cataclysmic foreboding of the Adamses, Norton, Barrett Wendell, John Torrey Morse, and William Sturgis Bigelow.[6] At this time the Brahmins were threatened by the same type of eclipse that New York's knickerbocker and mercantile elites began to experience two generations earlier.

Despite nouveau riche intruders, mid-nineteenth-century New York society retained a residue of tradition, graciousness, and modesty. Old Dutch and English families remained socially prominent. Famous hostesses, Mrs. James D. Roosevelt, Mrs. Hamilton Fish, Mrs. Henry Brevoort, and Mrs. William Schermerhorn, were linked by marriage and birth to old families. Compared to the frenetic dazzle of the post–Civil War smart set, society showed restraint in the frequency, splendor, and cost of its affairs. Recoiling from the excesses of the Four Hundred, commentators of knickerbocker descent, Edith Wharton, May King Van Rensselaer, and

[4] Tuckerman, *Hone Diary*, vol. 1, 88–89; McAllister, *Society*, 14–15, 129–33; Bristed, *Upper*; Morris, *Incredible*, 24; Nevins, *Strong Diary*, vol. 3, 39–50.

[5] A sketch of Fisher and a synopsis of his writings are in Burt, *Perennial Philadelphians*, 23–30, and Fisher is quoted on 26.

[6] For a discussion of the Brahmin sense of pessimism and decline, see Jaher, *Age*, 196–213, and *Doubters and Dissenters: Cataclysmic Thought in America, 1885–1918* (New York, 1964), 141–87.

William Ingraham Kip, celebrated the antebellum social establishment as a comparative model of polite deportment and patrician stability.[7] Perhaps their view was somewhat distorted by the perspective of their own displacement or by mellowed childhood memories. After World War I, when Newport and Fifth Avenue gave way to the performers, athletes, debutantes, and international adventurers of café society, vestiges of Mrs. Astor's circle, once considered vulgar interlopers, similarly complained about vanishing tradition, refinement, and established social rank.

Former carpenter Isaac Brown's appearance as the first of a series of déclassé arbiters of New York society offers the weightiest evidence of the advent of the *arriviste*. He was followed by Ward McAllister, a suave ex-bookkeeper, and Harry Lehr, a penurious Baltimore fop. During the 1840s the ex-craftsman from upper New York State became sexton of Grace Church, by his own admission "the most fashionable and exclusive of our metropolitan 'courts of Heaven.' "[8] Grace Church, as opposed to the old guard shrines of Trinity and St. Mark's, catered to the "pomps and vanities" of the rich set.[9] Through the 1850s and 1860s Brown reigned as *arbiter eleganterium*. He occupied an unprecedented position among the older eastern seaboard elites and played a role that remained unique to New York. Previous leaders of polite society, a Mrs. Phoebe Rush of Philadelphia, a Mrs. Harrison Gray Otis of Boston, or a Mrs. John Jay of New York, set the tone from within. Brown and his successors Ward McAllister and Harry Lehr originated as outsiders and remained in varying degrees employees and clients of the set they directed.

The social arbiter performed a vital function in New York's permeable and shifting society. Since the well-heeled were often not the well-born, these figures sorted out pretence from precedence and balanced wealth and birth in order to legitimate the fragile exclusiveness of the city's fashionable elite. Brown, and later McAllister and Lehr, counseled hostesses on every procedure from seating musicians to patronizing the proper florist. Brown's excellent memory for lineage, social credentials, and biographical details proved invaluable in his chief function, advising on invitations. A consummate snob, he separated society into "old family, good stock," or "a new man" who "had better mind his p's and q's, or I will trip

[7] William Ingraham Kip, "New York Society in the Olden Times," in William L. Stone, *History of New York City* (New York, 1872), 106; Edith Wharton, *A Backward Glance* (New York, 1934), 5–7, 21–23, 65–70, 79, 92, 95, 120, 143, and *The Age of Innocence* (New York, 1936); Van Rensselaer and Van de Water, *Social Ladder*; Martin, *Passing*, and *Things*, 77–80.

[8] Brown quoted in Morris, *Incredible*, 21.

[9] Nevins, *Strong Diary*, vol. 4, 148. Hone felt the same way about Grace Church. See Nevins, *Hone Diary*, 754. Cf. Sherwood, *Epistle*, 179.

him up." When employed by the recently arrived, the sexton cautioned guests from old families, "This [affair] is mixed, very mixed." But there were limits even to Brown's suzerainty. "I cannot undertake to control society beyond fiftieth street," he warned at the close of his reign.[10] Upper Fifth Avenue, beyond Brown's domain, became the center of postbellum fashionable New York.

In the 1880s and 1890s leading hostesses, Mrs. William Astor, Mrs. William K. Vanderbilt (later Mrs. Oliver Hazard Perry Belmont), and Mrs. Stuyvesant Fish, along with their major domos, Ward McAllister and Harry Lehr, made the final attempt to organize wealth, birth, and style into a coherent social system. Several basic traits differentiated this society from establishments in other East Coast centers. New Yorkers were unique in admission of new wealth, female domination, extravagant lifestyle, internal rivalry for social sovereignty, desire for publicity, and indifference to civic responsibility.

"Why there are only about four hundred people in fashionable New-York society," asserted Ward McAllister, who coined the term in 1888. "If you go outside that number you strike people who are either not at ease in a ball room or make others not at ease."[11] The ballroom to which he referred was, of course, Mrs. Astor's. After four years of incessant pressure, McAllister divulged the names of the members to the New York Times in 1892.[12] Actually the list contained 273 individuals that Mrs. Astor and her court chamberlain agreed constituted select society. For McAllister, the group represented the "crème de la crème" of New York, the leading members of Mrs. Astor's circle and the matrons and patriarchs of the assembly balls.[13] Much information about fashionable New York can be gleaned from an examination of the geographical origins, occupations, vintages of wealth, and family backgrounds of the Four Hundred.

Nineteenth-century urban patriciates along the Atlantic seaboard have generally been insular. The gentry of antebellum Charleston had for generations come from that city or surrounding low-country plantation parishes. Prominent Philadelphia clans were also geographically homogeneous. The Rosengarten, Etting, Markoe, and Boirie dynasties originated

[10] Brown quoted in McAllister, Society, 124. Accounts of Brown are found in Morris, Incredible, 21; Wecter, Saga, 209–10; Amory, Who Killed, 115–17; Sherwood, Epistle, 179.
[11] McAllister interview, in New York Daily Tribune, 25 Mar. 1888, 11.
[12] McAllister interview, in New York Times, 16 Feb. 1892, 5.
[13] See the guest list at Mrs. Astor's annual winter ball, in New York Times, 2 Feb. 1892, 5. See list of matrons and patriarchs in Social Register, New York, 1893, 7 (New York, 1892), 343.

in eighteenth-century German, French West Indian, and Portuguese birth-places, but this exotic trend ceased with Bavarian-born banker Francis M. Drexel in the 1830s. When the Four Hundred emerged, these clans had been Philadelphia-bred for several generations. Unlike their predecessors, post–Civil War family founders did not stem from distant lands. William Elkins, the utilities magnate, was from West Virginia, and Pennsylvania Railroad president Alexander J. Cassat was born in Pittsburgh.[14] Proper Boston was even more inbred. After the 1820s, when Abbot and Amos Lawrence and Nathan Appleton left rural New Hampshire and Massachusetts to become Brahmin textile titans, very few outsiders gained acceptance in blueblood Boston. Alexander Agassiz, the Swiss naturalist who came to the city in 1849, was a notable and virtually unique exception to Brahmin insularity.

Members of old knickerbocker families similarly sprang from New York City or from family estates in the Hudson River valley. But the Four Hundred was not exclusively derived from this group; hence its geographical origins were more diverse than those of other urban elites.[15] Of the 121 members of the smart set whose birthplaces have been definitely traced, 64 came from New York City, 50 from elsewhere in the United States (mostly New York State, New England, New Jersey, Maryland, Pennsylvania, and Ohio). Among the last-named group, 18 came from

---

[14] Burt, *Perennial Philadelphians*, 64–66; Baltzell, *Philadelphia Gentlemen*, 70–106. For a comparison of birthplaces of Boston and New York economic elites, see Jaher, "Nineteenth-Century Elites."

[15] Findings on the geographical origins, vintage of wealth, occupations, and genealogy of the Four Hundred were obtained by research into the biographical data of the names listed in the *New York Times*, 16 Feb. 1892, 5. The information came from these sources: Walter Barrett (Joseph Scoville), *The Old Merchants of New York*, 5 vols. (New York, 1885); Charles Morris, ed., *Makers of New York* (Philadelphia, 1895); Lyman H. Weeks, *Prominent Families of New York* (New York, 1897); Margherita A. Hamm, *Famous Families of New York*, 2 vols. (New York, 1902); W. R. Cutter, ed., *Genealogical and Family History of Southern New York and the Hudson River Valley*, 3 vols. (New York, 1913); L. R. Hamersly, ed., *Who's Who in New York City and State* (New York, 1905); John W. Leonard, ed., *Who's Who in America* (1899–1900) (Chicago, 1900); James Grant Wilson and John Fiske, eds., *Appleton's Cyclopedia of American Biography*, 6 vols. (New York, 1888–89); Teunis G. Bergen, *Genealogies of the State of New York*, 3 vols. (New York, 1915); Henry Hall, ed. *America's Successful Men of Affairs*, 2 vols. (New York, 1895); David Van Pelt, *Leslie's History of the Greater New York*, 3 (New York, 1898); *New York Genealogical and Biographical Record*, 1–101 (1870–1971); *New York Times* obituaries, 1851–1971; Allen Johnson, Dumas Malone, and Robert L. Schuyler, eds., *Dictionary of American Biography*, 1–22 (New York, 1928–58); "American Millionaires," *Tribune Monthly*, 4 (June 1892), 57–85.

For a similar study of the backgrounds of nineteenth-century economic elites in Boston and New York, see Jaher, "Nineteenth-Century Elites."

old New York families (11 of them from the 15 born in New York State), as did 3 of the 7 born abroad. The remainder, about one-third of those with ascertained birthplaces, had no connection with New York families. Thus a relatively large contingent of geographical outsiders was represented among the Four Hundred, especially when compared to the more insular patriciates of Charleston, Philadelphia, and Boston.

But the proportion of native New Yorkers in Mrs. Astor's circle increases when the component with probably known geographical origins is added. Another 99 birthplaces can be reasonably fixed: 4 members of the set came from families who did not live in New York City or State; 95 had parents who spent their entire lives in the city or who moved in childhood or adolescence. The addition of these 99 people makes the proportion of outsiders almost one-fifth of the total with reasonably or certainly known birthplaces. The birthplaces of 53 individuals on McAllister's list could not be discovered. The unknowns, one-fifth of the total number, could significantly affect the findings. In the unlikely case that all the undiscovered were either native New Yorkers or born elsewhere, geographical outsiders could constitute as little as about one-seventh or as much as one-third of the Four Hundred. Thus the proportion of outsiders in the smart set is probably higher than in genteel Philadelphia, and definitely higher than in the settled patriciates of Boston and Charleston. Nevertheless, the size of the native-born segment in New York high society is much closer to these elites than to its counterparts in newer cities like Chicago and Los Angeles.[16]

While the haute monde of New York drew people of diverse geographical origins, wealth was its one universal attribute. The impoverished gentility of post–Civil War Charleston could maintain a patrician social style in the Charleston Club and at the St. Cecilia balls, but South Carolina was not the cockpit of American capitalism. High society in other cities possessed ample fortunes. Many of the richest families in Chicago belonged to Mrs. Potter Palmer's entourage. Philadelphia's patriciate and the Boston Brahmins similarly included many millionaires among their numbers. New York, the economic capital of the nation, housed the most colossal of America's late nineteenth-century fortunes. Even more than in other places, its fashionable elite had large accumulations of money. Social prominence

[16] For an insider's account of Chicago society, see Arthur Meeker, *Chicago with Love* (New York, 1955). Another treatment of Chicago society is Emmett Dedmon, *Fabulous Chicago* (New York, 1963), 45ff. For the behavior of the fashionable sets in newer cities, see Amory, *Who Killed*; Gunther Barth, "Metropolism and Urban Elites in the Far West," in Jaher, *Age*, 158–88; Cornelius Vanderbilt, Jr., *Farewell to Fifth Avenue* (New York, 1935), 88–90.

in New York was also more costly than elsewhere. Unlike the more established urban patriciates, the Four Hundred needed conspicuous consumption for the publicity necessary to achieve and sustain status.

In 1892 the *New York Tribune* published a list of American millionaires.[17] Among the 1,368 New Yorkers in this compilation, 50 were from the Four Hundred. Another 92 members of the set were spouses or children or had married offspring of New York millionaires. Slightly over half of Mrs. Astor's circle married, or would probably inherit, great fortunes. This group included monied clans such as the Astors and Vanderbilts and the relatively new monied men like William C. Whitney. The *Tribune* study, based on opinions from bankers, lawyers, and trustees rather than on probate documents or tax lists, probably underestimates the number of millionaires. It is likely that many of the Four Hundred who did not appear on the list, or were not intimately related to those who appeared, were also millionaires. A case in point is Matthew Astor Wilks, an Astor grandson unlisted in the *Tribune* but almost certainly a millionaire.

If some of New York's great fortunes were represented in Mrs. Astor's circle, others were not. The great Jewish banking and mercantile families were absent from McAllister's collection. New money was sometimes disqualified for insufficient refinement; the Goulds and the Harrimans were thus excluded. Conversely, knickerbocker millionaire Roosevelts, Stuyvesants, and Hoffmans were not in Mrs. Astor's set, perhaps because they considered the group vulgar upstarts. Despite the absence of these mellowed millions, most of the wealth in high society was decently aged. Of the 191 with determined vintage of fortune, only 3 (lawyer Henry L. Burnett, banker Frank K. Sturgis, and McAllister) were possibly self-made. Another 24 inherited wealth made in the previous generation, and the remainder were bequeathed more ancient accumulations. About 14 percent of those with traced vintage of wealth could be considered nouveau riche, i.e., first or second generation. In the unlikely case that the 30 percent of unknown vintage were parvenus or their children, most of the Four Hundred would still have been rich for at least three generations.

This large segment of inherited wealth may account for the lack of vocational achievement within the group. Women composed 138 of the 273 people on McAllister's list. Novelist Mrs. Stephen Van Rensselaer Cruger (Julie Grinnell Storrow) was apparently the only woman with a vocation other than that of society matron. Thirty of the men had no profession. Biographical sources list them as retired businessmen, family trustees, gentleman farmers, clubmen, sportsmen, visitors from other cities, living on inherited income, or simply with no occupation. Discounting

17 "American Millionaires," *Tribune Monthly*.

Mrs. Cruger, these two groups make up 167 members of the smart set, three-fifths of the total number, with no occupation outside high society. The remainder were mostly lawyers, merchants, capitalists, and realtors. But some of these may have been primarily concerned with society. The five Cuttings in the Four Hundred were in law and real estate, but they also belonged to a group of affluent playboys called "the dudes."[18] Lispenard Stewart, another example of the difficulty in separating vocation from avocation, was designated as both lawyer and clubman.

Further evidence for lack of accomplishments beyond the world of society is the fact that only 23 on McAllister's list appeared in *Who's Who*. This finding is based on the 1899 edition, which included prominent figures deceased since 1 January 1895. Perhaps others, who died between 1892 and 1895, might have been in an earlier edition. Adding them, however, would not substantially swell the tiny segment of the Four Hundred that could be considered part of the national achievement elite.[19]

At first glance the Four Hundred appears to embody the qualities of an urban aristocracy. Most of them came from families of old and great wealth, and the majority were probably born in or near New York City. Only ten members of the inner circle of high society were absent from New York's *Social Register* of 1893, and intermarriage and common ancestry linked many in the group.[20] Closer examination of the social credentials of the Four Hundred, however, makes this initial impression somewhat misleading. Some families whose fortunes were at least three generations old were deemed déclassé into the 1880s. The Vanderbilts belonged to this group, and the Astors did not become socially prominent until after the Civil War. Others, such as Heber Bishop, inherited third-generation wealth from locally prominent clans with no social standing outside their immediate geographical area. McAllister himself, as we shall see, distinguished between affluence and high social status and included both in his compilation.

A listing in New York's *Social Register* was scarcely more indicative of social position than was wealth. The register contained approximately 10,000 names, including Jay Gould, Andrew Carnegie, and others unwelcome in Four Hundred homes. The widespread kinship that existed among members of Mrs. Astor's entourage similarly provided inadequate evidence of a legitimate patriciate. Historically, upper classes have intermarried, and the consequent interrelationships have been crucial in developing their ascriptive cohesion. The aristocratic structure of genteel Boston, Phila-

---

[18] Wecter, *Saga*, 219.
[19] *Who's Who in America* (1899–1900). For a similar use of *Who's Who* to discover the achievement elite within the Philadelphia patriciate, see Baltzell, *Philadelphia Gentlemen*, 28–45.
[20] See n. 13 for bibliographical reference.

delphia, and Charleston depended not on intermarriage alone but on union among old families. Many knickerbocker elements of the Four Hundred were related to each other through the clustering of old clans, but other figures in the group—the Baldwins, DePews, and Martins—were not products of such ties.

In order to measure the aristocratic component in the Four Hundred, four subgroups must be differentiated: knickerbockers, offspring of prominent patriciates in other places, descendants of mercantile families established in New York before the Civil War, and those belonging to none of these categories and therefore of relatively undistinguished lineage. Since four-fifths of the smart set fall into these subgroups, the unknowns cannot significantly alter the findings. Collateral connections have been excluded because these tenuous relations did not define social status. Henry L. Burnett, for example, was an Ohioan with a Van Cortlandt great-aunt, but he did not move in knickerbocker circles.

Family Background of the Four Hundred

	NUMBER	PERCENTAGE
Total	273	100.0
Total identified	220	79.5
Knickerbockers	83	37.7
Offspring of other patriciates	22	10.0
Great mecantile families	41	18.6
Undistinguished	74	33.6

The aristocratic core of the Four Hundred consisted of knickerbockers and patricians from other places. Among the former were four Livingstons, two Van Rensselaers, a Barclay, a Schuyler, and a DePeyster. Among the latter were three Baltimore Browns, three Philadelphia Willings, and three Boston Brahmin Otises. Descendants from these two enclaves represented nearly one-half of the known genealogies in Mrs. Astor's circle.

Members of great mercantile families composed almost one-fifth of those with discovered lineage. Liberally sprinkled among the smart set were Astors, Stokeses, Howlands, and other offspring of the early nineteenth-century overseas traders. After the Civil War, some of them, such as the Astors, were marrying into knickerbocker clans and attaining a social status denied them in antebellum New York.

The last identified subgroup consisted of society figures such as the Bradley Martins, the Chauncey DePews, and the William C. Whitneys. They sometimes belonged to local elites in New England and New York State, but their family backgrounds were considered mediocre, and they entered fashionable New York through wealth, personal fame, and/or supreme energy and skill in navigating the shoals and reefs of high society. Descendants of New York's antebellum merchants may or may not have passed muster in polite society, although their place in the Four Hundred was secure. Even if they are ranked with aristocratic core, however, one-third of McAllister's chosen were not among the manor-born. This attests to the relative permeability of Mrs. Astor's set when compared to genteel Boston, Charleston, and Philadelphia sets. Acceptance of *arrivistes* resulted from the traditional accessibility of New York elites, from the recent formation of the Four Hundred, and from the lesser importance of ascription in New York social circles than in those of other old cities. But the aristocratic element in fashionable New York makes it resemble the social establishments of the eastern seaboard rather than the parvenu society of newer cities like Los Angeles and Chicago.

The balance between old families and the newly risen is apparent in the backgrounds of the leading hostesses of the Four Hundred. Mrs. Stuyvesant Fish (Marion Graves Anthon), socially prominent through her family, wedded a scion of the knickerbocker gentry. Mrs. William K. Vanderbilt (Alvah Smith) married the old commodore's grandson and propelled her spouse's family to the pinnacle of select society. Mrs. William Astor (Caroline Webster Schermerhorn) drew on her own colonial antecedents and three generations of Astor money to become the undisputed queen of the smart set. In an ideal geometrical configuration, one of the hostesses sprang from and married into the patriciate, another of blueblood origins made the Astor millions socially esteemed, and the third, with no genealogical pretensions, elevated the Vanderbilts to high society respectability.[21] The same pattern repeated itself among secondary figures. Mrs. Ogden Mills merged the Livingston name with a California mining fortune; Mrs. Ogden Goelet, on the other hand, married into the old New York real estate family; and Mrs. Hermann Oelrichs, daughter of an Irish immigrant who made millions from the Comstock Lode, wedded the son of a Bremen-born shipping titan.

Shunted aside by this congregation of wealth and birth was the "Faubourg Saint-Germain set" of knickerbocker families. Mrs. Hamilton Fish, Mrs. Theodore Roosevelt, Sr., and Mrs. Lewis Morris Rutherfurd presided over the circle's modest, unpublicized activities. Their self-contained world of opera at the Academy of Music and quiet evenings in lower Manhattan brownstones differed greatly from the social swirl in

---

[21] For information on these figures, see Tully, *Era*, 3–9, 18–25, 41–53; Morris, *Incredible*, 144–47, 151–55; Amory, *Who Killed*, 489–93, 519–20, and *Last Resorts*, 208–14; O'Connor, *Astors*, 187–208; McAllister, *Society*, 126–28; Wecter, *Saga*, 332–42; Lehr, *"King Lehr,"* 80–90; Andrews, *Vanderbilt*, 250–69.

Mrs. Astor's circle further uptown. Inherited social status, worship of the past, smaller fortunes, an anonymous, modest lifestyle, and contempt and envy for the nouveaux riches who eclipsed them defined their set of values and attitudes. For the knickerbockers, fashionable society was no longer polite society.[22] Though the two groups diverged in customs, leaders, origins, vintage and source of wealth, and residential areas, they shared in a manner typical for New York certain experiences, personnel, and values. Fishes and Astors both went to Harvard in the 1880s, Philip Schuyler and George F. Baker served together as trustees of the New York Public Library, and a few descendants of old families associated with new wealth.

But it is simplistic to designate these examples of overlapping as indications of partially merging groups. Fellowship at school and at board meetings does not necessarily mean a commingling of family-structured social groups, though it may enhance the opportunity for such integration. Transferring membership from one social system to another does not inevitably signify a drawing together of the two structures involved. Caroline Schermerhorn Astor easily qualified by lineage and upbringing for the Faubourg Saint-Germain set, but this fact did not endear her enclave to knickerbocker critics May King Van Rensselaer, William Ingraham Kip, Edith Wharton, and Theodore Roosevelt. Renegades do not increase interaction between the deserted group and the group they join or form. The surest evidence of closeness between two social groups is the prevalence of dual allegiance and the exercise of appreciable influence in both sets. Available data show that the most powerful members of fashionable New York, Mrs. Astor, Mrs. Vanderbilt, Mrs. Fish, and Ward McAllister, did not belong to old New York. Whether the scions of old families that followed in the wake of these prominent figures maintained membership and significance in the Faubourg set is a matter for biographical analysis. Research to this point indicates a limited degree of interaction between the groups, specifically in the cooperation between the old and new elites in sponsoring the patriarch balls.

Mrs. Astor and McAllister were primarily concerned with fashionable circles that had wealth. To the degree that fashion required fortune, one might expect the elites of wealth and style to overlap; to the degree that fashion required leisure, taste, and a commitment of time and energy, one might expect many self-made or even second-generation millionaires and their families to be excluded from the smart set. The Four Hundred reflected the social strategy of balancing, as McAllister put it, "the nobs" (birth) and "the swells" (wealth). He praised Mrs. Astor for possessing

[22] Wecter, Saga, 331–32; W. Jay Mills, "New York Society before Its Great Transformation," Delineator, 64 (Nov. 1904), 747–52.

"a just appreciation of the rights of others." She valued "ancestry; always keeping it near her, and bringing it in, in all social matters," without failing to "understand . . . the importance and power of the new element; recognizing it, and fairly and generously awarding it a prominent place."[23]

The queen and her minister realized the dual risk of excessive exclusion and unselective inclusion. Barring new blood would displace the reigning order through the same process by which the Four Hundred had outflanked its predecessors. In rapidly growing New York a newer and richer class would inevitably emerge to overshadow the aloof establishment. Insufficiently high barriers presented another danger. New York, the center of American capitalism, attracted and produced hordes of freshly minted millionaires. Hence unrestricted entry would dissolve the distinction of the smart set in an unrefined mix of multitudinous parvenus.

McAllister functioned as traffic manager for the Four Hundred, incorporating the style and status of lineage with the vitality and riches of the *arriviste*. At Newport in the summer or during the social season in New York he patiently prepared candidates, guiding them over obstacles and coaching them in proper behavior. Failure to meet accepted standards in domicile, dress, manner, or dinner table blackballed anxious aspirants. Rejection was often abrupt, but entry was gradual. Admission to the larger fetes, where hostesses indulgently mixed guests from different enclaves, indicated preliminary approval and a further test. Invitations to more intimate soirées rewarded progress, and ultimate success meant a social call by Mrs. Astor.

Hierarchical selection culminated, for the few who penetrated the inner circle, in an invitation to the patriarchs' ball. McAllister, Cerberus of New York's smart set, vigilantly guarded the gates of entry. The patriarch balls, begun in 1872, were devised to organize New York society. These events imitated elite balls in other old cities, such as Charleston's St. Cecilia ball (1737) and the Philadelphia assembly (1748). But the differences between the patriarch affairs and those eighteenth-century institutions characterized the distinction between fashionable New York and the Atlantic seaboard aristocracies. The Charleston and Philadelphia dances were traditional and modest, and restricted in management and membership to old families. New York's counterparts were newly formed, costly, and accessible to *arrivistes*. The twenty-five directors of these dances represented old wealth through descendants of the King, Livingston, Fish, Rutherfurd, and Van Rensselaer families, comparatively recent but decently mellowed fortunes in C. C. Goodhue and John Jacob and William Astor, and new men in Ward McAllister and William R. Travers. "The object we

[23] McAllister, *Tribune* interview, 11.

had in view," McAllister declared, "was to make these balls thoroughly representative; to embrace the old Colonial New Yorkers, our adopted citizens, and men whose ability and integrity had won the esteem of the community, and who formed an important element in society. We wanted the money power, but not in any way to be controlled by it."[24] Under the leadership of the patriarchs, these brilliant, exclusive, and costly affairs, emphasizing wealth and birth, imposed hierarchical order upon New York society.

Georgia-born Ward McAllister was superbly qualified to succeed Isaac Brown as master of ritual for fashionable New York. Although a nephew by marriage of early nineteenth-century banker Samuel Ward, he, like Brown, did not stem from any segment of Gotham's upper class. Through Mrs. Astor's patronage, successful management of the patriarch balls, and expertise in cuisine, wine, dress, ritual, genealogy, and heraldry, McAllister became the major domo of the Four Hundred. McAllister's own money and acquired status led to membership in the patrician Union Club and Metropolitan Club and a listing in the *Social Register*, but the source of his power remained Mrs. Astor's backing. When age and senility unclasped her hold on society, Stuyvesant Fish, leader of the patriarchs and never a great admirer of the Astor crowd, ousted him from the patriarch balls. McAllister died shortly thereafter, largely unmourned by the Four Hundred he made famous. But the deposed arbiter was soon avenged, for several years later the patriarchs disbanded, and New York society in its usual whimsical way began to orbit about a new sphere.[25]

"I begin where Ward McAllister left off," said Harry Lehr. "He was the voice crying in the wilderness who prepared the way for me."[26] Reflecting the continued insecurity of the fashionable set, New York's next social arbiter, like his two predecessors, was an imported product. His party skills of mimicry, dancing, and piano playing, and above all, his wit, served as substitutes for wealth and inherited position. Often he remarked to Mrs. Astor or Mrs. Belmont, "How could anyone take me seriously, dear lady? I'm only your fun-maker, your jester."[27]

[24] McAllister, *Society*, 214. For McAllister on the patriarchs, see ibid., 209, 214–17, 224, and *Tribune* interview, 11. For society balls in other cities, see Amory, *Who Killed*, 90–91; Baltzell, *Philadelphia Gentlemen*, 163–64.

[25] The best source on McAllister is McAllister, *Society*. Other sources of biographical data are *Tribune* interview, 11; Morris, *Incredible*, 144–53, 248, 274; O'Connor, *Astors*, 192–93; Lehr, *"King Lehr,"* 22–24; Worden, *Society Circus*, 51–54; Wecter, *Saga*, 210–27; Amory, *Who Killed*, 118–23, and *Last Resorts*, 185–89; Martin, *Things*, 73–74, 257, 269.

[26] Lehr quoted in Lehr, *"King Lehr,"* 23.

[27] Lehr quoted in ibid., 53.

Despite enormous social skills and later marriage to wealth and family, Lehr never achieved the eminence of McAllister. Qualities of the buffoon and the mercenary did not encourage invitations from the clubs that had elected McAllister. But Lehr's shorter reign (at best fifteen years, compared to McAllister's twenty-five) and his inferior status (clown prince but never prime minister of the smart set) were due as much to structural changes in New York society as to personal defects.[28]

McAllister's preeminence was rooted in the absolute power of his patrons; similarly, Lehr's lesser position stemmed from the weaker source of his strength. Although launched by Mrs. Astor, Lehr forsook the serious-minded and aging queen for the younger and gayer Mrs. Stuyvesant Fish. Mrs. Astor dominated society in the 1880s; twenty years later Mrs. Fish shared influence with Mrs. Belmont, Mrs. Goelet, Mrs. Oelrichs, and other contenders. Mrs. Fish also suffered from anemia of the bank account. "We are not rich," she once said. "We have only a few million."[29] Society queens customarily enlisted tens of millions to finance their social conquests. Mrs. Fish, lacking the fabulous funds of Mrs. Astor and Mrs. Vanderbilt, could not always protect her interests. Her fortune was neither large nor, as in the case of other hostesses, independent from personal pressure by dint of investment in securities and real estate. Consequently Mrs. Fish could not prevent E. H. Harriman from removing Stuyvesant Fish from the presidency of the Illinois Central Railroad when she refused to sponsor the Harrimans in society.[30]

Client Lehr and patron Mrs. Fish harmonized in a manner reminiscent of the Astor-McAllister relationship of the 1880s. Lively Mrs. Fish disliked the stuffy balls, dinners, and nights at the opera that passed for entertainment in the reign of Mrs. Astor.[31] Aided by Lehr, she became the most imaginative hostess in town, the mistress of the high-class put-on. Her formal dinners ended in pranks, guests appeared in outlandish dress, and déclassé but interesting people like Marie Dressler, Irene Castle, and John L. Sullivan rubbed elbows with the fashionable set at Mrs. Fish's gatherings. Such proceedings scandalized Mrs. Astor. "Many women will rise up to take my place," said the leader of sober society. "But I hope that my influence will be felt in one thing, and that is, in discountenancing the undignified methods employed by certain New York women to attract a

---

[28] The best source on Lehr is ibid. Other information can be found in Amory, *Last Resorts*, 191–95, 227, and *Who Killed*, 123; Worden, *Society Circus*, 53–54; Wecter, *Saga*, 227–28.

[29] Mrs. Fish quoted in Amory, *Last Resorts*, 174.

[30] Ibid., 213–14.

[31] Martin, *Things*, 205.

following. They have given entertainments that belong under a circus tent rather than in a gentlewoman's house."[32]

Mrs. Astor lived by dubious values but possessed unerring instincts. She realized that Lehr's and Mrs. Fish's burlesque of the Four Hundred compromised the dignity of fashionable society. Ridiculing ritual and substituting fun for formality wounded the essence of social elitism. The two pranksters proclaimed the barrenness of their class by seeking the company of outsiders; they undermined its claim to exclusiveness by revealing the hollow nature of its customs and values. Their fun and games presaged the advent of a new set, café society. When actress Marie Dressler told Mrs. Fish, "I want to be able to tell my mother that I have had dinner with Mrs. Stuyvesant Fish," she replied, "I shall be proud to tell my children that Marie Dressler has dined with me." This exchange foreshadowed a regrouping of elites that fully materialized after World War I. Society figures, reversing the previous course of relations, began to pursue athletes and entertainers, and the search for sensation replaced that continuity of tradition which held the old guard together.[33]

A rapid circulation of elites created a mosaic of diverse and overlapping upper strata in New York. The anxiety and competitiveness caused by social climbing led to the sensational feuding that distinguished New Yorkers from the more secure and serene patriciates of other Atlantic cities. Caprice, luck, and strategy played a large role in determining admission to select circles, and a relatively high rate of turnover and permeability encouraged a state of turmoil. Tensions bred by unstable continuity and uncertain status gave rise to a variety of squabbles. Knickerbocker families snubbed the Astor set; outsiders, like Mrs. Harriman, feuded with those, like Mrs. Fish, who excluded them. Factional conflict did not unite the Four Hundred. Hostesses with different styles, but sharing a common aim, vied for social supremacy. Lehr's formula for "when the Queens start fighting among themselves" was withdrawal "until I feel it is the psychological moment for a truce. Then I do what I can to pour oil on the waters."[34] Internecine strife increased the instability that gave it birth. Intergenerational associations solidified upper orders in other Atlantic cities; the New Yorkers' contentiousness threatened to end their ascendancy before they could bequeath it.

Female domination is another striking difference between the smart

[32] Mrs. Astor quoted in Morris, *Incredible*, 253.

[33] Mrs. Fish and Miss Dressler quoted in Amory, *Last Resorts*, 218. For descriptions of Mrs. Fish's society, see Amory, *Who Killed*, 519–20, and *Last Resorts*, 213–28; Wecter, *Saga*, 341–43; Morris, *Incredible*, 252–54; Lehr, *"King Lehr,"* 168–73; Fish, *1600–1914*, 219–22.

[34] Lehr quoted in Lehr, *"King Lehr,"* 130.

set and established elites along the eastern seaboard. Ever since Sarah Van
Brugh Livingston Jay (Mrs. John Jay) presided over social affairs in New
York during George Washington's administration, the city's high society
had been run by females. A century later, society's queen bees still organized most of the social affairs, appointed the arbiters, and decided who
belonged and who received the lion's share of publicity. They attracted
around them male fireflies—drones might be a better designation—who
added luster to the circles, but the hostesses exercised social sovereignty.
New York's arbiters of elegance, whose existence depended upon sensi-
tivity to power alignments, recognized the primacy of women. "She had
the power that all women should strive to obtain," McAllister reminisced
about a leader of the 1870s, "the power of attaching men to her, and keeping them attached; calling forth a loyalty of devotion such as one imagines
one yields to a sovereign, whose subjects are only too happy to be subjects."
Lehr concurred in this judgment: "Samson's strength lay in his hair . . .
mine lies in the favor of women. All I have to do is to keep in their good
graces and everything comes to me." [35]

"Philadelphia, like London, is definitely a man's town," concludes one
historian of genteel Philadelphia, "and most of Philadelphia's characteristic phenomena, customs, institutions or even arts, are male dominated." [36]
As a result of achievements in business, the arts, and civic functions, upper-
class Boston and Philadelphia produced well-known society leaders and
civic figures in Henry Lee Higginson—banker, financier, founder of the
Boston Symphony Orchestra, and donator of Soldiers' Field to Harvard—
and George Wharton Pepper—prominent lawyer, Republican senator during the 1920s, president of the American Law Institute, recipient of fifteen
honorary degrees, and indefatigable director on numerous charitable, cultural, and business boards in Philadelphia. The style, services, and vocational triumphs of these "grand old men" perpetuated their groups' reputation for public leadership. If knickerbocker New York had retained the
vitality of patrician Boston and Philadelphia, its equivalent figure might
have been August Van Horne Stuyvesant, Jr. Stuyvesant, the ninth and
last direct descendant of Governor Peter Stuyvesant, died at age eighty-
three in 1953. An unmarried recluse and so withdrawn that his servants
went for days without seeing him, he had no friends, never appeared in
society, and shunned civic affairs. Stuyvesant's isolation symbolizes the
passivity and irrelevance of the old New Yorkers. [37]

[35] McAllister, *Society*, 128; Lehr quoted in Lehr, *"King Lehr,"* 154. Cf. Sherwood,
Epistle, 363–76.
[36] Burt, *Perennial Philadelphians*, 535; cf. Baltzell, *Philadelphia Gentlemen*, 336.
[37] Amory, *Who Killed*, 509–14.

Men played a larger role in what passed for high society in Boston and Philadelphia because of greater cohesion in the higher echelons in those cities. Style and fashion in New York had become the realm of a special segment of society led by Mrs. Astor. In Philadelphia and Boston no distinct groups embodied high society, polite society, and civic leadership. Cultural, intellectual, and a substantial vestige of economic leadership remained in the hands of a united group of families. The patriciate in those cities conceived of these functions as interrelated facets of a total class identity. The historical turnover of elites in New York fragmented roles that in other cities were combined in an urban aristocracy. New York intellectuals with genteel social origins, historian Theodore Roosevelt, astronomer Lewis Rutherfurd, and novelist Edith Wharton, came primarily from the knickerbocker enclave. Most of the great industrialist and investment-banking families, the Goulds, Harrimans, Seligmans, Morgans, Stillmans, Loebs, Rockefellers, and Andrew Carnegie, by either choice or exclusion were not members of fashionable social sets. Fashionable society (the Four Hundred) and polite society (the Faubourg Saint-Germain set) had adherents who traveled in both circles, but the groups themselves were separated by different values, leaders, and origins. Segmented New York society meant enclaves that dominated particular social functions. In these circumstances a group of wealthy heiresses could establish their own self-contained empire, and by emphasizing conspicuous consumption and leisure to the exclusion of civic responsibility and commercial activity, they could dispense with male leadership.

The confining Victorian world gave willful, energetic women few spheres other than society in which to display their talents. Conversely, the men, particularly the self-made variety, had neither time nor taste for social frivolity. Gentlemen of inherited wealth who traveled in the smart set or married its leaders were unlikely to be strong-willed activists. William Astor preferred the demimonde atmosphere he created on his yacht to the beau monde presided over by his wife. Stuyvesant Fish, dominated by his wife, tolerated society for her sake and even sacrificed his job to her social pretensions. The male Astors, Oelrichs, Millses, Whitneys, and Vanderbilts arrived chiefly because of the determined efforts of their formidable spouses.

Feminine leadership determined the type of males chosen for arbiters of the fashionable set. Brown, McAllister, and Lehr presented no distaff threat to the reigning queens; Brown never married, Lehr married rather late, and McAllister did not include his reclusive wife in the Four Hundred. Husbands who ordinarily might have suspected such intimate associations as McAllister with Mrs. Astor or Lehr with Mrs. Fish apparently had little to fear. Available evidence has uncovered no hint of scandal, or even of sexual interest, in the trio of social directors. One of Lehr's maxims for social climbers was "Never try to take any other woman's man, whether husband, lover or well-wisher."[38] At least the arbiters followed this advice. In a female-dominated, late Victorian group, the absence of sexual disruption from this quarter contributed significantly to community cohesion.

Merits other than the advantages of neuter gender recommended Brown, Lehr, and McAllister to New York hostesses. They were passionately concerned about ritual, lineage, manners, food, and fashion. But New York society's ornate ceremonialism cannot be solely attributed to female dominance. Ritual is important to all upper classes: it establishes group image, distinguishes the order from the rest of society, insulates the elite from impingement, thus strengthening inner cohesion, and enhances group reputation by providing visibility. Philadelphia, Boston, Richmond, Charleston, Baltimore, and many other cities have debutante dances, costume balls, formal dinners, and society cotillions. The difference between the post–Civil War smart set and other urban elites is not the importance but the *all* importance of these rites. Unlike other patriciates, the Four Hundred seems to have been undistracted by community obligations or cultural interests. At the height of its brilliance, during the 1882–83 social season in Manhattan, 849 affairs exclusive of weddings appeared in the society pages of the *New York Tribune*. The *Tribune* reported 205 dinner parties, 35 luncheons, 301 receptions and teas, 17 balls, 36 theater parties, and 23 musicals not counting the opera. Only 30 (4 percent) of these events were organized for charitable purposes. Among these hundreds of newsworthy activities appeared 3 art exhibits and 36 lectures. Culture claimed 12 percent of the publicized affairs. One of the worst depressions in American history intervened between the 1882–83 season and 1900. Turn-of-the-century society, however, only doubled its percentage of charitable affairs and increased its intellectual activities by 1 percent.[39]

If the bequests of the richest men in the group are any reflection of the disposition of smaller fortunes, the Four Hundred displayed no more sense of public welfare individually than as a unit. Mrs. Astor's husband left $145,000 (one-third of a percent) of his millions to public service organizations. William H. Vanderbilt, son of the old commodore, allowed philanthropy three-fourths of a percent of an estate of $200,000,000.[40] Although extravagant in other expenditures, these New Yorkers cannot be accused of lavish alms-giving.

[38] Lehr quoted in Lehr, *"King Lehr,"* 114; cf. Sherwood, *Epistle*, 379.
[39] Almond, "Plutocracy," 156, 158, 272.
[40] O'Connor, *Astors*, 231–32; Andrews, *Vanderbilt*, 236.

The bons vivants who composed fashionable New York contributed little to those civic functions commonly exercised by elites in other Atlantic cities. Men from financially independent families, such as Whitneys, Belmonts, Vanderbilts, and Astors, devoted themselves largely to clubs, casinos, the turf, and yachting. Other millionaires, still accumulating first- or second-generation fortunes, often rejected both the fashionable life and more responsible elite social roles. Men of the greatest force, like J. P. Morgan, Jay Gould, and Edward Harriman, shunned or were excluded from society, or as in the case of William C. Whitney and Chauncey De-Pew, they acted as ornaments rather than central figures.

Lacking noblesse oblige and intellectual involvement, unassociated with males interested in cultural and civic activities, and perhaps discouraged by Victorian legal and social inhibitions, the leading ladies of the Four Hundred added virtually nothing to the beauty or welfare of their city. Traditions of intellectuality and social responsibility and a more dominant influence in blueblood Boston encouraged genteel women to pursue a useful life. Even New York heiresses blossomed in the culturally stimulating atmosphere of proper Boston. Brahmin-wedded Isabella Stewart Gardner, daughter of a New York dry-goods merchant, became Boston's leading patroness of the arts. Julia Ward Howe, child of New York banker Samuel Ward and cousin of Ward McAllister, was another New York heiress transformed by Boston. Had she not married Boston reformer Samuel Gridley Howe, she recalled, "I should probably have remained a frequenter of fashionable society, a musical amateur, and a *dillettante* in literature."[41] In Boston she became involved in movements for women's rights, abolition, and penal reform, and joined a set of abolitionist and transcendental intellectuals consisting of Howe, Wendell Phillips, Theodore Parker, Charles Sumner, and Margaret Fuller. The smart set produced neither patronesses like Mrs. Gardner, reformer-intellectuals like Mrs. Howe, nor creative artists like Mary Cassat of Philadelphia or Amy Lowell of Boston. New York's noted lady of culture, novelist Edith Wharton, belonged to the knickerbocker enclave. The vacuum in upper-crust feminine influence in charity work, barring the notable exception of another knickerbocker, Louisa May Schuyler, is indicated by blueblood Josephine Shaw Lowell's moving down from Boston to become Gotham's celebrated social-work matron.[42]

Thoughtful members of this gilded group admitted the existence of a

[41] Julia Ward Howe, *Reminiscences, 1819–1899* (Boston, 1899), 80. For the great influence of Boston upper-class women in civic affairs, see Amory, *Proper Bostonians*, 95–142.

[42] William Rhinelander Stewart, *The Philanthropic Work of Josephine Shaw Lowell* (New York, 1911).

cultural vacuum. Mrs. Fish formed her own circle in order to escape the dullness of Mrs. Astor's enclave. Mrs. Winthrop Chanler, a hostess of the smart set, declared, "The Four Hundred would have fled in a body from a poet, a painter, a musician or a clever Frenchman."[43] Even McAllister realized the intellectual limitations of his associates. He recognized the presence of "any number of cultivated and highly respectable, even distinguished men outside of fashionable society." They mixed with the fashionable circle on permissive occasions like the large balls, when "we go outside of the exclusive set and invite professional men, doctors, lawyers, editors, artists and the like."[44]

Undeterred by other interests or obligations, society leaders wholly immersed themselves in social convolutions. Power in fashionable New York rested with the wealthy, the leisured, and the exclusively committed. "Society is an occupation in itself," said McAllister. "Only a man who has a good deal of leisure and a taste for it can keep up with its demands and with what interests it."[45] The fashionable life strained even those with abundant resources of time and material comfort. Mrs. Vanderbilt knew "of no profession, art, or trade that women are working in today as taxing on mental resource as being a leader of Society."[46] Judging from the mental breakdowns suffered by Mrs. Astor, Mrs. Oelrichs, and Harry Lehr, Mrs. Vanderbilt and McAllister did not exaggerate the enormous demands made upon social leaders.

Philadelphia and Boston included multimillionaires among their patricians, but New York, the center of commerce and banking, attracted most of the nation's titanic fortunes. This wealth, uninhibited by traditions that gave meaning to modest ancestral homes, old ways, and even old clothes, and undiverted by social obligations inherited from previous generations, flowed uninterruptedly into channels of colossal conspicuous consumption. The vast accumulations of the Astors, Vanderbilts, Whitneys, and Belmonts underwrote the splendor of fashionable New York.

Many members and observers of New York society dated the beginning of lavish expenditure to the 1870s, when multimillion-dollar imitation Renaissance palazzi or French châteaus first mushroomed at Newport or on Fifth Avenue. Splendid art collections, priceless jewelry, European antiques, yachts the size of ocean liners, lavish social gatherings, and stables of racehorses became socially necessary expense items. At this level of expenditure, Mrs. Fish's lamenting her paltry few millions and

---

[43] Mrs. Chanler quoted in Amory, *Who Killed*, 494n, 120–21.
[44] McAllister, *Tribune* interview, 11.
[45] Ibid.
[46] Mrs. Vanderbilt quoted in Andrews, *Vanderbilt*, 286.

McAllister's remark that "a fortune of a million is only respectable poverty" were not the hyperbole of rich snobs.[47]

Other East Coast patriciates lived in a less splendid manner. Their modest style reflected smaller fortunes, but also evolved from more traditional tastes and habits. The dress, architecture, and gastronomy of patrician Philadelphia and Boston were determined by historical customs, reverence for ancestral relics, and notions that material luxuries created vulgar impediments to the acquittal of cultural and social responsibilities. Lifestyles developed from the past of their class, city, and nation buttressed the status of genteel Boston and Philadelphia.[48] By contrast, M. E. W. Sherwood, a member of the fashionable set, knew "only . . . one family who are living in the same house which they occupied when I first came to New York [in the 1860s]."[49] Through costly antiques and replicas of the European nobility's style of life, New Yorkers sought to compensate for the traditions possessed by older elites. But buying or imitating the symbols of other aristocracies could not provide a genuine claim to aristocratic status. These objects might bring beauty and visibility to their new owners, but uprooted from their original places, they could not convey continuity.

Insecure in its own style of life, fashionable New York looked to old Europe for guidance and confirmation. Patriarch balls were modeled on London social events, Fifth Avenue houses on French châteaus or Venetian palaces, and hostesses' dinners on French cuisine. European antiques substituted for family heirlooms, and marriages between foreign titles and New York heiresses were arranged to fortify mediocre genealogies. An episode illustrating the uncertain and untraditional status of the Four Hundred was the tragic mismatch of Consuelo Vanderbilt with the duke of Marlborough. Mrs. Vanderbilt forced her daughter to forsake Winthrop Rutherfurd for a disastrous union with British nobility. The spectacle of parvenu wealth rejecting the scion of an old family for a European title caricatures the shaky pretensions of fashionable New York.[50]

[47] McAllister, *Tribune* interview, 11. For references to lavish expenditures, see Morris, *Incredible,* 239–56; Andrews, *Vanderbilt,* 264–68, 279–89; Amory, *Who Killed,* 519–20, and *Last Resorts,* 175–76, 209; Lehr, "*King Lehr,*" 70–71; Wecter, *Saga,* 336–45, 368–69, 438–39, 452–54; McAllister, *Society,* 349ff.; Tully, *Era,* 9–15, 53–54; Almond, "Plutocracy," 156–59; Martin, *Passing,* 29–58; Crockett, *Peacocks,* 68–80, 272–75; Van Rensselaer and Van de Water, *Social Ladder,* 160–61, 349.

[48] For the more modest upper-class lifestyle of Philadelphia and Boston, see Burt, *Perennial Philadelphians,* 514–22, 525–29, 579–86, 593–98; Baltzell, *Philadelphia Gentlemen,* 53, 57, 363; Amory, *Proper Bostonians,* 87–107.

[49] Sherwood, *Epistle,* 187.

[50] Almond, "Plutocracy," 162; Morris, *Incredible,* 204–8; Wecter, *Saga,* 386–427; McAllister, *Society,* 210–11, 305–19. The Four Hundred's adoration of prominent

The status anxieties of nouveau riche New Yorkers impelled the daughters of the Goulds, Astors, Whitneys, and Vanderbilts toward marriage with European nobles. Extravagant tastes and a widespread desire to save titles from poverty ensured success in this quest for coronets. New York heiresses far outscored poorer and more insular but more confident belles from Boston and Philadelphia. According to a compilation of 1915, 454 American women were married to titled or prominent Europeans. Of the 356 listed with birthplaces, 193 (47.5 percent) came from New York. Philadelphia and Boston trailed far behind with 20 and 17 women, respectively.[51]

The splendor of the smart set served purposes of self-glorification and publicity. Patricians in Philadelphia, Charleston, and Boston, secure in their inherited ascendancy and retaining other sources of celebrity, shunned sensational self-advertising. In their quest for notoriety, as in other characteristics such as lavish lifestyle, great wealth, and open entry, the New Yorkers more closely resembled the elites of new cities like Chicago, Denver, and San Francisco than did the mellower Atlantic seaboard aristocracies.[52]

Leading hostesses of the fashionable set craved publicity, and the metropolitan press and gossip sheets complied with their desires. Marriages of rich heiresses to European nobility, grand balls, and sumptuous dinners provided sensational copy for newspapers. An important source of the social power of Mrs. Vanderbilt, Mrs. Astor, Mrs. Fish, and their major domos, McAllister and Lehr, was an ability to draw attention to themselves and their associates.[53] McAllister performed a brilliant publicity stunt in dubbing Mrs. Astor's court the Four Hundred. He created instant public image by formally delineating an elite enclave whose numerical des-

---

Europeans caused Theodore Roosevelt to schedule a British fleet to forgo the usual visit to Newport, "simply because the antics of the Four Hundred when they get a chance to show social attentions to visiting foreigners of high official positions are sometimes a little embarrassing to the foreigners and rather humiliating to Americans." Theodore Roosevelt to George Brinton McClellan, 4 Aug. 1905, in Elting Morison, ed., *The Letters of Theodore Roosevelt*, 4 (Cambridge, Mass., 1951), 1299.

[51] A. E. Hartzell, *Titled Americans* (n.p., 1915); cf. Wecter, *Saga*, 406–15; Amory, *Who Killed*, 229–35; Elizabeth Eliot, *Heiresses and Coronets* (New York, 1959).

[52] See n. 16 for bibliographical references on elites in newer cities. For the reticence and aloofness of knickerbockers and other older patriciates, see Amory, *Proper Bostonians*, 19, 110–11, 352–53, and *Who Killed*, 83, 86, 90–92, 509–14; Wharton, *Backward*, 23, 55–56, 61, 79, 92, 150; Van Rensselaer and Van de Water, *Social Ladder*, 33.

[53] For the smart set's craving for publicity, see Wecter, *Saga*, 349, 357–58, 361–64, 369–70, 410; Worden, *Society Circus*, 313–15; Almond, "Plutocracy," 277–78; Amory, *Who Killed*, 121–24; O'Connor, *Astors*, 198; Van Rensselaer and Van de Water, *Social Ladder*, 48–53; Sherwood, *Epistle*, 197; Brown, *Golden Nineties*, 77–78.

ignation symbolized exclusiveness and cohesion. McAllister added mystery, thereby increasing publicity value, by refusing to disclose the names of the chosen until 1892.

Ardently sought celebrity ultimately embarrassed the smart set. Extravagant escapades, highlighted in the newspapers, made people aware of society's trivial, immoral, and irresponsible activities. Unique to New York was *Town Topics*, a scandal sheet that preyed on the bon vivant elite. Figures in fashionable society suffered an opprobrium that befell no other patriciate from older cities. Several of its members moved permanently to Europe to escape public criticism over their costly lifestyle.[54]

An infamous image of wasteful expenditure tarnished the reputation of the Four Hundred, but breakdown of family life endangered its very existence. Relatively rapid upward mobility, leisure, and luxury corrupted the wealthy New Yorkers in a manner and degree impossible for older elites disciplined by a more modest, settled, and busier way of life. Group cohesion suffered from episodes like the estrangement of the William Astors, the divorce and remarriages of the William K. Vanderbilts, and the well-publicized peccadilloes of indiscreet gentlemen. An elite cannot prolong its status unless it bequeaths its position. Continuity depends upon strong marital ties within the class. Flagrant violation of the taboos of monogamy resulted in intragroup conflict, and encouraged the development of those multitudinous and exogamous marital and sexual arrangements that diminished the fortunes and disintegrated the families of New York millionaires. Promiscuous involvements became characteristic in the Astor, Vanderbilt, and Whitney clans after World War I, but the degenerative antecedents began to appear in the 1880s.[55]

Extravagant flaunting of American conventions of productive labor, modest lifestyles, and sexual discipline drew indictments from knickerbockers, journalists, and conscience-stricken representatives of affluent New York. Theodore Roosevelt's 1901 critique epitomizes New York society's widespread disrepute, serves it as an unfortunately accurate epitaph, and previews the salient features of its successor, café society: "As for society people—the Four Hundred, the men and women who at this moment find their most typical expression at Newport—they lead lives which vary from rotten frivolity to rotten vice . . . they are not serious people even when

[54] For New York society's unfavorable publicity, see Morris, *Incredible*, 256–57; Wecter, *Saga*, 368–80; Amory, *Who Killed*, 123–24, 519–20; Crockett, *Peacocks*, 69–80, 272–75; Brown, *Golden Nineties*, 68–69, 77–79.

[55] The best account of the decline is Amory, *Who Killed*; see also Amory, *Last Resorts*, 7–62; Andrews, *Vanderbilt*, 296–305, 312–21, 365–66, 374–78, 381–401; Almond, "Plutocracy," 261–70; Wecter, *Saga*, 344–45; O'Connor, *Astors*, 321ff.

they are not immoral, and thanks to the yellow press, and indeed to the newspapers generally, they exercise a very unwholesome influence on the community at large by the false and unworthy standards which they set up."[56]

Plutocracy triumphed over aristocracy in New York's high society, thus opening it to the newly risen, denying it the refinement of ancient status, making it uncertain of traditions and prerogatives, preventing the emergence of noblesse oblige impulses that rise from consecutive generations of urban leadership, encouraging the pursuit of publicity, stimulating the emergence of cliques vying with each other for social leadership, narrowing the spectrum of community functions that it sought to dominate, transferring social sovereignty to strong-willed females, and creating a fashionable style of conspicuous luxury. These traits, already marked before the Civil War, became dominant by the 1870s.

Although it diverged in these important respects from more mellowed urban elites, high society in New York and the Philadelphia and Boston patriciates shared common attributes. Wealth, for example, is necessary for hegemonic enclaves. Without money they lose vital components, leisure, largesse, power, and so on, that enable elites to maintain internal cohesion and legitimate their community leadership. Some differences between the New Yorkers and these other groups were matters of emphasis rather than of mutually exclusive values. The smart set appreciated ancestry, but placed greater stress on wealth than did these other patriciates. In contrast to genteel Philadelphia, Boston, and Charleston sets, the Four Hundred was comparatively indifferent about source of income, occupation, and degree of civic or commercial power. The greatest disparity in belief and style between high society in New York and in Philadelphia and Boston occurred in the former's domination by females, dependence upon publicity and costly and conspicuous luxury to establish and sustain its status, marital disruptions, internal squabbling, lack of broad-gauged civic leadership, and importation of European titles, artifacts, and styles to substitute for its own lack of rooted credentials and conventions. Many of these dissimilarities also differentiated the Four Hundred and its successors from the knickerbocker contingent. Significant variations thus existed among elites in different cities, and within the same city, as in New York,

[56] Theodore Roosevelt to Cecil Arthur Spring Rice, 3 July 1901, in Morison, *Roosevelt Letters*, vol. 3, 107; cf. Roosevelt quoted in Nicholas Roosevelt, *Theodore Roosevelt as I Knew Him* (New York, 1967), 26. For similar evaluations, see Martin, *Passing*; Van Rensselaer and Van de Water, *Social Ladder*; Pulitzer, *Society*; Roosevelt, *Love*; Vanderbilt, *Farewell*, 91, 96.

where the circulation and fragmentation of elites prevented the development of an upper class. These divergences both reflect and condition the broader urban context in which the elites arose and in which they operated.[57]

[57] For an analysis of elite economic, political, and social behavior in Boston and New York and the relationship of this behavior to urban contexts, see Jaher, "Nineteenth-Century Elites."

Metropolitan Elites in the Midwest, 1907-29: A Study in Multivariate Collective Biography

RICHARD JENSEN

This investigation of the business, professional, and social decision-makers of midwestern cities in the early twentieth century shows how the interaction of variables such as age, occupation, geographic mobility, education, religion, party affiliation, and civic activism produces distinctive profiles of elite characteristics. A generous definition of "elite" is used in order to probe below the level of millionaire bankers and corporation executives to reach the leading five or ten thousand men in the cities studied. Multivariate statistical techniques and computerized data-processing make possible simultaneous analysis of three or four variables, while comparison of elites in several different cities suggests those profile characteristics unique to one city, and those generic to the region or the nation.[1]

This is a greatly revised version of a paper delivered to the American Political Science Association in September 1969. I am indebted to Thomas Kerwin, Barry Parker, and Ann Safier for coding and analyzing portions of the data.

[1] The previous handful of statistical profiles of historical elites simply described the distributions of a few characteristics taken one at a time. Hypothesis testing has been chiefly limited to the rate of intergenerational mobility. The most interesting older studies are: Henry Cabot Lodge, "The Distribution of Ability in the United States," *Century Magazine*, 42 (1891), 687–94—an early gem; Stephen Visher, *Geography of American Notables* (Bloomington, 1928); C. Wright Mills, "The American Business Elite: A Collective Portrait," *Tasks of Economic History*, 5 (1945), 20–44; Eleanor Bruchey, "The Business Elite in Baltimore, 1880–1914," Ph.D. diss. (Johns Hopkins University, 1967); and Thomas Alexander and Richard Beringer, *The Anatomy of the Confederate Congress* (Nashville, 1972). For further listings, see William Miller, ed., *Men in Business* (New York, 1952), 310–11, 381–82; Lawrence Stone, "Prosopography," *Daedalus*, 100:1 (1971), 46–79, which perpetrates a horrible term for collective biography; and Charles Dollar and Richard Jensen, *Historian's Guide to Statistics* (New York, 1971), 281–83.

The members of the elite were identified by the recognition bestowed by qualified contemporaries, not by the application of criteria set up by historical hindsight. These men were considered prominent enough at the time to merit inclusion in "who's who" directories compiled for several cities by John Leonard and Albert Marquis, the first and second editors of *Who's Who in America.* The compilers apparently sent standarized questionnaires to lists of prominent citizens nominated by a variety of business, professional, and civic sources. The autobiographical responses were then edited to a uniform format, that of *Who's Who in America,* and published in a single volume to be sold to the biographees.

No two investigators are likely to agree on a single list of prominent men in a community, so the directories can hardly be termed definitive. Nevertheless, the editors were experts at their work and built strong reputations on the basis of the fairness, accuracy, and comprehensiveness of their product. The first edition of Marquis' Chicago directory appeared in 1905. The second edition of Marquis' Chicago directory appeared in 1911. This edition, with 6,700 autobiographies, formed the basis of this study, together with the fourth Chicago edition (1926), Marquis' second Saint Louis (1912) and Detroit (1914) editions, and his only edition for the state of Minnesota (1907). Also used were the first edition of Leonard's *Who's Who in Finance* (1911) and the only edition of a directory for Wichita, Kansas (1929), which, while not compiled by Marquis or Leonard, also met high editorial standards and permitted fuller comparison with a smaller city.[2]

Although from 2,000 to 10,000 names appeared in the various directories, some very prominent men were missing, and doubtless many secondary figures were left out. A few eminences refused to cooperate despite repeated appeals; others were never invited. The omissions will not distort the overall results unless there was a systematic bias against certain classes of prominent men. A cross-check against various lists of civic leaders in Chicago indicates that the great majority of the city's upper crust found a place in the directory. Marquis did, however, discriminate against "disreputable" types, such as hack politicians and underworld characters.[3]

---

[2] The directories were: *The Book of Chicagoans* (Chicago, 1911, 1926), *The Book of St. Louisans* (St. Louis, 1912), *The Book of Detroiters* (Chicago, 1914), and *The Book of Minnesotans* (Chicago, 1907)—all published by A. N. Marquis and edited by Marquis or Leonard. Also John William Leonard, ed., *Who's Who in Finance* (New York, 1911), and Sara Mullin Baldwin, ed., *Who's Who in Wichita: 1929* (Wichita, 1929).

[3] This point is made explicit in the prefaces of the directories. In 1912 the 74,000 men arrested by the Chicago police included 102 lawyers, 318 physicians, 7 stock dealers, 109 brokers, and 10 clergymen. *The Daily News Almanac and Year-Book for 1914* (Chicago, 1913), 529; this yearbook also provided numerous lists of civic leaders.

Leaders of labor and ethnic communities were absent, unless they were also prominent in government or religion, or unless, like Demetrius Jannopoulo, the Greek leader in Saint Louis, they were "president of the Missouri Tent and Awning Co." or some other species of successful businessmen. Before the Nineteenth Amendment passed, no women, not even Jane Addams or Mrs. Potter Palmer, received separate entries.[4]

Keeping in mind these omissions, and the fact that men in their twenties and thirties rarely had acquired solid business or professional reputations, it is difficult to discern any other systematic biases that would make the patterns revealed by the directories significantly different from the patterns that would be displayed by some "ideal" list. The strongest criticism would be directed at the editors' choice of what proportions of men were included in each particular occupational or professional group. This criticism can be met by analyzing the data chiefly in terms of occupational categories.[5] The shortcomings, real or imagined, of the directories should not be allowed to obscure their immense advantages for the urban historian. They cover thousands of merchants, railroad managers, manufacturers, real estate operators, editors, corporate officials, educators, investors, philanthropists, consultants, civic leaders, physicians, traders, judges, lawyers, engineers, wholesalers, dentists, politicians, artists, social workers, brokers, bankers, and clergymen who ran the affairs of great cities but who otherwise would be totally unknown or obscure today. For the vast majority of these men the directories provide information that historians otherwise could obtain only by fantastically difficult searches through obituaries, clipping files, tax records, manuscript censuses, marriage licenses, and family Bibles.

No historian can digest 7000 autobiographies, however brief, just by reading through them. A systematic research strategy, relying primarily upon quantification, is necessary to deal adequately with this large body of men. The easiest decision is to punch all the data on IBM cards and let a computer do all the work. The rub is that computer programs are purely

[4] However, see John William Leonard, ed., *Women's Who's Who in America* (New York, 1914). Richard Jensen and Barbara Campbell, "How to Handle a Liberated Woman," *Historical Methods Newsletter*, 5 (1972), 109–13, is the first report of a study parallel to this paper.

[5] The directory listed half the bankers counted by the census of 1910 (350 out of 706), one-third of the lawyers (1,300 out of 3,866), one-seventh of the physicians (600 out of 4,032), one-eighth of the manufacturers (1,400 out of 11,116), and only one-ninth of the clergymen (200 out of 1,693). Obviously if these proportions had been changed, the aggregate elite would have a somewhat different profile, but the lawyers, physicians, and so on, would have about the same profile. Bureau of the Census, *Thirteenth Census* . . . 1910, 4: "Population: Occupational Statistics" (Washington, 1914), 157, 161, 163, 165.

mechanical devices, perforce lacking historical imagination and a sense of the past.

The challenge is to code the autobiographies so that numerical values stand for characteristics expressed in words, and then to use computers to perform routine statistical manipulations. Then the historian—not the programmer or statistician—must search the printout for meaningful patterns. If the historian wants to discuss urban elites on the basis of more than a handful of remarkable cases, he will have to adopt a quantitative research strategy equal to the exigencies of dealing with great masses of data.

Most painful, these exigencies demand the use of very simple codes. The computers that help land men on the moon can store any information a historian can find, but any coding scheme elaborate enough to retain one-tenth of the richness of the information in the stylized little autobiographies would be a hundred times too complicated to use in statistical analysis. The state of the art of statistics, not computers, is the limiting factor. Of course historians oversimplify complex attributes all the time— they must call a man who raises mules, sells corn, and speculates in real estate a farmer if they expect to understand agriculture.

Coding schemes have to be simple, but they do not have to be naive. The questions one asks determine the codes one uses. If migration patterns are of concern, it makes sense to set up a series of categories—place of birth, distance and direction from destination, size of birthplace, location of college, number of places lived in, year of arrival at destination, and so on. Such information may not be given explicitly in the source, but can be extracted with the help of gazetteers. If the historian has thought out his basic questions, he can approach the directories like a detective looking for implicit clues that can be made explicit by careful searching and ingenious codes.

The codes also must be prepared with an eye to the limitations of IBM cards and statistical routines. Each person receives one or more cards, with each bit of information recorded in one or more columns. To simplify rechecking, each Chicagoan received an identification code consisting of his abbreviated name and his directory page number. The first variable for analysis was the last two digits of his year of birth, which occupied two columns. (All the analysis divided men by decades, so the second column has not yet been used.) The second variable indicated place of birth, with the first column indicating region and the second identifying the state or foreign country. The third variable was a one-column code for size of birthplace when the subject was born.[6] In like manner, 65 of the 80 col-

---

[6] The code was 0 = unknown, 1 = farm, 2 = rural nonfarm, 3 = town (under

umns of a single IBM card were filled with codes for 48 different variables. To keep the printout manageable, to facilitate the use of library computer programs, and to avoid complicating the statistics, only the digits 0 through 9 were used in any one column after the name entry. (It is very undesirable to use symbols such as + and −.) The fewer the categories for any one variable, the easier the statistical analysis becomes. Hence frequent use was made of two-valued (dichotomous) codes and of geometric progression codes.[7]

It is unnecessary to code every name in every directory, since a systematic random sample provides nearly the same results with much less trouble. For Chicago one name in nine was selected at random (the first on each page), and for Wichita one name in five. The autobiographies that fell in the sample were then coded and the data punched on IBM cards; the coding process was by far the most time-consuming part of the study. The other directories were not coded or computerized. Instead, whenever a particular question arose, an ad hoc random sample was chosen and the desired information tabulated by hand. The manual tabulations provided both comparative perspective across cities and deeper explorations of particular groups, but could not generate new patterns as the computer did. Random samples produce patterns that closely resemble, but are not identical with, the patterns that would result from using every name in the directories. The larger the sample, the smaller the error, and for a sample size (or N) of 746 for Chicago in 1911, the average sampling error is reasonably small—of the order of a few percent. (Quadrupling the sampling size would quadruple coding time, but would only halve the already small sampling error.)[8]

The chief reward for computerizing a collective biography project is the ease in cross-tabulating variables, otherwise an extremely laborious process. Not only did the computer count the number of men in each category for each variable, but also it automatically counted the number of men in every possible combination of categories for two variables, and it generated thousands of special tables incorporating three variables. Thus the printout not only indicated how many men were in each age cohort, but it also told how many financiers, lawyers, manufacturers, and so on,

---

2,500 at time of birth), 4 = small city (2,500 to 20,000), 5 = city (20,000 to 200,000), 6 = metropolis (over 200,000).

[7] For example, 1 = Mason, 0 = not a Mason was a dichotomous code; 1 = lived one year or less in city, 2 = 2 or 3 years, 3 = 4 to 7 years, 4 = 8 to 15 years, 5 = 16 to 31 years, 6 = 32 or more years, 0 = no information was a geometric code.

[8] For a guide to sampling techniques, and further bibliography, see C. A. Moser and G. Kalton, *Survey Methods in Social Investigation* (London, 1971), 61–210, 440–47.

were in each cohort. Furthermore, it reduced the tabulations to percentages, computed chi-square, and calculated an "expected" number of men in each cell in the table. (The expected number of lawyers born in the 1850s equals the percentage of all men who are lawyers, times the total number of men born in the 1850s.) Every computer center has a library of "canned" programs that will easily perform these operations for a historian who does not know FORTRAN, and many have the super packages, SPSS, OSIRIS, and DATA-TEXT, which make computer work almost trivial.[9]

Computers can be *too* helpful—they will quickly print out, at low cost, all the possible cross-tabulations for each pair of variables. The total number of tables equals the square of the number of variables used—20 variables produce 400 tables (of which 210 are superfluous), 50 variables produce 2,500 tables, and 100 variables produce 10,000. When the ancillary tables are added, the number of tables increases by 300 percent, and a truck is needed to cart the printout home. The historian who has just transformed a small portion of one directory into a mountain of paper will wonder how he can possibly find the story of the past in such a mass of numerals. Essentially he needs a method for discovering the interesting tables in the printout. He can then take these tables and further analyze them by dividing the men into categories—e.g., young, middle-aged, and old—and generating the same cross-tabulations for each of the subgroups. Then it becomes possible to discover whether a third variable—age in this example—alters the patterns displayed by pairs of other variables. A fourth and even a fifth variable can be similarly used, though quickly the number of cases in the sub-subcategories becomes so small that artificially strong patterns may easily arise from a slight skewness in the sample.

The two key difficulties are finding the interesting cross-tabulations in the first place, and then devising a method of comparing patterns. At this stage, sophisticated mathematical statistics suddenly becomes critically important for the historian. The first problem he solves by identifying and ignoring largely random patterns, and the second he solves by use of an appropriate mathematical measure of statistical association. A random pattern occurs when each column of the table (in percentage form) is roughly identical. That is, the distribution of Republicans by age is parallel to the distributions of Democrats and nonpartisans by age. (See the two columns of Table 11 headed "Finance and Manufacturing" for an example of randomness.) In this case, age does not differentiate partisan

[9] Computations in this paper were done with house programs at the Washington University Computer Center, which generously provided free machine time. On the versatility of the super programs, see Edward Shorter, *The Historian and the Computer* (Englewood Cliffs, 1971), which describes DATA-TEXT.

attributes; age and partisanship are unrelated for the sample, hence we conclude for the entire elite. The historian, unless he is surprised by this result, should turn to the next table. If it is nonrandom, the columns differ sharply when put in percentage form. For example, the foreign-born might be old, the easterners middle-aged, and the Chicago-born young.

That is worth looking into. For a series of tables dealing with the same number N of men, the chi-square statistic will order the tables from low to high according to randomness.[10] But when it is necessary to compare tables with different Ns, the chi-square values are misleading. A variety of measures of association exist to bridge the gap, of which Pearson's contingency coefficient C seems to be the most useful.[11] The behavior of C somewhat resembles the well-known correlation coefficient r, which for technical reasons cannot be used with categorical data. The value of C ranges from o (randomness) to nearly $+1.0$ (very strong pattern). Table 1, for which $C = 0.85$, illustrates a strong pattern for the Chicago elite—a man's first occupation was, except for financiers, usually his current occupation. A high value of C does not mean that a particular table is important—there may be elementary reasons for the high value, but these can be observed quickly upon inspecting the table.

TABLE 1. *First Occupation by Current Occupation, Chicago 1911*

CURRENT OCCUPATION (READ DOWN)

FIRST OCCUPATION	FINANCE	TRADE AND TRANSPORT	MFG.	LAW	MED.	OTHER PROFL.	ALL
Finance	44.6%	2.6%	2.1%	0.8%	0.0%	0.0%	7.9%
Trade and transport	23.2	65.6	15.5	2.3	3.1	8.7	25.9
Manufacturing	1.8	3.1	59.2	2.3	0.0	0.0	12.9
Law	7.1	5.1	1.4	80.6	0.0	1.1	16.8
Medicine	1.8	0.5	0.7	0.8	84.4	1.1	8.0
Other professional	6.3	6.7	4.9	7.0	9.4	81.5	15.8
Manual	2.7	4.6	5.6	3.9	1.6	1.1	3.8
Other and unknown	12.6	11.8	10.5	2.3	1.6	6.5	9.0
Total %	100	100	100	100	100	100	100
N	112	195	142	129	64	92	746

Chi-square = χ^2 = 2,027; contingency coefficient = C = 0.85.

[10] On chi-square, see Hubert Blalock, *Social Statistics* (New York, 1960), 212–20. On the measurement of association, see Dollar and Jensen, *Historian's Guide*, ch. 3.

[11] The value of C equals $\sqrt{\chi^2/(\chi^2+N)}$ where χ^2 is chi-square for the table (computed by the computer!) and N is the number of men in the table.

The recommended strategy for a first scanning of the printout is to investigate the tables with values of C greater than 0.3. This reduces the double dangers of overlooking important patterns and of wasting time on uninteresting tables. The C values can also be used to compare the strength of patterns in entirely different tables, even different samples. Of course there is no substitute for common historical sense in interpreting patterns, so long as one has a precise pattern to interpret.

The most important result of the study was that the exact physiognomy of the elite emerged from the shadows of myth and guesswork. The elite naturally differed sharply from the general population. In 1910, 62 percent of all Chicagoans aged 45–64 had been born abroad, in contrast to only 14 percent of the elite. Fully 60 percent of the men attended college, a privilege denied to all but a handful of other Chicagoans of the same age. In a predominantly Catholic city, only 4 percent of the elite acknowledged a Catholic affiliation (only 3 percent were Jewish), while 35 percent belonged to Protestant bodies. (The remainder did not mention a religious affiliation, but were clearly of Protestant background.) The largest Protestant denominations, Methodist, Lutheran, and Baptist, were represented by only 60 men, in contrast to 164 members of the much smaller Congregational, Episcopal, and Presbyterian bodies. One surprise (see Table 2) was the relationship between religion and education, the Catholics being the most educated and the Jews the least. This pattern also held for Saint Louis, and was due to the prominence of Catholic lawyers and Jewish merchants and manufacturers.

Birthplace information proved to be among the most valuable. It showed that in 1911 the older men came from farther away (Europe and the Northeast), while younger men came from Chicago and the Midwest

TABLE 2.   *Education by Religion, Chicago 1911*

RELIGIOUS AFFILIATION

EDUCATION	NONE MENTIONED	PROTESTANT	CATHOLIC	JEWISH
Some college	54.8%	67.3%	80.0%	20.0%
High school or less	35.8	31.9	16.7	80.0
Not given	9.4	0.8	3.3	0.0
Total %	100	100	100	100
N	436	260	30	20

Chi-square = 84, C = 0.32, for entire table, of which this is a condensation.

(see Table 3). A similar pattern occurred in the smaller boom city of Wichita in 1929 (see Table 4).

TABLE 3. *Place of Birth by Age, Chicago 1911*

AGE

BIRTHPLACE	28–40	41–50	51–60	60+	ALL AGES
Chicago	26.2%	18.9%	10.2%	2.4%	15.1%
Other Midwest	45.3	36.8	39.0	16.0	35.2
Other U.S.	15.4	28.9	32.2	52.0	31.7
Foreign	13.1	15.5	18.7	29.6	18.0
Total %	100	100	100	100	100
N	137	264	177	125	723

Chi-square = 132, C = 0.39, for original table; 23 men omitted for lack of birthplace data.

TABLE 4. *Age by Nearness of Birthplace, Wichita 1929*

AGE	BORN WITHIN 500 MILES	BORN BEYOND 500 MILES
45 and over	36.9%	65.1%
44 and under	63.1	34.9
Total %	100	100
N	313	146

Chi-square = 37, C = 0.28, for this condensed table; for the original table, chi-square = 62, C = 0.34.

Three different hypotheses can explain the observed phenomena: (1) long-distance geographical mobility among the elite was declining in the late nineteenth and early twentieth centuries; (2) migration rates remained the same, but older men typically have had more opportunities to move in their lifetime, and so in 1911 tended to be farther from their birthplaces; (3) Chicago-born sons of the older members of the elite had an easier time entering the directory lists than did young men from outside who lacked local connections. There is no way to choose among the three alternatives on the basis of the cross-section of the elite in 1911. It is necessary to compare a cross-section taken at a later or earlier date; the 1926 edition of the directory provides this opportunity. Hypothesis (1) predicts additional shifts toward both Chicago and midwestern birth for each age category in 1926. Hypothesis (2) predicts a pattern in 1926 virtually identical to that of 1911. Hypothesis (3) predicts that Chicago-born will increase faster than any other category, and that paternal relationships should be observable. Table 5 shows the birthplaces of the 1926 elite by age, and Table 6 shows the percentage differences between each entry in Table 5 and the corresponding entries in Table 4, that is, the change in rates.

TABLE 5. Place of Birth by Age, Chicago 1926

AGE

BIRTHPLACE	28–40	41–50	51–60	60+	ALL AGES
Chicago	36.9%	28.5%	23.9%	13.3%	23.0%
Other Midwest	34.9	40.0	37.2	36.0	37.9
Other U.S.	22.8	20.0	27.5	32.0	25.9
Foreign	5.4	11.5	11.6	18.7	13.1
Total %	100	100	100	100	100
N°	149	270	113	75	282

* Ages sampled separately; do not sum horizontally.

The 1926 patterns of birthplaces show a marked movement toward Chicago in all age groups, and a lesser movement toward the Midwest for the oldest age group. The other American states and Europe supplied a decreasing proportion of the Chicago elite. Obviously hypothesis (2) must be rejected—the pattern of geographical mobility did change in the short span of 15 years. Hypothesis (1), in predicting the contraction of geographical mobility, is justified for each age group except the youngest. There the proportion of Chicagoans did go up 10.7 points, but the proportion of midwesterners fell 10.4 points, and the proportion of men from other regions increased 7.4 points, which was the opposite of the prediction. Only hypothesis (3) seems to be consistent with all the patterns in Table 6. Further checking indicates that 31 percent of the Chicago-born elite of 1911 had a relative (father, brother, father-in-law, or son) in the

TABLE 6. Change in Place of Birth by Age,
Chicago 1926 versus 1911

AGE

BIRTHPLACE	28–40	41–50	51–60	60+	ALL AGES
Chicago	+10.7	+9.6	+13.7	+10.9	+7.9
Other Midwest	−10.4	+3.2	−1.8	+20.0	+2.7
Other U.S.	+7.4	−8.9	−4.7	−20.0	−5.8
Foreign	−7.7	−4.0	−7.2	−10.9	−4.9

same directory, in contrast to only 16 percent of the 1911 elite born outside Chicago. For 1926, fully 33 percent (77) of a sample of 232 men born in the city after 1880 were sons of men listed in at least one edition of the directory (1905, 1911, 1917, or 1926); doubtless many others were nephews or in-laws of elite members. Thus hypothesis (3) is consistent with all the findings, but there is some doubt whether it alone can account for the magnitude of the shifts. It seems likely that two effects were operating simultaneously, that is, that both hypotheses (1) and (3) are correct.

Chicago was the only large city that was the birthplace of more than 3 percent of the 1911 elite. Of the 467 native-born (excepting the Chicago-born and those for whom birthplace data are missing), only 7 percent (32 men) were born in a city of more than 200,000 population, and 11 percent (50) came from medium cities of 20,000 to 200,000. The largest number came from small towns and cities. Small cities of 2,500 to 20,000 population contributed 18 percent (82) of the men, while towns and villages of under 2,500 population claimed 33 percent (155). It proved virtually impossible to distinguish between rural nonfarm, estimated at 27 percent (127), and the farm-born, estimated at 4.5 percent (only 21 men). Very probably more were actually born on farms. Even when the Chicagoans and the foreign-born are included, cities of more than 20,000 population were the birthplaces of only 30 percent of the Chicago elite. In Wichita the small-town bias was even stronger, with 19 percent of the city's total elite (90 out of 480) born on farms, another 45 percent (218) from towns of under 3,000 population, and only 6 percent (27) from cities of more than 100,000. The metropolitan leadership community was bred in the small town—but seldom on a farm.

It is not too surprising that old-stock, well-educated, rural- and small-town-bred white Protestant elites in the midwestern metropolises were Republicans, but the poor showing of the Democratic party is remarkable. Table 7 shows the breakdown by location. In Chicago, Detroit, and the twin cities Minneapolis-Saint Paul, the Democrats enrolled a meager 10 percent of the elite. In Wichita they did a little better (14 percent), but only in the border city of Saint Louis did they enlist a respectable one-quarter of the elite. The Republicans included about half the elite everywhere except Saint Louis, where they were held to a third. A substantial proportion, ranging from 30 percent in Wichita to nearly 50 percent in the larger cities, was presumably so politically apathetic that it listed no major party identification. This included a tiny handful of third-party members like the four Socialists and two Prohibitionists in Chicago, and a few men who specified they were "independent in politics."

TABLE 7.   *Partisanship by City and Occupational Group,*
Midwestern Business and Professional
Elites, 1907–29

CHICAGO (1911)	% REP.	% DEM.	% NONE, NA, AND OTHER	N
All*	47.4	9.2	43.1	698
Finance	58.9	5.6	35.5	107
Manufacturing	50.4	10.2	39.4	137
Trade and transport	46.3	7.3	46.3	179
Medicine	35.5	0.0	64.5	62
Law	61.3	22.6	16.1	124
Other professions	22.5	3.4	74.1	89
WICHITA (1929)				
All*	56.3	14.1	29.6	480
Business	57.8	14.8	27.4	303
Clergy	58.8	0.0	41.2	17
Education	38.3	14.9	46.8	47
Medicine	47.4	18.4	34.3	38
Law	71.9	18.7	9.4	32

* In Chicago and Wichita, all names were drawn from one systematic random sample, so the marginal totals can be added; in the other cities, separate samples were drawn for each occupation.

DETROIT (1914)				
All business	53.2	10.4	36.3	77
Automotive	47.5	7.5	45.0	80
Railroad	47.7	9.5	42.8	42
Heavy mfg. (ex. auto)	53.4	6.3	40.3	189
Construction	47.0	13.0	40.0	15
Real estate	66.1	7.1	26.8	56
Law	51.8	22.7	25.3	162
Medicine	41.5	6.2	52.3	65

SAINT LOUIS (1912)				
All business	36.2	19.1	44.7	544
Shoes	31.6	34.2	34.2	38
Beer	36.7	13.3	50.0	30
Real estate	37.4	33.3	29.3	75
Construction	50.0	14.3	35.7	28
Railroad	19.2	23.3	57.5	73
Law	37.6	44.7	17.7	170
Medicine	25.2	23.2	51.6	147

TWIN CITIES (1907)	% REP.	% DEM.	% NONE, NA, AND OTHER	N
All business	41.1	6.8	52.1	73
Banking	43.9	9.9	46.2	41
Lumber	46.7	0.0	53.3	30
Newspapers	42.5	2.5	55.0	40
Law	55.0	10.0	35.0	60

NINE MIDDLE-SIZED MINNESOTA CITIES (1907)
(8,000 to 75,000 pop.)

	% REP.	% DEM.	% NONE, NA, AND OTHER	N
All business	43.0	22.0	36.0	14
Banking	60.0	7.0	33.0	15
Lumber	50.0	7.0	43.0	16
Newspapers	55.0	35.0	10.0	20
Law	50.0	27.5	22.5	40

MINNESOTA: SMALL CITIES AND TOWNS (1907)

	% REP.	% DEM.	% NONE, NA, AND OTHER	N
All business	48.7	7.7	43.6	39
Banking	58.0	4.9	37.1	81
Lumber	43.0	0.0	57.0	7
Newspapers	53.1	18.4	28.6	49
Law	62.5	8.8	28.8	80

The Democratic showing was not much better in the various occupational groups, except that fewer lawyers were independent, and the Democrats picked up support there. Businessmen in fields that might seem dependent upon political favoritism, such as construction, real estate, and steam or street railroads, were no more politically involved than others. Indeed, steam railroad managers and owners, and especially physicians, clergymen, educators, and other professionals, clearly tended to avoid partisanship. Perhaps they considered themselves technical experts who stood above petty partisanship, or perhaps they moved around so much that they never acquired firm roots in local politics. In Wichita 35 percent of the 150 men who had lived there fewer than eight years were nonpartisan, in contrast to only 27 percent of the 327 longer-term residents. Only in Saint Louis did Democrats outnumber Republicans in certain occupational groups, but there the Democratic strength rested primarily on the large number of southerners and Catholics. If these two groups are excluded, the Saint Louis Republicans outnumbered Democrats by 3 to 1 or 4 to 1 in every category. The overall political complexion of the city does not seem to have been a decisive factor, since Republicans in those days outpolled the Democrats in most elections in every city except Chicago.

The Republicans fared no better among the richest members of the elites than among the average members. The "richest" were identified by lists of capitalists, bankers, corporate directors, and investors in another compendium similar to the Marquis directories. Table 8 gives the politics

T A B L E 8. *Partisanship by Location, Capitalists, 1911**

ILLINOIS	% REP.	% DEM.	% NONE, NA, AND OTHER	N
Chicago	55.6	8.7	38.4	403
Downstate	75.1	18.1	7.0	144
MICHIGAN				
Detroit	48.3	20.7	31.0	29
Upstate	71.0	21.1	7.9	114
MINNESOTA				
Minneapolis-Saint Paul	46.4	7.2	46.4	97
Nine middle-sized cities	43.2	0.0	56.8	44
Small cities and towns	61.4	8.6	30.0	140
MISSOURI				
Saint Louis	38.9	23.1	37.9	203
Kansas City	50.0	25.0	25.0	16
Outstate	37.1	59.1	3.8	159
IOWA	82.8	15.2	2.0	197
DEEP SOUTH (Alabama, Arkansas, Florida, Georgia, and Mississippi)	7.8	83.6	8.6	370

* Based on John William Leonard, ed., *Who's Who in Finance* (New York, 1911).

of the richest men in Illinois, Michigan, Minnesota, Missouri, and, for comparison, Iowa and five states in the Deep South. So few capitalists lived in Kansas City, Missouri, that a few names had to be taken from Kansas City, Kansas, including one Balzac Hoffman, one of the wealthiest millers in the country, owner of a chain of grain elevators in Kansas, and member of the Socialist party.

The most striking pattern in Table 8 is the heavy partisanship of bankers outside the metropolises. The exception is Minnesota, where partisanship seems to have become old-fashioned by 1907. The metropolitan capitalists in Table 8 represent, beyond doubt, some of the wealthiest and busiest men in the country. They apparently held so many directorships, presidencies, portfolios, and country club memberships that they had little time or inclination for politics (although some held high party or government posts). The evidence suggests that politics was most salient in the small cities, and least relevant to the metropolitan notables, who, as indicated above, tended to come from small cities; perhaps much of their remaining partisanship was the lingering effect of youthful indoctrination.[12]

The few Democrats who entered the elite may have had difficult relations with their peers—only 15 percent of the Chicago Democrats belonged to one or more of the three leading social clubs (Union League, University, Chicago), in contrast to 34 percent of the Republicans. One reason may have been their close ties to the notorious Chicago machine of Mayor Carter Henry Harrison, Jr. (who was himself a member of exclusive clubs and was naturally listed in the directory). Lawyers accounted for 41 percent of the Democrats, in contrast to only 15 percent of the other elite men, and 38 percent of all the Democrats had already been candidates for public office, in contrast to only 11 percent of the Republicans. Of course a few men like old Robert Hall McCormick of the reaper family, a noted collector of art and member of the best clubs, were Democrats; McCormick's son was a Republican. Only a handful of men in the various samples (just two in Chicago) identified themselves as "progressive Republicans," "insurgent Republicans," or "Progressives." Equally uncommon was the designation "gold" or "Cleveland" Democrat.

Robert Wiebe and Samuel Hays have suggested that a new middle class of businessmen emerged in the metropolis early in the twentieth century who were cosmopolitan rather than localistic in outlook, and for whom professional, technical, and trade associations, rather than political parties, served as vehicles for relating their expertise to social and political problems.[13] Traces of such a group showed up in the elite sample in Chicago, as Table 9 suggests. Over 40 percent of the Republicans and nonpartisans mentioned one or more association memberships, in contrast to only 28 percent of the Democrats, who were still wedded to machine politics. Of the men who listed memberships, one-sixth of the Republicans and

[12] For opposite results in the 1960s, see Everett Ladd, *Ideology in America* (Ithaca, 1969).

[13] Robert Wiebe, *The Search for Order: 1877–1920* (New York, 1967), 129; Samuel P. Hays, "Political Parties and the Community-Society Continuum," in William N. Chambers and Walter Dean Burnham, eds., *The American Party Systems* (New York, 1967), 152–81. Municipal reformers and good government activists in Chicago mostly belonged to the City Club, whose membership closely resembled the overall political profile of the Chicago elite: 50.7 percent were Republicans, 8.7 percent were Democrats, and 40.6 percent listed no affiliation. (N = 67, based on a random sample of 245 of the 1,780 members listed in City Club of Chicago, *Ninth Year Book: 1912* [Chicago, 1912].)

TABLE 9.   *Technical Associations by Partisanship,*
Chicago 1911

PARTISANSHIP	% WITH MEMBERSHIP IN TECHNICAL OR PROFESSIONAL ASSOCIATIONS°	% OF MEMBERS HOLDING LEADER- SHIP POSITION	N
Republicans	40.4	17.0	334
Democrats	28.4	15.8	67
Nonpartisans	43.0	33.6	312

° National, state, and local associations included for all occupations.

Democrats also held leadership positions, in contrast to one-third of the nonpartisans. Thus it would appear that professional leadership served as a substitute for political activism, as the hypothesis suggests.

The figures were somewhat deceptive, however. Physicians and educators, two highly nonpartisan groups, were by the nature of their work much more likely to join professional societies than were businessmen. Only 12.5 percent of the 64 physicians held no memberships, in contrast to 80 percent of the men in trade, transportation, and manufacturing. But each businessman averaged 2.5 memberships in social clubs, while each professional man (excluding lawyers) averaged only 1.1. Clearly, local medical and other professional societies served as substitutes for social clubs, in addition to their technical functions.

However, the hypothesis becomes dubious when a specific group such as physicians is considered. A hand-tabulated sample of 182 elite physicians in Saint Louis disclosed that one-sixth of the Republicans (7 out of 44) and one-sixth of the nonpartisans (17 out of 104) held leadership positions in medical affairs, in contrast to fully one-third of the Democrats (11 out of 34), or quite the reverse of Table 9.[14] In Saint Louis therefore, Democratic affiliation was associated with professional leadership among physicians; the two roles were mutually reinforcing, not mutually exclusive as the Wiebe-Hays interpretation would suggest. (Only 3 partisan and 12 nonpartisan physicians listed no memberships in medical societies, while the solitary Socialist turned out to be an eminent surgeon.)

The use of a computerized research design facilitates the investigation of the basic question of multivariate analysis: how does one variable affect the relationship between two other variables? For example, does the same

[14] Leadership positions included president of a medical society, member of the city or state board of health, editor of a medical journal, dean of a medical school, or delegate to an international conference.

relationship between occupation and partisanship hold for young, middle-aged, and old men? If different patterns emerge for the different age groups, then the historian must explain the patterns either in terms of the biological or life-cycle effects of aging or in terms of the different specific historical experiences encountered by each generation in its formative years. Since age seemed the variable most likely to have a multivariate effect, the Saint Louis (1912) and Chicago (1911) elites were divided into three cohorts, "old" (born before 1849), "middle-aged" (born 1850–69), and "young" (born after 1870), and every pair of variables was examined for each cohort.

An example of the life-cycle effects of aging appeared in the relationship between occupation and recreation. The physicians, educators, clergymen, engineers, architects, authors, artists, and scientists in the sample were so busy with technical activities that they enjoyed little leisure time for fishing, tennis, yachting, or gardening. Only 10 percent of the 30 young men in these categories specifically mentioned any form of outdoor or indoor recreation, along with 18 percent of the 97 middle-aged and 4 percent of the 24 old. What little time was available to these professionals for recreation came in middle age. By contrast, the corresponding rates for businessmen and lawyers were 54 percent for 107 young men, 46 percent for 344 middle-aged, and 33 percent for 108 old. Unlike the professionals, the businessmen enjoyed recreation more when they were younger, as would be expected from aging factors. The nonlegal professionals were also much less likely to be members of fraternal lodges (12 percent of 151 versus 26 percent of businessmen and lawyers).

The most intriguing result of the age cohort analysis was the changed relationship between occupation and partisanship. The partisanship patterns for each occupation are roughly the same across the cohorts, except for finance, manufacturing, and law. Table 10 shows the Chicago pattern.

TABLE 10.   *Partisanship by Age and Occupation,*
Chicago 1911

	FINANCE AND MANUFACTURING		LAW		ALL OTHER OCCUPATIONS	
	MIDDLE-AGED	YOUNG AND OLD	MIDDLE-AGED	YOUNG AND OLD	MIDDLE-AGED	YOUNG AND OLD
Rep.	58.4%	45.6%	54.4%	68.4%	37.3%	36.7%
Dem.	9.7	5.4	29.4	14.0	5.5	5.8
Ind.	31.8	48.9	16.2	17.5	57.1	57.5
N	154	92	68	57	217	120

The middle-aged financiers and manufacturers, born between 1850 and 1869, were 12.8 points more Republican than older and younger men in the same line of work. Lawyers born between 1850 and 1869, however, were 15.4 points more Democratic than other lawyers.

One plausible explanation is in terms of the different political experiences of each generation. Men born in the 1850s and 1860s came of age politically and entered their occupations between about 1874 and 1900, when the currency and tariff questions were the most salient issues in national politics, with the Republican party taking positions more often favored by banking and manufacturing interests. The middle cohort of bankers and manufacturers was therefore less independent and more Republican than the cohorts that came of age when other issues were more salient, and also more Republican than men in the same cohort but in occupations not so directly affected by monetary and tariff debates.

As for the lawyers, it is notable that the only decades in which promising young Democrats could reasonably aspire to high Illinois or national offices were precisely those during which the middle cohort came of age. Since most lawyers had a bent toward politics, it is plausible that the law was especially attractive to ambitious Democrats of the middle cohort, or conversely that the Democratic party was especially attractive to aspiring lawyers in that cohort. Upward mobility for a young Democrat was most likely in the legal profession rather than banking, commerce, manufacturing, or the professions, where his ideas might seem too heterodox; in law, Democratic principles were still orthodox.

Before accepting an interpretation of Table 10 based on political generations, it would be well to consider the corresponding patterns for Saint Louis, shown in Table 11. The partisanship of middle cohorts of financiers, manufacturers, and lawyers there was identical with that of young and old cohorts. For other occupations, however, the middle-aged cohort was significantly less Republican than the young and old cohorts. A revision of the generational hypothesis offered for Chicago applies to both cities

TABLE 11.   *Partisanship by Age and Occupation,*
Saint Louis 1912

	FINANCE AND MANUFACTURING		LAW		ALL OTHER OCCUPATIONS	
	MIDDLE-AGED	YOUNG AND OLD	MIDDLE-AGED	YOUNG AND OLD	MIDDLE-AGED	YOUNG AND OLD
Rep.	35.6%	36.5%	46.1%	47.6%	26.6%	41.7%
Dem.	18.4	17.6	46.1	42.9	18.1	10.7
Ind.	46.0	45.9	7.8	9.5	55.3	47.6
N	87	74	13	21	94	84

(except for lawyers, for whom the Saint Louis sample size is too small to allow reliable conclusions). In Chicago the age cohorts were politically similar except for a Republican bulge among middle-aged financiers and manufacturers. In Saint Louis the cohorts were also similar, except for a Democratic bulge among the middle-aged in *other* occupations. In both cities the middle-aged financiers and manufacturers were significantly more Republican, in terms of the combination of age and occupation, than might have been expected by looking at other occupations. Thus Republican party policy in the 1870s, 1880s, and 1890s seems to have influenced the partisanship of men who were then both young and engaged in occupations that were affected by national tariff and monetary policies.

This paper has touched on only a few of the questions that can be studied through quantitative collective biography. The relationships between age and geographic mobility, occupation and party, religion and education, partisanship and technical associations, and age-occupation-partisanship-city that have been discovered are only suggestive of the rich results made possible by computerized research. Of course collective biography has limitations beyond the biases and omissions that have already been mentioned. The directories were snapshots, at one moment in time, of lives that were not yet complete. No historian would ever guess from the Chicago data that the Republican party was about to split, or that the world would soon plunge into a great war. What reader of the optimistic autobiographies in the 1929 Wichita directory would guess that the city's economy was about to collapse? And what about the beliefs, attitudes, fears, aspirations, and calculations of the elite? How are they to be discovered, or if found, coded? Party, religion, and memberships provide "hard" data on activities, but are they adequate substitutes for individual attitudes? Clearly the directories cannot answer half the questions the historian can ask about metropolitan elites.

On the other hand, quantitative collective biography promises to answer half the questions that have been unanswerable before, and to free the historian from dependence on the haphazard generalizations of journalists, novelists, and biographers of famous men. Hunches can give way to numerically specific conclusions. Simple tabulations will show who comprised the elite, where they came from, and what their family structures, social activities, business connections, political involvements, and recreations were like. Cross-tabulations, multivariate analysis, linkages with earlier and later directories, and comparisons with other cities will reveal patterns that were never even suspected, and provide clues to the explanations of those patterns.

The Political Responses of the Chilean Upper Class to the Great Depression and the Threat of Socialism, 1931-33

PAUL W. DRAKE

The critical questions about upper classes in an underdeveloped country like Chile concern their responses to the challenges of modernization. Do the privileged groups promote, accommodate, distort, or prevent change? When industrialization, social mobilization, and mass politics take hold in developing areas, the ruling groups face simultaneous demands to produce economic growth and to include the lower classes in national life. The traditional power holders are not a constant factor but rather a key variable in this historical process. Their reaction to pressures for change may determine the outcome of change. The global Great Depression of the early 1930s strained the Chilean status quo and galvanized new political movements leading the workers under the socialist banner. The corresponding adjustments made by the upper classes and the right speeded resolution of the crisis. Furthermore, the new equilibrium reached in the 1930s forecast the outlines of Chilean political development for decades to come.

The Chilean upper class can be placed within the broader setting of Latin America. Societies in Latin America, throughout most of their histories, have been dominated by a privileged oligarchy. This self-perpetuating minority controlled the basic economic and power resources of society, exercised a veto power on fundamental issues, and restricted access to its ranks.[1]

[1] In particular, see discussions in Robert H. Dix, *Colombia: The Political Dimensions of Change* (New Haven, 1967), esp. 42–55; Seymour Martin Lipset and Aldo Solari, eds., *Elites in Latin America* (New York, 1967); Frank Bonilla, *The Failure of Elites* (Cambridge, 1970); John J. Johnson, ed., *Continuity and Change in Latin America* (Stanford, 1964).

Building on foundations laid in the colonial period, the Latin American upper strata in the nineteenth century rested mainly on ascribed, inherited laurels. Family names and lineage defined the upper class. In most cases it was a landed aristocracy, possessing vast underutilized estates and a preindustrial mentality that disdained labor and commerce. The core of the ruling class formed a trinity of landowners, clergy, and military. Their control of politics, as well as the economy, society, and culture, was facilitated by the weakness of the dependent middle sectors and the subservience of the rural and urban poor. Despite the existence of a thin middle stratum, a simple dual-class structure approximated reality. Firmly ensconced at the top of this edifice was a neocolonial upper class, looking to Europe and the United States for markets, styles, and intellectual cues. By the late nineteenth century, this portrait of social stratification and those at the top changed somewhat, for the middle classes grew in size, and emerging urban financial and industrial interests were added to the upper classes.

In the twentieth century, distinctions were made between the older landowning aristocracy and the newer plutocracy. These newcomers relied more on wealth and education for their upper-class credentials. The division between landed, rural elites and business, urban elites, however, may have been more conceptual than real. It has been argued that a web of mutual social and economic interests frequently bound the higher socioeconomic groups in the countryside and those in the cities rather closely together.[2] Even in modern times the upper classes have been characterized by diffuseness, by a multiplicity of family, kin, social, and economic connections. They maintain a wide range of occupations, resources, interests, affiliations, contacts, and defenses. The middle classes and the urban workers have multiplied and made many gains, but class lines are still sharply drawn. Although important political and even economic changes have occurred in Latin America, fundamental social changes have been rare. Perhaps above all, the upper sectors have sustained the traditional value structure. In fact Latin America has been called a "living museum," in which old ruling groups and forms of political authority persist, thriving side by side with more modern groups and institutions. In some cases the upper class itself has become a mixed group, blending archaic and modern attributes in a cumulative rather than sequential fashion. This mixture provides one explanation for the tenacity of original forms and for the persistence of profound conservatism beneath a veneer of ferment in Latin America.[3]

[2] See various studies on industrial and landed elites in James Petras and Maurice Zeitlin, eds., *Latin America: Reform or Revolution?* (Greenwich, Conn., 1968).

[3] Charles W. Anderson, *Politics and Economic Change in Latin America* (Princeton, 1967), 104–12. See also Richard N. Adams, "Political Power and Social Structures,"

306 The Rich, the Well Born, and the Powerful

Though some generalizations seem safe, they should not obscure the vast diversity within Latin America or the numerous questions remaining about Latin American upper classes. More detailed studies of upper-class composition and connections are still needed. And once the dominant groups have been identified, their institutions and resources should be studied, particularly to uncover changes over time. What are their defenses and assets? In Latin America the privileged groups pursue their interests both publicly—through parties, elections, and coups—and privately—through family links, social clubs, and economic organizations. These nongovernmental mechanisms have been called "private governments,"[4] and may be the principal instruments of upper-class control in the twentieth century. Such institutions deserve more research. As societies become more complex, these clubs and organizations can help institutionalize personal contacts and channels for furthering upper-class interests. These institutions may admit the upwardly mobile yet remain under the reign of the upper classes. It has been argued, for example in Peru, that the upper sectors seldom need coercion or overt pressure to achieve their ends, in part because social affiliations keep them close to ascendant middle-class leaders.[5]

There are other facets of the upper classes requiring further research. The maintenance of upper-class defenses suggests a relatively unified, cohesive upper sector, but still open to question is whether the higher social groups are more integrated or competing with one another, particularly since industrialization has created new privileged sectors. The scarcity of modernizing upper-class leaders in Latin America might be traced to the disunity of the privileged groups.[6] On the other hand, the absence of progressive leadership might be explained by the tight interpenetration of the upper strata. The degree of interlocking among upper-sector factions has significant political implications. For example, a pluralistic upper class indicates possibilities for incremental reforms, while a more monolithic upper

in Claudio Veliz, ed., *The Politics of Conformity in Latin America* (London, 1967); Anthony Leeds, "Brazilian Careers and Social Structure: A Case History and Model," in Dwight B. Heath and Richard N. Adams, eds., *Contemporary Cultures and Societies of Latin America* (New York, 1965).

[4] Robert E. Scott, "Political Elites and Political Modernization: The Crisis of Transition," in Lipset and Solari, 117–45.

[5] Carlos A. Astiz, *Pressure Groups and Power Elites in Peruvian Politics* (Ithaca, 1969), esp. 197–204; François Bourricaud, *Power and Society in Contemporary Peru* (New York, 1970). In addition, see Peter H. Smith, *Politics and Beef in Argentina* (New York, 1969).

[6] Scott, "Political Elites"; José Luis de Imaz, *Los que mandan* (Buenos Aires, 1964).

class might exclude all avenues to change except revolution.[7] Beyond the
ties of exalted groups to each other, their relationship to less fortunate
social sectors must be explored. How do they relate to the middle and lower
classes and to functional elites, such as military, church, and labor leaders?

Finally, the strategies and reactions of the upper classes, and the
effect of those responses on national politics, development, and integration,
provide a focus for study. Some Latin American aristocratic groups have
led and guided change, continuing to rule rather directly and providing
for conservative modernization. This has apparently been the case during
certain historical eras in Colombia and Brazil. Other upper classes have
acquiesced in the predominance of those from below in political offices. In
these instances the upper sectors have tried to compromise with, moderate,
accommodate, or co-opt middle-class reformers. Still other upper classes
have battled intransigently against renovating forces, and have either held
the line through repression or lost the fight. In Cuba the upper classes and
their allies lost and then opted for the ultimate strategy of withdrawal,
taking valuable resources and skills with them. Which strategies upper
classes elect may depend largely on the severity of the challenges that
face them. In turn, the strategies chosen will influence the likelihood of
national integration and stability. Through their techniques for protecting
what they have and securing what they want, are the upper classes able to
maintain continuities within change? Although the bases of the various
national upper classes in Latin America appear fairly similar, the national,
historical experiences of the upper classes have been distinguished by their
different responses to modern pressures for change.[8]

Within the Latin American context, Chile has been a deviant case.
The Chilean ruling groups have left a record of unusual political stability,
democratic continuity, and toleration for reform, or even radical, movements. The upper classes consolidated their ranks and a progressive political and economic system earlier than most Latin American countries. A
pattern of flexibility began forming early in the nineteenth century, when
important commercial elements developed among the landed elites. The
dominant landholders had interests at variance with those of the small
merchant-industrial-mining groups, but were also receptive to their partial

[7] James Petras, *Politics and Social Forces in Chilean Development* (Berkeley,
1969); C. Wright Mills, *The Power Elite* (New York, 1956).

[8] Bourricaud, esp. 13–20; Astiz, 203–4; Lipset and Solari, vii–viii; Dix, 42–55,
389–417; Hélio Jaguaribe, "The Dynamics of Brazilian Nationalism," in Claudio Veliz,
ed., *Obstacles to Change in Latin America* (London, 1965), 162–87; Bo Anderson and
James D. Cockroft, "Control and Cooptation in Mexican Politics," in Irving Louis
Horowitz, Josué de Castro, and John Gerassi, eds., *Latin American Radicalism* (New
York, 1969), 366–89.

inclusion in the aristocracy. Avoiding overt clashes or military interference, the Chilean upper classes developed a strong tradition of peaceful electoral political struggles long before the vigor of those institutions was seriously tested by social conflict. The twentieth century, however, brought the need to take new social and economic forces into account in the political arena, thus calling forth adjustments on the part of the upper class.[9] This study emphasizes the traditional political elite of the upper classes and their "private governments," how they operated through party and private institutions to respond to the Great Depression and the threat of socialist mass politics, and what these reactions meant for the perseverance of the Chilean political system under stress.

Erosion of Traditional Politics, 1912–31

Founded in 1891, the Parliamentary Republic of Chile served well the interests of the privileged sectors, especially in agriculture, through 1912. The stability of the republic resulted from limiting the participation of lower social groups, and prosperity rested on the precarious base of mining exports, not internal development. But the traditional political arrangements of the republic proved inadequate to deal with the forces of economic frustration and the changes sired by industrialization and urbanization. A conservative system designed to protect upper-class social values and economic prerogatives, the republic could not assimilate new pressures from the middle and lower classes and remain the same.

The republic conformed to the upper-class strategy of defensive politics. Because the privileged were sustained by social and economic bases largely independent of government support, they considered a potent, active state an undesirable, competing locus of power, except when aiding their particular interests. From the Parliamentary Republic, the aristocratic elements obtained a favored European political style and limited state action in economic development and social welfare. Since the upper class controlled the parliament in order to insure a powerless presidency, the republic was not designed to respond quickly to new economic forces or demands from other social groups. Nevertheless, the prosperity and social peace of the pre–World War I years, unmatched in later decades, limited dissatisfaction with the system.[10]

[9] Alberto Edwards Vives, *La fronda aristocrática*, 6th ed. (Santiago, 1966), 15–17; Maurice Zeitlin, "The Social Determinants of Political Democracy in Chile," in Petras and Zeitlin, 220–34; Frederick B. Pike, "Aspects of Class Relations in Chile, 1850–1960," in Petras and Zeitlin, 202–19.

[10] Edwards Vives, 15–19; Francisco José Moreno, *Legitimacy and Stability in Latin America* (New York, 1969), 145–46.

The parliamentary parties that most closely represented upper-class interests and divisions were the Conservatives and the Liberals. The Conservatives, united and disciplined, identified with the Catholic church and agriculture; the Liberals, frequently splintering into factions, appealed more to anticlerical and urban groups. The middle classes were usually associated with the centrist Radical party, and the laboring groups with the moderate Democrats and later the Socialists and Communists. The Liberals dominated Chilean politics in the early twentieth century by holding the center between the Conservatives, their social allies, to the right, and the Radicals, their political allies, to the left.[11]

Upper-class resources outside party channels included leadership of both the rural and urban economic sectors. The growth of urban and mining economies at the end of the nineteenth century had expanded business, industrial, and financial elements that shared the upper-class status associated with the large landowners. To avoid internal taxes and thrive on relatively effortless, established prosperity, the upper classes depended on exports, principally of nitrates; this mining was under foreign, mainly British, control. A hybrid oligarchy vulnerable to divisions, under the parliamentary republic the upper classes usually coalesced against interference with their control.[12]

The economic superiority of the upper classes was reinforced by their social prestige and connections. Extended families and social ties frequently crossed economic and rural-urban boundaries. The selective economic societies promoting agriculture and industry, the National Society for Agriculture (SNA) and the Society for Factory Development (SOFOFA), helped consolidate upper-class leadership. In addition, the upper classes were concentrated in the central region of Chile and interacted through exclusive clubs, such as the Union Club in the centrally located capital of Santiago. All these prestige organizations not only furthered unity among the upper sectors but also introduced them to rising members of the upper middle strata. The church, the military, and select schools still provided support for the dominant groups, although these linkages diminished after 1900 as the middle classes filled more prominent positions. Through all these avenues, the traditional advantaged groups exercised political as well as social and economic influence.[13]

[11] Julio Heise González, "La constitución de 1925 y las nuevas tendencias político-sociales," in Chile, Universidad, Anales . . ., no. 80 (4th trimester, 1950), 140–50; Federico Gil, The Political System of Chile (Boston, 1966), 47–56.

[12] Domingo Melfi, Sin brújula (Santiago, 1932), 75–77; Heise González, 134–43; Carlos Sáez Morales, Recuerdos de un soldado, 1 (Santiago, 1934), 46; Frederick B. Pike, Chile and the United States, 1880–1962 (South Bend, 1963), 121–22.

[13] Carlos Vicuña Fuentes, La tiranía en Chile, 1 (Santiago, 1938), 15–21.

Economic setbacks, combined with social pressures from the ranks of the discontented in the middle and lower groups, increased after 1912 and came to a head following World War I. Openings appeared for mass politics and reform movements, often led by middle-class political competitors. The rise of populist politics reflecting socioeconomic cleavages coincided with the decline of the traditional aristocratic political system. Partly as a result, Arturo Alessandri Palma, a charismatic, renegade, liberal reformer, became president through the landmark election of 1920. Alessandri's victory was based mainly on the Radicals and Democrats. Overreacting with intransigence to this mild reformer, the right (a majority of the Conservatives and Liberals) stymied President Alessandri through control of the congress. When their congressional supremacy slipped toward the end of Alessandri's administration, many among the upper classes hoped that the military would end its historic abstinence from open politics and halt the threat of reforms. The military did seize power in 1924–25, but the younger, more middle-class officers ousted their superiors and vowed to institute the reforms that Alessandri had been advocating. The conservative forces discovered to their dismay that the military, as well as the president and the parliament, was unreliable.[14]

The military, in effect, ran the government from 1925 to 1931. Through the passage of a new constitution in 1925, a presidential system replaced the Parliamentary Republic. At the same time, church and state were separated and new labor, welfare, and property provisions enacted. Carlos Ibáñez del Campo emerged as the military strongman of the regime, and ruled as a dictator until the international depression brought him down in 1931. Ibáñez contributed to the dismantling of the traditional political system but failed to construct a viable alternative to the parliamentary republic. When the depression hit, the essentially oligarchic system that had reigned at the turn of the century was cracking near its foundations.

From 1912 through 1931, the emergence of the middle and laboring classes and international economic reversals had exposed the weaknesses of the Parliamentary Republic. Politically the upper classes and the right had lost the security of the presidency, the parliament, and the armed forces. The social exclusiveness of the privileged groups had been diluted by the ascent of the middle sectors. The Constitution of 1925 had curtailed the perquisites of the church and other supports of the upper class. With their historic defenses and political recourses reduced drastically, the tra-

[14] For further information and bibliography on all the points in this essay, see Paul W. Drake, "Socialism and Populism in Chile: The Origins of the Leftward Movement of the Chilean Electorate, 1931–1933," doctoral diss. (Stanford University, 1971), esp. 21–43.

ditional leaders received an additional blow when the Great Depression shook their economic underpinnings. The resulting chaos in 1931–32 ushered in the modern, socialist phase of the leftward movement of the Chilean electorate, and the upper class adjusted to this new style of national politics.

The Great Depression

The Great Depression at the start of the 1930s was a bench mark in Latin American history. The tenuous order based on export of raw materials and import of manufactured goods threatened to disintegrate. Military coups and nationalistic political movements appealing to the masses appeared throughout the hemisphere. To conserve foreign exchange and more effectively insulate the domestic economy from foreign shocks, attempts at industrialization accelerated. These ventures in protected import-substitution marked a new epoch in the orientation of the Latin American economies. As efforts to foster economic growth and to pay attention to the common man coincided, the state expanded in both the economy and social welfare. As a result, the leaders of Latin America adopted new political strategies.

In Chile the Great Depression caused political instability and change unmatched in the twentieth century. At least in the foreign sector, Chile's economy suffered more than any other in the Western world. The collapse of the export economy, particularly in mining, and the devastating repercussions in agriculture weakened the traditional economic leaders and turned the emphasis inward toward greater industrialization. Consequently, economic organization, production, and distribution became primary political issues.[15]

The industrial sectors had grown in the 1920s, and were now heralded by the nation and their own spokesmen as the salvation from the depression. The depletion of foreign capital and markets was partially offset by the opportunities created when competitive foreign imports declined. Foreign exchange became scarce, not only for buying ingredients needed in manufacturing but also for purchasing finished goods from abroad. Since national production was amplified out of necessity, the depression was a boon as well as a bane for industry.[16]

[15] P. T. Ellsworth, *Chile: An Economy in Transition* (New York, 1945), 4–16, 26–35, 161–62, 175–76; Chile, Dirección General de Estadística, *Sinopsis geográfico-estadística de la República de Chile* (Santiago, 1933), 114–17, 134–236, 264–65, 270–75; La Sociedad Nacional de Agricultura, *Memoria de la Sociedad Nacional de Agricultura correspondiente al año 1931* (Santiago, 1932), 5–25, 126–58.

[16] La Sociedad de Fomento Fabril, *Plan de fomento de la producción* (Santiago,

The upper classes were displeased with the economic crisis, the fading of their traditional perquisites and social exclusiveness, and the threat of political anarchy. When protests erupted against Ibáñez, the higher social sectors offered support and helped topple the dictator in 1931. Even when the upper-class groups disagreed on economic priorities, they concurred on the need for a new president to restore peace and public confidence. Contrary to the situation in much of Latin America, the Chilean military was ruling at the time of the depression and consequently lost favor with the public. The armed forces could not offer themselves as an unsoiled alternative in the crisis, so civilian groups recaptured political leadership. This historical experience damaged the military's political image and ambitions and helped fortify civilian control of Chilean politics for the future.[17]

The first political strategy tried by the upper class in the crisis was to join the middle classes in electing a moderate Radical to the presidency in 1931 after the ouster of Ibáñez. The Conservatives and Liberals, through the flexible, unprecedented tactic of supporting a Radical for president, hoped to restore the calm and prosperity of the past. But this attempt to contain the national crisis within the orderly channels of traditional party politics and to return to pre-1920 political normality failed soon after the election. The continuation of the depression, the resultant misery of the majority of the people, and the lethargy of the government escalated discontent. A cadre of military and civilian conspirators ejected the new administration in June 1932 and installed the Socialist Republic of Chile.[18]

The Socialist Republic represented the high point of the political crises during the Great Depression. Led by Air Force Col. Marmaduke Grove Vallejo, the junta lasted only twelve hectic days. In spite of the Socialist Republic's brief tenure, it aroused enough hopes and fears to make a major impact on Chilean politics. Many leaders of the upper classes and the right at first tried to accept the Socialist Republic. Some argued that it was merely a new label for evolutionary reformism that could be tamed and tolerated. That attitude, however, quickly passed to one of resolute opposition. Agriculturalists resisted land colonization schemes. Industrial-

---

1932), 2–7; Chile, *Sinopsis* (1933), 214–35, 268–71; Ellsworth, 4–32, 161–62; Raúl Simón, *Determinación de la entrada nacional de Chile* (Santiago, 1935), 58–83; Oscar Álvarez Andrews, *Historia del desarrollo industrial de Chile* (Santiago, 1936), 246–330.

[17] Raúl Marín Balmaceda, *La caída de un régimen, julio de 1931* (Santiago, 1933), 16–63; René Olivares, *Ibáñez* (Valparaíso, 1937), 69.

[18] *El Mercurio*, 29 July 1931, 1; 30 July 1931, 9; 3 Aug. 1931, 11; 19 Aug. 1931, 3; 30 Aug. 1931, 27; 22 Sept. 1931, 15. *El Diario Ilustrado*, 3 Oct. 1931, 4; 4 Oct. 1931, 16; 5 Oct. 1931, 4. Eulojio Rojas Mery, *Recuerdos de un joven "octogenario"* (Santiago, 1958), 237; Ricardo Boizard, *La democracia cristiana en Chile* (Santiago, 1963), 116; La Sociedad Nacional de Agricultura, *Memoria* (1932), 29.

ists cut production plans. United States business and government representatives opposed banking reforms and withheld oil deliveries. The upper classes secretly began organizing armed defense groups. Above all, upperclass leaders tried to convince the regular military that the socialist junta was either infiltrated by or unable to control Communist agitators. The Socialist Republic fell, and new presidential elections were slated for October 1932. It was hoped that a new chief executive could restore political order so the task of economic reconstruction could commence. Out of these trying months emerged the Socialist party of Chile and the right's resolve to adopt new strategies in order to avert more ominous threats.[19]

The 1932 election, through which Chile overcame its greatest crisis in the twentieth century, produced a new electoral left and a redefinition of the political spectrum. The socialist forces, with the presidential candidacy of former Socialist Republic leader Marmaduke Grove, claimed a permanent place on the political roster and spearheaded a lasting shift of the electorate to the left. This shift involved a realignment of the wealthy as well as the workers. In other words, the entire political alignment moved toward the left, as the masses embraced Marxist-labeled instead of liberal alternatives, and the upper classes gravitated to more reformist positions to accommodate that change.

In 1932 sufficient numbers of voters formerly aligned with the right eschewed past antagonisms to assure ex-President Alessandri a victory over Grove. The conservative forces voted in large numbers for Alessandri because other alternatives were exhausted and formidable more leftist options had arisen. The belief was growing that only a dynamic, forceful president who could appeal to both the lower and the upper classes could restore tranquillity. The right hoped that the reelection of their former foe would avert social conflict. The strategy worked. Alessandri took office and held the presidency for a full six-year term, until 1938. On the surface, Chile returned to the security of traditional modes and entered a period of stability and recovery. For forty years after the 1932 election, constitutional,

[19] Sáez, Recuerdos, vol. 3, 185–208; Partido Socialista, 4 de junio (Santiago, 1933), 1–4; interview with Carlos Charlín Ojeda, a member of the socialist republic; Ernest Galarza, "Socialists Seize Government in Chile," Foreign Policy Bulletin, 11 (17 June 1932), 1–2; ¿Por qué cayó Grove? (Santiago, 1932), 1–13; Ricardo Donoso, Alessandri, agitador y demoledor, 2 (Mexico and Buenos Aires, 1952–54), 106–7; Pedro Luis González, "Socialización de industrias," in La Sociedad de Fomento Fabril, Boletín de la Sociedad de Fomento Fabril, no. 6 (June 1932), 269–70; Javier Vial Solar, El diluvio (Santiago, 1932), 11, 85–87, 123–43; Rafael L. Gumucio, No más (Santiago, 1932), 19–25; Dávila de cuerpo entero (Santiago, 1932); Jack Ray Thomas, "The Socialist Republic of Chile," Journal of Inter-American Studies, 6:2 (Apr. 1964), 203–20, and "Marmaduke Grove and the Chilean National Election of 1932," Historian, 29:1 (Nov. 1966), 22–33.

presidential turnovers were regular, and the military refrained from overt political intrusion. Changes at a deeper level in 1931–33, however, had remolded electoral politics and would continue to do so. To understand the full meaning of the adjustments in Chilean politics by the higher social groups requires further exploration of the parties and policies with which the upper classes identified in those years.[20]

Political Elites, 1931–33

To identify the leadership of the Conservative and Liberal parties, a sample of those leaders and of the heads of the centrist Radicals and the nascent Socialists in 1931–33 can be compared (Tables 1–4). Examining this sample of party leaders in 1931–33 shows that the social images that suffused Chilean politics had some basis in reality. There was a strong, though not absolute, social gradation from the right to the left. The leaders of the conservative parties (both the Conservatives and Liberals) tended to belong to higher-class occupational groups and organizations than did the leaders of the parties further to the left. The leaders on the right had high levels of educational attainment, and the Conservatives were noteworthy

TABLE 1.   *Percentage of Leaders Engaged in Various Occupations*

OCCUPATION	CONS.	LIB.	RAD.	SOC.
Agriculturalists (large landholders)	29%	35%	23%	6%
Businessmen and commercialists	28	19	14	11
Workers and artisans	0	0	0	7
Employees	2	1	7	20
Industrialists	7	7	7	2
Professionals	75	73	77	57

TABLE 2.   *Percentage of Leaders Who Attained the Following Educational Levels*

INSTITUTION OR LEVEL	CONS.	LIB.	RAD.	SOC.
University of Chile	49%	64%	65%	44%
Catholic University	42	2	0	9
Foreign	15	11	8	7
Below university level	11	11	13	24

[20] Drake, 109–63.

TABLE 3. *Percentage of Leaders Who Were Members
of the Following Organizations*

ORGANIZATION	CONS.	LIB.	RAD.	SOC.
Union Club	60%	78%	43%	0%
SNA	40	34	13	2
SOFOFA	9	13	7	4
Professional organizations	40	35	45	34
Employee or worker organizations	0	0	2	11

TABLE 4. *Number of Leaders in the Sample*

CONS.	LIB.	RAD.	SOC.
54	85	93	54

for possessing the highest percentage of leaders who had attended the Catholic University. It should also be noted that the heads of the Conservative and Liberal parties, far more than the dominant figures in the parties appealing to the middle and lower classes, came from the two central provinces of urbanization and vast landed estates. Close to 70 percent of the leaders in both conservative parties came from the influential core provinces of Santiago and Valparaíso. In sum, the composition of the right was strongly suggestive of the upper classes in politics.[21]

Nonetheless, these leadership profiles reveal some bases for coalitions as well as conflicts. For example, spanning the party spectrum were a predominance of professionals and professional organizations, a tendency to draw most leaders from the central provinces and from the middle to upper classes, and an attainment of a level of education higher than that of the general population. At all points there was scant participation by the less integrated groups from the more underdeveloped provinces and the lower-status occupations. There were socioeconomic traits that the leaders of the competing parties shared, but their differences were revealed in their political behavior during the Great Depression.

[21] The leaders and the data on them in the table were culled from a wide variety of sources. The percentages do not necessarily equal 100, because a leader may be tallied more than once, if, for example, he was significantly occupied as a lawyer as well as a landowner or had attended both the Catholic and a foreign university. These duplications have been kept because the purpose of the tables is to reflect the tendency of the various political groups to belong, for example, to workers' unions or to the Union Club. The figures are rounded to the higher whole percentage point. The term "leaders" in these tables signifies party heads, members of party directorates and leading committees, recognized opinion-leaders for parties, congressional representatives, and cabinet ministers. The figures presented here represent minimal findings. For further information on these leaders and tables, see Drake, 164–72.

The material, emotional, and intellectual shock of the depression years prompted Chileans from all social categories and political camps to import new models from abroad and venture new strategies at home. With myriad motivations and variations, Chileans looked to state intervention, industrialization, and economic nationalism as the keys to recovery. Disillusionment with free enterprise permeated the political spectrum. Divergent alternatives sprouted from the common ground of dissatisfaction with economic chaos and disorganization. The need for state expansion in the economy was agreed upon; how much expansion, who should control, and for whose benefit were not. Heterogeneous foreign influences mingled in every proposal to transform the capitalist economy. The left, however, emphasized socialist models, and the right stressed corporativist-fascist notions of state regulation. As the new left pressed for greater state action to help the masses, the right demanded that the state control restless social groups. The traditional groups' response to the new parties and policies growing out of the crisis in 1931–33 helped determine the outlines and outcome of the new contenders' entrance into the system.[22]

Upper-Class Economic Adjustments

The upper classes turned more toward state solutions, industrialization, and economic nationalism in 1931–33. Although these proposals were advocated more vehemently by the politicians leading the middle and lower classes, the policies were not opposed by the upper sectors except in minor instances. The privileged few envisioned natural benefits from promoting Chilean economic elites against foreign competition in the name of nationalism. The upper classes also accepted the concept of Chile's diversifying its exports and importing capital goods in preference to consumer and semidurable goods. At the same time, they moved ever closer to ties with United States instead of British capital. These changes in external economic relations might decrease instability and excessive dependency, thus curtailing the crises arising from the vulnerability of a small nation deeply enmeshed in international trade.

In a similar vein, many hoped that a relatively smooth transition in emphasis from a rural economy to urban industry would reduce conflict. The leaders of the upper strata saw that state intervention and the develop-

[22] Oscar Álvarez Andrews, *Bases para una constitución funcional* (Santiago, 1932), 14–97; Álvarez Andrews, *Historia*, 1, 351–56; Ellsworth, 16, 51; Daniel Martner, *Economía política*, 2nd ed. (Santiago, 1934), 171–78; Guillermo González Echenique, *Reflexiones de la hora presente* (Santiago, 1934), 45–59; Markos Mamalakis and Clark Winton Reynolds, *Essays on the Chilean Economy* (Homewood, Ill., 1965), 14–16, 70, 190, 227–36, 279–81.

ment of a larger industrial capitalist sector might breathe new life into their agricultural as well as commercial and industrial interests. The restoration of general order and legality, moreover, was likely to favor established economic interests. In addition, the upper classes thought that a more directed and industrialized economy would promote the paramount goal of social tranquillity. In retrospect it is evident that most upper-strata leaders were not defending the traditional structure of the state and economy as much as working to direct the emerging system to their needs.[23]

The rural, agricultural elites favored state aid to agriculture as their first goal, but they also advocated industrialization. They argued that boosting agricultural exports would garner more foreign exchange, while increasing industrial production would reduce spending for foreign goods. As industry expanded, so would its demands for primary materials, which came largely from agriculture. The agriculturalists also hoped that industrialization would ease population pressure on the land and dampen incipient demands for agrarian reforms. In sum, the large landholders felt that industry would absorb raw materials, labor, and social discontent.[24]

The landed barons were also concerned with cultivating political allies to help them prevent certain policies. For example, they wanted to retain a veto over national land policies to avoid redistribution of their properties. An equally pressing worry was the specter of an organized rural labor force. Both under Alessandri and later under the Popular Front—a coalition of Radicals, Socialists, and Communists that took office in 1938—the landowners were able to postpone Socialist and Communist threats to mobilize rural laborers and divide the great estates among the workers. Landholding, although declining in economic importance by 1932, still conferred great social prestige and sizable political power. Urban economic elites and rising members of the middle classes purchased land for status and as a hedge against inflation. This tendency helped diminish the enthusiasm of middle-class politicians for agrarian reform. The rural elites and the urban upper and middle classes also shared similar concerns because they depended on the state. They relied on foreign inflows to state coffers to provide credit and salaries. The landowners' indebtedness was huge. Therefore the disappearance of funds during the Great Depression

[23] Ellsworth, 16–32, 128; Mamalakis and Reynolds, 14–16, 70, 190, 227–36, 279–81; José María Cifuentes, *La propiedad* (Santiago, 1932), 26–80; Sáez, *Recuerdos*, vol. 3, 231; Heise González, 134–43; Guillermo Subercaseaux, *La política social nacionalista moderna* (Santiago, 1932), 6–15; Carlos Keller, *Un país al garete* (Santiago, 1932), 35–57; Jorge de la Cuadra Poisson, *La revolución que viene* (Santiago, 1931), 22.
[24] Keller, *Un país*, 122–25; Jaime Larraín, *Orientación de nuestra política agraria* (Santiago, 1932), 1–29; Charles A. Thomson, "Chile Struggles for National Recovery," *Foreign Policy Reports*, 9:25 (14 Feb. 1934), 282–92.

injured rural and urban economic sectors simultaneously. The rural elites consequently shared the urban upper and middle sectors' desires to find more dependable ways for the state to meet their needs. At the same time, as the voting population tilted toward the cities, control of the rural vote ceased to guarantee political domination. This also prompted the conservative forces to cooperate more with past political opponents, often with urban reformers.[25]

The activities of the National Society for Agriculture (SNA) illustrate the tendency of the privileged groups to expand and fortify their traditional organizations in the early 1930s while they sought new supports from the state. The SNA represented the large landowners. It was Chile's most powerful economic interest organization and the most directly involved politically. Traditional party leaders filled its membership ranks. The SNA founded both the Society for Factory Development and the National Society of Mining. These organizations were social clubs as well as pressure groups. Membership overlapped, but not inordinately. In any case, the rural and urban economic leaders were frequently connected by social, family, banking, and party ties as well as by the interest organizations. Although at odds on numerous specific issues, the rural and urban sectors could agree on larger goals. Necessity prompted all these interest organizations to turn more toward the state in the early 1930s. With old political parties weakening and new ones unreliable, the interest organizations sought new allies and defenses. They tried to attract more members while tightening the internal control of existing small groups within the organizations. Control within the SNA and similar institutions was even more oligarchic than the social profile of the members would indicate. At times, the SNA and its companion organizations influenced ongoing national decision-making on economic matters at least as much as did the

[25] La Sociedad Nacional de Agricultura, *Memoria* (1932), 5–29, 126–28, 158–60; Larraín, *Orientación*, 1–29. "In general, the aristocratic classes founded their pride on . . . the lands that belonged to them. The grand *fundos* [great estates] represented tradition, lordship, the blood and energy of the select social groups. A great *fundo* was a patent of aristocracy and dominion. It was the electoral department. Domination over the neighboring city. Command over the authority of Intendants or Governors. In sum, it was the seat of the senator, or, that which is the same, the predominance in the central government"; Melfi, *Sin brújula*, 76–77. George M. McBride, *Chile: Land and Society* (New York, 1936), 144–65, 219–71; Gene Ellis Martin, *La división de la tierra en Chile central* (Santiago, 1960), 91–94, 134–36; "El malestar de la agricultura y su curación," in La Sociedad Nacional de Agricultura, *Boletín de la Sociedad Nacional de Agricultura*, 64 (July 1932), 327–31; Robert R. Kaufman, *The Chilean Political Right and Agrarian Reform* (Washington, 1967), i, 1, 5–6, 41–46; André Siegfried, *Impressions of South America* (New York, 1933), 86; Carlos Keller, *La eterna crisis chilena* (Santiago, 1931), 233–49; Arturo Alessandri Palma, *Recuerdos de gobierno*, 3 (Santiago, 1952), 58–59; Almino Affonso, "Trayectoria del movimiento campesino chileno," *Cuadernos de la realidad nacional*, no. 1 (Sept. 1969), 15–31.

political parties. Since the political parties were not the only organizations exercising power, they were, to a degree, integrating people into an electoral, verbal aspect of the political process that was not always the center of national decision-making. On the other hand, parties provided some access for those not included in interest organizations such as the SNA.[26]

The industrial elites urged all political groups to help restore a stable, tranquil society so the state could mobilize for industrialization. The industrialists argued that, as in the United States, centralized, scientific industrialization with ample benefits and guarantees for the workers would avoid waste, poverty, and, above all, social conflict. Although agreed that assistance for agriculture was crucial, the industrialists stressed that it was time for Chile to move beyond its agrarian, mineral base to a more modern economy. The Society for Factory Development (SOFOFA) stated its case in nationalistic terms, mirroring on the surface the arguments of many middle- and lower-class leaders in 1932. These groups debated, however, whether the campaign to rationalize production and industrial relations meant greater benefits for the workers or more scientific use of the workers.[27]

The new stature of the industrial groups reflected changing upper-class attitudes as well as pressures for fresh economic directions from the new left. Even the archbishop of Santiago announced his support for a campaign of national industrialization. This campaign coincided with the rise of mass, populist politics in Chile for several reasons. Both industrialization and new forms of working-class politics were responses to the Great Depression. Industrialization aggravated social relations, which made new political alternatives, such as the Socialists, more attractive to labor groups. Even while immediate populist, leftist demands for changes and reforms mounted, the expansion of industry was seen as a way in the long run to promote social and political quiescence. Industrialization and social and political peace were viewed by many, including some industrialists, as mutually reinforcing. Industrialization raised incentives for bringing the

[26] La Sociedad Nacional de Agricultura, *Memoria* (1932), 5–31, 123–24; "Descentralización," in La Sociedad Nacional de Agricultura, *Boletín de la Sociedad Nacional de Agricultura*, 64 (Dec. 1932), 605–7; McBride, 227–31; Affonso, 16–19; Genaro Arriagada, *La oligarquía patronal chilena* (Santiago, 1970), 27–32, 49–82; Ricardo Lagos Escobar, *La concentración del poder económico* (Santiago, 1961), 95–165; Pedro Luis González, *50 años de labor de la Sociedad de Fomento Fabril* (Santiago, 1933), 3–4; Robert E. Scott, "Political Parties and Policy-Making in Latin America," in Joseph LaPalombara and Myron Weiner, eds., *Political Parties and Political Development* (Princeton, 1966), 331–67; Scott, "Political Elites."

[27] La Sociedad de Fomento Fabril, *Plan*, 1–2, and *Rol de industriales de Chile* (Santiago, 1932), 72; La Asamblea Nacional de Acción Cívica, *Primera memoria semestral* (Santiago, 1932), 4–6.

lower classes into politics and for enacting labor reforms; greater worker benefits and orderly participation of the masses might remove conflicts from the industrial arena. While the left pushed for better treatment of the lower classes, many industrialists also saw improvements as beneficial.[28] One advocate of industrialization advised industrialists not to fear the state, the organization of workers, or benefits for labor:

> We must not forget that without unions there would never be a corporative regime, nor control, and the danger of a social revolution would be permanent. . . . Without abundant population, there will be no internal market; even with population, but without good salaries and wages, neither will there be an internal market. . . . Such is the tight connection of the social and the industrial problem and the contribution that labor laws ought to make to industrial development.[29]

The upper classes, while flexible on certain economic issues, were adamant on others. They were prepared to fight for preservation of the banking system and the structure of rural land and labor relationships. Bank and state credit agencies were traditional nerve centers for the privileged groups; these institutions served as both political and economic bases. The upper segments and the right, for example, had successfully opposed plans for state interference with banking during Grove's socialist republic in 1932. In the early 1930s, the upper classes, while open to certain notions of reform, were still determined to defend essential bulwarks of the traditional economic and social structure.[30]

Social Preservation, Accommodation, and Transition

Although remaining distinctly socially aloof, the upper classes had lowered some barriers and lost some perquisites since 1920. Still in the 1930s the privileged groups showed repeatedly that they were more willing to

28 La Sociedad de Fomento Fabril, Boletín de la Sociedad de Fomento Fabril, 49 (Jan.-Nov. 1932); González, 50 años, 3–31; La Sociedad de Fomento Fabril, Plan, 1–7, and Rol, 4–75; La Sociedad de Fomento Fabril de Chile (Santiago, 1935), 1–3; James O. Morris, Elites, Intellectuals, and Consensus (Ithaca, 1966), 151–53, 268–69; Santiago Macchiavello Varas, Política económica nacional, 2 (Santiago, 1931), 100–102; El Mercurio, 24 Dec. 1931, 11, and all issues for Jan. 1932; Álvarez Andrews, Historia, 1–7, 246–81, 310–11, 348–57; Mamalakis and Reynolds, 14–17, 54–55; Ellsworth, 1–2, 29, 128, 161; Keller, La eterna, 169–85, and Un país, 127–29; Wilhelm Mann, Chile luchando por nuevas formas de vida, 2 (Santiago, 1935), 38–63.

29 Álvarez Andrews, Historia, 350–51.

30 El Mercurio, 13 Oct. 1932, 3; Alessandri, Recuerdos, vol. 1, 353–57; Vicuña Fuentes, La tiranía, vol. 1, 26, 63–64; vol. 2, 183; Lagos Escobar, 114–65; Boizard, La democracia, 25–29; Wilfredo Mayorga, "Crisis con sangre," Ercilla, no. 1682 (30 Aug. 1967), 15.

share political, and even economic, prerogatives than to sacrifice social exclusiveness. One observer remarked in the 1930s: "The change of social stratification signified for the aristocracy only the renovation of its components, but it could not take away its class character."[31] Nevertheless, upper-class flexibility and the dilution of its hegemony were also evident in upper-class social relations with the groups beneath. The upper sectors were neither monolithic nor closed to all outsiders. Their social and family institutions tried to preserve upper-class homogeneity but also admitted some newcomers. Organizations, schools, clubs, and political parties not only distinguished one social group from another but also provided for social exchange. Associations or even coalitions could emerge from these social contacts. Interaction among upper- and middle-class politicians reduced the likelihood that the upper sectors would be politically isolated or polarized; this was partly because interaction promoted compromises on new ideas and reforms, and partly because it helped the middle and upper classes close ranks in the crisis.[32]

The Union Club and its social-political role illustrated this mixture of continuity and change in aristocratic organizations. The club was the traditional epitome of upper-class exclusiveness in the public eye, but it was also open to the upwardly mobile. Among politicians who were club members, Conservatives and Liberals dominated. On a lesser scale, the Radicals were also well represented in the club, but the Democrats, Socialists, and Communists were absent. Thus social and political distinctions coincided in this organization. The club was a potent negative symbol to the excluded masses and the left. The numerous Radical members indicated both that the upper classes were welcoming the rising upper middle class into the club and that many Radical leaders were themselves upper class. The Union Club, not unlike the SNA and the SOFOFA, was expanding its membership by the early 1930s. Foreigners, particularly economic leaders from the United States and Europe, were prominent members. High military officers—some younger officers from the middle sectors and older ones close to the upperclass—also belonged. The Union Club, like other upper-class social institutions, was both a means and a reflection of social advancement. Partly through these social connections, political familiarity was formed and maintained.[33]

---

[31] Mann, vol. 1, 79–80.

[32] Vial Solar, 149–50; Vicuña Fuentes, *La tiranía*, vol. 1, 15–19; Juan Antonio Ríos, *Durante el gobierno del General Ibáñez* (Santiago, 1931), 19.

[33] When the club banqueted Ibáñez in the 1920s, allegedly for having saved Chile from Communism, he warned the upper-class members present to be more flexible and reformist in order to promote class cooperation. Ibáñez said, "This center was considered by the people as the monument which symbolized the injustice, the

Family traditions still figured in political participation, illustrated by the aristocratic names among the Conservative and Liberal party leaders. In the past, politics had been little more than a contest among prestigious families and clans, among "social tribes." Upper-class families continued to shun social exchanges with the middle classes even while dealing with them more in the political and economic spheres. While the family system continued to protect the upper classes, politics was slipping out of the control of families. Consequently, like other upper-class social mechanisms, families and marriages were occasionally used to bring newcomers into the fold.[34]

Educational institutions were another traditional bastion of social and political defense for the upper classes that was beginning to bring them into closer contact with the middle classes. The leaders of the traditional parties had more education than those of the leftist parties. The privileged groups, however, did not find a university degree as important to their status as did the middle sectors. Many upper-class families avoided the public universities and sought private schools in order to minimize contact with the other social groups. Aristocratic secondary schools, such as the Colegio de San Ignacio, traditionally defined and unified the upper class more than university affiliations did. They also served as breeding

indifference and the haughtiness of the ruling classes"; René Montero Moreno, *La verdad sobre Ibáñez* (Buenos Aires, 1953), 109–11. The social purity of the Union Club was diluted in the 1920s. "The Club was no longer formed by the restricted circle in which entered only the people of the [Catholic] mass, that is to say, with an *hacienda* [great estate], open or closed coach, house of two floors . . . theatre box . . . marriageable daughters and a grand spot in the Mortgage Department. It [the club] was sort of a peep-show compared with the old one . . ."; Emilio Rodríguez Mendoza, *El golpe de estado de 1924* (Santiago, 1938), 300–301. The Union Club maintained close relations with the Jockey Club of Buenos Aires and other South American upper-class organizations. El Directorio del Club de la Unión, *Septuagésima sexta memoria* (Santiago, 1932), 8–20; Guillermo Edwards Matte, *El Club de la Unión en sus ochenta años (1864–1944)* (Santiago, 1944), 7–69; *El Mercurio*, 13 Oct. 1932, 3; Vicuña Fuentes, *La tiranía*, vol. 1, 19, 63–64; vol. 2, 188.

[34] "A Chilean aristocrat is, generally, a grand lord, proud of his aged parchments, who lives on a superior plane, from which he looks . . . at the mass of his fellow citizens. Large landowners, associated at times with large industry, the men of our aristocracy have had in their hands for a long time the direction of national politics and the economy, by natural right, concealed behind an apparent delegation of popular sovereignty. To give orders has been for them a customary right. A man of blue blood can, in Chile, be an agriculturalist, perhaps an industrialist, manager of a great importing firm, but . . . he could not be an apothecary, shopkeeper or owner of a food business, without the danger of declining in the esteem of the persons in his social category. Between a lord of lineaged ranks and a man with no titles other than his own merits, there exists among us a distance which the former can shorten with signs of manifest benevolence, but which the latter could not annul except in very qualified cases"; Sáez, *Recuerdos*, vol. 1, 46. Keller, *Un país*, 17–19; Vicuña Fuentes, *La tiranía*, vol. 1, 15–19; vol. 2, 183; Domingo Melfi, *Dictadura y mansedumbre* (Santiago, 1931), 8–20; Petras, 62.

grounds for presidents. But the growing importance of professional skills in a more complicated, industrialized society brought more upper-class individuals and rising members of the middle classes together in the universities. Political associations sometimes grew out of these educational contacts.[35]

As a political issue, the church no longer kept the Conservatives and Liberals apart and had even lost its potency for the ardently anticlerical Radicals. The church's influence with the masses and its usefulness as a control device for the upper classes were small and primarily reduced to the rural areas. The clergy had flexibly cooperated with the 1925 separation of church and state, in hopes of both avoiding conflict and expanding their following among the middle and lower classes. After that separation, the church, although still wedded to the landed aristocracy, began adding reformist, material promises to its spiritual appeals to labor. Some Catholics saw the battle with the new leftist parties, particularly for the loyalties of students and workers, as a shift of the nineteenth-century political-religious clashes to new issues and new parties. Conservatives assumed more reformist postures partly because of more liberal, social encyclicals from the pope and the new concerns within the Chilean church. Conservatives also made adjustments because their leaders wanted to keep the Catholic vote united behind them. The church and the Conservatives hoped that a more reformist and charitable turn on the part of Catholic organizations would awaken the workers' religious sentiments in the urban as well as rural areas, and thus reduce class conflict. In the process, they hoped to undercut socialism and populism.[36]

The dwindling social and ideological strength of the upper classes in the military rendered the armed forces an undependable source of support. The upper sectors had hoped that the military, like the church, could be rebuilt as a pillar of tradition through cooperation with moderate reformers and the middle classes. After the Socialist Republic, however, the military was so closely associated with socialism and populism that conservative leaders both in the military and the traditional parties vowed to keep the armed forces removed from open politics. The right hoped to

[35] Melfi, Sin brújula, 81–83; René Olivares, Alessandri, precursor y revolucionario (Valparaíso, 1942), 66; interview with Raúl Urzúa, a sociologist at the Catholic University.
[36] Vicuña Fuentes, La tiranía, vol. 1, 170–71; Arturo Alessandri Palma, Mensaje leído por S. E. el Presidente de la República (Santiago, 1921), 19, 38–41; La defensa del obrero (Santiago, 1932), 2–16; Francisco Javier Ovalle Castillo, Hacia la política chilena (Santiago, 1922), 7; Rafael L. Gumucio, El deber político (Santiago, 1933), 1–19; Julio Gaete Leighton, Tarapacá y Antofagasta ante las consecuencias del pasado (Iquique, 1931), 3–13; Fidel Araneda Bravo, El Arzobispo Errázuriz y la evolución política y social de Chile (Santiago, 1956), 25–31, 152–54, 181–229.

unite all nonsocialist forces against the military and behind constitutional order. Far more than constitutionalism was at stake, for the campaign against militarism was simultaneously a campaign against the left.[37] A despondent Liberal said in retrospect: "it is in the nature of things that [military] interventionist actions lead to no other result than to clear the route by which socialism advances. . . ."[38]

Based on experiences from 1924 through 1932, most leaders of the right preferred to gamble on the uncertainties of electoral combat rather than take a chance with the unpredictable and volatile military in politics. Agreement on the desirability of preventing any future overt political action by the armed forces also united many segments of the upper and middle classes. The higher social groups formed white guards and joined the middle sectors in creating paramilitary republican militias to deter military incursions and intimidate the left. Severely divided but uniformly resentful of the criticism heaped upon them, the armed forces withdrew in bitterness from open politics in 1932. Although some upper-class leaders on the right later considered using the military in politics, from 1932 on there were severe constraints on the upper class's willingness and ability to call on the armed forces.[39]

Political Realignment on the Right

The traditional upper-class political parties liberalized their positions in the early 1930s, thereby easing the entire electoral spectrum toward the left. The upper-class parties now became increasingly willing to make concessions on certain nineteenth-century goals and prerogatives in the quest for coalitions to maintain political and social order. As demands rose for social and economic as well as political justice, the economic left of 1932, the Socialists and Communists, made the political left of 1920, Alessandri and the Democrats and Radicals, appear far preferable. The conservative parties, while continuing to defend social and economic essentials,

[37] Gumucio, *No más*, 3–11; Ricardo Cox Balmaceda, *Discurso* (Santiago, 1932), 4; *Unión Republicana* (Valparaíso, 1932), 2–31.

[38] Ladislao Errázuriz, *Los deberes del partido liberal en la hora actual* (Santiago, 1934), 5–6.

[39] Mario Bravo Lavín, *Chile frente al socialismo y al comunismo* (Santiago, 1934), 8–79, 130–89; Alain Joxe, *Las fuerzas armadas en el sistema político de Chile* (Santiago, 1970), 57–59, 72–73, 112–30; Ricardo Boizard, *Cuatro retratos en profundidad* (Santiago, 1950), 23–25, 54–57; La Milicia Republicana, *Albúm conmemorativo de su presentación pública* (Santiago, 1933), 1–44; Acción Nacionalista de Chile, *Ideología* (Santiago, 1932), 3–12; René Montero Moreno, "Los principios comunistas . . . ," *Memorial del ejército de Chile* (Jan. 1932), 45–53; Wilfredo Mayorga, "La milicia republicana, *Ercilla*, no. 1609 (6 Apr. 1966), 18–19; Gumucio, *No más*; Montero Moreno, *La verdad*, 148–49; Sáez, *Recuerdos*, vol. 1, 8; vol. 2, 138–41; vol. 3, 318–19.

came to accept the 1925 constitution, participation for all manner of parties and candidates, and coalitions with past opponents. The endorsement of various statist solutions by the Conservatives and Liberals, steeped in nineteenth-century orthodoxy, spelled the demise of traditional right-wing politics. Given the absence of great socioeconomic differences between the Conservatives and Liberals, resolving the church-state controversy in 1925 removed the major barrier to a close alliance between the two parties.

The leadership profile of these two rather homogeneous parties closely paralleled the composition of their constituency. More than with the Radicals or the parties on the left, a shared creed and social attributes united not only the leaders but also the leaders and the followers of the conservative parties. After a decade of reversals, the upper-class political leaders realized they were far more likely to retain indirect political influence than to rule directly. Following the clear erosion of its electoral strength in 1932, the right knew it would be hard pressed to control congress or to win a two-man presidential race without the aid of center parties. The right's percentage of votes for the lower house of congress had declined progressively: 76 percent (1912), 66 percent (1918), 55 percent (1921), 37 percent (1932). After the low point in 1932, the right's electoral percentages tended to level off.[40]

The traditional ruling groups also knew that their mere appearance in high public office, as during the short-lived government elected in 1931, automatically could spark discontent and disorder. Partly for these reasons, the upper classes aligned with reformist politicians, such as Alessandri and the Radicals, in 1931–33. These coalitions were facilitated by increased upper-class contact with the middle classes and by the fact that many Radical leaders were themselves upper class. Of course the Radicals and their middle-sector followers were not always available to the upper classes as allies, for their availability depended on their own current political strategy.[41]

The Conservative party was undecided on how much liberalization to assimilate, and during 1932–33 the party devoted considerable time and effort to an attempt to reconcile the traditional and progressive factions. A party leader gave this strategic advice:

[40] Chile, Tribunal Calificador, *Elecciones extraordinarias generales* (Santiago, 1933); Chile, Dirección General de Estadística, *Política, administración, justicia y educación* (Santiago, 1938), 1; Chile, *Sinopsis* (1933), 34–35; Ricardo Cruz-Coke, *Geografía electoral de Chile* (Santiago, 1952), 53; Germán Urzúa Valenzuela, *Los partidos políticos chilenos* (Santiago, 1968), 73; Zarko Luksic Savoia, *La conducta del votante y sus razones sociales* (Santiago, 1961), 48.

[41] González Echenique, 60–74; Melfi, *Sin brújula*, 15–16; Alessandri, *Recuerdos*, vol. 3, 48; Alberto Edwards Vives and Eduardo Frei Montalva, *Historia de los partidos políticos chilenos* (Santiago, 1949), 221–25.

The sad truth is that we do not have ... recourse to a movement of popular opinion. This is the painful reality; we are absolutely impotent to impede any legislative attack that one would want to mount. In order to obstruct or postpone, we must live [by] negotiating, making combinations, ceding constantly in order to save the basics, tolerating inconveniences, resisting impulses, subduing ... impetuous urges of those who do not recognize the bitter reality. We need to realize such distressing labor because to give battle today, without the forces to conquer, would be reprehensible madness.[42]

Consequently, Conservatives began to argue that they too were a centrist party advocating solutions that bridged individualism and state socialism. They offered themselves as added weight in any coalition against the socialist left. Some of the more optimistic Conservatives thought the party might have a great future combating the Marxist threat if they could convince the public that reform and conservation were compatible, indeed inseparable, concepts. To preserve social peace, they proposed, in effect, greater state and employer paternalism. In the early 1930s some Conservatives also advocated eliminating disorders by integrating all social, economic, and regional groups into more active national participation. These plans for inclusive politics were usually cast in a corporativist mold that favored hierarchical participation over populist, mass politics. Through these adjustments in their traditional political positions, the Conservatives hoped to accommodate the common man in politics.[43]

The clearest evidence of a turn to the left within the Conservative party was the emergence in 1931–33 of a nucleus of young reformers who later formed the Falange and then the Christian Democrats. Instead of trying to counter liberal reformism with Christian charity as their elders had done, the new Conservative generation hoped to outbid socialism and communism with Christian reform. Some even called for "Christian socialism." In the nineteenth century the clerical and anticlerical forces fought over who would lead the aristocratic system; now forces similarly opposed fought over who would lead the reform system. Like their counterparts in the secular socialist camp, the future *falangistas*—offshoots from the Catholic Conservatives—were motivated by the depression and foreign ideas.

[42] Gumucio, *El deber*, 17.
[43] Partido Conservador, *Programa y estatutos* (Santiago, 1933), 3–15; Ricardo Boizard, *Hacia el ideal político de una juventud* (Santiago, 1931), 3–15, and *Voces de la política, del púlpito y la calle* (Santiago, 1939), 43–45; Boizard, *La democracia*, 42–43; Marcial Sanfuentes Carrión, *El partido conservador* (Santiago, 1957), 57–102; Gumucio, *El deber*, 1–24; Morris, 126–207; Pedro Lira Urquieta, *El futuro del país y el partido conservador* (Santiago, 1934), iii–xii, 9–29, 35–72. *El Chileno*, 12 Nov. 1932, 4; 29 Aug. 1931, 1; 15 Aug. 1931, 1. *El Debate*, 16 Oct. 1932, 1; *El Mercurio*, 22 Oct. 1932, 3.

Along with Catholic influences, fascist ideas colored their early thinking. The young Conservatives aimed to win away from the Marxist left the supporters being lost by the Radicals and old reformers. In this way they intended to offer a reformist option to the Catholic middle class. The Conservative reformers advocated statist, nationalist, corporativist changes in the economy and society to achieve progress without class conflict.[44]

The leaders of this rebellion in the Conservative party resembled many of the Socialist leaders, not only in their youth but also in their roots among students and professionals. They were principally from the Catholic University. Some had participated in largely unsuccessful attempts in the 1920s and early 1930s to attract labor to a Christian union movement. The appearance of these future Christian Democrats in 1931–33, arising in opposition to the socialist left, forecast the battle lines in reform politics for a later time. The founders of the Falange also became a force leading the Chilean electorate toward more reformist positions.[45]

The Liberals had traditionally advocated a more urban, industrial, anticlerical program than the Conservatives. But the social similarities between the two groups facilitated the alliance that the two parties formed at the beginning of the 1930s, though the unification did not become official until many years later. The Liberals shared the Conservatives' desire to transform the upper-class parties into bulwarks of the center against the socialist left. Therefore in 1932 many Liberal factions also adopted more reformist, statist positions. The grafting of these palliatives onto their perennial program and opposition to the state marked a critical turning point for the Liberal party: "The Liberal party congregates its men in ... an hour that is an open parenthesis toward a future which one perceives indistinctly and which surely we will not be able to stop ... an instant ... accompanied by a necessity for change and reform, for social readjustment. ... In this hour of uncertainty.... the Liberal party initiates a new stage."[46]

Many Liberal leaders tried to reconcile corporativism and liberalism to provide participation for all groups within an orderly structure. They hoped thus to maintain the party's relevance in a postliberal era. National

---

[44] Ricardo Boizard, *Historia de una derrota* (Santiago, 1941), 67–68, 143–51, and *Doctrinas sociales* (Santiago, 1933), 4–14; Boizard, *La democracia*, 109–79, and *Cuatro*, 171–214; Luis Vitale, *Esencia y apariencia de la democracia cristiana* (Santiago, 1964), 105–7; Sergio Guilisasti Tagle, *Partidos políticos chilenos*, 2nd ed. (Santiago, 1964), 199–201; Bartolomé Palacios M., *El partido conservador y la democracia cristiana* (Santiago, 1933), 4–26, 86–87.

[45] Boizard, *La democracia*, 36–37, 167–79, 200–202, and *Cuatro*, 169–83; Edwards and Frei, 242–43; Frank Bonilla and Myron Glazer, *Student Politics in Chile* (New York, 1970), 82–100.

[46] Gabriel Amunátegui Jordán, *El liberalismo y su misión social* (Santiago, 1933), 6–7.

reorganization along functional lines was expected to produce efficiency and harmony between employers and workers, thereby obviating social conflicts. Functional concepts of reform among the Liberals and other political groups in Chile reflected similar thinking in Spain, Italy, Germany, and as the 1930s progressed, the United States during the New Deal. These corporativist reform ideas in Chile were also related to plans to reorganize regional participation along functional lines in order to eliminate conflict among the provinces. Most Liberals now agreed that measured state intervention and limited reforms were needed as counterweights to save the private economy and social structure from their own shortcomings.[47]

Two other significant, newly formed groups that attested to the ferment on the right in these years were the Agrarian party and the National Socialist movement, or Nazis. Affected like everyone else by the depression, these parties believed that reconstructing the economic system was the only way to end social upheavals in politics. The Agrarians and the Nazis were further examples of the search for a political path between a discredited liberal system and the new threat of a socialist order. Parties of the right, they hoped to take on a centrist image by challenging the left with a mixture of corporativism and reform.[48]

From 1931 to 1933, the upper classes and their economic, social, and political organizations eased the move of the electorate toward the left. The upper classes' expanded willingness to cooperate with the traditional politicians of the middle classes was one of several ways they demonstrated their flexibility. Upper-class contacts with the middle groups facilitated coalitions or at least tolerance of movements favored by the middle sectors, and also may have moderated middle-class antagonisms toward the privileged groups. Significantly, the upper classes sacrificed relatively little in order to accept middle-class aspirations, sharing more political perquisites but retaining the major levers of economic and social power in their hands.

[47] Partido Liberal, *Quinta convención* (Santiago, 1932), *La crisis* (Santiago, 1932), 1–8, *Proyecto de estatuto orgánico del partido liberal* (Santiago, 1931), and *Programa y estatuto* (Santiago, 1934); Edgardo Garrido Merino, *Espíritu y acción del liberalismo* (Santiago, 1934), 3–24; René León Echaíz, *Evolución histórica de los partidos políticos chilenos* (Santiago, 1939), 166–69; Enrique O. Barboza, *Los liberales democráticos y la candidatura de Don Enrique Zañartu Prieto* (Santiago, 1932), 1–3; Amunátegui Jordán, 6–14; Agustín Edwards, *Las corporaciones y la doctrina liberal* (Santiago, 1934), 3–14; Morris, 146–71; Errázuriz, *Los deberes*, 3–11; Sáez, *Recuerdos*, vol. 3, 120–21; Urzúa Valenzuela, 148.

[48] Edwards and Frei, 239–40; Partido Agrario, *Declaración de principios y programa* (Temuco, 1934); *El movimiento nacional-socialista de Chile* (Santiago, 1932); *El Imparcial*, 22 Oct. 1932, 11; interview with Carlos Keller, an early Nazi intellectual leader in Chile; Wilfredo Mayorga, "Jorge González von Marées," *Ercilla*, no. 1740 (23–29 Oct. 1968), 41–42.

Most of the middle groups responded by aligning with the higher social sectors in defense of order in 1931–33. The middle classes, however, had the ability to coalesce politically with the upper or lower classes, with the right or the left, and they would lead the Popular Front movement of 1938.[49]

Conclusions, 1931–33

By the 1930s the upper classes had shifted from ostentatious, direct rule to more indirect methods. After 1930, the state, and to a lesser degree the society and economy, became less oligarchic in form. Above all, the upper sectors no longer ruled electoral politics directly. The privileged groups had to take minimal mass needs more into account in order to safeguard their own foundations and the overarching goal of social stability. Both the grudging acquiescence of the upper classes and the allegiance of the masses helped populist, socialist, urban middle-class leaders succeed. Flexibility on the right contributed to political change as did militancy on the left.[50]

By opting for increased changes, albeit with varying degrees of reluctance, the upper classes were in effect acknowledging that concessions were the minimum price for social unity. When the conservative sectors backed a moderate, Radical president in 1931, they had sought to resurrect an earlier status quo. By 1932 they were trying to preserve the existing one. Now the upper-class leaders argued for "reform, not restoration," because the only apparent choice was between evolution and the dreaded socialism of Grove. Although pessimism drove some to endorse outmoded traditions, most of the upper-class politicians accepted attitudes, reforms, and alliances they had rejected in the past.[51]

The upper classes and the right, out of necessity and choice, became more flexible from 1920 to 1932. They simultaneously admitted new groups and ideas into old institutions while fortifying those institutions to defend their basic interests. Events since 1912, particularly the depression and the Socialist Republic of 1932, had been a learning experience. A former Conservative later observed: "The right, in our country, has one great virtue, and that is that it promptly absorbs experiences and succeeds in

[49] Mann, vol. 1, 70–72; Siegfried, 69–70, 174–75; Pike, *Chile*, 112–15; Melfi, *Sin brújula*, 74–80.

[50] José Antonio Viera-Gallo and Hugo Villela, "Consideraciones preliminares para el estudio del estado en Chile," *Cuadernos de la realidad nacional*, no. 5 (Sept. 1970), 3–24.

[51] Vial Solar, 193–96; Lira Urquieta, 9, 20; Amunátegui Jordán, 12–14; Subercaseaux, *La política*, 1; Cifuentes, *La propiedad*, 69–70; Errázuriz, *Los deberes*, 3–11.

grasping the form of events to introduce itself into them."[52] To a limited but significant degree, most upper-class leaders in 1931–33 tried to salvage the future, not by defending the past with intransigence but by accommodating the present with flexibility.

Upper-class willingness to bend with change was greatest in the political realm, less evident in economic matters, and minimal in the social order. Whereas during the Parliamentary Republic the upper classes had restrained the state as a potential threat to their private enclaves, now they feared more the threat of new groups against their interests and state stability. When the old republic held sway, the upper sectors relied on economic prosperity and social peace. They had counted upon the political subordination of excluded sectors, a passive, compliant, upper-class president, and an apolitical, loyal military. By 1932 the upper classes had adjusted to economic depression and social unrest. They operated with the political inclusion of new groups, a strong president, and a politicized, even leftist, military.

Building on a tradition of sophisticated flexibility, the upper classes accepted a powerful state led by an activist president as the best hope for accommodating countervailing groups and for managing economic and social conflict. The upper classes sought to mollify class antagonisms and voter unrest by stabilizing the economy under state auspices. They hoped to promote harmony by reducing their opposition to the incorporation of regional, social, and political groups that historically had remained on the fringes of national life. The flexibility of the privileged groups permitted peaceful political renovation and the inclusion of socialist leaders of the lower classes in the electoral system. These accommodations appear minimal today, but they were costly to the upper classes because such adjustments were tantamount to relinquishing future electoral preeminence to the middle-class politicians and their populist followers.[53]

In oversimplified terms, the bargain struck in the 1930s involved ceding officeholding to the middle classes and promoting industrialization, but preserving immunity for the countryside. Even in the Popular Front, reforms would be restricted to the cities. Throughout, the capacity of the upper classes to live with new leaders and ideas, coupled with their rela-

[52] The author was one of the young Conservatives who entered congress in 1932 and later became a Christian Democrat. Boizard, *La democracia*, 101.

[53] González Echenique, 5–8, 62–74; Edwards Vives, *La fronda*, 15–19, 207–8. One author's comment on the superficiality of some of the political changes: "Many of the same men of yesterday reappeared dressed in other clothes, applauding that which they had repudiated"; Melfi, *Sin brújula*, 112–13. Vial Solar, 197–98; Lira Urquieta, 25–29; Amunátegui Jordán, 12–14; Partido Liberal, *La crisis*, 1–8; Edwards, *Las corporaciones*, 6–7; Domingo Amunátegui Solar, *El progreso intelectual y político de Chile* (Santiago, 1936), 6–12; Viera-Gallo and Villela, 3–24.

tive unity and organization, contributed to political stability. The need for evolution and reform was proclaimed with varying intensity by the traditional right as well as more leftist groups. Many in the privileged sectors began to think that accepting state expansion, mass politics, selected reforms, and industrial economic growth offered perhaps the best way to soothe social antagonisms. In a sense, traditional and modern modes were blended in the upper class. It was not really a modernizing upper class, but neither was it opposed to partial modernization.

The Chilean upper classes favored more economic than social changes. In fact, despite developmental formulas postulating that economic alterations lead to social alterations, many of Chile's traditional leaders hoped that economic change would avert social change. They also hoped that moderate state capitalism would preempt state socialism. In the process of economic change, the integration of the rural and urban economic leaders was sufficient to avoid sharp conflict. Consequently there was a rather smooth transition in emphasis from declining rural to rising urban enterprises. This compromise between agrarian and industrial sectors helped forestall potential threats from below. This accord was constructed within democratic boundaries, buttressing continuities that contributed to political stability.[54]

The alliance between the two upper-class political parties in 1931–33 and the similarity of proposals from the agriculturalists' SNA and the industrialists' SOFOFA provide only indirect or fragmentary evidence of interlocking between the agricultural and business-industrial elites. Since this study focuses on the political elites, overlapping between the rural and urban economic leaders is only deduced from background information on party heads. Tables 1–4 established the Conservatives and Liberals as a rather homogeneous and distinct group compared to the parties further to the left. The leadership tables also showed that the right was very active in the interest associations representing the economic upper sectors. A closer look at the data behind the leadership tables reveals that six of the nine Conservative leaders who were either prominent in industry or the SOFOFA were also large landholders or members of the SNA. Of the sixteen Liberals in the sample who were important industrialists or SOFOFA members, twelve were also major landholders or SNA members.

These are inconclusive findings because economic affiliations were merely one set of variables, not the constants, in this analysis of political elites. Beyond the Conservative and Liberal leaders, it is not known precisely how much the top economic groups meshed. Only four of the twelve Radical leaders who were industrialists or SOFOFA members also pos-

[54] See Petras, esp. 53–55, and Dix, esp. 12.

sessed great estates or belonged to the SNA. Available evidence for the early 1930s proves neither that the upper classes were tightly interwoven nor sharply divided, but it does point to significant linkages and mutual interests. And it is worth repeating that the SNA had founded the SOFOFA in the nineteenth century. In other words, the shared values and political affiliations of the rural and urban upper classes had some basis in shared socioeconomic foundations.

The upper sectors were politically cohesive, their parties reached a new stage of unification, and there was enough interlacing of rural and urban upper groups to facilitate cooperation in order to surmount the crisis. Although the rural and urban upper sectors had displayed commonalities and cooperation in the past, the growing merger of the two upper-class parties during the Great Depression was symptomatic of the reaching of a major new understanding. But more detailed studies of familial and financial connections are needed to delineate fully the integration of the rural and urban upper classes in 1931–33. In all probability, both the interpenetration of the upper classes and their penetrability—both their solidarity and their diversity—contributed to their perseverance. Because the upper sectors were rather closely knit but neither monolithic nor closed to all newcomers, they were able to accept change without being overwhelmed by it.

Having arrived at a consensus that religion was no longer a paramount political issue and that protecting the social order was the most important objective, the Conservatives and Liberals basically agreed that both commercial-industrial and agricultural interests could be defended without grave damage to either. The right normally avoided futile confrontations and instead pursued a more indirect strategy from the 1930s on, trying to contain or limit reform efforts while countering the socialist threat. Their politics shifted from opposition to an activist state and liberalism to opposition to mass pressures and socialism.[55]

In the wake of the Great Depression, all political sides accepted limited compromises, partly because the military, burdened with the stigma of failure, had proven an unreliable instrument, whether installing the Socialist Republic or deposing it. The military's withdrawal from the public political process served notice to civilian politicians that they would have to maintain order and resolve conflicts within the electoral system. It deterred the Socialists from seeking and justifying nonelectoral routes to power, and it constrained the traditional groups from denying the Socialists offices won at the ballot box.

Though predominant in the political system, flexibility had its limits.

[55] See Gil, esp. 253; Petras, 97–101.

Both continuities and changes flowed from the political watershed of 1931–33. Upper-class willingness to tolerate Socialist and even Communist electoral leadership of the masses did not include bowing to all their reform demands. New political symbols were more acceptable than reordering society. New styles, ideas, and parties entered the political system without changing its basic orientation or eliminating past actors. Participation in a system of expanding electoral permissiveness did not necessarily lead to power. In some cases, expressing discontent through radical electoral options substituted for violent or anomic disruptions of the social order. Thoroughly competitive politics, with all ideological viewpoints participating electorally, could deflect attacks and grievances away from the system and direct them toward current officeholders. As Alessandri returned to the presidency, the fundamental contours of the social, economic, and political hierarchy were left relatively untouched. Chile survived the crisis. For the moment, expansion and alteration had not brought basic changes, but only held out possibilities.[56]

Perhaps the critical question for Chile's political system and history was not the immediate outcome but rather how opposing groups chose to conduct the contest for the future. Socialism became a legitimate voter alternative in part because of the essential flexibility of the Chilean political system. A fundamental accord on democratic, adaptive, accommodative norms avoided anarchy, violence, and the military. For example, the threat of a nonelectoral left, seen in the takeover by the Socialist Republic, made the electoral left more palatable to traditional groups. The various parties vigorously disagreed over the pace of change, but after 1932 rarely clashed over the rules of the game. At the same time, the leftward movement of the Chilean electorate remained a latent threat to the historic thought and positions of many in the privileged groups. This movement to the left continued, erratically but persistently, for the next forty years. The voting patterns and party alignments shaped in 1932 set precedents for the decades that followed.[57]

Future of Chilean Upper Classes and Political Change

The upper classes benefited more than any other social group in the 1930s from economic recovery under Alessandri, but the left grew rapidly in electoral strength. With their political influence mushrooming, the Social-

[56] Anderson, 87–137; Osvaldo Sunkel, "Change and Frustration in Chile," in Veliz, *Obstacles*, 116–44; Seymour Martin Lipset and Stein Rokkan, eds., *Party Systems and Voter Alignments* (New York, 1967), 4.

[57] Anderson, 87–114; Kaufman, i, 1, 25, 42–43.

ists and Communists backed a Radical for the presidency in the Popular Front victory of 1938. Although tempted to try to prevent the takeover of the Popular Front, the right chose flexibility. The military did not reenter politics to obstruct the voters' choice, and the leftist coalition took office. The transition to the Popular Front consecrated the tradition that the left, including the Socialists and Communists, could reach the national administration through coalitions and elections.[58]

A series of reform governments from 1938 to 1958 promoted industrialization but did not assault the system of land tenure or the social hierarchy. Meanwhile, studies of the upper classes in these later years indicated that their composition and strategies had altered little since 1933, although the middle sectors and some segments of labor had made great advances. Analyses in the contemporary era have portrayed the privileged groups fortifying their interconnections and defenses in land, industries, and commerce. For example, it has been estimated that in the 1960s nearly half of the large businessmen in Chile either owned large farms or were closely related to large farm owners. It has been argued that banking served as the nexus for all these linkages and operations. There is also some evidence that the upper sectors managed to become prominent in state enterprises created as reform measures. The industrial and agricultural leaders in these later years remained tied to each other and to government at many points. They squabbled over particular interest issues but usually united on larger questions, such as threats of redistribution. At the same time, the upper classes continued to guard their political flanks through the Conservative and Liberal parties and through trying to reach understandings with centrist parties, such as the declining Radicals and the rising Christian Democrats.[59]

In the mid-1950s the congressional leadership of the upper-class parties was still primarily aristocratic and homogeneous. The Conservatives

[58] Thomson, 290–91; Ellsworth, vii, 1–2, 18–52, 96–100, 128–65; Mamalakis and Reynolds, 15–17, 54–55; Boizard, *Historia*, 35–78, 147–50; Antonio Cifuentes, *Evolución de la economía chilena desde la crisis hasta nuestros días* (Santiago, 1935), 15–16; Arturo Alessandri Palma, *Rectificaciones al tomo IX* (Santiago, 1941), 118–52; Domingo Amunátegui Solar, *La segunda presidencia del Arturo Alessandri* (Santiago, 1961), 232–34; Carlos Sáez Morales, *Y así vamos . . .* (Santiago, 1938), 198–203; Julio César Jobet, *Ensayo crítico del desarrollo económico-social de Chile* (Santiago, 1955), 188–203; Wilfredo Mayorga, "La derecha deseaba la dictadura," *Ercilla*, no. 1693 (29 Nov. 1967), 15; John J. Johnson, *Political Change in Latin America* (Stanford, 1958), 81–83. For details, see John Reese Stevenson, *The Chilean Popular Front* (Philadelphia, 1942).

[59] See Petras, esp. 38–55, 100; Gil, 294–95; Lagos Escobar, 7–16, 95–172; Urzúa Valenzuela, 146; Dale L. Johnson, "Industrialization, Social Mobility, and Class Formation in Chile," *Studies in Comparative International Development*, 3 (1967–68); Constantine C. Menges, "Public Policy and Organized Business in Chile," *Journal of International Affairs*, 20 (1966), 343–65.

were overwhelmingly agricultural, though many party leaders also held professional titles and were active in banking. Their education still reflected the religious ties of the party and provided the major difference from the leadership of the Liberals. The Liberal party leadership resembled that of the Conservatives, though the Liberals were slightly more urban and commercially oriented. As the economic unity of the upper classes apparently progressed over the years, so did the political unity of the two parties associated with the upper strata. In the 1960s the Conservatives and Liberals finally officially joined to form the National party. In the same decades, the center and left parties still boasted far more leaders with less aristocratic occupations, schooling, and affiliations.[60]

There was a brief conservative revival in 1958, when the right succeeded in putting Jorge Alessandri Rodríguez, son of the earlier president, into office in a three-way contest. But the voting strength of the right continued to decline into the 1960s. Unless they were fielding a charismatic figure like Alessandri or supporting a center party, the conservative forces were in deep electoral trouble nationally. Electoral competition in the 1960s was waged primarily between the Socialist-Communist coalition and the progressive Christian Democrats. The electorate continued moving to the left, both because votes for the leftist parties increased and because those receiving leftist and even centrist votes adopted increasingly radical programs. The Christian Democrats won the presidential election of 1964 primarily because the right flexibly abandoned its preferred candidates to insure the victory of Eduardo Frei Montalva over the Marxist contender, Salvador Allende Gossens.[61]

Frei's administration instituted unparalleled reforms, but inflation, negligible economic growth, structural problems and inequalities, and lower-class discontent persisted. Even on the land-reform question, the right was now willing to bargain. The upper classes still hoped to manage conflicts rather than resolve them, and thus preserve national stability. The traditional conservative forces, however, would back the Christian Democrat reformers only so long as that support appeared mandatory to block the threat of socialism.[62]

In the presidential election of 1970, the right believed that they could return Jorge Alessandri to the presidency in another three-way contest. The Christian Democrats hoped to elect a successor to Frei, Radomiro Tomic Romero. On the left a coalition arose reminiscent of the combination of forces in 1938, but with the Radicals as minor members and the Socialists

---

[60] Urzúa Valenzuela, 125–54; Petras, 103–4.
[61] Federico G. Gil and Charles J. Parrish, *The Chilean Presidential Election of September, 1964* (Washington, 1965); Gil, 230–43, 298–313; Petras, 104–13.
[62] Kaufman, i, 41–46; Petras, 108–13, 158–255, 338–55.

and Communists dominating. The Socialist candidate of this coalition, Salvador Allende, won the presidency with 36 percent of the votes. The right had miscalculated. There were rumors that the military might act to prevent Allende's succession, but again the armed forces, to the disappointment of some civilians, stayed in their barracks. In November 1970 the Socialists, after nearly forty years, took office directly and democratically and began trying to fulfill decades of promises and expectations.[63]

By 1970 the political strategies pursued since 1932 had reached an apparent conclusion. The upper classes and the right were faced with at least three possibilities. First, it was possible that the Allende victory promised the demise of the traditional privileged groups as a national power. The limits of accommodation and flexibility may have been reached. The remaining upper-class leaders knew that the growth of the interventionist state since the 1930s meant that the capture of the state apparatus by the left was more ominous in 1970 than in 1932 or 1938. A government not just devoted to economic development and industrialization but specifically committed to redistribution could cut deeply into upper-class preserves during a six-year term. Many prosperous Chileans abandoned the country, though often with hopes of returning in the future. A second possibility for the upper classes was not surrender or withdrawal but an open fight against the regime. But most leaders on the right seemed reluctant to overthrow the constitutional stability that had served them so well for so long. Moreover, the upper sectors feared they might not be able to muster the forces to win an overt clash, whether through military or paramilitary means. Consequently, as in the past, many conservative groups tended toward a third set of strategies, between capitulation and counterrevolution.[64]

The third possibility for the upper classes was to rely primarily on more traditional tactics to help them survive the Allende experiment. The right tried to coalesce the anti-Marxist forces, align the middle classes and bureaucracy against Allende, and establish a working relationship with the centrist Christian Democrats. Some conservatives also hoped for assistance from the United States, Argentina, and Brazil. Through delaying tactics, hobbling Allende in congress, and perhaps contributing to economic and international troubles, many conservative groups thought they could contain change within tolerable limits until the next presidential election. In other words, although unusually difficult, it was possible that the traditional sectors would once again arrive at an unpleasant but bear-

[63] Carlos Núñez, *Chile: La última opción electoral?* (Santiago, 1970); Chile, Dirección del Registro Electoral, *Elección ordinaria de Presidente de la República* (Santiago, 1970); Eric J. Hobsbawm, "Chile: Year One," *New York Review of Books*, 17:4 (23 Sept. 1971), 23–32.

[64] See Hobsbawm, esp. 30.

able accommodation with the new political environment. During the opening months of the Allende government, the upper classes and other opponents of the regime pursued multiple strategies. In the final analysis, their choices and their success or failure would largely depend upon how revolutionary Allende proved to be.[65]

In the long view of Chilean history and politics, it would be daring to predict the elimination or final subordination of the existing upper classes in Chile. They have shown themselves in the past to be resourceful, sophisticated, determined, and resilient. Even though the Chilean situation under Allende was unique, it remained risky to assume that the upper classes and the right had conceded the future. The upper classes were, after all, skilled in the political art of preservation. In fact it might be argued that their relative flexibility in the 1930s helped preserve more of their privileges than overt intransigence would have. On the other hand, the accommodations to change made in the 1930s, while holding out the promise of stability, also held the possibility of gradual erosion of upper-class control and eventual takeover by the new forces on the left. And that takeover by the left came within the system legitimized by the dominant groups for decades. As a result, more than the 1930s, the 1970s posed one of the gravest challenges to the upper classes in Chilean history.

Chile and Latin America, as well as many other underdeveloped areas, appear to be restrained by the past from fully entering the modern age. The past seems to control the present, and continuities are more common than changes. The obstacles to progress often overshadow the impulses or openings for meaningful reforms. When historians of these countries study the instances of upheaval and innovation, it should be clear that they are focusing on exceptional cases in the broader sweep of history. So perhaps more attention should be devoted to the forces of conservation than to the forces of change. Without denying significant changes in the history of Latin America, it remains true that "whatever his area of interest or specialization, the Latin American historian will sooner or later find that he must come to grips with the tenacity of conservatism—the persistent flexibility of traditionalism. . . ."[66] In the historical treatment of developing countries, studies of the upper classes can help illuminate the forces of inhibition and tradition. To understand the dominant forces that have shaped the histories of the Latin American nations, it might be especially fruitful to analyze the guardians of the past, who have so repeatedly prevailed.

[65] Hobsbawm.

[66] Stanley J. Stein, "Latin American Historiography: Status and Research Opportunities," in Charles Wagley, ed., *Social Science Research on Latin America* (New York, 1964), 114.

The New Deal
Intellectual Elite:
A Collective Portrait

THOMAS A. KRUEGER AND
WILLIAM GLIDDEN

*"I am all in favor of government by experts—as long as they
are my experts."*

—Anon.

At the summit of his public career, Franklin Roosevelt forcefully attracted
the interest and loyalty of many American intellectuals, who flocked to
Washington to place their talents at his command and to realize their
long-standing reform ambitions. Perhaps no other administration since the
early days of the Republic brought so many intellectuals into its service.
During the Roosevelt years, intellectuals worked together with unaccus-
tomed unity for social, political, and economic objectives; moved from
their artistic and professional habitats into an alien political environment,
they confronted a variety of unfamiliar challenges to their collective existence and to their most cherished aspirations. The Roosevelt age affords a
rare opportunity to study an intellectual species fighting both for survival
and for environmental mastery.

So far the story has been only partially told. There are journalistic accounts, memoirs, and histories of the Brain Trust, the New Deal planners,
the service intellectuals in the Department of Agriculture, the Keynesians,
the Black Cabineteers, and the Brandeisians, but no comprehensive study
of the Roosevelt intelligentsia.[1]

[1] Raymond Moley, *After Seven Years* (New York, 1939), and Rexford G. Tugwell,
The Brain Trust (New York, 1968), are excellent accounts by the Brain Trust's two
most important members. A good general discussion is in Arthur M. Schlesinger, Jr.,

This essay attempts to fill that gap with a general analysis of the New Deal intellectual elite. It seeks to surpass previous accounts not only in scope but also in method. Supplementing the customary devices of narrative history with techniques borrowed from descriptive statistics, modes of analysis taken from prosopography, and theories adapted from the social sciences, we hope to contribute an original chapter to the social and intellectual history of the New Deal. We attempt to differentiate the New Deal intellectual elite from the rest of the American population and from other modern American elites. By specifying the group's distinctive characteristics, we seek to describe in part the social basis of American politics during the Roosevelt era. Our findings bear directly on the classic political problem facing every democratic society—the reconciliation of the interests of the theoretical rulers, the sovereign people, with the interests of their actual rulers, the leadership cadres exercising power and authority. Finally we try to describe and assess the New Deal intellectuals' political ideology. If successful, this essay could clear the way for similar studies of other political and economic elites active during the Roosevelt era; it might facilitate investigations of the role of pressure groups in the formation of New Deal policies; and it might lead to studies of the relation between the social and ideological characteristics of other elites in modern American society.

From general histories, specialized monographs, and a variety of official and unofficial sources, we compiled a list of some 1,500 persons active in government during the 1930s and 1940s.[2] From it, we selected

---

The Age of Roosevelt, I: *The Crisis of the Old Order* (Boston, 1956), 398ff. Ellis Hawley, *The New Deal and the Problem of Monopoly* (Princeton, 1966), considers planners, spenders, and trust-busters. Richard Kirkendall, *Social Scientists and Farm Politics in the Age of Roosevelt* (Columbia, Mo., 1966), describes the intellectuals in the Department of Agriculture. The Keynesians are portrayed in Herbert Stein, *The Fiscal Revolution in America* (Chicago, 1969), 91–168, and John Kenneth Galbraith's review in the *New York Times Book Review,* 16 May 1965, 1, 34–36, 38–39, also reprinted in his *Economics, Peace, and Laughter* (Boston, 1971). Jane R. Motz, "The Black Cabinet: Negroes in the Administration of Franklin D. Roosevelt," M.A. thesis (University of Delaware, 1964); Unofficial Observer [John Franklin Carter], *The New Dealers* (New York, 1934); and Joseph Alsop and Robert Kintner, *Men around the President* (New York, 1939), are also interesting.

[2] In addition to the works cited in n. 1, the following were used to compile the list of names: Arthur Altmeyer, *The Formative Years of Social Security* (Madison, 1966); Sidney Baldwin, *Poverty and Politics: The Rise and Decline of the Farm Security Administration* (Chapel Hill, 1968); Irving Bernstein, *The New Deal Collective Bargaining Policy* (Berkeley, 1950); Donald C. Blaisdell, *Government and Agriculture* (New York, 1940); Clarke A. Chambers, *Seedtime of Reform* (Minneapolis, 1963); Arthur Whipple Crawford, *Monetary Management under the New Deal* (Washington, 1940); Robert Eugene Cushman, *The Independent Regulatory Commissions* (New York, 1941); Milton Derber and Edwin Young, eds., *Labor and the New Deal* (Madi-

380 who seemed to fit into the vague category "intellectual."[3] We tried to get representatives from every reform tendency involved in the New Deal; those included either faithfully supported Roosevelt's programs, or at some important point during the period they preferred Roosevelt to any of the other available political choices. We think we have thus identified the most important intellectuals associated with the Roosevelt administration and some of the lesser lights as well.

The chief limitation of the method is that it does not permit us to generalize about a population larger than the group under analysis. Although we assume our descriptions would apply to New Deal intellectuals not on our list, we have no direct evidence to support the assumption, and our methods do not warrant confidence in it. Indeed, what statisticians call the ecological fallacy and logicians call the fallacy of division do not permit statements about aggregates to be predicated of their individual members, not to mention persons who do not belong to them.[4] Strictly speaking, our conclusions can neither be applied to a larger universe of New Deal in-

---

son, 1961); John M. Gaus and Leon O. Wolcott, *Public Administration and the United States Department of Agriculture* (Chicago, 1940); Donald S. Howard, *The W.P.A. and Federal Relief Policy* (New York, 1943); Jesse H. Jones, *Fifty Billion Dollars* (New York, 1951); Timothy L. McDonnell, *The Wagner Housing Act* (Chicago, 1957); Arthur W. Macmahon and John D. Millett, *Federal Administrators: A Biographical Approach to the Problems of Departmental Management* (New York, 1939); Edwin G. Nourse et al., *Three Years of the Agricultural Adjustment Administration* (Washington, 1937); Michael E. Parrish, *Securities Regulation and the New Deal* (New Haven, 1970); John A. Salmond, *The Civilian Conservation Corps, 1933–1942* (Durham, 1967); Lawrence F. Schmeckebier, *New Federal Organizations* (Washington, 1934); Lester Seligman and Elmer Cornwell, eds., *New Deal Mosaic: Roosevelt Confers with His National Emergency Council, 1933–1936* (Eugene, Ore., 1965); Edwin E. Witte, *The Development of the Social Security Act* (Madison, 1962); select volumes of the *United States Government Manual*, which first appeared in 1935. For whatever it may be worth, Paul Appleby later placed the total number of New Dealers at somewhere between 300 and 400; Appleby, memoir, Oral History Collection, Columbia University, New York City. The complete list of names is in the appendix at the end of this essay. We wish to thank Richard Barnet, Barton J. Bernstein, Frank Freidel, Otis L. Graham, John Herrick, John B. Kirby, William E. Leuchtenburg, and Arthur Schlesinger, Jr., for helpful suggestions; they are of course not responsible for any errors of fact or interpretation that may appear in the sequel.

[3] Our definition of "intellectual" was taken with some modifications from Edward Shils, "Intellectuals," *International Encyclopedia of the Social Sciences*, vol. 7, 399–415, and from Seymour Martin Lipset, *Political Man* (New York, 1960), 332–33. For a brilliant and contrasting analysis, see G. Eric Hansen, "Intellect and Power: Some Notes on the Intellectual as a Political Type," *Journal of Politics*, 31 (May 1969), 311–28. An earlier account of the New Deal intellectuals from a different perspective is Richard Kirkendall, "Franklin D. Roosevelt and the Service Intellectual," *Mississippi Valley Historical Review*, 49 (Dec. 1962), 456–71. On elites, see Suzanne Keller, *Beyond the Ruling Class* (New York, 1963).

[4] For the ecological fallacy, see Charles Dollar and Richard Jensen, *Historian's Guide to Statistics* (New York, 1971), 97; for the fallacy of division, see Ralph Ross, *Symbols & Civilization* (New York, 1962), 37.

tellectuals nor be predicated of persons who might have merited inclusion on the list but who were, for one reason or another, not placed on it.

The chief limitations of prosopography, in turn, are that it tends to convey a spurious sense of precision when in fact it relies on ambiguous and overlapping categories, and it generates a false sense of explanatory power when it accounts, by itself, for no more than traditional narrative history. It serves heuristic and descriptive purposes; it does not provide encompassing causal explanations.[5]

A clear delineation of the social and intellectual characteristics of the New Deal intelligentsia will not automatically explain the major developments of the Roosevelt era. Its explanatory utility lies outside the means used to obtain it. Whatever causal force it possesses depends upon the use of implicit or explicit theories to relate it to the history of the Roosevelt era. Its ultimate significance can be determined only by a synthetic analysis that weighs it in comparison to the other forces determining the events of the period. In the end there is no methodological substitute for imagination, theory, and intelligence.[6]

By the 1920s the age of the great folk migrations from Europe to the underinhabitated portions of the globe had entered its terminal phase. Of the nations founded or acquired during the millennium of European expansion, the United States may have been the most heterogeneous. Nearly every major ethnic, national, and linguistic subdivision of the human race had representatives in the American population: the aborigines were Mongolian; a sizable minority originated in black Africa; much smaller contingents stemmed from the Near and Far East; the Caucasians derived from every significant ethnic and political grouping in Europe.

[5] Lawrence Stone, "Prosopography," *Daedalus*, 100 (Winter 1971), 46–79; Lewis J. Edinger and Donald D. Searing, "Social Background in Elite Analysis: A Methodological Inquiry," *American Political Science Review*, 61 (June 1967) 428–45; Dankwart A. Rustow, "The Study of Elites: 'Who's Who, When and How,'" *World Politics*, 18 (June 1966), 690–717. All contain material on the benefits and the dangers of collective biographical analysis.

[6] The issues here are not entirely clear, in part because historians have largely ignored the philosophers, and the philosophers have analyzed the work of practicing historians through the wrong end of the telescope. Historians obviously attempt causal explanations of the phenomena they describe. The philosophers' mistake has been to look for causal statements in individual sentences. They would be better advised to analyze works of history as wholes—to see how much consists of description and classification and how much of causal, correlative, and other types of explanation. For illustrative material, see Arthur Danto, *Analytical Philosophy of History* (Cambridge, 1965), and Morton White, *Foundations of Historical Knowledge* (New York, 1965). For an interesting attempt at clarification, see Robert F. Berkhofer, Jr., *A Behavioral Approach to Historical Analysis* (New York, 1969), 270–321. On scientific method, see F. S. C. Northrop, *The Logic of the Sciences and the Humanities* (New York, 1947).

The country's ethnic diversity and the "melting pot" mystique have obscured the proportional composition of the American population. In 1920 the aboriginal and Oriental contingents each constituted far less than 1 percent of the 106,000,000 resident Americans. The largest minority, the Afro-American, was only 10 percent of the total. Although millions of southern and eastern Europeans had recently immigrated, the New Immigrants made up only 13 percent of the population. About three-fourths of the American people originated in northern Europe. The United States was a white man's country—a northern European white man's country.[7]

The New Deal intelligentsia reflected the nation's dominant ethnic character. The ancestors of at least 74 percent of its members came from northern Europe—the British Isles, Ireland, Scandinavia, Germany, France, and Switzerland—giving the northern European cohort random representation in the group.[8] Recent immigrants constituted 7 percent of the New Deal elite and, in 1930, 11 percent of the total population; they were therefore underrepresented by a factor of 0.6. The immigrant total included 21 persons from southern and eastern Europe, who were underrepresented in the elite by a factor of 0.5. Most of the eastern European immigrants were Jews; there were no Poles, only one-half a Czech (Beardsley Ruml), one Italian (Ferdinand Pecora), and two Russians. Taking up 5 percent of the group, the blacks made up about 10 percent of the population, and were underrepresented by a factor of 0.5; however, if all of the 35 blacks alleged to have been in the Black Cabinet had been included in the analysis, their proportion of the New Deal elite would have nearly equaled their

[7] Biographical information came mainly from standard sources: *Current Biography, Who's Who, Who Was Who, Who's Who in American Jewry, Who's Who in World Jewry, National Cyclopedia of American Biography, New York Times* obituaries, *Dictionary of American Biography*, and *American Men in Government*. Published biographies and autobiographies were also consulted, as were unpublished materials in the Oral History Collection at Columbia University and in the Franklin D. Roosevelt Memorial Library at Hyde Park. The data on the ethnic composition of the population in 1920 come from John B. Trevor, "An Analysis of the American Immigration Act of 1924," *International Conciliation*, no. 202 (Sept. 1924), 424–33.

[8] The analysis will subsequently suggest that the northern Europeans were slightly overrepresented. Indices of representation are calculated by dividing the percentage of the subgroup in the reference population into the subgroup's percentage in the New Deal elite; if 75 percent of the population and 75 percent of the New Deal intellectuals originated in northern Europe, then the index of representation for Northern Europeans in the New Deal elite is 1. Index numbers larger than 1 indicate overrepresentation; numbers less than one indicate underrepresentation; the index number is also the factor by which a subgroup is over, under, or equally represented. Unless otherwise indicated, percentages quoted in the text are calculated on the basis of the number of the total population for whom information was available. In the present instance, we found information for 362 of the 380 intellectuals.

share of the American population.[9] Although no one of Oriental, Near Eastern, Greek, or Indian origin appeared in the group, their respective shares of the total population were too far below 1 percent for them to have been represented on a random basis. The inequities fell most heavily on non-Jews of recent immigrant origin—mainly Italian, Slav, Hungarian, and Mexican.[10]

The two ethnic groups faring comparatively well have been unique among American minorities in the tenacity of their efforts to achieve power and distinction in American society. Despite years of systematic exclusion from honor and reward, then worsened by the effects of the depression, the black community contained educated leaders ready to act whenever they found weaknesses in the surrounding racist society. Whatever else may be said about New Deal racial policies, they gave black leaders more chance to exploit the weaknesses in the American caste system than they had had since Reconstruction. Skillfully pressing their advantages, they contributed to some useful if unspectacular changes in Washington's racial customs and in the federal government's racial policies. During the New Deal, black Americans held more important positions in a national administration than they had ever held before. Although most were race relations advisers or special assistants on Negro affairs, three of them acquired some power in government: Mary McLeod Bethune, the National Youth Administration's director of Negro affairs; William H. Hastie, federal Judge in the Virgin Islands; and Robert C. Weaver, special assistant to the administrator of the United States Housing Authority. By presenting a unified point of view, the Black Cabineteers provided a lobby for the Afro-American population within the federal government. Their presence in the Roosevelt administration marked a dramatic reversal of the decline in black appointments to upper-level administrative positions that had occurred under Roosevelt's Republican and Democratic predecessors in the twentieth-century presidency.[11]

[9] Motz, "The Black Cabinet," 23ff. The black ratio was calculated on a denominator of 380.

[10] Since most of the other identifiable groups were somewhat underrepresented, the northern Europeans were probably slightly overrepresented. For an illustration of how eastern Europeans feel about their exclusion from positions of power and prestige, see Michael Novak, "White Ethnic," *Harper's Magazine*, 243 (Sept. 1971), 44–51.

[11] In addition to Motz, "The Black Cabinet," the most recent analyses of New Deal race policy include Leslie Fishel, "The Negro in the New Deal," *Wisconsin Magazine of History*, 48 (Winter 1964–65), 111–26; Raymond Wolters, *Negroes and the Great Depression* (Westport, Conn., 1970); August Meier and Elliott M. Rudwick, *From Plantation to Ghetto*, rev. ed. (New York, 1970), 238ff.; John B. Kirby, "The New Deal Era and Blacks: A Study of Black and White Race Thought, 1933–1945,"

Suffering less from overt discrimination, emboldened by strong familial and communal organizations, and highly educated and urbanized, the Jews alone among American minority groups succeeded within the New Deal elite out of proportion to their share of the total population. With 53 members of the group, 15 percent of the total, and about 3 percent of the nation's population in 1930, the Jews were overrepresented by a factor of 5. Yet despite their numerical overrepresentation, they failed to fill more than their fair share of the most powerful positions held by members of the New Deal elite. The Jews in important positions—cabinet posts, assistant and undersecretaryships, heads of major department subdivisions, and chiefs of independent agencies—constituted no more than 2 percent of the entire elite. Only Jerome Frank, Felix Frankfurter, Henry Morgenthau, Jr., William Leiserson, David E. Lilienthal, Nathan Straus, Samuel Rosenman, and Abe Fortas held positions of power in the New Deal. All but Leiserson were German or western European Jews.

Immigrants to America have tended to adopt the country's manners long before they move into its centers of power and prestige.[12] They learn the language, take up the nation's platitudes, and dream the American dream; they seldom become cabinet officers, presidents or board members of large corporations, high-ranking military officers, or university presidents. The prestige and power they acquire lie within the immigrant community and cannot be transferred during the first generation to the larger society. Few members of recently immigrated minority groups achieve notable success in the American social system; aside from the Jews, the members of most recent immigrant groups remained largely beyond the pale of wealth, power, and prestige throughout the 1930s.

It is unlikely that any modern nation-state quickly incorporates alien or ethnic minorities into its leadership cadres. The Soviet Union, another polyglot country, is said to be governed almost exclusively by the Great Russians, who form only half of the total Russian population. Perhaps no

---

Ph.D. thesis (University of Illinois, 1971), and "The Roosevelt Administration and Blacks: An Ambivalent Legacy," in Barton J. Bernstein and Alan J. Matusow, eds., *Twentieth Century America*, rev. ed. (New York, 1972). Samuel Krislov, *The Negro in Federal Employment* (Minneapolis, 1967), 22–23, and Laurence J. W. Hayes, "The Negro Federal Government Worker," *Howard University Studies in the Social Sciences*, 3 (1941), esp. 153, have interesting information on black workers in federal employment; both clearly show that the proportionate decline in black employment at the federal level had been reversed by Roosevelt's Republican predecessors in the 1920s. On the eve of the New Deal, blacks constituted between 9 and 10 percent of the federal work force; by the end of the 1930s their proportionate share of total federal employment was still between 9 and 10 percent. The number of blacks employed rose from 53,000 in 1933 to 82,000 by 1938.

[12] See Milton Gordon, "Assimilation in America: Theory and Reality," *Daedalus*, 90 (Spring 1961), 263–85.

established society, no matter how open, moves immigrants immediately into its vital centers of influence. Considering the bitterness of the cultural conflict between northern European Americans and the New Immigrants in the first decades of the twentieth century, the underrepresentation of southern and eastern Europeans in the New Deal elite is not surprising. The fairest judgment may be that the New Deal elite was remarkably egalitarian. It included sizable numbers of blacks and Jews, a few non-Jewish New Immigrants, and an unusually large number of women.[13]

Nevertheless, the egalitarianism was numerical, not hierarchical. Within the New Deal elite the northern Europeans retained their political primacy. The ethnics, the blacks, and the women almost invariably occupied the least powerful positions filled by the group's members. Where positions of power and influence were filled, the northern Europeans usually filled them. With the notable exceptions of the Treasury and Labor portfolios, the northern Europeans held most of the cabinet posts, the assistant and undersecretaryships, the directorships of major department subdivisions, and the key posts in independent agencies. At the leadership level, the New Deal was not so much a coalition of ethnics, blacks, women, and older American stocks as it was a satellite system with the old American stocks at the center and the blacks, Jews, women, and a few ethnics in orbit around them.

Not only did the main ethnic colors of the American population map appear on the demographic map of the New Deal elite, but the two populations were also broadly similar in the length of time their constituent families had been in North America.[14] The families of 83 of the whites could be traced back into the colonial period, 44 percent of the total for whom precise information was available. With the 18 blacks added, the colonial group's share rises to 54 percent. At that, the ratio may be too low. Among the 193 persons for whom accurate information was not available were 176 who were at least second-generation Americans; they were

[13] The 37 women constitute around 10 percent of the group. Although the ratio of women in the total population was obviously much higher than that, the New Deal's record is impressive not only in comparison with the records of most other American leadership elites but also in view of the relative decline in the social and economic position of women since 1940. Mrs. Roosevelt herself was hardly the stereotyped all-American wife—the man's loyal and faithful servant, whose duties are merely to mend the clothes, mind the children, and make the dinner. She was the most liberated of all the wives of modern American presidents, and perhaps of all the wives of modern American husbands. See Joseph Lash, *Eleanor and Franklin* (New York, 1971).

[14] Since precise information was available for only 187 families, data for the 193 unknowns could totally invalidate the conclusions in the text. Thomas Krueger is now seeking additional information, and plans eventually to run successive random samples of the group to see whether this initial analysis is generally correct. See Dollar and Jensen, *Historian's Guide to Statistics*, 13.

all American-born, but the dates of their families' arrivals in North America could not be determined. Since most had British surnames, some of them were undoubtedly of colonial ancestry; if the proportion equaled the ratio of persons of colonial ancestry in the British-American population in 1920, then 85 percent of the 176 would have been able to trace their families back to the seventeenth or eighteenth centuries, a total of 150 persons.[15] An arbitrary deflation of the figure to 75 percent reduces the number with colonial ancestors to 132; adding that to the original 101 raises the colonial ancestral group to 233—64 percent of the 363 for whom some information was available. By comparison, 46 percent of the total population and 52 percent of the white population in 1920 were of colonial origin. Either way, persons of colonial ancestry seem to have been slightly overrepresented among the New Deal intellectuals.

Thirty-three members of the group were third-generation American, 18 percent of the total. Since the exact number of third-generation Americans in the total population is unknown, an index of representation for the group cannot be computed. For whatever it may be worth, the proportions of Old Immigrants—Germans, Irish, and Scandinavians—in both populations were about the same. The Old Immigration may therefore have been randomly represented in the New Deal elite. Second-generation Americans constituted 13 percent of the New Deal intelligentsia and 22 percent of the population; their index of representation was 0.59. As already noted, the southern and eastern European immigrants were even less well represented. The most plausible, if tentative, conclusions are that the colonial ancestral group was slightly overrepresented, the third generation probably equally represented, and the second and immigrant generations somewhat underrepresented in the New Deal elite.[16]

The New Deal intellectuals also originated with approximate equality in every major geographical subdivision of the United States. Thirty-seven of its members were born in New England, 86 in the Middle Atlantic states, 115 in the Middle West, 58 in the South, and 24 in the Far West.[17] In the

[15] Trevor, "Analysis of the American Immigration Act of 1924," classifies as colonial anyone whose ancestors arrived before 1820; in our analysis everyone who could trace at least one side of the family back into the eighteenth century or earlier was classified as colonial. Since few immigrants arrived in the United States during the first twenty years of the nineteenth century, the chances of significant error seemed slight.

[16] See Trevor, "Analysis of the American Immigration Act of 1924"; and *The Statistical History of the United States from Colonial Times to the Present* (Stamford, Conn., 1965), 56ff.

[17] The regions were defined as follows. New England—Maine, New Hampshire, Vermont, Massachusetts, Rhode Island, Connecticut. Middle Atlantic—New York, New Jersey, Pennsylvania, Delaware, West Virginia, Maryland. South—Virginia, Kentucky,

census of 1890, the year closest to the group's mean birth year of 1893, New England contained 8 percent of the nation's population; its share of the New Deal elite came to 10 percent. The comparable figures for the Middle Atlantic states were 24 percent of the population and 24 percent of the group; for the South, 28 percent and 16 percent, respectively; for the Middle West, 35 and 32 percent; and for the Far West, 5 and 7 percent. The slight overrepresentations of New England and the Far West do not seem to indicate any significant discrimination in patterns of recruitment. The greater underrepresentation of the South can probably be explained by the region's substandard levels of wealth, education, and urbanization—three indices on which the New Deal intellectuals were well above the national average.

The important distinctions between the New Deal intellectuals and the rest of their countrymen began along rural and urban lines. One-third of them were born in rural areas, while two-thirds of the population was still, by the census definition, considered rural.[18] In addition, 18 percent of the New Deal elite was born on farms when 42 percent of the national work force was still employed in agriculture. Conversely, two-thirds of the New Dealers were born in urban areas when only one-third of the population resided in them. The intra-urban breakdowns are even more revealing. In 1890, 6 percent of the population lived in urban clusters of more than 500,000; 19 percent of the New Deal intellectuals were born in metropolitan areas. Eleven percent of the population lived in cities ranging from 50,000 to 500,000; 21 percent of the New Deal elite originated in medium-sized cities. Sixteen percent of the population lived in the remaining urban areas of 2,500 to 50,000; 27 percent of the New Deal intellectuals were born in small cities. The indices of representation decline from about 3 for the metropolitan-born, to about 2 for those born in medium-sized cities, to 1.69 for those born in small cities, to 0.5 for the rural-born. The New Deal intellectuals originated as an urban elite in a rural society.

As they pursued their careers, they concentrated even more heavily in urban areas.[19] By 1933, 100 lived in metropolitan New York, 66 in Wash-

---

Tennessee, North Carolina, South Carolina, Georgia, Alabama, Florida, Mississippi, Arkansas, Louisiana, Oklahoma, Texas. Middle West—Ohio, Michigan, Indiana, Illinois, Wisconsin, Minnesota, North Dakota, South Dakota, Iowa, Nebraska, Kansas, Missouri. Far West—Montana, Idaho, Wyoming, Utah, Colorado, New Mexico, Arizona, Nevada, California, Oregon, Washington. Information was available for 354 of the 380. Included in the 354 but not classified were the 27 immigrants, 3 born in the District of Columbia, and 4 born abroad of American parents.

[18] These calculations were based on a denominator of 345.

[19] The analysis of pre–New Deal urbanization rests on data for 353 persons; for the post–New Deal, data were available for 337 persons.

ington, 35 in Boston, 24 in Chicago, and 12 in Philadelphia; on the eve of the New Deal, 237 members of the group, two-thirds of the total, had thus concentrated in the five largest metropolitan areas of the industrial and urban Northeast. The rest had also become more urbanized by 1933. With one or two exceptions, they were all working in sizable urban areas when recruited by the New Deal. Even the agricultural intellectuals were no longer rural; they were well-educated scientists and publicists seeking to place their talents and knowledge at the service of the nation's farmers.

Throughout the period, the intellectuals continued to concentrate in northern and eastern cities. At the end of World War II, 170 worked in Washington and 63 in New York, 76 percent of the group's surviving members; and the five largest metropolitan areas in the Northeast provided work for 81 percent of its members. The rest were dispersed across the country in medium-sized cities and in metropolitan areas outside the industrial Northeast. While two-fifths of the American population was still rural, almost 100 percent of the New Deal elite had become urbanized—heavily concentrated in a handful of large metropolitan areas in the northeastern quadrant of the country.[20]

The New Deal intellectuals were further differentiated from the rest of American society along class lines. The majority of them were born into the nation's middle, upper middle, and upper classes; by 1933 they were overwhelmingly concentrated in the upper middle class, with a few still middle class and a smaller number still upper class.[21]

Seventy-two of the intellectuals' fathers were businessmen. Among this group, 16 were big businessmen; they were multimillionaires, railroad barons, investment brokers, and merchant princes in large urban areas. Twenty-seven were engaged in merchandising: a few in sizable and lucra-

---

[20] In 1930 and 1940 the national population was 44 percent rural; in 1950 it was 33 percent rural. See *Statistical History of the United States*, 14.

[21] The analysis rests on data for 188 of the families and 357 of the group's members. The absence of data for 192 fathers and the difficulties involved in class analysis make this the most tentative part of the essay. The definitions adopted may not satisfy the reader's desire for analytical rigor, but we hope they will appeal to his common sense. Persons were considered upper class if they had incomes or accumulations of wealth in the millions; upper middle class rankings were given to all persons in prestigious professions and in affluent business occupations of high status unless other evidence indicated another classification was more appropriate; middle class was equated with middle status occupations; lower middle class was equated with low-paying low status white-collar work; aside from farmers, all who earned their livings by manual labor were considered workers. Farmers were classed as upper middle, middle, and lower middle class on the basis of income and standard of living. For discussion, see Robin Williams, *American Society*, rev. ed. (New York, 1960), 87ff., and Seymour Martin Lipset, *Revolution and Counter Revolution* (New York, 1968), 87ff. For a more sophisticated class analysis, see Sidney H. Aronson, *Status and Kinship in the Higher Civil Service* (Cambridge, Mass., 1964), 84ff.

tive concerns, but most as small retailers or proprietors of general stores. There were 2 contractors, 3 small-town bankers, 4 manufacturers, 6 engineers, and 9 in service enterprises: real estate agents, salesmen, hotel proprietors, and insurance brokers. The remainder included a partner in a papermill supply firm, 3 in miscellaneous occupations, and 3 listed in the sources simply as businessmen.

Twenty-one of the business fathers participated directly in the modern industrial sector of the economy, as employees of the large corporations that guided the nation's late nineteenth- and early twentieth-century drive to economic maturity; their share of the business fathers group was 29 percent, and 11 percent of the total parental group. The other business fathers were in preindustrial occupations. Mercantile and service enterprises are almost as old as the division of labor—although the Industrial Revolution undoubtedly affected their technology and their methods of operation. Banking is similarly preindustrial. The miscellaneous remaining business occupations were also not direct products of the Industrial Revolution. Nearly three-fourths of the business fathers were associated with preindustrial or nonindustrial sectors of the system.

The relation between the distribution of business occupations and the reformist careers of the New Deal intellectuals is not immediately obvious. No one has ever clearly shown how different parental business experiences shape the social and political attitudes of businessmen's children. Merchants in large urban areas may have more in common with industrialists than with their brethren presiding over general stores at country crossroads. The banking fraternity may be a fraternity no matter what the size of the banks within it; small-town banks may be linked to the economy's modern sector by their investments, the location of their reserves, and their interest in community economic development.

Even if lines of affinity and cohesion could be drawn around different subgroups among the business fathers, we would still not know how their children were affected by their fathers' careers. Some of them, after the fashion of Richard Hofstadter's progressives,[22] may have been moved to reform because industrial capitalism had undermined the status and power of their familes; hostility to the new economic order may have been part of their patrimonies. Or since they came from preindustrial sectors of the business community, they may not have understood or sympathized with the system; ignorance and lack of feeling may have driven them into reform careers. On the other hand, their fathers may have taken vicarious pride in the nation's industrial affluence; instead of bequeathing biases against it to their children, they may have conveyed a sense of patriotic

[22] *The Age of Reform from Bryan to FDR* (New York, 1960), 131ff.

esteem. The fathers' business occupations may also have been wholly unrelated to the children's subsequent social and political attitudes. Whatever the case, the line between parental business careers and filial reform interests has not yet been clearly drawn.[23]

The only supportable conclusion is that the proportion of business fathers in the parental group was higher than the proportion of businessmen in the national labor force.[24] In 1900, 14 percent of the work force was in business, while 39 percent of the New Deal fathers were so employed. In addition, persons in mercantile occupations constituted 7 percent of the labor force and 14 percent of the New Deal fathers. One percent of the labor force and 11 percent of the New Deal fathers were involved in large business enterprises. Since the mercantile fathers were overrepresented by a factor of 2 and the big business fathers overrepresented by a factor of 11, the big business fathers were disproportionately represented in comparison to the mercantile paternal group.[25]

Generally, the business fathers held positions of high rank and status. Without exception they belonged to the middle, upper middle, and upper classes. As local notables, small-town bankers stand high in prestige and usually earn incomes well above the community average. Less prominent perhaps, local manufacturers are usually affluent, and their economic power exceeds the communal norm. Formerly, the operators of general stores were figures of renown in their communities, with larger than average incomes and accumulations of wealth. If there was a national upper class at the turn of the century, some of the big businessmen belonged to it. Only the salesmen, the real estate agents, and the others in service enterprises were lodged near the middle levels of the social hierarchy. Some of them may have deserved higher rankings; although their occupations were probably of middling prestige, their incomes may have been well above average.[26]

---

[23] That goes for David Donald as well as for Hofstadter; see *Lincoln Reconsidered* (New York, 1947), 19ff.

[24] These calculations were based on the distribution of persons in occupations in 1900, as listed in *Statistical History of the United States*, 75–78.

[25] Sales and service personnel were 4 percent of both groups.

[26] In the late 1940s and early 1960s the status of 90 occupations was ranked after a sample of adult American opinion. In 1947 corporation board members ranked 18 out of 90, and in 1963 17.5 out of 90; the corresponding figures for bankers were 10.5 and 24.5; for accountants in large businesses, 29 and 29.5; factory owners employing 100 workers, 26.5 and 31.5; building contractors, 34 and 31.5; insurance agents, 51.5 in both surveys; traveling salesmen, 51.5 and 57. See Robert W. Hodge et al., "Occupational Prestige in the United States: 1925–1963," in Reinhard Bendix and Seymour Martin Lipset, eds., *Class, Status, and Power*, 2nd ed. (New York, 1966), 322–34. Unfortunately we do not know whether these rankings would have been duplicated by polls had they been taken at the turn of the century.

If middle class is equated with middle level occupational status, independent of the level of income, perhaps as many as 30 of the business fathers belonged in that social category. An additional 27 can be considered upper middle class: some of the business executives, the engineers, general store proprietors, merchants, bankers, and manufacturers. Nine of the fathers belonged to the nation's upper class: Edward Harriman, who could be counted twice, once for his daughter, Mary, and once for his son, W. Averell; David Eccles, multimillionaire and regional magnate with an empire of banks, lumber companies, sugar refineries, and railroads; the senior MacLeish, partner in Chicago's Carson Pirie Scott & Company; Nathan Straus's father, with Macy's in New York; Robert Straus's father, also a Macy's partner; Gardner Jackson's father, whose Colorado enterprises included banks, railroads, and mines; Josephine Roche's father, another wealthy and powerful Colorado businessman; Henry Morgenthau, Sr., financier, lawyer, prominent Democrat; and Warren Delano, Franklin Roosevelt's great-uncle, father of Frederic A., China trader, and New York aristocrat. Another six might also be considered upper class: John Collier's father, Atlanta banker, lawyer, and mayor of the city; Harold Loeb's father, stockbroker and relative of the Loeb of Kuhn, Loeb, Schiff and Co.; Francis B. Sayre's father, Robert H., engineer, railroad president, and Bethlehem Steel executive; Robert E. Sherwood's father, a stockbroker; the senior Ferdinand Silcox, cotton factor, naval stores broker, and president of Charleston Cotton Mill; Charles Stanley, father of William, landed aristocrat, bank president, Maryland state legislator, and state government official. If these 15 were in fact members of a national upper class, then 21 percent of the business fathers and 8 percent of the total number of fathers of the New Deal elite belonged to the upper level of the American social hierarchy.

The professional fathers also came from the upper echelons of American society, although fewer of them belonged to its upper class.[27] Constituting 27 percent of the parental group, the 8 doctors, 24 lawyers, 5 college professors, 6 journalists, 4 school administrators, 1 teacher, 1 judge, and 1 dentist occupied high or middle status positions. In 1900 their professions made up about 3 percent of the labor force; their index of representation is 9—a factor four times larger than the index of representation for business fathers.

The overrepresentation of clerical fathers was even greater. The 19

[27] See ibid. Physicians ranked 2.5 and 2; lawyers, 18 and 11; college professors, 8 in both polls; public school teachers, 36 and 29.5; county judges, 13 and 14; dentists, 18 and 14; ministers, 13 and 17.5; newspaper columnists, 42.5 and 46; newspaper reporters, 48 in both polls.

ministers—4 Unitarians, 4 Congregationalists, 2 otherwise unspecified Protestants, 2 Episcopalians, 2 Presbyterians, 2 Baptists, 1 Methodist, 1 Disciple of Christ, and 1 Methodist-Congregationalist—constituted 10 percent of the group, while the entire ministerial cohort was only 0.4 percent of the labor force in 1900; the ministers were overrepresented by a factor of 25.

Two of the professional and clerical fathers seem to have been upper class: the elder Acheson, Episcopal bishop of Connecticut, and the father of Edward S. Greenbaum, a New York state supreme court justice. Thirty-eight were upper middle class: the dentist, the doctors, the 18 remaining clergymen, the lawyers, and the college professors. The other 11 were middle class: the journalists, the school administrator, and the school teacher.

Altogether, business and professional fathers make up 75 percent of the paternal group. As many as 17 of them were upper class, 83 upper middle class, and 42 middle class.[28] If the New Deal intellectuals ran well ahead in the race of life, it was in part because so many of them began with a considerable head start. Their achievements may have rested on solid merit, but that merit in turn rested on the ascriptive advantages they acquired from their families.[29]

The remaining parents included 27 farmers, 8 government and business functionaries, and 11 workers. Three of the farmers were well-to-do and have been included in the upper middle class. The 19 who owned or farmed between 100 and 500 acres and earned comfortable livings have been placed in the middle class.[30] The remaining 5 were poor and have

[28] A more subtle analysis might alter some of the classifications. On the basis of family connections and prestige, for example, the parents of Adlai Stevenson, Michael Straight, and Thomas and Charles William Eliot II might have been considered upper class.

[29] Even the black New Dealers fit into this pattern. With few exceptions, they were light-skinned and well educated—not only better educated than their fellow blacks but also better educated than the average white. Their parents in turn belonged to the highest ranks of the black community. See Motz, "The Black Cabinet," 21ff.; Richard Bardolph, *The Negro Vanguard* (New York, 1959), 346–48; William Trent, Jr., to Thomas Krueger, 22 Sept. 1971.

[30] The New Dealers themselves, of course, overwhelmingly rejected farming as an occupation—perhaps an indication of the lower occupational status it has acquired in modern America. For an illustration of parental dissatisfaction with farm life, see John Carmody, memoir, Oral History Collection, Columbia University; and for an illustration of its rigors, see Chester Davis, memoir, also in the Oral History Collection. The difference between the total number of farm-born and the total number of farmer fathers results from the different criteria used to classify the data; farm-born means what it says, nothing more; fathers were classed as farmers if farming occupied most of their working lives or if they preferred farming to all other occupations they may have held.

been included in the lower middle class, along with the government and business functionaries.

The working-class parental group contained 5 artisans, men of special skills who operated their own concerns, 2 who combined work and farming, 2 who combined work and business, and 2 listed in the sources simply as poor workers. They take up only 6 percent of the group's parents, while at least 38 percent of the labor force at the turn of the century could be considered working class; at a minimum, workers were underrepresented by a factor of 0.16. They also represented a small segment of the nation's proletariat. With the possible exception of the two poor workers, they were completely uninvolved in the nation's growing heavy industries. Like so many of the business fathers, they were engaged in trades or employed at jobs that antedated the Industrial Revolution.

No more than 13 percent of the New Deal intellectuals made the quantum leap from the lower middle and working classes into the upper middle class prior to their recruitment into the New Deal. The few that made the leap jumped from the upper rungs of the lower social orders, not from the bottom.[31]

The New Deal intellectuals not only began with a head start, but they also widened the distance between them and the rest of the population as they ran. They attended college, completed graduate and professional training, and then entered the most respected professions in the country. By highest level of education attained, the New Deal elite was strikingly marked off from the rest of the American population. Thirteen attended college without graduating, 44 graduated, 27 had graduate work without obtaining a master's degree, 38 had the master's or its equivalent, 13 had graduate work beyond the master's, 75 had the primary law degree, and

---

[31] The totals and percentages for each class were: upper class, 17 parents, 9 percent; upper middle class, 86 parents, 46 percent; middle class, 61 parents, 32 percent; lower middle class, 13 parents, 7 percent; working class, 11 parents, 6 percent. The parents were more widely dispersed through the class system, the children more heavily concentrated in the upper middle class, and proportionately fewer of the children belonged to either the upper or middle classes. The data indicate nothing whatever about aggregate social mobility in twentieth-century America. The correct methods for measuring total social mobility are discussed in Stephan Thernstrom and Peter Knights, "Men in Motion: Some Data and Speculations about Urban Population Mobility in Nineteenth-Century America," *Journal of Interdisciplinary History*, 1 (Autumn 1970), esp. 16–23, and Daniel Scott Smith, "Cyclical, Secular, and Structural Change in American Elite Composition," *Perspectives in American History*, 4 (1970), 351–74. To measure aggregate mobility, we need to know how many potentially mobile there were, how far they went both proportionately and numerically, how many opportunities there were, and how these changed over time. For erroneous conclusions about aggregate social mobility based on studies of American business elites, see W. Lloyd Warner and James C. Abegglen, *Big Business Leaders in America* (New York, 1963), 31–33.

126 had Ph.D.'s. In addition, 4 had medical degrees, 4 others divinity degrees of various kinds, and one had a master of laws. The combined doctorate and professional degrees equal 209, 59 percent of the total group. Only 36 failed to attend college, no more than 10 percent of the 380. Conversely, 90 percent of the New Deal intellectuals attended college when less than 10 percent of the eligible 17-year-old population went beyond high school; almost three-fifths of the group had doctorate and professional degrees when less than one-tenth of a percent of the total number of high school graduates went on to the Ph.D.[32]

The New Deal intellectuals graduated from a scattered and diverse group of 133 educational institutions, ranging from the most prestigious Ivy League schools to the Chautauqua Institute. Harvard led in bachelor's degrees conferred with 31, followed by Yale and Wisconsin with 16 each, Columbia with 12, Cornell with 11, Chicago 10, Princeton, Amherst, and CCNY 9 apiece, Pennsylvania 6, and Texas and Williams 5 each. Fifty-two schools awarded the master's degrees: Harvard granted 28, Columbia 19, Wisconsin 15, Chicago, Cornell, and Michigan 4 each, and Berkeley, Pennsylvania, and Princeton 3 apiece. The doctorate and law degrees were conferred by a smaller number of institutions. The Ph.D.'s came from 26 schools, Harvard granting 31, Columbia 23, Wisconsin 17, Chicago 10, the Brookings Institute Graduate School 8, Johns Hopkins 5, Cornell and Michigan 4 each, Pennsylvania 3, and Yale, Princeton, and Berkeley 2 each. Twenty-three schools produced the New Deal lawyers: Harvard 38, Columbia 10, Chicago 8, Yale 4, New York University 3, and George Washington, National University, and Kent Law College 2 each.[33] Drawn from every section of the country, the New Deal elite was initially processed through a diverse group of colleges and universities, then further refined at about 40 prestigious graduate and professional schools. The end product was an educated elite remarkably similar in outlook, training, and lifestyle.

Their class origins predisposed the New Deal intellectuals to be interested in community affairs. Their professional training reinforced their preexisting inclinations by requiring them to be concerned about subjects directly bearing on matters of public policy. By the early 1930s most of them had demonstrated their commitments; they had taken part in civic crusades, embarked on careers in government, worked for voluntary organizations, written about questions with broad social implications, joined

[32] The denominator for these calculations was 355.

[33] Discrepancies between the total number of each degree awarded and the totals given by highest level of education attained resulted from the differences between the two indices. Highest level of education and number of each degree are partially separate and partially overlapping categories. Here information was available for 355 persons.

professional associations, and taken out membership in at least one fashionable urban club. In the twentieth century, civic consciousness, participation in voluntary organizations, and memberships in clubs and professional associations have been distinctive characteristics of the privileged members of American society.[34]

The class character of the New Deal elite emerges even more clearly from a consideration of the occupations of its members. The vast majority were recruited directly from the professions. One-third—or 115—came from universities: 60 from economics departments, 26 from law schools, 12 from political science, and 17 from an assortment of professorial occupations. The university professoriate was overrepresented in the New Deal elite by a factor of about 32,000. Social service organizations sent 40 persons to the New Deal elite; they were overrepresented by a factor of around 3,333. The 53 lawyers constituted 15 percent of the New Deal intelligentsia and about .003 percent of the labor force, giving the lawyers overrepresentation by a factor of 5,000. Taken together, the professors, lawyers, and social workers constitute 58 percent of the group. Many of their other colleagues were also professionals. Twenty-six came from journalism, including Henry Wallace, who could have been classed as scientist, economist, or businessman. Thirty-eight were already in federal government service by 1933, and another 20 left state and local government jobs to join the New Deal. There were also 24 businessmen, 15 students, 10 college administrators, 5 artists, 3 grade school teachers, 2 trade union economists, 2 politicians, 2 Roman Catholic priests, 1 high school administrator, and 1 doctor. Classifying the students, businessmen, politicians, priests, and artists as nonprofessional brings that group's share of the total to 15 percent. In addition, the unknowns are 5 percent of the total. At a minimum then, 80 percent of the New Deal elite came from the professions, the haven of the American upper middle class.[35]

To summarize: the New Deal intellectuals were scarcely distinguishable from the bulk of the American population in their ethnic, ancestral,

[34] Arnold Rose, *The Power Structure* (New York, 1967), 169ff.; G. William Domhof, *Who Rules America* (Englewood Cliffs, 1967), 18–19; E. Digby Baltzell, *The Protestant Establishment* (New York, 1964), 353–79.

[35] The denominator for these percentages was 357; ratios of different occupations were calculated on the basis of figures given for 1930 in *Statistical History of the United States*, 75ff. By 1933, 21 of the New Dealers were upper class, 307 upper middle class, and 31 middle class; the corresponding percentages were 6, 85, and 9. The sociology of intellectuals and their professions is a fascinating blend of narcissism, insight, and nonsense. For examples, see Karl Mannheim, *Ideology and Utopia* (New York, 1936); John Kenneth Galbraith, *The New Industrial State* (New York: Signet Book, 1968); Talcott Parsons, "Professions," *International Encyclopedia of the Social Sciences*, vol. 12, 536–46; and Everett C. Hughes, "Professions," *Daedalus*, 92 (Fall 1963), 655–68.

and regional origins. They were marked off from their countrymen by their urban and middle-, upper middle, and upper-class origins, by their high level of education, by their professional occupations, and by their upper middle class position in the social hierarchy.

Whether the group's unique characteristics determined the polices its members supported and automatically rendered it incapable of serving the interests of the rest of the population cannot be decided on *a priori* grounds; the iron law of oligarchy may or may not have worked its immutable will. The social composition of a leadership elite is one thing; the interests it furthers are another. Despite marked differences from the rest of the population, the New Deal elite might still have worked for the benefit of the American masses. Together with their political allies, the New Deal intellectuals tried, with some measure of success, to serve the nation's lower orders: workers, migrant farmers, sharecroppers, the New Immigrants, even blacks on occasion. They consciously desired to satisfy the test of utilitarian democracy: to provide the greatest good for the greatest number. Their failures can be ascribed only in small part—if at all—to the inexorable operation of the iron law of oligarchy. Indeed the New Deal elite could have been more unrepresentative than it was, but its policy proposals might still have satisfied the test of utilitarian democracy.

Democratic principle was, however, violated by the inegalitarian relation between the elite and the underrepresented and nonrepresented segments of the population. The relation was essentially asymmetrical. It lacked the parity of common life experiences, shared adult aspirations, and rough equality in power and prestige. When professional and humanitarian concerns moved the New Deal intellectuals to discover for themselves how the other half lived, the sympathy and understanding that developed were tinged with pity, the condescending attitude of a superior toward his less fortunate inferiors. The intellectuals from the sovereign realms of wealth, status, and power who extended their sympathies to the lower orders never asked the lower orders to reciprocate; nor would voluntary reciprocity have been welcomed. Although occasionally asked to have patience with their betters, the lower classes were not asked to understand the social, economic, political, and personal problems of the upper classes. The relation between the two groups was always unbalanced: sympathy and power flowed downward; gratitude and a little patience were all that were supposed to flow upward.

The lower orders have the problems; the upper classes have the solutions. The power to solve implies fate control; the upper orders must and will decide, even if occasionally the decisions clearly conflict with the interests of the lower classes. Here, if anywhere, the iron law of oligarchy applies; it is not so much that decisions are taken by a small inner clique as that when they clash with the interests of the nonrepresented, there is no way to counter them. The problem of the unorganized lower orders is that they ordinarily lack the power so readily at the disposal of the upper middle and upper classes: the power to initiate and the power to obstruct.[36]

Some of the New Dealers were acutely aware of the dangers inherent in the disparity in power between government bureaucrats and the lower-class beneficiaries of government programs. They sought with mixed success to increase popular understanding of government policy and popular participation in government programs: Mrs. Roosevelt's tireless attempts at public education, the fireside chats, local administration of crop-reduction programs, black and white voting in AAA elections, autonomous tribal councils for the Indians, and workers voting to select their own collective bargaining representatives. These remedial measures may have partially diminished the conflict inherent in the asymmetrical relation between the upper and lower orders. Complete resolution of it may have been politically impossible. Whether more could have been done to mitigate it is an open question; the evidence may be available, but no one has yet bothered to gather and analyze it.[37]

The New Deal intellectual elite not only differed from the rest of American society, but it was also distinct from other modern American elites.[38] It contained more blacks, more Jews, and more women. Although

[36] Robert Michels, *Political Parties*, tr. Eden and Cedar Paul (New York, 1959), 377ff. J. David Greenstone, *Labor in American Politics* (New York, 1969), 59ff., contains an excellent critique of the iron law of oligarchy. For an illustration of what the lower orders think of privileged intellectuals, see Robert Coles, "Understanding White Racists," *New York Review of Books*, 17 (30 Dec. 1971), 12–15.

[37] The dangers of participatory democracy at the grass roots are well described in Philip Selznick, *TVA and the Grass Roots* (Berkeley, 1953).

[38] Other modern American elites are analyzed in C. Wright Mills, *The Power Elite* (New York, 1956); G. William Domhof, *Who Rules America*, and *The Higher Circles* (New York, 1970); Donald Matthews, *The Social Background of Political Decision-Makers* (Garden City, 1954) and *U.S. Senators and Their World* (Chapel Hill, 1960); Warner and Abegglen, *Big Business Leaders in America*; Morris Janowitz, *The Professional Soldier* (New York, 1960); Ari Hoogenboom, "Industrialism and Political Leadership: A Case Study of the United States Senate," in Frederic C. Jaher, ed., *The Age of Industrialism in America* (New York, 1968), 49ff.; Andrew Hacker, "The Elect and the Annointed: Two American Elites," *American Political Science Review*, 55 (Sept. 1961), 539–49; W. Lloyd Warner et al., *The American Federal Executive* (New Haven, 1963); Reinhard Bendix, *Higher Civil Servants in America*, University of Colorado Studies, Series in Sociology, no. 1 (July 1949); David T. Stanley et al., *Men Who Govern* (Washington, 1967); Mabel Newcomer, *The Big Business Executive* (New York, 1955); Gabriel Kolko, *The Roots of American Foreign Policy* (Boston, 1969); Waldo H. Heinrichs, Jr., "Bureaucracy and Professionalism in the Development of American Career Diplomacy," in John Braeman, ed., *Modern America: Twentieth-*

its pattern of urbanization is comparable to that of big business elites, it differs significantly from the congressional elite in this respect; most senators and congressmen retain their regional residential affiliations, and many of them live in small and medium-sized urban areas. Despite the abnormally high level of education in every modern American elite, the educational level of the New Deal elite was much higher than that of other elite groups. The long-term rise in the educational level of American elites has still not brought some of them up to the level attained by the New Deal intellectuals forty years ago.

The New Deal intelleculs were also much younger than their chief political rivals. With a mean birth year of 1893, they were forty on the average when they entered Roosevelt's service. Since 224 were born after 1889, three-fifths of them were in their early forties or younger when the New Deal began. The members of most other American elites have been much older at the peaks of their careers. Federal civil service personnel and federal political executives reach the top in their late forties; business executives assume company presidencies and board chairmanships in their early fifties; admirals and generals obtain their ranks from their late forties to their late fifties; in the late 1930s the average age of United States senators was fifty-eight.

The New Deal intellectuals were also distinguishable from the conservative political leaders of the Progressive era and presumably distinct from their conservative contemporaries as well. If Republican leaders had not changed since the Progressive period, they would have been of old American and Anglo-Saxon stock, more urban than the national average, and members of the nation's upper and upper middle classes. Better educated than the average American, they would have been heavily recruited from banking, industry, law, and journalism. On these indices, they would have resembled the New Deal intellectuals.

On others, differences would have appeared. The Republican elite would have had fewer blacks and Jews, and probably fewer women. It would have contained a smaller percentage of Ph.D.'s. It would have been recruited more from business than from the professions. Its business recruits would have generally come from industrial and financial enterprises rather than from mercantile concerns. It would have more equitably repre-

Century American Foreign Policy (Columbus, Ohio, 1971); Richard Barnet, *Intervention and Revolution* (New York, 1968); James N. Rosenau, *National Leadership and Foreign Policy* (Princeton, 1963). For general bibliography, see Carl J. Beck and J. Thomas McKechnie, *Political Elites: A Select Computerized Bibliography* (Cambridge, Mass., 1968).

sented the different regions of the country and the smaller and medium-sized cities. As the Republican regulars of the Progressive era were older than their reform opponents, so probably would the regulars of the 1930s have been older than the New Deal intellectuals.[39]

In addition, the two groups served different political masters. Conservatives in Congress represented clearly defined geographical areas. Although drawn in large measure from the urban and industrial Northeast, the New Deal intellectuals represented the area in only a tenuous sense. They had been called, not sent, to Washington. They could not be voted out of office. They were responsible to the president, not to the region from which they came. Their only other obligation, if they had one, was to Congress, which could block their appointments, attack them with impunity, and try to prevent payment of their salaries. As the president's servants, they were caught up in the historic conflict between the executive and legislative branches of the government—a conflict inflamed in the 1930s by the New Deal's relentless executive activism, the doubling of the federal budget, and the two-thirds expansion in the total number of federal employees.[40]

The New Deal intelligentsia's distinctive characteristics provided the materials for the scarecrow that caught the conservatives' vision and stood at the center of so many of their polemics: the young and inexperienced college professor duping an unwitting president into leading the nation toward a collectivist apocalypse—fascism, socialism, or communism.[41] It was the stuff of much business hostility to the New Deal; light-headed academic theorists who had never met a payroll had been granted power at the expense of practical men who were accustomed to running the

[39] On the pre–World War I conservatives, see Norman Wilensky, *Conservatives in the Progressive Era: The Taft Republicans of 1912*, University of Florida Monographs, Social Sciences, no. 25 (Winter 1965). This should be supplemented by Jerome Martin Clubb, "Congressional Opponents of Reform, 1901–1913," Ph.D. thesis (University of Washington, 1963); David P. Thelen, "Social Tensions and the Origins of Progressivism," *Journal of American History*, 56 (Sept. 1969), 323–41; and William T. Kerr, Jr., "The Progressives of Washington, 1910–1912," *Pacific Northwest Quarterly*, 55 (Jan. 1964), 16–27. The New Deal elite also differs from the foreign policy and national security elites of the twentieth-century; both have been recruited almost exclusively from the nation's upper class, in contrast to the New Deal's heavier recruitment from the upper middle class, and neither group reached the average level of education attained by the New Deal elite. For details, see tne studies by Heinrichs, Rosenau, Domhof, Barnet, Kolko, and Stanley et al., cited in n. 38.

[40] Data on the budget and the bureaucracy come from *Statistical History of the United States*, 710–11.

[41] For examples, see Schlesinger, *The Coming of the New Deal*, 472ff., and *The Politics of Upheaval*, 544–45, 604ff.; and George Ira Wolfskill and John A. Hudson, *All but the People* (London, 1969).

government or having the government run to serve their interests.[42] At the leadership level, the political conflicts of the Roosevelt era were grounded in sharply defined cleavages in American society.

The pluralist character of American politics severely limited the New Deal intellectuals' ability to achieve their political objectives. In conflicts with others, their claims to hegemony in determining public policy were morally and functionally indistinguishable from the claims of rival political and economic interest groups. No mechanism existed to give automatic primacy to their analyses and policy recommendations. They lacked both the power and the authority to impose their views on other organizations or, in serious conflicts over policy, on the president.

Rival elites had developed superior financial and organizational resources to promote their interests and advance their vision of the general welfare. Business, agriculture, and labor worked through lobbies with hired staffs and independent incomes; through trade associations, farm organizations, and nonpartisan leagues they presented their case in public, fought for legislative objectives, and moved into electoral politics to reward their friends and punish their enemies. Deeply entrenched in the federal courts, American conservatives executed effective rearguard action against the New Deal until the middle of 1937; then they resorted to party and legislative agencies to frustrate New Deal aspirations.

The New Deal elite, on the other hand, lacked organizational coherence. Split into small subgroups, it failed to create an agency to coordinate its objectives and to enable it to survive adverse turns in its political fortunes. A band of self-conscious and self-styled idealists formed around Harry Hopkins, deeply convinced of its own rectitude and deeply suspicious of those who did not belong to it.[43] The social workers rallied behind the practical and unemotional reformism of Frances Perkins and Arthur Altmeyer.[44] Orbiting bicentrically around Mary McLeod Bethune and Robert C. Weaver, the Black Cabineteers developed unified positions on policy matters of concern to their people, but were seldom asked to coop-

---

[42] Roosevelt recruited proportionately more educators than either Truman or Eisenhower; see Stanley et al., *Men Who Govern*, 132.

[43] Aubrey Williams, "Draft Autobiography: A Southern Rebel," Williams Papers, in Franklin D. Roosevelt Memorial Library, Hyde Park.

[44] Ibid. See also the sketches of Miss Perkins and Altmeyer in *Current Biography*, *1940*, 643–46, and *1946*, 14–15. For a test of Altmeyer's quality, see his *Formative Years of Social Security*, and of Miss Perkins', see Frances Perkins to FDR, 12 Mar. 1935, PSF, Box 24, Roosevelt Library, Hyde Park, and her *The Roosevelt I Knew* (New York, 1946).

erate with the white grouplets within the New Deal elite.[45] The Brandeisians and legal technicians worked with Thomas Corcoran and Benjamin Cohen for immediate legislative objectives.[46] Ephemeral study groups formed to look for ways to revive the stagnant economy.[47] By the end of the 1930s, numerous Keynesians, both converts to the faith and novices in it, had become important in the councils of government; they were united by their personal connections with the great man and by their adherence to the doctrines and commandments of *The General Theory of Employment, Interest, and Money*.[48] Throughout the period, an amorphous group of planners waged a losing battle for economic rationality in the National Recovery Administration, the Bureau of Agricultural Economics, the National Resources Planning Board, and the Bureau of the Budget; on the fringes, the National Economic and Social Planning Association provided a forum for them in its journal, *Plan Age*.[49]

Whatever political unity these grouplets possessed was provided almost entirely by the president; he was the only one who ever came close to coordinating their divergent interests and programs. Unable to become masters of their own political destiny, they were far more dependent on Roosevelt than he was on them—emotionally as well as politically. He was their main strength; they were only a small part of his. As he often reminded them, he was obligated to many others: to powerful southerners on congressional committees, to a sizable part of the business community, to organized labor and organized agriculture, to the Democratic party.[50] If they embarrassed him, they could be dispatched on unimportant missions abroad, relegated to less consequential positions in the government, or

[45] Motz, "The Black Cabinet."

[46] Alsop and Kintner, *Men around the President*; also Schlesinger, *The Politics of Upheaval*, 386ff.

[47] Vol. 1 of Thomas I. Emerson's memoir in the Columbia Oral History Collection contains an example of one such group.

[48] For the Keynesians, see Stein, *Fiscal Revolution in America*, 91ff.; Galbraith, *New York Times Book Review*, 16 May 1965.

[49] Hawley, *New Deal and the Problem of Monopoly*; Kirkendall, *Social Scientists and Farm Politics*; Charles E. Merriam, "The National Resources Planning Board: A Chapter in American Planning Experience," *American Political Science Review*, 38 (Dec. 1944), 1075–88; Unofficial Observer, "Too Many Cooks: Big Bad Wolves vs. Little Hot Dogs," *Today*, 5 (2 Nov. 1935), 20–22; *Plan Age*, 1–7 (1934–40); Harold Smith, "Memos and Conferences: Daily Record," Smith Papers, Roosevelt Library, Hyde Park, especially the documents for these dates: 2 June 1939, 22 May 1943, 1 Oct. 1943, 31 Aug. 1944, 14 Mar. 1945, 13 Apr. 1945.

[50] Some of course were aware of Roosevelt's other obligations; Rexford Tugwell was perhaps most annoyed about them. For one who was less annoyed, see William E. Leuchtenburg, "The Great Depression and the New Deal," in John A. Garraty, ed., *Interpreting American History: Conversations with Historians* (London, 1970), II, 192.

simply dismissed from his service. When powerful congressmen went after them, he could do little to protect them. In the words of Lyndon B. Johnson, himself a New Dealer in his youth, he was the only president they had; they would not have another until the early 1960s.

Successful liberalization of the Democratic party in 1938 might have strengthened their position. With a progressive Congress, they might have had the political base they were never able to secure.[51] Some were on good terms with congressional progressives, others had staffed congressional committees, and their aspirations were in many cases shared by the Democratic left on Capitol Hill.[52]

The failure of the attempted purge and the advent of the war destroyed their chances of remaining close to power long enough to realize their broad objectives. As the world lurched toward war and the president lost control over the course of domestic events, reform declined in importance, and the New Deal became increasingly vulnerable. Under the cover of war, Congress killed the Civilian Conservation Corps, the National Resources Planning Board, the Work Projects Administration, and the National Youth Administration. It emasculated both the Bureau of Agricultural Economics and the Farm Security Administration. Public housing projects were built to house war workers, not the ill-housed one-third of the nation so prominent in the president's second inaugural. Minimum wages remained low, the social security system's coverage narrow, and its meager benefits held constant.[53]

Although most of the intellectuals stayed in government until 1945, they survived by avoiding notoriety or by adapting themselves to the war

[51] There is no comprehensive account of the so-called purge of 1938; the best description may still be in Basil Rauch, *History of the New Deal* (New York, 1944), reprinted in 1963 by Capricorn Books, 318–25. For an additional contribution to the history of the subject, see Thomas Krueger, *And Promises to Keep: The Southern Conference for Human Welfare, 1938–1948* (Nashville, 1967), 11–19.

[52] For illustrative material, see Rexford G. Tugwell, "Notes from a New Deal Diary," 10 Sept. 1935, Tugwell Papers, Roosevelt Library, Hyde Park; Schlesinger, *Politics of Upheaval*, 134ff.; Alsop and Kintner, *Men around the President*, 165. For evidence of common ideology, see J. Joseph Huthmacher, *Senator Robert F. Wagner and the Rise of Urban Liberalism* (New York, 1968), esp. 71, 292, 316; Frank Alan Coombes, "Senator Joseph Christopher O'Mahoney: The New Deal Years," Ph.D. thesis (University of Illinois, 1968), 207ff., and compare with the subsequent section of this essay.

[53] Salmond, *The Civilian Conservation Corps*, 215–17; Merriam, "The National Resources Planning Board." For the Farm Security Administration, see Baldwin, *Poverty and Politics*, 325–401. On the Bureau of Agricultural Economics, see Kirkendall, *Social Scientists and Farm Politics*, 218ff.; Altmeyer, *Formative Years of Social Security*, 118ff. On housing expenditures, see Nathan Straus, *The Seven Myths of Housing* (New York, 1944), 28n15. Other data were obtained from Richard Morris, *Encyclopedia of American History* (New York, 1953), vol. 1, 341ff.

effort. The controversial figures were humiliated, frustrated, or forced out. In 1942 Claude Wickard drove the irrepressible Gardner Jackson out of Agriculture. The following year, Clark Foreman left government, finding greater scope for his reform ambitions in Black Mountain College, the National Citizens' Political Action Committee, and the Southern Conference for Human Welfare. That same year, increasing congressional opposition to the Farm Security Administration forced C. B. Baldwin out of the government. By 1944–45, disgust at the difficulties of achieving reform in wartime Washington had driven many of the Black Cabineteers into private employment. In 1945, Congress blocked the appointment of Aubrey Williams, outspoken champion of the South's dispossessed, to the Rural Electrification Administration. First removed from the Board of Economic Warfare and then prevented from succeeding himself as vice-president, Henry Wallace was subjected to further indignity when his appointment as secretary of commerce was accompanied by removal of all loan agencies from that department; he was thereby prevented from using them as he had planned to stimulate postwar economic growth.[54]

During the transition from war to peace, the power of the New Deal elite diminished further. Although many joined the Truman administration, their hopes for careful planning to control the transition and to avert a postwar depression went unrealized as the inexperienced and badly informed president grappled ineptly with the massive problems of reconversion. Neither the Servicemen's Readjustment Act nor the Employment Act of 1945 met the planners' specifications. Price controls were ineffectively applied, large business dominated the reconversion process, and other powerful groups secured favors at the expense of the general interest.[55]

Even with a coherent organization of their own, the New Deal intel-

[54] On C. B. Baldwin, see S. Baldwin, *Poverty and Politics*, 390–96, and compare his interview in Studs Terkel, *Hard Times* (New York, 1970), 254–61. Dean Albertson, *Roosevelt's Farmer* (New York, 1961), 354–55, recounts Gardner Jackson's firing. For Aubrey Williams, see Leonard Dinnerstein, "The Senate's Rejection of Aubrey Williams as Rural Electrification Administrator," *Alabama Review*, 21 (Apr. 1968) 133–43. For Clark Foreman, see Krueger, *Promises*, 103–4; and *Current Biography, 1948*, 219–21. For the Black Cabineteers, see Motz, "The Black Cabinet," 31–33. On Henry Wallace, see Russell Lord, *The Wallaces of Iowa* (Boston, 1947), 497ff.

[55] On the difficulties of reconversion, see Barton J. Bernstein, "Clash of Interests: The Postwar Battle between the Office of Price Administration and Agriculture," *Agricultural History*, 41 (Jan. 1967), 45–57; "The Debate on Industrial Reconversion: The Protection of Oligopoly and Military Control of the War Economy," *American Journal of Economics and Sociology*, 26 (Apr. 1967), 159–72; "The Removal of War Production Controls on Business, 1944–1946," *Business History Review*, 39 (Summer 1965), 243–60; "The Truman Administration and Its Reconversion Wage Policy," *Labor History*, 6 (Fall 1965), 214–31; and "Economic Policies," in Richard S. Kirkendall, ed., *The Truman Period as a Research Field* (Columbia, Mo., 1967), 87–148.

lectuals would have had difficulty achieving all of their objectives. Without one, their chances of survival in the jungles of Washington politics were slim, and their hopes of attaining environmental mastery were utterly unrealistic. Their rudimentary organism was too weak. Aside from the strength they drew from the president and the power of their intellects, they were armed with little more than a set of broad human objectives.[56] Although these may have contained the force that inheres in the grandeur of noble aspirations, they were insufficient by themselves to enable the group to become dominant in the councils of the American government.

The New Deal intellectuals believed the United States had the natural resources, the technology, and the labor force to create an economy of abundance. The country had the potential to provide every American family with an adequate standard of living: a decent job, comfortable housing, proper diet, minimum health care, access to educational opportunity, and time for leisure and recreation.[57] After briefly trying for more equitable distribution of a stable national income, they came to agree with John Maynard Keynes on economic growth as the central objective of public policy—steady annual increases in per capita output and real income.[58] With great faith in professional intelligence and applied expertise, they expected federal policy shaped by specially trained experts to deliver increasing progress to the masses of the American people. Given a generation in power, they thought they could achieve their broad objectives: secure the gains of technological development for the public, and prevent oligopolistic industry from cornering more than its fair share of the yield

[56] The phrase "broad human objectives" appears in Schlesinger, *The Politics of Upheaval*, 385. Formation of the radical Independent Citizens Committee for the Arts, Sciences, and Professions during the war and the liberal Americans for Democratic Action after it illustrates American intellectuals' awareness of the need for a political organization of their own.

[57] The following composite statement is based on a sample of the published and some unpublished writings of President and Mrs. Roosevelt, Adolph Berle, Rexford Tugwell, Frances Perkins, Harry Hopkins, Thurman Arnold, Edgar Kemler, Corrington Gill, Harold Ickes, Donald Richberg, Hugh Johnson, Felix Frankfurter, Jerome Frank, Malcolm Ross, Aubrey Williams, Raymond Moley, Nathan Straus, Mary McLeod Bethune, Clark Foreman, John Dickinson, Harlow Person, Mordecai Ezekiel, Harold Loeb, John W. Studebaker, Robert S. Lynd, Morris Ernst, Robert M. Lovett, Clarence Pickett, Lawrence Hughes, Calvin Hoover, George Creel, and Mary K. Simkhovitch. In addition, the files of *Plan Age* and *Today* for the 1930s were thoroughly sampled. Unfortunately the data for comparative ideological analysis are extremely sparse. R. Joseph Monsen, Jr., and Mark W. Cannon, *The Makers of Public Policy: American Power Groups and Their Ideologies* (New York, 1965), analyze programmatic differences among elites.

[58] John Maynard Keynes, *The General Theory of Employment, Interest, and Money* (New York: Harbinger Books, 1965), vii, 372ff.; Robert Lekachman, *The Age of Keynes* (New York, 1966), 78–81.

of steady economic expansion. Guided by disinterested experts, public policy would stimulate business to produce more for less—to expand output while lowering prices. High-volume low-price production policies, together with government-generated increases in aggregate demand, would eventually abolish poverty within a widely reformed American economy.

More drastic and alien schemes, communism on the left and fascism on the right, would not be needed to satisfy popular cravings for justice. Under expert guidance, a reformed capitalism would be equal to the essential test of utilitarian democracy; it would produce the greatest good for the largest possible number of Americans.

With the satisfaction of every American's basic wants would come solutions to the problems of political obligation and of the relation between governors and governed in a democracy. Abundance would destroy the internal sources of social and political disintegration: class, ethnic, religious, and economic conflict. Completely loyal to their political and intellectual leaders, Americans would spontaneously honor and serve the men responsible for the satisfaction of their basic needs. Threats to the Republic could come only from external enemies who might make war on it or whose aggressive actions might menace the nation's vital foreign interests. A few of the New Dealers even dreamed that abundance would prepare the way for the fulfillment of the ultimate promise of the human personality. The abundant life would lay the basis for the good life. Plenty and leisure would give the average American time to enjoy the highest products of the human spirit and a chance to participate in their creation. The United States might give birth to the first renaissance in history where culture would be the property of the democratic many rather than a monopoly of a privileged few.[59]

The New Deal intellectuals' exalted aspirations have gone almost unrecognized in the history of the era. In a nation of short memories, even the professional curators of the past often forget nearly as much as they

[59] For examples, see Rexford G. Tugwell, *The Battle for Democracy* (New York, 1935), 178; Jerome Frank, *Fate and Freedom* (New York, 1945), 206ff.; David E. Lilienthal, *This I Do Believe* (New York, 1949), 25–31, 195–208; Hallie Flanagan, *Arena: The History of the Federal Theater* (n.p., 1940), 231ff., 325–27, 371–73; Harry Hopkins, *Spending to Save* (New York, 1936), 173–78; John Dickinson, *Hold Fast the Middle Way* (Boston, 1935), 238–39; Harold Ickes, *The New Democracy* (New York, 1934), 142–44; Adolph Berle, *New Directions in the New World* (New York, 1940), esp. 140–41; Henry Wallace, *Statesmanship and Religion* (New York, 1934). On the appropriate occasion even the president expressed himself in such terms; see Franklin D. Roosevelt, *The Public Papers and Addresses of Franklin D. Roosevelt*, 8 (1939), 335ff., and 10 (1941), 72–76. For an indication that Roosevelt's sentiments were genuine, see George Creel, "Roosevelt's Plans and Purposes," *Collier's*, 98 (26 Dec. 1936), 7–9, 39–40.

remember about bygone eras. Whether better and richer memories would raise the level of public discourse, they might reduce the volume of mis-information issuing from official and unofficial sources. The War on Pov-erty could have been announced with a sober acknowledgment of the previous campaigns against poverty during the Progressive era and in the subsequent reigns of Herbert Hoover and Franklin Roosevelt. The New Left could have arisen behind the banner of participatory democracy while tempering its disdain for the brittle and murderous liberalism of the Great Society with the recollection that some liberals had once been as con-cerned for democratic participation as the members of Students for a Democratic Society. The New Deal's genuine desire to enhance the quality of American life should also have earned it fonder memories.[60] The New Dealers may not have been able to give flesh to their hopes, but on this score there is little to choose between them and their latter-day radical critics, who are, if anything, much further from realizing their utopia than the New Deal intellectuals were when their brief moment of glory had come to an end.

The recent criticisms of the New Deal have been not only somewhat unfair but also partially misdirected. They have scored Roosevelt for fail-ing to do what he never intended to do—abolish capitalism, for example, and attack American racism. They have stressed the New Deal's failure to transcend certain ideological limits, without assessing the weaknesses within those limitations. Neither the critics nor the intellectuals ever sys-tematically analyzed the shortcomings inherent in the New Deal's broad aspirations.

Not until the intellectuals' moment in power was approaching its end did they begin to recognize the lack of a clear connection between abun-dance and the good life. Plenty is obviously preferable to poverty, but the relation between color television sets and the fulfillment of man's ultimate

---

[60] New Left historiography on the domestic New Deal consists of Howard Zinn's introduction to his edition of documents, *New Deal Thought* (Indianapolis, 1966); Brad Wiley, "Historians and the New Deal," mimeo distributed by SDS's Radical Education Project; Barton J. Bernstein, "The New Deal: The Conservative Achieve-ments of Liberal Reform," in his *Towards a New Past* (New York, 1967), 263–88; Paul Conkin, *The New Deal* (New York, 1967). The pioneer war on poverty is dis-cussed in Robert Bremner, *From the Depths* (New York, 1956). For indications that the quest for abundance was central for Progressive era reformers, see Daniel N. Fox, *The Discovery of Abundance* (Ithaca, 1967); Donald Richberg, *My Hero* (New York, 1954), 45; and Harold Ickes, *The Autobiography of a Curmudgeon* (Chicago: Quad-rangle Books, 1969), 164. For a different view of the role of abundance in American history, see David M. Potter, *People of Plenty* (Chicago, 1954), where it is considered basic to the formation of the American character rather than a central aspiration of modern American reformers.

promise remains obscure. Human beings may have to eat before they can become philosophers, but a nation of well-fed burghers may still fail to produce a single metaphysician of merit, not to mention a democratic cultural renaissance.[61]

Nor did the intellectuals attempt to check the confusion spread through the nation's consciousness by their faith in abundance. In the abstract, an abundant economy should be able to satisfy most wants simultaneously. Hard decisions about the allocation of scarce goods among competing claimants will seldom, if ever, be necessary. If American capitalism could satisfy human wants without conflict, the economy would function as a nonzero-sum game: everyone could win, no one would have to lose.

Unfortunately neither the nation nor the planet has the resources to satisfy wants without conflict. Difficult decisions about the allocation of scarce goods among competing consumers will have to be made regardless of the economic system, whether free market, regulated oligopolistic competition, or central planning.

If conflict is minimized, it tends to be reduced at the expense of those outside the system. Ignoring the pleas of an occasional maverick,[62] the New Dealers consciously sought expanded overseas markets and free access to foreign sources of raw materials.[63] With few if any exceptions, they ignored the problems freedom of access might create for the countries supplying the resources. With the gap between rich and poor nations widening,[64] the underdeveloped countries have been partially handicapped by lack of adequate resources; the resource-acquisitions policies of the rich nations have increased the strains under which they operate. To the

[61] For one who was aware of the missing link between material well-being and the good life, see Helen Hill Miller, *Yours for Tomorrow: A Personal Testament of Freedom* (New York, 1943), 124–26. For later concern, see John Kenneth Galbraith, *The Affluent Society* (Boston, 1958), and David Riesman, *Abundance for What?* (Garden City, 1964).

[62] Jerome Frank, *Save America First* (New York, 1938).

[63] Kolko, *Roots of American Foreign Policy*, 48ff.; Barnet, *Intervention and Revolution*, 16–17; Lloyd Gardner, *Economic Aspects of New Deal Diplomacy* (Madison, 1964).

[64] See L. J. Zimmerman, *Poor Lands, Rich Lands: The Widening Gap* (New York, 1965). For examples of New Deal resource policy, see David Cushman Coyle, *Roads to a New America* (Boston, 1938); Edgar B. Nixon, ed., *Franklin D. Roosevelt and Conservation, 1911–1945*, 2 vols. (New York, 1957); National Resources Planning Board, *National Resources Development: Report for 1943*, pt. II: *Wartime Planning for War and Post War* (Washington, 1943). The emphasis was on rational use, waste avoidance, and resource development, and the emphasis persisted after World War II; see J. Frederic Dewhurst and Associates, *America's Needs and Resources* (New York, 1947), which does not mention the possible adverse effects American resource-acquisition policies might have on the nations supplying us.

extent that rich nations' imports of raw materials reduce the resource bases of poor nations and their price policies worsen the poor nations' terms of trade, the affluence of the advanced industrial powers is in part a function of someone else's poverty.

The New Dealers' obsession with economic growth, a mania shared by Keynesian and Marxian economists alike, assumed an ever-expanding supply of resources to fuel an ever-growing economy.[65] They either begged or ignored the Malthusian question: Is there enough for all within the present organization of the international economy? If the answer was no, the abundance mystique and the growth mania prevented Americans from realizing that national and international economic systems were in part zero-sum games: somebody wins, somebody else loses.

The New Dealers similarly avoided a direct confrontation with the paradox of the general interest. Unlike special interests, the general interest lacks a specific group or class to support it. Even accepting the intellectuals' image of themselves as its guarantors, the most that can be said is that the general interest was entrusted to the care of an unorganized elite without the power to promote it.[66] Out of power, the New Deal intellectuals could do little to further the general interest beyond persuading those in power to accept their recommendations. Controversial recommendations had small chance of adoption; important policies are usually both controversial and a threat to some organized interest, so they cannot be effectuated without disciplined political support. Out of power, the intellectuals could do nothing more for the general interest than provide it with extensive verbal care; they could not lead it to victory over organized special interests.

In power, their connection to it was immediately severed. They joined agencies designed to execute specific policies for the benefit of narrowly defined groups: marginal farmers, the unemployed, blacks, migrant farm workers, the unorganized. Nor could their most important colleagues evade the dilemma. Henry Wallace became the secretary of agriculture, not the secretary of everything. Frances Perkins was appointed secretary of labor, not secretary of labor, consumer, and business cooperation. Functionally there was no difference between the intellectuals who came to Washington to promote the general welfare and the George Peeks who joined the New Deal to further the interests of commercial farmers.

[65] Keynes, *General Theory*, 245–46, contains a summary statement of the theory that fails to mention resources at all—not only among the system's dependent and independent variables, but also among the things it took for granted.
[66] See the studies cited in nn. 3 and 35.

Caught up in the most exciting and rewarding work of their lives, the intellectuals were able to avoid abstract intellectual dilemmas. Nevertheless, the dilemmas were genuine, and confronting them might have furthered their purposes. Their pretention to be the keepers of the national conscience and the guarantors of the public interest was unendurable to their business, labor, and agricultural rivals, and even to some of their allies who failed to see how the intellectuals were either morally or politically superior to them. The gap between their self- and public images contributed to the political acrimony of the era, and it may have prevented the New Deal from going further than it did. If lack of tact and want of careful persuasion ever made the difference between legislative success and failure, then the intellectuals' arrogance limited the New Deal's reform achievements.

In addition to being insufferable, their fight for government by intelligent experts was largely irrelevant. They waged a war that had already been won against opponents who fought alongside them. Government by experts was a bogus issue in the 1930s, as it was again in the 1950s when George F. Kennan and his allies in the State Department made so much of it. No American president, Andrew Jackson included, staffed technical and policy-making government positions with ignorant and untutored men.[67] By 1933 the United States had long filled its bureaus and civil service positions with trained experts of one kind or another. The Progressives had used experts to further government purposes, and so had Herbert Hoover.[68]

The problem was not to choose between government by experts and government by ignoramuses. The problem is that government by experts is no more a guarantee of good government than government by nonexperts is a guarantee of bad government. Expert knowledge is subject to neutralization, manipulation, and distortion; it can be put to uses unforeseen by the experts who possess it. It cannot determine whether the uses to which it is put will be wise or just. Expert knowledge serves the purposes of the dominant social and political forces making and executing public policy. In the best of all possible political worlds, the wisdom of public policy would not be proportional to the amount of expert knowledge invested in its formulation. Wisdom cannot be taught in graduate and professional schools. It is a rare commodity—not because it is the monopoly of the

[67] Aronson, *Status and Kinship*, 89, 94, 104, 124, 165–66.

[68] Kirkendall, "Franklin D. Roosevelt and the Service Intellectual," 456–58; Bary Dean Karl, "Presidential Planning and Social Science Research: Mr. Hoover's Experts," *Perspectives in American History*, 3 (1969), 347–409.

privileged classes but because it occurs so seldom. It is not an appanage of the rich, well-born, and well-educated. It can be found among the poorest and most ignorant peasants, as well as occasionally in the posh clubs of eastern, urbanized American intellectuals.

APPENDIX

Abbott, Edith
Abbott, Grace
Abt, John
Acheson, Dean
Agger, Eugene
Alexander, Will Winton
Alfred, Helen
Allin, Bushrod
Alsberg, Henry
Altmeyer, Arthur J.
Anderson, H. Dewey
Anderson, Mary
Andrews, Elmer Frank
Andrews, John B.
Armstrong, Barbara
Arnold, Thurman
Arthur, Henry Bradford
Baker, Jacob
Baker, Oliver Edwin
Baldwin, Calvin Benham
Ballinger, Willis Jerome
Bane, Frank
Barkin, Solomon
Barrows, Harlan Hiram
Bassie, V. Lewis
Bean, Louis
Beecher, John
Bell, Daniel
Bell, Spurgeon
Bennett, Hugh Hammond
Berge, Wendell
Berle, Adolph
Bethune, Mary McLeod
Biddle, Francis
Black, Albert Gain
Black, John D.

Blair, John M.
Blaisdell, Donald C.
Blaisdell, Thomas C.
Blakey, Roy G.
Blandford, John B., Jr.
Bledsoe, Samuel B.
Blough, Roy
Bowles, Chester
Brady, Robert Alexander
Brannan, Charles F.
Bressman, Earl N.
Brown, James Douglas
Brown, Josephine Chapin
Brown, Nelson Courtlandt
Brown, Richard R.
Brownlow, Louis
Bruere, Robert W.
Bullitt, William
Burns, Arthur E.
Burns, Eviline M.
Cahill, Holger
Caliver, Ambrose
Carmody, John M.
Carter, John Franklin
Catlett, Fred Wayne
Cavers, David F.
Chapman, Oscar
Clague, Ewan
Clapp, Gordon
Clark, Tom
Cohen, Benjamin
Cohen, Wilbur J.
Collier, John
Colm, Gerhard
Cooke, Morris L.
Corcoran, Thomas G.

Corson, John Jay
Cowles, Michael
Cox, Archibald
Cox, Oscar
Coy, Albert Wayne
Coyle, David C.
Creel, George
Currie, Lauchlin
Daniels, Jonathan
Darrow, Wayne H.
Davidson, C. Girard
Davis, Chester Charles
Davis, Elmer
Davis, William Hammatt
Dean, Gordon
Dean, William H.
Dearing, Charles Lee
Delano, Frederic A.
Dewhurst, J. Frederick
Dewson, Mary W.
Dickinson, John
Dimock, Marshall E.
Dorn, Harold F.
Douglas, Lewis
Douglas, Paul
Douglas, William O.
Durr, Clifford J.
Eastman, Joseph B.
Eccles, Marriner S.
Edwards, Corwin
Eliot, Charles W. II
Eliot, Martha May
Eliot, Thomas H.
Elliott, Foster F.
Elliott, Harriet Wiseman
Embree, Edwin R.
Emerson, Thomas I.
Emmerich, Herbert
Englund, Eric
Epstein, Abraham
Ernst, Morris
Evans, Joseph H. B.
Ewing, Oscar R.
Ezekiel, Mordecai
Fahy, Charles

Fainsod, Merle
Falk, Isidore S.
Feis, Herbert
Ferguson, Garland Sevier, Jr.
Fischer, John
Flanagan, Hallie
Fly, James Lawrence
Foley, Edward H.
Foreman, Clark H.
Fortas, Abe
Foster, William T.
Frank, Jerome N.
Frankfurter, Felix
Freund, Paul
Fuchs, Herbert
Galbraith, John K.
Gallagher, Rachael
Galloway, George B.
Garrison, Lloyd K.
Gass, Oscar
Gaston, Herbert
Gellhorn, Martha
Gellhorn, Walter
Gilbert, Richard V.
Gill, Corrington
Ginsberg, Charles David
Givens, Meredith B.
Gladieux, Bernard L.
Glavis, Louis
Goldenweiser, Emanuel Alexander
Goldschmidt, Arthur
Grady, Henry F.
Graham, Frank P.
Gray, Lewis Cecil
Greenbaum, Edward S.
Groves, Harold Martin
Gruening, Ernest H.
Gulick, Luther H.
Haas, Francis J.
Hall, Helen
Halpern, Nathan L.
Hamilton, Walton H.
Hamm, John
Handler, Milton
Hansen, Alvin H.

Harriman, W. Averell
Harris, Joseph Pratt
Harris, Seymour Edwin
Hart, Henry M., Jr.
Hastie, William H.
Hawkins, Harry Calvin
Hays, Lawrence Brooks
Henderson, Leon
Herrick, Elinore
Hewes, Lawrence I., Jr.
Hickock, Lorena
High, Stanley
Hinrichs, Albert F.
Hiss, Alger
Hoey, Jane M.
Holland, George Kenneth
Hoover, Calvin B.
Hopkins, Harry L.
Horne, Frank S.
Howe, Frederick C.
Hudgens, Robert W.
Hughes, James E.
Humphrey, Don
Hunt, Henry
Hunter, Howard Owen
Ickes, Harold L.
Ihlder, John
Jackson, Gardner
Jackson, Robert Houghwout
Jaszi, George
Johnson, Clarence R.
Johnson, Gove Griffith
Johnson, Hugh S.
Johnson, Sherman E.
Jones, Eugene K.
Jones, Roger Warren
Katz, Milton
Keenan, Joseph B.
Keezer, Dexter M.
Kellogg, Paul U.
Kemler, Edgar
Kerr, Florence
Keyserling, Leon
King, Cornelius
Kohn, Robert David

Kreps, Theodore, Jr.
Krug, Julius
Landis, James M.
Lane, Marie Dresden
Laning, Clair
Latimer, Murray W.
Lauck, W. Jett
LeCron, James D.
Leiserson, William
Lenroot, Katharine
Lerner, Max
Lilienthal, David E.
Loeb, Harold
Lorwin, Lewis L.
Lovett, Robert M.
Lubin, Isador
Lynd, Robert S.
Lyon, Leverett S.
McCamy, James L.
McConnell, Beatrice
MacKaye, Benton
MacLeish, Archibald
Madden, Joseph Warren
Maddox, James G.
Magdoff, Harry
Magill, Roswell F.
Magruder, Calvert
Maher, Amy S.
Malin, Patrick Murphy
Manly, Basil
Margold, Nathan R.
Maris, Paul V.
Marshall, Leon C.
Mathews, George C.
May, Stacy
Mead, Elwood
Means, Gardiner C.
Mellett, Lowell
Merriam, Charles E.
Merrill, Harold Arthur
Miller, Helen Hill
Millis, Harry Alvin
Milton, George Fort
Mitchell, Ewing Y.
Mitchell, George S.

Mitchell, Wesley C.
Moley, Raymond
Montgomery, Donald
Moon, Henry Lee
Morgan, Arthur E.
Morgan, Harcourt A.
Morgenthau, Henry
Morrison, L. A.
Morse, Wayne L.
Musgrave, Richard A.
Myers, William I.
Nathan, Robert Roy
Nienburg, Bertha
Niles, David K.
Nourse, Edwin G.
Ogburn, William Fielding
Olds, Leland
Oliphant, Herman
Oxley, Howard W.
Oxley, Lawrence A.
Packard, Walter E.
Padover, Saul K.
Parisius, Herbert W.
Parran, Thomas
Pasvolsky, Leo
Pecora, Ferdinand
Perkins, Frances
Perkins, Milo
Person, Harlow
Persons, W. Frank
Pickett, Clarence E.
Podell, David Louis
Porter, Paul A.
Poston, Theodore
Powell, Fred W.
Pressman, Lee
Price, Don K., Jr.
Purcell, Ganson
Rauh, Joseph L., Jr.
Reed, Stanley F.
Reilly, Gerard Denis
Richberg, Donald R.
Riefler, Winfield William
Riley, Roderick H.
Roche, Josephine

Rogge, O. John
Roos, C. F.
Rosenberg, Anna Marie
Rosenman, Samuel I.
Ross, Malcolm
Rowe, James H.
Rubinow, Isaac M.
Ruml, Beardsley
Rumsey, Mary H.
Ryan, John A.
Sachs, Alexander
Salant, Walter
Samuelson, Paul A.
Saposs, David
Sayre, Francis B.
Schneiderman, Rose
Seltzer, Lawrence
Shea, Francis Michael
Sheppardson, Gay
Sherwood, Robert E.
Silcox, Ferdinand A.
Simkhovitch, Mary K.
Simpson, Kemper
Slattery, Harry
Smith, Alfred Edgar
Smith, Blackwell
Smith, Donald Wakefield
Smith, Edwin S.
Smith, Harold Dewey
Smith, Hilda W.
Splawn, Walter M. W.
Sprague, O. M. W.
Stanley, William
Steelman, John Roy
Stephens, Harold
Stern, Bernhard J.
Stevens, William H. S.
Stevenson, Adlai Ewing
Stine, O. C.
Straight, Michael W.
Straus, Nathan
Straus, Robert K.
Strauss, Michael Wolf
Studebaker, John Ward
Sweezy, Alan R.

Taeusch, Carl F.
Tapp, Jesse W.
Taylor, Carl C.
Taylor, Telford
Thorpe, Willard L.
Tolley, Howard
Trent, William, Jr.
Tugwell, Rexford
Vann, Robert L.
Viner, Jacob
Vinton, Warren Jay
Wallace, Donald
Wallace, Henry A.
Wallace, Schuyler C.
Walling, Lewis M.
Ware, Caroline F.
Warren, George F.
Washington, Forrester B.
Watkins, Ralph J.

Weaver, Robert C.
Webbink, Paul M.
Wechsler, Herbert
West, Charles F.
White, Harry Dexter
Wickens, Aryness Joy
Wiecking, Ernst H.
Williams, Aubrey W.
Wilson, Milburn
Wing, Marie
Wirtz, Willard
Witt, Nathan
Witte, Edwin E.
Wolfsohn, Joel David
Wolman, Leo
Woodbury, Coleman
Woodward, Ellen S.
Woofter, Thomas J., Jr.
Wyzanski, Charles

Selected Bibliography

This bibliography consists of books and articles that have helped us in our research and that explore other aspects of the study of elites and upper classes. This collection is not exhaustive, and those wishing to investigate further are advised to consult the references cited in our footnotes and in the writings listed below.

1. Theory

Aaron, Raymond. "Social Structure and the Ruling Class." *British Journal of Sociology,* 1 (1950), 1–16, 126–43.

Barber, Bernard. *Social Stratification.* New York: Harcourt Brace & World, 1957.

Bottomore, Thomas B. *Classes in Modern Society.* New York: Pantheon Books, 1966.

———. *Elites and Society.* New York: Basic Books, 1964.

Centers, Richard. *The Psychology of Social Classes.* Princeton: Princeton University Press, 1949.

Clifford-Vaughan, Michalina. "Some French Concepts of Elites." *British Journal of Sociology,* 11 (1960), 319–32.

Dahl, Robert A. "Critique of the Ruling Elite Model." *American Political Science Review,* 52 (1958), 463–70.

Dahrendorf, Ralf. *Class and Class Conflict in Industrial Society.* Stanford: Stanford University Press, 1959.

Davis, Kingsley. "A Conceptual Analysis of Stratification." *American Sociological Review,* 7 (1942), 309–21.

———, and Moore, Wilbert. "Some Principles of Stratification." *ASR,* 10 (1945), 242–49.

De Tocqueville, Alexis. *Democracy in America.* Ed. Phillips Bradley. 2 vols. New York: Vintage, 1956.

———. *The Old Regime and the French Revolution.* New York: Doubleday, 1955.

Gordon, Milton M. *Social Class in American Sociology.* Durham: Duke University Press, 1958.

Halbwachs, Maurice. *The Psychology of Social Class.* New York: The Free Press, 1958.

Keller, Suzanne. *Beyond the Ruling Class: Strategic Elites in Modern Society.* New York: Random House, 1968.

Lasswell, Harold D.; Lerner, Daniel; and Rothwell, C. Easton. *The Comparative Study of Elites: An Introduction and Bibliography.* Stanford: Stanford University Press, 1952.

375

Lipset, Seymour Martin, and Bendix, Reinhard, eds. *Class, Status, and Power.* New York: The Free Press, 1953.
————. *Social Mobility in Industrial Society.* Berkeley: University of California Press, 1959.
Mannheim, Karl. *Essays on Sociology and Social Psychology.* New York: Oxford University Press, 1953.
————. *Ideology and Utopia.* New York: Harcourt Brace, 1949.
Marshall, T. H. *Citizenship and Social Class.* Cambridge: Cambridge University Press, 1950.
Mayer, Kurt B. *Class and Society.* New York: Random House, 1955.
Merton, Robert K. *Social Theory and Social Structure.* New York: The Free Press, 1964.
Michels, Robert. *Political Parties.* Glencoe, Ill.: The Free Press, 1949.
Mosca, Gaetano. *The Ruling Class.* New York: McGraw-Hill, 1939.
Pareto, Vilifredo. *The Mind and Society.* 4 vols. New York: Harcourt Brace, 1935.
Parsons, Talcott. *The Social System.* New York: The Free Press, 1951.
————. *The Structure of Social Action.* New York: McGraw-Hill, 1937.
Polsby, Nelson. "Community Power: Some Reflections on the Recent Literature." *ASR,* 27 (1962), 838–41.
————. "How to Study Community Power: The Pluralist Alternative." *Journal of Politics,* 22 (1960), 474–84.
————. "Three Problems in the Analysis of Community Power." *ASR,* 24 (1959), 196–203.
Reissman, Leonard. *Class in American Society.* New York: The Free Press, 1959.
Rossi, Peter H. "Community Decision-Making." *Administrative Science Quarterly,* 1 (1957), 415–53.
Schulze, Robert O. "The Role of Economic Dominants in Community Power Structure." *ASR,* 23 (1958), 3–9.
————, and Blumenberg, Leonard U. "The Determinants of Local Power Elites." *American Journal of Sociology,* 63 (1957), 290–96.
Schumpeter, Joseph. *Imperialism and Social Classes.* New York: Meridian, 1955.
Tumin, Melvin, "Some Principles of Stratification: A Critical Analysis." *ASR,* 18 (1953), 387–97.
Warner, W. Lloyd. "The Study of Social Stratification." In *Review of Sociology,* ed. Joseph B. Gittler. New York: John Wiley, 1957.
Weber, Max. *From Max Weber: Essays in Sociology.* Ed. Hans H. Gerth and C. Wright Mills. New York: Oxford University Press, 1946.
————. *The Protestant Ethic and the Spirit of Capitalism.* New York: Scribner's, 1950.
————. *The Theory of Social and Economic Organization.* Tr. and ed. A. M. Henderson and Talcott Parsons. New York: Oxford University Press, 1947.
Wrong, Dennis H. "The Functional Theory of Stratification." *ASR,* 24 (1959), 772–83.

2. Historical and Community Studies

Albion, Robert G. *The Rise of New York Port.* New York: Scribner's, 1939.
Amory, Cleveland. *The Proper Bostonians.* New York: E. P. Dutton, 1947.
————. *Who Killed Society?* New York: Harper, 1961.

Baltzell, E. Digby. *Philadelphia Gentlemen*. New York: The Free Press, 1958.
————. *The Protestant Establishment: Aristocracy and Caste in American Society*. New York: Random House, 1964.
Barber, Elinor G. *The Bourgeoisie in Eighteenth Century France*. Princeton: Princeton University Press, 1965.
Barth, Gunther. "Metropolitan and Urban Elites in the Far West." In *The Age of Industrialism in America*, ed. Frederic Cople Jaher. New York: The Free Press, 1968.
Bindoff, S. T.; Hurtsfield, J.; and Williams, C. H., eds. *Elizabethan Government and Society: Essays Presented to Sir John Neale*. London: Athone Press, 1961.
Burt, Nathaniel. *The Perennial Philadelphians: The Anatomy of an American Aristocracy*. Boston: Little Brown, 1963.
Cady, Edward Harrison. *The Gentleman in America*. Syracuse: Syracuse University Press, 1949.
Cole, G. D. H. "Elites in British Society." *Studies in Class Structure*. London: Routledge & Kegan Paul, 1955.
Dahl, Robert A. *Who Governs*. New Haven: Yale University Press, 1961.
Davis, John Cashman. *The Decline of the Venetian Nobility*. Baltimore: Johns Hopkins University Press, 1962.
Dobb, Maurice. *Studies in the Development of Capitalism*. London: George Routledge & Sons, 1946.
Domhoff, G. William. *Who Rules America*. Englewood Cliffs: Spectrum Books, 1967.
Dowdey, Clifford. *The Virginia Dynasties*. Boston: Little Brown, 1969.
Earle, Edward Mead, ed. *Modern France*. Princeton: Princeton University Press, 1951.
Everitt, Alan. "Social Mobility in Modern England." *Past and Present*, no. 33 (Apr. 1966), 56–73.
Ford, Franklin. *Robe and Sword: The Regrouping of the French Aristocracy after Louis XIV*. Cambridge, Mass.: Harvard University Press, 1953.
Forster, Robert. *The Nobility of Toulouse in the Eighteenth Century: A Social and Economic Study*. Baltimore: Johns Hopkins University Press, 1960.
Gelzer, Matthias. *The Roman Nobility*. Tr. Robin Seager. Oxford: Blackwells, 1969.
Gerschenkron, Alexander. "Social Attitudes, Entrepreneurship and Economic Development." *Explorations in Entrepreneurial History*, 6 (1953–54), 1–20.
Goodwin, Albert. *The European Nobility in the Eighteenth Century*. London: Adam and Black, 1953.
Henrietta, James. "Economic Development and Social Structure in Colonial Boston." *William and Mary Quarterly*, 22 (1965), 79–92.
Hoskins, W. G. *Industry, Trade and People in Exeter: 1688–1800*. Manchester: Manchester University Press, 1935.
Hunter, Floyd. *Community Power Structure*. Chapel Hill: University of North Carolina Press, 1953.
————. *Top Leadership, U.S.A.* Chapel Hill: University of North Carolina Press, 1959.
Jaher, Frederic Cople. "The Boston Brahmins in the Age of Industrial Capitalism." *The Age of Industrialism in America*. New York: The Free Press, 1968.

————. "Businessman and Gentleman: Nathan and Thomas Gold Appleton—An Exploration in Intergenerational History." *EEH*, 2nd ser., 4 (Fall 1966), 17–39.

————. "Nineteenth Century Elites in Boston and New York." *Journal of Social History*, 5 (Fall 1972).

Jennings, M. Kent. *Community Influentials: The Elites of Atlanta*. New York: The Free Press, 1964.

Johnson, John J., ed. *Continuity and Change in Latin America*. Stanford: Stanford University Press, 1964.

Kelso, Ruth. *The Doctrine of the English Gentleman in the Sixteenth Century*. Urbana: University of Illinois Press, 1929.

Kohn-Bramsted, Ernest. *Aristocracy and the Middle Classes in Germany*. Chicago: Phoenix Books, 1964.

Labaree, Leonard Woods. *Conservatism in Early American History*. New York: New York University Press, 1948.

Landes, David. "Social Attitudes, Entrepreneurship and Economic Development." *EEH*, 6 (1953–54), 245–73.

Lane, Frederic C. *Andrea Barbarigo, Merchant of Venice, 1418–1449*. Baltimore: Johns Hopkins University Press, 1944.

————, and Riemersma, Jelle C., eds. *Entrepreneurship and Secular Change*. Homewood, Ill.: Richard D. Irwin, 1953.

Lipset, Seymour Martin, and Solari, Aldo. *Elites in Latin America*. New York: Oxford University Press, 1967.

MacCaffrey, Wallace T. *Exeter, 1540–1640: The Growth of an English Country Town*. Cambridge, Mass.: Harvard University Press, 1958.

McKay, John P. *Pioneers for Profit: Foreign Entrepreneurship and Russian Industrialization, 1885–1913*. Chicago: University of Chicago Press, 1970.

Main, Jackson Turner. *The Social Structure of Revolutionary America*. Princeton: Princeton University Press, 1965.

Mingay, G. E. *English Landed Society in the Eighteenth Century*. London: Routledge & Kegan Paul, 1936.

Morison, Samuel Eliot. *Maritime History of Massachusetts, 1783–1860*. Boston: Houghton Mifflin, 1930.

Palmer, R. R. *The Age of Democratic Revolution*. 2 vols. Princeton: Princeton University Press, 1959, 1964.

Pessen, Edward. "Did Fortunes Rise and Fall Mercurially in Antebellum America? The Tale of Two Cities: Boston and New York." *Journal of Social History*, 4 (1971), 339–58.

————. "The Egalitarian Myth and American Social Reality: Wealth, Mobility and Equality in the Era of the Common Man." *American Historical Review*, 76 (1971), 989–1034.

Petras, James, and Zeitlin, Maurice, eds. *Latin America: Reform or Revolution?* Greenwich: Fawcett, 1968.

Ponsonby, Arthur. *The Decline of Aristocracy*. London: T. Fisher Unwin, 1912.

Queller, Donald E. "The Civic Irresponsibility of the Venetian Nobility." *EEH*, 2nd ser., 7 (1969), 234–45.

Redlich, Fritz, ed. "A Symposium on the Aristocracy in Business." *EEH*, 6 (1953–54), 77–130.

Rose, Arnold. *The Power Structure*. New York: Oxford University Press, 1967.

Rosenberg, Hans. *Bureaucracy, Aristocracy and Autocracy: The Prussian Experience, 1660–1815.* Cambridge, Mass.: Harvard University Press, 1958.

Sawyer, John E. "Social Structure and Economic Progress: General Propositions and Some French Examples." *American Economic History Review, Papers and Proceedings,* 41 (1951), 321–29.

Simpson, Alan. *The Wealth of the Gentry, 1540–1660.* Chicago: University of Chicago Press, 1961.

Sjoberg, Gideon. *The Preindustrial City: Past and Present.* New York: The Free Press, 1960.

Stephens, W. B. *Seventeenth Century Exeter: A Study of Industrial and Commercial Development, 1625–1688.* Exeter: University of Exeter Press, 1958.

Stone, Lawrence. *The Crisis of the Aristocracy, 1558–1641.* London: Oxford University Press, 1965.

———. "Social Mobility in England, 1500–1700." *Past and Present,* no. 33 (Apr. 1966), 16–56.

Syme, Ronald. *Colonial Elites: Rome, Spain and the Americas.* London: Oxford University Press, 1958.

Taylor, Georve V. "Noncapitalist Wealth and the Origins of the French Revolution." *AHR,* 72 (1967), 469–96.

Taylor, L. R. *Party Politics in the Age of Caesar.* Berkeley: University of California Press, 1961.

Thometz, Carol Estes. *The Decision-Makers: The Power Structure of Dallas.* Dallas: Southern Methodist University Press, 1963.

Thompson, F. M. L. *English Landed Society in the Nineteenth Century.* London: Routledge & Kegan Paul, 1963.

Thrupp, Sylvia L. *The Merchant Class of Medieval London, 1300–1500.* Chicago: University of Chicago Press, 1948.

Uslick, W. Lee. "Changing Ideals of Character and Conduct in Seventeenth Century England." *Modern Philology,* 33 (1932), 149–66.

Wecter, Dixon. *The Saga of American Society: A Record of Social Aspiration, 1607–1937.* New York: Scribner's, 1937.

Wilkinson, Rupert, ed. *Governing Elites: Studies in Training and Selection.* New York: Oxford University Press, 1969.

Wiseman, T. P. *New Men in the Roman Senate, 139 B.C.–14 A.D.* Oxford: Oxford University Press, 1971.

Yaney, George. *The Systematization of Russian Government: Social Evolution in the Domestic Administration of Imperial Russia, 1711–1905.* Urbana: University of Illinois Press, 1973.